Consumers' Imperium

Consumers'
Imperium

*The Global Production
of American Domesticity,
1865–1920*

Kristin L. Hoganson

The University *of*
North Carolina Press
Chapel Hill

Designed by Kimberly Bryant
Set in Scala by Tseng Information Systems, Inc.
Manufactured in the United States of America

This book was published with the assistance of the Thornton H. Brooks
Fund of the University of North Carolina Press.

⊛ The paper in this book meets the guidelines for permanence and
durability of the Committee on Production Guidelines for Book
Longevity of the Council on Library Resources.

Library of Congress Cataloging-in-Publication Data
Hoganson, Kristin L.
Consumers' imperium : the global production of American domesticity,
1865–1920 / Kristin L. Hoganson.
p. cm.
Includes bibliographical references and index.
ISBN 978-0-8078-3089-5 (cloth : alk. paper)
ISBN 978-0-8078-5793-9 (pbk. : alk. paper)
1. Consumption (Economics)—Social aspects—United States—History.
2. Consumer behavior—United States—History. 3. Social change—United
States—History. 4. Lifestyles—United States—History. 5. Cosmopolitanism—
United States. I. Title.
HC110.C6H57 2007
306.30973'09034—dc22   2006100121

Portions of this book appeared earlier, in somewhat different form,
as "Cosmopolitan Domesticity: Importing the American Dream,
1865–1920," *American Historical Review* 107 (Feb. 2002): 55–83; "Food
and Entertainment from Every Corner of the Globe: Bourgeois U.S.
Households as Points of Encounter, 1870–1920," *Amerikastudien/American
Studies* 48, no. 1 (2003): 115–35; and "The Fashionable World: Imagined
Communities of Dress," in *After the Imperial Turn: Thinking with and
through the Nation*, ed. Antoinette Burton (Durham: Duke University
Press, 2003), 260–78 and are reprinted here with permission.

cloth   11 10 09 08 07   5 4 3 2 1
paper   11 10 09 08 07   5 4 3 2 1

THIS BOOK WAS DIGITALLY PRINTED.

To Jerry, Annemily, & Edie Frances
In appreciation of the imaginative worlds
you create in every picture, story, dance,
and dream

Contents

Illustrations

Acknowledgments

Perhaps because this book originated around the time I had my first child and neared completion when I was awaiting what I fully expect to be my last, the maternalist association of authorship and gestation resonates with me: books, like children, do take a lot of time and energy to produce. But the comparison should not end there. Like children, books can keep you up all night. They can be messy and demanding. They do not always behave the way you want, and they take you to places you never even knew existed. When they go out into the world, they lead a life of their own. And, finally, it takes a village. I would like to thank that village here.

I began this book during a delightful interlude at Harvard University, where considerate colleagues—including Sven Beckert, Lizabeth Cohen, Cathy Corman, Ruth Feldstein, Jay Grossman, Akira Iriye, William Kirby, Ernest May, Lisa McGirr, Jan Thaddeus, and Laurel Thatcher Ulrich— helped me make the leap from clueless graduate student to hardboiled junior faculty member. Harvard provided me with ample support for research assistants, and Corinne Calfee, Jenny Chou, Daniel Chung, Kelly Hoffman, Charlotte Houghteling, Abby Fung, Sarah Little, Anadelia Romo, and Aparna Sridhar helped get this book off the ground. While in Cambridge, I also had the good fortune to belong to an extraordinary writing group, consisting of Elizabeth Abrams, Steve Biel, Cathy Corman, Jim Cullen, Hildegard Hoeller, Jill Lepore, Jane Levey, and Laura Saltz. This group never failed to eviscerate my writing and then envision wonderful new ways to put it all back together again.

This book has been shaped even more markedly by my colleagues in the History Department at the University of Illinois, Urbana-Champaign (uiuc), where I have been since 1999. uiuc has been a fabulously rich academic home for me, and this book bears its imprint in innumerable ways. I have learned much from departmental discussions across national boundaries and my colleagues' engagement with empire, migration, transnationalism, colonialism, and world history.

I owe particular debts to those who tore apart drafts in the History Workshop and the Gender and History reading group, and to those who provided me with citations, translation help, and more general advice and support. These colleagues include Jim Barrett, Adrian Burgos, Chip Burkhardt, Antoinette Burton, Vernon Burton, Clare Crowston, Ken Cuno, Augusto Espiritu, Peter Fritzsche, Keith Hitchins, Fred Hoxie, Fred Jaher, Diane Koenker, Craig Koslofsky, Mark Leff, John Lynn, Anne M. Martínez, Tamara Matheson, Kathy Oberdeck, Elizabeth Pleck, Cynthia Radding, John Randolph, Leslie Regan, Adam Sutcliffe, Ron Toby, Maria Todorova, and Juliet Walker. Among the graduate students who have pushed my thinking in new ways, in seminars, reading groups, and other contexts, are Kate Bullard, Michael Carson, Will Cooley, Jennifer Guiliano, Rebecca McNulty, Elisa Miller, Bryan Nicholson, Karen Phoenix, Melissa Rohde, and Michael Rosenow. I also appreciate the capable research assistance provided by Sandra Henderson, Dong-Keun Kim, Karen Phoenix, and Rachel Shulman. The UIUC History Department office staff, and especially Tom Bedwell, Sharon Findlay, Shelly Gulliford-DeAtley, Jan Langendorf, Judy Patterson, Nilufer Smith, Aprel Thomas, and Julie Vollmer, helped with everything from faxing to photocopying to explaining how things work. Without Danny Tang and his associates at ATLAS, this book would have been lost somewhere in my hard drive ages ago; countless are the times they have rescued me from computer emergencies.

The village to which I am beholden extends far beyond my recent departments to generous colleagues in the profession. I appreciate the conversations, close readings, email exchanges, comments, off-the-cuff remarks, letters of support, and invitations to present my work offered by Thomas Bender, Mary Blanchard, David Brody, Frank Costigliola, Susan Davis, Mona Domosh, Nan Enstad, Maureen Flanagan, Donna Gabaccia, Michael Grossberg, Dirk Hoerder, Michael Hogan, Akira Iriye, Bob Kingston, Paul Kramer, Mark Lawrence, Jackson Lears, Karen Leroux, Martha McNamara, Jeff Pilcher, Mary Renda, Daniel Rodgers, Christine Ruane, Jordan Sand, Susan Schulten, David Strauss, James Todd Uhlman, Pamela Voekel, Shirley Wajda, Allan Wallach, Jeffrey N. Wasserstrom, Laura Wexler, and Mari Yoshihara. This book also has been shaped by the insights of audiences at the Institute for Advanced Study, Tepoztlán Institute, Lewis University, Ohio State, Smith College, the University of Montana-Missoula, UIUC, Yale University, and various conferences, and by the observations of readers known to me only as "anonymous." I wish to offer particular thanks to Laura Wexler, Daniel Rodgers, and Mary Renda for their thoughtful comments on the manuscript and to Michael Hogan and Akira Iriye for their generosity as mentors.

I have been blessed by the assistance of numerous librarians and archivists, foremost among them Neville Thompson, Emily Guthrie, and Jeanne Solensky at Winterthur Museum and Library, Suzanne Gould and Morgan Davis at the General Federation of Women's Clubs, Halyna Myroniuk at the University of Minnesota, Margaret Schoon and Stephen G. McShane of the Calumet Regional Archives, Marcia Tucker at the Institute for Advanced Study, and Mary Stuart at UIUC. Proving that it really does take a village, Christine A. Jenkins, also of UIUC, alerted me to the work done by Progressive Era librarians when I fortuitously encountered her at a block party.

One of the great pleasures in working on this project was corresponding with and meeting clubwomen. Though scattered far and wide, together they constituted one of the most valuable archives for this project. Thank you, Nan Card, Doris Chipman, Helen Covey, Donna Davis, Madge V. Drefke, Beverly Hermes, Olive Hummel, Lillian Johnsson, Barbara Love, Elizabeth Moe, and Mary Sicchio for providing me with travel club records! And special thanks to Lillian Johnsson for interviewing the late Adelaide Dannenbring on my behalf and to Doris Chipman for letting me research armchair travel in the comfort of her living room.

For research support and the most valuable gift of time, I would like to thank the C. Boyden Gray fund, UIUC research board, Mellon faculty fellowship program, UIUC Center for Advanced Study, and Winterthur Museum and Library.

The final professional debts I'd like to acknowledge are to Chuck Grench, Amanda MacMillan, Katy O'Brien, and Brian R. MacDonald of the University of North Carolina Press for shepherding this book through the publication process.

And now for the more personal acknowledgments. This book would have been sorely neglected were it not for the caregivers who have given so generously of themselves for my family: Ann Millett, Jill Johnson, LuAnn Shirley, and, above all, Deanne Karr. I owe my musings on domesticity to their strenuous, but tender, domestic work. The other great enablers behind this book are family members: my sister, Ann Hoganson; my brother, Edward Hoganson; my parents, Barbara and Jerome Hoganson; and my partner in life, Charles Gammie. They have sustained me in so many ways, proving the adage it's not what you know, it's who you know. I could not have written this book without them.

Last of all, my children. Having started by comparing them to books, I will end with an appreciation of their differences from books. True, books don't have sticky fingers and they don't bonk each other in fits of rage or go tearing around hollering at the top of their lungs, but neither do they laugh, play, snuggle, or fabricate things out of boxes and junk. For all that, and more, I would like to thank Jerry, Annemily, and Edie Frances. I realize that you would prefer something more accessible, but this book, like your mother, is dedicated to you.

Beyond Main Street

*Imperial Nightmares and Gopher
Prairie Yearnings*

A decade before his icy death aboard the *Titanic*, the English journalist W. T. Stead grappled with destiny in a book titled *The Americanisation of the World*. As the title suggests, Stead painted a picture of growing U.S. assertion. He covered topics ranging from the expanding population of the United States to its support for overseas missionaries, commercial power, and military prowess (demonstrated in its 1898 war against Spain). Even the mighty British Empire could not withstand the onslaught—the U.S. heiresses who had triumphed in the aristocratic marriage market were just the tip of a far larger iceberg. Stead invoked some "prophetic pictures" from *Life* magazine to convey the magnitude of the challenge Americanization posed to British customs and institutions. Underneath a photograph of Parliament, the American publication had placed the inscription: "The residence of Mr. John B. Grabb, of Chicago."[1]

According to Stead, the inexorable Americanization of the world presented Great Britain with a momentous choice: to join in or be left behind. If the British Empire—the world's leading power with a colonial presence on six continents and numerous small islands in the Caribbean, Pacific, and elsewhere—did not merge with the United States, it would be displaced by it. Stead insisted that he faced the possibility of an English-speaking federa-

In the interest of readability, I use "American" instead of "U.S." throughout the text when the context makes it clear that I am referring to the United States and not all of North and South America.

tion with "joyful confidence" rather than a "spirit of despair." "The Briton, instead of chafing against this inevitable supersession, should cheerfully acquiesce in the decree of Destiny, and stand in betimes with the conquering American." But Stead's protestations that American ascendance did not necessarily mean the end of the world reveal just how deep anxieties ran. Indeed, Stead began his account by admitting that many of his countrymen resented "Americanisation." He went on to say that "the American invasion has somewhat scared Europeans. . . . When Prince Albert of Belgium returned from his American trip in 1898 he was said to have exclaimed to an American friend: 'Alas! You Americans will eat us all up.'"[2]

As Stead well knew, many Europeans regarded the prospect of being ingested by the United States as the stuff of nightmares. Such apprehensions found expression in tracts like "The American Invasion," "Die Amerikanische Gefahr" (The American Danger), and *Le peril américain* (The American Peril). Stead's countryman F. A. McKenzie captured many of the anxieties surrounding Americanization in *The American Invaders*. McKenzie characterized U.S. commercial might in military terms, claiming that "America has invaded Europe not with armed men, but with manufactured products." The extent to which American exports had transformed domestic life could be seen by following an Englishman through his day: "The average citizen wakes in the morning at the sound of an American alarum clock; rises from his New England sheets, and shaves with his New York soap, and a Yankee safety razor. He pulls on a pair of Boston boots over his socks from West Carolina, fastens his Connecticut braces, slips his Waterbury watch into his pocket and sits down to breakfast. Then he congratulates his wife on the way her Illinois straight-front corset sets off her Massachusetts blouse, and begins to tackle his breakfast, at which he eats bread made from prairie flour . . . tinned oysters from Baltimore, and a little Kansas City bacon."[3] And so on. In McKenzie's account, the United States comes across as an expansive empire. Its advance troops may have been commercial agents; and its occupying forces, manufactured goods; but it was an empire nonetheless. Sixty-some years before critics coined the term "cultural imperialism," McKenzie accused the United States of practicing it.[4]

Later historians have echoed such assessments of the United States as a commercially and culturally expansionist nation at the turn of the twentieth century. Their tendency to interpret this period through the Americanization of the world framework can be seen in book titles such as *America's Outward Thrust, Peacefully Working to Conquer the World, Spreading the American Dream, Exporting Entertainment,* and *Drive to Hegemony.*[5] This interest in the "outward thrust" of the United States originated with foreign-relations historians, who have found plenty of evidence of empire in U.S. military interventions in Cuba, Puerto Rico, the Philippines, Guam, Panama, Haiti, the Dominican Republic, China, and elsewhere. But internationally minded historians of the Gilded Age and Progressive Era have not stopped with U.S. occupations and political control. They also have turned their attention to the informal empire resulting from U.S. business expansion, philanthropic and missionary endeavors, and the export of popular culture, via such means as minstrel shows, Buffalo Bill spectacles, and Hollywood movies.[6]

The narrative of U.S. expansion at the turn of the twentieth century serves the useful function of setting up later instances of Americanization. Historians writing on the United States in global context after World War I have emphasized its expanding reach and influence. From military might to jazz, from economic clout to rock 'n' roll, the story of the twentieth-century United States is the story of the elephant in the world parlor. Especially in the period following World War II, the United States filled the room. Nobody could take their eyes off it, and everybody sidled warily around to avoid being crushed. Even the growing interest in globalization has not displaced the Americanization of the world paradigm, as seen in accounts that give globalization an American face.[7]

What makes this face all the more American is the sense that the United States has stood fairly aloof from global currents. A number of historical accounts have suggested that in contrast to the rest of the world, which could not ignore the American colossus (nor, in many cases, more proximate powers), the United States could choose to look inward. Suffering from an acute City on the Hill complex, the United States refused to welcome the foreign, or so run the narratives stressing American exceptionalism. To the extent that Americans looked outward, they did so largely with ambitions of transforming the world, not of transforming themselves.[8] Even as the United States instilled fears of being gobbled up, Americans continued to prefer Kansas beef and home grown potatoes to Belgian chocolate.

Of course, historians have recognized that the United States was never completely isolated from foreign cultural production and influence. Karen Ordahl Kupperman has noted that, as a product of transatlantic colonial encounters, the United States was international before it became national. Even after independence led to greater calls for national self-assertion, many Americans continued to venerate European high culture. Wealthy Americans departed on grand tours, ordinary people flocked to Shakespeare performances, and French films dominated the American market prior to 1910.[9] Orientalism also made a mark on U.S. culture, as seen for example in chinoiserie, the Egyptian revival, an interest in Buddhism, amusement park belly dancers, and the fin-de-siècle Japan craze. Black nationalists looked to Africa, the Caribbean, and Asia as sources of culture; Progressive Era reformers took inspiration from European social politics.[10] But fascination with foreign cultural production has played a minor role in histories of the late nineteenth- and early twentieth-century United States. Domestically produced mass culture and commercial amusements have occupied center stage.

The greatest exception to the narrative of turn-of-the-twentieth-century cultural aloofness can be found in the voluminous literature on immigration. Yet, until recently, these histories have focused on the assimilation of immigrants into American ways. Furthermore, historians have underscored the hostility that greeted many immigrants. As Matthew Frye Jacobson has written, "strains of xenophobia would become increasingly important in American civic life in the years between 1876 and World War I, as the successful export of American goods to all the world's peoples would also entail a massive *import* of the world's peoples."[11] Indeed, historians have shown how the antipathy toward immigrants, particularly those from outside of Europe, resulted in the passage of immigration restriction measures such as the 1882 Chinese Exclusion Act and the 1924 Immigration Restriction Act.[12]

Besides stressing efforts to maintain a narrowly understood national culture by changing immigrants or keeping them out, historians have marshaled the history of immigration in behalf of the Americanization-of-the-world argument. U.S. commercial expansion, they have argued, owed a huge debt to immigrant workers. Furthermore, historians writing on the many labor migrants who returned to their homelands have emphasized the American ways they brought back to their villages.[13] The massive human influx into the United States in the late nineteenth and early twentieth centuries has failed to shake historians' conviction that the United States was a predominantly exporting nation. To the extent that immigration was an exception, it was the exception that proved the rule.

Rather than stressing integration into the world, historians have tended to tell the history of the United States from the end of the Civil War through World War I as a story of national integration that enabled imperial expansion. This narrative emphasis fits with their coverage of other periods. According to Eric Foner, "Historians are fully aware of how American military might, commodities, and culture have affected the rest of the world, especially in the twentieth century. We know how the United States has exported everything from Coca-Cola to ideas about democracy and 'free enterprise.' Far less attention has been devoted to how our history has been affected from abroad."[14] To elaborate on Foner's point, we know more about tariffs than the goods that made it past them; more about the destruction of the tropical rain forest than the marketing of mahogany; more about the export of Singer sewing machines than about imported silks; more about the United Fruit Company in the Caribbean than about the consumption of bananas; more about the exercise of U.S. military power than how that power affected daily life and consciousness in the United States; more about efforts to Americanize immigrants than to preserve their cultural traditions.[15] That is, we know more about the outgoing tide than the incoming swells. Much of our understanding of the United States in the world in this period combines W. T. Stead's emphasis on U.S. expansion with a characterization of American culture straight from Sinclair Lewis's *Main Street*.

Lewis published this novel in 1920, following a horrific war that left a wide swath of Europe in ruins. Though ostensibly about the fictitious town of Gopher Prairie, Minnesota, Lewis intended his novel as a commentary on small-town American life in general. "Its Main Street is the continuation of Main Streets everywhere. The story would be the same in Ohio or Montana, in Kansas or Kentucky or Illinois, and not very differently would it be told Up York State or in the Carolina hills." Rather than looking out, Main Street looked in. The residents led dull, unremarkable lives, marked by a smug sense of superiority. As Lewis ironically commented, "Main Street is the climax of civilization. That this Ford car might stand in front of the Bon Ton Store, Hannibal invaded Rome and Erasmus wrote in Oxford cloisters. What Ole Jensen the grocer says to Ezra Stowbody the banker is the new law for London, Prague, and the unprofitable isles of the sea; whatsoever Ezra does not know and sanction, that thing is heresy, worthless for knowing and wicked to consider." The sturdy farmers of Gopher Prairie might have had hundreds of years of European culture behind them, but for naught: their intellectual lives revolved around gossip and trivial daily matters; they manifested little curiosity about the wider world. Even in the middle of the Great War, the people of Main Street yawned and said the conflict was none of their business. For the stalwart local boosters and nationalists of Gopher Prairie, the good life meant a day at the lake. Main Street symbolized American provincialism.[16]

This does not mean that the denizens of Gopher Prairie were utterly isolated, of course. Not only did the farmers in the surrounding countryside export their grain to the far corners of the earth, but they also had culturally expansive ambitions. Lewis casts the provincialism of Gopher Prairie as slightly dangerous for precisely this reason: "A village in a country which is taking pains to become altogether standardized and pure, which aspires to succeed Victorian England as the chief mediocrity of the world, is no longer merely provincial, no longer downy and restful in its leaf-shadowed ignorance. It is a force seeking to dominate the earth, to drain the hills and sea of color. . . . Such a society functions admirably in the large production of cheap automobiles, dollar watches, and safety razors. But it is not satisfied until the entire world also admits that the end and joyous purpose of living is to ride in flivvers, to make advertising-pictures of dollar watches, and in the twilight to sit talking not of love and courage but of the convenience of safety razors."[17] The people of Gopher Prairie wanted to make everybody else just like them; to turn the entire world into one big Gopher Prairie, characterized by mass production, high levels of consumption, and commercial outlooks.

Along with harboring expansive tendencies, Gopher Prairie engaged with the wider world through the immigrants who settled there. Its Norwegians had colorful costumes and they cooked delicious food in their charming kitchens. But even these newcomers did not draw Gopher Prairie from its quintessential localism, for within a generation, they "Americanized into uniformity . . . losing in the grayness whatever pleasant new customs they might have added to the life of the town."[18] The ethnic heterogeneity of Gopher Prairie meant little in the long term, for its residents faced intense pressures for conformity.

Thanks to this novel, Main Street has become a synonym for American provincialism. But there is more to *Main Street* than navel-gazing, moralizing, and commercial assertiveness. What makes this book more than a caricature of local boorishness and imperial ambitions is Lewis's understanding that provincialism has another meaning. Yes, it can mean narrow-mindedness and homogeneity, the opposites of cosmopolitanism. But it also means being part of a province, that is, existing on the periphery of some larger, greater entity.[19] The main character, Carol Kennicott, brings this second dimension of provincialism to the fore.

Carol longs, with poignant desperation, for engagement with the wider world. As a young woman, she became enthusiastic about missionary work and dreamed of living in a settlement house. She read sociology texts covering village improvement in France. She went to the theater, to symphonies, to the Art Institute, to a bohemian party where a Russian Jewess sang the Internationale and free-mannered beer drinkers discussed Freud, feminism versus haremism, Chinese lyrics, and fishing in Ontario. And she continued to read: volumes of anthropology, Parisian imagistes, Hindu recipes for curry, voyages to the Solomon Isles. Once she even thought she might give up her work as a librarian and "turn a prairie town into Georgian houses and Japanese bungalows." Her friends liked to have her over because she could be depended upon to appreciate the Caruso phonograph record and the Chinese lantern from San Francisco. Yet for all of her fantasies, Carol wears sensible shoes. "Never did she feel that she was living."[20]

Then she married Dr. Will Kennicott and moved to Gopher Prairie, where she tried to cast herself as a counter to small-town insularity. She professed to prefer café parfait to beefsteak. She hired a Swedish maid, Bea, who served visitors from a Japanese tea set. For her first party, Carol turned her front and back parlors into an Orientalist spectacle, with a Japanese obi, a divan, and a vermilion print. She commanded her guests to don Chinese masquerade costumes from an import shop in Minneapolis. "Please forget that you are Minnesotans, and turn into mandarins and coolies and—and samurai (isn't it?), and anything else you can think of." Carol stunned her guests by appearing in trousers and a coat of green brocade edged with gold, her black hair pierced with jade pins, a languid peacock fan in her hand. She led the assemblage in a "Chinese" concert and then served "blue bowls of chow mein, with Lichee nuts and ginger preserved in syrup."[21]

Carol is noteworthy not only for her struggle against the village virus that turned her neighbors' gazes inward but also for her enthusiasm for the exotic. Unlike many of her neighbors, she regards the foreign with more appreciation than disdain. When her women's club covered Scandinavian, Russian, and Polish literature, one member condemned the "sinful paganism of the Russian so-called church." But Carol, ever in search of the picturesque and romantic, took pleasure in the Norwegian Bibles, dried cod for Ludfisk, and Scandinavian farmwives in a local store. She reveled in the "mild foreignness" of a Norwegian Fair at the Lutheran church. Whereas her friend Vida suggested presenting the high school with a full set of Stoddard's travel lectures because of their educational value, Carol saw the rest of the world as a means to pleasure. A visiting Chautauqua series made her fantasize about Syrian caravans. She dreamed of Venice, Buenos Aires, Brussels, and Tsing-tao. In contrast to Vida, who remarks, "I imagine gondolas are kind of nice to ride in, but we've got better bath-rooms!" Carol desires "startling, exotic things." She longs to be "a part of vast affairs, not confined to Main Street and a kitchen but linked with Paris, Bangkok, Madrid." She professes solidarity with the "Negro race and the Asiatic colonies" and finds happiness in a Chinese restaurant in Minneapolis that made her feel "altogether cosmopolitan."[22]

Looking back over the previous decades, Lewis tapped into a tension between small-town insularity and yearnings for connection to the wider world. His characterizations of Gopher Prairie do not refute Stead's depiction of the Americanizing juggernaut, but they complicate it. Through Carol, Lewis tells the other side of Stead's story: even as the United States gained a formal empire of direct political control and an informal empire of commercial and cultural influence, it was not impervious to the offerings of the rest of the world. Carol represents an intense desire to connect with larger currents. History is a matter of perspective as well as fact, and Lewis reminds us that the matter of Americanization might look somewhat different from home.

This book tells the story of the United States in the world at the turn of the twentieth century from a domestic perspective. It looks at quintessentially domestic places—middle-class American households—to find evidence of international connections. Rather than treat these households as thoroughly domestic, it treats them as contact zones. Appreciating the extent to which real homes served as places of encounter can help us reconsider the idea of the United States as home. Thus this book explores the foreign inflections of "home" in both senses of the word: households in particular and the nation more broadly.[23]

Recognizing that homes did not decorate themselves or invite their friends over for Orientalist teas, this book is also about the women charged with producing U.S. domesticity. These women did more than dumbly respond to prescriptive literature and the marketplace; they asserted agency through their shopping, decorating, and dining preferences and their choices of leisure and reform activities. I do not write about all American women, however. I focus on native-born, white, middle-class to wealthy women. These women were less likely to work outside their homes than American women in general and more likely to have the financial resources to lavish large sums on their houses, wardrobes, and entertainments. They were more likely to employ household help so they would be free to pursue leisure activities, and they were more likely to gain prominent positions as reformers, thanks to their social standing. So why do I focus on such a privileged, atypical group? Because these women served as symbols of U.S. domesticity, exercised considerable power in the marketplace, and raised many of the leaders of the American century.

I first came to appreciate the international dimensions of white, middle-class American women's daily lives when, in the course of researching my first book, I noticed numerous references to foreign people and countries on the women's pages of turn-of-the-century U.S. newspapers. Intrigued, I started sampling women's and family magazines from 1865 to 1920. There too, I found an abundance of international allusions: advice on buying imported products in the shopping columns, extensive coverage of Paris fashions in the sewing columns, news of European aristocrats in the gossip columns, recipes for dishes identified as foreign in the cooking columns, instructions for producing exotic theme parties in the entertainment and etiquette columns, and reports on overseas travel in the features pages. This surprised me, because I had always thought of the women who read such publications as somewhat narrow-minded and parochial. To be sure, I knew of upper-crust women's transnational activism on behalf of suffrage, temperance, peace, and other causes, but I nonetheless thought of white, middle-class housewives as primarily local in their leanings. After all, they were charged with responsibility for homemaking, inculcating patriotism in their children, and perpetuating the race. Furthermore, like their male associates, white, well-to-do women in this time period are known for their racism, nationalism, and missionary zeal for cultural transformation. Indeed, the same publications that brought the world into middle-class parlors contained articles on women's Americanizing endeavors at home and abroad. The tension between seemingly cosmopolitan and more limited outlooks begged for explanation.[24]

After further research, I divided this book into five chapters, focusing on international sensibilities as manifested through imported household objects, fashion, cooking and entertaining, armchair travel clubs, and the immigrant gifts movement. The first investigates how foreignness in household decoration came to seem desirable as an end in itself, both as an expression of cosmopolitanism and as a means to participate in empire. Besides linking cosmopolitan household interiors to U.S. political and commercial expansion, it attributes their rise to European, and especially British, imperialism. American housewives decorated their living rooms in Orientalist fashions because Europeans did so. Copying European styles provided opportunities to experience empire secondhand.

The second chapter covers the United States following of the Paris-based fashion system and the imagined communities it implied. Through their choice in clothes, fashionable women strove to demonstrate their affiliation with European aristocrats and other wealthy women from across the Western and westernizing world. But communities are about exclusion as well as inclusion. Just as their choices in dress helped women proclaim far-flung affinities, they also helped women proclaim their differences from less fashionable women, at home and abroad. In contrast to studies of identity formation that have emphasized the importance of local milieus, this chapter argues that fashionable women asserted their class, racial, national, and civilizational standing with an eye on far wider contexts. It finds that their sense of entitlement had global dimensions.

The third chapter considers imported foodstuffs, foreign recipes, and entertainments such as national theme meals and around-the-world dinners. It argues that food writings and cooking served as forms of popular geography, for they conveyed ethnographic lessons. Although some of these lessons taught contempt for other peoples (who reportedly ate disgusting, barbarously prepared foods), others stressed the foreign as a source of novelty and pleasure. Guides to producing exotic entertainments, which went far beyond foods to include decorations, costumes, and music, encouraged hostesses to celebrate their standing as privileged consumers in a global marketplace by faking foreignness in their homes.

The fourth chapter, on women's armchair travel clubs, builds on the theme of geographic consciousness. It explains the popularity of these clubs by situating them in a larger culture of fictive travel—involving everything from circuses to museums, travel lectures, worlds fairs, and church bazaars—and it discusses their role in advancing a tourist mentality, meaning a tendency to see the rest of the world as service providers.

The last chapter examines the Progressive Era immigrant gifts movement. This involved enthusiastic displays of immigrants' dances, songs, costumes, and handicrafts, in events typically directed by "old stock" Americans. Focusing on the gifts events produced by settlement house residents, Young Women's Christian Association (YWCA) affiliates, playground workers, librarians, and clubwomen, this chapter argues that colorful song and dance routines advanced pluralistic conceptions of citizenship by appealing to the consumerist valuation of novelty and difference. It contends that gifts promoters cherished difference all the more because they feared that the relentless tide of Americanization was effacing it.

The various chapters may hold particular appeal for those interested in household decoration, fashion, food, travel, and folk arts. But the point of these chapters is not curtains, clothing, or cooking per se. It is what such phenomena can tell us about the United States in world context. This preeminently female, domestic, consumption-oriented approach to understanding the United States in the world stands in stark contrast to foreign-relations histories emphasizing the preeminently male topics of diplomacy, the military, and manufacturing. But the fundamental premise of this book is that the traditional choice of subjects has advanced the Americanization-of-the-world argument while deflecting attention from the globalization of the United States. In focusing on the outward thrust of American power, historians have overlooked the extent to which the United States should be seen as a consumers' imperium.

What do I mean by "consumers' imperium"? First, this term refers to the importance of imports in shaping American domesticity. Histories of consumption tend to be national in scope, but this book reminds us that the national pie had foreign ingredients.[25] Even as it centers on the ingestion of that pie, this book urges us not to forget the foreign cooks who helped produce it and the foreign culinary traditions that influenced its flavor. It maintains that the much-vaunted American standard of living has depended on an imperial system of consumption.

While acknowledging that diplomacy, the military, and manufacturing affected consumers' abilities to buy imported goods, this book shifts our gaze from these relatively well-studied topics to the relatively unknown subjects of the imports themselves and their reception. Without rejecting the importance of policy making, military might, and economic expansion to U.S. power, it insists that consumption constituted a form of interaction with the wider world. Although in most cases consumption did not mean face-to-face encounters with foreign producers, each marketplace transaction provided a point of contact for people situated within vast webs of production, commerce, and wealth. Beyond reflecting larger relations of power, each purchase helped sustain a particular international political economy. Although this book does not pursue the ways in which consumer demand affected policy making, military engagement, and capital flows, it is of great relevance to those topics. Without the material desires of the consumers' imperium, there would have been no cause for policies, interventions, and investments aimed at gratifying consumer demand.

Given that the late nineteenth and early twentieth centuries were a heyday of empire, purchasing imports in this period can be seen as an act of imperial buy-in. Exporters, investors, missionaries, and militarists were not the only groups with an interest in empire: countless middle-class Americans had quite a lot at stake as well. Consumers participated in the formal empire of U.S. political control, the informal empire of U.S. commercial power, and the secondhand empire of European imperialism through shopping for trifles and savories. In contrast to those who experienced imperialism as a more menacing development entailing exploitation, impoverishment, and bloodshed, the consumers in this account experienced it as a collection of goods.

In addition to referring to the material base of American domesticity, consumer's imperium refers to an imagined realm of fantasy fulfillment. The following chapters pursue this aspect of the consumers' imperium by investigating the elaborate webs of meaning spun around imported household objects, Paris fashions, foreign foods, ersatz travel experiences, and immigrant performances. They find that consumerist outlooks led to a self-centered kind of engagement with the rest of the world that emphasized pleasure and novelty. Regarding empire from the perspective of stockholders rather than workers made it possible to ignore the costs of production incurred by distant, unseen peoples. Insofar as consumers acknowledged a less savory side to the rising U.S. empire, it was as a reference point to remind themselves just how fortunate they were.

Whereas the first meaning of consumers' imperium alludes to a literal but often tacit process of imperial buy-in, the second treats imperial buy-in as a more figurative but also more conscious process. If the first interprets empire as a matter of material goods, the second centers on the belief that imperialism was itself a good because of its role in creating distinction. Although the women I write about exercised social, cultural, and economic power over others, they were not political leaders or, in most cases, fully enfranchised citizens. Even as they seized the opportunities that were available to them, they had grounds to doubt whether they were in control of their own destinies. This explains much of the attraction of the consumers' imperium. The pleasure of boundless consumption deflected attention from the inequities encountered on the home front by reminding these women that, on a global scale of things, they occupied a position of privilege. The women who bought into the consumers' imperium sought not only tangible items but also a sense of empowerment.

For those interested in "big" topics like the United States in the world, this book may seem to deal in trivia: pottery, party dresses, recipes, travelogues, and pageants. But these things provide telling insights into U.S. history unappreciated by Stead and others who have stressed the Americanization of the world. By shifting attention from production to consumption, exports to imports, high politics to culture, pivotal events to daily life, and men to women, this book urges us to rethink the Americanization-of-the-world narrative. As it provides a historical grounding for the desires of the fictional Carol Kennicott and her real-life kindred spirits, it makes a case for the globalization of the United States reaching back well before the twentieth century. It maintains that empire was not just located out there, but that it had purchase at home, thanks to consumerist desires and fantasies. Ultimately, it collapses the distinction between "abroad" and "at home" by showing how they came together in the domestic realm of the consumers' imperium.

1

Cosmopolitan Domesticity, Imperial Accessories

Importing the American Dream

In the late nineteenth and early twentieth centuries, middle-class Americans commonly regarded household interiors as expressions of the women who inhabited them. As the author of a 1913 decorating manual put it, "We are sure to judge a woman in whose house we find ourselves for the first time, by her surroundings. We judge her temperament, her habits, her inclinations, by the interior of her home."[1] Motivated by that logic, American women with money to spend turned to their homes to define themselves.

One such woman, more typical in her taste than her extraordinary wealth, was Bertha Honoré Palmer. After the 1871 Chicago fire gutted the Palmer holdings, she and her millionaire husband invented themselves anew. They first rebuilt the Palmer House, a downtown hotel. In 1882 they started on a private residence, Palmer Castle, built on landfill fronting Lake Michigan. Contemporaries described the exterior as early English battlement style. Italian craftsmen laid the mosaic in the front hall, which set off the Gobelin tapestries on the wall. From there visitors could wander into the French drawing room, the Spanish music room, the English dining room, the Moorish ballroom, and the Flemish library. Upstairs, Bertha Palmer slept in a bedroom copied from a Cairo palace.[2] The Castle, no longer standing, was a Gilded Age spectacle, but a curious one in light of the principle of self-revelation. Given the tendency to regard domestic interiors as an expression of their occupants, what explains Bertha Palmer's efforts to stage the world in her household?

The story of the Palmers' Lake Shore Drive mansion, rising from a former swamp, dripping with tapestries and heavy chandeliers, is in part a story about class—of the desire to display abundant wealth, the ultimate intent being to secure a hold at the top of the social pyramid. Acquiring the mellowed trappings of aristocracy was a means to compensate for the rawness of post–Civil War fortunes, to distance one's dwelling from the vulgar commercialism that had enabled it to be built in the first place. (The Palmers' fortune rested on retailing, real estate, and their hotel.) In choosing to shop abroad as well as in the United States, Palmer underscored her purchasing power, for interiors filled with costly foreign goods arranged against seemingly foreign backdrops signified wealth. Elegant European rooms won particular favor, but high-style Oriental rooms also could be extremely expensive. In an 1897 story by novelist, society writer, and domestic advice purveyor Constance Cary Harrison, the poor Virginian has only to see the "Oriental magnificence," the "cushioned divans and filigree Moorish arches" of a New York apartment to fully comprehend its owner's fortune.[3]

Even though Palmer was extraordinarily affluent, her tastes were not limited to the super rich. Countless middle-class women adorned their parlors with Turkish curtains, French styles of furniture, and knickknacks from around the globe. Though millions of dollars away from Palmer's unattainable luxuries, these women nonetheless exhibited a relatively modest version of her far-reaching appetites. The housewife who draped a packing box with gaudy fabric in hopes of making an Oriental cosey corner was, as one decorating article pointed out, part of a trend that had, at its extreme, the "sumptuous and elegant affair found in the mansions of the wealthy."[4] No less significantly, this housewife was part of a design trend that encompassed Europe and that purportedly looked to the Near and Far East for its original inspiration.

Palmer and like-minded women undoubtedly wished to convey their economic standing through exhibiting imported objects and replicating distant styles, but their story is about more than just class. Through their households, these women strove to convey a cosmopolitan ethos—meaning a geographically expansive outlook that demonstrated a familiarity with the wider world. Their cosmopolitanism implied an appreciation of other peoples' artistic productions. But theirs was neither a universalist nor an egalitarian cosmopolitanism. It was a cosmopolitanism that contributed to particularistic racial, class, and national identities. Not only did it emerge from U.S. commercial and political expansion, but it helped promote it. This was a cosmopolitanism that celebrated empire, on the part of both the United States and the European powers.[5]

Cosmopolitan domesticity, seemingly paradoxical by definition, was at odds with some core nineteenth-century ideas about households. Tract writers commonly presented the home as a haven from the outside world. As John F. W. Ware, author of an 1866 treatise on home life declared, "A home is an enclosure, a secret, separate place, a place shut in from, guarded against, the whole world outside." Suburban homes in particular appeared as safe havens from the immigrants who swelled the cities and entered the most private sanctums of urban households in their capacities as servants. Yet urban homes also stood as bulwarks against the surging masses of city streets. Besides keeping the wider world out, homes were expected to keep middle-class women in. Ware, in full accord with many of his contemporaries, went on to pronounce the home "the peculiar sphere of woman. With the world at large she has little to do. Her influence begins, centres, and ends in her home."[6] Even those who found this vision of the home too restrictive, arguing instead that middle-class women should reach out from their homes to reform the wider society, joined with moralists such as Ware in presenting homes as fonts of racial, ethnic, local, and national identity. The shared assumption that homes were sheltered has obscured the extent to which they were firmly embedded in an international market economy. Nineteenth-century homes were loci not only of cultural production and reproduction but also of consumption, and in the period after the Civil War, much of this consumption had international dimensions.[7]

As the various theme rooms in Palmer's castle suggest, cosmopolitan domesticity encompassed design choices as well as imported objects. In the late nineteenth century, U.S. decorators looked primarily to France and Britain for inspiration. Contemporaries regarded many of the rococo styles of the Victorian period as fundamentally French, and they snatched up empire and Louis XIV, XV, and XVI furniture, done in varying degrees of accuracy. The press paid considerable attention to French design, and imported French goods could be counted on to seem chic. "The French have the flavor and the delicate discrimination that, as a nation, young America still lacks," wrote one Francophile in the *Art Interchange*.[8] British styles had an equally loyal following, especially after Charles L. Eastlake published his *Hints on Household Taste* in 1868. By 1881 the book had come out in its sixth American edition and U.S. shops were stocked with furniture passed off as "Eastlake style." Further testimony to Britain's influence can be seen in decorating magazines' glowing descriptions of English country homes.[9]

Along with French and British designs, other European styles found adherents. Among the sights found in U.S. houses were Italian, German, Dutch, Russian, Spanish, and Scandinavian theme rooms. The latter in-

this is happening again now

cluded Sara Bull's Norwegian room, the centerpiece of her colonial house in Cambridge, Massachusetts. From the red and black corner fireplace to the bread baskets and milk jugs, the room evoked the atmosphere of her late husband's Norwegian home.[10]

Although Europe exercised the greatest influence over U.S. decoration, not all theme rooms mimicked European dwellings. Decorators also drew on the Americas for inspiration, as seen in a "American Indian room" featuring curios from Mexico and Guatemala. "Many women of fashion have developed of late a fad for odd Oriental, South American, and Mexican belongings," noted the *Atlanta Constitution* in 1896. "Today no woman with a charming home considers it complete without some bits of Mexican ornament." This interest in seemingly traditional Central and South American objects intersected with the better-known enthusiasm for Native American rugs, pottery, and baskets.[11] Whether from New Mexico or across the border, craft objects with Native American inflections appealed to Anglo purchasers.

More common than Latin American themes and objects were Eastern ones, especially during the Orientalist craze that swept the nation from the 1870s to the turn of the century. Late nineteenth-century domestic Orientalism generally entailed fanciful productions passed off as Moorish, Turkish, Chinese, Japanese, or a combination thereof. This was not for everyone. Harriet Prescott Spofford made that clear in her 1877 book on home decoration, in which she said that Oriental designs would always seem fantastic in American homes and were best suited for "the very young and gay, and for those cosmopolitan people who are able to feel at home anywhere."[12] Despite—or what seems more likely, because of—its cosmopolitan associations, Orientalist design attracted a following among trendy homemakers. One enthusiast was Mme Theophile Prudhomme, a resident of New Orleans. She returned from a trip to the Far East entranced by what she had seen. So she created a Japanese room with screens, fans, mats, vases, and tea sets. It was so "rich in the colors and perfumes of the land of the 'cherry blossom'" that a visiting reporter imagined herself as "indeed in Japan instead of a boudoir in far-off New Orleans."[13] A simpler interpretation of Japanese style can be seen in a five-room California bungalow profiled in the *House Beautiful*. This had sliding doors, walls painted in bamboo color, woven floor matting, and Japanese lanterns (ill. 1.1).[14]

Decorators who lacked the wherewithal to turn an entire room into an Orientalist spectacle could still partake of the craze by producing an Orientalist "cosey corner." These typically consisted of an upholstered divan, a profusion of cushions, a rug, a Turkish coffee table, a few decorative ob-

Sliding Doors to Resemble Fusima   Walls Painted Bamboo Color   Old Rush Furniture Painted Black

1.1. Mary Rutherford Jay, "A Bungalow in Japanese Spirit," *House Beautiful* 32 (Aug. 1912): 72. Courtesy of the Winterthur Library: Printed Book and Periodical Collection, Winterthur, Delaware.

jects (such as screens, fans, lanterns, and pottery), and lush draperies to frame the entire ensemble. (Textiles played such an important role that a fabric company—sensing profit—published a booklet with instructions for making four different cosey corners.)[15] Some cosey corners struck viewers as essentially Japanese or Chinese, but most looked primarily to the Middle East for inspiration. It is difficult to gauge the exact extent of their appeal, but they did spring up across the country. In 1897 a New York City couple constructed an Orientalist platform on one side of their apartment's parlor. Another New York City apartment clustered tropical plants and Eastern textiles around a corner divan (ill. 1.2). A Chicago householder added a large parasol, spears, and fans to the basic arrangement (ill. 1.3). A Houston cosey corner had a pile of inviting pillows and an inlaid Turkish chair and table. A Denver cosey corner took up the bulk of a front hall. In the cold reaches of Montana, a teenager created a modest one in her bedroom. A woman heading to Argentina to work as a schoolteacher may have tried to produce one on shipboard, judging from the comments of an English passenger: "An American girl could contrive to make a desert look homelike, with a couple of Japanese fans."[16] Even the *Good Housekeeping* article that denounced cosey corners as a tasteless fad provides evidence of their popularity (ill. 1.4).[17]

The interest evinced by U.S. decorators in far parts of the globe differentiates the post–Civil War period from earlier eras. This is not to overlook the China trade and the enthusiasm for chinoiserie stretching back to the time when porcelain served as ballast for homeward-bound sailing ships or

1.2. New York cosey corner, from William Martin Johnson, *Inside of One Hundred Homes* (1898), 44. Courtesy of the Winterthur Library: Printed Book and Periodical Collection, Winterthur, Delaware.

1.3. Chicago cosey corner, from William Martin Johnson, *Inside of One Hundred Homes* (1898), 54. Courtesy of the Winterthur Library: Printed Book and Periodical Collection, Winterthur, Delaware.

1.4. "This is the Bride's Cozy Corner," *Good Housekeeping* 41 (Oct. 1905): 385. Courtesy of the Winterthur Library: Printed Book and Periodical Collection, Winterthur, Delaware.

¶ This is the Bride's Cozy Corner. Is it Cozy? No, the Corner is not Cozy. Then why is the Bride Pleased? Be-cause it is a Fad. The Bride has not learned that Fads in poor Taste pass soon.

the scattered experimentation with other "Oriental" styles before the Civil War. But Chinese imports and chinoiserie of Western manufacture had been available to a comparatively narrow segment of the population, and other non-European design traditions failed to attract more than a modicum of interest.[18] In the last decades of the nineteenth century, by contrast, a wider section of the American public had access to non-European imports, and taste makers touted products and styles from a broader expanse of the globe.

The popularity of Orientalist designs makes Bertha Palmer's Moorish hall and bedroom seem somewhat less extraordinary. Novel though they may have appeared to the unsophisticated, they were fully in keeping with the design trends of her day. So was her mixing and matching of styles. Although some home furnishers favored a particular style, others turned their homes into virtual world tours. Like Palmer, these decorators crafted a series of nationally styled theme rooms.

Fashionable middle-class housewives (on whose shoulders fell the brunt of decorating responsibility) could struggle to produce a theme room or two, but only with great difficulty, and an entire ensemble of them lay far beyond grasp. But there was no need to despair. Just as a cosey corner could substitute for an Orientalist salon, a parlor stuffed with things from around the world could stand in for a series of national theme rooms. Late nineteenth-century design writings favorably profiled dwellings that mixed German tankards with French chairs and Persian embroideries; an Egyptian ceiling with Celtic ornaments and statues of Buddha; Moorish grillwork with a Louis XV chandelier, Swiss clocks, and a Florentine cabinet.[19] "All nations are represented" enthused a *Good Housekeeping* article on a Philadelphia dining room.[20] That such mixing was not limited to the mansions of the very wealthy can be seen in a profile of a small city apartment that combined Turkish brass, Japanese tables, a Chinese cabinet, carved gourds from Central America, a Mexican fan, a Breton vase, a Bohemian chalice, and posters from Paris and London. "Decorative art in this country is essentially eclectic, drawing from every available source," claimed an 1886 essay.[21]

An eclectic mixture might be easier to pull off than a series of theme rooms, but it still took money to gather the Buddhas, the furs, and the feathers. The housewife who found even an eclectic ensemble out of her grasp might have been tempted to throw her hands up in despair or fill her parlor with cattails, ferns, and ivy. But there was hope for the would-be decorator with just a modest discretionary income. Individual items, including such small decorative pieces as ceramics, fans, and pillows, could give a humdrum household a cosmopolitan aura. Only the richest of the rich could afford a series of lavish theme rooms done in various national styles, but photographs and descriptions of middle-class households from the late nineteenth century typically reveal at least a handful of objects that served as symbols of far-reaching tastes.

The appeal of imports, particularly from outside Europe, seems to fly in the face of the claims that households should represent the women within them. It seems even odder given the provincialism associated with white, native-born, middle-class American women in this period. This was, after all, an era of rampant white supremacist ideas and practices, lynchings, the disfranchisement of African American voters, and the entrenchment of Jim Crow. Historians have characterized the 1870s as a decade in which native-born Americans had faith in the assimilation of newcomers, but rising xenophobia in the 1880s and 1890s led to calls for immigration restriction. Many white Americans worried about the "yellow peril," that is, about being overrun by Asian workers so poorly paid that they would undercut American wages. The 1882 Chinese Exclusion Act prohibited practically all Chinese from immigrating to the United States, and in the 1908 Gentleman's Agreement, President Theodore Roosevelt arranged to limit immigration from Japan. Chinese Americans and Japanese Americans faced hostility and discrimination; they were ineligible for naturalized citizenship and, in many cases, isolated from European Americans in Chinatowns and Japantowns. In keeping with this anti-immigrant backlash, nativistic "purity" campaigns took off in the late nineteenth century. Concerned about the moral corruption of women and children, the antivice crusader Anthony Comstock blamed foreigners and immigrants for obscenity. The Woman's Christian Temperance Union had a Department of Purity in Literature and Art that campaigned against "Parisian indecency" and Oriental dancers at carnivals and fairs.[22] The fin-de-siècle obsessions with racial separation, immigration restriction, and purity all represent boundary-building efforts aimed at keeping difference at bay.

Along with circling the wagons, those who regarded difference as dangerous worked to make the world around them more like home. Reformers strove to "Americanize" Native Americans, immigrants, and others by teaching them their own narrow-minded visions of American domesticity. Americanizers expounded their visions of domesticity outside the United States as well. U.S. missionaries shipped household goods all the way to China so they could model their versions of home life to potential converts. Similarly, American colonizers in the Philippines strove to reproduce the homes they had left behind in order to insulate themselves from the surrounding culture and to teach what they saw as proper domesticity to the Filipinos.[23]

Given this context of shoring up domestic boundaries and Americanizing the world, why did so many late nineteenth- and early twentieth-century U.S. decorators embrace foreign theme rooms, eclecticism, and imports? Leisure travel deserves some of the credit. Although foreign tourism remained a hallmark of wealth, rising numbers of Americans ventured abroad in the late nineteenth century. "There was nothing remarkable in going to Europe," said novelist Robert Herrick in his characterization of a wealthy Chicago woman. "One went to hear an opera, to order a few gowns, to fill out an idle vacation."[24] And as the unfolding story made clear, one went to shop for household goods. Bertha Palmer had some company when she toted her treasures back to Illinois.

Indeed, numerous writings aimed at would-be tourists drew attention to the shopping opportunities that awaited them at their destinations. Such writings commonly noted that tourists could purchase costly items for a small fraction of their domestic price if they traveled to the point of origin. *Harper's Weekly*, for example, reported on the nominally priced pottery in Egyptian bazaars and the charming baskets to be had for a few centimes in Martinique. The *Chicago Tribune* strayed even farther afield when it provided advice on the porcelain in the "Pekin" curio market. More commonly, metropolitan newspapers ran advertisements for London and Paris shops that sold Oriental carpets, Irish linens, and other household goods. These advertisements targeted the growing number of Americans who had the means to cross the Atlantic, called the "six-day pond" by knowing travelers who had made the trip. Articles and advertisements that provided counsel on overseas shopping destinations assumed that middle-class and wealthy Americans were in a position to take full advantage of the world's marketplaces.[25]

Along with pleasure-seeking tourists, the missionaries, government agents, professionals, and businessmen who made overseas trips brought back furniture and smaller decorative items. In service of the consumers' imperium, naval officers doubled as purchasing agents: Ulysses S. and Julia Grant had a friend, Captain Daniel Anmen, order them a 315-piece Cantonese dinner service on an 1868 voyage to China.[26]

Globe-trotters might have been able to find the greatest bargains, but even stay-at-homes found imported wares increasingly within their grasp. After falling by more than half during the Civil War, ocean shipping rebounded in the postwar years. Although domestic manufacturers supplied the majority of household goods, an unprecedented amount of imports entered the country. According to official trade figures, U.S. imports of wool carpets rose from less than $900,000 in 1865 to more than $2.7 million in 1900 and $13.6 million in 1920. (This factor of fifteen increase dwarfed the factor of two increase in the consumer price index from 1865 to 1920.) As for earthen, stone, and china ware, the United States imported roughly $2 million worth in 1865, $8.6 million in 1900, and $11.6 million in 1920. Imports of household furniture rose too—from less than $200,000 in 1865 to almost $400,00 in 1900 and $1.9 million in 1920.[27] And these are just some of the categories of imported goods: baskets, cutlery, brass, silver, curtains, laces, glassware, towels, linens, clocks, and so forth also entered the United States.

In the late nineteenth century, middle-class and wealthy American consumers had access to products produced around the world, ranging from Argentine lamp shade covers to Aztec relics, Belgian linen, Bohemian glass, Brazilian hammocks, German cooking ware, Hungarian pitchers, Javanese batiks, Norwegian pottery, Puerto Rican drawn work, Singapore malacca, and Zulu baskets. Recognizing the abundance of imported goods in American shops, the *New York Tribune* counseled Europe-bound tourists not to spend too much time hunting for distinctive gifts. "There are not many things, after all, to be bought in Europe which cannot be found in our own shops."[28] The woman who hauled the skins of various antelopes back from South Africa provided a lesson to the unsophisticated traveler as well as a testimonial to American abundance: upon her return, she reportedly discovered that she could have secured identical pelts "with less trouble and expense" in a local department store.[29]

Although antelope pelts and other imports could be found most readily in the department stores that were gaining a prominent role in American retailing, intrepid shoppers also found imports off the beaten retail path. Specialty shops that sold Oriental goods sprang up in a number of cities. A. A. Vantines sold everything from Russian finger bowls to Japanese dinner gongs, Egyptian bookends, and Chinese teakwood furniture in its New York emporium and Chicago branch. (Bertha Palmer purchased her Oriental goods at Vantines as well as at the Oriental Importing Company and the Japanese Trading Company.) Other cities had their own establishments. New Orleans shoppers, for example, had at least three vendors of Oriental wares: Hop Kee and Company, Wokee and Company, and Tackita Loy's. In 1884 another New Orleans store, Shwartz and Son, had a "Grand Oriental Exhibition" featuring novelties imported for the World's Exhibition.[30] Besides visiting Chinatown for the best selection of Oriental shops, New Yorkers could purchase household goods from cash-strapped European immigrants who peddled family heirlooms on the street. World's fairs did more than expose tourists to design trends; they also offered shopping opportunities. The closing days of expositions offered bonanzas to bargain seekers, who snatched up samples that had once been on display.[31]

Outside of large cities, shoppers had fewer choices, but they nonetheless had access to a wide variety of imported and foreign-seeming household products. An article in the *New York Tribune*, aimed at shaming city sophisticates, maintained that small towns actually sold higher-quality Oriental items. The explanation for this surprising assertion was that purchasers for large urban establishments pounced on mongrel goods, vitiated for the American taste, leaving the more genuine items for merchants from smaller towns. Catalogs offered another way for small-town residents to purchase imported products. Vantine's presented its catalog as an aid to those who could not "personally visit" their establishment. The John Wanamaker's catalog had a section titled: "From the Japanese Store." The Matsumoto-Do

Company mailed goods direct from Tokyo for an advertised postage rate of twelve cents a pound.[32] In 1915 Denver had twenty-six curio shops. A New Mexico mail-order firm that sold Mexican and American Indian handicrafts attracted buyers from more than twenty different states, ranging from Alaska to New Hampshire, Alabama to Wisconsin. The thousands of pack peddlers—Syrian immigrants prominent among them—who crisscrossed the country hawked exotic bric-a-brac as well as practical supplies.[33]

Along with an increasing availability of material goods, this period was notable for rising awareness of foreign conventions of interior design. One writer attributed the sudden popularity of cosey corners to the seemingly benign phenomenon of geographic awareness: "Only within the last decade have we become sufficiently well acquainted with these same neighbors to feel at liberty to borrow from them."[34] Ignoring how it was that American women had managed to become acquainted with their Eastern "neighbors" and what forms this acquaintance took, this writer tried to locate cosey corners in the realm of the sentimental. But there was nonetheless something to her claims of feeling well acquainted. The middle-class public learned about decoration from a variety of sources, including paintings, photographs, museums, missionary presentations, manufacturing displays, ethnographic writings, and arts and crafts of the homelands exhibits focusing on immigrant folk arts. World's fairs showcased foreign goods to such an extent that a visitor to the 1876 Philadelphia exposition reported feeling that he had "landed in some large Chinese bazaar" (ill. 1.5).[35]

Just as overseas travel provided greater access to goods, it also played an important role in disseminating decorating knowledge. Tourists did more than fill their trunks with foreign treasures; they became conduits of information. They saw new styles in hotels and homes alike, and their sightseeing expeditions took them to upscale manufacturing establishments. Upon their return, they reported on what they had seen. The numerous travel accounts published in newspapers and magazines exposed wide circles of Americans to disparate styles. An *Outing* magazine article on Canton, "The Paris of China," serves as an example. It reported on the silver filigree work, lacquered ware, porcelain, and sandalwood found in local shops. As for households, it took note of the shrines, ebony chairs, mattings, and silken lanterns they contained. Decorating articles credited tourism with influencing domestic design when they argued that travel would inevitably lead to greater variety in furnishings. "Travel broadens the mind and makes it more hospitable to new ideas," claimed one such article, "hence the furnishing accessories of foreign countries, with their unexpected designs and colorings, become more and more appreciated."[36] The more that Ameri-

1.5. "The Chinese Court—Celestial Exhibitors Explaining Their Wares," in
Frank Leslie's Illustrated Historical Register of the Centennial Exposition (1876), 84.
Courtesy of the Rare Book and Special Collections Library, University of Illinois
at Urbana-Champaign.

cans ventured beyond their borders, the more they learned of the wider
world, and the more they coveted what they saw.

Interior decorators, then the path-breaking members of a new profession that catered to the wealthy, played a particularly important role in pro-
mulgating knowledge of foreign design. The most sought after professional
decorators had traveled as part of their education, and they were more likely
than the average householder to stay current with European tastes. A fea-

ture on decorator Virginia Brush, from New York City, mentioned that she liked the French method for salons and English style for libraries. She also excelled "marvelously" in Japanese designs. Every year she spent a few months in Europe, visiting London, Paris, and Vienna. In these cities, she collected the "newest of materials—the fashions that prevail in furniture."[37] If familiarity with foreign styles helped decorators such as Brush promote their craft, the elegant rooms they created furthered the appeal of foreign styles.

Those who could not afford to hire a decorator could still find plenty of professional advice. There was an explosion of writing about interior decoration in the late nineteenth century, in keeping with the expansion of the popular press. The *Decorator and Furnisher* (aimed at both trade readers and householders) depicted exquisite interiors starting in 1882; the *House Beautiful* and *House and Garden* followed on its heels. Women's magazines that did not specialize in decoration, including the *Ladies' Home Journal*, *Godey's Magazine*, and *Good Housekeeping*, offered decorating advice on occasion, as did family magazines such as *Frank Leslie's* and art magazines such as the *Art Amateur*, the *Art Interchange*, and *Arts and Decoration*. Daily newspapers addressed the subject too, especially on their women's pages, and publishers turned out handsome decorating treatises and straightforward handbooks. In contrast to decorating guides from the mid-nineteenth century, which tended to advocate the creation of distinctly American homes, those of the post–Civil War period had wider outlooks. Purveyors of decorating advice reprinted stories from European design magazines and reported on foreign design developments, thereby widening readers' horizons. And they advocated foreign styles for American households, including those of modest means.[38]

The role of decoration writings in making the tastes of the rich accessible to middle-class readers can be seen in their treatment of cosey corners. The *Ladies Home Journal* described one that could be made for ten dollars. And there were even cheaper versions. Julia Darrow Cowles—who boldly proclaimed that "Cozy corners have come to stay" in an 1898 book on household decoration—counseled the cost-conscious to stuff their pillows with milkweed if possible, new-mown hay and pine shavings if necessary.[39] But what to use for upholstery? Experts encouraged women with Indian shawls, in vogue before the Civil War, to dig them out of their trunks and cut them up. Even a woman without a corner could put something together, as a piece on fixing one up on the back of a piano demonstrated (ill. 1.6).[40]

Along with instructing middle-class decorators on matters of style, decoration writers taught them to be cognizant of provenance. Instead of "cur-

1.6. "Cozey Corner Decoration for Back of Piano," from James Thomason, "Piano Decorations," *Decorator and Furnisher* 25 (Oct. 1894): 31. Courtesy of the Winterthur Library: Printed Book and Periodical Collection, Winterthur, Delaware.

tains" they favored "Baghdad curtains," instead of rugs, "Oriental rugs," or even better, Turkish, Persian, Bukhara, Caucasian, and other geographically identified rugs. (This is not to say that a Bukhara rug was necessarily from Bukhara—some were just shipped from there, others were made elsewhere in Central Asia but in designs that rug dealers thought typified the Bukhara region. A Bukhara rug might even be made in the United States, after the Bukharan fashion.) Although its accuracy could be questioned, the expansive decorating literature of the postwar period made a point of identifying origins, and many of the products it featured were foreign. Agnes Bailey Ormsbee, author of *The House Comfortable*, provided the kind of purchasing advice typical of late nineteenth-century domestic writing. She counseled her discriminating readers to buy Irish and French damask, Scottish linen, English porcelain, Japanese china (she warned against the imitations from New Jersey), Turkish towels, Indian fabrics, Chinese rattan, and Turkistani, Daghestani, Smyrna, and other Oriental rugs.[41] By paying so much attention to origins, decoration experts heightened the appeal of products manufactured outside the United States.

Merchants too touted the attractions of foreign goods and styles. "Rare Specimens of Ceramic Art from All Countries," proclaimed one *Atlanta Constitution* advertisement. "The Cairo rug which has only lately been imported to any extent, is coarse and heavy, but it conveys an unmistakable sense of the orient," counseled a shopping guide that assumed readers would want a "sense of the orient" to emanate from their floors. Likewise, a catalog company that sold Mexican handicrafts assumed that consumers appreciated foreignness, for it maintained that its "zerapes" had "a distinctly foreign air."[42] The John Wanamaker's catalog that drew attention to the "large number of Wanamaker buyers who crossed the ocean looking for goods to stock" and the F. P. Bhumgara and Company furniture advertisements that mentioned the company's offices in Bombay, Madras, Calcutta, and London also reflected the assumption that American buyers appreciated imports.[43] Rather than downplaying its location, for fear that xenophobic consumers would shy away, a Japanese mail-order firm cast its foreignness as its greatest asset: "'Things Japanese,' that are peculiarly characteristic of Nippon, or as we call them, *wasei* (native make) can not be obtained in other countries. The original articles must be bought here."[44] Even goods manufactured in the United States—like a suite of Boston-made bedroom furniture advertised as being made of Cuban mahogany, following English ideas, with Egyptian cloth—lured consumers with the cachet of cosmopolitanism.[45] The bedroom suite may have been manufactured domestically, but it brought to mind connections with distant parts of the world.

Although advertisements and decoration writings sometimes stressed the cost savings offered by imports, they more frequently associated imports with quality. In an age of machine-made products, many imports seemed appealingly handmade—one-of-a kind rather than standardized.[46] But if decorators just wanted handmade items, they could have surrounded themselves with cross-stitch, Shaker chairs, and the like. Advertisements that stressed the desirability of having genuine foreign articles rather than merely attractive or expensive ones assumed that foreignness itself was a large part of the appeal of imports.

In keeping with this appreciation of foreignness, decoration experts urged shoppers to buy goods that expressed authentic foreign taste. Japanese goods, maintained decorating expert Harriet Prescott Spofford, appealed to Americans because they had not been "injured by European demands . . . in buying a Japanese article we are tolerably sure of getting something according to the aboriginal idea."[47] The attractions of authenticity also can be seen in statements lamenting the tendency to buy Japanese goods made especially for the Western market. Decoration writers urged shoppers to buy authentically foreign objects because of the "change they impart to the mind. . . . The effect is somewhat similar to that of travel, in which the strangest things have the greatest charm."[48] Almost as important as design authenticity (or, at the least, the assumption of authenticity) was seemingly authentic display. Hence one decorating manual counseled readers to place their Oriental rugs about "in true Eastern style."[49] The point went well beyond taking advantage of foreign artistic capacities to entail crafting a house that was not really domestic, in the national sense, at all.

1.7. Whittall Rugs advertisement, *House Beautiful* 28 (Oct. 1910): xiii. Courtesy of the Winterthur Library: Printed Book and Periodical Collection, Winterthur, Delaware.

Imports had so much cachet that decorating magazines reported on high-end retailers who duped purchasers as to the provenance of their goods, "representing them as from England, France, almost any country excepting our own."[50] Realizing the prestige of European affiliations, devious retailers spuriously claimed connections with a home office in London or Paris. "These foreign offices are often entirely imaginative," reported a supporter of domestic manufacture, who was disgusted by consumers' gullibility and craving for European gloss.[51] In a similar effort to capitalize on foreignness, purveyors of Oriental rugs embellished their advertisements with pictures of berobed and turbaned men, camels, pyramids, and reclining Oriental women. Even the Whittall Rug Company, a Worcester, Massachusetts, firm, filled its advertisements with pictures of Arabs, camels, and palm trees in order to cash in on the desire for products that seemed exotic (ill. 1.7).[52] If the decorating objective was foreignness, then the more foreign the better, and non-European touches struck Euro-Americans as the most foreign of all.

Although decorators, design writers, and merchants certainly deserve credit for advancing domestic cosmopolitanism, to attribute its popularity solely to their influence is to downplay the choices made by countless middle-class women. To understand more fully the appeal of cosmopolitan interiors, we need to go beyond the urgings of design experts and vendors and attempt the difficult task of determining what foreign goods meant to consumers. Shopping, at once so commonplace and so ephemeral, did not result in routine record keeping of what attracted buyers to their purchases. Nor did most householders keep notes on why they decorated as they did or what effect they were trying to attain. The intentions and resonances of household interiors no doubt varied as much as the individuals who crafted them. But even without the help of voluminous shopping and decorating diaries, descriptions of household interiors and the objects they contained can help us deduce much about their meanings. And even if we recognize the multiplicity of motives behind particular decorating choices, we still can draw conclusions about larger patterns.

What did foreign interiors evoke? Householders who mixed goods from around the globe had grounds to regard their interiors as daringly artistic. Decoration magazines often raved about the mismatched contents of avant-garde studios, thus associating eclecticism with artists, actresses, and other bohemians. An expatriate American painter living in Rome lived up to the stereotype of the cosmopolitan artist: the walls of his studio were "covered with many and many a thing of beauty, every part of the earth from Norway to Japan having contributed something."[53] Sarah Bernhardt, the famous French actress who made nine triumphant tours of the United States between 1880 and 1918, had a notably artistic studio in Paris. Indian weapons, Mexican hats, and Chilean umbrellas crafted from feathers adorned the walls. Furs of bears, beavers, and buffaloes lay strewn on the divan, along with a less inviting alligator skin. Separated from the drawing room by a curtain of beads was a little Japanese salon. Mabel Dodge Luhan demonstrated a comparable catholicism in her tastes. After keeping a palacio in Florence, she became a prominent member of the Greenwich Village avant-garde. But at the end of World War I, she left New York for the Southwest. In Taos she built a house that mixed French sofas and Mexican chairs, Navajo rugs and Italian tables, Buddhas and Virgins. The striking mix identified her as a woman not beholden to narrow conventions, as a woman open to the artistry of the world.[54]

Although artistic studios resembled museums and department stores in their eclectic display, they were not intended as symbols of scientific rationality or commercial values. Instead, contemporaries understood them as protests against conventionality, as expressions of a sometimes shocking open-mindedness, ease, sensuality (think of Bernhardt's divan with the pile of pelts on it), and even decadence. Instead of exhibiting a strong desire for conformity to standards of respectability, such interiors showed a powerful desire to flaunt these standards.[55] These interiors conveyed not just class authority but also individual personality. There is a certain irony in expressing one's individuality through exotic goods admittedly disassociated with the self, but the householders who strove for a cosmopolitan decor aimed to express a fluid individuality, notable for its receptivity to wider currents and outside influences.

Admonished to maintain group boundaries through their sexual purity, social exclusiveness, and standards of consumption, the women who favored cosmopolitan interiors crossed racial, class, and national boundaries in their search for individual expression. Their decorative schemes revealed a desire for autonomy. Ironically, the yearnings for personal freedom can be seen most clearly in harem-like Orientalist settings. An American woman who recounted how she learned to sit on a divan illuminates the tendency to regard Orientalist design as a means of female liberation. She acquired the skill in Constantinople, at a reception given by an Armenian lady, recently emancipated and consequently able to receive mixed company. When the American woman "proceeded to seat herself," she did so "gingerly upon the very edge, with two neat little toes carefully balanced to touch the floor." At this point a Greek guest laughed and "begged permission to give a few lessons in the art of using a couch. 'Sit on your foot,' he commanded; 'curl it comfortably under you, so. Now be seated, far back, build a wall of cushions about your shoulders, and know true happiness.'" The daringness of this pose can be seen by contrasting it to an essay, "A Proper Way to Sit," published in the *Ladies Home Journal*. This admonished readers to seat themselves stiffly, their spines straight. The divan-sitter was well aware of prevailing rules of deportment, but she had the temerity to pooh-pooh them: "Once visit the far East, and old prejudices concerning the vulgarity of sitting on your foot are promptly dissipated." With practice, she concluded, the Turkish mode of sitting was more graceful and comfortable than the proper Western way.[56] In this account, the Oriental interior is not the locus of oppression—the Armenian woman, after all, was recently emancipated—but of the liberation of the American woman who overcame her primness, old prejudices, and aloofness by following a command to assume an Oriental posture.

Another account that illuminates the attraction of Orientalist niches for American housewives is the story of "Miss Muffin and Mr. Turk," printed in the *House Beautiful*. "Our big stuffed armchair . . . is openly polygamous," asserted the anonymous author. "Why shouldn't he be? He is a Turkish chair. He typifies the Pagan attitude toward life. We cannot openly approve of him, but we can't help liking him in our heart of hearts. He is so good-humored. . . . He is as comfortable as a summer day, as cosy as a winter evening." In the process of redecorating, the author purchased another chair, an antique of black walnut. "She was evidently a lady, for furniture, of course, has sex. She was amusingly homely, and perfectly self-satisfied with her looks; dowdy without being snuffy, clean without being dainty, she reminded us of nothing so much as a dependent dowager or an upper class London land-lady, insistent on her respectability and her social rights. In fact, she was inexpressibly British, and we weren't surprised to learn that, when a young chair, she had come from England to the States." After introducing the two anthropomorphized characters, the author moved on to the dilemma: "We had planned to place Miss Middle Class Muffin next to our fat old Turk, but how would they get along together? We could imagine British respectability oozing from every pore. To relieve the reader's suspense we hasten to say that they took to each other at once, and that they get on famously. Perhaps in the depths of Miss Muffin's linsey-woolsey heart, there burns a spark of desire for a free, wild life of adventure, and probably our fat old Turk long since grew tired of perfumed, sweetmeat-eating odalisques, and he appreciates the toast-browning, slipper-warming, domestic virtues. To us, the friendship between the pair seems quite romantic."[57]

This story of cultural mixing illuminates what American housewives saw in their Turkish acquisitions: shock value, difference, physical pleasure, and a "free, wild life of adventure." The household Turk could serve as a foil to middle-class status, respectability, passionlessness, industry, and domesticity. When uprooted from their pagan and English contexts and placed in an American household, the Turk and Muffin engendered romance. They offered an imaginative escape from the strictures that bound white, middle-class American women's lives. They promised an unbounded world of romantic self-fulfillment. They promised cosmopolitanism.

It may seem logical to associate cosmopolitan sensibilities with New Yorkers and other eastern sophisticates, with their vast emporiums and transatlantic ties, but as Palmer's example suggests, cosmopolitanism may have had a particularly urgent appeal to people who regarded themselves as being on the fringes of culture. In "Social Life in Chicago," an article aimed at establishing that the Windy City was not so backward after all, the author insisted that there were more beautiful houses in Chicago than in Boston, New York, and Philadelphia. To prove this point, she insisted that the

Chicago woman "travels the world over" to decorate her house. The result? "Rooms correct in every detail in the Indian, Japanese and Pompeiian manner, and in the well-known French periods."[58] A San Francisco writer made similar claims about her city in a report on a recently built mansion, modeled after the Chambord castle in France. "Nothing used in its construction is of Pacific Coast production. The marble is from Italy, the oak carvings from England, the woods from France, San Domingo and the Indies, the plate glass from Belgium, the tapestries from Germany . . . the furniture from Paris and New York, and New York decorators ransacked Europe for designs and art treasures for the interior."[59] If residents of Chicago and San Francisco felt a more pressing need to demonstrate Europeanness than New Yorkers, who could take pride in older money, world-class furniture outlets, and nationally known decorators, then residents of smaller towns and rural areas may have felt the desire to display cosmopolitan sophistication more keenly still. Women who sat on their porches on stifling small-town summer evenings, listening to the drawn-out whistles of distant trains, had depths to their cosmopolitan yearnings that city dwellers could only imagine.

Carol Kennicott, the frustrated housewife in Sinclair Lewis's *Main Street*, illuminates such feelings of dissatisfaction. Feeling like she is stuck in dullsville, she longs for mystery and romance, for a feeling of connectedness with the wider world. On a more prosaic level, she craves consumer choices unavailable in Gopher Prairie. When not dreaming of escaping from her conventional and predictable surroundings, she adds Orientalist touches, such as a Japanese tea set, obi panel, and a divan to her home. "Every one in town took an interest in the refurnishing," commented Lewis, but Carol eventually finds out that they did not unequivocally approve of it. On first glance at the vermilion print hanging against the Japanese obi, Julius Flickerbaugh, the attorney, gasped: "Well, I'll be switched." Later, a neighbor asks if her divan "is too broad to be practical?" Her friend Vida informs Carol that the local housewives not only "think the broad couch and that Japanese dingus are absurd" but regard her as eccentric. (This is the same friend who later says: "I don't want to see any foreign culture suddenly forced on us.")[60] Such criticisms stung, but they also confirmed Carol's point: unlike her neighbors, she appreciated the artistic currents of the day. She refused to be satisfied with local standards, for her frame of reference was global.

In response to those who claimed that women's appropriate sphere was the home, cosmopolitan decorators reconceptualized their homes so they encompassed the world. Their exotic interiors brought to mind men's ability to travel. Through purchasing foreign goods, homebound women could associate themselves with globe-trotters. As for those who actually had traveled, stuffing their households with souvenirs was a way to reify their rambling. The knickknack acquired in a foreign bazaar served not only as evidence that one had the financial means to travel but, just as importantly, that one had the freedom, inclination, and physical ability to do so. The Atlanta woman who mixed Persian silk, Spanish leather, French china, and Venetian glass in her dining room could feel confident that her neighbors regarded her as cultured and adventuresome as well as rich when her local paper noted that she had brought her china and glass back "from abroad."[61]

Besides evoking overseas destinations, cosmopolitan interiors evoked public spaces within the United States. Ostensibly foreign styles appeared in, among other places, world's fairs, amusement parks, department stores, music halls, casinos, and theaters. The Montana Club in Helena had a Turkish room. The New York Armory had Moorish rooms; Masonic temples sometimes had Persian themes. Murray's Restaurant, on Broadway in New York City, had Roman, Egyptian, and Gothic banquet rooms. Nearby, the Hoffman House Hotel had Oriental apartments on the first floor—one Chinese, one Indian, one Persian, one Moorish, and one Turkish. The Waldorf also had a Turkish salon, and the Palmer House Hotel in Chicago mixed Egyptian and European touches.[62] Cosey corners brought to mind public places of pleasure within the United States.

If cosmopolitan interiors can be read as protests against the constraints of women's domesticity, they also can be read as protests against the narrowness of *American* domesticity. In contrast to those who regarded homes as citadels or as launching pads for Americanizing campaigns, cosmopolitan decorators evinced relatively greater receptivity to difference. They professed new allegiances, based more on taste than nationality. A 1910 *Good Housekeeping* article on pottery from Provence showed how wide these imagined communities of consumption could be. Italy, Egypt, Spain, and the South American republics imported the most, but the manufacturers exported their wares to "all ports of the seven seas"—to San Francisco, Petersburg, Hong Kong, and New Orleans. Devotees had supposedly "formed a cult—whether they be on Broadway, Picadilly or the Nevsky Prospekt."[63] Casserole owners could regard themselves as members of an international community of like-minded consumers. Just as the national marketplace drew late nineteenth-century Americans closer together, the international marketplace led them to imagine still wider connections.

An article in the *House Beautiful* went so far as to characterize good taste as inherently cosmopolitan. "A thing may be Chinese or German, Norwegian or from the South Seas, and still be recognized by good judges as beautiful or ugly. There is far less diversity of opinion between different nations than one is led to believe, far less than is found in fact in people of the same nation, or even in the members of the same family. An American with a keen sense of beauty is able to appreciate the artistic product of the whole world. There is no geography in art."[64] Despite the protestation that art knew no geography, this article taught a geographic lesson: those with truly discriminating tastes paid little heed to the boundaries that more narrow-minded people held so dear. Indeed, other decoration writings dismissed local tastes as a holdover from the past. According to one decorating pamphlet, the interiors of "our forefathers" were relatively simple, from poverty and "from the fact that they were not a much traveling people, and their curiosity about other lands and their inhabitants was not very great." To be modern meant to be comparatively cosmopolitan: "We, on the contrary, take a very great interest in other peoples and in other countries. . . . In our houses we give our love of adventure free play, and like to be reminded at every turn, of the fact that America, big as is her territory, is but a small part of the world."[65]

Rather than stalwartly defending local manufactures, or posing as the guardians of local or national decorative traditions, the American women who sought foreign objects for their households demonstrated an eagerness to engage with the world. And rather than striving to completely Americanize it, they positioned themselves at the receiving end of cultural transmission. Admitting that their country could learn from others, cosmopolitan decorators looked abroad for design inspiration. Through their decoration choices, they sought to transcend the local. Above all, they strove to seem European.[66]

Bertha Palmer illustrates the longing to claim Europeanness. The daughter of one retailer who sold imported goods and the wife of another, Palmer derived her financial status in part from transatlantic commerce. She spoke fluent French and belonged to a group called the Tuesday Art and Travel Club. She maintained houses in Paris and London as well as Chicago, and she rambled on the continent and the watering grounds of North Africa, making friends along the way with European aristocrats, authors, actors, and artists. In the early 1890s, she chaired the Board of Lady Managers of the World's Columbian Exposition. In this capacity, she traveled to Europe to win support from her socially prominent contacts. The resulting exhibits favorably contrasted European to American women on several counts, including political power, education, and scientific attainments. Although the women's exhibit was not as universal as she liked to think—it focused primarily on the accomplishments of white American and European women — she proudly described it as the most cosmopolitan of the fair's displays.[67]

Despite the European emphasis of cosmopolitan domesticity, it also encompassed an appreciation of goods and styles produced outside of Europe. In an age of white supremacist thinking and practice, cosmopolitan decorators stood out for lauding the artistic attainments of people of color. Or at least they applauded those who crafted the things they coveted. Significantly, household goods made by Africans living south of the Sahara and other groups assumed to be at the very bottom of the racial hierarchy received little favorable mention in decorating columns. Cosmopolitan decorators may have prized antelope skins, but they scorned black Africans for failing to produce attractive domestic accoutrements.[68] Yet cosmopolitan decorators' enthusiasm for Asian, Middle Eastern, and Native American items led them to challenge some racial stereotypes. The most broad-minded cosmopolitan decorators insisted that the production of desirable household goods demonstrated racial and civilizational attainments.

The Japanese in particular won favor because of their manufactures and artwork. One article praising Japanese design said the "ingenious" Japanese deserved the title "Yankees of the East." Another lauded the Japanese for their "western quickness."[69] In contrast to these assessments, which continued to hold up Western standards as the ideal, some praised the Japanese for the alternative they offered, for having taught people in the West "a new way to look at life; the beauty of simplification and elimination."[70] "The Japanese way is best," asserted an article extolling Japanese simplicity.[71] The opening of Japan to export trade revealed, as one writer put it, "how absurd were our own systems of decoration with all their barbarous mannerisms and conventionalities, compared to the simple and natural methods employed by these men of the East, whom for ages we had, in our bigoted ignorance, supposed to be little better than savages."[72] Some of this praise reflects the condescending attitudes of people so confident in their own racial and civilizational superiority — seen as resting to a large degree on scientific and technological achievements — that they could concede the minor virtue of artistic skill to others. But decoration experts put more stock in the value of artistry than the American people at large, and their proclamations also reveal heartfelt admiration of Japanese attainments. Some fans of Japanese creations insisted that they could infuse U.S. households with positive moral values and spiritual qualities.[73]

Rather than pursue such moments of appreciation, studies of Orientalism have tended to focus on its function of distinguishing Western people from the racial and cultural "other." Yet Oriental and European decorative schemes also provided moments of identification, however distorted by ignorance or romance, with distant peoples. This can be seen in the strange phenomenon of enacting otherness, of using exotic domestic interiors as a stage for performing difference. Rebie Lowe, an Atlanta woman with an Oriental reception room, exemplifies this phenomenon. She liked to appear in it in "soft, clinging draperies and a Zouave bodice richly embroidered in gold." Her intent was picturesqueness, but this was a picturesqueness premised on pretending to be Algerian.[74]

The transgressive possibilities offered by non-European theme rooms and displays can be cast into relief by looking at the boundaries cosmopolitan decorators refused to cross. White householders may have displayed a Zulu shield or basket as part of an eclectic ensemble, but they did not aim to produce a black southern African decor. It would have been unthinkable for a white woman in late nineteenth-century Atlanta to make a central African reception room so she could better pretend to be Congolese. To embrace foreign styles, to fake foreignness in American homes, meant to acknowledge that the foreign had something to offer. To be sure, it did not necessarily mean untrammeled admiration for foreign producers, but it did mean acknowledging that they had some redeeming features.

Along with presenting positive portrayals of some nonwhite (and especially Japanese) producers, design writings sometimes played a transgressive role by criticizing imperial policies. In particular, they claimed that Western influence was ruining Oriental art, "tainting it with the poison of false ideas, and polluting it with the refuse of worn out vanities."[75] Despite their enthusiasm for eclecticism at home, decoration experts expressed dismay at Egyptian interiors done in French styles and Persian homes with bentwood chairs imported from Austria.[76] Rather than associating such interiors with progress, they associated them with cultural loss. This sense of nostalgia also surfaced in complaints that Western commercialism had degraded craftsmanship and corrupted artistic production. Just as bad as the implications for artisanship were the implications for workers: according to a *House Beautiful* article on Indian rugs, Western commercialism had turned the workman into "a mere living machine, a human automaton."[77] The desire for "authentic" goods made cosmopolitan decorators reproach imperial relationships for debasing the goods and fostering a regrettable international uniformity.

Perhaps the best evidence for the transgressive dimensions to cosmopolitan domesticity can be found in the heated opposition it elicited. The eagerness with which late nineteenth-century shoppers filled their households with imported objects troubled the economic nationalists who supported high tariffs. Tariff proponents worried that imports would undercut American industry, that they would benefit distant foreign workers at the expense of their compatriots. Nor did the passion for imported products make sense to cultural nationalists, who thought that American women should surround themselves with American objects to better foster patriotism and good citizenship in their children.[78]

Opponents of cosmopolitan domesticity regarded exotic interiors as inappropriately heterogeneous. They echoed the British and French cultural critics who maintained that taste should be national, by which they meant that it should be shared by everyone in the nation and that it should indicate specifically national sensibilities. Taste, they argued, was a marker of national progress. Calls for households decorated in a particularly American way were in keeping with calls to purge domestic servants (generally understood to be African American or foreign born) from American (understood, in this context, to mean white, middle-class, and native-born) households. They also were in keeping with efforts to persuade immigrant women to reject Victorian decor for a more "American" esthetic. Amelia Muir Baldwin, a Boston-born interior decorator and needle tapestry designer who as an older woman taught Americanization courses to immigrants, called for racially and culturally appropriate interiors in a 1916 essay. "In our own houses we are certainly happier if we have a background which expresses something of ourselves, racially and individually . . . a Turkish harem, however well done from a decorative point of view, is ill adapted to the uses and ideals of domestic life in this country." She went on to object to the French style as "foreign to our genius."[79]

The objections to cosmopolitan interiors led some proponents of cosmopolitan domesticity to argue that their interiors were, in their very cosmopolitanism, quintessentially American. In contrast to other nations, which had evolved distinctive design styles over time, Americans, "the most conglomerate of all peoples," free from a limiting design history, were, according to the advocates of cosmopolitanism, able to pick and choose.[80] "The people of the United States are not trammeled by history and tradition; they are not childishly bound by the limitation of ancient plastic forms; their imagination is not haunted by ancient models. Theirs is an entirely liberal spirit of accommodation," asserted one of the more open-minded articles published in the *Decorator and Furnisher*.[81] According to this point of view, the appreciation of novelty was a virtue, something that distinguished Americans from more hidebound peoples, content to stick to their own design traditions. Though ostensibly foreign, eclectic interiors were really American after all.

Critics were not convinced. Implying that households should convey local and national sensibilities through their design and the objects they displayed, they bewailed the modern drawing room for being, as one put it, "a mass of heterogeneous articles imported from all lands, instead of being an organic design." They urged householders to remove foreign influences from "the intimacies of domestic life."[82] Warnings of European goods so infested with microbes and insects that they seemed "lively enough to transport themselves across the ocean, independent of any steamers," suggested that imported products endangered national purity in more ways than one.[83]

Domestic Orientalism came under particularly heavy fire. Alice and Bettina Jackson, authors of a book on interior decoration, captured the core of the protest in their claim that "Oriental peoples and their art are so utterly different from Occidental peoples and their art that the two are not particularly congenial when brought together. . . . With rare exceptions Kipling was correct in saying, 'East is East, and West is West, and never the twain shall meet.'"[84] Such critics argued that disdain for producers should translate into disdain for their handiwork. The suspicion that Eastern goods, though perhaps fine in artistry, might bring too much of the Orient into hygienic American homes led one turn-of-the-century rug-shopper to say: "I don't want any half-ragged dirty specimen that has come out of some filthy Turk's house."[85] The particularly vehement opposition to domestic Orientalism reveals that those who advocated narrowly national styles did not just want to preserve national boundaries; they felt even more strongly about preserving racial and civilizational boundaries. Those who equated Turkish homes with filth feared that Turkish corners would degrade American homes. They feared that Orientalist interiors would make the Orient seem less objectionable.

As their denunciations of foreign influence suggest, critics of cosmopolitan domesticity called for greater nationalism in U.S. household decoration. At the most extreme, they advocated maize art, meaning corn-inspired designs (ill. 1.8). Despite some contests to encourage the theme, maize art did not catch on, but another style with nationalistic appeal did: the colonial revival, which arose in the 1870s and became the most popular U.S. style by World War I. The simple lines and relatively sparse interiors of the colonial revival represented a rejection not only of excessive ornament and clutter but also of foreignness. In an article on American versus foreign art, the *Decorator and Furnisher* imagined a conversation between a colonial house and its mismatched neighbors. Said the former: "I can afford to overlook their ridiculous airs, for I alone can claim pure blood and style,

1.8. Emery Roth, "The Price 'Maize' Competition," *Decorator and Furnisher* 15 (Feb. 1890): 138. Courtesy of the Winterthur Library: Printed Book and Periodical Collection, Winterthur, Delaware.

the rest are a heterogeneous mass of no one knows what, imported from every country under the sun."[86] Mary Logan, widow of a Union general, had similar reasons for endorsing the revival. "I am delighted to see a growing taste for the Colonial period," she said. "It is our legitimate style. Oriental decorations harmonize with the Oriental atmosphere, and with Eastern tastes and habits of thought."[87] Colonial furniture stood for ethnic purity in an age of immigration, for national boundary setting and assertion in an age of international connections.[88] Decorators who advocated colonial furniture were wont to stress the especial desirability of inherited pieces, the point of which surely did not escape the notice of those whose ancestors had been elsewhere, impoverished, or enslaved during the seventeenth and eighteenth centuries.

Along with the colonial revival style, the mission and arts-and-crafts styles gained popularity as reactions to cosmopolitanism. The mission style can be seen as a southwestern version of the colonial revival. In keeping with the concern for purity, one proponent of New Mexican furnishings praised them for their "chaste, artistic designs expressive of American genius and environment."[89] For their part, arts-and-crafts devotees favored designs that had evolved from local traditions and products made from local materials.[90] They saw the movement as particularly Anglo-Saxon.

The irony of these nationalistic and racially inflected styles was, of

Cosmopolitan Domesticity, Imperial Accessories

course, their mixed antecedents. Both fans and critics of the colonial revival acknowledged that its origins were really more English than American and that it also reflected Oriental influences—the East India company had introduced lacquer, porcelain, and Chinese rugs to England in the sixteenth century, and Chippendale furniture was heavily influenced by Chinese design. As for the mission style, it stemmed from Spanish taste and traditions, which in turn had Moorish antecedents. The arts-and-crafts movement likewise had British origins and Japanese inflections.[91] Yet however much these styles reflected outside influences, contemporaries persisted in viewing them as American. And that explains much of their appeal: they were part of a protest against the cosmopolitan ethos.

Home economists joined in this protest by pronouncing hygienic American interiors, stripped of bric-a-brac, ornate furniture, and heavy draperies, as models to the world. As Nancy Tomes has noted in *The Gospel of Germs*, "around the turn of the century, the hygienic criticism of the American home finally began to bear fruit. Architects and home designers promoted new looks—including the colonial revival, modernist, and arts and crafts styles—that eliminated dust lines and facilitated a more bacteriologically informed cleanliness."[92]

Ostensibly national styles seemed to be not only more hygienic but also more masculine. Despite men's prominence as purveyors of decoration advice and as high-end interior designers, critics regarded cosmopolitan tastes as essentially feminine.[93] Even worse, they saw cosmopolitan interiors as inappropriately feminine. Those who believed that white, middle-class, American women should maintain racial, class, national, and civilizational boundaries by modeling and expounding a narrow kind of domesticity regarded cosmopolitan preferences as an inappropriate kind of female self-assertion. Rather than staying in their sphere or extending its influence, cosmopolitan decorators admitted the world into their homes. They exhibited dangerous yearnings for liberation. They used the foreign as a backdrop for enacting their own desires. Hence critics presented colonial, mission, and arts-and-crafts designs—characterized by simplicity, solidity, and pared-down upholstery—as manlier alternatives to interiors characterized by lush draperies, abundant adornments, and soft cushioning. Unlike cosmopolitan interiors, these relatively spare homes left no doubt as to the occupants' racial, class, and national allegiances.

Some of the support for plain national styles emerged from a commitment to democratic principles. Peace activist Lucia Ames Mead condemned cosmopolitan interiors because she believed they reeked of imperial power. She associated the luxurious interiors of the late nineteenth century with

Old World corruption and empire, as opposed to new world simplicity and republican virtue. "In the home of American citizens," she wrote, "imperial splendor is a menace to democracy."[94] Mead was unusually outspoken in her denunciation of empire, but other critics of cosmopolitan domesticity denounced aristocratic sensibilities as inimical to American democracy. An article on the poor taste of the rich drew attention to the "droll incongruity of transplanting royal furniture to a democratic land." Such furniture was "untrue to American life, to American thought, to American ideals." It observed that "if a home is merely an exhibition place, wherein may be gathered the remnants of European palaces; a place to house works of art and the spoils of foreign travel," then those furnished with European goods and in European styles were eminently successful. But if the home was to stand for "something in our national life," then such houses were "rank failures."[95]

Critics who rejected cosmopolitan domesticity for its aristocratic and imperial inflections were the exception rather than the rule, however. Rather than denouncing cosmopolitan interiors for being insufficiently democratic, most critics denounced them for being insufficiently patriotic. As one opponent put it: "Your true cosmopolitan is rather a colorless person. He proudly proclaims his lack of prejudice and will not bind himself with ties of race or country. And yet I think that love of country is a wisely fostered instinct."[96] The unapologetic imitation revealed in eclectic interiors was an embarrassment for a rising power. "It is humiliating, and a national disgrace that rich Americans should build palaces and spend millions of dollars in adornment that is exclusively foreign, both in idea and execution," editorialized the *Decorator and Furnisher* in 1895.[97]

Critics worried that too much mixing would undercut national boundaries rather than affirm them, that it would reduce rather than uphold racial and civilizational hierarchies. Rather than seeing cosmopolitan decorating efforts as a means to assert cultural standing, they saw them as an admission that the United States was culturally deficient. Try as they did to associate themselves with the European ruling class, cosmopolitan decorators struck their critics as akin to colonial subjects. After all, at least one French writer regarded the export of French goods as a means to "civilize barbarous peoples."[98] Like the wealthy Latin Americans who regarded European styles as a means to prove their civilizational standing, cosmopolitan decorators within the United States showed their provinciality by looking elsewhere for guidance on how to arrange their homes.[99] According to the most common vein of criticism, the problem with cosmopolitan decoration schemes was not that they were too imperialistic, it was that they were not imperialistic enough.

B ut just how cosmopolitan were cosmopolitan decorators? Were they really colorless people, devoid of ties to race or country? Hardly. Like those who favored the colonial revival, mission style, and arts-and-crafts interiors, cosmopolitan decorators expressed strong commitments to racial, national, and imperial distinctions. They just followed a different path to this end. Instead of keeping the foreign out or trying to eliminate it, cosmopolitan decorators appropriated it. Unlike those who saw the wider world as a threat, cosmopolitan decorators positioned themselves as enthusiastic beneficiaries of Western imperialism and global trade. Unlike those who wanted to remake the world in their image, cosmopolitan consumers wanted what the world had to offer. Their greater receptivity to foreign (and particularly European) cultural production did not imply a commitment to an egalitarian world order, however. Cosmopolitan decorators reveled in the power of the pocketbook, the power of knowledge, and the power of social distinction.

As they wallowed in the plenitude of the marketplace, cosmopolitan householders flaunted the power of their purses. A woman shopper who offered advice in the *House Beautiful* attested to the sense of privilege afforded by commercial forays: "The chief thought in the mind of the woman who goes out to buy curtains and draperies . . . must be one of thankfulness that she lives in this particular age of the world, for never before were there so many interesting things from which to choose." She went on to mention Japanese, Persian, Scottish, and Madagascar fabrics. Shifting her attention to dishes and cutlery, she continued in awe: "From the four corners of the earth come marching long processions of tableware." The mistress of the house could "make of her dining-table, spread with appropriate wares, a part of a Dutch room, or a Spanish room, or a German room, or a Japanese or a Chinese room. Or, if she wants to make her dining room merely quaint and homey, with a bit of the *bizarre* flavor that seems always to add just the necessary tang to bungalow furnishing, she can pick and choose from the offerings of half the nations of the earth."[100] As envious window shoppers well knew, not everybody could bring the world home. But cosmopolitan decorators could and did.

The assumption that American shoppers could buy whatever they wanted exaggerated the strength of all but the fattest pocketbooks. Nevertheless, the abundance of the U.S. marketplace did reflect financial power. Only the rich could fill their houses with imported decorative items, and the United States, in aggregate, was rich. Decoration writings and laden shop counters taught American consumers that their nation's relative wealth put them in a position of power in the international marketplace. Decorating experts acknowledged American purchasers' economic power in descriptions of specific transactions. They recounted stories of precious Oriental rugs that had come onto the market because of the dire poverty of their original owners, who had no choice but to relinquish their treasures to Western buyers. Missionaries in Persia found opportunity even in famine: "It is wonderful how every commodity is sold for a mere song," one reported.[101] That international exchanges were not always regarded as equal can be inferred as well from the words used to describe them. Contemporaries claimed that the markets of the East had been "ransacked" for products, that Europeans relinquished their many treasures to the "hordes of Americans who come armed with the invincible dollar." They referred to foreign goods as "plunder" and "trophies of travel." "It is not unusual for a buyer to invade the dwelling of a Persian gentleman and bid for his dishes or the rugs on his floors or walls," claimed an article in *House and Garden.* "The wretched part of it is that he very often gets them. Persia is being stripped with all the rapidity possible."[102]

Accounts focusing on production threw the power American consumers wielded over foreign workers into particularly sharp relief. News of low foreign wages, as little as three cents a day for a Chinese laborer, might have worried American manufacturers and workers, but they provided grounds for American consumers to see themselves as fortunate. Consumers could feel even more fortunate upon reading how foreign producers toiled on their behalf. Writing in the *Decorator and Furnisher,* Emma Thacker Holliday reported that women provided most of the labor in the manufacture of Oriental carpets, starting at age six or seven. This burdensome labor was "the cause of physical degeneracy of what would otherwise be a fine race of people." To make things worse, the weavers were ill-paid, subject to epidemics, and victimized by rapacious officials. The source of her discomfiting assertions? Vantine's, the retail establishment (ill. 1.9).[103] Rather than advocate social change, such acknowledgments of poverty, hard working conditions, and exploitation made the consumer feel fortunate in the existing global scheme of things.

Those who celebrated imported goods and foreign fashions luxuriated in American consumers' enviable status. They saw little need to question the international distribution of wealth, although they did sometimes allude to it. "One could moralize here by the hour . . . on the distance between the price paid to the poor artisan and that to the seller," wrote Hester M. Poole,

1.9. "Weaving Oriental Rugs," *Decorator and Furnisher* 27 (Nov. 1895): 48. Courtesy of the Winterthur Library: Printed Book and Periodical Collection, Winterthur, Delaware.

a frequent contributor to *Good Housekeeping*, in reference to Oriental goods. Yet Poole chose in the end not to moralize, dismissing the issue with a brisk "but that is subject to the social economist, not to the decorator," thus implying that her readers could continue to shop duty free—that is, without any sense of obligation to producers.[104]

Although shoppers could find reports of grim working conditions, decoration writings were more likely to turn a blind eye to the upheavals caused by export-oriented production, the redistribution of wealth within and across national boundaries, and the environmental consequences of massive resource extraction. (To take one example, the American-Guatemalan Mahogany Company cut more than 16 million board feet of mahogany between 1907 and 1930. Each tree shattered numerous smaller ones as it fell; only in our day are the replacement trees coming to maturity.) Instead of elaborating on such unsavory aspects of international trade, decoration writings struck a blither tone, more conducive to commerce. They romanticized the conditions of manufacture. Hence one account on Persian rugs described the weavers working at home in pleasant courtyards, accompanied by singing nightingales. "Here are no sweatshop methods!" exclaimed a catalog of Mexican handicrafts that touted the pleasant home-based manufacturing conditions of its workers.[105] Shoppers could actually watch ostensibly contented Irish lace makers, Persian rug weavers, and other crafts people ply their trades at world's fairs and manufacturing exhibits.[106] The result of such rosy accounts and appealing displays was to make the U.S. position within the world marketplace seem benign. By ignoring conflict and obscuring unsavory working conditions, such accounts made the inequitable distribution of international power seem unexceptionable. They thus helped forestall critiques of imperialism based on evidence of exploitation.

Some acquisitions even appeared benevolent, a charitable transfer of wealth to the needy. Claimed an article on Mexican drawn work: "Save a meager livelihood through the natural products of the soil, with many Mexican families the sale of this work furnishes the only means of subsistence."[107] Relief agencies that sold handiwork to support destitute peasants likewise made the benevolence of buying explicit. In these contexts, the American consumer came across as a patron, not a plunderer. Whether envisioned as booty or charity, the imported products in such accounts conveyed a sense of unequal power relations between U.S. consumers and foreign producers. Guided by such accounts, cosmopolitan shoppers could understand their forays into the marketplace as an act of national mastery. In reading the John Wanamaker catalog's exultant "Nowhere in all the world is there another such variety of furniture," they could count their blessings. Disregarding their compatriots who might have mopped Wanamaker's floors but could not buy its wares, they could feel thankful to live in a nation with unparalleled riches. Indeed, American women were often told to regard consumption as a sign of national strength, to thank their lucky stars that they had been born into a country where women were "spenders" not "earners."[108] Accounts heralding the march of goods from the four corners of the earth to the United States suggested that U.S. consumers benefited from their national standing. Such articles taught readers that they could take full advantage of the world's marketplaces thanks to their nation's growing power.

In addition to conveying economic power, cosmopolitan interiors conveyed the power of knowledge. In contrast to colonial revival and other seemingly national designs, which maintained hierarchies by keeping difference out, cosmopolitan interiors maintained hierarchies by teaching lessons about difference. Like the museums they resembled, cosmopolitan interiors imparted geographic knowledge. Indeed, cosmopolitan decorators insisted that foreign design schemes and imported objects had great educational value. This can be seen in a *House Beautiful* article that counseled setting the dining room table with items from around the world: "Each item upon a table thus spread from so many different sources has its own story to tell of the country whence it comes, the way it was made, and the uses to which it would have been put in the homes of peasant or artisan had it not journeyed to America instead."[109]

But how was a housewife to read the objects upon her table? Shopping columns and decoration essays devoted so much attention to provenance that it seems likely that a large part of middle-class women's awareness of the wider world was associated with the goods they purchased for their households. Design writings that provided information on foreign objects in use in their original surroundings provided consumers with a sense of knowing what the rest of the world was really like, a sense made especially powerful because of its material grounding. Having seen a picture of a Moor using a prayer rug in the course of worship, a U.S. homemaker might feel that she knew more than the intended usage of her hall rug, perhaps that she also had some understanding of Islam. Having seen pictures of Cairo households, she could do more than arrange her cushions in what struck her as an authentic way; she could draw some conclusions about Egyptian family life.[110]

These conclusions were no doubt informed by other contemporary sources of geographic information, which tended to provide classification schemes that placed the classifiers on top. Although decorating literature sometimes waxed enthusiastic about the cultural attainments of foreign artisans, articles on provenance did not always depict producers favorably. Many repeated the denigrating assessments that could be found in other forms of popular ethnology. Others struck an ambivalent note. An article that called the Arab "the greatest of decorators," "romantic and splendor-loving," also called him "the fiercest of fanatics . . . the most treacherous of foes."[111] Another article that mixed admiration and disdain contrasted the Oriental, "steeped in moral degradation, but with intuitive perception of grace of line and harmony of color," with the Scot—"noble, true, generous—but whose highest art achievement has been the combining of ugly checkered squares."[112] As this assessment of Oriental artistry suggests, the ability to produce beautiful things did not necessarily imply upstanding character. Indeed, practical-minded Americans tended to regard artistic handiwork as only a minor attainment. At the turn of the century, many white Americans supported industrial education for people of color at home and in U.S. dependencies, thinking that manual work would teach discipline and work habits without challenging racial hierarchies.[113] Much of the appreciation of handicrafts made by poor, colonized, and dark-skinned workers can be seen as consistent with this logic.

By making consumers feel like geographic experts and by confirming their racial and cultural prejudices, decoration writings enhanced their sense of superiority. According to the president of the New York School of Fine and Applied Art, the more one knows, the less he limits himself to one furniture style: "the broader becomes his concept, the wider his experience and the more versatile and refined his expression."[114] Following this reasoning, cosmopolitan consumers could consider themselves exceptionally knowledgeable. They could look down on those who exhibited local tastes as relatively ill-informed. Gazing at the rugs upon their floors, American consumers could smugly conclude that they knew the Orient. Contrasting themselves to the women who had been weaving carpets since the age of six, they had reason to think that this knowledge was not reciprocal.

Knowledge of foreign decoration traditions and trends denoted the outlook of the traveler and the connoisseur. It also indicated imperial power, for imperial rule played a crucial role in bringing non-European goods to Western attention. The story of Major Kettle, published in *House and Garden*, illustrates this point. The major, who had presumably traveled to the Orient in service of the British Empire, introduced Persian and Indian antiques to the people in the author's small town. Although the neighbors initially regarded the newcomer with suspicion, some came to appreciate his strange artworks. Among them was the author, who attributed his lifelong love of the "curious and beautiful things of the Orient" to the influence of the major.[115]

And what were the implications of this love for Oriental objects? Knowledge did more than reflect power relations; it also helped produce them. Knowledge of the natives helped manufacturers gain markets. It helped imperial officials govern. And it helped prompt expansionist ambitions. Cosmopolitan decorators embraced the idea of homes as museums because they endorsed the racial, class, national, and imperial ends that museums served. They needed to look no further than their mantelpieces and corner tables to appreciate the benefits that accrued to them as the wives and daughters of the ruling class of a powerful nation in an imperial age.

Yet however much their homes evoked museums and department stores, cosmopolitan decorators did not really want to live in galleries or retail outlets. Neither did they want to position themselves as curators or clerks. Through their decorating choices, they strove to associate themselves with the global elite, which they understood to be primarily white, wealthy, and Western. Above all, cosmopolitan decorators wanted their homes to evoke upper-crust European dwellings. The desire to produce a European look can be seen most noticeably in ostensibly French, British, and other European theme rooms. But even eclecticism conveyed European tastes. True, some accounts claimed that eclecticism was particularly American. Others proclaimed eclecticism a sign of the age, not of a particular place. In a book on her Egyptian travels, Emmeline Lott described harem rooms *à la Europe* along with those stacked high with pillows. Travel lecturer Burton Holmes reported finding "installment-plan" furniture in Algeria. *House and Garden* ran a story on Baron Sumito's three houses, in Osaka, Tokyo, and Kyoto, all of which had Occidental rooms for the reception of Westerners. Those who visited the Filipino village in the 1901 Pan-American Exposition in Buffalo could see such mixing for themselves: the thatched roofed huts sheltered American-made chairs, tables, and stoves.[116]

But most decoration writings did not identify nations such as Egypt, Algeria, Japan, and the Philippines with cutting-edge eclectic tastes. To the contrary, design writings, like other geographic writings, depicted non-Western peoples as relatively traditional and local. Despite scattered efforts to cast eclecticism as a U.S. style, eclecticism signified Western, and particularly European tastes. The *Art Amateur*, for example, reported on a French design writer who "holds it possible to combine the most incongruous objects — a cabinet of the Italian Renaissance, surmounted by a trophy of Oriental arms and a group of grimacing Japanese masks; a Spanish console leaning against a porter of point d' Hungry; a Persian carpet on the floor."[117] With such writings to guide them, eclectic decorators could conclude they had far more in common with the European elite than with the Filipinos on display in Buffalo. Imperial encounters affected the decorating practices of both rulers and subject peoples, but eclectic decorators strove to identify themselves with those who seized trophies of Oriental arms rather than those who had only recently obtained cookstoves.

As this affinity with Western imperialism suggests, the desire to seem European can be seen even in the enthusiasm for Orientalist schemes. It was no coincidence that Orientalist rooms became popular in the apogee of European imperialism. In the 1870s Russia intervened in Turkey, leading to the 1878 Congress of Berlin. In that gathering, the European powers kept the Ottoman Empire politically free (regarding it as too important to be dominated by any one power) but allocated opportunities for concession hunters. This maneuver was part of a much larger, and in many cases more invasive, pattern. The British had annexed the Punjab to their Indian holdings in 1849, and they occupied Upper Burma in 1885, thereby consolidating their control over South Asia. Russia established its dominance over Central Asia in 1885, when it defeated the Turkomans. Russia and Britain divided Persia into spheres of influence in 1888. In 1882 British troops marched into Cairo and the French fully occupied Algeria. Admiral Perry's 1854 display of power opened up trade between Japan and the West. By 1900 the European powers, Japan, and to a lesser degree, the United States, obtained trading rights in China.[118] In buying the Baghdad curtains, the Turkish rugs, and the Indian brass work, American shoppers positioned themselves with the grasping Western powers. This can be seen most clearly in the appeal of Oriental rooms in the 1870s and 1880s.

Oriental rooms were a cultural manifestation of imperial politics. They resulted from Western knowledge of Eastern styles (however jumbled and perverted) and Westerners' ability to obtain Eastern products. Russian conquests, for example, brought railroads that facilitated the export of rugs, previously transported on caravan routes. Imperial rule also brought the manufacture of numerous products under Western, especially British, control. In 1877 decorator Harriet Prescott Spofford acknowledged the imperial connections that brought foreign products to American households. She said that American shoppers could obtain finer goods than ever before, due to "our better acquaintance with the Eastern countries, the farther depth to which we have penetrated them."[119] The British furniture factory that advertised the Chinese and Assyrian cloths, Moroccan leather, American birch, and Spanish mahogany that went into its products hinted at the networks of trade, linking north and south, east and west, that resulted from years of imperial expansion. So did the column in the *Atlanta Constitution* that identified London as "the place to buy East India things cheap."[120] If the exotic objects that filled American households could speak, the rooms would reverberate with stories of empire.

Some of these stories—especially those on compelled labor—should have made conscientious decorators blanch. One article on Oriental rugs noted that in Mirzapore, India, "the [British] Government has, by engaging as many of its convicts in the jail as soon as it could find space for [them] at carpet weaving, set the fashion for the whole neighborhood." Convicts reportedly made carpets in Bangalore and Vellore, too, including ones on order for Americans.[121] Yet rather than condemn such prison labor, those who reported on it were more likely to cast it as an efficient means of enforcing discipline. This can be seen in the story of a Hindu workman, more skilled than Tiffany's best artisans, who worked for a mere twelve cents a day. He had a fondness for drink, which had the unfortunate result of reducing his productivity. But his clever British taskmasters had a strategy: they had him locked up for disorderly conduct whenever they wanted a job completed.[122] The acceptance of coercive labor practices—indeed, the tendency to regard them as evidence of superior British managerial skills rather than as shocking evidence of exploitation—reveals an acceptance of the imperial power relations that made a wider range of goods available to American decorators.

These power relations were particularly visible in Orientalist smoking rooms and bachelor's apartments. The apartment of a New York banker illuminates why. An awestruck reporter admiringly compared its Turkish room to the harem of the Pasha. Its walls were bedecked in tapestries "representing Eastern dancing girls in the most luxurious attitudes." Beside the door stood a life-size nude statue in bronze of an Odalisque. In one arm she held a tray, heaped with luscious figs, apples, oranges, and nuts.[123] It was a sensuous room in which men could enjoy eroticized Eastern women. Such rooms provided the Western bachelor with access, if only in his imagination, to the prohibited harem. If, in its inaccessibility, the harem symbolized the limits of Western men's power to fully grasp the Orient, its duplication suggested that nothing was beyond Western men's reach.

Yet erotic reveries were not the only escapes offered by Turkish dens. The bankers, doctors, industrialists, and merchants who retreated to their confines also surrounded themselves with the thrill of violence: many such rooms had weapons prominently displayed on the walls.[124] The weapons might convey masculinity, but as far as Oriental men were concerned, it was a cowed masculinity, for these daggers, swords, and spears had been unable to prevent the European seizure of power. The most potent masculinity inhered in their current possessors—the men who could hang them on their walls along with college banners and hunting trophies.

What about cosey corners? Did the women who made them see them as shrines to empire? The American women who constructed Oriental cosey corners had, in all likelihood, been exposed to information on Oriental products and their manufacture, and, beyond that, to ethnographic writing on the harem, whether in missionary bulletins, daily newspapers, travel accounts, or women's magazines. Those who purchased household items at world's fairs could recall their display in "the Streets of Cairo" or other supposedly ethnographic concessions. Fiction, too, provided imaginative imperial contexts for imported goods. *The Garden of Allah*, a 1904 novel by Robert Hichens, included elaborate descriptions of Egyptian interiors, noting everything from the colors of the rugs to the patterns on the divans and the ashtrays on the smoking tables. And, of course, decorating literature provided information on household items as well. That exposure only intensifies the mystery of cosey corners' appeal, however, for evangelical and secular ethnological literature alike presented harems as virtual prisons, as symbols of women's degradation in male-dominated societies.[125]

A decorating article that praised the "exquisite workmanship" of the embroidery pinned to the wall of an Iranian harem but then went on to mention opium smoking, a sickly baby, child marriage, superstition, jealousy between wives, and the sheltered women's utter ignorance of the world captures the tension between the admiration for Eastern products and the abhorrence of the East.[126] If men were likely to regard the harem as the symbol of unattainable pleasures, the bastion of resistance to Western imperial surveillance and control, women were more likely to see it as a symbol of oppression.

This denigration of the harem fit into a larger pattern of condemnation for the Middle East. Just as white, middle-class Americans tended to regard East Asians as inferior, they tended to disdain the Middle East as backward. Rather than criticizing European aggression against the sultan's dominions, Americans increasingly saw Turks as oppressors of subject Christian minorities. They deplored Turkish massacres of Bulgarian Christians in 1876 and Armenians in 1894–95. They protested the slave trade, which continued to flow from inner Africa, through Tripoli, to Constantinople in the early 1870s. And they sent missionaries to the region: in the 1880s, the Ottoman Empire was the largest foreign mission site for the United States.[127] Yet all the while, middle-class housewives were sewing cushions for sensuous Oriental niches.

Given the tendency to regard the harem as a locus of male pleasure at the cost of female oppression, and the widespread contempt for and desire to uplift "heathen" peoples, Middle Easterners supposedly among them, why did Euro-American women tolerate any hint of the harem in their parlors? Why did they attempt, through their domestic surroundings, to become "as they are"? One possibility is that they disregarded the vast majority of harem writings and latched on to the idea of the harem as a protective or delightfully eroticized space for women. Another is that they draped Turkish fabrics in their doorways to manifest a sense of sympathetic identification with oppressed harem denizens. In either case, their efforts to add Oriental touches to their households can be interpreted as an expression of their own dissatisfactions, whether with male-dominated social spaces or their own sexual repression and domestic captivity. Despite admonitions to be thankful for their privileges, these women may have felt that they still had all too much in common with women of the East. Even confident, capable, socially powerful women such as Bertha Palmer had reason to identify with women of the harem: Palmer's husband reportedly locked her in her room from time to time.[128]

But just because the harem served as a symbol of women's oppression, it does not follow that its reconstruction in Western households necessarily did too. White, middle-class American women did not get their Orientalist ideas straight from Turks or Egyptians. They got them via Europe, which had a long history of Orientalist design, with aristocratic cachet. Perhaps the best-known Orientalist spectacle was Brighton Pavilion, built by King George IV in the 1790s. As those who had heard the popular travel lecturer John Stoddard well knew, the Russian royal family had a Chinese room in one of its summer homes. Following the royal lead, aristocrats added Arabian halls, Indian drawing rooms, and Moorish billiard rooms to their mansions in the late nineteenth century. Maude Andrews, who wrote a series of travel articles for the *Atlanta Constitution* in 1896, was struck by a Turkish room in London: "sumptuous, restful, exquisite—nothing in it, I assure you, like the cozy oriental corners we see copied out of newspapers and fashion books."[129] She may have disdained cosey corners for being lowbrow, but these too had European connections—the 1892 Exhibition of Rooms at London's Crystal Palace had one on display.[130]

Constructing a cosey corner meant more than mimicking the wealthy within the United States: like the rich who hired decorators to compose lavish Oriental retreats, the middle-class American women who draped their corners in fabric and piled cushions on the divan demonstrated a sense of European sophistication through their exhibitions of Oriental exoticism. The couple that added an Oriental platform to their French-style apartment did so as part of an effort to seem Parisian. The American housewives who constructed Orientalist cosey corners did not produce an unmediated Eastern decor but a colonial decor, one that emerged from the crucible of empire and was as much European as "Oriental." Just as the spreading reach of Western ships had contributed to the rage for chinoiserie in the eighteenth century, a sense of affinity with Western imperialism contributed to the Orientalism of the nineteenth. Like the public exhibitions that endorsed Western imperial power, Orientalist cosey corners revealed an enthusiasm for empire, if only secondhand.[131]

Western women may have regarded the harem as a locus of oppression for its denizens, but they saw it as a tourist destination for themselves. The ability to travel, if only imaginatively through their household interiors, marked them as privileged. Their imagined mobility had a social as well as a geographic dimension. Those who read about white women in the Orient read stories about empowerment: memsahibs reported on a level of authority unavailable to them in the metropolis. Memsahibs also reported on unaccustomed levels of luxury and on households teeming with servants.[132] In the context of empire, middle-class Western women could become upper-class. Like the bachelors who lounged around in Turkish smoking rooms, the women who reclined on plush divans could appreciate the power dynamics implicit in their cosey corners. Though members of the subordinate sex at home, they could claim affiliation with a dominant race, nation, and civilization. Cosey corners may seem to have been private places of female repose, but they revealed a desire to enjoy the satisfactions of the ruling class in an imperial world order.

In buying foreign goods and creating foreign interiors, American women no less than American men accepted, whether knowingly or tacitly, the relations of power that brought these products to their doorsteps. Middle-class American women might never be as rich as Bertha Palmer, but they nonetheless had something in common: they could demonstrate their standing through their household acquisitions. As beneficiaries of an imperial economic and political order, they could regard their purchases as a means to demonstrate privilege. And what was the point of the nation, the point of empire, if not to preserve that privilege? Cosmopolitan interiors produced as well as reflected international relations, in the sense that wide-ranging tastes added impetus to commercial expansion.[133] International trade depends on consumers as well as producers, and cosmopolitan American housewives proved remarkably eager to purchase imports for their parlors.

In sum, cosmopolitan decorators showed just as much interest in social distinction as their critics; they just disagreed over how best to achieve it. They may have collected some foreign handicrafts, but they did not want their homes to look too peasantlike. They may have attempted to evoke the Orient in richly draped niches, but they did not identify with Asian immigrants in their communities. They may have fancied tropical hardwoods, but this does not mean they recognized the full humanity of the workers who felled the trees. Their decorating preferences did not demonstrate truly universal outlooks. The issue that divided them from their detractors was not whether to be national and imperial, but how. In contrast to colonial revivalists and their allies, who placed more of an emphasis on racial and national inheritances, cosmopolitan decorators embraced novelty. In contrast to the arts-and-crafts emphasis on production, cosmopolitanism centered on consumption. Whereas those who preferred the stark beauty of the mission style and other "American" interiors chose restrained display, cosmopolitan decorators favored an air of abundance. When confronted with the foreign, cosmopolitan decorators cast their lot with engagement. But their receptivity to difference served exclusionary ends. Cosmopolitan households, no less than more narrowly nationalistic ones, reveled in U.S. commercial power and celebrated Western imperialism. Whereas inward-looking critics saw cosmopolitan domesticity as a potential threat to racial, class, national, and civilizational hierarchies, cosmopolitan decorators saw the entire world as the terrain that constituted these privileges.

Cosmopolitan domesticity did not imply a belief in the essential equality of all human beings or a profound understanding of other nations and cultures. Nor did it necessarily imply a willingness to open the nation's borders to immigrants. Those who lamented the vitiation of "authentic" styles in the non-Western world thought that cosmopolitanism should be a testament to *Western* knowledge, openness, and modernity. Those who mixed and matched imported objects fabricated the exotic. Those who sought imported items that had been crafted to suit their tastes or who arranged them so that they felt familiar, domesticated the wider world, denying its difference and asserting their own appropriative power. And even those who strove for authenticity furthered imperialist ends, at least according to the reasoning that commercial supremacy demanded greater understanding of potential markets.[134]

The cosmopolitanism of consumption, premised on unequal economic and political relations between people of various countries, was a cosmopolitanism in which American consumers only superficially and in some cases only imaginatively engaged with distant producers. And they did so as a privileged, purchasing class. Despite the nostalgia for a preimperial past evinced in some decoration writing, cosmopolitan domesticity did not spark concerted opposition to the relations of power that structured the international marketplace. Langston Hughes's later musings that mahogany grand pianos and chests of drawers were made of "wood and life, energy and death out of Africa" cast a more critical light on the origins of imported goods than turn-of-the-century white design writers ever did.[135] Though inherently political, cosmopolitan domesticity was more a posture than a movement to effect change, and though it made gestures toward universalism, it remained closely intertwined with the hierarchies of its day.

So why were critics so incensed? They found cosmopolitan domesticity objectionable because its advocates did not sing the praises of a distinctive and unified American culture. Instead, they suggested that one of the defining aspects of that culture was its openness and the variety that it encompassed. Notwithstanding its limitations, cosmopolitan domesticity illuminates something far more complex than the self-assertion generally thought to characterize the United States in this period. For those who embraced the cosmopolitan ethos, homes were not so much bunkers as entrepôts. Cosey corners and sundry imported objects provided a way to demonstrate a broad outlook, wide experience, and engagement with the world. Eclectic decorative endeavors suggest that late nineteenth-century middle-class American culture can be characterized by more than just insularity and efforts to remake the world; it also involved a search for novelty and difference, a materially rooted geographic consciousness, and a desire to associate with powerful Europeans. Rather than serving exclusively to separate homes from the world around them, domesticity provided a locus of material and imaginative interaction. In the late nineteenth century, cosmopolitan consumers imported the American dream.

2

The Fashionable World

Imagined Communities of Dress

Xenophobic nationalists in the Gilded Age had plenty to worry about besides Turkish carpets and Bohemian glass. Among other things, they fretted over the wave of marriages between wealthy U.S. women and European noblemen. As one opponent wrote in a heated letter to the *Chicago Tribune*: "It is distressing as well as disgusting to see our beautiful, pure, and accomplished girls thus stoop and throw themselves away on such wretched scum as this bartering, conscienceless, and immoral class comprises. . . . The forte of this class is hauteur, pomp, exclusiveness, and pleasure-seeking." The critic dismissed the would-be husbands, with their titles, finery, and frivolous pursuits, as mere men of fashion, unworthy of American women. The pursuit of titled husbands struck the Chicago protester as a national disgrace but, fortunately, one limited in scope: because the "titled fellows" were only interested in money, most of "our girls" were safe.[1]

The outcry against transatlantic matches, sometimes sneered at as gilded prostitution, may have centered on the brides, but it was aimed at their entire class and its European allegiances. Faultfinders—including some old-money elites—used the marriages to condemn the social striving and questionable patriotism of the nouveau riche.[2] They censured those who sought to affiliate themselves with the European nobility for putting ambitions of social climbing above national loyalties. In so doing, they defined themselves as comparatively patriotic. Middle-class critics could sniff at such marriages secure in the knowledge that pecunious dukes and counts would not come pounding on their doors, hoping to spirit a bride away. But claims of a class-based immunity to the attractions of European aristocracy rang hollow, for the desire to participate in an international world of fashion extended well into the middle class. Women who could not afford a prince or lord spent extravagant sums on hats made in Paris and gowns à la mode. Unable to procure the titles, they settled for the clothes. No less than the brides who hoped to enhance their social standing through foreign matches, stylish American women expressed a desire to be part of a transatlantic world of fashion. Like the heiresses who cast about for coronets, they sought to position themselves as the most entitled members of the consumers' imperium. The difference was that the vast majority of fashionable women had only imaginary connections to aristocratic circles.

Benedict Anderson coined the term "imagined community" to explain the nature of modern nationalism. He used it to refer to a group of people who did not know each other personally but who still felt a sense of affinity with each other.[3] U.S. fashion writings in the late nineteenth and early twentieth centuries underscore Anderson's point that the press fostered a sense of national belonging, for fashion writings looked beyond particular localities to discuss national standards of taste. But most fashion writings did not stop at the nation's borders. Nationalism was not the outermost ring in the series of concentric circles that constituted fashionable women's identities. Like other facets of the consumers' imperium, the Paris-based fashion system reveals imagined communities that extended far beyond the nation. In addition to showing the inadequacy of a strictly national framework for encapsulating affiliative yearnings, focusing on the world of fashion shows the need to look beyond the nation in explaining how American women differentiated themselves from other women. Women's dress played a major role in marking who belonged inside and who outside the imagined community of imperial consumption. In both its inclusionary and exclusionary functions, fashion reminds us not to take nationalism for granted but to consider just how fabricated imagined communities have been.

Style-conscious women of the late nineteenth century could not remember a time in which fashion was not an international phenomenon or France a leader in women's dress, for these two developments were well in place by 1800. Although the grip of French fashion led to scattered calls for U.S. fashion independence throughout the nineteenth century, most U.S. fashion writing in the late nineteenth and early twentieth centuries reveals an acceptance of, if not complicity with, French fashion dominance. In 1888 Jane C. Croly, until recently the chief staff writer of *Madame Demorest's Mir-*

ror of Fashions, assessed the state of American fashion from an insider's perspective: "It is true that in America we are as yet only an echo. We do not originate our clothes, not in fashionable circles. To-day, we echo La Belle France."[4] The *New York Tribune* could similarly declare in 1912 that the fashion openings in Paris "are always awaited with keen interest all over the world. Buyers from far and near have been camping for weeks as near as possible to the ateliers of the great French designers, who, despite all protestations and arguments, govern the world of fashions to-day."[5] When the Parisian designer Madame Paquin sent dresses on a tour of five U.S. cities in 1914, 60,000 people paid to view them in New York alone. Headlines such as "Fashion's Dictates from Paris," "The Last Word in Paris Fashions," "Seen in the Shops of Paris," and "Paris Notes" revealed, even as they promoted, the reach and allure of Parisian fashion. The grip of French fashion also can be seen in the French terms that cropped up in fashion writing — *de rigueur, bouffant, cachemire des Indes, crêpe de Chine, faille Française* — to list a few from one report on "Seasonable Styles."[6]

High-end retailers often joined with fashion writers in proclaiming Paris "the style center of the world."[7] Stores that imported blouses, suits, hats, robes, trimmings, and other items of dress emphasized the French origins of their goods. One such company, J. M. Giddings and Company, a tony Fifth Avenue establishment, advertised itself as "The Paris Shop of America." It claimed to "introduce the Correct Paris Fashions in America — first."[8] John Wanamaker's was just as forthright in stressing the imported origins of its wares: "When our commissioner stepped off the S.S. *Rotterdam* ten days ago she brought with her six trunks straight from Paris." Promised another dress goods retailer: "You can almost catch the odor of their recent ocean voyage."[9]

Along with fashion writers and department stores, milliners and dressmakers (the latter made most high-end dresses in an age when ready-made wear for women was just catching on) emphasized their French connections if they were lucky enough to have them or brazen enough to fabricate them. When Madame Nicole, creator of millinery styles for the Maison Georgette of Paris, set up shop in New York, she publicized her store as "Nicole de Paris Chapeaux Parisiens." Her advertisements, in mixed French and English, emphasized the recent arrival of her hats and their "true French accent."[10] Equally aware of the value of French connections, an Atlanta milliner announced her impending trip abroad in the newspaper. She promised to return from her summer travels in Paris, London, and Berlin with "new ideas and pretty goods."[11] According to one fashion writer, cutting-edge dressmakers traveled to Europe not only "to sharpen up their wits" but to "make the most of our snobbish American delight at anything that is 'imported.'"[12]

Despite long hours and exacting work, most milliners, dressmakers, and seamstresses earned far too little to travel abroad. Nevertheless, many strove for a French cachet by copying French fashion plates and by fabricating French personas. The Tirocchi sisters, immigrant Italian women who owned an upscale dressmaking establishment in Providence, read *Vogue* and *Harper's Bazaar* (full of news of French fashion), consulted the magazine *Les Créations Parisiennes*, referred to model books on Paris designs, and purchased luxury fabrics from France.[13] Dressmakers whose only ties to France were fashion bulletins did not hesitate to refer to themselves as "modistes," and the boldest among them prefixed their names with "Madame" and "Mlle." One woman who recognized the economic value of a French persona was Ellen Demorest. Born in Saratoga, New York, she passed herself off as Mme Demorest when she became head of Demorest's pattern company. So many dressmakers affected French roots that the *Atlanta Constitution* praised one local modiste for being the genuine article. "Madame la Modiste is not called so just because she is a dressmaker. She is not a lady with a French name and a strong German accent, neither is [she] a Parisian from Cork or a New Yorker whose accent proclaims her from the wild and woolly west. She is a genuine Parisian."[14]

Although U.S. publications tended to acknowledge Paris as the world capital of women's fashion, they recognized other European cities as players. London won particular acclaim for tailored goods such as walking jackets, riding habits, and bicycling costumes. But coverage of London fashion did not stop there. Society reports from London also provided details on party dresses and theater wear. Other European cities, from Brussels to Vienna, appeared in fashion reports as well. Gowns from Nice, Monte Carlo, and Cannes, all watering holes of the affluent, likewise won favorable mention.[15] But Paris still reigned supreme in the imaginations of most Americans who followed women's fashions: when *Harper's* republished styles from the Berlin *Bazar*, the rival *Demorest's* scored points by claiming to copy from the "fountain-head—from Paris alone, rather than Paris adapted to Berlin." And even in its coverage of the fashions worn across Europe, *Harper's* acknowledged the dominance of Paris, as seen in its assertion that "London is so very near to Paris that *le dernier cri* (the 'latest thing out') appears in Bond Street about as soon as it does in the Rue de la Paix."[16]

Photographs of the clothes worn by American women between the Civil War and World War I bear witness to the widespread following that French fashion attracted. After analyzing a wide range of such photographs, Joan L.

Severa concluded that by the 1840s, all but desperately poor women knew about and adopted aspects of French fashions within a year of their introduction in Paris. It became difficult to procure dress goods during the Civil War, especially in the Confederate states, but American women nonetheless continued to follow French designs, and some women were able to buy imported buttons, fabrics, hats, and laces. Paris maintained its hegemonic grip on middle-class and wealthy women's fashion until the 1890s, when the tailored look popularized by Charles Dana Gibson attracted a large following. But even as U.S. clothing manufacturers exported shirtwaists, French fashion tenaciously maintained its appeal, above all in elegant dresses, better suited for leisure than work.[17]

Although French fashion had upper-crust connotations, working-class women were well attuned to it. Urban working-class women discussed the latest fashions at work, read the fashion columns, kept an eye on the clothes they saw on the streets, and distressed status-conscious reformers by imitating the dress of wealthier women. This is not to say that they copied every detail. Whereas middle-class women preferred dark or subdued colors, working-class women favored brighter palettes. Whereas middle-class women wore more sensible shoes, working-class women favored high French heels. Whereas middle-class women saved their fancy dresses for festive events, working-class women wore them to work, in some cases because they had no other clothes. Despite displaying distinctive tastes, working-class women nonetheless followed the main trends emanating from Paris. They adapted rather than rejected *haute couture*.[18]

For immigrant women, fashion became a means of demonstrating Americanization. This is not to say that there was no ethnic costume in the United States: many Chinese and Mexican immigrant women, for example, continued to dress as they had at home. Yet European immigrants commonly sought to acquire ready-made American clothes upon their arrival to the United States. They purchased these garments both to demonstrate their new identities and to obtain work, for many employers refused to hire immigrants in old country clothes.[19] Cheap ready-to-wear dresses clearly differed from the pricier dresses worn by wealthy women, but they were far more in keeping with the trends of the fashionable world than immigrant women's discarded shawls and kerchiefs. There is some irony to expressing Americanization through the display of French fashions, but to dress American in this period meant to dress with Paris in mind.

French fashion crossed racial and geographic lines as well as ethnic ones. Like working-class white women, working-class black women sometimes drew attention for showy, brightly colored dresses, but wealthy black women followed European fashion trends just as avidly as wealthy white women. As for rural women, they enrolled in government-supported Agricultural Extension Service classes starting in 1914 to learn how to sew stylish clothing following paper patterns. The reach of French fashion sometimes surprised contemporaries, including two home economists visiting a small town in upstate New York. They pegged the residents as backward country folk, so behind the times that they drank unclean water from a well. But to their astonishment, when the women made calls, they were "habited in silk, and their hats drop over their eyes in quite the fashion of Paris."[20] Fashion enabled working-class, immigrant, black, and rural women to appear like ladies, or at least upwardly mobile, and, in some cases, to effect their mobility.[21]

Strangely, all this attention to French fashion played out against a backdrop of U.S. fashion productivity. By 1855 the clothing industry had become New York City's largest; by 1900 more than 134,000 New York men and women made their living as dressmakers, tailors, and garment workers. The U.S. fashion industry made its mark in ready-made clothes, which included tailored jackets and skirts as well as shirtwaists. Whereas the French still regarded women's suits as revolutionary in 1901, they had become common in the United States in the 1860s and extremely popular by the 1880s. "Even Paris concedes our tailored frocks the best in the world," bragged the *New York Tribune* in 1916.[22] Abraham Cahan also discounted Paris fashion dominance in *The Rise of David Levinsky*, a novel about immigrant acculturation and the New York City clothing trade first published in 1917. According to Cahan, recent Jewish immigrants had made the "average American girl a 'tailor-made' girl." The ascent of the ready-made market between 1890 and 1910 had, in his assessment, made Russian Jews more important in American women's fashion than Parisian modistes. Indeed, by 1910 Jewish and Italian immigrant women composed the majority of garment industry workers in the United States. These women met much of the booming domestic demand for clothing.[23]

Besides manufacturing clothing, the United States had a strong pattern-making industry. Demorest started her pattern-making business in New York City in 1860. Her company churned out an average of 23,000 patterns a day in 1871 (the year her catalog first came out simultaneously in London and New York). The more popular designs soon sold as many as 50,000 copies. In marketing her patterns, Demorest highlighted her international connections and appeal. She pointed out that her patterns had won prizes in international exhibitions, and she claimed that "The best Dress-makers in this country, in England, France, and other foreign countries," used them.[24]

Demorest had some stiff competition from Ebenezer Butterick, who started issuing patterns for women's dresses in the late 1860s. In contrast to Demorest, who marketed her patterns primarily to professional dress-makers and their middle-class clients, Butterick marketed his patterns to the masses. In 1871 his company sold more than 6 million patterns. In 1874 he left New York to direct his company's European agencies. In explaining the move, he said that it had "resulted in the establishment of our business on a firm and successful basis in Paris, Vienna, and Berlin. We are even now perfecting arrangements in Dresden and St. Petersburg."[25] Butterick's international ambitions can be seen in the *Delineator*, the fashion magazine he published to sell his patterns. It ran ads in Spanish and German, and it gave prices for Mexican customers. Butterick also published a "cosmo-politan" edition of his magazine, called the *Metropolitan Catalogue of Fashions*, which provided full descriptions in English, Spanish, and German. Confident that his patterns had no equals, Butterick challenged the "united world" to excel them.[26]

As the international markets obtained by U.S. pattern makers suggest, the U.S. fashion industry started to reach beyond the nation's borders in this period. Government trade data for 1870 reveal more than $680,000 in clothing exports, mostly to Asia, the Pacific (especially Hawaii), and the Americas. By 1910 clothing exports had risen to more than $10.4 million, and by 1920 the United States was exporting more than $113 million in clothes.[27] Clothing exporters trumpeted their international successes to their domestic audiences. B. Altman and Company, for example, proudly announced in its 1880 catalog that it mailed goods to "all parts of the United States and Territories, Canada, Central and South America and West Indies, etc."[28] Fashion experts likewise gloried in their international following. In 1896 *Vogue* claimed sales in Canada, Mexico, Japan, Great Britain, continen-tal Europe, India, South America, and Australia. "When a fashion changes in New York, its influence is felt from the Atlantic to the Pacific, and from Canada and British America to the Gulf of Mexico," boasted fashion writer Frances Faulkner in the pages of the *Ladies World*. Yet even Faulkner had to admit that the original source of these fashions was exogenous. "The chief cities of the United States, more especially New York and Boston, are in constant touch with the great fashion centers of Europe, and they seek out the best and most graceful modes, while American genius modifies, adapts and develops them to suit the beauty-loving instincts of our people."[29]

Faulkner's invocation of the "great fashion centers of Europe" serves as a reminder that despite the productivity of the U.S. garment industry and the predominantly regional export markets for U.S. fashion, much of the design inspiration for U.S. fashions came from Paris, frequently passing through New York before being disseminated more broadly. Indeed, into the teens, the United States remained a net importer of clothes. In the fiscal year ending June 30, 1869 (on the eve of the Franco-Prussian War), the United States imported close to $20 million of finished clothing items, roughly $4 million of that from France (compared to about $680,000 in total clothing exports). By 1910 clothing imports had doubled to almost $40 million, roughly $8.5 million from France (compared to approximately $10.4 million in total clothing exports).[30]

Although import figures overshadowed export figures until the advent of World War I, they discount the true influence of French fashion, for domestic goods could seem essentially French, as seen in clothes touted as "Expressive of Paris" or as having the "Cachet of Paris."[31] Above all, France exported styles—something that U.S. Commerce Department statisticians could not quantify, to the great regret of French designers who accused Americans of shamelessly pirating their clothes. Even Demorest and Butterick based their patterns on European designs. Demorest emphasized that her patterns reflected the "latest designs from the highest and best authorities on Fashion in Europe, including Paris, London, Berlin, etc."[32] For his part, Butterick advertised his European presence as a means to keep up-to-date on the fashions. Rather than shrinking the reach of French fashion, the success of U.S. pattern manufacturing helped spread it by enabling home sewers to craft garments that echoed couture clothing.[33]

Regardless of the actual origins of their clothes, fashionable women strove to look French. The Atlanta woman who boasted that she "had a Frenchwoman in New York who made her best things" illustrates the tenacious allure of French fashion, even in an age of New York fashion ascendance.[34] So does the New York merchant who admitted to sewing copies of Paris labels into his domestic dresses because "American women have been brainwashed into thinking French clothes are superior."[35] Recognizing the allure of Paris fashion, department stores pronounced their Paris modes "authentic," fashion writers praised fabric for being "characteristically French," women's magazines provided pictures of French dresses for home sewers to copy, and advertisers trumpeted their wares as "more 'Frenchy' than ever and very 'chic.'"[36] Rising exports notwithstanding, in the late nineteenth century U.S. designers continued to defer to Paris as the ultimate arbiter of style.

So what explains the cult of French fashion in the United States? Material reasons undoubtedly contributed to its appeal. Paris had a sophisticated fashion industry with long-standing connections to aristocratic circles and growing patronage from new-money elites who wished to show that they had arrived. Charles Frederick Worth, an Englishman by birth, became the leading light of this industry in the late nineteenth century, after rising to fame as the couturier to Empress Eugénie in the 1860s. Worth took advantage of the highly skilled workers and wealthy international clientele found in Paris to establish *grande couture*.[37] The dresses made by Worth and other leading couturiers were truly works of art. Small-town seamstresses would be hard put to duplicate them.

But the appeal of French fashion went far beyond couture dresses. Few women could actually afford a couture gown. As the emphasis on looking French suggests, Frenchness implied a sense of style. According to numerous fashion reports, the elusive phenomenon of French taste extended from the humblest shopgirl to the wealthiest lady.[38] In this respect, fashion seemed to be a national or racial, rather than a class, aesthetic.

But what was taste? The fashions changed every season. Their instability showed just how subjective taste could be. If French taste was not timeless, neither was it necessarily even French, for Paris designers drew on styles from around the world. In their search for novelty, they looked far beyond the bounds of the wealthy, Western communities they catered to, thus popularizing a wide range of materials and styles. Closest to home, they revived and reinterpreted folk designs from around Europe. As European peasants forsook local and regional dress for Paris fashions, leading designers incorporated aspects of the discarded garments, thus aligning themselves more closely with nostalgic exponents of ethnic dress than with the peasants themselves.[39]

Occasionally French designers looked to the United States. One passing fad involved skunk skin. Designers reportedly offered it to shoppers "with a great flourish," calling it "*skonce américaine*" and assuring them that it was "*très haute môde*." "Of course," said one less than enthusiastic American, "it costs more here than at home, but its odor, when it has been out in the rain, is no whit improved by importation."[40] After the Buffalo Bill show stopped in Paris, milliners made hats with wide rolling brims that they dubbed "Buffalo" and "Annie Oakley." Following the U.S. entrance into the Great War, French designers drew on Native American motifs to express their appreciation (ill. 2.1).[41] In these cases, to favor French design meant to favor ostensibly American tastes.

In their search for inspiration, French designers more commonly looked

2.1. Daring Indian Gown
(detail), from Anne
Rittenhouse, "What Well-
Dressed Women Will
Wear," *New York Tribune*,
Feb. 10, 1918. Courtesy
of the Rare Books, Manu-
scripts, and Special
Collections Library,
Duke University,
Durham, North Carolina.

to the East, crafting brightly colored Orientalist garments. In 1880 *Godey's* reported on the popularity of Turkish jackets in Paris, noting that even women "who have hitherto avoided everything like eccentricity or conspicuousness in dress" had adopted them. The following month, it discussed Eastern influences on textiles, saying that French manufacturers had beautifully imitated the colors and patterns of Chinese, Indian, and Japanese goods.[42] In 1896 a visit of the shah of Persia suggested "embroideries and soft eastern colors to the dressmakers."[43] The Japanese victory in the Russo-Japanese War led to the introduction of the kimono sleeve, and, according to the Paris correspondent of the *Ladies' Home Journal*, the Japanese influence extended to draped bodices too. The Orientalist costumes of the Ballets Russes, which performed in Paris in 1909, sparked yet another Eastern craze. In 1920 the popularity of North Africa as a source of inspiration led the *Times Picayune* of New Orleans to characterize French design as "One Step from Savage, But Fashionable."[44]

By covering such borrowings, U.S. fashion writings made it clear that Parisian fashion was eclectic in its origins. Fashion reports published between 1880 and 1912 mentioned Breton bonnets, Spanish mantillas, Irish cloaks, Bulgarian embroidery, Italian lace-edged ruffles, Scotch plaid shawls, and the like. In a page of drawings labeled "Fashion Gleanings from Abroad," *Demorest's* included four outfits described as "Russian" in inspiration and one Swiss-looking waist (ill. 2.2).[45] In 1914 the *Ladies' Home Journal* ran an article on "The New Spanish Dresses," identified as "picturesque in color, fabric, and design" (ill. 2.3).[46] The desire to attribute distant origins to dress goods affected even the names given to colors. Geographic descriptors such as "Swedish tints," "Turk red," "bluish Russian green," and "Abyssinian shades of brown" typified much fashion reportage. An 1892 report in the *New York Tribune* expressed awe at the bricolage of fashion: "Never assuredly have there been so many different styles inaugurated by that autocrat known by the name of 'La Mode.' In one and the same drawing-room or salon one sees to-day costumes in the style of Louis XIV, of Russia, of the French Empire, of Walachia, of Greece, and of Japan."[47] American women who kept up with fashion writing knew very well that *La Mode*, though ostensibly French, was based on appropriation.

As the coverage of the far-flung origins of French design indicates, couturiers did more than create style, they validated it. Rather than inhering just in the dresses themselves or in the appearance of any particular item, the appeal of French fashion inhered in its connotations. In writings on fashion, clothes never just stood for themselves; they signified affiliation with particular groups. Fashion served as a way to assert social belonging. It signified inclusion in an imagined community of consumption.

This is not to say that the fixation on French fashion reveals a deep-seated Francophilia among American women or a sense of exceptional affinity with the French people. The women who sought French fashions may have regarded the French favorably, but in all probability this was as much a *result* of their fashion preferences as a cause of them. The imagined community implied by French fashion was not France per se. French peasant women had no place in this community, and French working-class women existed only on its periphery. Nor did French fashion necessarily evoke images of wealthy French women: fashion writings were just as likely to associate it with the *haute monde* from other nations. Like other women committed to the Paris-based fashion system, American women looked to Paris because they thought that meant being world class. Guided by fashion writers and purveyors who spoke of "the newest and best the world has to offer" and couturiers "of world wide fame," they embraced the idea of fashion as an international (albeit overwhelmingly European) system that happened to be centered in Paris.[48]

Fashion Gleanings from Abroad.

(For Descriptions, see Page 62.)

WE DO NOT GIVE PATTERNS FOR ANY OF THE DESIGNS ON THIS SUPPLEMENT.

2.2. Fashion Gleanings from Abroad, *Demorest's Family Magazine* 29 (Nov. 1892): 61. Courtesy of the Winterthur Library: Printed Book and Periodical Collection, Winterthur, Delaware.

2.3. Augusta Reimer, "The New Spanish Dresses," *Ladies' Home Journal* 31
(Mar. 1914): 29. Courtesy of the Winterthur Library: Printed Book and
Periodical Collection, Winterthur, Delaware.

Writings on France as a fashion mecca made it clear that American women were not the only ones who looked to Paris for their clothes. The *Delineator* reported that "some of the wealthy Russian ladies have standing orders with the leading Parisian *modistes* and dressmaking establishment to furnish them forthwith the latest *cri* of fashion."[49] Greek women "ape Paris fashions," reported popular travel writer Burton Holmes. Even German women, often stereotyped as dowdy, reportedly recognized the superiority of French designs. This represented a coup for French fashion, because German women were known for being "loyal to home fashion, home manufacture."[50] Wealthy Englishwomen too reportedly coveted French fashions. An American woman who shopped at Worth's reported recognizing and being recognized by "many familiar friends—for it is at these places [Worth's and Doucet's] beyond all others in Paris that the best dressed English and American women meet to look at new styles, to gossip and to enjoy themselves generally."[51] If the clothes marked membership in an exclusive transatlantic club, the designer's salon served as a clubhouse in which wealthy women could meet their compatriots—of varying nationalities—in the realm of fashion.

Although the imagined community of fashion united primarily American and European women, its reach extended much further. In addition to mentioning the various nationalities of the European women who shopped in Paris, fashion writings made it clear that wealthy Latin American women also purchased their clothes there. In 1892 the *New York Tribune* ran a gossipy account of a family of well-dressed "South Americans" who lived in Paris a good part of the year. The newspaper's U.S. informant found them "charming" and "noticeable for their perfect taste in gowns." Having established their impeccable taste, she relayed their advice, which further marked them as insiders to the world of fashion: "They tell me that they now get everything from Doucet, finding him much to be preferred to Worth, who, it is whispered, is getting rather old fogyish."[52] One need not travel all the way to Paris to find well-dressed Latin American women, however. In another travel report, Burton Holmes noted that "feminine Buenos Aires naturally takes Paris for her model." (Indeed, the French designer Mme Paquin had a branch in that city.)[53] In the teens, Havana won a reputation for being a "transplanted Paris," slightly behind the times in women's dress, but still brilliant. Those hoping to spot some local color looked in vain for mantillas at elite Cuban gatherings, for French fashion reigned supreme. Observed the *Tribune*: "The Havanese, like her Spanish neighbors in Argentina, Brazil and Chili [sic], lives for and has her very being in beautiful clothes."[54]

Just as the commitment to French fashion proved the modernity of Latin

American women—or at least of those who discarded their mantillas and other items of traditional dress—U.S. fashion writing presented the spread of European fashion as an index to civilization in Asia, the Pacific, and the Middle East. Coverage of Japan's efforts to claim a place "among modern civilizations" emphasized that "a chief phase of the movement is the decision of the Japanese women to adopt the European dress."[55] The empress herself ordered gowns from Worth. Similarly, accounts of the modernizing Young Turk movement highlighted Turkish women's Parisian tastes in clothes. The U.S. press also reported favorably on the appearance of Queen Lili'uokalani, who dressed in a tiara and fashionable gowns to prove her royal status to westerners inclined to see Hawaiians as savages.[56] If women from around the world were looking to France for fashion, not to do so would mean being stuck in a provincial backwater, outside the major currents of the time. It would mean settling for second-rate in an era of international standards. Through fashion, American women affiliated themselves with the entitled and the trendy, the civilized and modern, from around the world.

Fashion writers sometimes obscured the role of fashion in determining social distinction by invoking feminine universalism. In an 1889 article subtitled "Cosmopolitan Styles," a fashion writer for the *Ladies' Home Journal* said that "the universal desire to dress becomingly is essentially feminine and natural." A year later, another contributor to the *Journal* expressed similar sentiments: "I write and I talk to the general woman. She is the woman all over the world who is interested in looking her best."[57] In foregrounding the seemingly borderless world of femininity, the universalist understanding of fashion assumed a world in which common values and aesthetics framed rivalries over beauty. Rather than dwelling on the ways that race, class, nationality, and culture contributed to the divisions among women, this approach to fashion emphasized how taste united them. But such references to a worldwide feminine essentialism notwithstanding, most writings on fashion drew attention to its exclusive character. To begin with, fashion signified class.

The world of fashion, in its quintessential form, was an aristocratic world, a world of independently wealthy pleasure seekers who lived in close proximity to and yet, in terms of their life-styles and status, far apart from ordinary people in places like Paris, Monte Carlo, Newport, and stately English country houses. Rather than being defined by distinctive boundaries that could be drawn onto a map, the fashionable world divided near neighbors and spilled over national lines. As *Vanity Fair* said of the fashionable women at Monte Carlo: "They belong to Paris, to Vienna, to St. Petersburg. They are the citizens of the world."[58] The U.S. press, which covered its doings in great detail, acknowledged the domestic component of the fashionable world but made it clear that its center lay in Europe. Society pages presented Europe as the wellspring of fashion, the source that influenced even U.S. elites. Those at the top of the U.S. social hierarchy might enjoy enviable riches and aloof status, but as their embrace of European dress and emulation of European aristocrats indicated, they were at best peripheral representatives of the fashionable world.

The aristocratic character of the fashionable world inhered not only in its Europeanness but also in its tastes. Significantly, fashion reportage devoted disproportionate coverage to fancy dress, intended for social events rather than work. Restrictive corsets, trailing skirts, massive hats, and delicate laces advertised a woman's removal from hard labor. Beyond that, they indicated an ability to command labor: that of the workers who made the effusion of textiles, who sewed the elaborate patterns, and who helped clean, mend, and otherwise maintain garments characterized, in many cases, by stunning artistry. (*Demorest's* bluntly pointed out that Parisian ladies preferred light colors because they "cost a fortune to launder" and because black served as "almost a uniform" among working-class women.)[59] The names given to dresses—tea gowns, evening gowns, ball gowns, casino gowns, yachting costumes, watering-place costumes, and so forth—spoke of the social functions they were intended to grace. The imagined world of fashion was a world of consumption, not production (or reproduction, judging from the pinched silhouettes), even though producers could claim fleeting affiliation through emblematic purchases.[60] These might not root them firmly in the fashionable world, but they could at least express a commitment to belonging.

Just as contemporaries saw fashion as aristocratic in its internationalism and its extravagance, they regarded it as aristocratic in its origins. *Cosmopolitan* magazine attributed the origins of the fashion system to Empress Eugénie of France. It noted that the fashion system had become more oligarchic since the fall of the second empire in 1870, but it still credited "members of the old nobility" with sanctioning the fashions. Department stores then popularized their decisions. "But this gives the death blow to the garment; for, just as soon as it becomes common, the great people discard it."[61] Though more democratic than it had been in the days of Eugénie, fashion still bore the imprimatur of aristocracy and great wealth. The recognition that a garment ceased to be fashionable as soon as it became common revealed a clear understanding of its exclusionary intention.

As the *Cosmopolitan* article recognized, department stores played an important role in disseminating fashion because of their prominence as retail outlets. But it was fashion reportage that took the lead in affixing the connotations to the goods. To authenticate particular styles as truly fashionable, some reports cited exclusive dressmakers and designers. Others proceeded from the premise that society functions offered the strongest proof of fashionability. Hence U.S. fashion writings alluded to the outfits seen at weddings in London, the races at Ostend, the casinos on the Riviera, the fetes at the Paris Grand Opera, the trendy bridge teas of Paris, the country clubs of France, and "the fashionable promenades where smart French women take their daily airing." In the effort to convey what should be worn when, fashion writers provided extensive coverage of the "idle set."[62] And the more they did so, the more the clothing they profiled came to evoke this set. Rather than just selling dresses, fashion writings sold aspirations of belonging. The vast majority of American women who copied French fashions could but dream of sojourns in Paris and seasons in London, but they too could participate (if only vicariously) in the upper-crust world of fashion by copying the costumes that signified inclusion.

Despite the ascent of a merchant, banking, and manufacturing elite in Europe, U.S. fashion reports highlighted the role of aristocrats within the international idle set. (After all, if American consumers were going to copy plutocrats, they need not look abroad.) Titled women, such as the "pretty young duchess" who wore a "tailored costume of beige and tan silk" to the Bagatelle Exposition and the duchess who wore a "lovely gown of white tulle hung in tunic skirts over gold gauze" to a Paris theater, made the fashion columns of U.S. newspapers. Likewise, to demonstrate the fashionableness of one of the dresses it featured, *Frank Leslie's* described it as "recently made in Paris for an English lady of rank attached to the Court of Queen Victoria." For its part, *Vogue* laid claim to fashionable credentials by profiling dresses worn by duchesses, countesses, vicomtesses, princesses, and other titled "grandes dames."[63] By-lines such as "Comtesse de Champdoce," "Baroness Salsee," and "Lady Duff-Gordon" that accredited fashion reports underscored the aristocratic pretensions of the fashionable world.[64] The European women of fashion featured in the U.S. newspapers did not always possess titles, but even those who did not displayed strikingly aristocratic life-styles, characterized by leisure, display, and exclusiveness.

Although some royals failed to make the roster of the ultrafashionable, royals often topped the list. As *Cosmopolitan's* explanation of the fashion system suggested, Empress Eugénie featured prominently in fashion writings in the 1860s. Especially when younger, Queen Victoria received notice too. In 1855, for example, *Frank Leslie's* cited her appearance in tartan to explain its popularity in London and Paris. A generation later, *Vogue* called Queen Alexandra "the legitimate head of fashion throughout the vast British domain." Lesser royals—such as Princess Suzanne Czartorisky, spotted wearing a dress adorned with Turkish embroidery—also attracted attention. "Royal princesses often set a fashion," noted an article in *Vogue*. A fashion reporter for *Godey's* knew that she had an enviable scoop when she was afforded the opportunity to inspect the trousseau of a princess—"a real princess, that is to say, one of undoubted royal blood—the damsel in question being the Princess Marie Alexandrina of Saxe-Weimar, niece of the King of Holland."[65]

Associating fashion with aristocracy meant shifting attention away from more than just plutocrats. High-end courtesans purchased dresses from Worth and other French couturiers, and they flaunted their fabulous costumes in public promenades. But, with scattered exceptions (mostly on the part of dress reformers who rejected the world of fashion and on the part of buy-American advocates, who wanted to nationalize it), the U.S. press overlooked their role in establishing trends. It did, however, acknowledge another group of socially suspect women: actresses. An article on Sara Bernhardt, for example, carefully described the outfit she wore to a champagne breakfast. The nature of the coverage can be seen in its description of her hat: "a modification of the Gainsborough mode of dark green plush with a distinct lustre, and trimmed with a heron's aigret, a crow's wing, and two squirrels' heads, which had been so trimmed as to counterfeit the head of a wolverine." This hat presumably came from Felix, of the Rue Boissy d'Anglais, Paris, identified in the article as Bernhardt's choice for millinery and dress. But not all her clothes came from Felix: the article mentioned a girdle given to the actress by the Prince of Wales. Along with her beauty and clothing budget, Bernhardt's life-style—her champagne breakfasts, costly standards of personal display, and connections to royalty—identified her as fashionable.[66] Bernhardt may not have been an aristocrat, but she played the part, on stage and off. The styles she modeled conveyed a whiff of aristocracy along with the bohemianism of the stage.

Few actresses enjoyed the social stature that Bernhardt commanded, but even the costumes worn by lesser actresses conveyed the glamour of the social elite. Fashion writings reported on the clothing worn by theater and opera patrons, and some of this glitter rubbed off on actresses by association. Furthermore, fashion writers often attributed actresses' dresses to the most exclusive designers. Just as frequently, fashion writers presented the costumes worn on stage as the inspiration for designer gowns.[67] And, like aristocrats, actresses occupied the public eye, providing personalities on which to drape the clothes. To dress like an actress might imply dressing seductively or outrageously to some, but to others, it meant to dress like a society woman.

Although actresses won some credit for initiating fashions, aristocrats provided the essential stamp of approval. Thus, another *Cosmopolitan* article on the origins of fashion attributed marked innovations in fashion to actresses but noted that the "correct style" filtered down from the "more fortunate peeresses." Its assertion that Queen Alexandra had "naturally . . . always been a leader of the mode" reveals the assumption that title and rank played a major role in determining fashionability.[68]

Aristocrats had so much weight in the world of fashion that even the dress reformers who rejected fashion for hygienic, moral, aesthetic, and economic reasons turned to royals to popularize their proposals. One praised Queen Victoria and the Russian royal family for introducing sensible outdoor and vacation wear; another promoted greater simplicity in dress by arguing that American women spent too much and appeared too dressy in comparison to European aristocrats. "The American husband, if he has the money, will never limit his wife. An English husband always does. Duchesses, trusting to old lace and jewels, are often extremely shabby as to their gowns, not caring a pin what any one says."[69] The point? To be truly fashionable, American women must dress less lavishly. This seemingly contradictory strategy made some sense to those versed in the logic of the fashionable world: to look truly aristocratic, American women must look less plutocratic.

Historians have found the nineteenth century to be a democratizing age in women's fashion—largely because of the spread of paper patterns—but the wider dissemination of the latest fashions should not blind us to fashion's undemocratic associations.[70] Fashion writings made it clear that the world of fashion encompassed the titled, tremendously rich, and the trendy (even shabby duchesses could be seen as harbingers of more restraint in dress). Though not limited to aristocrats, fashion appeared to emanate from their circles. Through couture clothing and lower-cost copies alike, American women claimed membership in a class-stratified world that placed European aristocrats at the pinnacle.

This desire to associate with European aristocrats, if only imaginatively, seems inconsistent with republican traditions of antipathy to inherited privileges. The outcry against European aristocracy was so great at the time of the American Revolution that the U.S. Constitution forbids hereditary titles. The opposition to aristocracy continued to echo through the nineteenth century. Opponents dismissed aristocrats as degenerate and exploitative, as throwbacks to a feudal past rather than as harbingers of a democratic future. The transatlantic marriages between aristocrats and heiresses fueled the invective, leading to complaints that the fortune hunters were libertines, debtors, and debauchers.[71] To underscore their points about aristocrats' immorality, patriotic critics did not hesitate to censure aristocratic women's dress. One critic denounced gowns seen at court functions for giving the women the appearance of the demimonde. If not immodest, their dress struck critics as ridiculously extravagant, as seen in the charge that Hungarian court ladies had turned charity visits into an "affair of fashion." Dress reformer Abba Goold Woolson denounced fashion itself as an absurdity of "duchesses and queens, whose daily lives are of little value to the world or to themselves, and who can afford to give their time to the display of costly follies."[72] In light of such republican sentiments, what explains the popularity of a fashion system understood to be fundamentally aristocratic?

The most obvious answer to this question is that women who imagined aristocratic connections imagined affiliations with power and privilege. Would-be denizens of the world of fashion scorned national boundaries in their efforts to identify themselves with an entitled transnational elite. Rather than opting out of the fashion system on nationalistic grounds, the American women who followed European styles cast their lot with upperclass internationalism. Aristocrats might not have had as much money as plutocrats—hence their need for transatlantic marriages—but they had considerably greater cultural capital. However small their economic reserves, their cultural prestige made them symbols of what Europe as a whole seemed to offer the United States. To Americans who felt their country lacked tradition, history, and culture, European aristocrats offered standards of taste. Beyond this, they offered examples of power that inhered not just in pocketbooks and political might but in social positioning. In an article titled "Queening It over Ireland," for example, *Vogue* rhapsodized about the social brilliance of Lady Wimborne, wife of the British viceroy to the Emerald Isle. The article made it clear that more than her wealth and the political reach of the British Empire underlay her stature; her title and couturier were also significant.[73]

Besides representing cultural capital, aristocrats represented racial standing. Plutocrats might have Jewish or other socially disparaged backgrounds, but even penniless aristocrats had distinguished pedigrees. In an era marked by increasing interest in family histories and genealogies and the rise of hereditary societies like the Daughters of the American Revolution, aristocrats had enviably long lineages. Those concerned about racial boundary maintenance appreciated aristocrats' ostensibly pure stock.

What made aristocracy particularly attractive to *women* was the conviction that the perquisites of rank were not limited to aristocratic men; women of the aristocracy could wield cultural power even when other forms of power eluded their grasp. Especially during the reign of Queen Victoria, it was hard to escape the conclusion that monarchies offered something that was unavailable in the United States: the possibility that a woman could become head of state. Furthermore, aristocratic women exercised significant power in guarding the boundaries of their class. Men might lead in politics and business, but social life revolved around women. In contrast to American high society, in which men's accomplishments in the marketplace seemed relatively more important in determining status, aristocrats seemed relatively less devoted to the masculine world of commerce than to the feminine world of ritual and display. By expressing allegiance to the world of fashion, American women could thus express a commitment to a social system that seemed to offer women — at least those lucky enough to belong to its inner circles — seemingly unrivaled opportunities to exercise power.[74]

If part of the appeal of the fashionable world stemmed from its difference, from its ability to offer imaginative entitlement and escape, another part of its attraction lay in its familiarity. U.S. newspapers and magazines wove aristocrats into the fabric of everyday life. They devoted considerable attention not only to the royal families of the great powers — Britain, Russia, and Germany foremost among them — but also to minor courts and royals, from Denmark to Bulgaria. Now obscure figures such as the Princess of Bourbon-Sicily, the Prince d'Orleans-Braganza, Prince Victor of Thurn and Taxis, and Princess Louise of Coburg flitted in and out of the pages of the U.S. press. When the Queen of Sweden suffered ill health, U.S. newspapers took note. They also followed the tsarita's trip to the Crimea, Prince Wilhelm's marriage, Baroness des Groches's elopement, Archduchess Isabella's annulment, and Countess des Garets's suicide.[75] The most intimate affairs of European aristocracy made headlines in the United States. Such tell-all coverage may have bred contempt, but it also bred fascination. Aristocrats came across as foreign enough to merit interest and familiar enough to retain it. Those who placed aristocrats at the heart of the imagined community of fashion placed discrete individuals, known for particular habits, tastes, and histories, into the center of the circle. Their individuality helped make the world of fashion seem like a real community and not just a collection of disembodied dresses.

Aristocrats did more than validate fashion; they provided figureheads with which to associate the clothes. Like the actresses who were receiving increasing amounts of press coverage, aristocrats made the imagined world of fashion seem more tangible by associating it with real people. This can be seen in the tendency among fashion writers to shift into gossip mode. The full title of the ladies' magazine *Frank Leslie's Gazette of Fashions and the Beau Monde* showed the conflation of fashion with high-society gossip. So did headlines such as "Dress and Gossip of Paris."[76] Indeed, gossip writing could be viewed as the most effective fashion writing, for if the point of fashion was to prove belonging in society, what better way to learn of what it took to belong than in the society pages? Just as fashion writing often strayed into the realm of gossip, gossip columns devoted considerable attention to clothes. The articles in *Vogue* that mixed descriptions of social functions attended by the "exclusive set" with sketches of the latest toilettes illustrate this trend (ill. 2.4).[77]

The blurry line between fashion and gossip writing enabled the women who followed the fashionable world to buy the connotations along with the clothes, foremost among them, aristocratic distinction. The names attached to various styles denoted the aristocratic longings they helped satisfy: princess gown, duchesse skirt, Empress walking-suit, Queen Margot polonaises. The same held true for brands: Czarina corset, Princess chic supporter, Empress skirt.[78] Fabrics came in shades of Metternich (after the princess who took credit for discovering Worth) and Bismarck. Retailers fueled the affiliative ambitions of their customers by advertising their modistes in terms such as "Costumer to Royalty" and "Costumer to Courts of Europe." "Aristocratic Overcoats at Democratic Prices" proclaimed a 1913 ad.[79]

Along with the tension between foreignness and familiarity, the tension between exclusiveness and accessibility contributed to aristocrats' allure. Hereditary exclusiveness had its attractions to those who felt displaced by new immigrants and the nouveau riche. Nor was it necessarily anathema to those on the fringes of society, who could enjoy the spectacle of their superiors in the local pecking order joining them on the social margins. Furthermore, cracking the aristocratic circle could provide a thrilling challenge, as attested to by the abundance of romantic fiction on this theme. What made this challenge all the more tantalizing was the possibility of success. In the fifty years or so leading up to World War I, U.S. magazines and newspapers painted a picture of wealthy Americans being welcomed, to an unprecedented extent, into aristocratic European circles. The transatlantic brides provided the foremost evidence for this acceptance. Between 1870 and 1914, more than 450 American women married European aristocrats, many of them making headlines in the process. Like European couture clothing, aristocrats came to seem within the grasp of well-heeled debutantes. As an article on shopping for a titled husband noted: "There has been nothing between her [the American girl] and the thing she wanted since she learned to walk. To steadily approach the tree and pluck the peach has been her manifest destiny . . . she has gone to the best shops and has bought the best goods and the latest fashion. So, when she goes to Europe she intends to take the best she can get, Kings and Queens, Dukes and Princes included."[80] The world of fashion, tantalizing to begin with, became doubly so when it offered a chance—however slim—of reaching its innermost sanctums.

Influenced by the impression of purchasability, U.S. press accounts sometimes presented European aristocracy as more open to mobility than the old guard of U.S. high society. According to an article in the *Ladies' Home Journal*, an American woman "who has left her nebulous surroundings in the western continent" might catch the eye of someone at a continental watering place and be proclaimed the new American beauty, "arriving speedily in the inner circle of that portion of the British aristocracy which is safe to welcome, with like fervor, a black bishop or a champion lady-whistler. And what London has endorsed, New York will never put aside. We, in our turn, and despite our bewildered protest that really she was never heard of here, accept little Miss Nobody at second-hand. She and her family, upon re-touching their native shores, shine with a new lustre in our sight. The cavillers who decry English influence upon our manners ought really to be grateful to them for teaching us to practice the democracy we preach."[81] Therein lay much of the attraction of aristocrats: as an exogenous, well-established, and yet occasionally welcoming elite, they countered domestic hierarchies without countering hierarchy itself. They promised to legitimate people on the margins. They functioned, in essence, like fine clothes, for they provided social aspirants with a means of entrée. They ratified worth and confirmed status, offering even the low-born outsider an opportunity to become the consummate insider. Of course, most fashionable American women never mingled with aristocrats outside of their imaginations. But the fewer American women who mingled with aristocrats, the fewer there were who had felt snubbed or slighted in real encounters. The more distant aristocrats were in actuality, the more intimate they could become in fantasy.

What made these fantasies of inclusion so enticing was that aristocrats stood for exclusion. Not everybody could be an aristocrat; not everybody could even socialize with them. American women tried to dress like European aristocrats both to signal their affinities with the social elite and to signal their distance from those lower on the social scale. Along with promoting geographically expansive feelings of affiliation, fashion demarcated borders that separated "us" from "them." These lines divided fashionable women from most other women on more than just the basis of class. Insofar as it emanated from Europe and was particularly associated with the hereditary nobility, fashion signified whiteness. And insofar as observers took careful note of the geographic origins of participants, fashion served as an index of national and civilizational standing.

Those who looked to Paris for fashion believed that other styles of dress signified marginality. This can be seen particularly clearly in ethnographic writings, including ones adjacent to fashion columns on women's pages. Rather than presenting all dress as ethnic, that is, as geographically and culturally bounded, ethnographic accounts drew a line between fashion (by which they meant the styles emanating from Paris) and the clothes worn by most of the world's women. A *National Geographic Magazine* article on Bulgaria, for example, juxtaposed pictures of women college students in "Euro-

2.5. Photographs from Hester Donaldson Jenkins, "Bulgaria and Its Women," *National Geographic Magazine* 27 (Apr. 1916): 382. Courtesy of the University of Illinois at Urbana-Champaign Library.

Photo by Theron J. Damon

UNEDUCATED BUT HAPPY : BULGARIA

Photo by Hester Donaldson Jenkins

BULGARIAN COLLEGE STUDENTS : IS NOT EDUCATION WORTH WHILE?

"Often the daughter of an unlettered peasant, living in a remote village, after some years of schooling, will take her place in Sofia or Varna as a teacher or leader in civic betterment. Her peasant costume and knitted footwear she exchanges for a European dress in excellent taste. The heavy, falling braids of her hair she now arranges in the fashion of the day. Her manner becomes assured, yet modest, and she takes her place as a leader of a woman's reading club or a member of a hospital board with proper dignity. . . . I was told in Sofia that women from the college were the greatest influence for higher ideals that the city possessed" (see text, page 398).

pean dress" with "uneducated" peasant women in local styles, the point clearly being to demarcate the vast gulf in culture and outlook between them (ill. 2.5).[82] Folk costumes might be picturesque, admitted these accounts, but in contrast to fashionable dress, they were parochial, backward, and lower-class. If the fashionable world was the world of the appropriators, the rest of the world was appropriated. To buy into the fashion system centered in Paris thus meant to distinguish oneself from penurious, colored, and colonized people.

The distance between fashionable women and those who did not don Paris styles also could be seen in stereographic shows of native costumes from around the world and in advertisements that used women in local dress to represent other countries. The Singer sewing machine company drew attention to the global hierarchies of fashion in trade cards that depicted people (mostly women) in "typical" clothing, with descriptive text on the back. As their label, "Costumes of All Nations," suggests, these cards purported to teach geography through dress. One set, distributed at the World's Columbian Exposition in 1893, contained no cards for the United States, England, France, or Germany—nations where women presumably donned "fashions" rather than "costumes." But Europe was represented, by Bosnia, Hungary, Naples, the Netherlands, Norway, Portugal, Rumania, Spain, and Sweden. The non-European cards included Algeria, Ceylon, China, India, Tunisia, and Zululand.[83]

Taken as a whole, the Singer cards suggested that the "natives" of Naples and Norway had something in common with those of Algeria and Ceylon: "peculiar" local dress. Despite the advent of the sewing machine—heralded as a great aid to all the women on the cards—native dress seemed essentially unchanged and hence located outside of the world of fashion, which was, by definition, ephemeral. The women pictured on Singer's cards were incorporated into an international capitalist system to the extent that they now sewed their clothes by machine, but their continued adherence to seemingly traditional dress revealed them to be oddities on the fringes of modernity and high culture. Zululand provided the one exception, at least as far as adherence to traditional dress was concerned: the women on that card wore simple versions of Western fashions, the point being that the British Empire, with help from Singer, had done them the favor of covering their nakedness. The Zulu women may have abandoned their customary habiliments, but according to the Singer cards, they resembled the women who had not, in that they received rather than initiated modernizing developments.

To be sure, U.S. observers often described folk costumes as picturesque. They appreciated their historical roots and, no less significantly, their current ephemerality. By the late nineteenth century, U.S. fashion writing made it clear that folk costumes were passing, especially in Europe. An article on the costumes worn by "stolid Dutch fisherfolk" described them as carryovers "from a by-gone age."[84] Most reports on folk clothing assumed the nostalgic, sentimentalizing tone of the wealthy Europeans who strove to preserve the remnants of ethnic dress. A piece on Switzerland, published in *Godey's* in 1876, was no exception. It recalled that in times gone by, nearly every valley "prided itself on some distinguishing feature of dress or ornament." But in recent years, the railroad had penetrated even the most secluded spots, bringing the styles with it. The Swiss women who still wore their traditional costumes apparently did so only for the benefit of the tourist trade. "It is a thousand pities, that costume has disappeared all over Europe. It is a loss to the painter," mourned an equally regretful article in the *Ladies' Home Journal*.[85]

2.6. "A Forecast of Fall Fashions in the Balkan War Zone," *Vanity Fair* 3 (Sept. 1914): 38. Courtesy of the Winterthur Library: Printed Book and Periodical Collection, Winterthur, Delaware.

The sentimentalizing of folk clothes did not mean untrammeled enthusiasm for them, however. Fashion writings tended to treat folk costume as indicative of provincial sensibilities and tightly constricted communities. An ironical photo montage in *Vanity Fair* titled "A Forecast of Fall Fashions in the Balkan War Zone," went so far as to associate folk costumes with ethnic conflict. Published in 1914, at the start of the fighting in Europe, it featured twelve women, including "A Girl of Turkish Bosnia," "A Magyar Girl," and a "Girl of Croatia," each in a distinctive dress. The irony resided in labeling these dresses "fall fashions," for they appeared more timeless than trendy. Indeed, the very existence of a Balkan war zone seemed related to the disparity in the women's dresses. Their traditional costumes bespoke such narrowly bounded lives that even near neighbors had little in common. The failure to follow a unifying fashion system helped explain the failure to live together in peace (ill. 2.6).[86]

In addition to connoting localism, folk costumes connoted lower-class standing. Travelers who noted the persistence of local costumes might regard them as attractive, but they almost invariably described them as peasant garb. Geographic accounts published in the United States did provide images of picturesque peasant women happily frolicking in village fetes and carnivals, but these were shadowed by images of desperately poor, miserably uncomfortable, prematurely aged, and frightfully ugly peasant women. In one account, a Rumanian bride appeared "richly dressed in gold embroidered costume, with head-dress of orange blossoms and long threads of gold." But even as the article called the "costume" of the Rumanian peasant "perhaps the most artistic in the world," it deplored the sorry condition of the peasantry.[87] The Russian women of another account wore "nothing but handkerchiefs upon their heads while working in the field and their feet are generally bare. . . . Their dresses are short and they tuck them up when they are working. They wear little or no underclothes and their summer dress consists of this shirt, a chemise and a short sack, which extends only to the waist. . . . The peasant woman knows nothing of the corset and she has no idea of fashion. The people wear the same costumes from year to year, and the peasant dress of today is the same as that of generations ago."[88] As this account indicates, folk costumes, however attractive at their finest, were also suspect, for they connoted poverty, hard labor, ignorance, backwardness, and stagnation to the observers who eyed them from the perspective of the fashionable world.

Perhaps worst of all, folk costumes signified affinities with non-Western women, who also wore clothes that seemed strange to middle-class American women. The association between European and non-European folk costume can be seen in a *Chicago Tribune* article on Easter hats. "How would you like to attend a reception or go to church today wearing any of the strange bonnets printed on this page?" questioned the article, which featured hats from "those places where women still wear their native costumes." These places included Switzerland, Alsace, the Netherlands, Naples, Turkey, Algiers, and Tunis.[89] From the white Dutch headdress to the close-fitting Tunisian "fez" (a misnomer, because only men wore fezzes in Tunisia), all the hats came across as ethnic curiosities. However disparate the women, they nonetheless had something in common: they were all outsiders to the world of fashion. Their headdresses marked them as local anomalies in an age of growing international connections.

Though European peasant women struck many ethnographic writers as throwbacks to a more localized age, women in Africa, Asia, Latin America, and the Pacific generally struck them as most backward of all. To be sure, some won recognition for adopting Paris fashions, but these women came across as elite path breakers. As an article on Mexican women noted, "The people who can afford it wear the Frenchiest of French creations in the way of hats," but the majority of women just wore light scarves. Indeed, the "great middle class," clad only in sandals, still went without stockings.[90] These Latin American women were a far cry from their compatriots who shopped in Paris. The same held true for Hawaiians. Despite Queen Lili'uokalani's impressive wardrobe, the dress worn by most of her country-women, joked travel writer Burton Holmes, "would not be tolerated in the state of Kansas."[91]

A more sinister tone characterized much writing on Eastern women's dress. The horrors of foot-binding proved particularly compelling to those who reported on China. Though not as physically constricting, veils also came to symbolize bondage. Travelers to the Middle East reported disparagingly on concealing headdresses, claiming that Muslim fathers sometimes went so far as to beat their daughters for appearing unveiled at the windows of their homes. On the opposite end of the spectrum from excessively constricting and obscuring clothing lay scanty dress. This too struck Western observers as being beyond the pale. During the 1904 St. Louis Fair, an official declared that Igorrotes from the Philippine exhibit should not go out in society because of their exposed skin. This led a journalist to humorously characterize top-free Igorrote fashions as "extremely décolleté."[92] The skimpy coverings of tropic peoples clearly called for Western sartorial intervention. Indeed, as the Zulu card in the Singer collection suggests, the Christianizing and civilizing project embraced by Western missionaries, governments, and corporations included reclothing non-European women in the garb of Western modernity, or at least a simplified version thereof.[93]

Even critics of the Paris-based fashion system shared the assumption that fashion indicated civilizational standing and modernity. One of the most perceptive commentators on fashion in the late nineteenth century was Thorstein Veblen, known for his observation that ostentatious dress demonstrated membership in the leisure class. But Veblen did not limit his remarks to the class implications of fashion. "It is well known that certain relatively stable styles and types of costume have been worked out in various parts of the world; as, for instance, among the Japanese, Chinese, and other Oriental nations; likewise among the Greeks, Romans, and other Eastern peoples of antiquity; so also, in later times, among the peasants of nearly every country of Europe," he wrote. "These national or popular costumes are in most cases adjudged by competent critics to be more becoming, more artistic, than the fluctuating styles of modern civilised apparel."[94] According to Veblen, ancient people, Orientals, and European peasants all existed outside of the world of fashion. This did not mean that their clothes were unattractive—to the contrary—but it did mean that they did not change from year to year. They also had limited appeal, as seen in their only having a national or local following.

Dress reformers allied with the women's rights movement tended to agree with Veblen's assessments that fashion was a modern, upper-class, Western phenomenon. Writing in the *Ladies' World* (a women's magazine with extensive fashion coverage), Frances E. Fryat presented China as a welcome alternative to the Western fashion system. "Fashion is the great modern Juggernaut which crushes under its massive wheels tens of thousands of victims. . . . I think that the Chinese have the advantage over women of the western world. Their costumes are regulated by ancient custom and do not change. There are no apings and envyings; each class has its regulation dress; consequently there is a restfulness among them which is not known to their western sisters. The modern Chinese women of the better classes have more leisure to devote to study and improvement than American women of the same classes can compass. Here it is a race to keep up with the requirements of the ever-changing fashions."[95]

Whereas Fryat deplored fashion for constricting women's minds and channeling their energies, other dress reformers stressed the health benefits of Eastern modes of dress. These reformers blamed confining corsets for female invalidism and, because of their implications for reproduction, racial degeneracy. Looking for alternatives to the Western silhouette, they frequently invoked Oriental women as models. Responding to those who found Eastern dress unattractive, one reformer shifted perspectives, claiming that Oriental women regarded the corseted "civilized" woman as "ugly and stiff and unnatural."[96] Another asserted that "Paganism and the Chinese women only bandage their feet, while Christian women bandage, with equally unrelenting self-sacrifice, the vital organs."[97] Western fashion abuses seemed all the more appalling given that even supposedly inferior peoples—known for their mistreatment of women—did not stoop that far. The Western woman might recoil at the bound feet of the Chinese woman, but she should envy her unfettered waist. (Indeed, she ended up copying this waist. Aesthetic women in the Gilded Age adopted a corsetless dress, influenced by Eastern costumes, that served as a precursor to the fashions of the teens.)[98]

Although dress reformers shared the widespread belief that a huge gulf separated the world of fashion from other systems of dress, their favorable assessments of other forms of dress put them far from mainstream thinking on fashion. A contributor to the *Ladies' World*, Frances Faulkner, revealed a more typical attitude toward women outside the purview of the

2.7. "Superb Chinese Coat," *Vogue* 29 (Feb. 7, 1907): 189. Courtesy of the Winterthur Library: Printed Book and Periodical Collection, Winterthur, Delaware.

Paris fashion system. "The higher the civilization, the more important is the part played by costume, and the more subject to marked changes and fluctuations in its fashioning. This is due to the mental activity, the spirit of invention which is abroad, as well as to the culture and refinement of a highly civilized people. . . . In Oriental countries there is no change in costume; law, custom, tradition and necessity forbid it." According to Faulkner, fluctuations in dress signified the superiority of Western civilization, rather than its wastefulness and frivolousness. Fashion indicated mental activity and an inventive spirit.[99]

Faulkner's efforts to draw a line between Western and Eastern dress overlooked not only the ways that Eastern dress had changed over time but also the debts that Western fashion owed to Eastern designs. In marketing Asian imports, silk purveyors stressed more than cost and quality. They presented the Orientalism of their fabric as an important part of its appeal. Vantine's trumpeted the "pretty Oriental designs" on its silk; Simpson Crawford

Company advertised that its silks displayed "all the noted Oriental effects for which the Japs are famous." Mme Najla Mogabgab, a New York importer (with branches in Palm Beach, Newport, and Hot Springs, Virginia) touted the "originality" of her wares, saying "the clever use of genuine Oriental fabrics and ornaments is what distinguishes many of Mme. Mogabgab's creations from models made by dressmakers who lack her direct connection with the centers of Far Eastern art and commerce."[100] Vendors and fashion writers touted even French silks—sometimes decorated with conventionalized poppies, great lotus leaves, or other seemingly Asian touches—as Eastern in character.[101] And if French goods won acclaim for looking Eastern, then surely Eastern goods could be seen as French, and hence all the more desirable to fashionable U.S. consumers.

Along with welcoming fabrics that struck them as essentially Oriental, fashionable American women wore garments that struck them as Oriental in their cut. Like aristocratic European women, they wore Chinese mandarin coats to the opera, assuming a kind of theatricality in their persons equivalent to that shown on stage (ill. 2.7).[102] By the teens, Orientalism had made a significant mark on women's everyday wear. Starting around 1910, corset-determined curves gave way to straighter lines. Observers often acknowledged that the new silhouette owed a debt to Eastern dress. The *New York Tribune*, for example, maintained that the French "did not originate the sheath gown," but that it resembled the national costume of Burmese women. In 1914 the *Ladies' Home Journal* noted that "this season we are borrowing from almost every Oriental country and the effect is most picturesque. We have adapted the Persian lampshade tunic and headdresses, the Chinese colors and embroideries, kimono effects and collars from Japan, and burnoose draperies from Arabia. Evidently all is grist that comes to the fashion mills."[103] The *Atlanta Constitution* also credited the East in a 1912 report on the latest Paris fashions. "Months ago the whole feminine world was wondering what the Fashions were to be. Then they were told the secret—*Orientalism*. One 'warms up' at the world—the pulse beats faster—the impulse is stronger. 'Ah, this is what we love,' comes pouring from every woman's finery-loving heart. So soft and flowing in line, so peculiarly beautiful in color, and yet so simple and easy to wear, as to be nothing short of lovable. To the woman concerned about her wardrobe for the coming social season they are an inspiration, a revelation, a joy."[104]

The links to Eastern fashion won fullest acknowledgment in writings on "boudoir attire." Whereas other Orientalist garments tended to be acknowledged as adaptations, boudoir attire tended to be cast as more authentic. In 1916 Bonwit Teller advertised Oriental house robes "executed on

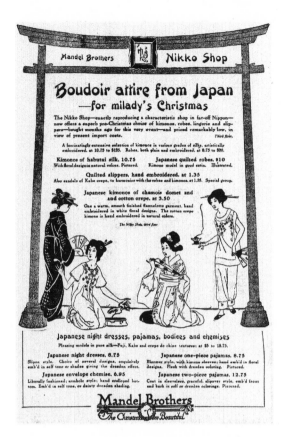

sinuous Egyptian lines." Two years later, fashion columnist Anne Rittenhouse reported on "Charming boudoir sets" that were "really Chinese mandarin costumes or clever imitations of them. They consist of trousers and jacket, slippers and cap all made of the same material."[105] Most popular of all were Japanese-inspired kimonos, which one fashion writer admonished women not to wear outside their bedrooms (ill. 2.8).[106] Although purveyors frequently proclaimed their authenticity, the kimonos available in the U.S. marketplace diverged markedly from those worn in Japan. Nonetheless, the American versions evoked the originals in their loose fit, colors, and decorative motifs. Expensive versions sold for fifty dollars and up, but as the *Times Picayune* of New Orleans observed, "Large stores in every city in the country are selling real hand-embroidered kimonos at $1.50 and $2. . . . They are the real Japanese shapes, with the full, loose sleeve, and they are universally becoming."[107] Montgomery Ward's sold kimonos—some with Persian designs—starting at seventy-eight cents. Sears, too, sold low-cost versions. Particularly price-conscious women could find patterns for sewing their own, and those willing to throw authenticity completely to the winds could follow directions for crocheting one.[108]

The appreciation of Asian fabrics and Orientalist designs seems strange given the turn-of-the-century measures to keep Asian immigrants out and the hostility shown toward people of Asian ancestry living in the United States. But wearing Chinese silks or crocheted kimonos did not mean identifying with Asian women. In choosing to wear kimonos at home, American women could identify themselves with what they imagined to be Eastern—and above all, Japanese—elegance, grace, sensuousness, and eroticism. But in choosing not to wear them in public, they signaled their distance from the Japanese women who did. Drawing on Eastern dress did not mean that fashionable Euro-American women wanted to associate themselves with Asian women. Indeed, Euro-American women only rarely cut and sewed their Chinese silks into the tunics and pants favored by Chinese women. What ultimately enticed many American women into a limited Orientalism—an Orientalism of small decorative touches, a less constricted figure, and exotic-looking fabrics—was that the Paris-based fashion system validated it. The acceptability of Asian motifs in U.S. fashion depended, in large part, on the French imprimatur. American women could dress "Asian" and still be fundamentally European. Indeed, because French designers looked to the East for inspiration, American women had to do the same to maintain a chic, European demeanor.

The selective embrace of fashion Orientalism underscores the point that the affiliative urge was not the only one that extended beyond the nation; the need to draw distinctions did as well. American women adhered to the Paris-based fashion system with such loyalty to prove their civilizational distance from the lowest of the world's dispossessed as well as their equivalency to the highest of the world's *haute monde*. If non-Western dress could be seen as unduly restraining or as inappropriately revealing, and hence indicative of low racial and civilizational standing, Western dress supposedly conveyed high racial and civilizational status. This extended beyond the financial power demonstrated by consuming goods produced by others to include the social power of standard setting and display.

According to writings on dress, clothes did more than reveal power; they helped constitute it. This can be seen in the example of May French-Sheldon, a New Yorker by birth, a Briton by residence, an adventuress by inclination. Leaving her husband behind, she traveled extensively in Africa in the early 1890s, accompanied only by African servants, described in one account as "her savage escort." A prolific writer and an entertaining speaker, she attracted a following among white, middle-class women in the United

States, who thrilled to her stories of exotic adventures and her claims of having visited places never before seen by a white man, much less a white woman.[109] In relating her successes, she credited not only her race and her bearing, but also her wardrobe, and the press picked up on this theme.

In an account of an expedition from Zanzibar, *Housekeeper's Weekly* cut right to this point. "What did she wear?" it asked. The answer? "Mrs. Sheldon's mind was firmly made up that she would show the African tribes, who had never seen a white man save in a travel-stained and bedraggled condition, that a white *woman* could look fresh, neat, and even dainty under all disadvantages. Accordingly she took with her thirty-six wash-dresses of silk, outing cloth, and flannel . . . and a court dress!" On the march she wore a "jaunty white flannel suit" but when she approached a village she stopped to change. She then "received" the chief in a "magnificent trained court dress of white silk covered with silver gauze, collar and girdle of jewels, and a blonde wig whose curls fell to her waist. The simple natives thought her a goddess, and loaded her with gifts on her departure."[110] Those who followed her adventures had grounds for regarding women's dress—and above all, garments such as her court gown that signaled aristocratic privilege—as an instrument of imperial power. According to French-Sheldon, gauze could be more effective than guns in winning the homage of scantily clad natives. Western fashion, she believed, articulated power in a language intelligible to "savages" and the readers of *Housekeeper's Weekly* alike.

The irony of identifying more with the aristocratic French-Sheldons of the fashionable world than with the natives who had never seen a court dress was that the latter group tended to have more tangible connections to fashionable women's clothes than the ladies of leisure who merely modeled the styles. The tendency to associate fashion with European aristocrats deflected attention from the linkages between the women who purchased stylish dresses and the ever widening circle of workers who produced them. Western fashion was becoming more and more international in this period, not only because Paris designers looked far beyond their national boundaries for design inspiration, but also because goods from around the world flowed into Western markets. In the year ending June 30, 1915, for example, the United States imported more than $2 million worth of ostrich feathers (mostly from the United Kingdom and South Africa) and $1 million worth of buttons (mostly from Austria-Hungary, Germany, Japan, and France).[111]

Although they focused on consumption, U.S. fashion pages did acknowledge this increasingly expansive system of production. Department stores and catalogs offered dress goods identified as imported from far-flung corners of the earth. Proclaimed a Pennsylvania textile company: "From the production of makers the world over we have selected the best." A Bon-wit Teller advertisement picturing imported blouses mentioned "German Valenciennes insertions," "French crepe," "English eyelet embroidery," and "real baby Irish insertions." The 1902 Sears catalog hawked Chinese and Japanese silks and "Duchesse a Parisian Novelty Silk." John Forsythe, a New York retailer with a catalog department, sold waists with "fine Mexican hand embroidery and drawn work" and "Japanese hand embroidery." Revillon Frères, a fur merchant with establishments in New York, London, and Paris, advertised that its furs originated in northern Siberia, Bukhara, and Chile, to list just a few places. To help consumers visualize the geography of production, Vantine's ran ads with maps showing where its dress goods originated—including China, Southeast Asia, Japan, India, Morocco, and Egypt.[112]

Some of these trade connections had great economic significance for foreign producers. In the late nineteenth and early twentieth centuries, China and Japan exported more silk than any other commodity, including tea. The silk trade financed at least 40 percent of Japan's imports of foreign machinery and raw materials from 1870 to 1930, thus contributing significantly to its industrialization. And the leading market for this silk? The United States.[113] But regardless of the importance of such trade relationships to foreign producers, U.S. fashion writings continued to center on aristocratic consumers. As the realm of production became ever more global, the imagined community implied by fashion stayed tightly bounded. The fashions themselves bespoke far-flung networks linking consumers and producers, but fashion writers refused to acknowledge that stylish American women had common interests with those who made or inspired their clothes. As a result, those who imagined themselves as part of the world of fashion lived in a realm of fantasy. Instead of fully acknowledging their reciprocal relations with real-life producers, they relegated the world of production to their social unconscious.[114]

Racial and civilizational presuppositions played a major role in keeping nonwhite and non-Western women outside the imagined community of fashion. In contrast to the gossipy reports on European high society, fashion reports aimed at white American readers rarely individuated women of color. To find detailed information on these consumers, American readers would best look in ethnographic writings rather than fashion pages. Yes, occasional articles might mention the rich embroideries and royal designs worn by elite Chinese women, but they labeled such clothes "mandarin costumes," not fashion.[115] Yes, the Queen of Hawaii and Empress of Japan dressed in the latest French styles, but few non-Western women appeared

Wind the threads deftly, little maidens of far Japan; fair ladies must have the silk-worm's coverlet of silver down, that their ankles may shimmer and gleam and lure men to say—"You just know she wears them!" Interesting Booklet sent free on request.

McCALLUM HOSIERY COMPANY
NORTHAMPTON, MASS.

2.9. McCallum Silk Hosiery advertisement, *Vanity Fair* 10 (Oct. 1918): 105. Courtesy of the Winterthur Library: Printed Book and Periodical Collection, Winterthur, Delaware.

in the fashion pages of the white press, and this dearth of coverage in turn militated against imagining communities with them.

Along with racial and civilizational presuppositions, assumptions about class kept nonwhite and non-Western women on the outskirts of the fashionable world. This can be seen in an ad for silk hosiery that showed a Japanese woman and girl spinning silk from cocoons so that the ankles of "fair ladies" would "shimmer and gleam." The advertisement did not include an image of the fair ladies with shimmering ankles, but their implied life of pleasure stood in contrast to the toil of the Japanese workers, one a mere child, both with sturdy ankles and bare feet (ill. 2.9).[116] As the silk stocking ad suggests, fashion purveyors often cast Asian women and other women of color as working-class producers rather than upper-class consumers. Whereas fashionable women's doings and personalities merited detailed coverage, the daily lives of producers received relatively little, and their personal qualities, virtually none.

The refusal to acknowledge a sense of community with Asian workers carried over to situations in which Western women actually knew the producers of their garments. Writing in *Harper's Bazar*, Laura B. Starr said that the dressmakers whom she had known while living in China and Japan were "pretty much the same, except in the one case he wore a queue, and in the other a perpetual smile." Having de-individuated the "boys" who sewed her frocks, she highlighted the gulf between herself and her employees. They arrived in odd clothing, used their "prehensile toes" in their work, and exhibited a striking lack of intelligence. Further differentiating herself, Starr commented: "They lack style, and style is an intangible and inexplicable thing that refuses to be put into words, but which must be put into clothes if they are to mark the well-dressed man or woman." On the positive side, the men were inexpensive to hire, but this too served to differentiate them from their prosperous employer.[117] Starr's remarks show how racial prejudice combined with an upper-class disdain of workers to deny any kind of intimacy with—indeed, to deny any shared humanity with—Asian dressmakers.

Although nonwhite and non-Western peoples seemed particularly distant from the fashionable world centered in Europe, the association of fashion with aristocratic circles also served to differentiate white women within Western nations from each other. True, French designers often drew on peasant motifs. But this does not mean that the fashionable women who donned peasant blouses identified with women working in the fields. Rather than coming to the attention of U.S. fashion purveyors from the passengers disembarking from steerage, such items came to their attention from Paris correspondents and from first-class travelers. The peasant blouses on display in U.S. department stores were supposed to imply the tastes of moneyed consumers rather than of working-class producers. Fashion writers did acknowledge the wide-ranging origins of goods and styles—they would have been blind to have missed this—but they did not present the ever more integrated world of production as a true community and certainly not as a community that American consumers would want to imaginatively affiliate themselves with. Indeed, rather than signaling affinities, the adoption of folk motifs from Europe and elsewhere could signal distance, for pastiche displayed the power of appropriation.

Sometimes the power relations conveyed by appropriation were readily apparent, perhaps nowhere more so than in a European diplomatic reception described by the widow of an American diplomat. Shortly after the Chinese ambassador arrived, an American woman entered. "The ambassador caught sight of her instantly, and his agitation was painful to see. For she wore the coronation robes of the Empress of China!" These robes had recently been, as the ambassador and many of the assembled guests well knew, looted from the imperial palace by foreign troops in the aftermath of the Boxer rebellion. As the ambassador sank trembling into a chair, on-lookers led the woman away. "We all thought it was the most disgraceful thing we had ever witnessed. But in speaking about it in America, I was astonished to find many people take the woman's part." Their reasoning: "If a woman wanted to wear them to a party instead of a Paquin gown—they wouldn't especially admire her taste—but why wouldn't she?"[118]

The logic of "why wouldn't she" helps explain the appropriation of folk motifs. Rather than signifying exclusion from the fashionable world, they signified the fashionable woman's ability to take whatever pleased her from around the globe. The ability to borrow from other design traditions could signal distance from the originator just as readily as it could signal prox-imity. Just as decorators who favored Orientalist touches aimed to align themselves with European imperialists, the fashionable women who favored peasant motifs aimed to associate themselves with Parisian couture. An article on the popularity of Russian designs made this clear. "The mujiks might stare some to see their blouses, which they wear of fur and merely turn inside out in summer, made up in gauze, but they won't know any-thing about it, any more than they know about the restless desire for novelty that sends us westerners to the ends of the earth for a new design."[119] Fash-ionable women who wore adaptations of Russian blouses could feel confi-dent that their energetic search for novelty—a fundamental premise of the modes—differentiated them from ignorant peasants and non-Europeans with little understanding of the wider world. They could regard their ability to grasp other people's products as proof of their racial, class, and national standing.

Fashionable women could also see their ability to purchase imports as a result of imperial power. Donning burnoose draperies meant donning the trappings of European imperialism. Slipping on imported silks meant luxu-riating in the expanding empire of U.S. commerce, backed up by U.S. politi-cal and military might. The violence that undergirded the world of fashion can best be seen in the case of imports from the Philippines. The Philippine-American War resulted in, among other things, the establishment of a sig-nificant lingerie trade with the islands. By 1920 clothing imports from the Philippines topped $7 million, and judging from the advertisements that appeared in metropolitan dailies, much of this was underwear.[120]

Playing to an interest in exoticism, Bonwit Teller advertised its Philip-pine lingerie as Oriental in nature, "made from their own distinctive de-signs, under their own supervision, by native needle workers. Every seam and embroidery done entirely by hand."[121] But hoping to differentiate its lingerie from the other Philippine products on the market and hedging its

2.10. Bonwit Teller advertisement, "The May Sale of Philippine Lingerie," *Vogue* 49 (May 1, 1917): 5. Courtesy of the Winterthur Library: Printed Book and Periodical Collection, Winterthur, Delaware.

bets with those suspicious of too much exoticism, Bonwit Teller soon ran ads very different in emphasis, which claimed that their Philippine lingerie had been made by "native needle-workers under the direct supervision of Bonwit Teller and Co. representatives."[122] By 1918, when French undergarments had become scarce because of the war, John Wanamaker's advertised that its Philippine underwear copied French designs and that some was trimmed with Valenciennes lace—"made on the Islands by the pupils of the lace makers exiled from the old world." (Hidden in this narrative of European tutelage was the history of the Philippine textile industry. In the early 1800s, Iloilo had been a textile center, renowned for fine hand-woven cloth. But by the 1850s, a British manufacturer had pirated the patterns. He had them mass-produced in Britain, shipped back to Iloilo, and then fraudulently reexported as hand-woven. By the late nineteenth century, textiles were the islands' biggest import.)[123]

The Philippine case was not unique. A second island acquisition, Puerto Rico, also exported lingerie to the United States. Many of the women who sewed the garments had been forced into the job market after the U.S. invasion led to a devaluation of the Spanish peso and hence an economic crisis on the island. As in the Philippine case, the U.S. occupation reduced the costs of imports by bringing Puerto Rican goods within the duty-free zone. And the U.S. occupation affected the supply of Puerto Rican textiles in yet another way: U.S. needlework corporations paid home economics teachers from the United States to offer sewing classes in Puerto Rican public schools.[124] As a result, seemingly traditional handiwork came via imperialist intervention. But even though Philippine and Puerto Rican producers made export garments under the U.S. flag, that still did not win them inclusion into the imagined community delineated by fashion.

As Philippine lingerie evolved from being an emblem of Oriental exoticism to an example of the finest European craft traditions, it never lost its connotations of handiwork done by patiently toiling Asian women for white Western consumers. The Bonwit Teller advertisements contributed to a sense of imagined community to the extent that they affixed women's names to the garments—Ana, Amalia, Mercedes, and so forth—but the illustrations effaced Filipina women, in that they depicted women of European origins wearing the undergarments (ill. 2.10).[125] Furthermore, the given names of imaginary Filipina women did not advance a sense of community in the same way that the full names of real (often aristocratic) individuals did. Instead of fostering feelings of empathy with Filipina needle workers, the Bonwit Teller ads repressed any such leanings. Though connected to Filipina women by political as well as commercial ties, the American women who looked to the Philippines for intimate wear felt far more intimacy with European ladies of rank who had never sewn a stitch on their behalf.

The boundaries drawn around the imagined world of fashion were so firm that few critics called them into question. One notable exception was Edward Knoblauch, an expatriate American playwright who had spent most of his adult life on the Continent and in Britain. In *My Lady's Dress*, which made its U.S. debut in the New York City Playhouse in October 1914, he took the wealthy women in his audiences to task for refusing to acknowledge a sense of community with the workers who fabricated their toilettes. The play told the story of a dress in a series of vignettes. Starting with the British woman who had purchased the featured gown and fully intended to wear it despite her husband's protestations of its risqué cut and extravagant cost, the ensuing scenes took the audience on a continental tour of the origins of the component parts. After depicting Italian peasants who raised silkworms near Lake Como, the play moved on to weavers in Lyons, France, a lace tatter in Holland, a flower maker in the East End of London, a fur trapper's stockade in Siberia, and back to London, to a pretentious dress-

2.11. "My Lady's Dress,"
Vanity Fair 3 (Dec. 1914):
38. Courtesy of the Win-
terthur Library: Printed
Book and Periodical
Collection, Winterthur,
Delaware.

maker's establishment (ill. 2.11). Even as it suggested the universality of
themes such as vanity, jealously, and self-sacrifice, the play drew attention to
a specific historical development: the increasing internationalism of Western fashion. Said the astounded Sir Charles upon visiting the dressmaker's:
"Strikes me you have to rummage all over the world to put a dress together
nowadays."[126] Knoblauch began and ended the play in his adopted city of
London, never venturing across the Atlantic, but he dramatized trends that
fashionable American women could hardly miss — stylish dresses and other
articles of clothing documented astonishing international linkages.

During the play, the owner of the gown in question comes to appreciate
its history in a dream sequence. Upon awakening, she regards her purchase
in a new light, as an emblem of labor. The drama underscores her new-
found sense of identification with far-flung workers by having the same
actress who plays the modish Anne also play a character in each of the other
scenes. Not coincidentally, each of these characters has a name that is a vari-
ant of Anne — Annette, Annie, Anita, and so forth. Moved by the struggles
of the people who helped produce her dress, she professes a desire to try to
make the world better — or at least to improve the lot of European workers.

Anne acknowledges China's role in silk production but then dreams about Italian silkworm breeders. The community evoked by her dress did not extend beyond Europe. (This unwillingness to have the Anne character play an Asian woman is particularly striking given Knoblauch's own adventures in cross-cultural masquerade: in 1913 he staged an "Oriental" feast for Gertrude Vanderbilt Whitney and several other friends. Everyone dressed in Orientalist costumes and lounged on cushions around the food-laden coffee table.)[127]

Critics regarded the play's efforts to uncover the history of the dress favorably. The *New York Times* praised it for demonstrating the "interdependence of our modern, co-operative civilization."[128] It presented Anne's new awareness of those who labored on her behalf as a novelty, and it was indeed novel, because the overwhelming majority of fashion writing at the time did not promote feelings of affiliation with the silk makers, seamstresses, and other workers who enabled fashion. In contrast to Anne's imagined affinity with European workers, most fashion writings did little to associate the latest looks with any workers other than the leading couturiers. And even Anne could not fully escape the urge to regard her dress as a ticket to aristocratic society. Despite her husband's protests, she insists they keep a dinner engagement with Sir Charles so that she can display her gown. In the course of the play, Anne had come to realize how her dress linked her materially to European workers, but she could not escape the powerful hold of the imagined community of aristocratic consumption.

Although Knoblauch's efforts to inscribe workers within the imagined community of fashion failed to spark a revolution in fashion writings, his critique of its narrow class dimensions did find some sympathizers in the fashion pages. Those who deplored the hold of the Paris-based fashion system over U.S. women commonly denounced its aristocratic leanings. As Helen Gilbert Ecob, author of *The Well-Dressed Woman*, put it: "Our fashions originate among the frivolous if not shameless classes of the Old World, who have no true moral sense."[129] Denouncing fashion's aristocratic connotations did not mean urging a truly democratic fashion system, however, for most critics of the imagined community bounded by Paris fashion shared Knoblauch's race-based vision of inclusion. Although the *Ladies' Home Journal* ran a piece on dresses inspired by Native American designs (featuring decorative silver buttons and geometrical embellishments), its editor called for American fashion "since no Latin race can ever understand an Anglo-Saxon people in clothes or in any other need."[130] When the "harem skirt" came out in 1911, the *New York Times* argued that its Turkish origins "should be enough to set women against it . . . it suggests the customs of a country where women go about with veiled faces and are valued according to their weight."[131] A delegate to the 1912 General Federation of Women's Clubs convention also played the race card in her crusade against French fashion: she deplored its "immoral and decadent" Orientalist influences.[132] Fashionable women might see their tastes as a sign of belonging in a transnational community of wealth, but their opponents suggested that this community lacked sufficient racial discrimination.

As the particularly vehement opposition to Orientalist designs suggests, most critics of the imagined communities delineated by Paris fashion aimed not so much to democratize fashion as to nationalize it. The specter of American women looking to Europe, and above all Paris, for the modes flew in the face of the conviction, widespread among white, native-born, middle-class Americans, that women should model nationality. Just as white women's bodies marked racial boundaries by being sexually off limits to all but white men, American women's bodies marked national boundaries by serving as metaphors for the nation. Just as geographic accounts often represented national distinctiveness via pictures of women in traditional dress, depictions of "The American Girl" presented her as physically distinctive—a symbol of national youth, vigor, and beauty. In nationalistic drawings and cartoons, she towered over foreign men and women, puny aristocrats among them. Dress reformers, too, contributed to this understanding of American women's superiority. The freedoms of American women had made them physically distinctive from modern European women, ran one of their arguments, and so they needed less constricting clothing. According to the nationalist line of thought—and it had a significant following at the turn of the twentieth century—women's bodies and bodices alike should delineate national difference. As the *New York Times* put the matter in 1909, "Our national character is more reflected in the clothes of our women than in anything else."[133]

Those who admonished American women to favor U.S. designs and U.S. products maintained that their devotion to French fashion reflected poorly on their nationalism. The *New York Tribune* article that called on American women to "abstain from slavish imitation" of Parisian and London dress objected to the relationship of domination and subordination that this imitation implied. Similarly, Edward Bok characterized the women who favored French fashion as "meekly submissive" to the French purveyor's "soul-destroying, initiative-killing empire."[134] If European fashions turned American women into the victims of empire, favoring U.S. fashion would show that the United States was itself a great power. "As we imitate less . . . ," avowed one article in support of American fashion, "we are announcing to the world nothing less important than our mental, moral and physical development."[135] Like the Europeans and Latin Americans who called for greater fashion nationalism in this period, and like the Indian nationalists who started a swadeshi campaign in 1905 that advocated homespun as a replacement for British cloth, U.S. fashion writers who advocated national fashions saw them as a highly visible mark of national standing and a route to greater economic self-sufficiency and wealth.[136]

Those who urged American women to put national identities above class ones, to align themselves with American producers rather than European consumers, cast themselves as fashion nationalists. But just as they had no monopoly on racism or class-consciousness, they did not have a monopoly on nationalism. The women who looked to Paris insisted that participation in the world of fashion enhanced the nation's standing. As one essay in the *General Federation of Women's Clubs Magazine* that rejected the "exclusive use of American fabrics and costumes by American women" put it, "At the very moment when we have become an international power it would be worse than foolish to advocate a narrow nationalism."[137] Just as the U.S. press often interpreted American women's successes in European high society as an honor to their country, as, in the words of one diplomat, a boost to "the dignity and accepted importance of the United States," the American women who modeled the latest fashions won recognition for being credits to their country.[138] That elegant clothing marked national standing can be seen in the proud reports of the dresses worn by transatlantic brides in European functions, including what the Duchess of Marlborough (née Consuelo Vanderbilt of New York) wore to the opening of Parliament, what Lady Paget (née Minnie Stevens, also of New York) wore to a garden party at Windsor Castle, and what the Countess of Yarmouth (née Alice Thaw of Pittsburgh) wore to her nullification hearing. At the races at Ostend, in the Palace Hotel tea rooms, American women of the leisure class could be counted on to appear "beautifully gowned, furred and hatted, with exquisite attention to detail," claimed the *New York Tribune*.[139] Money and marriages won these American women entrance, but dress marked their full belonging in the fashionable world. And dress was something that a much wider circle of American women could make use of in their efforts to prove their nation's status. The *Atlanta Constitution* was no less nationalistic than the buy-American campaigners when it reported an Englishwoman's grudging admiration of American women's appearance. "Why, they dress as handsomely as our aristocracy."[140]

Fashion writers who embraced the styles emanating from Paris commonly claimed that the best evidence of American superiority could be found in the fashionability of its middle-class women. Unlike European and other societies more riven by rank, a greater proportion of American women supposedly looked like ladies. As one 1870 fashion guide claimed, "There are no such universally well-dressed people in the world as the Americans."[141] Rather than seeing the fascination with European fashion as a sign of national deference, supporters of the fashionable world saw it as proof of their ability to take advantage of the best offerings of the world. Reporting from London, the *Atlanta Constitution* correspondent Maude Andrews made this point. "The American woman seems to me, the more I think of her, to be the best dressed woman of this day and generation. She resembles the Parisian more than any other, but she even improves on that much-vaunted model, in that her toilets are never trimmed to a degree of frivolous fussiness. She has adopted the best and most desirable modes from both London and Paris."[142] Supporters of the world of fashion insisted that it showed just how connected American women were. As *Godey's* noted in 1868: "In former years travelers, on their return home, were immediately struck with the antiquated appearance of their friends. This is no longer the case; they now find that we are posted up in all the latest novelties and are as well dressed as most Parisians."[143] According to such proud assessments, those who regarded the United States as provincial need look no further than women's wear to realize how mistaken their assumptions. Women's fashion proved the nation's standing by showing that the United States was no longer a colonial backwater. It demonstrated Americans' social worthiness, their ability to fit into the most exclusive European circles.

Given the shared nationalism of those who condemned and those who embraced Paris fashion, why were they at loggerheads about women's dress? Just like cosmopolitan decorators and their detractors, they approached nationalism differently. Those who urged support for the U.S. fashion industry applied the values of self-made manhood to the nation. They regarded the accumulation of wealth as the key to national standing. That is, they believed that national standing stemmed from production, not consumption; from financial capital, not social capital. They equated national power with autonomy, self-reliance, and commercial success. This was an approach to nationalism that lent itself to exceptionalist outlooks. Looking abroad, they saw workers who might labor on their behalf, consumers who might purchase their goods, and degenerate aristocratic types who lacked Americans' manly virtues. This disparaging assessment of the wider world helps explain why they criticized their countrywomen who followed Paris fashions. They regarded transnational loyalties as oppositional to national ones because they believed in American preeminence. To want to affiliate with other peoples, if only imaginatively, meant to lower one's sights.

Those who followed Paris fashions, in contrast, applied the values of sociability to the nation. Although the debates over fashion nationalism did not follow strict gendered lines, the emphasis on sociability reflected more feminine sensibilities than the self-made manhood approach to nationalism. Given that middle- and upper-class Americans of the period regarded entrepreneurial accomplishment and moneymaking as fundamentally male, and given the barriers to women's independent accumulation of wealth, most well-to-do women recognized that their path to prominence lay in family connections and social success. This approach to social positioning undergirded the dedication to Paris fashion. Rather than just valuing economic capital, the women who saw their Parisian dresses as credits to the nation valued social capital. Rather than just valuing production, they valued consumption. When they looked out at the wider world, they saw not only potential sources of supply and potential markets but also social insiders, standard setters, and peers. Even as their nation came to play an increasingly dominant role in the international marketplace, their consumption choices show how they continued to look to Europe for culture. Through their clothes, fashionable women wished to show their identification with an entitled race, class, and civilization that refused to be constrained by national boundaries. Rather than just wanting to lord it over others, they wanted to lord it with others. In sum, rather than equating national power with national self-sufficiency, they equated national power with participation in global high society.

Those who favored French styles regarded fashion as fundamentally transnational; parochial fashion struck them as oxymoronic. "There is, we hope, no such thing as an American fashion," insisted an article in *Vogue*. "It would be too awful to contemplate. All art worthy of the name is universal, not local and provincial."[144] Instead of embracing superiority through difference, fashionable women claimed stature through inclusion. If, for individuals, fashion promised incorporation into an exclusive community with aristocratic pretensions, for the nation it promised inclusion in the modern, civilized world. Fashionable dress showed that the nation had cultural standing worthy of its economic standing. It revealed belonging in the ranks of the great powers that ruled so much of the globe.

If, on the one hand, adherence to the Paris-based fashion system signaled empowerment, on the other, it reflected profound anxiety over maintaining cultural hierarchies in an increasingly interconnected world. Just as the affiliative urge extended beyond the nation, so did the desire to draw distinctions. As media connections, commerce, and imperial governance drew far-flung consumers and producers ever closer, fashionable American women clung to the Paris-based fashion system in part to prove their civilizational distance from the world's dispossessed. Ultimately it was the desire for differentiation from those outside the circle of fashion that explains why the Paris-based fashion system proved so compelling. Given the increasingly global terrain in which feelings of individual, racial, class, and national superiority played out, not to be fashionable meant keeping very low company indeed. In response to the charge that those who followed Paris designs were insufficiently national, those who looked to Paris for the styles had merely to play the trump card of the consumers' imperium and dismiss their critics as insufficiently fashionable.

3

Entertaining Difference

Popular Geography in Various Guises

In 1796 Amelia Simmons published the first American cookbook in Hartford, Connecticut. Its title, *American Cookery*, made national claims for New England cooking. Just as boldly, it put forth the idea that the young nation had its own cuisine. Her instructions for roasting beef, mutton, veal, and lamb and baking chicken and tongue did little to distinguish her recipes from European cookery, but her directions for "pompkin" pie, "cramberries," and "Indian pudding" did underscore the *American* in her title.[1]

Simmons's nationalistic pretensions were echoed in nineteenth-century cookbooks featuring recipes for New England chowder, Maryland cold slaw, Boston brown bread, Philadelphia groundnut cakes, and southern gumbo soup. These manuals also resembled *American Cookery* in their hearty, if not heavy, fare. The larded liver, roast mutton, mashed potatoes, and boiled onions of Marion Harland's *Cookery for Beginners* (1884) would have seemed familiar to Simmons, as would Harland's instructions to boil green peas for half an hour before serving them (or what was left of them) with butter, salt, and pepper.[2]

If Simmons provided precedents for later food nationalism, she also provided precedents for nineteenth-century culinary internationalism. Her references to "pumpkin" and "cramberries" notwithstanding, Simmons revealed that it was hard to contain food within national boundaries. Many of her recipes owed an unacknowledged debt to European and especially British cookery, and, beyond that, Simmons made several explicitly international references. She sang the praises of the Irish potato, describing it as mealy, rich, and superior to "any known in any other kingdom." She drew on French nomenclature when she told readers how to "alamode a Round of Beef." And Simmons called for imported ingredients in some of her recipes: for Madeira wine in cooking turtle meat, almonds in her cream pudding. Even her "pumpkin" was flavored with allspice, an ingredient imported from the tropics.[3] However much Simmons wanted to capture an American cuisine in the pages of her cookbook, she could not avoid the attractions of the exogenous.

The international component to colonial American cookery should not be particularly surprising, because cross-culinary contacts have had a long history. Chinese rice came from the Middle East around 5,000 years ago; the meso-American tomato originated in Peru. At the time of the Roman Empire, merchants transported garum, a prized sauce made from the salted, decomposed intestines of fish, around the Mediterranean. Arab traders introduced bananas to Africa in the seventh century, and nobles in medieval Europe cherished Eastern seasonings, thinking they grew near Paradise.[4] The search for spices helped turn European kingdoms into colonial powers, and this colonialism fostered even greater culinary mixing. The Columbian encounter profoundly shaped cooking from Puerto Rico to the Philippines. As historian Raymond Sokolov has noted, modern Mexican cuisine "bears only a faint resemblance to the verminous, milkless, almost meatless food of the Aztecs."[5]

The food of what became the United States was no exception to this larger tendency toward culinary mixing and flux. Colonial North American cooking conjoined Native American, European, and African ingredients and methods; the tea that set off the American Revolution came from Asia. But the overwhelming majority of food consumed in the antebellum United States was local, if not homegrown. Nationalist sentiments meant that those who advocated foreign foods did so defensively. In *House and Home Papers*, first published in 1864, Harriet Beecher Stowe felt compelled to claim that taking some leaves from foreign cookbooks should not result in accusations of "foreign foppery."[6]

After the Civil War, cookbook writers who looked abroad for inspiration became less defensive. The international component of American cookbooks, present from the beginning, became more pronounced in the late nineteenth century. Rather than taking pains to justify foreign influences, cookbook writers assumed that foreignness had cachet. Instead of justifying her inclusion of foreign recipes ranging from "Asparagus, Spanish Style" to "Zwieback (Berliner Frau)," cookbook writer Janet McKenzie Hill assumed that her readers would appreciate such fare. Indeed, she reassured readers taken aback by cosmopolitan trends that hostesses did not have to serve "Flamingoes from Sweden, game from Africa and South America, and pears from Assyria," that exoticism need not be the main ingredient of a good dinner. The *New York Tribune* acknowledged the sea change in middle-class American attitudes in an 1880 article that mentioned "the growing interest and even enthusiasm of housekeepers in all parts of the country in acquiring the secrets of foreign cooks and learning their manner of preparing the economical, wholesome and appetizing dishes of which Americans have been so curiously ignorant."[7]

This is not to say that the bland, well-done, and heavy food of *American Cookery* disappeared, but that there was an infusion of new dishes identified as foreign. The majority of these dishes were European in origin. Cookbooks and other food writings aimed at middle-class American women provided instructions for everything from English peas to Flemish fish, Hungarian goulash, Russian piroga, Dutch pudding, Venetian fritters, Vienna bread, German liver dumplings, Spanish olla podrida, Swiss eggs, and oatmeal stuffed haddocks as eaten in Aberdeen and Limerick.[8]

Rather than expounding on regional and national cuisines, cookbooks included only a smattering of "foreign" recipes. The great exception to the tendency to publish a narrow range of dishes from any given place was France. "It cannot be denied that the French excel all nations in the excellence of their cuisine," wrote Fannie Merritt Farmer in *The Boston Cooking-School Cook Book*, and many of her contemporaries agreed.[9] As a result, cookbooks contained a slew of recipes identified as French. Besides inserting the word "French" into recipe names, food writers conveyed French origins through nomenclature—as in *hors d'oeuvres, bouquet de corsage, consommé,* and *filet de boeuf.* Even manuals professing to teach American cookery gave advice in a French accent. *Miss Corson's Practical American Cookery*, published in 1885, illustrates this trend. It referred to *entrées, entremets, fondus,* and *soufflés.* Its sample bill of fare started with *Huîtres* and moved on to *Potage* and *Poisson.* French recipes and terms were so pervasive that some experts provided glossaries to aid those who needed linguistic assistance in preparing their meals.[10]

Although European foods predominated in U.S. cookbooks, foods attributed to other parts of the globe appeared as well. A 1918 housekeeping manual with a chapter titled "Foreign Cooking" provided recipes for Turkish kabobs, Mexican frijoles, East Indian sholah pullow, Cuban corn pie, Bengal chutney, and English tea cake from the Bermudas. Elsewhere, cooks could find instructions for Persian salad, Peruvian chantisa, Tartary koumiss, curried radishes as eaten in Ceylon (described as "very 'snappy' in flavor"), and chop suey.[11] Mexican foods occupied a prominent place in this smorgasbord of recipes: in 1910 *Good Housekeeping* published an article on producing an entire Mexican dinner, with a menu including chili bisque, tomate con queso, chilies relleno, and cidracayote (squash and corn). Elsewhere (including in cookbooks published far from the Southwest, in states like Pennsylvania, Ohio, and Massachusetts), women could find recipes for chili sauce, chili con carne, Mexican stuffed peppers, gaspacho, enchiladas, pollo con arroz, and tamales de dulce. The most common dishes from outside of Europe hearkened not from neighboring Mexico, however, but from distant India. This was the age in which curry became a fixture of American cookery. One magazine article provided instructions for "Chicken Curry, as made in India," mutton curry, curry of eggs, curry of rice, curry of canned lobster, and curry sauce. "With this sauce as a basis, many otherwise discouraging left-overs may be transformed into tempting and satisfactory dishes," noted the author.[12] The advent of chop suey, chili, curry, and other dishes added a whiff of the exotic to Euro-American food ways.

Some of these recipes merely provided new ways for cooking familiar foodstuffs, but others introduced altogether new ingredients. In an 1887 cookbook, Maria Parloa (founder of the Boston Cooking School and a leader in the home economics movement) described the "aguacate, or alligator pear" to readers who had never encountered one: the pear-shaped aguacate grew on trees in the West Indies and could be identified by its pear shape, thin rind, and extremely large seed-stone. Parloa also told readers about Russian caviar, French truffles, India chutney ("a sauce that is held in high favor by gentlemen"), and Chinese and Japanese soy. In addition to introducing their audiences to new foods, cooking writers provided advice on which foods were superlative, telling readers that the preferred vanilla pods came from Mexico, the best olives from Spain, the best olive oil from Italy, the best chutney from the Vale of Cashmere. And for those uncertain where to find new foodstuffs, cookbook authors provided shopping advice. To find the novel aguacate, Parloa recommended specialty produce shops. Her counsel for New Yorkers was more precise: go to the fruit store on Fulton Street, near Fulton Market, "where this fruit can almost always be had."[13]

There were other ways to learn about imported foodstuffs besides cookbooks. Retailers and manufacturers advertised products ranging from chyloong Chinese preserved ginger to Norwegian cod liver oil, German wafers, Spanish nougat, and French table water. In the teens, Macy's announced that it sold "all the rare tropical fruits and vegetables, irrespective of sea-

3.1. A. R. Ward, "Landing Tropical Fruits at Burling Slip, New York," *Harper's Weekly*
14 (June 1870): 388. Courtesy of the Rare Book and Special Collections Library,
University of Illinois at Urbana-Champaign.

son."[14] But shoppers need not visit upscale department stores to find tropical produce. The *New York Tribune* sang the praises of the city's well-stocked
markets in 1884: "The contents of the horn of plenty seem to have been
spilled into the lap of Manhattan Island, and on every side the eye meets
great hampers of vegetables and countless barrels of fruit, both domestic and foreign." The *Tribune's* lists of locally available foodstuffs included
items such as Cuban yams, Canadian smelts, Chinese drilichinuts, Japanese
persimmons, Egyptian cantaloupes, and chayotes, yucas, and malangas of
unspecified origins (ill. 3.1).[15] Across the continent, shoppers in the Pacific
Northwest could purchase Peruvian sugar, Chilean peaches, Sandwich
Island syrup, and Liverpool salt when passing ships resupplied local merchants. In the mining town of Carson City, merchants stocked tea, coffee,
vanilla extract, olive oil, and canned sardines. Sears, Roebuck and Company
sold imported coffees, spices, canned fish, cheese, table relishes, olives,
salad oils, cookies, crackers, and candy to consumers across the nation.[16]

Grocer's manuals provide further insights into the provenance of American foodstuffs. One 1878 manual attributed allspice primarily to Jamaica,

noting that Americans were consuming more than a million and a half pounds of it yearly. It traced the U.S. almond supply to Spain and southern France, its capers to Sicily, its coconuts to the Pacific. A 1911 Grocer's Encyclopedia published in New York City had entries for "Baobab, or Monkey Bread" (from Africa and India), brie (France), cherimoya (Mexico, Central America, and Peru), ghee (India), Iceland moss (Norway and Iceland), canned kangaroo tails (Australia), maté (Paraguay), penguin eggs (Cape Colony, South Africa), pine nuts (Italy and southern France), pulque (Mexico), quinoa (Chile and Peru), and wasabi (Japan). Whereas prior to the Civil War, the ingredients for curry had to be obtained at a druggist's, by the late nineteenth century they were widely available in grocery stores.[17]

Trade data collected by the U.S. government can help quantify the rising tide of imports. In 1865 the United States imported around $55.7 million worth of food; in 1900 it imported more than $226 million, a fourfold rise. By 1920 the figure was about $1.84 billion, an eightfold increase over the 1900 amount. From 1865 to 1920, imports of coffee rose from about $11 million to $252 million; herrings, from $36,000 to $3.78 million; olives, from $4,000 to $4.9 million; bananas, from less than $112,000 to more than $19 million; cloves, from around $31,000 to more than $2 million. By far the largest category of food imports throughout this period was sugar and molasses, which accounted for roughly half of the total. Government data also reveal the extended production and trade networks that supplied the United States. Customs agents attributed the 1.2 million pounds of vanilla beans imported in 1920 to eighteen places, including the French West Indies, Mexico, French Oceania, and Madagascar. The 13.8 million pounds of fish packed in oil were attributed to twenty-five countries, foremost among them Norway, Portugal, France, Italy, and Spain. The 32 million pounds of dates came from seventeen places, above all Turkey, the United Kingdom, France, Egypt, and British India. The nearly 16 million pounds of cheese and cheese substitutes were shipped from thirty points of origin, led by Argentina, France, the Netherlands, and Switzerland, with some coming from as far as Australia and New Zealand. In the pickles and sauces category (valued at $1.5 million, no quantities given), Japan, Italy, England, and Hong Kong took the lead.[18]

As the internationalization of the American culinary repertoire—that is, the internationalization of both recipes and ingredients—indicates, in the late nineteenth and early twentieth centuries, middle-class American kitchens had become places of global encounter. Though symbols of domesticity, kitchens were far from being thoroughly domestic. Rather than serving as bastions of provincialism, they were at the cutting edge of globalization. Writings on food acknowledged as much. It is possible to be at a cultural crossroads without realizing it—to buy a yam or a smelt with no clue as to its origins, to eat curried eggs without associating them with anything beyond a neighbor's lunchtime offerings. But the same writings that encouraged women to broaden their culinary horizons drew attention to the geographic linkages that would imply. By alluding to the distant origins of particular foodstuffs and methods of preparation, the food writings found in cookbooks, home economics manuals, women's magazines, ladies' pages, and elsewhere became sources of geographic information. The food writings that taught about commercial and informational networks constituted a form of popular geography, a geography that prompted homemakers to buy in to the consumers' imperium.

Some of the popular geography conveyed by food writings was as simple as a foreign-language name, as in *bouillabaisse*, or a geographic appellation, as in French artichokes, Russian turnips, Brussels sprouts, and Spanish onions. Such naming practices suffused even domestically grown foodstuffs with a hint of the foreign. They heightened geographic consciousness by suggesting distant origins. Other food writings went much further, expounding on the provenance of foodstuffs and recipes. The 1867 housekeeping manual that identified tapioca as "a starch extracted from the root of the *Janipha manihot*, a growth of Brazil," was not at all uncommon in its effort to explain where exogenous foods originated. A 1915 guide to "practical cooking and serving" explained that the green turtle consumed in soups came from the tropical waters near the West Indies; Fannie Merrit Farmer's *Boston Cooking-School Cook Book* traced peppercorns to the West Indies, Sumatra, and "other Eastern countries." In elucidating origins, food writers acknowledged that some foodstuffs had complicated international histories. As an 1875 book on food pointed out, the Irish potato was indigenous to Chile and the path of the sweet potato had gone from India to Spain, England, and beyond.[19]

If one way to approach the geography of food was to trace the circulation of particular items, another was to consider the provisioning of a particular place. In 1916 the *National Geographic Magazine* ran an article, "How the World Is Fed," that investigated the origins of the U.S. food supply. "Where once all roads led to Rome," it remarked, "now they come directly to our dinner tables." The article invited readers to contemplate how those roads converged on a dinner menu. Many of the components of the elaborate feast had U.S. origins—the pecans came from Texas, the ribs from Kansas City, the potatoes from Maine. But other items came from further afield: the olives from Spain, the pepper from Africa, the rice from China. The importance of imports to the American diet became particularly clear as the meal progressed. "Next comes our salad, and it contains—if a man may guess at the contents of salads and dressings—Mexican peppers, Hawaiian pineapple, Sicilian cherries, Pennsylvania lettuce, Iowa eggs, Spanish olive oil, Ohio vinegar, California mustard, and Guiana red pepper. When we get down to the ice-cream, we eat Virginia cream, Cuban sugar, Ecuadorean vanilla, and Mexican chocolate. . . . When it comes to coffee, if we are fastidious we will have issued a draft on both Turkish Arabia and Dutch Java, or if we are only folk of every-day taste we will content ourselves with the Brazilian product."[20] By acknowledging the far-flung origins of American abundance, this article encouraged U.S. consumers to recognize how they were embedded in webs of international commerce.

In contrast to antebellum Americans, the vast majority of whom made their livings by farming, Americans living in the years following the Civil War were increasingly urban. Rather than producing their own food, they were more likely to purchase it; rather than eating primarily local items, they were more likely to eat things that had traveled long distances. A growing proportion of the meats, fish, fruits, and vegetables that graced American tables came from specialized farms and factories. By the turn of the century, Chicago meatpackers employing thousands of workers took advantage of national railroad networks and refrigerated cars to market their dressed meats across the nation. In 1860 the U.S. canning industry put up around 5 million cans of food; by 1870 it produced 30 million cans, and by the 1880s it was producing 90 million cans a year. Food processing companies such as Borden, H. J. Heinz, Pillsbury, Campbell's, Kraft, and Del Monte won national brand recognition for their condensed milk, pickles, flour, soup, processed cheese, and canned fruit.[21]

The growing industrialization of American food led to new ways of distributing it. Before the Civil War, shoppers purchased the foodstuffs they did not grow themselves from local merchants. But after the war, chains started to reshape the retailing landscape. In 1865 the Great Atlantic and Pacific Tea Company added a grocery line with twenty-six stores. By 1919 there were more than 4,785 A&P groceries, which competed with rival chains including Grand Union, Kroger, and Jewel Tea.[22]

In some respects, these changes in U.S. food provisioning led to greater uniformity. This can be seen by looking at apples: big commercial growers favored only a fraction of the 8,000 varieties listed by the Department of Agriculture in the late nineteenth century. But even as concentrated production and distribution diminished local offerings, they led to more variety, for shoppers could purchase foods that were out of season in their own locality and foods that were not produced locally.[23] The new arrangements reduced diversity across the entire consumer's imperium, but they enhanced it in particular households. In so doing, they helped alienate urban eaters from their daily bread.

Although it reveled in the geographically expansive abundance found on American tables, the *National Geographic* article on the American food supply took this alienation for granted. It started from the premise that its readers neither produced their own foods nor knew whence they came. But its readers may not have been as uninformed as the article assumed. Although the male author of this piece seemed awed by the global origins of his dinner, his findings would not have been particularly revelatory to inquisitive housewives. Any grocer who had studied his manual could have told shoppers as much. As the references to green turtles and peppercorns suggest, cooking writings aimed explicitly at women had long referred to the origins of foodstuffs. Indeed, domestic literature went even further than the *National Geographic Magazine* by covering the origins of recipes. Rather than stop with commercial links, domestic writings revealed webs of cultural exchange.

What gave rise to these webs? In many cases, cooking writers attributed their foreign (and especially French) recipes to wealthy travelers and expatriates. A *Good Housekeeping* article on society cooks maintained that they deserved to be emulated because, having "feasted in many lands," they understood "the combining of ingredients almost intuitively."[24] (Recognizing that the rich relied on others to do most of their cooking, the *Times-Picayune* gave credit where it was due: it attributed a piece on European cookery to Nellie Murray, a colored cook who had just returned from an extended tour through England and the continent in the capacity of a lady's maid.) In addition to broadening their repertoires on jaunts abroad, the wealthy learned from local travels—from trips across town to bohemian feasts, upper-crust restaurants, and fashionable dinners. Society and cooking pages alike reported on the preferences of the rich—sometimes printing the recipes favored by their French chefs—thus exposing a wider public to their gastronomic world. As a result, continental and especially French food became thoroughly associated with luxury. If home cooking smelled of middle-class provincialism, European *cuisine* evoked the cosmopolitanism of high society.[25]

The rich and their entourages were not the only ones who took pleasure trips abroad. Growing numbers of middle-class Americans traveled overseas in the late nineteenth century; still larger numbers traveled vicariously. The 1876 world's fair in Philadelphia had a range of eateries, including a Parisian restaurant, Viennese Bakery, and Swiss dairy. Visitors to the 1893 Chicago fair could eat corned beef and freckle bread in the Irish village, zelebiah and pita bread on the streets of Cairo; stuffed cabbage and boiled dumplings in the Polish café. Even stay-at-homes could find information on foreign foods in the abundant travel writings of the time. One guide to Mexico recalled both "piquant and excellent" meals (among them, chili-con-carne and tamales) and "some very unappetizing messes, reeking with grease and filled with red peppers, chilis and other fiery condiments." Whether favorable or not, travel writings could be highly informative: the guide to Mexico explained enchiladas, tortillas, and frijoles to U.S. readers.[26] Whereas in many cases cooking expertise resulted from travel, in others it provided grounds for travel. Food writers started to report from Mexico, China, and other distant spots. Jane Eddington wrote a series for the *Chicago Tribune* titled "The World's Cooks" with datelines from London and Edinburgh. Sarah Tyson Rorer, author of numerous cookbooks and head of the Philadelphia Cooking School, traveled to Europe in the summer of 1892 to learn new cooking methods. She spent the following summer at the Chicago World's Fair, where she had Turkish, Singhalese, Spanish, and other exhibitors instruct her on the preparation of their native dishes.[27]

In addition to acknowledging the importance of conspicuous consumption and tourism, food writers credited imperial connections with introducing new ways of cooking. Most notably, they attributed the chutneys, curries, and other Indian-derived items in the U.S. culinary lexicon to British imperialism. One article explained the transmission of Indian condiments as follows: "The Englishman resident in India takes very readily to the peppery chutneys and sauces so much in vogue in that sun-parched land, and when he returns home he usually brings with him some treasured formula for concocting at least . . . one of its varied relishes." Some of these treasured formulas appeared in U.S. cookbooks, others made their ways into the hands of English manufacturers who then exported their concoctions to the United States. The British labels pasted on the curry jars found in American groceries underscored their imperial origins.[28]

Imperial influences on the American palate were not always secondhand. Cooking writers pointed out that chili owed its presence to U.S. continental expansion in the mid-nineteenth century. They waxed equally enthusiastic about the culinary repercussions of later U.S. interventions in the Caribbean and eastern Asia, well aware that U.S. territorial expansion after the Spanish-American War had promoted the importation of tropical produce. As a 1910 *Good Housekeeping* piece noted, peppers had "become more common since the Spanish war, as they are used in our new territories so much that Americans are beginning to use them as the English learned curry from India."[29] Several months later *Good Housekeeping* ran another article rife with imperial imagery: "Uncle Sam is literally ransacking every corner of the globe for dainty and novel foods. . . . The Bureau of Plant Industry is sending agricultural experts to the uttermost ends of the earth to bring to us foods that the people of other countries find excellent, and of which we are ignorant." These foods included the chayote and mangosteen from the West Indies and Panama canal zone and the leitchee from China.[30] Upon reading such accounts, a U.S. housewife could conclude that the curry-eating British were not the only ones with an imperial cuisine, that the United States was busy producing its own.

The spreading reach of American commerce (something that accompanied military interventions and data-gathering government agents) likewise explained the growing range of foodstuffs. The *New York Tribune* attributed the availability of guavas to the "enterprising American canner who had planted his foot in Cuba and other Southern countries."[31] The United Fruit Company and its competitors transformed bananas from a Victorian luxury item into the most commonly consumed fruit in the United States in the early twentieth century. By 1900 the United Fruit Company—a U.S. conglomerate that owned plantations in five Caribbean countries and in the British colony of Jamaica—exported more than a million stems of bananas to the United States.[32]

Manufacturers joined with importers in introducing new tastes. The Campbell's Soup Company, for example, drew on European as well as American cooking traditions for its line of soups. Its turn-of-the-century selections included bouillon, consommé, julienne, and vermicelli-tomato. It also offered the more exotic mulligatawny soup, which combined coconut, chutney, mangoes, curry sauce, chicken, apple, and cayenne pepper. By the early 1900s, the Chicago-based Armour and Company and Libby, McNeill and Libby were producing canned chili con carne and tamales. The importance of commercial products in advancing new tastes can be seen in recipes that referred to specific brands. How to cook "Rice and curry a la Indienne"? According to *Everyland* (a mission-oriented children's magazine), with "two heaping teaspoons of Cross and Blackwell's curry powder."[33]

The last major means of disseminating food ways was immigration. "To us Americans come every year hordes of foreigners who have foods and different ways of cooking and preparing them that are new to us. If we are ready to learn from all of them we can enrich our diet incalculably," wrote the authors of a 1914 cooking manual. "The thrifty French, German, Italian, Slavic, or Scandinavian housewife, who has for generations considered cooking an art and who knows how to get the greatest return for the money spent, has a contribution to make to our national life."[34] This contribution could be seen in published recipes attributed immigrants, such as a *Good Housekeeping* article on cooking macaroni *à la Napoletaine* by Mrs. Monachesi of New York City. She concluded her instructions with: "My Italian name is sufficient guarantee for the genuineness of the above."[35] Flipping through the 1910 cookbook compiled by Milwaukee settlement workers, one can find recipes for sauerkraut, mandel kloese, kischtke, and Swedish timbale cases. Evidence of immigrant influences could also be seen on the tables of avowedly assimilated Americans—in the form of foods prepared by immigrant cooks. Treatises on home economics assumed that household help, if not African American, was likely to be foreign-born. This was not necessarily a cause for celebration, as employers' penchant for complaining about their servants made clear. But at times, charges of slovenliness, irresponsibility, inefficacy, emotionality, and so forth were countered by the claim that immigrants should be welcomed enthusiastically as domestic help because of their skill in cooking.[36]

Native-born women who lived in settlement houses or worked with immigrants in other benevolent and reform capacities had exceptional opportunities to sample immigrant foods. Sarah Tyson Rorer extolled the delights of garlic after learning about it from the Italian students in her cooking classes. An Italian neighbor taught Jane Addams and Ellen Gates Starr some rudiments of Italian cooking, including not to lump everything into one dish, but to "cook the macaroni in enormous quantities of boiling water and then to take it out and pour the gravy over it."[37] In the early 1920s, the San Francisco International Institute (a YWCA affiliated organization, much like a settlement house) concluded its board meetings with lunches prepared by its foreign-born workers. These included a Japanese luncheon "presided over by Mrs. Abiko" and a Greek luncheon "served under the supervision of Miss Antanacopoulos."[38] Even better than board lunches was home cooking. Reformers cherished their invitations to their clients' homes as evidence of their acceptance in the neighborhood. Elizabeth Howe, the executive secretary of the International Institute of Niagara Falls, took note of a meal with some Syrian neighbors featuring roast chicken stuffed with rice and nuts and sweet Turkish coffee. She later attended an international day party, with food provided by Armenian, Polish, and Italian neighbors. "Nothing American was served except the furnishings for the tea proper; milk, sugar, lemon," she reported.[39]

Another venue for enjoying immigrants' cooking skills was the ethnic restaurants that began to proliferate in the 1890s. While she was training

to be a YWCA worker, Ruth Crawford Mitchell worked to familiarize herself with the immigrant communities of New York City. One day she ate
at a Greek restaurant, where she had "chopped meat and rice done up in
grape leaves—a queer dish of thick slices of fried eggplant and lamb—rice
pilaf and a sweet wine made of white grapes and the gum of white pine."
All this she considered to be "an insight into the Greek character which
was quite new to me and fascinating."[40] Such ethnic eating opportunities
abounded in large cities. "It is altogether possible to dine in India, in Italy,
in Spain or Turkey or Japan—anywhere fancy suggests—without going beyond the confines of our own little Island of Manhattan," enthused the *New
York Tribune* in 1918.[41] Another city booster agreed: "There is surely no city
on earth where such elaborateness and variety distinguish the menus. . . .
Almost every nationality is represented by a dining-room and a cook."[42]
Boosters for other cities made comparable claims. A 1914 guidebook to
southern California praised Los Angeles for its culinary cosmopolitanism,
saying that "each tourist, no matter where his home, can find viands to suit
his taste." In addition to restaurants featuring European cuisine, the book
mentioned the New China Restaurant, the Oriental Restaurant, the Fosgate
and Rees' Mission Restaurant (with Mexican specialties), and the George T.
Marsh Japanese tea garden. Likewise, a guide to New Orleans held up its
range of restaurants as a sign of the city's status: "You can dine in any fashion, or in any country you wish, Spain, France, Italy, the United States, or
even China, without going half a dozen squares from your room."[43]

Reports on city restaurants stressed delectability as well as variety. Some
of the savories mentioned in a 1910 article on ethnic restaurants in Chicago
included egg and lemon soup in a Greek restaurant, the cakes in a Swedish
establishment, the spiced noodles in an Italian eatery, and the beer and rye
bread in a Bohemian café. A guidebook to Philadelphia rhapsodized over
the gustatory pleasures to be found in Little Italy. "Christian Street breathes
the Italian genius for good food. After lunching in a well-known Italian
restaurant on Catharine Street, where the Epicure [the author's friend] instructed me in the mysteries of gnocchi, frittura mista, rognone, scallopini
al marsala and that marvelously potent clear coffee which seems to the un-
instructed to taste more like wine than coffee, we strolled along the pave-
ment stalls of the little market."[44] Descriptions of ethnic restaurants often
associated quality with authenticity. Hence the *Atlanta Constitution* lauded
a German restaurant for being "in the real European German tavern style."
Likewise, the Garcia Cafe in Atlanta advertised itself as "A Genuine Spanish Restaurant for Ladies and Gentlemen." Newspaper articles that printed
choice recipes from such restaurants helped popularize their fare.[45]

Among the most visible ethnic restaurants on the U.S. culinary land-scape were Chinese chop suey establishments. Although European Americans often derogated Chinese Americans as rat eaters, these restaurants had become a central tourist attraction in U.S. Chinatowns by the 1890s. Euro-American slummers visited joss houses and opium dens and then sat down for steaming plates of pork, onions, rice, bamboo sprouts, beef, and chicken, "served with much gravy." Particularly adventurous eaters could try more than chop suey. *Good Housekeeping* reported on a twelve-dish meal at a Chinese restaurant in San Francisco that included Chinese winter radish, an "exquisitely flavored" squab stew, boiled rooster legs, fried abalone, pickled eggs "of extreme antiquity," and "pumelo, or grape-fruit, one of the largest fruits of the citrus family." It went on to note that "various sauces for the meats were on the table, all strange to Americans, some agreeable, others decidedly otherwise."[46] The influence of these restaurants radiated out beyond the Chinatowns where they were situated. A *Ladies' Home Journal Article* titled "Rice as the Chinese Prepare It" announced: "Here is the detailed process, learned firsthand from a Chinese restaurant proprietor." The article went on to tell readers to "Buy at a Chinese shop, or restaurant, a jar of the sauce that they always serve with the rice to their countrymen. It is a strange, dark reddish brown liquid, very salty and pungent."[47]

As this advice on Chinese rice indicates, immigrants won acknowledgment as retailing resources as well as bearers of cooking knowledge and skill. In 1888 home economist Juliet Corson noted that "formerly no good macaroni was made in America." Purchasers had to visit Italian stores to find the high-quality Genoa brand. But thanks to increasing numbers of Italian immigrants, good macaroni had become easier to find. "Macaroni is now largely manufactured in San Francisco, Philadelphia, and New York by Italians, who can produce a quality equal to the imported."[48] Much of the writing on procuring novelty foods counseled readers to seek out immigrant vendors. Louise Rice, author of *Dainty Dishes from Foreign Lands*, provided typical advice: "Those who live in the large cities should seek out the Italian Quarter, and buy their spaghetti, Roman and Parmesan cheese, and olive oil, in an Italian grocery, where they may be procured of a better quality, for less money, than anywhere else."[49] In an article on marketing in "Little Italy," where "but little English is spoken," Jeannette Young Norton advised shoppers to carry a pad, pencil, and camera. "These will flash the word, like an electric current 'Board of Health' along the entire market, and only the best it affords will be offered to you" (ill. 3.2). In a later article, Norton directed readers in search of water chestnuts, lily bulbs, dried shrimp, bean sprouts, and elephants' trunks (a vegetable) to Chinatown, noting that

GOING MARKETING IN "LITTLE ITALY"

3.2. Jeannette Young Norton, "Going Marketing in 'Little Italy,'" *New York Tribune*, July 23, 1916. Courtesy of the Rare Books, Manuscripts, and Special Collections Library, Duke University, Durham, North Carolina.

it was "perfectly safe" to go marketing there. Alternatively, a housewife could follow a cookbook's advice to procure bamboo sprouts from "your Chinese laundryman."[50]

Little Italy and Chinatown were just part of a vast world of immigrant retailing ranging from Tuscan peddlers in San Francisco to Jewish delis in New York City. Food writers told shoppers to find kohlrabi in markets supplied by German gardeners and brioche in pastry shops owned by Frenchmen. In 1899 there were 140 groceries in the Lower East Side of New York City that stocked foods familiar to immigrant patrons. Immigrant truck farmers raised produce for nearby city dwellers. Near New York City's Fulton Market, a Brazilian immigrant ran a store catering "to the patriotic appetites of South Americans and the natives of the West Indies." Although most of his customers came from South America and Cuba, the proprietor noted that people "born in colder climes" sometimes purchased his tropical fruits as curiosities. In San Antonio, recent immigrants from northern states could buy tamales, chili con carne, enchiladas, and other food from residents of Mexican ancestry; presumably these residents regarded the groceries in the newcomers' shops as equally exotic.[51]

Located in household writings addressed to women, information on the dissemination of foodstuffs purported to be more domestic than geographic. But writings on the origins of foodstuffs and recipes were thoroughly geographic, for they covered transnational networks of knowledge and exchange. They connected households and housekeepers to the wider

Try a Cup of Real Indian Tea
The clever hostess attracts interesting people to her drawing room by the art of serving unusual things.
And, first of all, she knows that she must serve a tea that is different — one that her friends will appreciate and remember. Such a tea is
Darjeeling Golden Orange Pekoe Tea
from the hills of Darjeeling, in Bengal, India
Because of the infinite pains of its slow raising—because of a climate and soil like no other in the world—Darjeeling is a tea for those who appreciate fine shades of quality. We have arranged to get small shipments of the rarest and choicest Darjeeling Tea imported into this country—and shall be glad to send it to you in its original Indian sealed tin.
Its price, delivered, is $2.00 the pound in the United States.
All orders promptly filled while our supply of Darjeeling lasts. We believe that this is the most expensive and rarest tea procurable. If you do not agree with us that this is also the best tea you ever drank, we will refund your money without question.
G. F. HEUBLEIN & BRO.
500 TRUMBULL STREET HARTFORD, CONNECTICUT
Importers of the Famous Brand's A-1 Sauce

3.3. G. F. Heublein and Brothers advertisement, "Try a Cup of Real Indian Tea," *Vogue* 44 (Nov. 14, 1914): 113. Courtesy of the Winterthur Library: Printed Book and Periodical Collection, Winterthur, Delaware.

world, in the process promising power to middle-class consumers. Through cooking "foreign" dishes, middle-class women could become like wealthy globe-trotters and male restaurant goers. (Not only did restaurants cater to a male clientele, but at least one etiquette manual from the 1890s warned that women who ate in public lacked refinement and propriety.) The belief that spicy food appealed most to the male palate meant that women who tried "piquant relishes" could savor the delights of gender transgression as they enjoyed the benefits of empire. And they could profit from the immigrants who in other contexts appeared so threatening in their difference. An advertisement for Indian tea that depicted an Indian man serving a white Western woman encapsulated the lessons of writings on food distribution (ill. 3.3). To consume novel foods was to become the woman in the advertisement—the beneficiary of global networks of wealth, power, and labor. This woman would appreciate the *National Geographic Magazine's* choice of headings for its article on food provisioning: "The World Our Servant."[52]

In addition to mobilizing legions of unseen servants on behalf of the middle-class U.S. household, the consumers' imperium claimed the best foods and methods of cooking from around the world. What made the imperial consumption even more enticing to American housewives was that it appeared to come without costs. The endorsement of exoticism smoothed the alienation from local produce. The embrace of novelty deflected attention from the uniformity of industrial food. The rapt attention to the lifestyles of the rich fueled fantasies of abundant consumption and leisure. Consumerist geographies' coverage of empire emphasized the pleasures that it promised to middle-class Americans rather than the human and environmental toll it extracted.[53]

To be fair, consumers were not completely oblivious to this toll. In the early twentieth century, the National Consumers' League launched a campaign against slave-grown cocoa from the Portuguese islands of San Thomé and Principe. However, this campaign was an unusual one for the Consumers' League, which focused on domestic working conditions. Furthermore, in choosing to campaign only against the most egregious overseas labor arrangement—outright slavery—the league overlooked issues of landownership, debt peonage, political coercion, and dependency that also rendered labor unfree.[54] By condemning only one case of forced labor, the league reassured the housewife who boycotted cocoa that her conscience could be clear as she consumed the other fruits of empire. Indeed, it would be easy for a housewife to dismiss charges of misgovernment as none of her business, because U.S. imperialism in this period had a strong informal component—meaning it consisted largely of commercial domination rather than direct political control.

However informal, the U.S. empire of trade was by no means equitable. Although Latin America produced as much as 95 percent of the world's coffee between 1850 and 1930, the lucrative retailing, wholesaling, roasting, grinding, and packaging operations were centered in North America and Europe. Of the roughly twenty-five cents a U.S. consumer paid for a pound of coffee, about a penny went to the workers who had cultivated the beans.[55] None of her business indeed. But the lack of critical attention to the international distribution of wealth and power that characterized food writings meant that the U.S. consumer could sip her coffee oblivious to the poverty of coffee workers, as well as to the smoldering stumps of Brazilian forests, burned to make way for coffee groves. If it was too bitter, she could sweeten it, equally heedless of the devastating toll sugar monocropping took on Caribbean ecosystems, the proletarianization of farmers on the part of large corporate producers, the international migration of sugar workers, and the long history of slave labor that had built the sugar industry. She might be a righteous woman, a warmhearted woman, a charitable neighbor and friend. But the coffee drinker was also a stakeholder in an inequitable — if not exploitative — political economy. Awakened by her brew yet still unmindful, she could nibble a banana grown by a U.S. company in league with authoritarian dictators who terrorized political opponents, conscripted Indians into deadly railroad building projects (how else to bring the fruit to market?), and violently suppressed strikes.[56]

The rosy outlook on the world that characterized writings on global trade networks held true for immigration as well. Writings on the origins of desirable new food ways presented immigrants as a cultural resource, thereby glossing over the antipathy toward them. By downplaying the possibility of misunderstanding, exploitation, and conflict, writings on food distribution presented the kitchen as a point of encounter in a fairly conflict-free world. They encouraged middle-class women to celebrate the international trends that were connecting their households to distant locales. They presented a joyful geography of globalization, one so palatable it could be characterized as sugarcoated.

Despite their enthusiastic tone, celebratory writings on food distribution did not necessarily lead to trips to Chinatown or macaroni dinners. The continued appeal of old New England fare reveals considerable resistance to novel foods and recipes. The continued preference for brown gravy over chow-chow or boiled custard over kipfel suggests that many native-born, white, middle-class women regarded the smell of garlic with more anxiety than satisfaction. Rather than reveling in their positions as the privileged beneficiaries of transnational systems of production and distribution, they hunkered down with familiar comfort foods. Even the writings that celebrated foreign foods fueled anxiety, for they reminded those wary of foreignness just how close the foreign was — across the harbor, down the street, in the pantry, on the table. Women who felt threatened by this onslaught did more than churn out soothingly bland sauces; they also mobilized in resistance, by supporting the home economics movement.

This movement aimed to rationalize and homogenize the American diet. Putting nutrition above taste, it evaluated foods in terms of digestibility and food value. Prizing social control over self-expression, home economists struggled to remake immigrant and working-class diets according to their own ethnocentric, nationalist, and class-based visions. Positioned as they were in a moment of unprecedented culinary contact, home economists used the language of science to try to distance the United States from the rest of the world. (Never mind that Sweden, Germany, France, England, and other Western European nations also jumped on the domestic science bandwagon in this period.)[57] In the process, they taught a different set of lessons about food than those offered by the writings that reveled in networks of exchange.

Home economists joined with other food writers in teaching lessons about the local. That is, they provided ethnographic information on people living in different parts of the world. Like other forms of popular ethnography—such as the *National Geographic Magazine*, travelers' accounts, world's fairs, and museums—cooking writings helped make geographic knowledge available to a wide swath of the American public. But unlike the *National Geographic Magazine* and travelers' accounts, cooking writings lacked highbrow pretensions. Unlike museums and fairs, they did not require their audiences to depart from daily routines. Food writings were part and parcel of ordinary life, inseparable from the mundane details of domesticity. Cookbooks and related writings turned kitchens into sites of ethnographic education and, in so doing, made curiosities commonplace.

At first glance, the ethnography of the kitchen appears to be a particularly feminine form of ethnography. It focused on a sphere of activity widely considered to be women's domain—cooking and entertaining. Women had advantages in gathering this type of information, for they knew what to look for. According to *Good Housekeeping*, women travelers noticed things that men hardly saw, including cooking methods. Furthermore, in comparison to other realms of geographic exploration, they had access. The military, political, commercial, and scientific structures that positioned men at the forefront of geographic exploration did not necessarily win them entrance into domestic gatherings. In some cases, domestic circles were closed to men by virtue of their sex. In other cases, social skills—that is, skills women could claim at least as readily as men—determined entrance to domestic folds. As food writers' accounts of their strenuous efforts to win invitations indicate, knowledge of foreign domesticity depended on acts of hospitality. Success in this kind of exploration rested less on physical prowess, technological skills, specialized education, and elaborate support staffs than on the ability to wrangle invitations.[58] Food writers obtained firsthand insights into foreign domesticity by posing as guests, a role fully in keeping with understandings of femininity.

But even as they posed as guests, the food writers who dished out ethnographic observations identified with explorers. Women food writers, no less than their male associates, depicted their visits to inner rooms and warm hearths as voyages of discovery. They portrayed their destinations, however homey, as being on the cutting edge of geographic exploration because of their inaccessibility to the unconnected traveler. Although their subject matter and methods of obtaining information might seem quintessentially feminine, the food writers who ventured ethnological insights wrapped themselves in the supposedly male mantle of scientific expertise. These food writers identified with the domestic science movement insofar as they sought to enhance their professional standing through displays of erudition. In their search for scientific authority, these writers went far beyond emphasizing their travels to foreign lands. They also took pains to say that they had poured over foreign manuals, translated foreign recipes, boned up on international commerce, and consulted ethnological and travel accounts.[59] By spelling out their research methods, these authors made it clear that they were not just homebodies but experts.

Lest anyone question the value of their subject matter, these writers maintained that culinary habits were some of the most revealing sources of ethnographic knowledge. As an article in the *Chautauquan* noted, "Perhaps different nations show their identity more in regard to preparing and eating food than in any other particular."[60] To know a people's cuisine was to know their culture, a point underscored by an article calling French sauces "representative of French character and wit, as subtle and piquant."[61] Food writers' search for characteristic national dishes reflected their belief that food provided a key for understanding cultural difference. "What is the French-Canadian dish . . . that would correspond to the Italian's spaghetti, the Mexican's hot tamales, the roast beef of old England—the national dish as it were?" questioned an article in *Table Talk: The National Food Magazine*. In identifying this dish as either *perdrix aux choux* (pork pie) or *soupe aux Pois* (pea soup), the author revealed how French-speaking Canadians differed from their erstwhile compatriots in France. In contrast to their Parisian cousins, the Canadians came across as relatively simple, with more robust rural life-styles.[62]

The assumption that cooking and eating provided evidence of civilizational attainments led many ethnographers to pay some attention to it. This can be seen in a *National Geographic* article, "Dumboy, the National Dish of Liberia." The author fondly recalled the "pleasures of Liberian dumboy," saying that the mere name brought to mind "a picture of some little native town at sunset, surrounded by the somber tropical forest, where the stillness is broken only by the appetizing crack of the pestle. The thought of a chicken dumboy with 'whaney' and 'kiffy' seed will obliterate all impressions of the steaming heat and the mad fevers, and leave only a desire to taste again this most fascinating dish." Having sung its praises, the article admitted that the "uninitiated" would no doubt regard it as a "barbarous concoction." Underscoring the seeming barbarism of the dish, the author noted that the "natives" used hardened pieces of dumboy as shot in their

3.4. "Pounding the Cassava to Make the Dumboy," in G. N. Collins, "Dumboy, the National Dish of Liberia," *National Geographic Magazine* 22 (Jan. 1911): 85. Courtesy of the University of Illinois at Urbana-Champaign Library.

long muzzle-loading guns and that dumboy casings stiffened the leather sheaths of the native swords and knives. (Presumably, they used plain dumboy, not the kind containing monkey meat.) Most white residents of Liberia reportedly disliked the dish, but those who formed the habit could boast that their "tenderfoot days" were over. Lest there be any doubt that dumboy represented the dangerous delights of barbarism, the article included a photograph of a barefoot, bare-chested, dark-skinned Liberian woman beating the cassava for the dumboy in an outdoor pestle (ill. 3.4).[63]

The logic of "you are what you eat" had the potential to underscore the similarities among people—everybody, after all has to eat, and most people eat common staples like rice, wheat, corn, and potatoes. But it also had the potential to underscore their profound differences, for not everybody eats the same thing. Ethnographically minded food writers often emphasized the latter point. According to cookbook ethnography, the cultural insights provided by a group's dietary habits were significant enough to indicate its level of civilization. An article that called the Japanese "the fine flower of the Orient, the most polite, refined, and aesthetic of races," clinched its case for Japan's polish by noting that "there is a native cuisine of great excellence."[64] Conversely, countries with questionable food ways (this category sometimes included Japan) came across as less advanced. Harriet Beecher Stowe claimed that the line between the savage and civilized could be determined by the lightness of bread. "The savage mixes simple flour and water into balls of paste, which he throws into boiling water, and which come out solid, glutinous masses, of which his common saying is, 'Man eat dis, he no die,'—which a facetious traveller who was obliged to subsist on it interpreted to mean, 'Dis no kill you, nothing will.'" Even the British, who had provided much of the basis for New England cooking and who wielded unparalleled global power in the late nineteenth century, did not escape criticism. An American woman physician traveling in London sent home a snippy report published in the *Chautauquan*: "I don't like their customs, such as cutting your own bread at table off a big, unwieldy loaf, and hulling your own strawberries. I object to doing the cook's work, especially as they don't use finger-bowls. But what grieves me most is the entire absence of ice cream soda water. It cannot be procured for love or money, and yet these people call themselves civilized!"[65]

As the comments on cutting the bread and hulling the strawberries indicate, it was not just the foodstuffs that provided telling insights as to civilizational levels, but also the ways in which they were consumed. Reports that West Africans ate without tablecloths, knives, forks, or plates suggested that such uncouth eaters were barbarous in comparison to those who did. Likewise, articles claiming that Hindu women had to watch their men folk eat and then make do with the leftovers presented India as a backward place, devoid of chivalrous respect for women. (Contemporary etiquette in the United States demanded that the men should never sit down until the women had taken their places.)[66]

Cookbook ethnographers may have claimed the centrality of food ways to civilization in order to enhance their own professional standing, but their references to tablecloths and seating arrangements serve as a reminder that the domestic never disappeared from the new field of domestic science. Paid professionals did not monopolize expertise in domesticity—this was a field with skilled practitioners in millions of households. The topics, including cooking, serving, and sociability, addressed by cookbook ethnographers resonated with their readers because of their own daily familiarity with them. Hence domestic scientists' search for authority empowered their readers as well. By making food ways a criterion for civilizational standing, the popular geography of cooking made the homemakers who read kitchen ethnographies expert judges of other peoples. After all, who was better situated to evaluate others based on their food preparation than those responsible for the same task at home? What cooking writers called upon their readers to judge were some of the most intimate things about other people—the secrets of the family dinner, the yearnings of the palate. And thanks to the abundance of cookbook ethnography aimed at white, middle-class housewives, these women had plenty to judge.

Like the domestic scientists who were working so hard to rationalize and control American cooking, cookbook ethnographers claimed that other people had curious habits that contrasted with the implicitly normative ones they espoused. According to their accounts, other people ate strange things, like Japanese miso—"a peculiar affair." They ate certain foods at odd times: the Norwegians finished off leftover fish at breakfast; the Swedes ate their soup at the end of dinner, instead of at the start. They ate inappropriate amounts: the English sipped so much heavy port and brandied sherry that it proved "most pernicious and dangerous." They ate in unusual ways—sitting on mats, with chopsticks, to return to the Japanese case.[67] Even when such writings purported to be neutral in tone, their implied comparisons conveyed the impression that divergent food ways should be regarded as aberrations from the white, middle-class, U.S. norm rather than equally meritorious customs.

If some accounts just depicted foreign foods and eating habits as non-normative or, beyond that, as a trial to the traveler, other writings on foods conveyed the impression that foreign foods were far beyond the pale. Like the European explorers who had earlier shocked readers with reports of cannibalism, late nineteenth- and early twentieth-century food writers made others seem barbarous by reporting on their tastes. "Many animals and insects are used as food in different parts of the earth, of which the mere mention is enough to create disgust and abhorrence," noted a treatise on "curious dishes and feasts of all times and all countries." "The flesh of the sloth, lizard, alligator, snake, monkey, and kangaroo are eaten in South America; the grasshopper is roasted and eaten by the North American Indian, and the eggs of various insects are prepared and eaten by other savages."[68] Eskimos and other people of the Arctic were often targets of such criticism. An 1867 housekeeping manual described their diet as "oleaginous to a degree that sounds revolting and almost incredible to a person that rarely sees ice more than six inches thick."[69] The Chinese also won particular opprobrium for eating rats, bats, snails, shark fins, dogs, cats, and living shrimp, still jumping in the bowl. ("I could not put one of these live things into my mouth," commented the author.)[70] Although the eating habits of non-Europeans received the most unfavorable publicity, disdain for foreign foodstuffs applied to Europeans as well. The French, Spaniards, Italians, and Belgians troubled some sensibilities because of their fondness for snails. German sausages filled with horse flesh and French *patés de foies gras* concocted from enlarged goose livers (a dish described as "fatal to many epicures") also elicited disgust.[71]

Critical appraisals of foreign food ways went beyond coverage of taboo ingredients to include stomach-turning methods of preparation. Or lack thereof. Groups ranging from the Abyssinians in the South to Eskimos in the North and Japanese in the East reportedly ate raw animal flesh. Even the English favored "large bleeding, steaming lumps of almost raw meat."[72] If some favored foods that had barely ceased breathing, others ate foods aged to the point of spoilage. Hindus supposedly ate rancid butter, the Chinese feasted on rotten eggs, and Norwegians enjoyed a cheese more moldy than milky. One particularly sickening article in the *New York Tribune* reported on a Paris restaurant that served woodcock and pheasants killed six weeks earlier to a patron fond of high game. The decomposing flesh had to be eaten with a spoon. Besides criticizing raw and putrefied foods, U.S. writers provided critical appraisals of dishes—such as the "nauseously sweet" soups found in Scandinavia—that they considered to be inappropriately cooked or seasoned. The critiques of foreign-food preparation went so far as to involve cruelty. To make whiter veal, claimed one account, French butchers hung calves up by the hind legs and let them bleed slowly to death. The author's comment—"This barbarious [*sic*] method is practiced universally in France, but the laws of this country prevent its open practice here"—conveyed a sense of national superiority typical of many writings on foreign food ways.[73]

This sense of national superiority carried over to writings emphasizing a lack of sanitation in foreign food preparation. Housewives concerned with cleanliness could only be repulsed by assertions that Italians exposed their macaroni to dust and "odors of every kind" when they hung it up to dry. "A traveler says that one look at the making of macaroni was enough to prevent him from ever eating any more of it," reported *Good Housekeeping*. "The workmen were seen to carry the tubes on their naked, dirty, sweaty shoulders and backs." (One result of such assertions was the practice of washing macaroni before cooking it—something deplored by cooking writers more concerned with taste than sanitation.)[74] Another traveler reported on the disgusting methods of the tea manufactory in Foochow. After weighing the tea, the workers passed it to "the man at the fires, who spread it on a dirty stained cloth laid over the boiling water." Once heated, it was "thrown at a man some feet distant, who emptied the smoking contents into a wooden

CEYLON AND INDIA TEA ... ALL UP-TO-DATE GROCERS SELL THESE TEAS ..

HOW THE CHINESE ROLL THE TEA LEAF.

CEYLON AND INDIA TEA is prepared entirely by machinery, which eliminates all contamination from nude perspiring "yellow men" and preserves its purity, natural aroma and flavor. MARK THE CONTRAST

INDIA and CEYLON TEAS can be obtained from us as Agents of the growers, in one-pound lead packets, at 35c., 50c., 60c. and $1.00 per pound. Sent, post-paid, on receipt of price. EAST INDIES TEA COMPANY, 121 Front St., New York. "TAZA-OHAR" (TEAS OF PURITY)

3.5. East Indies Tea Company advertisement, "Interior of a Chinese Tea Factory, Ceylon and India Tea," *Ladies' World*, Feb. 1897, 7. Courtesy of the Winterthur Library: Printed Book and Periodical Collection, Winterthur, Delaware.

mould. A fellow workman placed this under a ponderous lever, moved by a gang of almost naked men."[75] The Ceylon and India Tea Company played on such suspicions of filthy foreign conditions by depicting Chinese tea being prepared by hand, a pig at the heels of the scantily clad workmen. The accompanying text hawked tea from Ceylon and India, saying that, because it was prepared by machinery, it was free of "all contamination from nude perspiring 'yellow men'" (ill. 3.5).[76]

If the specter of bodily contamination was not enough to thoroughly nauseate the middle-class housewife, another ground of criticism had to do with poisonous fixatives. Cooking expert Maria Parloa warned that French and English companies relied on harmful copper sulfates to preserve the color of their tinned peas. Similarly, grocer's manuals denounced adulterated imports—such as cayenne tainted by brick dust, ferruginous earths, vermilion, and red lead. Significantly, U.S. cooking writings neglected to mention the European restrictions on American foodstuffs on the grounds that they were adulterated and diseased. The pitiful state of U.S. manufacturing standards can be seen in the nineteenth-century ketchup industry. Tomato canneries made the sauce from the rotten, worm-ridden, and green leavings collected from the floor, throwing in some toxic preservatives to keep the mixture from spoiling. An 1896 study of preserves and ketchups in California found that forty-eight out of fifty-five contained injurious ingredients. American consumers were not oblivious to domestic manufacturing conditions. Over half the states had passed pure food and drug laws by 1895; *The Jungle*'s horrific depiction of the meatpacking industry prompted Congress to pass a Pure Food Act in 1906.[77] And yet food writings persisted in associating impurity and filth with foreignness.

The suspicion of foreign food ways extended beyond those living outside the United States to the foreign-born within. "The clammy stuffing of the average Hibernian cook is a thing which cannot be eaten," complained one article deploring immigrant servants.[78] Social workers joined disgruntled employees in grousing about and attempting to rehabilitate foreign-born cooks. Their concern went well beyond their own kitchens to what immigrants cooked for themselves. The litany of their supposed evils included feeding coffee to three-day-old babies, a food habit thought to result in juvenile delinquency. Opposition to immigrant food ways helped fuel domestic scientists' calls for a national cuisine around the turn of the century.[79]

The writings emphasizing the unsavory nature of foreign foodstuffs and the problematic ways of preparing them made it seem that white, native-born, middle-class U.S. housewives were worlds away from other people and fortunately so. In contrast to other people given to disgusting tastes, barbarous habits, unsanitary conditions, and dangerous practices, these cookbook readers could regard themselves as more tasteful, cultivated, clean, and educated. They also could see themselves as comparatively wealthy. In explaining why foreigners ate foods that middle-class Americans would not touch, cooking ethnographers blamed taste, the caloric demands of extreme climates like those found in the Arctic, and scarcity. Italian peasants are so abstinent, claimed an article in *House Beautiful*, that one almost forgets that they eat. "The bit of black bread may be washed down by a flask of thin sour wine, but macaroni is a luxury; and that there is even an actual dinner in any American or English sense is quite problematical."[80] The American housewife who read such accounts could feel blessed to reside in a land of abundance (and, in defining her nation as one of abundance, she could overlook the hungry within it).

Even European travel writings—a genre that often exalted the allure of the foreign—waxed sentimental on the appeals of American cookery. "The German family table, with its mysteries and abominations, is the severest trial which the American has to undergo who submits himself to the domestic life of the country," reported one dyspeptic traveler. It may be fun for tourists to eat in taverns hundreds of years old, admitted an article in the *New York Tribune*, "but after a while it seems good to come back to America and stop at an inn which, as it is not three hundred years old, does not serve a menu of the same age."[81]

As such travel reports indicate, the cookbook ethnographers who trumpeted the superiority of U.S. foodstuffs could find plenty of supporting evidence in other writings on food. Some of the most effusive paens to U.S. foods had a commercial bent. According to the *New York Tribune*, the supposedly superlative Albert biscuit, imported from Scotland, "has long since been superseded by the dainty, delicious American crackers made in Albany."[82] An 1878 grocer's manual insisted that American cheeses were as good as the European ones whose names they bore. Perhaps the most compelling evidence of the superiority of American food could be found in its growing international following. In a counterpoint to the *National Geographic* piece on the origins of a U.S. dinner, the *New York Tribune* ran an article, "How England Is Fed," that traced its plum puddings to firms in Pennsylvania and New Jersey, its cheeses to New York and New Jersey, its hams to Chicago, and its beef to Nebraska and Texas.[83] U.S. food manufacturers advertised their success in the export market as evidence of their quality. The Quaker Company, for example, maintained that "Lovers of oats, of every race and clime, now send here for Quaker. Even Scotland sends here for the utmost in oatmeal. Not a country on earth produces oat food to compare with it, as evidenced by this world-wide demand."[84] Advertisements trumpeting the savoriness, wholesomeness, and wide distribution of U.S. foodstuffs marketed groceries through nationalism and nationalism through groceries. According to such advertisements, U.S. foodstuffs demonstrated the superiority of the United States, a message fully in keeping with that of cookbook ethnographers.

Cookbook ethnography had the potential to overturn ethnographic assessments promulgated elsewhere because it based its evaluations strictly on food and cooking, not on assessments of abstract reasoning, engineering feats, economic productivity, military might, political organization, and the like. Indeed, cookbook ethnography sometimes proved very critical of nations such as Great Britain, France, and Germany that usually won top positions in the supposed hierarchy of nations. The vagaries of the palate explain why food assessments sometimes located peoples a few rungs above or below their usual position in ethnographic hierarchies. Yet, in conveying a world in which the United States represented civilization at its peak—as opposed to both overcivilized countries like France and uncivilized ones like Abyssinia—cookbooks taught lessons that supported and in turn were supported by other sources of popular ethnography. Like other ethnographies, cookbook ethnography presented the United States as a superior nation. The European nations and their settler colonies lagged behind, and the lands inhabited by non-Europeans lay still further to the rear. The general rule was the darker the people, the lower their location on the civilizational scale. Rather than meriting attention because of its world view, which was fully in keeping with other forms of popular ethnography, cookbook ethnography deserves notice because it helped spread the reach of ethnographic thought and because it empowered the women who wrote and used such cookbooks. Even as ethnographic assessments helped authors position themselves as scientific experts — and hence to claim authority over ordinary homemakers — their assertion that food ways served as a criterion for civilizational standing positioned their readers as expert judges of other peoples.

Casting judgment upon the world may have been empowering, but it was not very polite. Knowledge of foreign food ways came from bygone meals. In maligning these meals and those who had served them, food writers betrayed their former hosts. This betrayal can be seen in the report of a dinner given by the British consul at Luxor, "a genial and cultivated Arab, who had traveled extensively in Europe, and fluently spoke several languages." The host, a man named Mustapha Aga, gave an Arab dinner so his guests "might observe the peculiar table etiquette maintained among the better class." And observe the guests did. One of them published a report criticizing the lack of tableware. Eating in true Arab fashion, she observed with disdain, entailed eating with the fingers.[85] Another guest lambasted a dinner consumed in a Chinese house in Peking. Admittedly, the doves with mushrooms and split bamboo-sprouts were "delicious," the "Chinese bird's-nests with ham-chips and bamboo sprouts (a mucilaginous dish) — excellent." But the "slices of sea-fish and shark's fins, with bamboo and mushrooms . . . was rather bad than good," "land-turtles with their eggs in castor-oil — abominable," "stale eggs . . . a terrible dish."[86] The merchant, though generous in his hospitality, came across as repulsive in his tastes. Similarly, a woman who had gone to great lengths to obtain an invitation to eat in a Norwegian home displayed scant appreciation in her assessment of the two soups: "neither very desirable." The sturgeon? "Coarse and oily."[87] Having received hospitality and, presumably, having smiled and nodded and thanked their hosts, the departed guests slighted the hands that had fed them. The food writers who claimed civilization for middle-class American women by disparaging their erstwhile hosts revealed a striking lack of civility. In trying to carve out a role for themselves in the "scientific" world of ethnography, they forsook the courtesy and warmth associated with domesticity.

Given that ethnographic writings on foreign food ways were so judgmental, one might expect the women who read them to have retreated into a bland but safe provincialism. No less than national identity was at stake, at least according to claims that food shaped, as well as reflected, national attributes. If the rest of the world failed to measure up to the United States, why run the risk of resembling it? Indeed, the belief that food had cultural as well as physiological ramifications helps explain why American missionaries to China went to great lengths to eat foods from home, going so far as to import canned goods, grains, and sugar from Montgomery Ward. According to the Lamarckian theories of racial formation that still had a following at the turn of the century, environmental influences could lead to heritable changes. That is, somebody who ate Chinese foods might become more Chinese herself and then pass these attributes on to her children. The belief that "white bread, red meat, and blue blood make the tricolor flag of conquest" made a low-fiber, high-protein "American" diet seem necessary to the quest for national power.[88]

Yet, as we have seen, domestic literature published in the late nineteenth and early twentieth centuries was full of advice stories on preparing "foreign" foods. Newspapers, magazines, handbooks, and cookbooks all provided recipes attributed to the places maligned in ethnographic accounts. Indeed, the same publications that disparaged foreign food ways provided instructions for cooking foreign dishes. Despite the contempt so often manifested toward others, recipe purveyors did not shun foreign foods. To the contrary, they embraced them.

The incongruity of adopting recipes from people deemed to have inferior culinary customs was not lost on the cookbook writers who urged the adoption of "foreign" dishes. Confronted with assertions that foreign methods should be regarded with suspicion, some turn-of-the-century recipe purveyors, like Harriet Beecher Stowe a generation earlier, felt compelled to justify their geographically expansive coverage. Efforts to explain the inclusion of "foreign" recipes and cooking methods resulted in a countervailing ethnography of food, more appreciative than most ethnographic food writings. Hence, in response to the assertion that the German family table was a severe trial, *Good Housekeeping* published an article that appraised German cooking more favorably: "Now I should like to know in what part of Germany the writer got all those queer things that are talked about—the vegetables floating in grease, the roast beef which is first boiled, then baked, etc., etc. I never met with such things in any German family that I have visited."[89] Such favorable appraisals of foreign cookery make the popularity of "foreign" recipes seem a little less incongruous.

The defenses of foreign cookery often centered on its nutritional advantages. According to the food writers who marshaled the language of science in support of foreign cooking methods, American abundance had a downside, insofar as it led to careless and wasteful cooking. As one household handbook put it: "We have so much that we undervalue it."[90] In contrast to Orientals, "the Occidental boils all the essence or life out of the vegetable and throws it away, retaining the mere waste for food." Whereas American abundance had led to overly rich foods and dyspepsia, foreign scarcity had given rise to more nourishing and healthful meals. "In general," an essay on food conservation claimed, "the foreign born man or woman has a higher regard for the value of food than the native born American."[91] *The General Federation Bulletin* agreed with this assessment. U.S. housekeepers, it claimed, could "take lessons in economy and thrift from the methods of foreign cooks, who know how to use up odds and ends in the most nourishing and appetizing ways." Especially after the First World War brought the issue of conservation to the fore, food writers praised foreign cookery for the savings it afforded.[92]

Although some food writings extolled foreign food ways for their nutritive value or economy, most "foreign" recipes did not come with explanatory notes. The occasional testimonial to the civilized status of foreign cooks or the health benefits of foreign practices cannot explain the proliferation of foreign recipes. To understand this proliferation, we must understand that not all food writings emphasized science and economy; many instead stressed taste, novelty, and pleasure. A *Good Housekeeping* article shows how these two standards of judgment could lead to very different conclusions. It acknowledged the critical sensibility cultivated by ethnographic writings. But it called the tendency to denounce "everything cooked by foreign rules" a mistake, for foreign housekeepers possessed the art of "concocting sauces of a deliciousness that, as Balzac says, would make a mother eat her own baby."[93] As a review of a collection of recipes from East and West put it, the foreign names were "enough to excite the appetite." Besides offering exquisite culinary experiences, foreign food ways offered variety. A review of Adelaide Keen's *With a Saucepan over the Sea* spoke to the thirst for novelty: "The constant cry of the jaded housekeeper is for something new wherewith to tempt the family appetite; and here is a cook-book that meets this long felt want."[94]

If those who wrote disdainfully of other people's eating habits seemed to long for an Americanized world, those who advocated foreign recipes and novel foodstuffs bought into the consumers' imperium. Instead of shouldering the heavy burden of uplift, they sought to have a good time. In contrast to those who struggled to keep foreignness at bay, the women who actually tried the curry recipes they found in their ladies' magazines worked through whatever anxieties they had by ingesting the foreign. This is not to say that they tossed their comfort foods aside for a steady diet of exotic fare but that, from time to time, they experimented with new foods and methods of cooking that domesticated danger even as they added adventure to daily life. They turned the foreign into the harmless stuff of pleasure that posed no significant threats to their sense of racial, class, national, and civilizational privilege. In the process, they created their own geographies, characterized less by anxiety than by self-assertion; less by feelings of vulnerability than by a sense of encompassing power.

At first glance, yesterday's recipes may not seem like a form of popular geography. Their main purpose, after all, was not to impart geographic information but to facilitate eating. And how could eating itself be a form of geography? What did diet have to do with geographic knowledge? Plenty. Like other forms of geography, food provided insights into the earth and its inhabitants—insights that often differed from those provided by other geographies. Unlike geographies that took an aloof, promontory perspective, the geography of cooking constituted a kind of participatory geography.[95] And in contrast to forms of geography that fostered a sense of distance from other peoples, eating encouraged imaginative identification. The housewife who duplicated dishes produced in other lands elided the gap between herself and the natives who had originated her recipes. By eating the best that foreigners had to offer, native-born Americans could experience foreignness (or so they were encouraged to believe) firsthand. They then could draw their own conclusions about the foreign, conclusions informed but not dictated by other ethnographic writings.

It is possible, of course, that those who actually followed the recipes identified as foreign gave little or no thought to any place beyond their own dining tables. Geography may have been the last thing on the minds of menu planners who just wanted to cook a savory supper, a novel lunch, or an inexpensive breakfast. However, recipes encouraged readers to identify specific dishes with foreignness by including geographic markers such as "Delhi curry" and "Polish sauce," by labeling them in languages other than English, and by insisting on their authenticity.[96] Louise Rice demonstrates the commitment to culinary cosmopolitanism particularly clearly. In her 1911 cookbook, *Dainty Dishes from Foreign Lands*, she insisted that the "cosmopolitan menus" she presented were "thoroughly typical of the countries which they represent" (ill. 3.6). Like other recipe purveyors who claimed authenticity—sometimes going so far as to provide native testimonials—Rice advanced the belief that more than taste and economy were at stake. She urged housewives to experiment with new recipes so that they could escape ordinary domestic life.[97]

Like the recipes they accompanied, instructions for serving and eating also taught lessons in foreignness. Hence one cookbook told readers not to cut their spaghetti, so that it could be eaten Italian fashion, wound around

X

SOME COSMOPOLITAN MENUS

(Italian)
Anchovies

Olives   Radishes
        Cabbage Soup
Beef Polentas   Peas
        Salad of Romaine
Gorgonzola Cheese   Crackers
        Demi-Tasse

(Italian)
Salami *

Leeks   Radishes
    Spaghetti with Beef Sauce
    Thin slices of Cold Ham
Asparagus, sprinkled with grated
        Parmesan Cheese
    Salad of Dandelion Leaves
Neapolitan Ice Cream   Demi-Tasse

    * Salami is a sausage similar to but much finer
than Bologna.

(German)
Carrot and Bean Soup
Bismarck Herring   Rye Bread
        Sauer Braten
Potato Salad   String Beans
        Pickled Beets
Swiss Cheese   Pumpernickel *
    Coffee, with sugar and milk

(French)
Clear Onion Soup
Sardines   French Bread
    Entree of Peas and Carrots
        in pasty cups
Veal Cutlet with Leeks and Potatoes
        Lettuce Salad
Camembert Cheese   Toasted Crackers
        Demi-Tasse

* Black bread.

3.6. "Some Cosmopolitan Menus," from Louise Rice, *Dainty Dishes from Foreign Lands* (1911), 56–57. Courtesy of the Winterthur Library: Printed Book and Periodical Collection, Winterthur, Delaware.

the fork. Others urged chopsticks for Chinese food and Japanese tea cups for Japanese tea. Entertaining guides counseled grouping foods together to provide theme meals — for example, combining rice, chopped cabbage with red pepper, drop cakes, and tea to produce a "Chinese Affair" or serving Vermicelli Soep, Snijboontjes (Schnitt beans), Aardappelen Met Room Sause (creamed potatoes), and gevulde lamschouder (stuffed shoulder of lamb) to make a Dutch dinner. "National suppers" were "much in vogue," claimed *Good Housekeeping* in 1888.[98] Advice on eating supposedly foreign foods in an appropriately foreign way and in appropriately foreign combinations underscored the premise that one attraction of foreign foods was their very foreignness. They offered an opportunity to experience the exotic.

But what was the nature of this experience? Trying to analyze food as a form of popular geography poses methodological problems. How can we erase our own palates to understand how a particular dish tasted to any one person, much less a range of people, a century ago? How can we get at the thoughts of those who twirled their spaghetti round their forks, Italian fashion? Indeed, how can we even determine how many Americans attempted the feat? Where is the archive that contains this information? Where are the remembrances of what it meant to eat "foreign" foods? Although it is difficult to find evidence on the experience of eating, there is an indirect way to approach the meanings attached to culinary cosmopolitanism—looking at the contexts in which foods were consumed. Consuming the foreign involved much more than cooking, serving, and manipulating forks. It involved costumes, performances, and stage settings. Therein lie clues to the contents of this performative geography.[99]

In the late nineteenth and early twentieth centuries, middle-class housewives staged more elaborate dinner parties than their mothers had, and they did so more often. These comprised far more than abundant eating, for they often involved impressive amounts of masquerade and display. Rather than just being precursors to an evening at the theater, dinner parties were themselves theatrical. Since the mid-nineteenth century, middle-class Americans had relished theatrical entertainments such as charades, pantomimes, and tableaux vivants. In *Confidence Men and Painted Women*, Karen Halttunen offered three explanations for the nineteenth-century rise of parlor theatricality: the increasing material prosperity and leisure enjoyed by the middle class, the tendency of genteel propriety to foster artificiality and performance in all aspects of social life, and the existence of helpful guidebooks.[100] As the century progressed, the expansion of ethnographic consciousness also promoted pretense. Thanks to geographic mobility (above all, to immigration, travel, and trade), to the great institutions of popular geography (such as the press, museums, fairs, and amusement parks), and to the ephemera of daily life in an increasingly interconnected world (for instance, bric-a-brac, postcards, product labels, trade cards, advertisements, shop windows, and cookbooks), middle-class Americans could not escape difference and representations of difference.

Ethnographic exposure often prodded white, native-born middle-class Americans to try and differentiate themselves from the multicolored, multilingual, and multicultured masses. But differentiation was not the only byproduct of ethnographic consciousness—exposure also sparked emulative impulses. We have seen these already in cosey corners and fashion trends. They flourished as well in social gatherings. Nineteenth-century Americans had sometimes adopted foreign personae in their frolicsome charades and more formal tableaux. By the late nineteenth century, this tentative experimentation with difference had become a virtual movement.[101]

The masked balls put on by the wealthy for their moneyed associates epitomized theatrical gatherings. In his 1890 account of high society, the New York socialite Ward McAllister reported on a Turkish ball to aid the wounded Christians in the Russian-Turkish War. He also mentioned an Oriental ball given by the emperor Napoleon III and a Newport variation involving "old Japanese objects of art," "cunning cane houses," and costumed Japanese "boys" serving tea, all illuminated with Japanese lanterns. Everything at this ball, he reported, "was to be European"—a statement that illustrates the tendency to regard Orientalism as a European import, as a way to experience empire secondhand.[102] Society pages covered comparable functions in cities across the country. These included a 1900 Chicago ball attended by more than 400 merrymakers disguised, among other things, as a Turkish lady, Rumanian peasant, Devonshire lass, Bulgarian peasant, and Gypsy. In 1916 New Orleans society gathered for a Spanish ball at the Hotel del Coronado. A month later, more than 1,000 people received invitations for an oriental ball in Santa Monica. "It will be the big fashionable event of the year and beach society is agog with anticipation," claimed the *Los Angeles Times*. "[The hostess] is having the ballroom and lobby of the hotel gorgeously decorated with the trappings of the Far East. The Veranda will be made into a bower of Chinese cosy corners. The palm court will be hung with Japanese lanterns to resemble the interior of the court in the royal palace at Tokio. Many beach residents have ordered costumes from San Francisco's Chinatown, some of which are said to have been smuggled from the Imperial palace at Peking."[103]

Although the masked balls of the late nineteenth century connoted the exclusivity of the social elite, the excitement offered by disguise garnered a following among middle-class American women as well. Their efforts to tone down the excesses, elevate the morality, and fit the whole spectacle into their dwellings resulted in the phenomenon known as the costume party. "Won't you come to my party as your other self?" ran an invitation for one such gathering covered by *Vogue*. What did "other self" imply? One woman came "dressed as a typical Irish maid-servant, in heavy shoes, coarse dress and woolen gloves." Taking the plea to come as her other self seriously, she acted the role suggested by her costume. The *Vogue* correspondent caught her, dust brush in hand, talking in brogue to a "swarthy little Italian in a red sweater."[104] Whereas some hosts gave guests the latitude to pick their own personas, others prescribed a theme. Most notably, the Orientalism that so appealed to the wealthy also appealed to the middle-class hosts of costume parties.

The appeal of costumery spilled beyond the purview of the parlor into middle-class women's fund-raising fairs. In her book on these events, Beverly Gordon notes that fair givers introduced costuming during the Civil War, and soon after it became typical for salespeople to dress up. Although some fairs emphasized historic themes taken from the nation's past, international themes peaked at the turn of the century. "Italian 'peasants' and wholesome 'Dutch girls' could probably be found at church bazaars in any

THE CHOCOLATE TABLE.

3.7. "The Chocolate Table," from Caroline French Benton, *Fairs and Fetes* (1912). Courtesy of the Winterthur Library: Printed Book and Periodical Collection, Winterthur, Delaware.

community in the country," comments Gordon (ill. 3.7).[105] Ersatz Dutch and Italian maidens had plenty of costumed company. New Orleans's *Times-Picayune* reported on a fair where women "personated" America, Mexico, Turkey, Japan, China, and eleven European countries in a "booth of all nations." Pageants and tableaux provided further opportunities to don foreign costumes on behalf of a cause. In one production, Chicago women posed as women from India, Japan, Korea, Africa, Burma, and China; in another, New York beauties posed as England, Japan, Ireland, Spain, Cuba, Egypt, and other nations.[106]

These functions resembled immigrant folk festivals in their reliance on distinctive dress and efforts to evoke an ethnic milieu; where they differed was that the women on display in church bazaars and charity tableaux generally purported to represent what was foreign to them instead of their own ethnicity. There were, of course, some exceptions to these tendencies. Immigrants sometimes faked foreignness in their own gatherings: a German charity ball held in Chicago featured not only beer-serving "German peasant girls" but also booths representing "every nationality from the Japanese to the Russians." Around-the-world fairs put on by native-born Americans sometimes included foreign-born participants. According to the *New York Tribune*, the wife of the Turkish consul general, Mme Mundji Bey, "clad in a bewitching pink kimona arrangement of shimmering silk, with a filmy veil pretending to hide her mouth," dispensed coffee at the Turkish booth of a 1908 fund-raising fair.[107]

The popularity of costume parties gave rise to a supporting infrastructure. Costume shops rented outfits, charging steep sums for the first use and increasingly lower amounts for subsequent rentals. One such company, described in the *Delineator* in 1876, had an inventory that included outfits identified as Greek, Eastern Queen, Gypsy Queen, and Italian Brigand. The advice literature that helped give rise to the costume party mania also provided assistance in preparing costumes, many of them foreign in intent. Butterick's published descriptions of "popular" party costumes ranging from Indian to Moorish and Hungarian dresses in its *Metropolitan* magazine. "There is an endless variety of conspicuous costumes to represent the apparel of different nations," it noted.[108] A more comprehensive guide to fancy dress published in London described how to make national costumes ranging from Albanian to Venezuelan, with Bahaman ("the face should be colored"), Circassian, Dutch, and others in between. For the final touches, partygoers could make use of cosmetics, advertised in the nineteenth-century United States through images of American Indian, Egyptian, Turkish, Japanese, and European women.[109] Of course, cosmetics manufacturers had their eyes on larger markets than the party trade, but the exotic women of their advertising campaigns underscored how makeup could help women transform themselves.

Though a leading way of staging foreignness, masquerades were by no means the only way. Party givers turned to games, music, and other activities to transport their guests beyond the realm of the local. An article on "Midwinter Entertainments" published in *Harper's Bazar* reported on a Scottish party in which "scenes from Scotch books were charmingly acted, Burns's verses were sung, and good selections from Scott given." For the finale, everyone sang "The Bluebells of Scotland." In a similar vein, "Kaffeeklatches" complete with German instrumental music, songs, and recitations provided afternoon escapes, and Tyrolean singers in national costumes enlivened garden parties.[110]

Just as costumery spilled out of private households into fund-raising events, so did "foreign" entertainments. To raise money for the Chicago Lying-in Hospital, patrons produced a "Pageant of the East" featuring dancing girls in an East Indian courtyard. In the Oak Park suburb of Chicago, a women's club put together a "Jahrmarket" in which "members in the garb of many countries presided at the booths." Diversions included a Dutch band, Hindu palmist's booth, and Indian war dance. Women's groups sometimes put on foreign entertainments for reasons other than profit. For its "Japanese Day," another Chicago-area club brought in two Japanese women, "dressed in the picturesque costumes of their native land," to entertain the club members with "Japanese songs and talk on the home life and customs of Japanese women." Then the two women demonstrated how to serve a cup of tea according to Japanese etiquette.[111]

Like the stage performances they echoed, theatrical gatherings involved scenery and props as well as costumes and performances. By festooning their houses with themed decorations, hostesses evoked not only foreign lands but also the "foreign" settings provided by public spaces such as world's fairs, amusement parks, theaters, and restaurants. Orientalist costumes and other displays seemed to demand theatrical backdrops. From Los Angeles to New Orleans and New York, hosts invited guests to "Japanese" parties that featured costumed party givers in Orientalist settings.[112] An 1892 Japanese tea "given by a family who have made the fashionable trip to Japan and brought back a choice variety of Japanese costumes and bric-a-brac," serves as an example. According to the report in *Demorest's*, "The ladies of the family, a mother and three daughters, have a charming boudoir off the drawing-room, which they have fitted up with mementos of their trip, supplemented by judicious selections from Oriental stores of this country, and the effect is charmingly Japanesque. In this artistic apartment they received their friends in a delightfully informal manner, each of the hostesses wearing a veritable Japanese dress, of *crêpe*, magnificently embroidered, and their heads bedecked with pins galore. Each had her tiny table from which she dispensed delicious tea in rare Japanese cups, both the cups and their contents eliciting enthusiastic exclamations from the recipients."[113] Such events were not limited to white women. African American clubwomen threw Japanese teas to raise money for charitable causes. In Brownsville, Texas, women of Hispanic descent came to a party dressed in Japanese style. Japanese teas were so popular that they struck some as hackneyed by the early twentieth century, but they nevertheless proved persistent. "While there is nothing very new in the Japanese scheme, it is always effective and people never seem to tire of it," noted the author of a 1912 party guide.[114]

If Orientalist costumes demanded Orientalist backdrops, the reverse was also true: Orientalist interiors invited Orientalist entertainments. Women who had decorated their parlors in Orientalist splendor completed the fantasy by throwing parties. Putting on costumes, lighting lanterns, and using their imported china enabled them to realize the fullest potential of the sets they had erected. For some, producing the foreign went well beyond the occasional theme party to become a part of daily life. Atlanta resident Rebie Lowe illustrates this point. She had an Oriental reception room where, according to the *Atlanta Constitution*, "she always makes the most picturesque appearance in soft, clinging draperies and a Zouave bodice."[115]

Exotic interiors lent themselves particularly well to theme parties and costumed displays, but they did not serve as necessary preconditions. Even hostesses with colonial revival interiors and little bric-a-brac could get into the spirit thanks to businesses that provided inexpensive decorations and party favors. One firm of this type, B. Shackman and Company, sold imported novelties and "quaint conceits" in a New York City store and through the mail. In addition to supplying Japanese napkins, lanterns, fans, and parasol favors, Shackman's stocked items such as miniature Dutch shoes and windmills, flags from assorted nations, Chinese hats with attached pigtails, Tyrolean hats decorated with a feather, and Turkish fezzes.[116]

Decorative Dutch shoes and comparable props played a central role in fund-raising fairs, where they served simultaneously as atmosphere and inventory. Women's fund-raising fairs predated the great international exhibitions held in the United States, but by the late nineteenth century they had come to include the same souvenir objects found at world's fairs. A common gimmick for turn-of-the-century fairs was an around-the-world theme, with small items for sale by costumed vendors at each booth. The Paris booth might have fans, perfume, handkerchiefs, and gloves; Amsterdam might have blue-and-white Dutch china, chocolate, cheeses, doughnuts, and crullers. Moving on to Nuremberg, a fairgoer was likely to encounter dolls and carts with wooden horses. At Constantinople shoppers could procure Turkish coffee in tiny cups and assorted "oriental goods." The maidens of Tokyo and Shanghai sold china cups, straw baskets, embroideries, umbrellas, prints, tea, rice wafers, crystallized fruits, and nuts. There might even be a Chinese restaurant serving chop suey. Coming at last to Manila, fairgoers might find oranges and bananas, shells, beaded bags, pictures of the islands, carved picture frames, soldier dolls, and "little brown dolls representing savages." In an odd admission of the brutalities of empire, Manila might also feature hospital supplies, sold by a woman dressed as a Red Cross nurse.[117] To better market their sundries and trinkets, fair givers displayed them in elaborately decorated booths. For one fund raiser, the Macon Ladies' Aid Society constructed an "immense pagoda, illuminated by electric lights." For another, the New York and Brooklyn branches of the American Federation of Women constructed a Japanese booth and an Oriental cosey corner.[118]

As the presence of chocolate, cheese, coffee, rice wafers, and oranges at these events suggests, food played an important role in fund-raising fairs. In some events, it played the central role. Caroline French Benton, the author of a handbook on fund-raising fairs, provided instructions for a "Market Day among All Nations." This event involved saleswomen clothed in peasant dress selling "as many kinds of food as possible, just as is customary in the real markets of Europe, held in the country towns by the peasants." The Swiss booth should sell honey; the German booth pretzels and sausages; the French booth cakes and candy; the English booth tea, cheeses, and marmalades; the Dutch booth crullers and doughnuts.[119] Church suppers also provided opportunities to mix fund raising with geographic adventure. One guidebook urged church women to decorate the hall with flags of all nations, photos, and views of foreign countries. Food should be served at two tables, representing the Western and Eastern Hemispheres. The recommended menu? German coffee cake, Wiener wurst, Japanese rice wafers and tea, mocha and Java coffee, English roast beef, oolong tea, Irish potatoes, Scotch oatmeal cakes, Italian macaroni, Turkish delight, French pot au feu, Chinese chop suey, Spanish olla podrida, Boston baked beans, Philadelphia scrapple, and Maryland biscuits.[120] Through eating, church members could have what they regarded to be a cosmopolitan experience. They could assess the differences between West and East and then bring the two hemispheres together on their own encompassing plates.

Just like church bazaars, theme parties relied on food to convey foreignness. At Japanese tea parties, guests drank tea. At St. Patrick's Day parties, they ate potato dishes. At "Kaffeeklatches" they enjoyed coffee, iced or hot, and German cakes and sweets. Guests at a tea "a la Russ" ate black bread; at an Italian dinner, spaghetti, cheese, and olives; at a "Chinese frolic," rice and chop suey, "with dainty bread sticks in place of chop sticks." Those who favored the advice proffered by the Sears catalog had canned meats, dill pickles, and rye bread at Dutch lunches (ill. 3.8).[121]

Sometimes home entertainers attempted the round-the-world scheme seen so often in church halls. One young ladies' mission band had a party in which each house represented a different country and several automobiles conveyed the guests to and fro. At each house, there was a five-minute paper about the host country, with music, amusement, and attendants in costume. Of course, there were refreshments "peculiar to the country": in Greece, guests ate olives; in Italy, spaghetti; in Germany, kafe kuchen; in Japan, meshi (rice); in France, vin rouge (red punch); in Russia, caviar canapés; in England, plum pudding; in the United States, pie. "With good committees this scheme may be enlarged," noted the party book that described the event.[122]

The Charm of a Dutch Lunch

NO HOSPITALITY can exceed the charm and sociability of a Dutch lunch. These lunches are so easily and inexpensively prepared, and are usually gotten up on the spur of the moment. It's easy enough to serve a Dutch lunch when you keep a supply of our potted and canned meats. They are just the thing for these occasions, and they keep indefinitely on your pantry shelf. They are packed by the largest and most reputable packers in America, are pure and deliciously well flavored.

Veal Loaf

Potted or Deviled Ham Sandwiches   Hot Frankfurters
Dill Pickles   Montclair Brand Stuffed Olives
Dutch Rolls
Pineapple Cheese   Montclair Brand Soda Biscuits
Rye Bread   Coffee

3.8. "The Charm of a Dutch Lunch," from Sears, Roebuck, and Co., *Your Grocery Store* (1916), 38. Courtesy of the Winterthur Library: Printed Book and Periodical Collection, Winterthur, Delaware.

A "club of young married people" did expand on the idea by organizing a series of themed meals. Every other week, members met to eat home dinners carried out in the style of different nations, "and extremely pleasant and successful functions they were." The hosts of the Mexican party served foods "highly peppered and spiced in Mexican style," including tamales and "frigoles [*sic*], the brown Mexican beans cooked in butter." After these came Mexican chocolate, flavored with a combination of vanilla beans and cinnamon. On the German evening, the refreshments included rye bread, frankfurters, and sauerkraut. On the Chinese evening the group gathered beneath lanterns to partake of chop suey "composed of chicken, mushrooms and rice" served with "a Chinese sauce like our Worcestershire," lychee nuts, kumquat and ginger preserves, and tea. At the Russian party, guests encountered a samovar, caviar, and bliny cakes. "The Japanese evening was especially easy to prepare, because of familiarity with costumes and manners," noted the account. Other evenings, "all observed in characteristic style," centered on Turkey, Rumania, Persia, Ireland, Scotland, and the United States.[123]

If the organizers of round-the-world dinners are to be believed, food could transport those who tasted it to other places. This was particularly true when it accompanied costumery, performance, and stage settings, but food could also signify foreignness by itself. According to an article in *Good Housekeeping*, the mere sight of macaroni "calls up visions of the blue Bay of Naples, the great smoking peak of Vesuvius in the background." "Will you ply across the ocean?" questioned an article on English dinners that invited readers to use food as a vehicle for fictive travel.[124] Even when consumed in the course of an ordinary family meal, a dish regarded as foreign added a taste of the exotic. Eating spaghetti meant eating Italian, eating frijoles meant eating Mexican. Through food, native-born Americans could learn— in a visceral way—about the foreign. Recalling how her children used to say "I can smell the West Indies" when they ate a coconut, the author of a domestic advice book commented: "No doubt, under its influence, those palm trees, monkeys and negroes, who figure in their illustrated geography, enlarge in their inner consciousness into life and motion."[125]

Indeed, those who produced foreign-theme parties and other events often understood them in educational terms. The literature on producing themed gatherings is full of admonitions to do research. One domestic manual instructed novices to prepare foreign costumes for masquerades by studying pictures representing the inhabitants of different countries. Another counseled the hostess who wished to produce a correct Japanese tea to study a book on Japanese customs. A third reported that a round-the-world club had obtained "needed information" by "consulting books of travel relating to the special country under consideration, or interviewing returned travelers."[126] As such proddings to prepare for theme parties by boning up on foreign customs suggest, middle-class social attainment lay in the ability to demonstrate geographic knowledge.

In fact, the games played at these parties sometimes pitted guests against each other in geographic competitions. At a Japanese party, guests might encounter envelopes containing jumbled letters of some of the largest cities on the islands. The task was to determine the names by straightening out the mixtures. At a Dutch party, guests might be asked to write down as many interesting facts about the Netherlands and its people as they could recall. At the end of twenty minutes, their papers would be read aloud and a prize may be awarded for the cleverest. Another challenge would be to "distribute squares of cardboard, with pencils, and see who can in fifteen minutes draw the most complete map of Holland." At a postcard party, guests vied with each other to determine where the pictures were taken and they raced to reassemble postcards cut into puzzle shapes.[127]

Theme parties might even represent the culmination of geographic study. Armchair travel clubs often ended their fictive tours of foreign countries with celebratory feasts. A Detroit women's club that reported becoming "so thoroughly Teutonized that its members think in German and eat in German" held a "genuine German luncheon with Kartoffel Salat, Schinken, Wiener Wurst, Schweizer Käse, Brödchen, Kaiser Semmel, Butter, Kaffe mit Schlagsahne, Eingemachte Birnen, Kaffee kuchen, Wasser, and Pfeffer Nüsse."[128] Another club concluded its studies of Spain and Portugal by decorating a parlor in red and yellow and hanging pictures of paintings by Spanish artists and a portrait of King Alphonso, draped in the Spanish flag. Then they sat down to eat chili con carne, served by maids in Spanish costumes. In conclusion, they sang Spanish songs and several young girls who "had been taught the steps by a teacher of fancy dancing" danced Spanish dances.[129] In the case of these clubwomen, the theme party served as an opportunity to display hard-sought geographic knowledge.

The tendency to regard theme parties as means to foster geographic awareness suggests that women had plenty of grounds to regard family meals as ways of exploring the foreign as well. By serving "foreign" foods, housewives strove to provide a taste of life in other lands. Through their efforts, mealtimes served as lesson times, and dining rooms became classrooms. But of course, dining rooms were much more—and much less—than classrooms. They were places to entertain and be entertained, and the lessons they taught were often fantastical. Much of the geography they presented was entirely imaginary; most of the rest was highly distorted as the Spanish function featuring Mexican chilis suggests.

The women who turned other peoples' cultures into the stuff of amusement could feel they knew the world, for, after all, they had ingested it. But, of course, rather than really engaging with difference, they merely engaged with their own approximation of it. The liberties taken in theme parties illuminate the creative cast to "foreign" entertainments. Australians did not really paint kangaroos on their bodices, but American women sometimes did when they dressed as Australia. The Dutch did not really speak in mangled English, but American hosts might in composing invitations: "Mine Frent: Come oudt und make pooty much fun with us at a Dutch Treat."[130] Japan consisted of much more than porcelain and cherry blossoms, Japanese cuisine of more than tea, but talismanic objects and familiar foods displaced more complicated or unsettling depictions. In the geography of entertainment, misperceptions and stereotypes reigned supreme.

The enormous liberties taken in depicting the foreign extended to food. The recipes passed off as foreign in American cookbooks would have amazed (if not horrified) their supposed originators. The dish that ostensibly represented Chinese cooking—chop suey—would have been completely foreign to Chinese cooks, regardless of region, for it originated in the United States among Chinese restauranteurs with Euro-American patrons. Similarly, the dish thought to represent traditional Indian cooking—curry—really reflected Anglo-Indian inventiveness. Besides passing off recent innovations as traditional cuisines, writings on foods that had originated elsewhere recommended astounding substitutions in ingredients. One *Good Housekeeping* recipe for chop suey said that, if unable to procure "Chinese sauce" (available in Chinese shops), a cook could substitute Worcestershire sauce. To be truly accurate, counseled a book on Japanese events, the menu should include raw fish and edible seaweed. "But it is not likely that such a menu would be received with very much enthusiasm by our American young people, so we shall substitute fish salad and lettuce or water-cress."[131] A macaroni recipe titled "The Italian Way of Cooking It," counseled "a clove of garlic chopped fine" but added, "if garlic is objectionable, an onion chopped and fried brown may be added instead." Besides replacing core ingredients, American cooks meddled with cooking methods. How long to cook the novel spaghetti? "Boil about one hour till all the water is exhausted," advised a cookbook published in 1888. In sum, the cooks who experimented with "foreign" recipes Americanized them. They minimized difference even as they appropriated it. What came in the guise of the outlandish was really home cooking after all. An article on Indian food admitted as much when it said that the curries of India were "no more like so-called curries made in Europe and America than coffee is like champagne."[132]

Admitting that the popular geography of food presented a highly distorted picture of foreign customs does not make it any less of a geography, however. Even immigrant cooks substituted local ingredients, blended food traditions, and invented new dishes. Not only in the United States but overseas as well, the foreign foods that American housewives were trying to evoke were themselves in flux. What should count as true Italian food in a time when migrant Italian workers were returning home, bringing new tastes with them?[133] How could anybody accurately represent fluid and variable practices? The issue extends beyond the feasibility of reproducing the elusive outside its native habitat to encompass the very nature of geography. All geographies involve some distortion. What matters—what makes them geographies—is that they purport to represent the wider world. And the geography of food certainly did that. Despite the wholesale substitutions and gross misrepresentations, "foreign" recipes represented efforts to bring the world into American households.

Like cookbook geographies, geographic entertainments led women to appreciate difference in two senses. First, they valued differences by making them the stuff of enjoyment, fantasy, and play. Second, around-the-world events put middle-class American women into other peoples' shoes—sometimes literally so in the case of the "Dutch" women who clumped around church bazaars in wooden clogs. In the process, they encouraged a sense of imaginative identification with people from beyond the nation's boundaries. Disregarding the artifice, superficiality, and underlying inequalities of household encounters, some contemporaries regarded the common ground of food as a means to facilitate true international understanding. As a cookbook writer who confessed to having "incorporated into my daily life, the habits of eating of French, Germans, Italians, Swiss, and even Chinese" phrased the matter, "the simple fact of eating the dishes of The World has seemed to bring us into closer sympathy with mankind, even in its most foreign guise."[134] However touching in its sentimentality and self-serving in its politics, such conclusions indicate that some women regarded their culinary forays as a counterpoint to geographies aimed at delineating hierarchies. The housewife who breakfasted on bananas, lunched on macaroni, and dined on curry could regard herself as benignly cosmopolitan.

But, as the reference to "even Chinese" suggests, there were significant limits to this cosmopolitanism. These limits can be seen in the boundaries left uncrossed. Instead of serving cocoa in Javanese booths, the women who produced round-the-world fairs served it in Dutch ones, thus revealing a preference for identifying with Dutch colonial masters rather than darker, colonized peoples. The white housewives who hailed difference through their cooking, entertaining, and masquerades were only willing to go so far. They might countenance Asianness, but blackness remained beyond the pale. They might temporarily remake themselves as distant others, but not by risking the boundaries that divided social groups at home. White women who ate foods with black African origins did so only after downplaying their Africanness, safely defining them as dishes from Dixie. Similarly, white women might cook Indian pudding, but by the turn of the twentieth century, this had become a vestige from colonial days, not in most cases a means of identifying with living and perhaps proximate Native Americans.[135] Cookbooks published numerous recipes attributed to British India, but not to the Philippines, thus suggesting the difficulties in quickly ingesting those islands. Despite the nation's increasing ties to the Caribbean and Philippines, white American women masqueraded far more as Europeans than as people from the nation's new island acquisitions and other economic dependencies. (Recall the Red Cross nurse as the occupant of the Philippine booth.)

Along with asserting whiteness, the women who savored foreign foods asserted class, national, and civilizational power. By preparing foreign dishes, a housewife could, in the words of the *General Federation Bulletin*, "give to her table a truly cosmopolitan distinction."[136] That is, she could differentiate herself from less cultivated neighbors, or from those who lacked the wherewithal to throw exotic entertainments. Situating herself in time, she could pride herself on being more worldly than her mother. Situating herself in space, she could regard herself as more worldly than the locals who labored on her behalf. By throwing foreign entertainments, white, middle-class American women could display their privileged positions in the global scheme of things. Like the world's fairs that celebrated the U.S. ability to profit from global production, ostensibly foreign meals expressed a conviction that those gathered around the table benefited from engagements with the world.

Although foreign entertainments had an outward-looking, appreciative dimension that differentiated them from the bland repasts urged by domestic scientists, their messages about racial, class, national, and civilizational differences resonated with the lessons found in home economics textbooks. Like the most nationalistic domestic science texts, foreign entertainments taught white, middle-class women how they differed from others. However much they may have seemed to elide difference, foreign entertainments reinforced it. Like the white people who played Indian or put on blackface, those who faked foreignness in themed entertainments distanced their real selves from their more colorful, playful, primitive pretend selves.[137] They could take comfort in the thought that their real selves were not like these other selves at all, that only in rare moments of playacting or revelry did they bear any resemblance to the other peoples of the world. Through self-consciously positioning themselves as "foreign" at special dinners and jovial fetes, they could pretend that their true selves were not in the least foreign, that they were as quintessentially American as their everyday fare.

Foreign entertainments enabled native-born women to position themselves as true representatives of Americanness in another way as well. By demonstrating an encompassing palate, these women showed that they were not bound by particular Old World traditions. By eating a bit of everything, they denied that they too were ethnics. Experimenting with multiple identities enabled them to show that they were so fully American they did not have to prove it.

Although immigrants too added new recipes to their repertoires, often borrowing from other newcomers, home economists and domestic advice purveyors generally did not value their cosmopolitanism. Rather than encouraging immigrant women and other women whom they regarded as insufficiently American (such as Mexican American women) to learn from their ethnically diverse neighbors, Americanizers tried to persuade them to forsake their favored foods for old New England fare. Tellingly, the New York Cooking School taught wealthy women to master French recipes and working-class women to boil haddock.[138] Regarding foreign entertainments as a way to prove sophistication and cosmopolitanism, native-born women tried to reserve them for themselves.

The role of culinary cosmopolitanism in reinforcing difference can perhaps most vividly be seen in the issue of invitations. In 1869 *Harper's Weekly* published a Thomas Nast drawing depicting African Americans, Native Americans, Chinese Americans, Irish Americans, and other ethnic types sitting around Uncle Sam's Thanksgiving table. Speaking to Reconstruction-era debates over national belonging, this drawing endorsed universal suffrage and equality. What matters is not so much the food—most of the dishes remained covered, only the turkey stands out—as the democratic vision of inclusion (ill. 3.9).[139] For all their celebration of culinary diversity, turn-of-the-century food writings failed to present a comparable sense of inclusiveness. The voluminous advice literature on producing foreignness did not counsel hostesses to invite immigrant guests. And, indeed, it appears that the native-born hostesses who strove so hard to produce the foreign in their households made virtually no effort to invite actual foreigners to represent themselves. In many cases, they overlooked the foreign-born women already in their households, hard at work in their kitchens. True, settlement house and International Institute workers held numerous parties for their immigrant neighbors, but these typically took place in the settlements and institutes, not in private parlors. This distinction was not lost on immigrant women. After mingling with native-born YWCA activists and supporters in an "international party," a group of Italian women told an inquisitive International Institute leader that they still felt slighted. The gist of their complaint? "The American women will patronize but not receive them into their homes."[140]

As the role of food and cooking in sustaining social distinction suggests, the increasing internationalization of American cookery has implications that go far beyond the gustatory pleasures of bygone dinners. Food writers provided more than advice on cooking supper, they provided geographic guidance. Taken together, the popular geographies of cookbooks and of cooking played a significant role in shaping the world views of white, middle-class, native-born women and those who consumed their creations. Many Americans never saw a world's fair, but meal planning, marketing, cooking, and eating were central parts of daily life. In 1898 the fledgling National

3.9. Thomas Nast, "Uncle Sam's Thanksgiving Dinner," *Harper's Weekly* 13 (Nov. 20, 1869): 745. Courtesy of the Rare Book and Special Collections Library, University of Illinois at Urbana-Champaign.

Geographic Society had fewer than 1,400 members, but cookbooks were common fixtures on kitchen shelves and cooking columns were regular features in ladies' magazines and on women's pages of daily newspapers.[141] Like writings on household furnishings and fashion, cookbooks and entertaining guides brought the rest of the world home, infusing daily life with geographic consciousness and helping white, middle-class Americans define themselves as cosmopolitans in a world full of locals. The women who read this literature may have continued to concoct their grandmothers' favorite dishes, but the increase in food imports and growing interest in foreign foodways after the Civil War exposed even the most parochial to new ingredients and recipes. Despite their association with women and the household, cookbooks and cooking were far from being exclusively domestic. If you are what you eat, then the women who experimented with new recipes and ingredients tasted of the consumers' imperium.

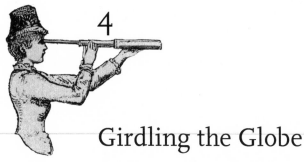

Girdling the Globe

*The Fictive Travel Movement and the
Rise of the Tourist Mentality*

In November 1889 a young reporter employed by the
New York World set forth on a dash around the globe, intent on matching
the feats of the fictional Phileas Fogg, the main character in Jules Verne's
Around the World in Eighty Days. Writing under the by-line Nellie Bly, she
sent back thrilling dispatches chronicling her race against the clock. In the
suspenseful stretches between cables, the *World* ran sensationalized reports of the dangerous conditions she would encounter. It offered round-
trip passage to England and spending money to the person who could come
closest in guessing the time of her return. The idea of a young, unescorted
woman, sprinting around the world with only a valise in hand caught the
imaginations of many of her contemporaries. Newspapers across the country covered her story. Sales of the *World* picked up outside New York City
and fan mail poured into its offices. *Cosmopolitan* magazine sent a competitor, Elizabeth Bisland, on her own round-the-world jaunt, to see if she
could beat Bly by traveling in the opposite direction. She could not, for Bly
made good time, seeing little other than the passing views from trains and
steamers. As she crossed the United States on the final leg of her journey,
crowds cheered her at her whistle stops. She arrived home after seventy-
two days, six hours, ten minutes, and eleven seconds underway. But Bly
did not stop moving. She published a best-selling book on her travels and
embarked on a forty-week lecture tour. Clothed in the dress she had worn
around the world, she regaled her audiences with stories of her adventures.
The globe-trotting Bly became a symbol of the spunky independence of the

late Victorian New Woman and the compression of time and space in an age of railroads, steamships, and transoceanic cables.[1]

Despite the *World's* insistence on the novelty of her feat, Bly was not the first American woman to circle the earth. Nor was she the first to pen an account of her round-the-world adventures. Her predecessors included Ellen Hardin Walworth, Lucy Seaman Bainbridge, and Anna P. Little, who published books on recently completed trips in 1877, 1882, and 1887, respectively. Bly's well-publicized feat promoted still more round-the-world tours by American women. These included Eliza Archard Conner, a journalist who circled the globe in 1899; Mabel Loomis Todd, who related her adventures in a 1901 issue of *Club Woman*; and a pair of "plucky newspaper girls" who set off in 1906 after arranging with several American newspapers to send back syndicated articles. Those who worried that all this globe-trotting was coming at the cost of domesticity could take heart from reports that two years into their trip one of the "girls" married a U.S. Army lieutenant stationed in the Philippines, leaving the other to continue on her own. Nuptials notwithstanding, world tours challenged the assumption that women's place was in the home. Recognizing their value to the cause, suffragists Maud Wood Park and Carrie Chapman Catt jumped on the bandwagon.[2]

The gimmick refused to go away. In 1910 *Travel Magazine* chronicled the trip of a New York woman who drove around the world in her motorcar, racking up 20,000 miles on her odometer and exhausting five sets of tires. In 1918 *Good Housekeeping* sent Madeline Z. Doty on a journey around the world that took her to Japan, Russia, France, and England. In 1920 Bainbridge published *Jewels from the Orient*, an account of her second round-the-world expedition. For total number of miles logged, Jessie Ackerman surely held a record: she completed the trip six times. Most globe-girdling women preferred leisurely schedules to Bly's whirlwind pace. But in 1911 a group of Chicago women circumnavigated the globe in forty minutes, with no luggage at all.[3]

The Chicago women did not really travel around the world, of course. They did so imaginatively, with the help of stereographic slides. In so doing, they participated in a virtual movement. In the late nineteenth and early twentieth centuries, tens of thousands of U.S. women organized themselves into travel clubs. Most of these women never boarded a ship. But all of them met on a regular basis to listen to travelogues and present travel briefings. Although many club members did their own research, others hired expert leaders or adopted commercially prepared curricula. To enliven their tours, club members presented special programs with music, national foods, costumes, decorations, and dances. Women who studied Germany feasted on

Berliner Pfannkuchen, saure Gurken, and heisze Wienerwurst. A group "touring" Spain sampled Burgos soup and Madrid tamals. To "add interest" to a lecture on Persia, a Chicago-area club decorated its meeting rooms with lamps, rugs, and "other articles of Persian manufacture or design." The members of one club made souvenir scrapbooks, complete with photographs, engravings, and colored pictures, to record an imaginative journey.[4] The most common destinations for these clubs lay in Europe—especially Great Britain and France—but after covering the beaten European track, many clubs ventured further afield, to Asia, Latin America, the Middle East, and North Africa, and sometimes on to destinations such as Australia, the Congo, and Guam.

Imaginary travel clubs show that the around-the-world movement involved more than a handful of globe-trotters and that it was more than a media production. Armchair travel helped give globe-trotting a popular purchase that extended beyond the small number of individuals who actually circumnavigated the earth. The late nineteenth-century fascination with travel helps explain why Bly became such a sensation and how the feats of world travelers permeated the wider culture.

The fictive travel movement also speaks to a central concern among those who wish to historicize globalization: the origins of global consciousness. When did various groups begin to situate themselves on a planetary scale of being? How have people conceived of the world far beyond their localities? What contributed to more geographically expansive world views?[5] Like the foreign foods and entertainments that made a distinctive mark on American domesticity, the proliferation of armchair travel clubs suggests that global consciousness gained a significant hold among white, middle-class American women in the late nineteenth and early twentieth centuries. These clubs reveal an awareness of substantial swaths of the earth and some sense of how disparate places were connected to each other. They show the importance of leisure travel, even among people who never left the country, for spreading geographic knowledge. They testify to the ascent of a culture of international travel and the importance of women in advancing this culture. Furthermore, imaginary travel clubs illuminate the spread of a tourist mentality, something that intersected with anthropological, governmental, missionary, and commercial outlooks on the wider world but that also had its own distinct emphases. In sum, the imaginary travel movement contributed to the rising global consciousness of the era, and it influenced the nature of such consciousness by advancing consumerist appraisals of the world.

How widespread was fictive travel? In her 1898 *History of the Woman's*

Club Movement in America, Jennie June Croly reported that of the eighty-three clubs in the Minnesota state federation, ten were "distinctly travel or tourist clubs." Others took on travel topics from time to time. In 1912 a report by the General Federation of Women's Clubs (GFWC) listed travel along with civics and sociology as one of three leading topics studied by affiliated clubwomen.[6] By searching the records of the General Federation from its inception in 1890 to 1920, I have found more than 320 affiliated clubs with a travel emphasis or travel department (see the appendix of travel clubs).

But this number greatly underestimates the total number of women's travel clubs, for most women's clubs did not or could not (in the case of African American clubs) affiliate themselves with the segregated General Federation. Furthermore, the GFWC's records are not fully forthcoming. Published registers provide club names but contain no information on club activities. Unless I could find specific information on the contents of club programs, I counted only clubs with names such as Travelers' Club or Tourist Club. Yet many clubs that embarked on imaginary journeys did not label themselves as travel clubs. The Thursday Literary Club of Selma, Alabama, discussed "foreign cities"; the Ladies' Literary Club of Kalamazoo, Michigan, enjoyed a trip though Mexico. The tendency for large clubs to divide into smaller sections also makes it difficult to pinpoint the number of clubwomen embarked on fictive travels, for most GFWC rosters did not elaborate on the doings of travel and other subgroups.[7]

That many clubs with travel themes did not identify themselves as travel clubs becomes particularly clear if we go beyond GFWC records. Most of the women's clubs that adopted the Bay View course—a travel-oriented study course that came with an informative magazine, readings lists, and exams—did not label themselves as travel clubs. Among the 203 clubs that signed on to the Bay View program in 1901 were the Ottawa, Illinois, Progressive Club; the Hesterville, Mississippi, Woman's Club; the Galena, Kansas, Shakespeare Club; the Greenville, Texas, Saturday Culture Club; and the Exeter, Nebraska, Happy Home Reading Circle. In 1902 about 8,000 people—the vast majority of them women—belonged to clubs that followed the Bay View Reading Circle programs (ill. 4.1). As the group set forth for Greece, the editor of the *Bay View Magazine* exulted in the magnitude of the movement: "If every Bay View club were an ocean steamer, the residents of Athens would view with wonder, and perhaps alarm, on the first morning in May, the presence of nearly five hundred ships in their harbor of Piraeus."[8] By 1914 the number of Bay View reading circle members had risen to 25,000, an estimated 95 percent of them women.[9]

4.1. The Classical, of Washington, Indiana, *Bay View Magazine* 6 (June 1899): 372.
Courtesy of the Michigan State University Libraries, Lansing.

Further complicating efforts to quantify the number of travel clubs is
the question, What counts as armchair travel? If we return to the records of
the General Federation, we find that art, language, history, literature, and
current-events clubs all had touristic inflections. The English Literary Club
of Bridgeport, Connecticut, had "occasional evenings of travel"; the Shrews-
bury Reading Club of Eatontown, New Jersey, intermingled tourist trips
with its study of literature and music. Though identified as an art and history club, the Society of Art and History of Cleveland characterized its 1898
program as a flying trip through Holland. The same tendency held true for
African American women's clubs: Anne Meis Knupfer has found that African American women's literary clubs in turn-of-the-century Chicago took
up a range of topics, including travel.[10]

Even if we added history, literature, art, and other clubs to the total,
we might still undercount the number of imaginary travelers, for general-
interest clubs also got caught up in the travel craze by tackling travel topics
now and then. The New Century Club of Philadelphia, which brought in
native teachers of French and German, also sponsored talks on travel in
Spain and Africa. In 1898 the Hull-House Woman's Club offered a series
of lectures on foreign cities; in later years it continued to sponsor travel
talks. The *Official Register and Directory of Women's Clubs* is full of similarly
named clubs—the Cosmopolitan Club, the Tuesday Club, the Study Club,
the Self Culture Club, the Wanderers, the Peregrinators, and so forth—that
may have focused on travel or taken up travel topics in some meetings.[11] Although it is impossible to pinpoint the number of women who participated
in the fictive travel movement, it is safe to say that tens of thousands joined
in from the 1880s to 1920.

Travel clubs sprang up from Alabama and Arkansas to Montana and California. But the densest concentrations lay in the Northeast and Midwest—in states such as Ohio, Minnesota, and New York. The Tourist Club of Minneapolis can provide some insights on the type of women who joined. It was founded in 1891 by Martha C. Wells, the valedictorian of the Rockford College class of 1866. Wells married in 1872 at what struck her family as the late age of twenty-five. After living in Michigan, she moved to Minneapolis in 1880. She had two daughters, one of whom died in infancy. Not overly pressed by maternal obligations, Wells turned her considerable energies and talents to art education. She contributed to magazines, prepared club programs, organized a traveling art library, and taught courses in private schools for girls, the Minneapolis Art Institute, and Hamline University. She visited several world's fairs in the United States and, although she had never been outside the country upon the founding of the Tourist Club, later made four trips to Europe. On the last three, she accompanied parties of women, lecturing to them in the galleries they visited. In 1910 Wells became state regent of the Daughters of the American Revolution. She also held leadership positions in the Minnesota Federation of Women's Clubs and served as president of her church's missionary society.[12]

In a reflection on the history of the club, one member recalled that Wells had insisted on keeping it exclusive:

And some—alas—were not admitted—
Through all the years they should be pitied.
But Sister Wells was adamant;
And cried—You see we really can't
Let people in who have not class.
We'll say to them—You shall not pass.
We're sorry but we clearly see
You haven't quite the family tree.
And then perhaps—too sad—we find
You have not quite that master mind.[13]

Who struck Wells as fit to include among the charter members? Isabella Reid Buchanan made the cut. The daughter of a schoolteacher, Buchanan graduated from the Fond du Lac high school in Wisconsin and taught primary school for sixteen years. After marrying in 1881, she moved to Minneapolis. She organized Bible classes and wrote several books on the women of the Bible. She too held offices in the Federation of Women's Clubs. A eulogist remembered her as being a student all her life and as having a passion for maps. She preached female self-assertion insofar as she admonished the women who presented their papers inaudibly to "speak out boldly." Once she made a three-month trip to Europe.[14]

Another charter member was Elizabeth Fish, a niece of Yale University president Noah Porter. Born in Green Farms, Connecticut, she moved to Minneapolis in 1880 but demonstrated some nostalgia for her birthplace by joining the Colony of New England Women. She also belonged to the Daughters of the American Revolution, the Women's Christian Association, and the Congregational Church. Like Wells, she graduated from Rockford College in Elgin, Illinois. Her husband practiced law and later served as a judge. She had four daughters, one of whom became a high school principal, and a son. Like Wells and Buchanan, Fish belonged to the local elite. These women were able to hold their meetings on Monday—wash day—because they employed laundresses.[15]

How typical were the Minneapolis Tourist Club members? With its DAR affiliations and transatlantic travelers, the Minneapolis club seems more exclusive than many others, but travel club members do appear to have been overwhelmingly native-born and white. Despite their interest in foreign countries, travel club leaders apparently did not seek out immigrant women as members. Nor did they admit women they considered to be colored into their clubs. When a Chickasaw woman established a Bay View Reading Club in Indian Territory, the Bay View Magazine played up the news value of this unusual event by describing it as "most interesting." It then went on to characterize the founder as "a refined and educated person," presumably to dispel the suspicion that an Indian woman would not be.[16] Although some African American women's literary clubs took up travel topics, the only African American women's club devoted primarily to travel that I have been able to locate is the Oak and Ivy Club of Springfield, Ohio, which toured China in 1895. Rather than entertain themselves with imaginary international jaunts, African American clubwomen were far more likely to make *real* travel a priority by protesting the Jim Crow laws that restricted their mobility and denied their full humanity.[17]

What about class status? Like the members of the Tourist Club of Minneapolis, many travel club members belonged to the local elite. Founding members of the McGregor, Iowa, tourist club included the Oberlin-educated wife of the school superintendent, the wife of a carriage factory operator, and the wife of a lawyer. A member of the Bay View travel club in Sioux Rapids, Iowa, described her group as "twenty of the city's best women." The roster of the Chamberlain, South Dakota, Travel Club reads like a who's who in local society—the founder, Susan Laughlin, was the wife of the mayor. Other women were married to a postmaster, judge, drugstore owner, hardware store owner, banker, and storekeeper. Yet travel club members could not always take their lofty social positions for granted. The roster of the Chamberlain club included farm women and ranch women. The only member who had traveled outside the United States had gone to Scotland to meet her immigrant husband's family. These women were pillars of their community, but they were not women of leisure. One member, Cora Watson, joined the club before she had children; two years after giving birth to her first child the demands of managing her household caused her to stop coming. After her children had grown, she moved to a nearby reservation where she ran a family store and pumped gas. Just as the Chamberlain club members knew what it meant to work for a living, many Bay View Reading Circle members supported themselves as teachers.[18]

As these examples suggest, most travel club members were busy homemakers and workers. Unlike the Minneapolis Tourist Club members, with their multiple memberships, many travel club members do not appear to have belonged to other women's clubs. They regarded the time devoted to club activities as precious time carved out from their daily routines of housework, tending to the needs of others, and, in some cases, earning a living. Yet even the exceptionally privileged members of the Minneapolis Tourist club had to defend themselves from charges of neglecting their homes and families and stepping outside their sphere. Despite their ability to hire domestic help, their travel club commitments meant that their families sometimes had to make do with shredded wheat and milk for club night dinners.[19] One tourist club program booklet hints at how hard women had to struggle to make time for club work. "If you gain fifteen minutes a day, it will make itself felt at the end of the year," it counseled. And for the really pressed: "Resolve to edge in a little reading every day, if it is but a single sentence."[20] Travel club members congratulated themselves on rising to the challenge. "All will bear witness to the excellence of the papers given," ran the annual report of another travel club, "and when we remember that this work has been done by busy women—wives, mothers, heads of families, each with manifold duties incumbent upon her, the Travel Class is indeed to be congratulated that among its members there are so many ladies not only willing, but competent, to interest the company gathered here from week to week." Travel club members regarded their journeys as hard-earned breaks from daily obligations, their programs as a source of pride.[21]

Historians who have written on the women's club movement that burgeoned at the turn of the twentieth century have emphasized the late nineteenth-century rise of clubs devoted to cultural matters and the twentieth-century ascendance of clubs devoted to civic betterment. They have not explained the proliferation of travel clubs, however. What explains the attraction of imaginative travel to women who could only read a sentence at a time? Why did busy women systematically set about pretending they were tourists? Raw escapism—the desperate desire to flee the dirty dishes, the crying children, the demanding husbands for the most distant reaches of the earth—no doubt played a role.[22] But art and literature offer their own escapes. So why travel?

One explanation is that travel club members were enticed by commercial agents who sold professionally prepared imaginary study tours. This began with the John Stoddard Travel Series. Stoddard was born in Brookline, Massachusetts, in 1850. He graduated from Williams College, studied theology for two years at Yale Divinity School, and then taught Latin and French in the Boston Latin School. After touring Europe, Asia Minor, Palestine, and Egypt in 1874, he began a career as a travel lecturer. In the 1880s he started to pen travel accounts as well. By 1898 his lectures were available in a ten-volume set, covering Norway, Switzerland, Athens, Venice, Constantinople, Jerusalem, Egypt, India, Japan, China, The Passion Play, Paris, France, Spain, Berlin, Vienna, St. Petersburg, Moscow, the Rhine, Belgium, Holland, Mexico, Florence, Naples, Rome, Scotland, England, London, California, the Grand Canyon, and Yellowstone Park. Over the next thirty years, Stoddard revised and reissued his lectures a number of times. He also published several folios of photographs and supplementary volumes on Canada, Malta, Gibraltar, Ireland, Denmark, Sweden, South Tyrol, the Dolmites, Sicily, Genoa, and the Engadine.[23]

Stoddard marketed his books as study guides for future travelers, as souvenirs for returned travelers, and, most importantly, as substitutes for those unable to travel. That he assumed a budget-conscious readership can be seen in promotional statements trumpeting the low cost of his volumes. His use of traveling salesmen to sell his books also suggests that he sought to reach a wide market. These agents had much to gain by encouraging the formation of travel clubs. Women who could not afford the entire series might cover part of the cost if they could persuade some of their friends to join them. Salesmen could reap a bonanza if each member of a newly formed club purchased a set. If in some cases the purchase of books sparked the formation of a travel club, in other cases existing travel clubs adopted Stoddard materials. Stoddard's popularity derived not only from his marketing efforts but from his compelling presentations. His vivid recountings of his touristic experiences and lavish use of photographs (at least one per page in his lecture series) encouraged his audiences to imagine themselves in foreign destinations (ill. 4.2).[24] Preferring colorful anecdotes to dry analysis, he made travel seem enticing.

One of the travel lecturers who followed in Stoddard's footsteps was Burton Holmes. Born in Chicago in 1870, Holmes became a travel buff at age nine, when he accompanied his grandmother to one of Stoddard's lectures. Seven years later, his grandmother took him to Europe, where he was thrilled to see Stoddard in the lobby of a German hotel. An accomplished photographer, he presented some of his travel pictures to the Chicago Camera Club in 1890. Club members suggested that he mount his negatives as slides and show them to the general public. After short-lived ventures selling real estate and working as a photo supply clerk, he obtained financial backing from his family to travel to Japan. Using material gathered on that trip, he began his career as a professional travel lecturer in 1893. At first he toured the Midwest, but when Stoddard retired Holmes established courses in eastern cities. In 1897 he enlivened his talks by adding motion-picture clips—running about twenty-five seconds each. (These depicted Italians eating spaghetti and other exotic sights.) His well-to-do audiences paid around $1.25 a ticket and came attired in evening dress.[25]

In a 1904 lecture tour in England, he started using the word "Travelogues" to describe his entertainments. By 1919 he appeared annually in New York, Brooklyn, Boston, Philadelphia, Washington, Pittsburgh, Chicago, Milwaukee, Saint Louis, and San Francisco, giving from ten to twenty performances in each city. Truly peripatetic, he spent five to eight months of the year traveling the world to gather material. Like Stoddard, he published his lectures in lavishly illustrated volumes. The fourteen-volume set released in 1920 (consisting mainly of reprints of earlier volumes) included lectures on Morocco, Cities of the Barbary Coast, Athens, Egypt, Italy, Switzerland, Paris, Berlin, Norway, Sweden, St. Petersburg, the Trans-Siberian Railway, Peking, Seoul, Japan, Manila, Rio de Janeiro and Brazil, Buenos Aires, and Over the Andes to Chile. Ultimately he sold more than 40,000 copies of his lecture series. The rave review offered by one fan, New York resident Mary E. Smith, can help explain his appeal: "Mr. Holmes charms you and retains your attention while you are drinking in the great benefits of travel."[26]

The Bay View reading courses emulated the Stoddard and Holmes series. These were produced under the auspices of the Bay View Association, a Methodist summer encampment on the shores of Little Traverse Bay in northern Michigan. An affiliate of the Chautauqua Literary and Scientific Circle since 1886, the Bay View Association ran a vacation university around the turn of the century. In 1893 John M. Hall instituted a reading

4.2. "Climbing the Great Pyramid, Egypt," from John L. Stoddard, *A Trip around the World* (1894). Courtesy of the Tutt Library, Colorado College, Colorado Springs.

program that members could follow at home. For the next twenty-five years, the reading circle went around the world, designating each year the English year, German year, and so forth. Hall commissioned brief, synthetic books such as *A Short History of Russia* and *South American Life* for circle members. He also edited the *Bay View Magazine*, devoted exclusively to fictive travel. Its writings on foreign sites encouraged the reader to assume a tourist's perspective. When the cold air comes down from the glacier, "you become enthusiastic," ran one article. "Before we enter the city, I want you to visit a most interesting place in the suburbs," ran another.[27] Reports of club activities published in the magazine furthered the conceit by pretending that stay-at-homes really had traveled. "After a year of unalloyed delight in Germany, eleven Danvers, Illinois ladies sailed for Spain a month ago," noted a typical entry.[28]

In conjunction with the travel course, members could proceed to the summer encampment at Bay View to hear travel talks and participate in "foreign tourist conferences." Hall marketed his travel programs by describing them as "suited to the busiest club woman and a very great labor saving help. All the essential studies are ready prepared, saving club people days and days in hunting up literature and digging out helps." Club members who were pressed for time or who found it difficult to produce their own programs (some travel club members struggled so hard to find relevant materials that they ended up founding libraries) could join a Bay View tour for convenience.[29]

One of the *Bay View Magazine*'s competitors was the *Mentor*, published twice a month out of New York City starting in 1913. This provided reading courses on a broad range of subjects, ranging from music to science, current events, and, of course, travel. Travel lecturer Dwight L. Elmendorf provided a "trip around the world" in the inaugural volumes. The twenty installments included "Scotland: The Land of Song and Scenery," "Paris, the Incomparable," and "Egypt, the Land of Mystery."[30] Given that each issue contained only one in-depth article, this represented a significant commitment to armchair travel. No doubt responding to surveys that ranked travel along with fine art and literature as readers' three favorite topics, the *Mentor* continued to focus on travel in later issues, publishing travel-oriented issues on Mexico, the Danube, the Canadian Rockies, Korea, and other places. Each issue came with a collection of six related prints with detailed descriptions on the back. By 1916 the *Mentor* had close to 100,000 subscribers, many of them clubwomen.[31]

Why stop with packaged materials? Professional travel lecturers sparked the formation of some travel clubs by offering to present the talks. One such lecturer was Professor Charles Farrar, a former instructor of mathematics and astronomy at Vassar, who became president of Milwaukee College in 1874. By the 1880s his interests had shifted to art history. He published a guide to the study of sculpture, painting, and architecture and started delivering lectures titled "Imaginary Tours of Europe." These proved to be such a hit that Farrar resigned the college presidency and devoted himself to "the cause of popular art education." As part of this endeavor, he set up several midwestern travel clubs, including the Hyde Park Travel Club, founded in 1888. Farrar charged the club $400 a year for a series of twenty illustrated travel lectures.[32] Recognizing clubwomen's interest in travel topics, a number of professional lecturers advertised their services in GFWC publications. Emeline Weld Kennan, for example, announced her talks on everyday life in Russia and "Forty Ideal Days in Jamaica"; other speakers promised to illustrate their talks with watercolor paintings and "stereopticon projections."[33]

Professional program providers had a financial interest in developing travel clubs and no doubt deserve some of the credit for their popularity. But to attribute the rise of travel clubs solely to the advent of packaged "tours" and professional lecturers means ignoring the clubs that predated these tours and those that did not rely on packaged information or lectures. Some clubs turned to professional materials only after a spate of do-it-yourself years, while others continued to travel even after dropping professional programs. When Farrar tired of presenting complete programs, the Hyde Park Travel Club kept on going. In 1895 Farrar gave ten lectures and club members the other ten. Upon Farrar's resignation in 1898, the group hired Agnes Ingersoll as his replacement. Ingersoll and the club members took turns conducting meetings. When Ingersoll stepped down in 1913, the club replaced her with the Reverend R. A. White, but club members continued to deliver talks and to invite outside speakers (many of them identified as "Dr." or "Prof." in their programs).[34]

As club members' strenuous efforts to produce their own material reveal, package tours and professional lecturers can only partially explain the popularity of imaginative travel. To understand why so many women favored this particular kind of escape we need to turn to the culture of international travel that arose in the late nineteenth century. By culture of international travel, I mean a culture permeated with reports and images of foreign travel, a culture rife with ersatz travel experiences. More than a random outpouring of unrelated developments, a culture of travel implies connections between, say, postcards, ethnographic displays, travel accounts, hotel advertisements, and published passenger lists. These connections were both causal (advertisements promoted travel, travelers wrote postcards) and synergizing (travel accounts fostered interest in ethnographic displays, ethnographic displays fostered interest in travel accounts). By a culture of travel, I mean a culture in which the sum was greater than the constituent parts—a culture in which a board game here, a trade card there, a lecture last week, and a window display glimpsed this morning—resulted in a sense of living in a time and place marked by mobility and touristic encounters. And finally, by a culture of international travel I mean a development that drew even those who did not have the means—or the inclination—to truly go abroad into its net. Although the culture of travel owed a huge debt to the rising tide of real travelers and their ever-broadening itineraries, it reached far beyond them, for it brought the world home, thereby adding a significant touristic aspect to the consumers' imperium.[35]

The travel culture of the late nineteenth century did not spring out of the blue. Popular travel literature developed in Britain in the seventeenth century. Eighteenth-century Americans wrote and purchased travel guides. U.S. publishers brought out about 325 travel books between 1800 and 1850 and close to 1,500 between 1851 and 1900. These attracted an enthusiastic readership. In the late 1840s, travel books constituted 19 percent of the books charged from the New York Society Library by men and 15 percent of those charged by women.[36] Travelogues featured prominently in lyceum offerings; the travel lecturer Bayard Taylor commanded $50 a talk, or about $5,000 a season, in the 1850s. Moving panoramas portrayed European battles and scenes of the Holy Land. All these phenomena help explain Lewis Perry's assessment of American culture between 1820 and 1860: "To a striking extent, intellectual activity in antebellum America consisted of travel and writing or speaking about travel."[37] But this was only a foretaste of what was to come. Rather than receding, the production of international travel accounts, imagery, and experiences expanded in the post–Civil War period, giving middle-class U.S. culture a distinctly touristic cast.

Whereas a minister preparing for a European trip in 1851 could not find relevant advice books in the best Boston and New York bookstores, Baedeker volumes and other guidebooks aimed at the cost-conscious tourist had become readily available by the end of the century. In addition to finding how-to advice, readers could find updates on the enabling infrastructure of international travel and analyses of world travel trends. Even those who had no plans to go abroad could find plenty of travel information in newspapers and magazines. Besides reporting on tourist attractions, expatriate society, overseas shopping opportunities, adventurous travelers, and foreign lands and peoples, they also professed to take the reader on imaginative journeys.[38] The *Chautauquan*, for example, copied the *Bay View Magazine* by providing study trips such as "A Reading Journey through Mexico" and "A Reading Journey in London." Periodicals focused on travel, such as *Around the World, Travel Magazine,* and *Outing,* provided a steady diet of travel writings for the hopelessly addicted. Fiction, too, exposed readers to distant places. Among the most tourist-oriented novels were Elizabeth W.

4.3. "The Wide and Winding Rhine," from Lizzie W. Champney, *Three Vassar Girls on the Rhine* (1887). Courtesy of the University of Illinois at Urbana-Champaign Library.

Champney's stories about traveling Vassar girls. These came with maps and pictures of local attractions (ill. 4.3). Travel writings generally made travel seem pleasurable, desirable, even normative. "Are you going to Europe?" questioned an ad for *Scribner's Magazine*. "Everybody has been or expects to go some time."[39]

The culture of travel was so far-reaching that domestic sanctums fell into its orbit. Indeed, ladies' pages and women's magazines became prime venues for travel writings. Information on transoceanic travel surfaced in writings on fashion, high society, cooking, entertaining, and household decoration. Although it was ostensibly devoted to "home" topics, the *Ladies' Home Journal* published a series of travelogues by Burton Holmes, editorials on the virtues and dangers of overseas travel, and other travel-related pieces. In the culture of travel, international travel knowledge became a component of domestic knowledge. What kinds of toilet facilities would a traveler find in Mexico? What should she wear to tea in the tropics? These were domestic questions and yet travel questions. The answers could be found both in travel writings that proffered domestic advice and in household manuals that proffered travel advice.[40]

We can see just how far the travel culture reached by looking at the minutiae of fin-de-siècle middle-class culture. Manufacturers hawked clothes, toys, and games by associating them with Nellie Bly. Her photograph appeared in advertisements for soap, medicines, and other products. Songs and poems memorialized her feat. And Bly was just the tip of the iceberg. Little girls (including Frances Lawton, my maternal grandmother, who passed on her well-worn collection) introduced their U.S. paper dolls to ones in national dress from an around-the-world series published by the *Ladies' Home Journal*. A set of trade cards produced by the Arbuckle Brothers coffee company depicted typical people and famous sites on one side and provided travel information on the other (ills. 4.4, 4.5).[41] In 1902 the Sears Roebuck catalog devoted five pages to its trunks and traveling bags. Etiquette books expounded on travel decorum; entertaining manuals provided advice on bon-voyage parties. As ocean liners prepared to depart, well-wishers crowded their public rooms to bid farewell to friends and family members. Every week the mail brought hundreds of letters from missionary women to the church circles that supported them.[42] Staying home offered no escape from the culture of travel, for its sweep was broad, its presence ubiquitous.

The travel industry played an important role in helping to make globetrotting part of daily life. Major daily newspapers ran advertisements for European hotels and shops. Ocean liners and cruise ships (including Caribbean fruit lines in search of more lucrative human cargo) also advertised heavily, luring would-be travelers with lists of distant ports (ill. 4.6). Travel agents and multinational tour operators such as Thomas Cook (with offices in New York, Boston, Chicago, Philadelphia, and San Francisco and subagencies in another fifteen U.S. cities) hawked their services, as did individuals who conducted groups abroad.[43]

4.4. Rome, Edinburgh, Stockholm, and Luzerne, Arbuckle Brothers Coffee Cards. Courtesy of the Winterthur Library: Joseph Downs Collection of Manuscripts and Printed Ephemera, Winterthur, Delaware.

4.5. Ecuador, Guatemala, Buenos Ayres, and Lima, Arbuckle Brothers Coffee Cards. Courtesy of the Winterthur Library: Joseph Downs Collection of Manuscripts and Printed Ephemera, Winterthur, Delaware.

4.6. The Royal Mail Steam Packet Company advertisement, "In Jamaica it is Summertime," *Travel Magazine* 13 (Jan. 1908): 161. Courtesy of the University of Illinois at Urbana-Champaign Library.

The growing visibility of travel in the cultural landscape of the middle class accompanied a rise in genuine overseas travel. Improvements in the infrastructure of travel—especially in railroads and steamships—made travel safer, faster, and less expensive. By the 1870s it took only a week to cross the Atlantic; by the 1890s, five days. "The broad Atlantic has now dwindled to an ocean ferry," claimed Stoddard at the turn of the century. "Europe is measured, not by weeks, but by hours. Constantinople, once so remotely Oriental, is but three days from London,—Cairo only five. Even the vast Pacific glides beneath our keel in thirteen days.'"[44] The completion of the Suez and Panama canals, the growth in consular services, easing of European passport restrictions, and proliferation of currency exchange bureaus also facilitated international excursions. So did Western imperial expansion, which played an important role in opening up more of the world to the Western tourist, and especially the white Western tourist in this segregated age. Americans could stop in Japan thanks to Commodore Matthew Perry's 1854 visit; they toured the East on British vessels that serviced the empire. When Holmes visited the Philippines in 1899 to gather material for his travel lectures, he stayed in U.S. Army quarters. Taken together, all these developments extended the reach of the tourist track. As Stoddard noted, "Two centuries ago, the man who had achieved a journey around the globe would have been called a hero. One century since, he would have been remarkable. To-day the name he earns is merely — 'Globetrotter.'" By 1892 the Thomas Cook travel agency had conducted nearly 1,000 sightseers all the way around the world; by 1912 the Hamburg-American line was advertising around-the-world tours starting at $650.[45]

Whereas once leisure travel was reserved for the very rich, growing numbers of middle-class Americans went abroad after the Civil War. In 1880 about 50,000 U.S. tourists went to Europe. By 1900 roughly 125,000 made the trip. In 1913, on the eve of war in Europe, the number had risen to nearly 250,000.[46] Potential travelers were encouraged by reports that "foreign travel is not alone for the favorites of fortune." Cost-conscious women could travel in respectable second-class accommodations and stay in inexpensive pensions. Those who preferred the security, ease, and fixed rates of group travel could take a Thomas Cook's tour specifically for teachers. According to the *Ladies' Home Journal*, even a teacher with a salary of $500 or $600 could go to Europe if she could manage to save $300. If she were very thrifty, she could go for $225.[47]

The would-be traveler could also turn to a growing pool of budget-conscious travelers for advice. In 1891 Alice Brown (an author), Maria Gilman Reed (her friend), Louise Imogen Guiney (a poet), and Anna Murdock (a teacher) wrote a fifty-page book on their summer travels in England. It included local information and a list of lodgings. Thus began the Women's English Rest Tour Association. All 500 copies of the publication sold out in less than six weeks. In 1892 the women brought out a second edition of 1,000 copies and founded a magazine, *Pilgrim Scrip*. This included lodging lists for continental Europe and, starting in 1895, countries in the Western Hemisphere too. Their publications were full of practical advice along the lines of do not sit by the wall in the dining saloon if seasick, because those seats were "not easily vacated in a hurry." They listed tariff duties, information on tipping, and contact information for groups such as the Cyclists' Touring Club in Europe.[48]

The tour association did more than just publish travel tips. The women elected officers and established membership criteria. Besides mustering two letters of recommendation, applicants had to manifest "social acceptability as evidenced by refinement, intelligence, good manners, good taste and an instinct for fair dealing." Members had to credibly represent their country abroad and pledge to "bring home, for the use of the Society, some information which can be utilized to the advantage of others who are look-ing forward to a foreign trip." On the first Thursday of the month, the group had teas, so the women could discuss their journeys, past and future, and find traveling companions. At their annual meetings, returned travelers talked about places they had visited; some showed slides. The group also gave and lent money to women who would profit from a trip abroad but could not otherwise afford it. Using the commission money from their trav-eler's check purchases, they gave a total of $750 to three women in the first year of the program. By 1910 the club had about 2,700 members, hailing from more than thirty states. Most came from the East Coast, but some from places like Oconomowoc, Wisconsin, and Pocatello, Idaho.[49]

The growing stream of international travelers won plenty of media atten-tion. Newspapers and society magazines regularly published lists of upper-deck passengers. Americans who traveled abroad reported on the omnipres-ence of their compatriots. "Everywhere we see Americans," reported one tourist from Paris. A traveler writing for the *Atlanta Constitution* concurred: "Not only are there flourishing American colonies in the larger cities of Europe, but they are found in its most remote corners. The desire to visit the old country is not confined to the Atlantic seaboard or to the people of large wealth."[50] The stay-at-homes who read these accounts had increasing grounds to think that they were missing out on something big. Recognizing the appeal of international travel, marketers and publicists dangled it as a prize. During Bly's race against the clock, the *New York World* offered en-thralled readers the chance to win a trip if they could guess the time of her return. *Vogue* magazine offered passage to Europe and "ample allowance for a two week's stay abroad" for readers who procured 125 new subscrip-tions. In 1906 six women—none from a large city—took advantage of this offer. *Travel Magazine* copied the gimmick in 1908, pledging to pay all the expenses of a summer vacation anywhere in the United States, Canada, or Europe. To lure nurses to the war-torn Philippines, the U.S. military prom-ised that those who arrived via the Pacific could return via Europe, "thus completing the circle of the globe and gaining an experience which is the desire of many, but which comes to but a few."[51]

The rise in tourism sent ripples through the wider society that went beyond the travel reports in the popular press. The golden age of the pic-ture postcard began around 1895, when printing developments permitted high-quality cards to be mass produced at low cost. Well-connected stay-at-homes could collect images of popular tourist destinations, often with effu-sive descriptions—"This is quite a lovely old place—very German and very interesting"—on the back. Postcard collecting became such a fashionable hobby (especially among women) that exchanges, newsletters, and magazines sprang up to aid enthusiasts.[52] Stay-at-homes could see further evidence of travel in the household items, fashionable clothing, recipes, and gifts brought back by their friends. And those who knew returned travelers no doubt heard all about their experiences. For every returnee, there was a circle of associates who experienced the trip vicariously.

The popularity of travel lectures meant that some of these circles of vicarious travelers were quite large. The 1902 Hull-House lecture series included a "tour Around the World." The *New York Tribune* frequently advertised free travel lectures such as "Life in the Philippines" and "Life among the Kaffirs" presented in public school assembly halls. Chautauqua Assemblies also offered travel talks. Even the working-class girls enrolled in the North Bennet Street Industrial School in Boston could supplement their courses in dressmaking, carpentry, and gymnastics with "delightful imaginary trips to Rome, Venice, Algeria, and other distant lands, by means of photographs and vivid descriptions."[53] Clubwomen proved to be a particularly appreciative audience. The year the Tourist Club of Minneapolis studied Mexico, three women who had visited the country gave guest lectures. Every year the Hyde Park Travel Club had a globe-trotter's day, on which it invited people who had traveled around the world.[54]

Not all travel lectures were presented by people who went abroad as tourists. Government officials, academic experts, visiting diplomats, and other foreign dignitaries spoke on foreign locales. The secretary of public instruction of France provided French lecturers to talk on "La Bastille et ses secrets" and similar topics before U.S. branches of the Alliance Française. Returned missionaries relied on travel talks to raise funds for their mission endeavors. To build support for international programs, the YWCA sent out speakers to discuss their overseas experiences.[55]

The development of the stereopticon, also known as the "magic lantern," contributed to the popularity of travel lectures. These lanterns were filled with gas or alcohol and then ignited to make a light. Placed six to eight feet from a white sheet or wall, they projected photographic images from glass plates. A good one cost around $25, but they could also be rented for an evening. Magic lantern vendors marketed them as a wonderful way to entertain friends and raise funds for charity. Sears, Roebuck and Company hawked a "stereopticon outfit"—complete with photographic views, stereopticon, burner, screen, bound lecture book, 1,000 advertising posters, 2,000 admission tickets, instruction book, and carrying cases for $53. It promoted the package as an honorable way to "make money with little effort." Plate purveyors advertised views on religious topics, portraits of distinguished

Americans, temperance, and so forth. But the heart of the business was the travel trade. In addition to marketing individual slides of places ranging from the Arctic to the Sahara, slide manufacturers advertised package tours. The "journeys" arranged by the Benerman and Wilson Company consisted of sets of 100 slides, "in geographical order." Along with each set, the company supplied "'Something to say' about each slide."[56] The C. T. Milligan Company offered an "Around the World" tour for $1.50 a slide. Sears beat this price, offering an 80-slide "Around the World in Eighty Minutes" tour and 500 posters for $25. Many of the dime museums that sprang up in the 1880s and 1890s offered stereopticon tours, narrated by a "doctor" or "professor" for nothing more than the basic admissions fee.[57]

Along with magic lanterns, stereoscopes facilitated imaginative travel. Unlike ordinary photographs, taken by a single camera lens, stereographic photo cards contained side-by-side images taken by adjacent lenses. Viewed through the stereoscope, the two nearly identical images merged, creating a three-dimensional impression. The sides of the viewing apparatus blocked the viewer's peripheral vision, adding to the feeling of immersion in the scene. According to a description published by Underwood and Underwood, a leading stereoscope purveyor, "the objects are seen standing out in natural perspective, natural size and at natural distances. Color alone excepted, the object is seen exactly as it would appear looked at through a window at the same distance from it as the actual distance of the camera."[58]

Stereoscopes traced their origins back to the early years of photography. In the 1850s American tourists returning from Europe used the novel contraptions to show their friends the scenes they had witnessed on their travels. By the 1880s companies such as Underwood and Underwood made stereographic pictures of foreign sites readily available even to stay-at-homes. In its advertising materials, Underwood and Underwood emphasized the verisimilitude of its travel experiences. "The Underwood Travel System . . . consists in travel of the truest kind, yet it does not utilize either ship or railroad, or any of the ordinary bodily conveyances. . . . The Underwood Travel System is largely mental. It provides travel not for the body, but for the mind, but travel that is none the less real on that account. It makes it possible for one to feel oneself present and to know accurately famous scenes and places thousands of miles away, without moving his body from the armchair in his comfortable corner. . . . To experience all this is to travel truly." To add to the sense of being there, Underwood and Underwood developed maps that located every standpoint and guidebooks that strove "to answer the very questions that would be likely to be asked in regard to the objects seen, the questions which (if you knew their language) you would ask of the people themselves."[59] The individualized nature of the stereoscope (only one viewer could use the apparatus at a time) meant that it did not lend itself to large groups, but smaller groups could pass it around the room. High school principals praised it for teaching geography, Sunday school teachers credited it with raising attendance, and librarians testified that their patrons called for them constantly.[60]

By the early twentieth century, Underwood and Underwood, with offices in New York, London, Ottawa, Kansas, and Toronto, had around 250,000 stereographic negatives in its inventory. It offered more than 300 prepackaged tours plus many more assembled to order.[61] Among the most comprehensive tours it offered were ones to China, Cuba and Puerto Rico, Egypt, England, Japan, Mexico, Norway, Palestine, and Spain, with 100 standpoints each. Shorter tours included Austria (84 standpoints), France (72), Korea (48), Manchuria (36), Ceylon (30), Panama (24), and a Trip around the World (72). Customers also could order individual slides, and slide series on racial types, women's occupations around the globe, typical homes and interior furnishings of the world, and modes of travel. Catering to an interest in current events, Underwood and Underwood produced a series on the Philippine-American War that included Admiral Dewey on his flagship, high school boys in Manila, and Spanish meztiza girls in native dress.[62]

Like magic lanterns and stereoscopes, cycloramic pictures promised to transport viewers. These are often associated with the early nineteenth century, but they continued to be displayed after the Civil War and gained new popularity in the 1880s. Upon its opening in 1874, the Chautauqua Assembly in upstate New York displayed one such sweeping spectacle in its main auditorium: a thirteen-by-thirty-foot panoramic landscape of the Holy Land. A Paris-by-night painting exhibited in the mid-1870s occupied nearly 40,000 square feet of canvas. After passing through a covered archway, viewers ascended a tower, emerging upon a shaded balcony, from which they could look down upon the city. Its promoters hawked the experiences as "equivalent to seeing Paris itself, without the perils and unpleasantness of a sea voyage, at a trifling cost, and without loss of time." Other cycloramas displayed in the late nineteenth-century United States included *The Mirror of Ireland*, *Paris under Siege*, and *The Battle of Manila*.[63]

As the popularity of magic lanterns, stereoscopes, and cycloramic pictures suggests, there was a strong visual component to the travel culture of the late nineteenth and early twentieth centuries. The culture of travel involved multifold opportunities to view the foreign. Travel buffs could purchase pictures of colonized people and distant vistas or view them in public expositions. The Massachusetts Art Club, for example, exhibited 125 prints of Australia, Tasmania, and New Zealand, lent by the Woman's Educational Association of Boston. Many travel writings came illustrated with photographs and engravings. The well-known cartoonist Charles Dana Gibson published amply illustrated volumes on Paris and London. His *Sketches in Egypt* featured pictures of American tourists in the land of the Sphinx. Henry Bacon and other painters captured touristic experiences such as life on shipboard.[64] Aspiring U.S. artists who studied in Europe filled canvas after canvas with the surrounding sights; U.S. travelers returned from abroad with foreign landscapes to hang on their walls.

By the early twentieth century, moving-picture producers touted the transportive possibilities of their productions. In vaudeville theaters, audiences watched short clips of trains arriving in French stations, Queen Victoria's funeral, bullfights, and other touristic matters. Among the Biograph films shown in 1902 were *A Quiet Hookah* ("A vivid and characteristic bit of local color from Constantinople"), *The Grand Fountain* ("Longchamps Palace, Marseilles, France"), and *The Black Sea* ("A beautiful panorama"). In the next few years, films such as *Picturesque Canada* and *Roosevelt in Africa* continued to expose moviegoers to foreign sights.[65]

Whereas nickelodeons catered primarily to working-class audiences, the traveling motion-picture exhibitors who toured the country in the first two decades of the twentieth century attracted a more upscale clientele. Many of these films were touristic—as *The Coronation Durbar at Delhi, Ireland and Her People, The Land of the Midnight Sun, Southampton to Cape Town by Sea, Fiji and South Seas Islands, Through Central Africa*, and other titles suggest. In response to itinerant film screeners' efforts to capture the travel market, travel lecturers claimed the new medium for themselves. The weekly travel lectures sponsored by the Brooklyn Institute in 1910 and 1911 featured films as well as slides. From 1915 to 1921, Burton Holmes produced fifty-two travel shorts a year for Paramount.[66]

Even the feature films that emerged in the teens sometimes had touristic tones. D. W. Griffith advertised his *Hearts of the World*, released in 1918, with the commanding: "Go to France Today!" Capitalizing on the transportive possibilities of film, the ad continued: "Stop at a little village; see the peaceful life—the lovers with their gentle wooing—the twilight minstrels under the moonlight—the happy homes—the contented villagers—AND THEN: Hear War's alarms; see the troops go marching off, sweethearts parted. . . . And so be with those NOW waging that terrific drama of the Western Front—FRANCE."[67] Just as stereoscopes blocked peripheral vision, darkened movie theaters focused the viewer's attention on the screen, thereby adding to a feeling of immersion. (One particularly sensational film, *A Ride on a Runaway Train*, struck audiences as so realistic that cleaning crews came to expect some patrons to wet their seats in panic each time it was shown.)[68]

For those in search of realism, world's fairs provided exceptionally rich opportunities to travel imaginatively, for they engaged all the senses. In the fairgrounds, visitors could see formal—sometimes elaborate—exhibits depicting artifacts from Argentina to Zanzibar, usually cased in regional architectural trappings. National exhibits presented attractive pictures of foreign countries, in some cases with the explicit intention of promoting tourism. On the pleasure grounds outside the fairs, visitors could see commercial attractions purporting to resemble foreign sites. The Midway Plaisance outside the 1893 Chicago fair included a Chinese opera house and Irish, Turkish, Algerian, Austrian, Dahomean, and South Seas Islands villages. The Streets of Cairo concession, run by an Egyptian entrepreneur, featured a mosque, coffee shops, residences, camels, snake charmers, dancing girls, and wedding processions. The Javanese village had eighty buildings and 300 natives on display. The German village had a castle, bands, and Bavarian beer. In the Bernese Alps Electric Theater, spectators went on a fifteen-minute trip to Switzerland through scenery, sound, lights, and icy temperatures. Fairgoers commonly proclaimed that the exhibits made them feel that they were truly visiting foreign lands (ill. 4.7).[69]

Despite occasional protestations that it would be "as unfair to take [the displays on the Midway] as representative of their respective nations as to take Buffalo Bill's 'Wild West' show as typical of American life," descriptions of world's fairs often played up the premise that they offered a genuine overseas travel experience. "In Switzerland we find rare and beautiful wood-carvings, in Brazil, dazzling collections of mosaics, gems and precious stones," wrote a traveler who had been no further than the Chicago's Columbian Exposition. About a tenth of the American population saw this fair in 1893. The 1876 Centennial Exhibition in Philadelphia, 1901 Pan-American Exposition in Buffalo, 1904 Louisiana Purchase Exposition in St. Louis, and others also attracted large crowds.[70]

Although they were the most prominent events on the fictive travel landscape, world's fairs were not alone in providing multidimensional fictive travel experiences. Their highbrow exhibits had multiple analogues elsewhere. Museums presented their novel habitat dioramas and life-size ethnographic displays, sometimes accompanied by travel narratives, as surrogates for the real thing.[71] Zoo designers in the late nineteenth century increasingly favored natural backdrops over cell-like cages. Although the surroundings they created often bore little resemblance to the animals' original

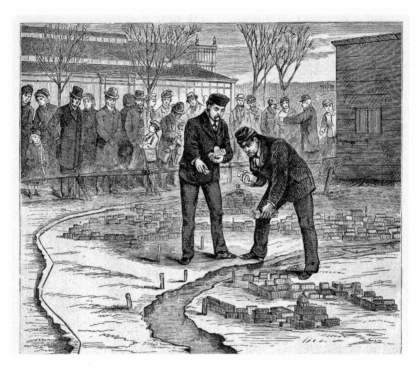

4.7. "Laying Out the Model of the City of Paris," in *Frank Leslie's Illustrated Historical Register of the Centennial Exposition* (1876), 74. Courtesy of the Rare Book and Special Collections Library, University of Illinois at Urbana-Champaign.

habitats, the landscaping encouraged zoo goers to imagine themselves in the wild. Botanical gardens displayed flora from the far reaches of the globe, commonly arranged so as to evoke exotic settings. (To produce an "Oriental atmosphere," the Huntington botanical garden hired a Japanese family to live in a Japanese house in the midst of its Japanese-style lily ponds.) All such displays referenced not only the "original" scene, but also the second-hand experiences offered by European museums, zoos, and gardens.[72]

Just as the highbrow aspects of world's fairs found analogues in museums, zoos, and gardens, the colorful and commercialized midways had echoes in more popular entertainments. Since the mid-nineteenth century, Barnum's "Traveling World's Fair" had presented Fiji cannibals, Circassian girls, and other foreign curiosities to the American public. The large railroad circuses of the late nineteenth and early twentieth centuries presented an even wider assortment of supposedly foreign attractions. They featured ethnological congresses of "strange and savage tribes," dramatizations of imperial military campaigns, exotic animals, South Asian *nautch* dancers, and Hindu housewives, who, according to a 1906 circus program, went about their duties, "baking, cooking, washing and sewing in their own Oriental and primitive way." At the turn of the century, the popular Buffalo Bill's Wild West Show added farther-flung scenes of empire to its basic repertoire of cowboy and Indian shows. Viewers could watch purportedly authentic enactments of the Battle of San Juan Hill, Boer War, and Boxer Rebellion, and they could gawk at ethnological displays of "Strange People from our New Possessions." Amusement parks, too, offered glimpses of exotica. Twenty-four Italian gondoliers plied the canals of Venice, California, in the early twentieth century.[73] Coney Island had a "Streets of Cairo" attraction that copied a concession at the 1893 Columbian Exposition. Elsewhere on the island, Dreamland had a reproduction of the Doge's Palace, a "Coasting through Switzerland" railway ride, and an "authentic" Bantoc village, featuring 212 tribesmen from the Philippines. Luna Park had a Japanese garden (reportedly built by Japanese architects and woodcarvers), Dutch windmill, Chinese theater, Durbar of Delhi, and Irish and Eskimo villages. Similar pleasure grounds appeared across the country: in 1905 Illinois had thirty-seven amusement parks; Ohio over seventy.[74]

Business establishments such as department stores, restaurants, theaters, and hotels offered their own glimpses of the foreign. In hopes of enticing shoppers, merchants decorated their establishments to look like French salons, Japanese gardens, and tropical wonderlands. In the 1890s the import firm Vantines constructed Persian, Japanese, Indian, Chinese, and Moorish interiors in its Broadway warehouse. In the early teens, Marshall Field's displayed Japanese-style goods in front of Japanese landscape paintings; Gimbels arranged its linoleum department to look like an "oriental mosque." For one fashion show, Gimbel's transformed its tearoom into the Monte Carlo de Paris; for another, Wanamaker's built Guatemalan Indian huts as a backdrop for the Mayan-inspired clothing.[75]

Weary shoppers could stop for lunch at a department store's German rathskeller or take lighter refreshments in its Oriental tearoom. The more sybaritic might enjoy a department store's Turkish baths. Come dinnertime, women accompanied by male escorts might dine at a place like Murray's Restaurant, a New York City establishment known for its Roman, Egyptian, and gothic rooms (ill. 4.8). (A visit to Murray's, claimed one patron, was equivalent to seeing the "exhumed ruins of Pompeii, the excavations made on the sites of ancient Nineveh or Babylon, or the palm-fringed banks of old Nile.")[76] After a day in the big city, an out-of-town shopper could retire to a hotel with rooms decorated in Persian, Italian, Dutch, Turkish, Japanese, and other ostensibly foreign styles.[77]

4.8. Murray's Restaurant, in Charles R. Bevington, *New York Plaisance* (1908). Courtesy of the Winterthur Library: Printed Book and Periodical Collection, Winterthur, Delaware.

The list goes on. Commercial displays such as the Japanese village and the Olde London Street erected in New York City in the 1880s purported to produce the foreign as well. Church bazaars and fund-raising fairs, with their national booths and "Around the World in Ninety Minutes" themes, offered still more versions of imaginary travel (ill. 4.9). Along with its panoramic painting, the Chautauqua Assembly had a 400-foot-long topographical replica of Palestine. Even county fairs might have a Swiss inn or Japanese pavilion.[78]

Though generally intended to serve community needs, not touristic desires, immigrant neighborhoods and festivals provided further opportunities to encounter the foreign. Guidebooks, travel magazines, and city boosters presented ethnic neighborhoods as tourist destinations, saying that they offered a glimpse of the Old World. A 1909 guide to Chicago triumphantly proclaimed that it had surpassed Constantinople as the world's most cosmopolitan city. Rather than shun immigrants as social dangers, urban tour-

4.9. George Full et al., "Around the World in Ninety Minutes," *Ladies' Home Journal* 25 (Oct. 1908): 33. Courtesy of the Rare Book and Special Collections Library, University of Illinois at Urbana-Champaign.

ists sought them out as colorful attractions. An advertisement for a "Land Show" in the Chicago Coliseum promised that a visit would "have many of the attractions of a trip to Europe," including "beautiful girls in picturesque peasant costumes" and "Scandinavian choruses." Sightseers visited opium dens in Chinatowns and markets in Little Italy. They viewed the foreign in ethnic celebrations, fund raisers, dances, and pageants; they tasted it in immigrant restaurants.[79]

Even those who did not seek out the foreign could not avoid finding traces of it in their everyday surroundings. Although U.S. architects were more likely to modify foreign styles than to copy them directly, they designed buildings that brought distant locations to mind. The Greek revival movement of the early nineteenth century had dotted the landscape with white pillared houses and banks. Gothic influences from northern Europe could be detected in cottages, churches, prisons, and university buildings. Italian villas inspired residences, firehouses, and town halls. Egyptian elements appeared in cemeteries and prisons. The mansard roofs that gained popularity in the 1860s and 1870s followed the Second Empire style popular in France and elsewhere in Europe.[80]

This passion for foreign styles continued through the late nineteenth century. A sharp-eyed Englishman who walked along Broadway and Fifth Avenue in New York in 1901 reported seeing "an extraordinary medley of incongruous styles . . . an architectural pot-pourri which almost rivals the Rue des Nations at the Paris Exposition of 1900. There are some excellent copies of European buildings, such as the Giralda of Seville, Venetian palaces, châteaux from Touraine, Palladian loggie, and here and there a German schloss."[81] Miles from New York, gleaming new Florida resorts and booming California beach towns quoted Spanish and other Mediterranean motifs. From the mansions of the wealthy to public buildings (such as castellated armories, art museums gussied up as Greek temples, railroad termini modeled after Romanesque cathedrals, and the full-scale reproduction of the Parthenon that graced Nashville's Centennial Park), U.S. architecture presented glimpses of Europe. Architectural Orientalism was less common but on the rise. The Washington Monument, completed in 1884, resembled the Egyptian obelisks on display in Paris and London. Bandstands, synagogues, and theaters also conjured up the East.[82]

As the built environment suggests, the culture of travel made distant places part of the landscape of everyday life. Historians have noted that the great imperial city of London provided evidence of empire at every turn. From the busy port to the exhibitions, monuments, music hall entertainments, and colonial subjects who appeared on the streets, London radiated empire.[83] But one need not travel to the heart of the British Empire to find imperial trappings. Turn-of-the-century U.S. cities had their own imperial referents, some carried over from the nation's colonial past, some derived from U.S. expansion, some intended to associate the United States with the European nations that controlled so much of the globe. The imperial world system helped create the culture of travel that gripped the United States in the late nineteenth century. Indeed, the culture of travel was a component of imperial culture, for an important way that empire came home was in the touristic guise. The culture of travel spun the economic, military, and political power of the United States and its European models as a matter of mobility and pleasure. It commodified the entire world for the privileged beneficiaries of the consumers' imperium.

Surrounded by messages touting the encompassing joys of travel, club-women looking to divert themselves jumped on the touring bandwagon. "We leave New York on an ocean steamer with the comfort in the feeling that we are leaving all circumstances of time and routine and have nothing to do but be amused, to float on a city of the world without caring a straw about the world," effused a Hyde Park Travel Club member upon commencing an imaginary journey.[84] "To travel is to live," claimed another fictive traveler, quoting Stoddard's assertions to that effect. "Travel is attractive as a means of acquiring happiness."[85] The culture of travel persuaded the clubwomen desperate for a break from daily routines that travel offered unparalleled opportunities for excitement. As one Bay View club reported, imaginary expeditions "relieved the monotony of the quiet village life." Captivated by the promise that leaving home could offer emotional fulfillment and personal gratification, clubwomen looked to fictive travel to do the same. Some, at least, were not disappointed. Members of a Nickerson, Kansas, travel club reported that their trip to Italy "will be forever one of the brightest spots in their lives."[86]

But the earnestness with which travel club members set about their journeys suggests that theirs was not a frivolous, lighthearted pleasure. One travel club complied a list of thirty-one reference books for its year on Scandinavia and the Netherlands. For a trip to India, another club referred to a bibliography of fifty-nine books. Acknowledging the importance of research to its programs, the Minneapolis Tourist Society held its meetings in the public library. Hyde Park Travel Club members insisted that theirs was not merely a social club "nor does it exist merely as entertainment for its members."[87] Fictive travelers frequently described their endeavors as fundamentally educational in nature. Rather than stressing pleasure, they highlighted mental cultivation.

No less than the pleasure-oriented aspect of the travel club movement, the educational aspect reflects the wider travel culture. Along with evoking self-indulgence, travel evoked self-improvement, as it had done at least since the grand tours of the Renaissance. "There is a liberal education in a European trip, an investment which will pay the investor," claimed the *Ladies Home Journal*.[88] Underwood and Underwood ads also extolled the educational value of travel: "Leading authorities consider the Underwood Travel System as nothing less than epoch making in the educational field, because it brings travel, with all its infinite possibilities of culture and education, within the reach of those of humble means as well as the more fortunate few." When a group of students at the University of Wisconsin formed a Globe Trotters club, *Travel Magazine* lauded the organization's educational function, saying that "knowledge of the world we live in, whether it be gained at first hand by actual travel or through associations and publications, is a part of education which no institution of learning should overlook."[89]

Travel clubs strongly endorsed the premise that travel—even of the imaginative variety—had educational value. Like other study clubs, travel clubs offered intellectual enrichment to women who spent much of their time managing their households and taking care of their families. Like other clubwomen, armchair travelers regarded their clubs as "the middle-aged woman's university."[90] Some women turned to group study as a substitute for an undergraduate education; those who had attended college regarded group study as a means of maintaining an intellectual life. According to a report in the *General Federation Bulletin*: "An eager mind enters gladly and wanders in new worlds, in the carefully treasured still hours, when the children are asleep. This is what the club gives to women." The report continued: "Many a little woman whose life has been, and still is, narrow and confined, has spoken to me feelingly of what her club has been to her. . . . She needs the club to lead her feet for an occasional hour out of the blessed but confining home rut of daily duty into the open fields of outside thought and work."[91]

Thanks to the surrounding travel culture, women looking to broaden their intellectual horizons, to leave the "rut of daily duty," saw imaginative travel as a prime way to do so. The Lewistown Tourist Club characterized itself as a club for "self improvement." "Why stay we on earth unless to grow?" ran the motto of the McGregor Tourist Club. An Indiana tourist club described its program as "the next best thing to actual travel for improving and enlarging the mind." The *Bay View Magazine* published a moving account of a subscriber who lived in the country, far from a public library. "The story of this woman in humble life, yet thirsting for culture, was full of tender pathos," it asserted.[92] Luckily, the Bay View reading program provided the enrichment she craved.

For the very fortunate, fictive travel served as a means to prepare for real travel. Reported one travel club: "We have found it of mutual pleasure and benefit, and a very good preparation for foreign travel. Our motto has been Dr. Johnson's saying: 'He who from travel would bring home knowledge must take knowledge with him." As experienced travelers knew, knowledge could be transported in one's head free of charge, "while between the covers of books it pays its price per pound."[93] But if some women embarked on imaginative study tours in preparation for real travel, most fictive travelers went no further than their local libraries. As a history of Arizona women's clubs pointed out, the Prescott Monday Club listened to papers such as "The Streets of Paris, and How to Get About in Them," even though a real visit to Paris "was the remotest thing imaginable." Their armchair excursions served as ends in themselves. For women leading circumscribed lives, fictive travel beckoned as a means to expand their outlooks. The desire to feel more connected may have been particularly acute on the part of women who lived far from major cities. The members of the Prescott Monday Club, for example, regarded their rough and dusty mining town as a marginal outpost, far from the cultured eastern states from whence they had come.[94]

Yet any kind of systematic study could expand a woman's outlook. There were particular reasons for embarking on fictive travels, and these had much to do with the culture of travel. The women who set sail on imaginative study tours believed that they needed to know about travel to be culturally literate. Living as they did, surrounded by international travel writings, advertisements, displays, amusements, ephemera, and perhaps even returned globe-trotters, travel club members regarded systematic study tours as a means to become conversant on a leading preoccupation of their day. A woman who had achieved basic travel literacy had no reason to fear party games such as "The Traveller's Tour," in which guests were called upon to provide information to a pretend tourist or "A Trip around the World," in which contestants had to guess the stops.[95] Stay-at-homes might ramble on about canning and curtains, but a world traveler could fascinate in conversation and prove her sophistication in parlor games. In sum, she could prove herself a quintessential clubwoman.

To belong to the General Federation of Women's Clubs meant to circulate in a world of leisure travelers. Profiles of club leaders often commented on their European journeys as a means of establishing their class standing, refinement, and cultural attainment. One such piece characterized a prominent Atlanta clubwoman as "handsome, dignified, graceful, womanly, cultivated and well-gowned" and then noted that she had traveled extensively. It declared her "thoroughly cosmopolitan."[96] Like GFWC publications, the African American clubwomen's journal, the *Woman's Era*, published articles on international travel and alluded to clubwomen's Euro-

pean tours. Besides invoking travel to demarcate class standing and cultivation, African American clubwomen used travel references (and especially
the warm receptions offered to their associates by European society leaders)
to discredit the racist denigration of all African Americans as lower-class,
uncultured, and socially inferior.[97]

If travel club records are any indication of larger trends, the GFWC's membership became increasingly likely to travel abroad as well. Upon the founding of the Minneapolis Tourist Club, only one member, an Englishwoman,
had been overseas. Yet, according to a club report, "In a few years there was
hardly a member who had not, one or more times, made the trip to Europe
and others who had made world tours."[98] Similarly, in the early years of the
Bay View program, the *Bay View Magazine* presented traveling members as
a novelty. But in 1901 it alerted readers to a departing tour that would "cover
the ground included in the Bay View Course this year." By 1902 it reported
that "Many of our students have recently gone to Italy, or will be there next
summer, and many have written that they have found in our Magazine an
invaluable preparation for the tour." There were so many clubwomen on a
1911 cruise around the Mediterranean that they held a meeting for "acquaintance and mutual benefit."[99]

The GFWC's publications recognized and catered to clubwomen's interest in travel by reviewing travel books and publishing study guides on foreign countries. In flipping through the General Federation's publications,
a clubwoman might also encounter ads for winter cruises, societies that
organized tours, and the World Art and Travel Club, which published its
own magazine and ran a reference library in Paris.[100] "Send Your Daughter
to Europe" trumpeted one ad placed by a clubwoman, Helen M. Winslow.
In her tantalizing description, she promised to chaperone a "select party
of ten girls" to Britain and Italy, providing them with daily conversation
lessons in French and German and the cultivated guidance of a genteel
escort. Another woman who hawked her guide services advertised herself
as a "prominent club woman . . . [who] understands what will interest club
women in a trip abroad." She had the extra advantage of twelve years' experience in managing and conducting European parties.[101] What messages did
these GFWC publications convey? To be a clubwoman meant to be a traveler,
either literally or by association and outlook.

Many travel club members felt that theirs was a democratic movement,
for it enabled people of modest circumstances to see the world. Because
venturing abroad for pleasure was associated with male privilege, upper-
class status, and the prerogatives of whiteness, there was an element of
transgression when people other than wealthy white men claimed travel

for themselves. The Travel Class of Albert Lea, Minnesota, got started when a local doctor departed for a long trip to Europe, without his wife. Upon being queried, "What are you going to do while he is away?" she replied: "I shall travel at home." The Travel Class was born when her friends joined her imaginary ramblings, thus refusing to be left behind.[102]

If the Albert Lea club traced its origins to a moment of female assertion, the hardworking teachers and other middle-class women who could not afford to cross the Atlantic but went to Europe anyway asserted their cultural parity with the upper class. The African American women who joined the travel-oriented Oak and Ivy Club and the Native American women who formed a Bay View travel club asserted racial as well as gender and class standing: their ramblings helped prove the cultural attainments and hence full humanity of women of color. The suffragist and pacifist Lucia Ames Mead tried to broaden the base of the travel movement even further by urging her well-to-do readers to organize courses for domestic servants, "where current events, foreign travel, illustrated with pictures, or other matters may be presented by a tactful woman in such wise as to break the monotony of housework and give her hearers a glimpse of culture that of right belongs to them as well as her."[103] Patronizing, to be sure (especially given that some of these servants had experienced border crossings firsthand), but in its reference to cultural rights and its assumption of sisterhood, this proposal also had a radical edge.

Not all armchair travelers saw their efforts as essentially democratic, however. For many, the allure appears to have been social distinction. Just as real travel marked out social divisions, imaginary travel differentiated those who professed touristic outlooks from earlier generations of home-bound women, from their neighbors who were not as attuned to the culture of travel, and from the presumed locals encountered on the way. Mastering travel culture was a way to evince a kind of civilized modernity that was not available to everybody. Travel knowledge served as evidence of upper-class standing, the privileges of whiteness, and the freedoms of men. An aphorism printed in a Lewistown Tourist Club program book admitted as much: "Knowledge is that which, next to virtue, truly and essentially raises one man above another."[104] A woman versed on travel could sparkle in local society.

Yet, ultimately, the stakes were much greater than local positioning. Through traveling, American provincials could remake themselves as world-class cosmopolitans. Like other women from European settler colonies, American women regarded European travel as a means to claim metropolitan culture. Having claimed it, travelers went beyond it, often concluding that their transnational perspectives set them above ordinary Europeans, such as the Venetian women who, according to Stoddard, filled their water buckets in the courtyard of the Ducal Palace, "unmindful of the history with which each stone in this old building seems at time so eloquent." Rather than just laying claim to the European metropole, armchair travelers regarded their travels as a means to establish an affinity with the moneyed elite from the entire Western and westernizing world. In an age when Thomas Cook had a whole department devoted to arranging European tours for Indian princes, international travel conjured up the cosmopolitanism of global high society. Touristic accomplishments identified one not only as upper-class but as world-class. As Charles Farrar admonished the Hyde Park Travel Club, keeping up with their studies would enable the assembled women to "become cosmopolitan on the eve of the cosmopolitan era which 1900 would usher in."[105] Imaginary or not, leisure travel would identify women as members of the global elite and prepare them for a bright future in an increasingly interconnected world. It would enable them to occupy the leading ranks of the consumers' imperium.

What travel knowledge meant can be inferred by looking at those left behind. An advertisement for the Hamburg-American Line's around-the-world cruises showed two turbaned men standing in a palm grove, next to a kneeling camel, watching a steamer cutting through the waves offshore. Presumably the passengers on the ship were busy enjoying the elevator, gymnasium, electric baths, and other modern amenities hawked in the ad, while the onlookers, with their flowing robes and resting camel looked like figures from a biblical tableau. If the gleaming Hamburg-American Line evoked northern European whiteness, the shaded viewers associated localism with darkness. The ship, with billows of steam pouring from its smokestacks, signaled male technological achievements; the draped garments of the quiescent natives implied a certain amount of effeminacy. The two men look at the ship with longing, as if they appreciated the shipboard comfort and pleasure promised by the ad. Movement versus stasis, modernity versus the past, northern European whiteness versus tropical darkness, masculine accomplishment versus feminine passivity, personal fulfillment versus desire and envy—the choice was clear (ill. 4.10).[106]

A woman who could claim the expertise of a tourist could do more than demonstrate her own alignments and standing. The ability to travel testified to national strength and power. A traveler might even help her country advance its interests. In explaining why its travel programs did not focus on the United States, the *Bay View Magazine* explained: "America has expanded, and now our commerce, our interests, and our diplomatic relations

4.10. Hamburg-American Line advertisement, "Around World Cruises," *Travel Magazine* 16 (Nov. 1910): 41. Courtesy of the University of Illinois at Urbana-Champaign Library.

are becoming world-wide. And so we must know the history, the life and conditions of the peoples of Europe and remoter lands. Americans must become cosmopolitan in learning, else they will take narrow views, prejudice, and misunderstanding into their discussions and judgments of foreign questions. . . . Those who fit themselves for the new age will make the most of its opportunities."[107] In sum, travel knowledge could be translated into useful commercial and political as well as social knowledge. To enhance their position in the international arena, Americans must turn tourist.

In saying that the culture of travel prompted women to join travel clubs, it is important to recognize that these women did more than respond to the culture of travel; they helped produce it. Besides heightening their own touristic sensibilities, travel club members introduced their families, friends, and neighbors to the wider world. Some clubwomen insisted that their studies made them better companions for their children, better comrades for their husbands. Others insisted that clubwomen had become "the centre of the intellectual activity of townships and neighborhoods all over the country." A Hyde Park Travel Club yearbook proudly reported "that the

Class has for more than a decade been recognized as a helpful factor in the educational and social life of this community."[108]

Such claims were more than mere puffery. Many travel clubs sponsored public lectures. Others held entertainments to which they invited friends and family members. At the end of its first year, the McGregor, Iowa, club invited guests to enjoy a program of Scottish music, literature, costumes, and dances. Similarly, an Indiana club gave an "Afternoon in Spain to a large company of delighted friends." Yet another club threw a banquet after touring Germany. What transpired at this event? "Gentlemen friends were taken in and civilized." The Travelers' Club of Portland, Maine, decorated school rooms. A Denver club gave a "stereopticon entertainment" on Holland to "the children from the orphan asylums."[109] By founding libraries, providing an avid audience for travel writings, and popularizing and disseminating travel knowledge, travel club members advanced the culture of travel, particularly in small towns in the Northeast and Midwest.

In their weekly meetings and beyond, women's travel clubs contributed to the rise of a tourist mentality, that is, the tendency to understand the rest of the world in terms of its touristic offerings. Although touristic outlooks cannot be fully disentangled from other approaches to the wider world—including missionary, commercial, governmental, and anthropological ones—they bore the clear mark of the consumers' imperium insofar as they promoted a sense of geographic consciousness more focused on consumption than were other lines of geographic thinking. The importance of the tourist mentality to geographic consciousness should not be underestimated. Whereas nineteenth-century atlas manufacturers emphasized the utility of their product for businessmen and students, by the 1920s they targeted armchair travelers.[110] Women's travel clubs were not alone in advancing the tourist mentality. The entire culture of travel did so. But focusing on women's travel club programs can help us understand the nature of the tourist mentality. Travel club records reveal the ways in which enthusiasts processed and promulgated the messages of the wider travel culture. To understand how, we need to pay more attention to their programs.

Where did club members go? Travel clubs that developed their own agendas typically visited European countries such as France and England first. The Hyde Park Travel Club picked France for an early tour because, as one member put it, "Every one is interested in France, everyone goes to France." To clinch her case, she pointed out that there were "many items of reference easily accessible upon France," and that Professor Farrar had "a large number of slides upon the topic, 20,000 in all." The Minneapolis Tourist Club said of its first destination, England: "We love thee dear mother, for giving us birth." The Tourist Club of McGregor, Iowa, chose Scotland to inaugurate its travel-by-proxy program because both the town's founders and one of the member's families hailed from there.[111]

After hitting the most popular tourist destinations, members looked further afield. The offerings of commercial outlets sometimes guided their choices. Originally the Bay View directors planned to provide a four-year cycle, rotating American, German, French, and English years. But club members who had completed the course wanted to keep going. So the directors added new countries, from Spain on to Russia, the Netherlands, Italy, Greece, and Switzerland. Eventually it left Europe to visit places such as Australia, Canada, China, the Congo, Haiti, India, Japan, Madagascar, Mexico, Panama, Peru, the Philippines, and Zanzibar. Current events guided some program decisions. The Bay View program focused on Spain in 1898 as a result of the U.S. intervention in the Spanish-Cuban War. Upon the outbreak of war in Europe in 1914, many clubs spotlighted the belligerent countries. Organizational directives influenced other decisions. After the president of the GFWC recommended the study of Latin American peoples in 1916, the GFWC Bureau of Information was inundated with requests for travel outlines on South and Central America.[112]

Yet even as we acknowledge the external forces that shaped program decisions, it is also important to acknowledge the inner workings of particular travel clubs. Club members sought novelty. Having toured a place, they moved on. Hence the dynamics of perpetual study prompted club members to wander ever further off the beaten track, with occasional returns to favorite destinations. Women such as Mary Phelps Ewan, who belonged to a travel club for fifty-two years, traipsed through a considerable swath of the globe. After twenty-six years of travel, the Hyde Park Travel Club yearbook of 1914 pronounced that "The Class has visited almost every country through study."[113] The Heliades Club of Illinois, organized in 1881, went from New Zealand to Micronesia, Melanesia, Australia, Polynesia, East India, Japan, China, "Mantchooria," Cochin-China, British India, "Beloochistan," Afghanistan, "Toorkistan," Siberia, Russia in Europe, Nova Zembla, Spitzbergen, Sweden, Norway, Denmark, Scotland, Ireland, Wales, the Roman Empire, Persia, Turkey in Asia, Turkey in Europe, Greece, Italy, Switzerland, Austria, Prussia, Holland, Belgium, England, France, Spain, Portugal, Egypt, Arabia, Nubia, Abyssinia, the Sahara, Soudan, Senegambia, the Guineas, the Congo and its countries, the east coast of Africa, Madagascar and the islands of the Indian Ocean, southern Africa, Atlantic Islands, Grahams Land, Patagonia, "etc., to the north pole."[114]

Such wide-ranging itineraries notwithstanding, there were limits to the scope of fictive travel. Most notably, tourist clubs tended to shun Africa south of the Sahara. Furthermore, coverage was by no means even. The Fremont Cosmopolitan Club spent a full year in most of the European countries it studied, but when it turned to the Pan-American republics, it did one or two a week.[115] Even as they strove to broaden their geographic consciousness, travel club members favored destinations thought to offer superlative touristic experiences. In picking their itineraries, trip planners were guided by more than just geographic curiosity; they were guided by the logic of tourism. The point was not to study the entire world, or to study any given place because it was there. Rather, the point was to study the places thought to have something noteworthy to offer to a tourist and to study them to find out exactly what that was. This touristic outlook can be seen in the contents of club presentations.

There was a physical geography component to tourist club programs. The *Bay View Magazine* encouraged travel club members to invest in maps, and some of its member clubs did, indeed, hold map contests to test basic geographic knowledge. The Tourist Club of Minneapolis likewise covered "Map questions" in its study of India. These included "Effect of the Himalayas on climate" and "The three river systems of North India."[116] But more than anything, tourist club geographies focused on the geographic features of particular interest to tourists. This meant the particularly spectacular mountains, the extraordinarily beautiful landscapes. To describe these features, club members turned to aesthetic terminology. Hence one club member reported on the "beautiful scenery of Switzerland with its snow-capped mountains, which were so pure and chaste in contrast to the green mountain sides." Speaking of a trip to Italy, another club member reported: "Our finest sensibilities were touched by the beauties surrounding us on every side."[117] The Lewistown Tourist Club heard a talk, "Hidden beauty spots of Mexico," and Hyde Park Travel Club members learned that "India is an endless panorama of interesting pictures." To grasp the loveliness of Japan, travelers turned to poetry: "The cherry blossom gleams, a pearly haze. Across the landscape, far as eye can see. Like mist-wreaths veiling in their shifting maze. Yoshino's mountain-gorges mystery."[118]

Not surprisingly, famous tourist sites loomed large in travel club geographies. In London, the Hyde Park Travel class visited Westminster Abbey, the National Gallery, and the Houses of Parliament. Other club members heard papers on the Eiffel Tower, the Pyramids, and the Taj Mahal. When touring Germany, an Ohio travel club member presented a paper titled "Popular Resorts."[119] On occasion, clubs visited workplaces and ordinary dwellings, but their interests lay more in the pleasurable and spectacular than in the troubling or the quotidian. Although travel clubs were all about movement, members did not want to become too unsettled. A Hyde Park Travel Club report sums up the travel club emphasis: "Miss Ingersoll as leader has taken us, during the season now closed, through Germany; not to show us, indeed, the Imperial Empire of the Kaiser so much as the Germany dear to the heart of the lover of art, romance and story and the picturesque."[120] A touristic outlook meant seeing the world through the lens of art appreciation. It meant searching for the sublime, the marvelous, the pleasurable. And it meant narrowing one's vision so that it centered on the attractions deemed worthwhile to a transitory viewer.

Because not everything nor every place mattered in tourist club geographies, tourist club members could congratulate themselves on knowing it all. Holmes advertised his "Around the World" volumes by asking: "Why not indulge your desire for going *everywhere* and seeing *everything*? *You can do this.*" The sense of truly knowing foreign lands, or at least all the worthwhile ones, was encapsulated by the Hyde Park Travel Club motto: "No country is unknown to us."[121] But what was known? The world was known for what it offered tourists. When the Bay View travel class completed its Italian tour, the *Bay View Magazine* reassured members who were reluctant to say good-bye that "we visited all the most interesting places. To have remained longer would have been only to fill the mind with more of the same kind of ideas." Having seen the greatest hits, tourists moved on, pleased with their sense of mastery. The test came when club members really traveled. Yes, reported returnees, they found what they had expected. As a Hyde Park Travel Club yearbook noted: "Many members of this class have testified to their surprise, in visiting foreign lands for the first time, to often find their surroundings strangely familiar, made so by their study in this Class."[122] Touristic endeavors led fictive travelers to believe they had developed encompassing perspectives.

In keeping with the touristic emphasis on cultural appreciation, tourist clubs had a significant cultural component. Papers on art, music, literature, religion, and history featured prominently in their presentations. Club members spoke on the paintings, sculpture, handicrafts, folk dances, costumes, and architecture to be found in their destinations. They prepared talks such as "Polish Music and Musicians" and "Chinese Music and Theaters,"[123] and they listened to music originating in the countries under consideration. In its trip through India, one club discussed the Bhagavat Gita, "Islamism," Buddhism, Jainism, and Hindu sects. Other travel clubs heard presentations on "Scandinavian Mythology and Sagas," "Winning the Canadian

West," "Holidays and Festivals in Aztec Land," and "Primitive Germans." The historical topics taken up by the Minneapolis Tourist Club during its trip to India included "The Greek Invasion to 750 AD," "Mughal, Maràthà and India as founded by Europeans," "Organization of East India Company and History to 1750," "History to 1859," and "History since 1859."[124]

If the tenor of the Stoddard travel lectures, *Bay View Magazine* articles, and other materials aimed at fictive travelers serves as any indication, travel club presentations lauded the cultural production of the world. They also encouraged an anecdotal approach to history that emphasized the common humanity of all peoples. The further from Protestant Europe, the greater the exceptions, but the demands of tourism muted critiques. Why bother to visit a place with no redeeming virtues? A basic premise of the tourist mentality was that any place worth visiting must have something to offer. Hence touristic accounts countered condemnation with more appreciative assessments. Mexican hotel rooms might lack baths and other modern amenities, but the costumes were picturesque and the people hospitable. So-called old-stock Americans might think little of the Italian immigrants who were pouring into the United States in the late nineteenth century, but tourists raved about their homeland. As a member of the Atwater, Ohio, Monday Afternoon Club enthused: "We are perfectly in love with our first glimpse of Italy."[125]

Their emphasis on cultural appreciation put travel clubs squarely in line with other study clubs. But travel clubs differed from clubs devoted to cultural subjects such as literature and art in having a significant ethnographic component. Like real tourists, armchair travelers paid close attention to the natives. Club members manifested particular interest in royalty and peasants, for they regarded them as especially indicative of national character. In one Hyde Park Travel Club meeting, a member spoke on "life among the different classes in England . . . from the Queen and her court, through the soldiery and the many classes of commoners, laborers or sailors." When the club journeyed to Lucerne, another member noted: "We rested at the hut by the way, we saw and heard the alpine horn, we visited the picturesque home of the peasant maid, examined the stone-edged roofs and minutely scrutinized the unique costumes of the laboring women."[126] Travel club ethnography was full of sweeping stereotypes. Club members learned that "The women peasants of Brittany are considered the most beautiful in France." Valencians could be identified by their "reserved, suspicious indolence," Andalusians by their "grace and wit," and Basques by their "pride but gentleness."[127]

Clubwomen's ethnographic papers often paid particular attention to women and domesticity. A member of the Pocasset, Massachusetts, Travelers' Club spoke on "The Emancipation of Mohamedan Women"; a Lewistown Tourist Club member held forth on "The Women of France." Speakers addressed such topics as "Housekeeping in Japan" and "Home Life of Russian People." They touched on dwellings, furnishings, dress, and marriage.[128] Although some accounts emphasized foreign women's benighted status in juxtaposition to the enviable position occupied by white, well-to-do U.S. women, travel club members reported favorably on foreign decoration styles. As one clubwoman said of Japan, "The simple furnishing and decoration of their homes are in much better taste than the crowded vulgarities of many of our drawing rooms." Speaking about Palestine, another fictive traveler maintained that "the interior of the homes of the better classes are very beautiful, there is a court in the center of which is a fountain around which are flowers, and orange and lemon trees."[129]

Like assessments of tourist attractions and cultural productions, clubwomen's ethnographic assessments often emphasized the romantic, the sentimental, the harmonious, and the attractive over the harsh, the political, the discordant, and the ugly. But clubwomen's ethnographic assessments were not always so glowing. Echoing the evolutionary hierarchies so pervasive in contemporary ethnological thought, travel club members reported on the backwardness and degeneracy of Latin American, Asian, African, and other peoples considered to be racially inferior. Hyde Park Travel Club members learned that Jamaicans "are very lazy and still use the old methods of working, plowing the ground with a crooked stick." On their trip to Morocco, they focused on the "melancholy proof of the degeneracy of the race which built the famous Alhambra of Spain." Turning to the Philippines, club members dismissed the natives as nomadic in habits and "very indolent." As for the Mexicans, "it is hoped they will progress."[130] Not even Europeans were immune from criticism. Clubwomen who followed the Stoddard lectures would have found sharp critiques of Russians and Spaniards—people understood to be Slavs and Latins rather than Anglo-Saxons.[131]

Travel club ethnography had a notable missionary component too. In studying China, the Hyde Park Travel Club heard a lecture touching on "the influence of Christianity upon the lives of women and children." In 1900 the Tourist Club of Minneapolis held a meeting at the home of a woman who had grown up in China, where her father and sister were missionaries. After showing her collection of costumes, pictures, idols, furniture, and ornaments, she gave a talk on Chinese customs and manners. This included a demonstration of the foot binding process. She then served tea on small tables "in the Chinese fashion." The ethnographic lessons? Chinese culture may be fascinating, its artistry enchanting (some of the women purchased curios before leaving). But a people who would cripple girls for aesthetic reasons undoubtedly needed uplift. The travelers contributed to their hostess's missionary fund.[132]

Although some travel club assessments emerged from and reinforced the racial and cultural hierarchies espoused in other forms of ethnography, travel club ethnography had its own distinctive emphases. Whereas commercially oriented ethnographies focused on the productive capacities of various peoples and politically minded ethnographies focused on their potential for self-governance, travel ethnographies paid relatively greater attention to how other peoples would affect the tourist experience. Would they delight the eye? Would they prepare good meals? Would they provide clean rooms? Would they deal honestly with a stranger? Could an English-speaker understand them? Like all ethnographies, tourist ethnography assumed an implicit audience, and in this case, the judge was the leisure traveler.

By no means a transparent eyeball, by no means neutral, tourists evaluated others with their own desires in mind. The rough-looking, inebriated, and slatternly Scots in one highland inn were redeemed when the traveler discovered that his room was decently furnished and clean. Tourist ethnography valued the knowledgeable guide, the accomplished cook, the indefatigable chair-carrier, the efficient porter, the dirt-chasing hotelier, and the helpful official. It valued them all the more if they came cheaply.[133] While tourists might admire artistic, technological, spiritual, military, and other accomplishments, they reserved some of their most heartfelt appreciation for the pleasingly servile native. "Search the world through, and where will you find servants such as these?" questioned Stoddard in a lecture on Japan. "From the first moment when they fall upon their knees and bow their foreheads to the floor, till the last instant, when they troop around the door to call to you their musical word for farewell—'Sayonara,' they seem to be the daintiest, happiest, and most obliging specimens of humanity that walk the earth" (ill. 4.11). Conversely, travelers damned those who had not gratified their desires. A Bay View book on Mexico characterized "peons," especially those in small towns and country places as "usually very stupid." What gave rise to this impression? "When visiting Puebla, I asked several if they could direct me to the post-office, but was unable to make any of them understand."[134]

The touristic accent that characterized ethnographic assessments carried over to economic coverage. Club members presented papers on the main

4.11. "Your Little Maid Brings in a Tray with the Tea Things," in May B. Rasmussen, "Hotel Life in Japan," *Travel Magazine* 13 (Jan. 1908): 173. Courtesy of the University of Illinois at Urbana-Champaign Library.

industries and exports of their destinations. They learned about harbors, agricultural production, electrification, business methods, and ground transportation.[135] They spent time on American commercial expansion in Latin America and Asia. But still touristic outlooks prevailed. Fictive travelers sought out the pleasantly dramatic stories of production, as seen in talks such as "The Romance of Rubber." They deplored economic developments that came at the cost of historic preservation and local color.[136] And among the most favored economic topics were those touching on the tourism infrastructure. Travel club members spoke on the amenities (or lack thereof) they might encounter on their travels. They paid particular attention to the manufacture of items favored by visiting shoppers and to the markets and shops that awaited tourists.[137] Even their reports on harbors, agriculture, electrification, business practices, and transportation spoke to the touristic experience. Where would the steamer dock? What would the tourist eat? Would the rooms be lit?

Political assessments too came colored by the tourist mentality. In their efforts to be comprehensive, travel clubs devoted some attention to domestic politics, social welfare, international relations, and current events.[138] Yet rather than grapple with the troublesome dimensions to these issues, the travel club members who touched on them tended to present superficial analyses consistent with their touristic assessments. How to evaluate the lovely Belgium? Completely overlooking the atrocities in the Congo, one traveler reported that it "cultivates the arts of peace." (Less typically, the *Bay View Magazine* drew attention to Belgian cruelties by publishing a photograph of a man whose hands had been chopped off, captioned "A Victim of the Belgian King's Inhumanity.")[139] Another travel report held up Holland, a nation of placid rural landscapes, as a model country, for it "has no civil or social struggles, no scandals in the government; one writer has said of Holland that it is the most civilized country in Europe." But poor Morocco, a land of corrupt customs officials, degenerate Oriental splendors, and bothersome beggars, was to be pitied: "It is hoped that with a good government it will soon be restored to a higher state of prosperity." How about Japan? Regrettably, reported a Hyde Park Travel Club speaker, it was "making encroachments on Chinese territory in the vicinity of Korea, taking advantage of Russia, England and France and snapping her fingers in the face of the United States." Westernization came at a cost. But it was inconceivable that such a fairy land could become a full-fledged imperial power. "It is not believed, however, that she will be the governing power of the Orient."[140]

Travel clubs' forays into political analysis generally fit with artistic, ethnographic, and other assessments to produce a coherent vision of a place. The point was not to critique the power relations that undergirded the consumers' imperium or to effect change. For the dedicated tourist, a rudimentary knowledge of governmental systems and international relations served as background to understanding a destination. As a travel topic akin to local dress or national holidays, political issues informed but did not dominate discussions. Fictive travelers tended to consider political matters important primarily because of their relevance to the travel experience. Would a country that snapped its fingers in the face of the United States remain pleasingly accommodating to tourists?

There were exceptions, to be sure. As they whirled around the world, some women began to feel that foreign affairs were their business. The Corning Clionian Circle began its studies in 1903 with papers on topics such as Delft ware and Dutch lace. By the teens, however, members were hearing talks on the League of Nations, the war in Turkey, and "Why Japanese Emigration Is a Failure." As we already have seen, travel club members supported missionary endeavors. The Chamberlain, South Dakota, club raised money for Near East Relief and briefly supported a child in Armenia. In contrast to the traveler who heralded Belgium for its peacefulness, a member of the Hyde Park Travel Club urged her associates to attend the

Congo Reform Committee meetings on "the distressful conditions existing in the Congo district."[141] During World War I, the club raised money for the American fund for French wounded and the British, French, and American blind fund. Like a number of other clubs, it reinforced the current events component of its program by scheduling talks on the conflict.[142]

These examples of growing engagement with world affairs notwithstanding, the focus on the touristic experience meant that even as travelers became more versed in current events, most did not alight from their trains to immerse themselves in distant struggles. The story of Cora M. Watson illustrates this point. According to her daughter, Watson had joined a travel club because she was interested in other countries. Yet Watson did not talk much about pressing international issues at home. She had pacifist leanings but did not become an antiwar activist.[143] Like many of her sister travelers, Watson managed to distinguish between political and touristic matters, to travel the world without coming to believe that the two were inextricably intertwined. For women such as Watson, seeing the world through the eyes of the tourist implied observation rather than activism, personal consumption rather than political engagement.

Saying that imaginative travel did not, in many cases, result in international political engagement is not to say that tourist club programs were apolitical. To the contrary, they were suffused with politics. Travel clubs taught a politically fraught way of viewing the rest of the world. Whereas the anthropological mentality centered on classifying, the commercial mentality on selling, the political mentality on governing, and the missionary mentality on converting, the tourist mentality centered on consuming. The thing to be consumed? Not a particular product or movable good but the world itself. The tourist mentality taught Americans to regard the rest of the world as service providers, if only by providing the service of spectacle. It made the needs and interests of the tourist paramount. Tourist club geographies had ethnological, commercial, political, and missionary inflections. But at the center of tourist club geographies lay the tourist. The core question addressed by the tourist club was, "What's in it for me?" Touristic endeavors positioned tourists and would-be tourists at the center of the world.

According to the tourist mentality, the value of a place was not so much inherent as it was mediated through the eyes of a prospective consumer of its riches. How did the Hyde Park Travel Club encapsulate its findings on Germany? "A summer in Bavaria is a delightful holiday, full of restful, silent peace which will always cling in your memory." What struck members most about France? "Paris is preeminently the city of pleasure."[144] Looking back on a recent trip, an Ohio travel club member concluded: "Spain is no longer an uninteresting spot on the map, but a living reality." Of course, Spain had been a living reality before the Ohio women embarked on their study tour. What had changed was not Spain itself, but the clubwomen who had visited it in their imaginations. Instead of seeing Spain as a decrepit power recently defeated by the United States, they had learned to comprehend it as a place worth visiting. Spain had come to matter because they had been there. The tourist mentality may have turned the world into a living reality, but it also reduced it to the personally meaningful.[145]

This view of the world as something to be consumed was intrinsically political, insofar as it situated the tourist in a privileged international position, as a beneficiary of the consumers' imperium not as somebody who toiled on its behalf. Stoddard explicitly encouraged travel club members to understand their new knowledge as a form of power. "Travel enables us to make the conquest of the world," he claimed. Merely viewing his photographs could make foreign lands "PERMANENT AND INTELLIGIBLE POSSESSIONS OF OUR MINDS." Following Stoddard's prompting, armchair travelers could exult: "The world is mine!"[146]

This sense of ownership was all the more political because of the limits to real travel. Within the United States, upscale hotels made it clear that Jews were not welcome. White southerners created significant impediments to travel by segregating doorways, ticket windows, waiting rooms, toilets, and other facilities. African Americans who journeyed to Europe found that their racist compatriots were pressing for segregated facilities there as well.[147] Would-be immigrants likewise found new obstacles in their paths. In 1882 the United States passed the Chinese Exclusion Act, which severely limited immigration from China. This legislation marked the start of a campaign to restrict entry into the United States. The effort to keep out "undesirables" soon resulted in the Gentleman's Agreement between the United States and Japan. As the United States began to develop a segregated travel infrastructure and police its borders more strictly, it made it clear that gaining entrance to and moving within the United States were freedoms reserved for the few.

In this context, identifying oneself as a traveler meant identifying with far more than male privilege and the pleasures that wealth could command. It meant identifying with whiteness, Western civilization, and national power. Tourist club members' sense of entitlement can be seen in a paper presented before the Lewistown Tourist Club in 1910: "Increased Immigration a Menace to Our Country." Even as they relished the rest of the world, the Lewistown ladies sought to keep it at bay. In the Colorado village of Erie, where, according to a Bay View Travel Club member, "most of the people are foreigners," a "band of a few choice spirits" joined together in a Bay View circle.[148] Rather than opening their circle to their "foreign" neighbors, tourist club members traveled with their social peers. Their desire to encounter the foreign did not imply welcoming foreigners. To the contrary. The Colorado clubwomen traveled the world in part to distinguish themselves from people who were in truth more cosmopolitan than they. Surrounded by people who regarded them as locals, they claimed the mantle of world travelers for themselves. In a town full of people who had migrated to earn a living, they chose to feel displaced for fun.

In addition to promoting a sense of personal entitlement, the tourist mentality had specific political implications. Seeing the world through the eyes of the tourist meant endorsing developments that enabled tourism. Foremost among these were European and U.S. imperial endeavors, which were opening up more of the world to Western tourists. Clubwomen who relied on the *Mentor* would have learned that the Barbary Coast had been a "nest of pirates" until its capture by France. Its tourist-minded assessment? "The French have greatly improved the place." Soon after the United States acquired the Virgin Islands during World War I, the *Mentor* published an issue on their touristic potential. The title of a paper presented in a tourist club's week on "wards of the United States" is just as telling: "Hawaii, a New Winter Resort."[149]

Tourist club reports emphasized that imperialism was resulting in expanded shipping and railway lines and the development of local service infrastructures catering to Western expatriates. They credited imperialism with making non-European travel safer and more pleasant for the Western, and particularly the white Western, traveler. Stoddard attributed the agreeable promenade in Canton to foreign influences; Holmes left for the Philippines on the first anniversary of Admiral Dewey's naval victory, fully expecting that once the war against the Filipinos had ended, U.S. tourists would flock to the islands. Stopping in China, Holmes was able to visit the Forbidden City because it was temporarily in the hands of the Ninth U.S. Infantry. In its study of the Philippines, the Hyde Park Travel Club "learned with pride that America has done more for the Filipino in fifteen years than Spain did in three hundred years. Manilla [sic] is for the most part a sanitary city." Ditto for Panama: "Under the Americans, the City of Panama became very much more sanitary and some very substantial buildings were built."[150]

The lessons of such observations proffered in a touristic context? Along with benefiting the locals, U.S. interventions benefited the traveler. Holmes, who witnessed shelling during his 1899 Philippine trip, regretted that circumstances prevented him from venturing far beyond Manila, but he departed "with the firm resolve to return on the conclusion of the war to study the Americanized Luzon of the near future and to explore the other islands of the archipelago when peace shall have made them accessible to the traveler." The enabling implications of U.S. interventions were not lost on the members of the Bay View Club of Irvington, Kentucky. In 1898 the club debated whether to retain the Philippines. I have found no record of the argument. Most likely, members touched on the religious, racial, civilizational, strategic, economic, and constitutional considerations that dominated contemporary discussions of the issue. But it also seems likely that in learning to view the world through the eyes of a tourist, club members had learned to appreciate the imperial order that enabled wealthy, white westerners to travel. They voted in favor of retention.[151]

The touristic conviction that the world should be readily accessible to the traveler colored travel club members' reactions to the Great War as well. Travel club speakers emphasized the destruction, horrors, and havoc of the conflict. They deplored the damage done to tourist sites and the disruption done to tourism. This coverage was not neutral: the devastated sites featured in these accounts tended to be Allied sites, the culprits, the Central Powers. Hence the tourist mentality contributed to pro-Allied sentiments. In assessing the links between travel and U.S. intervention in World War I, Christopher Endy has argued that "Americans fought to make the world safe not just for democracy but also for elite conceptions of culture and charm."[152] That is, they fought for the landmarks and experiences they associated with beleaguered France. They also fought for access. Everybody knew that the greatest threats to transatlantic travelers were German submarines. No less than real travelers, fictive travelers resented the forces that interfered with their avocation. Among the democratic rights at stake in the conflict was their right to travel.

The touristic mentality did not necessarily promote overseas intervention, however. Seeing the world through the eyes of the tourist meant assuming the aloof stance of the transient, a person whose fundamental loyalties lay at home. Unlike emigrants and exiles, tourists traveled with return fare. No matter how enticing their destinations, tourists did not stay. Even as they crisscrossed the globe, tourists remained locals at heart. The Hyde Park Travel Club minutes of 1910 reported that after touring the world, the group had returned "with a vivid and thankful appreciation of our own country." (Never mind that the group had just "landed" in Vancouver, Canada.) Its members sang "America" at the start of meetings.[153]

Like the geography schoolbooks that taught U.S. superiority, travel club reports often held up the United States as the standard against which other countries should be evaluated. A 1912 Bay View book on South America noted that the Western Hemisphere had twenty-one republics, "the most important, of course, being our own United States of North America."[154] Although travelers sought out the best that other places had to offer, their travels fueled national pride.

Travel club nationalism became most visible during World War I. Although some clubs raised money for French and British relief, travel clubs devoted even more energy to the American war effort. The Chamberlain, South Dakota, club served meals and lunches to U.S. soldiers on passing trains. The Hyde Park club dedicated itself to "National Defense."[155] At the height of the conflict, a number of travel clubs heeded the patriotic admonitions to see the United States first, and they abandoned their imaginary steamers for vicarious travel in their own country. The Lewistown club, for example, filled its 1917 calendar with talks such as "Our Capital City," "Our Scenic Wonderland" (on national parks), and "United States and Her Possessions."[156]

A telling sign of fictive travelers' local leanings can be seen in their insistence that their mode of travel had advantages over the real thing. A stay-at-home traveler could speak freely in Russia, without having to fear arrest and detention. She could traipse through Germany "without becoming foot-sore and weary." She could wander at will, gaining access to royal apartments and stately homes. She could scale tall peaks with no fear of danger. She could circle the entire world in a matter of days, "without the harrowing incidents connected with extended travel, such as parting with loved ones, looking after baggage, to say nothing of seasickness and other troubles incidental to traveling."[157] And, of course, she could do it all quite economically, keeping her money at home.

Club members extolled the virtues of fictive travel in part from a sense of defensiveness. Women who were unable to really travel hesitated to admit the shortcomings of the only mode of travel available to them. But the claims that fictive travel was best also underscore armchair travelers' domestic outlooks. Like tourists who actually traveled, the dedicated armchair traveler wanted to see the world without being bothered by it. If the point of tourism was the gratification of the tourist, there were advantages to imaginary travel. Stay-at-home travelers were never followed by curious natives. Unlike real travelers, they were never frightened, humiliated, or humbled. They could look without ever becoming a spectacle for the locals. They could traverse the globe without ever having to question whether their presence was welcomed or without ever becoming unsettled. If passengers on package tours had at most limited interactions with the locals, imaginative travelers were even more sheltered.[158] Those who sang the praises of imaginary travel took a central component of the tourist mentality, the gratification of the tourist, to its extreme. If what mattered most was the traveler, then the world could be left out without fatally compromising the endeavor. Indeed, the real world might only mar the touristic experience by suggesting an alternative cosmology in which the tourist was not the center of the universe.

Given that travel clubs fostered such local and national sentiments, it is ironic that contemporaries criticized them for being too cosmopolitan. Family members (including some cereal-eating husbands) and others who thought ill of the women's club movement complained that women ought to stay home rather than venturing abroad. At its fortieth anniversary celebration, a Minneapolis Tourist Club member recalled the opposition the club had provoked in its early years:

> The men with Tourist families blest
> Soon cried aloud—We're sore distressed.
> The woman's place is in the home;
> Good women never thus did roam.
> For when the countries far and near
> They know too well, alas we fear
> They'll go abroad and leave us cold;
> Abroad they'll spend our hard earned gold.[159]

Imaginative travelers were not the only clubwomen accused of stepping outside their sphere. All clubwomen were vulnerable to accusations that they were neglecting their households. But imaginative travelers were particularly vulnerable. Women who founded libraries could claim to do so for their children's well-being. Those who fought for temperance could call their efforts "home protection." Agitating for sewer systems and pure food legislation could be passed off as an extension of women's role in safeguarding family health. But globe-trotting seemed antithetical to women's labor on behalf of others and, indeed, to domesticity itself. Travel club members' focus on international travel seemed particularly egregious during World War I, when national boosters launched a "see America first" campaign that made an interest in foreign travel—if only imaginary—appear to indicate a want of patriotism.[160]

Faced with such criticism, imaginative travelers had ample grounds to regard their endeavors as a struggle against male efforts to enforce womanly domesticity. Despite their growing access to higher education, professional employment, civic involvement, and political influence, women continued to be subordinate to men. Even the wealthy, white clubwomen who exercised considerable social, economic, and political power still lacked opportunities open to men of their race and class. Despite their active participation in public life, they continued to be associated with the home. The tourist mentality encouraged women to see their ability to travel, if only vicariously, as a mark of women's increasing freedoms and rising status. To claim, as the motto of the Lewistown Tourist Club did, that "The World Is Woman's Book" meant to claim the unbounded vistas of elite men.[161] Mindful that women who really traveled challenged assumptions about women's frailty, timidity, dependence, and inherent domesticity, armchair tourists could dismiss outsiders' criticisms as narrow-minded and retrograde.

They found it harder to stand up to the pressures from within the women's club movement. At the turn of the century, the leadership of the GFWC became increasingly critical of clubs devoted to self-cultivation, travel clubs among them. Bessie Leach Priddy, chair of the GFWC civics committee, exemplifies this new attitude. In 1919 she told clubwomen to abandon their "pink tea programs, with a half hour to art, a half hour to the pyramids of Egypt, and twenty minutes for civics." Instead, members should build programs that would lead to substantial community work. Admonitions to become politically involved resulted in a seismic shift within the club movement. Whereas late nineteenth-century women's clubs tended to pursue literary and cultural topics, by the twentieth century a rising number of clubs focused on reform.[162] Tourist clubs were not oblivious to these developments. Although there was a resurgence of interest in forming travel clubs in the teens, the peak years for travel club formation were between 1890 and 1905.

Charged with being self-seeking cosmopolitans, unmindful of community affairs, armchair travelers made local activism an important part of their programs. The McGregor Tourist Club organized a "Clean-up Day" in the town's parks. The Lewistown Tourist Club voted to expand its purpose to include the promotion of civic welfare.[163] The Hyde Park Travel Club provided a scholarship for a Chicago Art Institute student. Its philanthropy department distributed blankets, clothes, Christmas dinners, and milk to needy members of the community. Once it paid for a Chicago woman's operation, another time it underwrote the treatment for a tubercular boy in an Illinois sanatorium. The club's political activism—involving such things as letter-writing campaigns in regard to the age of consent, women's suffrage, and libraries—likewise centered on local and national issues.[164]

Like club leaders a century ago, historians have heralded activist club-women for their role in advancing Progressive Era reforms. Rather than seeing clubwomen's turn to local activism as a retreat from the wider world once encountered in literary, artistic, historical, musical, and touristic studies, historians have characterized this shift as a broadening of women's visions. According to this line of thought, political and civic engagement did more than self-cultivation to expand clubwomen's outlooks and undermine Victorian tenets of domesticity.[165] There is undoubtedly much truth to this argument. Civic involvement literally brought women out of their homes and broadened their vistas, capacities, and ambitions. But social reform did not necessarily imply a rejection of domesticity. Indeed, local reformers often justified their efforts by referring to them as civic housekeeping. Furthermore, even as activist women became less domestic in the sense that they immersed themselves more fully in public affairs, many became more domestic in the sense that their horizons began to recede from the global to the national, state, and local.

To travel abroad, however, meant to leave the domestic (particularly in the national sense of the word) behind. It meant abandoning homes, and it meant abandoning home—the nation—for a more rootless state. It may seem that fictive travelers posed only a mild challenge to domesticity because most never really went anywhere beyond their community libraries. Yet the point of their endeavors was to envision a life beyond the confines of home—that is, beyond their households and neighborhoods. Like other study club members, imaginary travelers claimed the entire world as their sphere. Despite their self-centeredness, travel clubs fostered a sense of global consciousness, fused to aspirations of extending women's realm.

Travel club members embraced a central premise of the culture of travel, that travel was broadening. They insisted that their trips had made them open-minded. After five months of studying Italy, a Bay View club reported: "Our prejudices have disappeared." Other club members echoed these sentiments, insisting that their travels had taught them to sympathize with the nations under study. Indeed, some club members went so far as to say that they had learned to identify with the people in the lands they visited. As a Marne, Iowa, correspondent wrote: "Since our circle has taken up the Bay View course, the enthusiasm has grown so strong that it threatens to convert us all into Germans." At the close of the Spanish tour, the *Bay View Magazine* questioned: "Have not all noticed how that study and closer acquaintance made us all but Spaniards?"[166] By teaching travelers to appreciate and even identify with other people (especially with Europeans), imaginary travel planted the seeds of cultural relativism.

Even as we recognize the ethnocentric, racist, and nationalist dimensions of touristic programs (particularly when clubs ventured beyond northern Europe) and the ethnic, racial, and class homogeneity of the travel club movement, we also need to acknowledge that travel clubs cultivated more cosmopolitan sentiments. In this respect, imaginary journeys may have been as broadening as local activism. Although community activism exposed women to real differences, it often involved an effort to eliminate these differences—to Americanize immigrants, to reform delinquents, to teach hygienic principles to the poor, and so forth. In contrast to activists, bent on social change, tourists approached the world more passively, as consumers. Tourists did not always appreciate difference, but they did not seek conformity.

Besides fostering a sense of feeling foreign, imaginary travel led club members to literally want to become foreign, by going abroad. Insist as they did that theirs was a preferable mode of travel, club members recognized that their endeavors were a superficial imitation of the real thing. True, imaginary travel spared tourists the seasickness, the fatigue, the danger, and the expense. But fictive travelers knew that they were missing out on the shopping, the food, the color, the smells, the 360-degree vistas. Fictive travelers never met the locals; they never carried on a conversation with a stranger. Their presentations were only as good as the materials available to them. They knew that theirs was a derivative experience.

Recognizing the limits of fictive travel, a number of travel club members professed a desire for actual travel. According to the Hyde Park Travel Club minutes, a lecture on the Bay of Naples "inspired all present with a longing for a sail along the beautiful Bay." Another armchair traveler claimed that her club had developed a bad case of wanderlust: "So far our only unsatisfied desire is for some fairy to convert our poverty into $350, so we can go sailing around the world with Prof. G. W. E. Hill [a tour leader who went to the places covered by the Bay View program] next summer."[167] Club members may have been drawn into the fictive travel movement because of preexisting longings to travel, but over and over again they claimed that their imaginary journeys had bred stronger yearnings. As a Bay View traveler reported, "We are anxious now to be among the first tourists to Spain, after our reading, which has created an intense desire."[168] Such professions indicate that imaginary travel fostered nondomestic aspirations.

As their critics realized, women's travel clubs subverted domesticity in both its senses. First, they brought middle-class women out of their homes, into libraries, lecture halls, classrooms, and other women's parlors and, on occasion, onto trains and steamships. These forays won fictive travelers a place in newspaper stories, club movement annals, archival collections, and, ultimately, the historical record. But that was not all. More significantly, imaginary travelers redefined what it meant to stay home. Through their concerted efforts to learn about, experience, and even reproduce the world, they made the boundaries between the household and the world, the domestic and the foreign, far more permeable. They turned homes into points of departure and points of encounter. And, in so doing, they made a mark on the wider travel culture. Even as travel club members became somewhat less domestic in their pursuits and even less domestic in their outlooks, they gave the culture of travel a more domestic cast. They helped bring ersatz travel experiences from the realm of public amusements into the very heart of domesticity. By positioning women as prime promoters of the culture of travel and prime exponents of the travel mentality, travel clubs made women's desires for escape, status, enlightenment, and fun important considerations in understandings of the rest of the world. They fostered a consumerist global consciousness that put the interests of the white, Western, woman tourist center stage. Through fictive travel, homebound women could escape the confines of domesticity and explore the far reaches of the consumers' imperium, without ever having to fundamentally change perspectives.

5

Immigrant Gifts, American Appropriations

Progressive Era Pluralism as Imperialist Nostalgia

In 1916 Chicago celebrated the Fourth of July with its usual orgy of patriotism. Bands played stirring tunes, marchers belted out nationalistic anthems, and the huge crowd gathered in the Coliseum rose to sing "The Star-Spangled Banner." Representatives from various immigrant groups made three-minute speeches attesting to their loyalty. Six thousand "Americans of foreign birth" pledged their allegiance to their adopted nation. Celebrants forswore ties to all other countries and pledged to make the United States their "first and only object of devotion."[1] Such effusions of nationalism—and Chicagoans were not alone in waving the Stars and Stripes—grew even more fervent after the United States marched into the Great War the following year. The war resulted in more vociferous expressions of patriotism, an upsurge in nativism, sedition laws, deportations, and calls for 100 percent Americanism. It added urgency to the Americanization efforts already well underway in the Chicago Coliseum in 1916.[2]

The Progressive Era Americanization campaign had a broad organizational basis. Hereditary groups such as the Daughters of the American Revolution, National Society of Colonial Dames, and Sons of the American Revolution regarded themselves as particularly suited for Americanization work and made it a priority even before the United States entered the European fray. In 1918 the General Federation of Women's Clubs board resolved that the most pressing issue facing the nation was the "conservation, development, and absorption of American ideals of National, Civic, and Social Life, particularly among the foreign born." Following its urgings, all eleven GFWC departments—from art to library extension—developed wartime programs that concentrated on Americanization.[3] Manufacturers ran Americanization classes for factory workers; the Chamber of Commerce promoted it via a Committee on Immigration. Churches and religiously affiliated groups such as the Young Men's Christian Association, Woman's Christian Temperance Union, and Council of Jewish Women took up the cause. Civic leagues, philanthropists, librarians, settlement house residents, labor activists, and social workers did as well. The federal government also promoted Americanization among military recruits and through agencies such as the Women's Division of the Council of National Defense, the Committee on Public Information, and the Bureau of Naturalization. State and local governments joined with the federal Bureau of Education to bring the crusade into public schools. Even ethnic groups worked to assimilate recent arrivals.[4] Whatever Americanization was, it seemed that the nation needed plenty of it, and that there was no shortage of volunteers for the task.

What was Americanization? Recent interpretations have emphasized day-to-day acculturation on the part of immigrants, including their work experiences, consumption practices, and leisure activities. Progressive Era reformers, however, regarded this kind of acculturation dismissively. Regarding daily life and the marketplace as insufficient for the task at hand, they insisted that a more purposeful approach was necessary. But they did not always agree on means or ends. There were many strains within the Americanization movement. Business leaders taught antiradicalism and anti-unionism along with higher productivity; union leaders agitated for American working conditions and an American standard of living. Nativists pressed for immigration restriction, patriots sought loyal citizens, English-only advocates demanded linguistic uniformity, social workers attempted to alleviate the wretched conditions of industrial America, and immigrants mobilized for full inclusion.[5] Any given Americanizer might have several objectives; Americanizing programs typically had multiple components. Take the GFWC. Along with offering English classes to nonnative speakers, clubwomen affiliated with the GFWC endeavored to turn immigrants into U.S. patriots through song, flag veneration, and pledges of national allegiance. General Federation leaders also argued for "sound immigration laws," by which they meant legislation that would restrict immigration and raise the standards for naturalization. The hostility to immigrants that informed some Americanization programs can be seen in a Georgia club leader's report to GFWC headquarters: "In reply to your inquiry as to what has been done in Georgia for Americanization of foreigners, I have only

heard of one club which has a class for this purpose. We have only one percent of foreigners in Georgia, I am glad to say."[6]

In addition to its economic, political, and social components, the Americanization movement had a significant cultural thrust. Americanization
often implied cultural conformity. This ideal was captured in Americanizers' most powerful metaphor, the melting pot. This metaphor had a range
of meanings. Some Americanizers sought to pour newcomers into Anglo-
American molds; others saw the melting pot as a means to mix ethnic ingredients from across Europe into a flavorful new concoction. In either case,
the melting pot stood for homogenization and triumphant Americanism.
The Progressive Era melting pot was not a multicultural stew pot. It symbolized the desire to forge unity from diversity by eliminating difference.
In most renditions, it had no room for African Americans, Chinese Americans, or others with non-European ancestors. If people of color could not
join in, "old stock" white Americans need not jump in, for most Americanizers saw the melting pot as a crucible for immigrants alone. Those with
proper pedigrees could stand to the side and stir.[7]

One way Americanizers attempted to achieve their melting pot ideal
was through real pots and pans. Believing that Americanness lay in family
life as well as civic practice, in taste as well as loyalty, in consumption and
cleanliness as well as in citizenship and patriotism, Americanizers marched
into immigrant households and demanded change. Never mind that native-
born, middle-class women were experimenting with macaroni and chop
suey, Americanizers admonished immigrant women to cook blander, old
New England fare. When confronted with difference, melting-pot Americanizers preached the virtue of Yankee-style meat and potatoes. Their insistence on culinary uniformity testifies to a deeply felt disregard for the
foreign.[8]

The homogenizing impulse did not stop at the nation's borders. Domestic Americanization efforts had analogues across the globe. In numerous
overseas outposts, missionaries preached American home life as ardently
as the gospel. Americanization—always with a domestic dimension—lay
at the heart of the U.S. colonial enterprise in the Philippines, Puerto Rico,
Haiti, and elsewhere. Writing from Paris—which she characterized as a
city of indecent literature, alcoholism, and germs—*Harper's* correspondent
Flora McDonald Thompson called on American clubwomen to build on
the "imperialistic tendency of the American people" and reform the Old
World.[9] If the Americanizing impulse sometimes had a personal face,
more commonly it had a corporate one. Singer sewing machines spread
American fashion; Post cereal, American diets; Hollywood movies, Ameri-

can consumer culture. It was even possible to buy American homes in the international marketplace, for the Aladdin Company, of Bay City, Michigan, exported prefabricated bungalows at the turn of the twentieth century.[10]

The Americanizers' dream of girdling the globe with homes much like their own was an assertive dream in keeping with the expanding economic and political power of the United States. Their homogenizing ambitions seem to clinch the case that white, native-born, middle-class Americans remained narrow-minded and provincial even as their nation absorbed millions of newcomers; that they engaged with the rest of the world as exporters, not importers; that they struggled to establish dominance, diversity be damned.[11] But is this the whole story? Should we draw our maps of cultural influences with only one-way arrows? Of course not. As the previous chapters suggest, to focus only on Americanization is to miss out on a larger, more complicated, picture. In an age of increasingly global linkages—including unprecedented labor migrations, trade networks, communications breakthroughs, and imperial bonds—the arrows of cultural influence flew in many directions. Americanizers were well aware of this. Many of them tried to stoke the fires of the melting pot because they feared the United States was becoming too foreign. But the incoming arrows did not always generate panic. Along with the melting-pot metaphor, the Progressive Era produced an immigrant gifts movement that was closely allied with calls for pluralism. Whereas the melting pot had xenophobic overtones, the immigrant gifts movement was in full accord with the appropriative tendencies of the consumers' imperium.[12]

The belief that immigrants brought valuable cultural gifts to the United States can be seen in the Fourth of July celebrations described earlier. Even as the various Chicago events stressed the importance of patriotism and national loyalty, they depicted immigrants as culturally distinctive. Immigrant and ethnic Chicagoans, dressed in "gay-colored native costumes," paraded in divisions representing their Old World nationalities. They may have pledged allegiance to the United States, but they also danced their national dances, sang songs from the old country, and played folk tunes from home. As the Chicago festivities indicate, those who extolled immigrant gifts maintained that immigrants (by which they meant mainly European immigrants) could contribute to American life by transmitting Old World cultural traditions. Although native-born, socially prominent men orchestrated some displays, native-born white women played major roles in heralding immigrant gifts. Their prominence in the immigrant gifts movement owed much to the belief that women's realm included cultural guardianship.[13] If women claimed culture as their province, they claimed folk culture in particular. And gifts events centered on folk culture, especially the performing arts and handicrafts.

Folk songs occupied a prominent role in the assortment of gifts welcomed by native-born Americans. According to an article on music in the *General Federation Magazine*, "The foreigner brings to us a gift in which America is to an extent deficient, 'Folk Song.' He comes to us with an innate love of music, a born rhythm, and more than often with a talent that sometimes amounts to genius. Whether he be from sunny Italy or the steppes of Russia, we find him eager for the opportunity to sing."[14] And sing they did, often for audiences that did not understand the lyrics. Advertisements for and coverage of concerts produced by ethnic choral groups can be found in major English-language newspapers. In 1908, for example, the *Chicago Tribune* reported on a German music festival. Two thousand people took part, including several hundred children, "in costumes representing the different sections of the 'fatherland.'" In 1916 the *Los Angeles Times* alerted its mostly Anglo readership to a forthcoming Mexican independence celebration conducted by the Cura Hidalgo Club. The article promised an enticing program, featuring "music of Old Mexico" sung by a "chorus of fifty senoritas and caballeros."[15] In addition to attending concerts produced by members of particular ethnic groups, native-born music lovers produced and listened to concerts that mixed performers from different lands. The program for an evening of European folk songs and dances in Gary, Indiana, provided English synopses for songs such as the Bulgarian "Pred Bashtinata Kushta" (In Front of the Father's House) and the Russian "Da Zdravstvoet Rossyi" (Long Live Russia).[16]

Musical programs often included a second immigrant gift: dance (ill. 5.1). In 1908 as many as 10,000 people watched a festival of folk and national dances in New York City's Van Cortland Park. The following year, about 30,000 spectators witnessed a Chicago festival featuring residents of the city's foreign colonies. The 3,100 dancers, representing fourteen nationalities, included Bohemian Turners, members of a Gaelic Dancing Association, and Italian settlement children. And just as major English-language newspapers reported on concerts produced by particular ethnic groups, they also reported on ethnic celebrations that featured dancing. When Italians living in New Orleans celebrated Italian Independence Day with a big festival, the *Times-Picayune* printed pictures of the twirling children, thus enabling even those who had missed the event to appreciate their costumes and lithe figures.[17]

Drama did not play such a prominent role in the immigrant gifts movement as music and dance—no doubt related to reasons of language and

5.1. Slovak Dance in "Europe in America" program, International Institute of Northwest Indiana Records. Courtesy of the Calumet Regional Archives, Indiana University Northwest, Gary.

translation—but it did play a role. The Little Country Theatre in Fargo, North Dakota, produced a tableau entitled *A Farm Home Scene in Iceland Thirty Years Ago*, starring young men and women of Icelandic descent. According to one review, "The effect of this tableau was tremendous. It incited other students of foreign descent who were in attendance at the institution to present tableaux and scenes depicting the national life of their fathers and mothers."[18] In *Twenty Years at Hull-House*, Jane Addams noted that the settlement had lent its "little stage" to immigrant neighbors. On occasion, the native-born reformers joined with immigrant neighbors to dramatize Jewish religious stories, perform Irish plays, and enact ancient Greek tragedies. The latter included Sophocles' *Ajax*, staged at Hull-House under the direction of Mabel Hay Barrows, who had experience working with New England college students. But at Hull-House, Barrows cast Greek neighbors who felt that Americans did not appreciate their history and "classic background." The performers harbored high hopes of reaching out to non-Greek audiences. Addams described the play as an unqualified success in this respect: "It was a genuine triumph to the actors who felt that they were 'showing forth the glory of Greece' to 'ignorant Americans.'"[19]

All three of these performance arts—music, dance, and drama—came together in pageants. Although some ignored recent arrivals in their depictions of local history, ethnic displays helped make the early twentieth century the golden age of the pageant.[20] A Festival and Pageant of Nations conducted by the People's Institute of New York City serves as an example. Every evening for a week, groups of Irish, Bohemian, Croatian, Polish, Ruthenian, Jewish, and Italian children and adults performed their "national art" in Public School 63, on the Lower East Side. At the end of the week, they staged a culminating performance, outdoors, with additional participants from Holland, Germany, and Hungary. In assessing the pageant, one observer remarked that it "showed, first, that foreigners in New York are willing to show their native songs, dances, costumes—in a word, to reveal their national art—to Americans. And it showed that Americans, with no folklore of their own, no traditions, no specific expressions of mood in music, movement or color, are willing to come and see." Although the "foreign" participants had been fearful of low attendance, and particularly fearful that none but their own people would come, "great numbers of foreigners and non-foreigners looked on and clapped" (ill. 5.2).[21]

Beyond the performing arts, handicrafts played an important part in the immigrant gifts movement. As one GFWC program guide admonished members, "Every possible means should be taken to preserve and encourage the handicrafts which the foreigners bring to this country, such as embroidery, knitting, crocheting, hooked or hand woven rugs, basketry, bead work, woven table covers, coverlets and draperies . . . and an organized effort should be made in each community where they exist to develop these industries and make a market for them. Clubs can assist by giving exhibitions of the work and purchasing the articles."[22] Museums too exhibited European handicrafts. At the end of the Great War, the Boston Museum produced a series of exhibits entitled "The Nations Come to America Bringing Gifts." Each week it displayed items from different countries—Italy, Syria, Japan, and others. The intent? To make children "appreciate and love the beautiful things of the world."[23]

Hull-House's well-known Labor Museum arose from this larger celebration of immigrant handicrafts. In addition to presenting exhibits on agriculture, cooking, copper work, and pottery, the Labor Museum depicted the "historic development of the processes of spinning and weaving," from the early spindle and medieval wheel to the fly shuttle loom. This was not just a

A PAGEANT OF AMERICA IN THE MAKING

*H*OW patriotism may be taught in a neighborhood inhabited by aliens in such a way as to stimulate rather than repress their love for the cherished traditions of their home countries, was demonstrated recently in a street pageant organized by the Neighborhood House in Harlem [New York city]. It was the first venture in community drama in that populated area and strictly home-made. A Slovak group in picturesque costume presented a lively pantomime, based on the life of Janosik, a peasant hero of the eighteenth century, and Slovak children danced a folk dance. The Hungarian neighbors, in four tableaux, represented scenes from the lives of John Hunyadi, Louis Kossuth and Helen Zrinyi, and in song and dance made live again the village life of their native plains. Italian girls, also in peasant dress, danced the tarantella. From Julius Caesar to Victor Emmanuel, the heroes of popular tradition passed in revue. The closing episode brought these various groups together in common appreciation for their new home. Columbia, surrounded by figures representative of American history and of the present guardians of her military power and civil liberties, was followed by a procession of Allegiance, symbolic of the children of an older world pledging their loyalty and devotion to the new.

collection of equipment. Immigrants—including ones from Syria, Italy, and Ireland—demonstrated how to use the objects on display (ill. 5.3).[24] At least one of the spinners, Signora Annunziata, also appeared before the Chicago Arts and Crafts Society, which met in the Hull-House Lecture Hall. Besides showing how to use the distaff and wheel, she sang Italian folk songs. Other settlement houses that promoted immigrant handicrafts included Boston's Denison House, which held an Italian Arts and Crafts exhibit; New York's Richmond Hill House, which sponsored a Scuola d'Industrie Italiane,

5.3. "Keeping Old World Customs Alive," *Survey* 28 (Aug. 24, 1912): front cover. Courtesy of the University of Illinois at Urbana-Champaign Library.

aimed at reviving traditional Italian artisanship; and New York's Greenwich House, which exhibited items such as rugs, laces, peasant costumes, and religious paraphernalia from many countries. In 1913 the Jewish Settlement House in Cincinnati produced a homelands exhibit that displayed more than 500 objects—ranging from samovars to embroideries and ritual objects—brought by the Jewish diaspora to the United States. Costumed men and women presided over the booths. The program also included traditional songs, dances, and foods.[25]

As these events suggest, the immigrant gifts movement exposed innumerable Americans to ethnic and national difference. Judging from their attendance, reportage, and roles in producing gifts events, native-born Americans had a tremendous appetite for such displays. Their fascination with ethnic performances and handicraft exhibits resonated with other aspects of the consumers' imperium, such as the enthusiasm for imported household objects, Paris fashions, exotic recipes, and armchair travel. But the taste for foreignness seems at odds with the Americanization impulse. The tension between the appropriative urges of the consumers' imperium and the campaign for 100 percent Americanism begs for explanation. How can we reconcile the homogenizing thrust of the period with the surge of interest in immigrant folk culture?

Immigrants themselves deserve much of the credit for the immigrant gifts movement. By their mere presence, they familiarized native-born Americans with difference. Ethnic associations played a particularly prominent role in displaying difference to native-born Americans because most immigrants rapidly shed the Old World dress that marked them as distinctive when they went out and because they closed the doors behind them when they came home. Ethnic organizations, in contrast, made great efforts to publically assert difference by organizing concerts, parades, festivals, religious processions, and other events. Their celebrations sometimes attracted tens of thousands of spectators, many of them not members of the ethnic group at all but outsiders in search of foreign touristic experiences. Hence northern tourists attended Cuban entertainments while vacationing in Tampa, and special trains carried hundreds of spectators to the Swiss festivals in New Glarus, Wisconsin.[26]

Besides exhibiting ethnicity in national events, immigrants worked with native-born Americans and other immigrant groups to produce pan-ethnic events. Women from thirty-three national groups got together in Chicago to produce a "Gifts of the Nations" pageant in 1919. What motivated these women? No doubt a desire to dispel prejudice and win respect help explain their collaboration. In ethnic gatherings and elsewhere, immigrant spokesmen went beyond honoring their own groups to wax eloquent about the value of ethnic difference in and of itself.[27]

But immigrant agency alone does not explain the enthusiasm for immigrant gifts. Ethnic nationalists had to struggle to maintain interest in their activities; many of their functions suffered from low attendance. Immigrant leaders commonly bewailed the cultural declension of their children. The "old stock" Americans who produced immigrant gifts events echoed these jeremiads, often speaking of the need to teach immigrants to appreciate their own gifts and to preserve the foreign customs rapidly being abandoned by newcomers.[28] In addition to advocating cultural preservation, native-born reformers took an active role in teaching accomplishments later passed off as immigrant gifts. Playground supervisors taught songs and dances that appeared on programs as Old World carryovers. Festival guides provided information on authentic foreign costumes; schoolteachers taught ethnic handicrafts. Sicilian women in Gary, Indiana, sold Italian embroideries sewn upon stamped material provided by the YWCA; the "immigrant arts" displayed at New York's Greenwich House originated in the settlement's handicraft school.[29]

Native-born Americans who wished to produce an immigrant gifts event could find plenty of published advice. Handbooks for event organizers listed the immigrant gifts that should be displayed: Swedes should do a weaving dance; Scots, a highland fling; the Irish, a jig; Italians, the tarantella. The folk song collections used by music teachers typically included the music and lyrics for a number of European airs. Further evidence of fabrication can be found in the tendency to have immigrants depict traditions other than their own. Fabricating gifts was so common that the promoter of a Chicago festival took pains to insist that its tarantella performance would be authentic: "This dance had not been drilled into them, but had been taught them as a matter of course by their peasant parents."[30]

That the immigrant gifts movement had more complicated origins than the mere presence of immigrants also can be seen in the selective reception of gifts. The presence of gifts does not mean that they will be welcomed; indeed, the Progressives who enthused about immigrant gifts did not appreciate all gifts. Many of the migrants who came to northern cities in the Progressive Era hailed from the U.S. South, not from abroad. But African American folk culture found a relatively cold reception among white Americans. Similarly, immigrants arriving from Mexico and Asia found it harder to cast themselves as gift-bearers than immigrants from Europe. Anti-Semitism also dampened welcomes: Hull-House reformers shied away from sponsoring Yiddish cultural events, even though Eastern European Jews constituted about a third of their clientele.[31]

This is not to say that only Europeans found a place in gifts celebrations, however. According to the New York Tribune, "China eclipsed all other nations" in a 1908 spectacle put on by the Woman's Branch of the New York City Mission Society. In New Orleans, the City Federation of Women's Clubs worked with the Syrian Girls' Get-Together Club to produce an Oriental entertainment, characterized as "lovely" by one spectator. Another group of clubwomen included Mexican women's work in their handicraft exhibit and sale. The judges of a 1918 Chicago celebration involving sixty-four "racial" groups also applauded the contributions of non-Europeans: among the groups they singled out for special recognition were the Syrians, Chinese, Japanese, and Venezuelans. After the Chinese delegation bested twenty-five other nationalities to win first prize in a Columbus Day pageant, one non-Chinese observer commented: "The applause that greeted them as they passed was evidence of the immediate value of the celebration in removing race prejudice."[32]

Even though white Americans did not always associate immigrant gifts with whiteness and sometimes awarded top honors to what struck them as the most exotic displays, European origins tended to make gifts more palatable. Yes, a YWCA harvest pageant in Gary, Indiana, had "Assyrian maidens" represent Oriental harvest customs. But the next event put on by the group bore the title: "Europe in America in Folk Songs and Dances."[33] Neither performance included representatives from Gary's Mexican community.

CARNIVAL OF THE NATIONS

T HIRTY-SIX nationalities were represented in the tableau, the Star Spangled Banner, which was the closing scene in the annual Carnival of the Nations at the Philadelphia Y. M. C. A. The carnival marks the end of each year's work by the classes in citizenship which are conducted in all parts of the city. More than 400 people took part, dressed in native costumes and singing together the national hymns of nearly every tribe of men

5.4. "Carnival of the Nations," *Survey* 36 (July 15, 1916): 405. Courtesy of the University of Illinois at Urbana-Champaign Library.

When dance expert Luther H. Gulick warned that some dances should be avoided, he spoke specifically of erotic Oriental dances. "The love dances of the East, however beneficial they may be from the standpoint of the body movements, are entirely unsuitable from the standpoint of their emotional content and their relation to the morals of our civilization." Rather than welcome all gifts indiscriminately, gifts promoters extended their warmest welcomes to the gifts that helped them claim a European and Christian heritage for the United States. Regarding gifts as a way to integrate newcomers, they heartily embraced only those that fit in with their restrictive conceptions of who truly belonged to the nation.[34]

Although the immigrant gifts movement might seem to be at odds with the Americanization campaign, its exclusionary visions of national belonging reveal common ground. Far from standing in opposition to Americanization, immigrant gifts events advanced it. Just as the Chicago Fourth

A LIBERTY LOAN COMMITTEE FROM MANY LANDS

Coming together one evening in their native costumes, these Liberty loan campaign workers from Italy, Sweden, Poland, Finland, Armenia, and many other countries, discovered that in helping the cause of America they were helping not only that of their individual nationalities, but that of freedom-loving peoples everywhere

5.5. "A Liberty Loan Committee from Many Lands," *Survey* 40 (June 15, 1918): 311. Courtesy of the University of Illinois at Urbana-Champaign Library.

of July celebrations combined flag veneration and foreign dances, Americanization pageants mixed oaths of allegiance with "Gifts of the Nations" performances (ills. 5.4, 5.5).[35] However paradoxical it might seem, some Americanizers celebrated immigrant gifts even as they worked to assimilate immigrants and promote national homogeneity. Instead of shunning gifts events, these Americanizers produced them.

Settlement house workers took the lead in approaching Americanization through immigrant gifts. Mina Carson makes this point in *Settlement Folk*. She maintains that even as settlements offered classes in English, civics, and the like, "settlement workers were among the first to appreciate the Old World cultural survivals in the immigrant colonies."[36] Thus Boston's Denison House promoted Italian arts and crafts, and its "Circolo Italo-Americano" featured Italian songs and recitations. The Henry Street Settlement on the Lower East Side of New York City, long a supporter of immigrant dances, costumes, and other ethnic arts, produced an immigrant gifts pageant in 1913 that attracted an estimated 10,000 viewers. Several years later, Neighborhood House in Harlem produced its own "Pageant of America in the Making," with folk dances, songs, and pantomimes of national heroes.[37]

The GFWC also incorporated immigrant gifts into its Americanization crusade. Much of the federation's interest in immigrant gifts can be attributed to its ties to settlement house workers. Jane Addams, for example, addressed the 1906 GFWC convention, declaring that: "America needs the immigrants on the cultural side, quite as much as it needs the immigrants on the labor side."[38] Following Addams's admonitions, the GFWC lauded immigrant gifts in its book on Americanization. One of the essays urged clubwomen to hold "*Community Gatherings* of American and foreign born, at which the foreign born shall show the gifts of their nation in music, art and the crafts."[39] Another essay, on homemaking, suggested asking "any immigrant or person of foreign blood to make an exhibit of their best foods" to display alongside "good, nutritious, inexpensive, simply prepared American foods." Given the homogenizing ambitions of the home economics movement, one might expect the point to be the superiority of "American" food. But the article instructed the women to distribute recipes for *all* the concoctions. This essay also advocated exhibits of foreign handiwork, displays of "Musical Instruments of All Nations," and folk dances and games "illustrated by women or children in native costume."[40]

Did women's clubs follow through on these suggestions? At least some did. Along with starting English-language classes and establishing kindergartens in foreign quarters, clubwomen in Massachusetts pursued Americanization through exhibiting needlework and other handicrafts loaned by the "foreign women of the community." Clubwomen in Albany, New York, reached out to immigrant women by holding a song-and-dance event in a public school. A member of a mothers' club that offered an Americanization tea thought it so successful that she wrote a how-to account that was published in the *Woman's Home Companion*. The original event had costumed attendants at the various national booths, displays of embroidery borrowed from "foreign neighbors," folk dancing by public school children, and food cooked by immigrant women.[41]

Another major women's organization that approached Americanization through immigrant gifts was the YWCA. It did so primarily through its International Institutes. Edith Terry Bremer established the first of these in New York City in 1910. It functioned like a settlement house, providing educational classes, recreational programs, and assistance in matters such as housing, employment, and naturalization to immigrant women and their daughters. Institute employees aided young women who were traveling alone and they made "friendly visits" to immigrant homes. YWCAS in other cities—including Trenton, Los Angeles, Pittsburgh, and Lawrence, Massachusetts—soon copied Bremer's model. Although most of the institute clientele had European origins, institutes on the Pacific Coast and in Texas had significant contacts with women of Asian and Mexican ancestry.[42]

Following the urgings of the national board, YWCA members established a number of new institutes at the end of World War I. By the 1920s the YWCA had more than fifty International Institutes, mostly in the Northeast and Midwest. Bremer shaped the character of these institutes by helping to set them up, paying them visits, providing them with books, pamphlets, and other written materials, sending handicraft instructors and program advisors, and holding annual meetings that brought institute workers together. Starting in 1919, the YWCA published a magazine entitled *Foreign-Born* to aid Americanization workers. To help in the establishment of cultural programs, it ran articles such as "Nationalities in Their Home Countries" and "Foreign Holidays, Festivals and Saints Days."[43]

Unlike many of the Americanizers affiliated with the GFWC, Bremer had considerable firsthand experience with immigrants. Before becoming the head of the YWCA's Immigration Department, she had worked in the University of Chicago's settlement house, at Union Settlement in New York, and as an agent for the United States Immigration Commission. These experiences—and her ongoing work with the institutes—made her much more of a cultural pluralist than the melting-pot-oriented members of the Americanization movement. Bremer's choice of names is telling. She ruled against calling her organization "Immigrants YWCA" or "Immigrant Girls League" and settled on "International Institute for Young Women" because she intended it as "a place which is inaugurated by Americans out of friendliness to women of all nationalities not one before another, but all equally; because we respect our foreign neighbors and wish them to realize it."[44] To include the word "immigrant" in the name meant to label it an organization for outsiders; to choose the world "international" put all participants in institute programs on an equal footing.

Under Bremer's leadership, the native-born women who directed the various institutes hired immigrant women—known as nationality workers—to go into the surrounding neighborhoods. They combined homogenizing activities, such as English and homemaking classes, with programs aimed at cultural preservation (ill. 5.6). Although local chapters received some financial support from the Colonial Dames, they did not venerate eighteenth-

What the International Institute Does

HOW	Explains laws and customs of America to non-English speaking women.	THE
THE	Interests the foreign born in American institutions.	NATIONALITIES
INTERNATIONAL	Facilitates the best use of community resources by foreign speaking women. Interprets and translates for all nationalities.	SERVED
INSTITUTE		ARE
WORKS	Refers applicants to reliable doctors, lawyers, real estate agents, et cetra.	

Takes those in need of material help to relief giving stations.

Organizes classes of women, meeting in homes, neighborhood centers and schools, for the study of English, of citizenship, of home and health problems.

IN CO-OPERA-
TION WITH ALL
SOCIAL AGENCIES
AND FOREIGN
ORGANIZATIONS

THROUGH AN
INTERNATION-
AL STAFF OF
AMERICAN AND
FOREIGN LAN-
GUAGE WORKERS

Establishes mothers' clubs.

Encourages wholesome recreation.

Assists national groups with entertainments and pageants.

Strengthens the ties between old world mothers and new world daughters.

Offers to Americans opportunities for enjoying and assimilating the arts and handicrafts of other countries.

Aims in every way to establish mutual understanding and sympathy between native and foreign born.

ALBANIAN
BULGARIAN
CROATION
CZECH
FRENCH
GERMAN
GREEK (ON CALL)
HUNGARIAN (ON CALL)
ITALIAN
MEXICAN (ON CALL)
POLISH
ROUMANIAN (ON CALL)
RUSSIAN
SERBIAN
SLOVAK
SPANISH
SYRIAN (ON CALL)
UKRAINIAN

5.6. "What the International Institute Does" (ca. 1920), International Institute of Northwest Indiana Records. Courtesy of the Calumet Regional Archives, Indiana University Northwest, Gary.

century Anglo-America. Instead, they organized concerts, dances, festivals, pageants, plays, banquets, and exhibits that showcased the gifts of recent arrivals.[45] Along with offering classes in U.S. history and government, they offered classes in old-country languages (other than English), history, and culture.

The programs produced by the International Institute in Lewistown, Maine, illustrate the range of institute activities. In 1918 it sponsored a dinner of all nations that brought "non-English speaking people" together with "Americans of older generations." Greek, Lithuanian, and Italian women decorated national booths, cooked national specialties, and then served the food dressed in old-country costumes. After dinner, they sang and danced. The same year, the institute displayed crochet work, rugs, and bedspreads handcrafted by Greek and Lithuanian women, and it threw an international party that, according to an institute report, brought French, Lithuanian, and Greek girls together with "our own house girls." After each group sang its national song, a representative participated in a tableau portraying America as "one from many." Building on this success, it gave an "entertainment" the following year that combined European folk dances and music with a Pilgrim Play, Thanksgiving Drill, and Flag Song. This took a month to prepare, but the full seats at each of the two performances gratified the

5.7. "The Pageant of Nations and of the Public School," *Survey* 36 (July 1, 1916): 348. Courtesy of the University of Illinois at Urbana-Champaign Library.

directors.[46] As Raymond Mohl has written of the institutes, "Rather than undermining or destroying the immigrant heritage—the approach pursued by most agencies working with immigrants—the institutes fostered ethnic awareness, consciousness, and pride." (By the 1920s, this approach put them at odds with the national YWCA, which assumed a more assimilationist stance toward immigrants.)[47]

Educators also contributed to the immigrant gifts movement, thanks in part to Addams's prodding. Just as she admonished clubwomen to appreciate immigrant gifts, she urged teachers to nurture immigrant arts. Although public schools served as major agencies of assimilation (Americanizers tried to push immigrant children from parochial schools into public schools for precisely this reason), some teachers did follow Addams's admonitions. They produced "Pageant of Nations" events and, drawing on folk song books produced expressly for educators, led their students in European airs.[48] They promoted folk dancing, too. By 1909 Elizabeth Burchenal, author of several guides to folk dances and chairman of the Committee on Folk-Dancing of the Playground Association of America, had trained more than 2,000 public school teachers who in turn taught folk dances to more than 55,000 public school girls. In the 1908–9 school year, more than 30,000 elementary school girls in New York City learned folk dances under the auspices of the Public Schools Athletic League. Some public schools had folk dancing clubs, others included European folk dances in their end-of-year exercises (ill. 5.7).[49] Each grade in the Dubuque public schools learned a different dance in its physical training period. In 1914 first-graders learned a Swedish Klap dance; sixth-graders mastered a Hungarian Czardas. About 3,000 children participated in a 1908 Pittsburgh play festival that included folk dancing; another 500 danced in a Providence playground festival the following year. Chicago's Playground Association sponsored an annual Play Festival, featuring "the dances of people after people."[50]

Librarians too regarded immigrant gifts events as a means to advance their Americanizing ambitions. Even as libraries sponsored English and citizenship classes, they also acquired foreign-language reading materials and held cultural events such as folk dances. The library in Mt. Vernon, New York, offered performances of Italian vocal and instrumental music. The Cedar Rapids public library held an evening devoted to Bohemian folk songs and then sponsored a photographic exhibition on Prague and its environs. Besides producing events within libraries, librarians used their professional expertise to help with community pageants and other displays of immigrant gifts.[51]

The folk art exhibits that appeared in a number of cities during the teens served as another major venue for promoting Americanization via immigrant gifts. The Department of Immigrant Education in New York State joined forces with several other groups, including the American Federation of Arts and the Buffalo Board of Education, to produce one of the most influential of these exhibits. Although men won much of the credit for producing the Buffalo Arts and Crafts of the Homelands Exhibition, women also played prominent roles. Ella Cecilia McKinnon, president of the Buffalo Guild of Allied Arts, assumed the responsibility of selecting, assembling, and arranging the exhibits, and she helped with the entertainment program. Cornelia B. Sage Quinton, director of the Albright Art Gallery, offered the use of that building and the assistance of her staff. Other prominent native-born women who had been working with immigrant communities served as liaisons with the exhibitors.[52]

What was the exhibit like? Upon entering, visitors encountered upright glass cases with fans, laces, and jewelry from the various countries represented. The first gallery provided a "kind of association of nations"—that is, it brought together items from each of the twenty-two homelands represented in the exhibit as a whole, all of them European, except Syria. The assemblage turned the artistic productions of Buffalo's immigrants—a Belgian tapestry, a Norwegian woodcarving, an Irish harp—into one har-

5.8. "Hungarian Booth at the Buffalo Exhibition," in Allen H. Eaton, *Immigrant Gifts to American Life* (1932). Courtesy of the Michigan State University Libraries, Lansing.

HUNGARIAN BOOTH AT THE BUFFALO EXHIBITION
OLD PEASANT EMBROIDERIES SHOWN ON THE PILLOWS AND BEDSPREAD; MAN'S APRON ON THE LEFT

monious unit. But not all of the displays celebrated mingling. The bulk of the items in the exhibition, ranging from Scottish plaids to Russian stacking dolls, Czechoslovak Easter eggs, and Italian church vestments, were arranged in national booths divided into two galleries: one representing northern and eastern Europe and one representing southern, central, and eastern Europe (ill. 5.8). Then the various nations came together again in a room full of paintings from many lands.[53]

Although the Buffalo exhibit centered on handicrafts, it also had a performing arts component. Foreign-born groups provided entertainment supposedly characteristic of their homelands. Scandinavians depicted home scenes, Poles played instrumental music, and Hungarians danced country dances until the lights went out. On the closing night, immigrants returned in Old World dress for a pageant of the nations. In keeping with the Americanization purposes of the exhibit, the national representatives, from Armenia to Ukraine, gathered around Columbia and sang "America." More than 42,000 people came to the Buffalo exhibition during its two-week run. Later exhibits in Albany, Rochester, and elsewhere generated similar enthusiasm.[54]

Gifts events might seem to counter Americanization efforts, but the settlement house residents, clubwomen, International Institute staff members, educators, playground workers, librarians, and arts-and-crafts promoters who staged them appreciated the multiple ways they advanced the Americanization cause. To begin with, gifts events were great fund raisers. Hull-House, for example, had a benefit consisting of a series of national dances, "performed as far as possible by natives of the countries represented." The International Institute of St. Louis added to its coffers by contributing an exhibit of foreign handicrafts to a local carnival; the director of the Niagara Falls Institute proposed to raise money by producing a concert of folk songs, performed by girls in national costumes.[55] The Americanization tea mentioned earlier was a fund-raising tea. The native-born women who attended paid for the pleasure of experiencing foreignness. What made the affair even more lucrative was that expenses were low—at least for the clubwomen who staged it. Immigrant women who did not belong to the mother's club contributed food and costumes as well as entertainment. In such cases, immigrants themselves financed the Americanization crusade. The more spectators appreciated displays of artistic difference, the more they donated to the organizations that were working to efface linguistic, political, and other manifestations of difference. In reference to the Arts and Crafts of the Homelands exhibit held in Buffalo, one official noted: "Before the exhibition we had experienced considerable difficulty in raising funds for Americanization work, but just following it we raised with ease some $20,000."[56]

Americanizers also supported immigrant gifts because they saw them as a way of building relationships with immigrants. Realizing that more hidebound Americanization efforts alienated the intended targets, they sought to build trust and an interest in their programs through gifts events. Convinced that newcomers sought sympathy and understanding among "their own kind" because they failed to find it among native-born Americans, settlement house workers and other reformers welcomed immigrant gifts to show that not all Americans were cultural philistines or unsympathetic deracinators.[57] Immigrants who feared Americanization, thinking it meant a total rejection of their pasts, were supposed to conclude that they could cling to apolitical folk traditions, so long as they learned to speak English, mastered hygienic, civic, and other principles, and transferred their loyalties to their adopted country.

At the very least, celebrations of immigrant gifts brought immigrants into friendly contact with ambitious Americanizers who could then proceed with their transformation efforts. Hazel MacKaye, author of an article on "Americanization via Pageantry," praised pageants as the best "means of 'getting-together' . . . since the old-fashioned festivals of our forefathers on the village green." A report by the GFWC Sub-committee on American-ization commended handicraft exhibits for promoting "the acquaintance which is the beginning of a friendliness that flowers into cooperation."[58] One would-be Americanizer, frustrated by her inability to "get acquainted with the Italian girls," finally took her violin to factories for the noon-hour break. In keeping with her Americanizing ambitions, she taught the girls to sing the national anthem, but recognizing that the girls spoke little English, the rest of her programs consisted of Italian folk songs. Other American-izers produced performances starring schoolchildren in order to establish contact with multiple generations of immigrant families. As one Interna-tional Institute secretary noted of pageants, "Not only do they interest the younger girls who take part in them, but they often serve to bring out the older members of the family when everything else has failed. If 'Maria' is to take the part of Italy's gift-bearer to the new world, then surely Maria's mother must see her daughter in this important role. . . . Once she has come to the International Institute, she will most certainly come again." Institute workers who orchestrated an evening of folk songs and dances must have relished the write-up in a local paper: "Never in Gary's history has there been such a turn out of native and foreign born Americans. It was a real getting together of the north and south sides. And that is the basis of Americanization."[59]

In addition to embracing immigrant gifts as a means to reach out to immigrants, many Americanizers favored them because they regarded the very idea of gifts as instructive. The innumerable functions in which immi-grants presented offerings to Columbia showed immigrants what to do with their gifts: they were supposed to dedicate them to their new nation. A 1920 pageant produced by Nora Van Leeuwen, of the New York People's Insti-tute, illustrates this point. The participating nationalities paraded through the Lower East Side, with banners, music, and floats. Upon arriving in a great, bare field on Eleventh Street, each foreign society gave a "brief, strik-ing presentation of that which they consider most worthy of their national name and national pride." But before exhibiting their national glories, the various groups proceeded one by one to lay "an appropriate gift at the feet of a great triad of figures representing the three races whose amalgamation is producing the new America—the Teutonic, Latin and Slavic—with a rep-resentation of liberty rising above them all." The point was not lost on the performers or audience. Each national story was a gift to an even greater nation, the liberty-loving United States (which this tableau took pains to define as strictly European in its origins). The finale underscored the point that the European nationalities should honor the country that was absorbing them all: the children formed a huge American flag that the foreign societies then saluted with their own banners.[60]

All the talk of immigrant gifts notwithstanding, such spectacles hinted at a different kind of offering—tribute. It was not just the nature of the spectacles (the mandatory salutes to Columbia, the wreath laying at Liberty's feet, the kneeling before the "Altar of America") that evoked tribute but the fact that Americanizers often demanded gifts. As one GFWC convention speaker said, "we can demand of our illiterate immigrants that they become worthy representatives of their ancestral culture." Never mind that immigrants gave their sweat, skill, and sometimes lives to their adopted country; that Americans profited from their presence in innumerable ways long before immigrants paraded their gifts on stage.[61] The demand for gifts resonated with claims that, on balance, immigrants got more than they gave. As Horace J. Bridges wrote in his book on becoming an American, the immigrant ought to ask "What can I give?" rather than "What can I get?" Even as they insisted that immigrants did "give America something in exchange for what they receive," gifts promoters deflected attention from contributions other than handicrafts and the performing arts.[62] The celebrations of immigrants' cultural gifts rendered their labor, their low wages, and the hardships of their daily lives invisible. A sympathetic spectator might conclude that the gifts on display symbolized larger immigrant offerings, but the gifts movement also fueled the conviction that everything immigrants had already given was insufficient, that they needed to give still more. However much it acclaimed colorful songs and embroideries as national assets, the immigrant gifts movement promoted the belief that immigrants owed a great deal to their adopted country.

The immigrant gifts approach resembled other Americanization strategies not only in demanding more from immigrants but also in casting them as people who could greatly benefit from Americanization. For all its talk of contributions, the gifts movement encouraged condescending attitudes. Its focus on rural folk productions rather than urban high culture contributed to the tendency to see immigrants as lowly peasants. Furthermore, although immigrants pioneered in mass culture—in the commercialized productions of Tin Pan Alley, vaudeville, and Hollywood—Americanizers did not celebrate these gifts. The gifts movement focused on what were perceived to be timeless traditions, not recent innovations. As a result, it positioned immigrants and their homelands as less modern than their new compatriots and nation. Jane Addams, for example, described the women who spun in Hull-House's labor museum as relics from premodern Europe: "The women of various nationalities enjoy the work and the recognition which it very properly brings them as mistresses of an old and honored craft, but the whir of the wheels recalls many a reminiscence and story of the old country, the telling of which makes a rural interlude in the busy town life." In this respect, the immigrant gifts movement resembled urban tourism, which encouraged tourists to see immigrants as cultural artifacts rather than full participants in industrial America.[63]

The tendency to see immigrants more as Old World artisans and laborers than, say, as highbrow Wagnerites, contributed to the tendency among native-born reformers to look down on their foreign-born clients. The gifts movement thus abetted the practice of channeling immigrant children into vocational programs rather than the academic classes that would prepare them for higher-paid and higher-status white-collar jobs. The social worker who advocated manual training for Italian children because of their artistic national heritage—"It is not for nothing that they have lived for centuries in the land of beauty"—shows some of the conclusions that could be drawn from the display of ethnic arts.[64]

Besides helping Americanizers to position recent arrivals in hierarchies of aptitude, culture, and class, the immigrant gifts movement helped Americanizers position themselves. Americanizers who determined which gifts to display claimed power over ethnic life—over which aspects of ethnicity would be valorized and what purposes ethnicity should serve. As a review of Hull-House's *Ajax* put it: "It has remained for an American woman to discover our Greeks to us—to rediscover him to himself." Despite the convoluted phrasing, the point was clear. Director Mabel Hay Barrows, not the Greek neighbors, was in charge.[65] Immigrant gifts events did not highlight industrial work or the activities of labor unions. They shied away from eroticism and unruliness. They were overwhelmingly secular displays that stood in contrast to the religious festivals of non-Protestant newcomers. They downplayed the nationalist politics that were so important to ethnic celebrations within immigrant communities. Whereas the ultimate goal of ethnic celebrations within ethnic groups was ethnic preservation, Americanizers placed more emphasis on U.S. national cohesion. They applauded specific ethnic arts as a national resource, not ethnicity per se. Finally, all the talk of gifts associated immigrants with festivity. Although some in the immigrant gifts movement were sympathetic to labor struggles and many others worked to alleviate squalid living and working conditions, the joyful displays they produced made these endeavors seem less urgent. Appreciating immigrant gifts posed little threat to the existing social order; it could and did exist in the midst of homogenizing crusades.[66]

In addition to asserting power over immigrants, gifts promoters asserted power over rival Americanizers from the more melting-pot-oriented branch of the movement. The native-born Americans who produced exhibits and festivals celebrating immigrant gifts used them to demonstrate their own insider status, their access to and knowledge of immigrant communities. Taking credit for such events let them show off their own expertise—to justify their claims to be expert mediators between natives and newcomers, the most fit leaders of the Americanization crusade.[67]

The Americanizers who embraced immigrant gifts certainly had much in common with the melting-pot school of Americanizers—including a desire for national unity, a zeal for transforming others, an eagerness to enhance their own power, and a belief that the United States represented modernity and progress. But the tendency to lump all Americanizers together deflects attention from the very real—and meaningful—differences between them. In the context of the early twentieth century, and especially of the World War I years, when calls for exclusion and 100 percent Americanism reached a fevered pitch, the celebration of immigrant gifts had radical implications for understandings of nationality. The immigrant gifts approach to Americanization differed from efforts to pour immigrants into Anglo-American molds. Whereas many melting-pot pageants featured immigrants who entered the pot in ethnic dress and emerged in ready-made American outfits, the participants in gifts pageants did not shed their colorful costumes. Instead, they marched down Main Street or danced across stage in folk clothing to show that they could contribute to national life without being completely melted down. The gifts approach—with its positive dramatizations of ethnic difference—provided a more pluralistic alternative to the homogenizing melting pot.[68]

Historians who have written on Progressive Era pluralism have focused on the writings of a handful of male intellectuals, Horace Kallen foremost among them. Few of the women who participated in the immigrant gifts movement have won comparable recognition. Nonetheless, their work did at least as much as Kallen's writings to advance pluralism among their contemporaries. Through their celebration of immigrant gifts, they taught their audiences—sometimes counting in the tens of thousands—to appreciate European and, to a lesser extent, other exogenous cultural productions. Through colorful, laudatory, displays of foreignness, they taught the value of difference.[69] They made pluralism palatable to native-born Americans by making it a matter of consumption.

In keeping with the consumerist appreciation of novelty and variety, immigrant gifts proponents criticized the pursuit of conformity. As institute founder Bremer said of the homogenizing strain of the Americanization movement: "There was ignorance in it; there was the arrogant assumption that everything American was intrinsically superior to anything foreign. There was fear in it. There were the germs of hate in it." Similarly, Esther Johnston, a New York City librarian, critiqued the melting pot for having "something that was a little chauvinistic about it." A GFWC booklet on Americanization went so far as to offer a replacement for the melting-pot metaphor: "We like to figure Americanization, not as a melting pot, but as a glorious garden plot where varying types of human beings can grow and develop each in his own good way on a common liberty-loving soil."[70] Instead of sterilizing the past, Americanizers should cultivate the future. And this, the GFWC booklet made clear, meant self-cultivation as well as the cultivation of transplants.

Immigrant gifts advocates went far beyond the argument that there should be room in American culture for imports to insist that native-born Americans needed Americanization just as much as anybody. As Bremer put it, "the need for a more sensible understanding and a more intelligent sympathy between Americans and foreigners is mutual." The president of the Nevada Federation of Women's Clubs revealed similar sentiments when she proclaimed: "Let us Americanize our American homes."[71] What did she mean by that? Surely not lessons in cooking and hygiene. No — American homes needed lessons in pluralism. This conviction can be seen in a GFWC tract that defined Americanization as "the adjustment of the American mind to admit the foreign born into democracy."[72] This tract placed much of the burden of Americanization on native-born Americans. Before immigrants could be assimilated, insular clubwomen and their social peers had to broaden their minds.

How could native-born Americans become more pluralistic? First, they needed to educate themselves about difference. In keeping with one GFWC leader's claims that Americanization entailed "sympathetic knowledge of the treasure brought to us by the races we seek to assimilate," GFWC publications urged potential Americanizers to study immigrant customs and contributions. "Know our immigrant races by knowing their literatures," admonished the GFWC's chairman of literature.[73] Martha S. F. Bent instructed would-be Americanizers to instill "the American spirit" by teaching "respect for alien history, tradition, and abilities." Yet another GFWC program guide advocated studying a particular national group for a deeper sympathy of the foreign-born. Although much of this literature focused on European immigrants, some Americanization programs encouraged members to study those with roots in China, Japan, and Mexico.[74]

The GFWC did more than urge greater knowledge; it took steps to disseminate it. The 1916 GFWC convention included a session titled: "And They Come Bearing Gifts." Six women of European birth delivered talks on their homelands and the contributions of their fellow hyphenated Americans. Further information on the foreign could be found in GFWC publications. Its Americanization bibliographies included books such as L. Villari's *Italian Life in Town and Country*. GFWC program guides urged members to invite immigrants to their meetings to provide insiders' perspectives on their communities. They also referred members to social workers, ethnic associations, teachers of foreign-born students, and, of course, immigrant gifts events.[75] The intent of Americanizers' study programs may have been to turn native-born women into more effective Americanizers, but the irony remained: to become better Americanizers, native-born women must first learn about the foreign. As a *General Federation Magazine* article that urged "an acquaintance and comprehension of the alien" put it, "our Americanization programs may profitably begin with ourselves."[76]

Yet opening minds was not enough. Americanizers must open their hearts. A GFWC program guide emphasized this point. It defined Americanization as "the preparation of the hearts of the native born to receive into full fellowship the foreign born." Those who would do Americanization work must do it in a spirit of sisterhood. "No one can do good Americanization work who has not a real love for human beings," asserted Caroline Hedger in another GFWC booklet. ". . . You cannot make Americans by going at the foreign born either in a hostile spirit or with an idea that you are a superior being, about to confer wisdom."[77] Like other Americanization experts associated with the GFWC, Hedger preached the need for greater tolerance among "old stock" Americans.

How could an eager Americanizer best open her mind and heart? By establishing contact with newcomers. The *General Federation Magazine* urged clubwomen to reach out to "enlightened and educated" immigrant women. "Invite them to club meetings and to become members. Invite them to tell the story of their race, to make plain the needs of their people. . . . Americanization cannot be imposed on a community, cannot be from the top down. It must be a getting together of all the elements, with exercise of the principles of give and take. . . . The time for studying the foreign-born within our gates by means of books from the shelves of libraries has passed, and the hour for personal, human contact has come." A later article in this magazine continued this theme: "If Italians are most numerous in your neighborhood . . . bring Italian neighbors into your meetings. Take from them what they have to give, and give to them your sympathetic appreciation."[78]

Some clubwomen followed through on these admonitions to mingle. One Massachusetts club reported that after it offered cooking classes for Italian women in the community, "these women in turn held classes for American women, giving instruction in the Italian methods of cooking chicken, pasta and macaroni."[79] In the absence of further details, we can only imagine how these meetings unfolded: condescension and hurt feelings in the first encounter (what do you mean we need to improve our cooking?); reciprocity, appreciation, and perhaps amazement in the second (you don't boil them for an hour?). But it was easier to preach sociability than to practice it. Etta Gifford Young, chairman of the Arizona Americanization committee, reported that club leaders' calls for outreach were not always heeded. "Plans for social contact are still in rather a nebulous stage, the 'love ye one another' doctrine being still of somewhat feeble growth in the hearts of many native Americans." The *General Federation Magazine* likewise revealed members' resistance to mingling with immigrants when it chastised mothers who kept their daughters from participating in pageants, "for fear that they will meet their social inferiors."[80]

Settlement house residents, International Institute workers, teachers, and librarians had greater success than most clubwomen in befriending immigrants, for their working lives often centered on such contacts. Like other settlement house leaders, Addams tried to provide for give-and-take between native-born residents and immigrant neighbors. Among its many activities, Hull-House sponsored social events intended to foster a sense of neighborliness. The YWCA's institute workers also threw parties in hopes of developing relations with neighborhood women. When friendships blossomed across ethnic lines, YWCA agents counted them as triumphs. Randilla Willard, of the Lewiston International Institute, gratefully reported that Lithuanian "girls" had invited her and other YWCA workers to one of their houses for a "banquet of real Lithuanian food." She took note of this invitation in her official report because it struck her as better than a royal feast: it represented "a union of the native and foreign-born people." A pamphlet on home teachers also waxed enthusiastic over friendly socializing. It commended a teacher for establishing such good rapport with her students that they drew musical instruments from their hiding places, dragged costumes "from the seclusion of foreign-looking trunks and boxes," and overcame their timidity to show the exquisite pieces of handwork they had made.[81]

However much settlement residents, institute workers, teachers, and librarians asserted that it was possible for upper-crust, native-born women to reach out to working-class immigrant women on a friendly basis, most would-be Americanizers who sympathized with the GFWC's strictures found it difficult to do so. Never mind that many clubwomen employed immigrant women in their kitchens—the power dynamics that characterized these relationships (not to mention gulfs of ethnicity, language, and custom) created significant barriers to understanding, open-heartedness, and friendship. But the immigrant gifts movement provided safe, sanitized, and structured contacts removed from the patterns and politics of daily life that few could find objectionable. As one clubwoman said, "It can't hurt any normal, healthy girl to see how the other half of the world lives, or thinks, or how a Swedish Fjallmas-polka is danced or a Spanish scarf is made."[82] Such contacts would not throw the social order into turmoil, but they might broaden the girl's mind and expand her heart, in the process making her more fully American.

The emphasis on Americanizing "old stock" Americans casts a new light on gifts events. The Americanizing ambitions that motivated them extended well beyond the immigrants who laid wreaths at Columbia's feet, for they were intended to make better Americans of the native-born spectators as well. As the former absorbed the spirit of patriotism, the latter would learn the lessons of pluralism. A description of a "festival and pageant of nations" went so far as to single out the native-born as the group in need of education when it claimed that the event aimed "to interpret, not America to the foreigner, but the foreigner to America."[83] What better way to foster an open mind and heart than through immigrant gifts?

The presentation of gifts could be profoundly moving. A pageant titled "The Gift-Bearers" led at least one spectator to feel an intense sense of empathy with the immigrant performers. "And as each girl, representing a different nation, moved forward in the bright costume of her native country, the spectators realized that here was something deeper than pageantry. . . . For a sudden moment one's imagination left the stage with its brilliant groups clad in strange foreign costumes, and pictured the devious ways and long weary journeys by which these courageous little immigrants had traveled to appear in this Pageant of Nations. And when the performance was over, a deeper understanding had been implanted in the hearts of both Americans and foreign-born peoples."[84] We might question the nature of this "deeper understanding"—and especially its suggestion that immigrants traveled to the United States in order to participate in gifts events. But it is harder to discount the viewer's surge of emotions. For all that they obscured, gifts events rendered immigrants sympathetically. They could move even those disinclined to see any value in diversity. Supporters could only rejoice in testimonials like the one offered by a visitor to an Arts and Crafts of the Homelands exhibit. He had entered reluctantly, convinced that the money would be better spent on Americanization speakers. But after seeing a spirited Old World dance he reconsidered his homogenizing impulses: "I don't know . . . how much good this exhibition has done the foreign born but I do know that it has made a better American of me."[85]

The emphasis on changing native-born Americans along with newcomers reveals that the gifts movement arose not only from the practical concerns of moneymaking, relationship building, and self-positioning, but also from ideas about citizenship. By insisting that native-born Americans needed Americanization as much as newcomers, the immigrant gifts movement advanced a conception of nationality that was far more pluralistic than competing understandings of nationality at the time. Taken together, the calls to think, feel, and act in a more cosmopolitan fashion generated an understanding of what it meant to be American that stood in sharp contrast to the conviction that true Americanness lay in cherishing a collection of local traditions inherited from white colonists and their upper-crust heirs or that true Americanness lay in homogeneity. According to the immigrant gifts line of thought, true Americanism meant less nativism on the part of the natives. It meant receptivity to some forms of cultural difference and a willingness to welcome immigrants (especially those perceived as white) even if they retained some Old World trappings. Indeed, it meant welcoming them precisely because they brought vestiges of the Old World to the United States.

What explains this pluralistic approach to citizenship? Progressive Era internationalism deserves some credit. Many settlement house workers saw international understanding as a means to promote peace, and they situated their work with immigrants in this larger context. Jane Addams applauded "cosmopolitan neighborhoods" such as the one surrounding Hull-House for producing "an unprecedented internationalism which is fast becoming too real, too profound, too widespread, ever to lend itself to warfare."[86] U.S. YWCA leaders developed a greater appreciation for internationalism through their organization's association with the world YWCA, then headquartered in London. One International Institute worker described the organization's activities as a precursor to "international government work." The General

Federation also had strong internationalist leanings. Even as it committed itself to Americanization at its 1916 convention, it also embraced the "cultivation of the true Pan-American spirit." Speaking before the assembled delegates, William Norman Guthrie urged women's clubs "to study and create in us all a more hospitable frame of mind towards all things noble, tending so to make us truly cosmopolitan."[87] Two years later, peace activist Lucia Ames Mead repeated the call for cosmopolitanism in the *General Federation of Women's Clubs Magazine*. "The American woman must say: I am first of all a human being, a citizen of the world, a child of God; second, I am a woman; third, I am a privileged woman, more privileged than most other women on the globe in opportunity, security and education and far more privileged than women of past ages." Only after professing these three identities should she see herself as a "citizen of this beloved land."[88] Such cosmopolitanism lent itself to pluralism.

If internationalism went hand in hand with pluralism, the reverse was also true. The outbreak of war in Europe posed a significant challenge to pluralism not only because of the militant patriotism it engendered but also because contemporaries commonly traced the origins of the war to ethnic difference within the Austro-Hungarian Empire. This reading of history contributed to the antiethnic leanings of melting-pot Americanizers who demanded that Irish-Americans, Italian-Americans, and others drop their hyphens and fully assimilate. But there were alternative interpretations of the war more conducive to pluralist visions. These held that the conflict had originated in cultural intolerance, not ethnic difference. As Julius Drachsler wrote in his book on democracy and assimilation, "the fateful antecedents of the war can be traced back step by step, until the roots of the great conflict are discovered in national policies of coercion, cultural and economic."[89]

Drachsler's line of reasoning had a strong following among immigrant gifts supporters. GFWC publications, for example, devoted considerable attention to oppressive nationalism within Europe. In a suggested program for Americanization, Mary Gibson wrote: "No study is complete which does not carefully consider the results of language compulsion and restriction in Alsace-Lorraine, Poland, Croatia, Czecho-Slovakia, Serbia and Armenia." A GFWC Americanization tract annotated a bibliography on "Language Restriction and Compulsion," with the terse comment: "Shows how America may profit by oppressor's mistakes." Another GFWC program, on the Bohemian people, covered government suppression of language, schools, and national customs. The consequences? Bitterness and a lack of loyalty.[90] The lesson was clear: ethnic tensions and national discord could be traced to the kinds of policies advocated by Americanizers of the 100 percent American school. Rather than solving the problem of diversity, they were contributing to it.

The issue went beyond the origins of the war to include the nature of the adversary. Pluralists claimed that the Central Powers stood for an autocratic denial of self-expression. In the words of one Americanization tract: "Teutonic egotism and imperialism conspired during the last quarter century against the cultures of peoples whom they sought to absorb or assimilate. Like a ravaging reptile they covered their prey with the slime of contempt in order the easier to swallow them." Similarly, the *Survey* equated wartime English-only policies with the Germans' efforts to stifle the Polish language.[91] Pluralists compared the melting-pot approach to nationality to the coercive tactics of the Central Powers.

The United States and its allies, in contrast, stood for national self-determination. Although this is often taken to mean ethnic rights within Europe, the commitment to national self-determination had a domestic corollary: national self-expression within the United States. Settlement house worker Grace Abbott made this point in her book, *The Immigrant and the Community*: "The demand for 'nationalism' in Europe has been a democratic demand that a people shall be free to speak the language which they prefer and to develop their own national culture and character. . . . Here in the United States, we have the opportunity of working out a democracy founded on internationalism. If English, Irish, Polish, German, Scandinavian, Russian, Magyar, Lithuanian, and all the other races of the earth can live together, each making his own distinctive contribution to our common life . . . we shall meet the American opportunity."[92] Just as democracy in Europe meant the realization of national ambitions, democracy in the United States meant the ability (among European immigrants at least) to retain some ethnic distinctiveness. The achievement of this goal depended on open-mindedness, tolerance, and even an appreciation of ethnic expression—precisely the values the immigrant gifts movement worked to convey.

To gifts promoters, events in Europe did more than prove the soundness of their relatively pluralistic approach to nationalism. In their eyes, the war gave their efforts to promote pluralism global significance. Many of those who espoused U.S. pluralism claimed that it provided a model for international understanding. As Randilla Willard, secretary of the Lewistown International Institute proclaimed at the end of a "one from many" pageant, the gathering had "brought out the spirit of internationalism."[93] If the outside world, and particularly the warring European powers, could only emulate the United States, then international understanding and cooperation would triumph over nationalistic animosity and conflict. If all the peoples of the world would only learn from U.S. pluralism, then the world would become more harmonious without becoming completely homogeneous.

By holding up an idealized vision of the United States as a model for the world, Progressive Era gifts promoters resembled the melting-pot Americanizers who were equally convinced of American superiority and its world-regenerative destiny. Where they differed was in arguing that American greatness inhered less in its aloofness—in its city-on-the-hill qualities—than in its capacity to absorb the best from around the world. Rather than seeing foreignness as threatening, they saw it as a potential source of novelty, pleasure, and entertainment. This appropriative outlook suggests that internationalist sensibilities and wartime thinking about self-determination can only partially explain the pluralist visions of gifts promoters. Their receptivity to difference emerged from the context of cosmopolitan domesticity, the fashionable world, exotic entertainments, and fictive travel—that is, from the consumers' imperium. This does not mean that every gifts promoter had a cosey corner, spent enormous sums on Parisian styles, attended Dutch teas, and read Stoddard's travel lectures, but that the surrounding values of the consumers' imperium contributed to their appreciation of foreignness.

Even busy reformers could not ignore these values. *Charities* magazine, the journal of record for social workers, ran ads admonishing readers: "Now is the time to have your cosy corners fixed up in true Oriental style A LA PERSIA OR INDIA." The *Survey* (the successor to *Charities*) also taught reformers the appeal of foreign artistry by running advertisements for "Art Embroidered Linens from Italy." The various exhibits put on by Hull-House show that reformers got the message. The Chicago Arts and Crafts Society displayed boxes, trays, vases, and other artifacts with Persian, Japanese, Chinese, and Arabian motives, along with objects inspired by European designs. The Hull-House Labor Museum showcased a collection of foreign textiles that would have been the envy of an eclectic decorator: German embroideries, Norwegian fringes, Mexican serapes, and Venetian velvets. Hull-House shops catered to cosmopolitan tastes by selling textiles and other handicrafts to decorators in search of Old World craftsmanship.[94] Like the Hull-House affiliates who promoted immigrant handicrafts, clubwomen also stressed the value of the goods made by immigrants and the pleasure they would bring to the native-born purchaser. As the GFWC's chairman of art wrote in a piece on preserving immigrant handicrafts, "The products of many of these industries are needed by us."[95] Gifts promoters knew the tastes of the cosmopolitan decorator.

The craving for aristocratic cachet also resonated with the immigrant gifts movement. True, gifts promoters celebrated humble peasant arts — but so did European lords and ladies. French designers took inspiration from peasant dress in part because European elites patronized ethnic arts. The immigrant gifts movement owed a great deal to the European discovery of ethnicity. Across Europe, local boosters worked to attract tourists with displays of national folk culture. From Germany's Volkkunst museums to France's provincial museums and Sweden's open-air Skansen museum, institutions sprang up in the late nineteenth century to preserve and exhibit handicrafts, local music, and traditional life.[96]

Such preservation efforts spread from Europe to its imperial domains. In India, British officials collected Indian arts and crafts, established museums to aid cultural preservation, and made Indian soldiers set aside their Western uniforms for turbans, sashes, and tunics. Although many of the Western women resident in India worked to "civilize" the natives through missionary activities, teaching, and social reform, some supported endeavors to promote local culture and traditions. This interest in ethnic arts extended well beyond India. In 1906 Canadians formed a handicraft guild to preserve and promote the cottage industries of Canada and to "encourage and assimilate the varied beautiful crafts which newcomers were bringing in from countries world famed for a proficiency in the manual arts." Folkloric exhibits in Europe, India, and elsewhere often represented an invention of tradition as much as an attempt at cultural preservation, but contemporaries understood them as preserving their local and national pasts, or, in the Canadian case, the local and national traditions of newcomers.[97]

These wider attempts at cultural preservation influenced the immigrant gifts movement within the United States. Who did Viggo Bovbjerg credit for his manual on Danish folk dances, published in Chicago? The Danish Folk Dance Society of Copenhagen. What inspired the Italian Industrial School located in the Richmond Hill House in New York City? Similar schools in Italy. Indeed, the founders invited Caroline Amari, a patroness of the society of Italian Feminine Industries at Rome to come to New York and organize classes in embroidery and lace making among young Italian women. They also recruited Queen Margherita, a patron of the Roman school, to lend her name to the one in New York.[98] Immigrant gifts proponents marketed their handicraft displays by noting some of the items had won prizes in European exhibitions. They situated their folk festivals in the context of

5.9. Advertisements from *Peasant Art in Austria and Hungary*, ed. Charles Holme (1911), vi. Courtesy of the University of Illinois at Urbana-Champaign Library.

Bayreuth, Oberammergau, and the Tuscan Palio. They clinched their case for ethnic dances and festivals by pointing out that the large towns of Scotland and England were already promoting such recreations.[99]

Just as fashionable women imagined ties to well-dressed aristocrats, immigrant gifts promoters saw themselves as associates of the titled women who presided over handicraft schools, the wealthy collectors of peasant crafts, and the founders of folk museums. It was no coincidence that Hull-House's Labor Museum brought in Italian women to demonstrate spindle usage around the time a volume on peasant art in Italy (published in London and Paris as well as New York) informed its readers that "the spindle and distaff are returning to their place of honour despite the ever increasing progress of machinery."[100] Americans who extolled immigrant gifts could, and did, imagine themselves as part of a transatlantic community that included the distinguished members of countless European folklore, folk dance, and arts and crafts societies (ill. 5.9). They sought out arts promoters on their travels to Europe and invited them to visit the United States. And, at times, they collaborated: the Hull-House Players, for example, traveled to Ireland to perform with the Abbey Players.[101] Just as wearing Paris fashions implied an affiliation with the haute monde, so did promoting immigrant gifts.

The immigrant gifts movement also can be linked to the enthusiasm for exotic foods and entertainments. It should come as no surprise that Americanization teas featured immigrant cooking, for the clubwomen who produced them moved in the same social circles as those who prepared foreign-themed meals. The numerous International Institute parties featuring the national songs and dresses of the immigrant guests can be seen as the ultimate in exotic entertainments. Recognizing the European tastes of native-born reformers, G. Ricciardi advertised his "Torrone — Italian Nougat Christmas Pastetti" in the YWCA magazine, *Foreign-Born*. Like the hostesses and costumed partygoers who feigned foreignness, members of the immigrant gifts movement sometimes pretended to be foreign themselves. In 1902, for instance, the Public Schools Athletic League raised more than $2,000 in a folk dancing performance at the Waldorf-Astoria. It started with an English maypole dance and ended with the Swedish Fjainaspolska. The performers were not the girls the organization served, however, but affluent volunteers, who "became for the time Italians, Danes, Russians — a regular congress of nations."[102]

Finally, the interest in immigrant gifts owed a significant debt to the culture of travel. Travel writings and lectures told tourists, or would-be tourists, to journey with an open mind and appreciate the new customs they encountered. They gloried in native costumes, peasant life, folk dances, folk songs and other manifestations of local distinctiveness (ill. 5.10). Those fortunate enough to really travel abroad did, indeed, seek out ethnic events. As folk dance promoter Luther Hasley Gulick pointed out, "one of the most keenly sought after enjoyments of those who visit the old countries, is to watch the people on their holidays; holidays that are marked by the national dances."[103] These admonitions contributed to the conviction that foreign travel served as a credential for work among immigrants. What qualified Elizabeth Howe to serve as director of the International Institute of Niagara Falls? According to a colleague, "Her long residence in Europe, France, Russia, a journey around the world and twelve years in Rome, Italy, have given her just the necessary background for work of this kind."[104]

Beyond urging an open-minded approach to the world, the culture of international travel encouraged Americans to view immigrants as a touristic resource. Those who could not voyage abroad could take advantage of foreignness at home. Reporting on a Midsummer's Eve festival seen in

DANCING THE TARENTELLA.

This joyous and favorite dance in Naples, originated long ago in the Tarentine district and quickly spread throughout Southern Italy. 'Tis a pretty scene as the dancers move in graceful curves to the music of the castinets, with much posing and bowing. But to enjoy its picturesqueness you must supply the bright colors of the costumes, purple breeches and red turbans, the scroll work of gold lace on the coats of the men, and the equally showy costumes of the women.

5.10. "Dancing the Tarentella," *Bay View Magazine* 16 (Feb. 1909): 278. Courtesy of the University of Minnesota Libraries, Minneapolis.

Sweden, Chicago high school teacher Mary Wood Hinman called for a similar spirit of festivity in the United States. Refusing to be jealous of such folk traditions, she exclaimed: "Think of the opportunity for variety we have—greater than any other country. Think of the number and variety of our foreigners!" When the Cosmopolitan Club of Fremont, Ohio, studied Scandinavia, members presented papers on peasant life in Norway, folk life in Sweden, and "Scandinavians in America."[105] In a similar vein, a guidebook to the "real New York" claimed that "New York is the fourth greatest Italian city in the world, and contains more Italians than Florence and Venice put together." Those who had not had the opportunity to do the Italian tour—a tour in which Florence and Venice figured prominently—could at least enjoy the spectacle of Italians performing Italianness within the United States. Just as the advertisements for international travel that ran in *Charities* magazine prompted readers to associate their clients with picturesque Europeans, the folk dance teachers who reported having learned their dances abroad associated these dances with tourism. The tendency to see immigrants through touristic lenses can explain why Addams proposed to have the workers in the Hull-House Labor Museum dress in national costume. More than just representing preindustrial labor practices, costumed spinners and weavers would afford glimpses of the Old World akin to those sought out by globe-trotters.[106]

To say that the immigrant gifts movement emerged from the consumers' imperium is to tell only part of the story, however, for gifts events in turn contributed to consumerist appraisals of the foreign. Like Orientalist interiors, Paris fashions, exotic entertainments, and armchair travel, gifts events taught that the wider world had much to offer the United States. Like other components of the consumers' imperium, they encouraged a sense of imagined community that crossed national lines. Like other components, they taught Americans to view the foreign through the eyes of the consumer. Like other components, they shaped touristic outlooks. And like other components, they crystallized around a sense of loss.

This discontent with modern American culture is overlooked in writings—both by immigrant gifts proponents and later historians—that present immigrant gifts as a means of generational reconciliation within immigrant families. The generational thesis is not without merit. Native-born reformers who taught Old World folk arts often described such efforts as a means of bringing immigrant parents together with their over-Americanized children. Writing in the *Survey*, Mary McDowell claimed: "The too rapid Americanization of these children into pert young people without respect for authority is a dangerous problem. We should make every effort towards encouraging the children of the foreign-born to appreciate the culture of their parents' native land." McDowell worried that children who disdained their parents would not develop an appropriate respect for authority. Addams too advocated immigrant gifts as a way to overcome generational gulfs. She regaled her audiences with touching stories of Americanized sons and daughters who were astonished to learn of their mothers' skill in handicrafts or music. In these stories, the chastened children learned to respect their mothers and their Old World culture, and they ended up questioning whether "the new was the best."[107]

No doubt gifts promoters such as McDowell and Addams did believe that a proper valuation of folk culture could remedy the extraordinary generational tensions between immigrants and their Americanized children. But their stories of estrangement tell us as much about themselves as about immigrant family dynamics. They spoke so movingly about generational gulfs because they too experienced them. They questioned whether the new was best because they yearned for the old just as much as any immigrant mother. Like the stereotypical immigrant parents alienated from their Americanized children, immigrant gifts promoters regarded mass culture with a skeptical eye. They promoted folk arts so enthusiastically because they saw them as a remedy for U.S. commercial entertainments. Playground workers in Milwaukee, for example, hailed folk dances as a counter to amusement parks and penny arcades. Likewise Addams's enthusiasm for European folk dances can be understood more fully in light of her condemnation of popular dance halls.[108] In an address on the public school and the immigrant child, Addams expressed a preference for immigrant folk culture over commercial amusements: "We send young people to Europe to see Italy, but we do not utilize Italy when it lies about the schoolhouse. If the body of teachers in our great cities could take hold of the immigrant colonies, could bring out of them their handicrafts and occupations, their traditions, their folk songs and folk lore . . . they would discover that by comparison that which they give them now is a more meretricious and vulgar thing."[109]

This antipathy to commercial amusements emerged from a larger sense of dissatisfaction with the staggering changes that were remaking the United States. Addams revealed her opposition to the surrounding industrial order when she lauded immigrant gifts as "a wonderful factor for poesy in cities frankly given over to industrialism."[110] A Hull-House report blaming the loss of immigrants' "distinctive national features" on "the city's busy life" can be read as a critique of urbanization. Ultimately, the immigrant gifts movement lamented modernity itself. Why support folk dancing? Because, as one playground worker put it, folk dances offered an opportunity to express a "love of beauty and rhythm for which modern life seems to afford little opportunity."[111]

As these critical assessments of commercial amusements, industrialization, urbanization, and modernity suggest, immigrant gifts promoters valued immigrant offerings all the more because they were dissatisfied with modern American culture. Gifts promoters found that the most compelling way to articulate their own longings for the past was through the figure of the deracinated immigrant who had experienced changes in a matter of years akin to those that reformers born in the mid-nineteenth century had experienced over decades. Wrote settlement house worker Lillian Wald: "Great is our loss when a shallow Americanism is accepted by the newly arrived immigrant, more particularly by the children, and their national traditions and heroes are ruthlessly pushed aside."[112] The pageant producer who expressed shock at finding that among the thousands of Serbians in New York, not a single national costume could be found, also latched onto the immigrant as a touchstone for cultural change. And so did Florence Nesbitt, author of a handbook on household management that questioned how far the United States should go in reducing immigrants to sameness. She admitted that the Italian and Polish women who gave up making decorative lace had more time for housekeeping, but these women lost something as well, for "Americanization is too often a ruthless destroyer of beauty and charm."[113] Immigrant women were not the only ones who were spending less time on handicrafts and more living up to the strictures of domestic scientists, but the image of the rootless immigrant threw the issue of disappearing traditions into particularly sharp relief.

The immigrant gifts movement had much in common with other manifestations of antimodernism, but it also had its own distinctive inflections. Latching onto immigrants as symbols of the rapidly disappearing past provided a unique lens through which to express discontent with modern life. The specter of the deracinated immigrant suggested that the problem was not just industrial capitalism, mass culture, standardization, and urbanization. It suggested that the problem had a specifically national dimension: Americanization.[114] Too much Americanization, that is, not too little. The more the United States made its mark on the world, the more precious local variations became. Members of the immigrant gifts movement took the antimodern critique of economic rationalization and joined it to a critique of the homogenizing impulses and militant nationalism that fired the melting pot. Reformers welcomed immigrant gifts not just because they were there but, perhaps more importantly, because they were afraid they would disappear. The immigrant gifts movement promoted cultural pluralism as both the apotheosis of Americanization and the antidote.

Their reservations about Americanization aligned immigrant gifts advocates with antimodernists outside the United States. From England to Australia, Mexico to France, commercialism, mass production, mass culture, and mass consumption struck many observers as quintessentially American. True, these developments did not originate in the United States, but the United States was well on its way to becoming a leading exporter of industrial management techniques, goods, capital, and entertainment. Returned migrants added to the impact of American corporations by introducing new clothing styles, culinary preferences, and house designs to their villages. Whereas admirers saw the United States as a harbinger of abundance, critics saw the United States as a dangerous economic competitor and a portent of the demise of high and folk culture.[115] Yes, European capitalism and imperialism also threatened local color, but the ever-spreading reach of American commercial might and political power focused attention on Americanization.

Although the immigrant gifts movement was primarily concerned about over-Americanization within the United States, members did express con-

5.11. "Americanized Italians," in Burton Holmes, *Burton Holmes Travelogues* (1920), 4:194.

cern about the global trend toward Americanization. Echoing the innumerable travel accounts that reported on Americanization overseas, they situated the changes they witnessed at home within a larger context of cultural loss. As one folk dancing advocate said of Europe, "The traveler sees less and less of that which is picturesque and different."[116] The relationship between European and American cultural loss struck gifts proponents as causal, not just coincidental. Colorless foreigners made colorless immigrants. Longtime immigrant gifts proponent Allen H. Eaton underscored the urgency of his cause by insisting that "folk culture is being destroyed at its source"—that "standardizing influences in the homelands themselves" were destroying the "simple home arts of the people" (ill. 5.11).[117]

Immigrant gifts proponents may have resembled European antimodernists in their concern about over-Americanization, but there were important differences between them, too. When people outside the United States deplored Americanization, they cast themselves as defenders of the local against outside influences. But antimodernists within the United States did not blame the ills of modern life on foreigners, for like antimodernists abroad they tended to regard the United States as being at the forefront of progress. Instead of blaming foreigners for modernism, the immigrant gifts movement held them up as the cure, by presenting them as representatives of the traditional world that was being left behind. For antimodernists outside the United States, defining the problem as Americanization enabled them to seek refuge in national self-assertion. But U.S. antimodernists did not regard any power as capable of colonizing the United States. For members of the immigrant gifts movement, opposition to Americanization took the form of imperialist nostalgia.

Anthropologist Renato Rosaldo coined the term "imperialist nostalgia" to explain the yearning feelings that agents of colonialism have displayed toward the "very forms of life they intentionally altered or destroyed." Rosaldo argues that those who suffer from imperialist nostalgia "mourn the passing of what they themselves have transformed." Although Rosaldo focuses on transformations within overseas colonial contexts such as the U.S. occupation of the Philippines, the concept can be broadened to include efforts at cultural transformation within the United States—including the Progressive Era Americanization campaign. In sum, Rosaldo's concept of imperialist nostalgia can be applied to the settlement house residents, YWCA workers, clubwomen, teachers, librarians, and other Americanization proponents who took the lead in the immigrant gifts movement. Like the colonial agents he discusses, they mourned the passing of what they saw as traditional cultures, even as they advanced cultural change through their Americanization activities. Like the colonial agents he discusses, they waxed nostalgic to avoid their own complicity.[118] Rather than countering their Americanizing ambitions, their immigrant gifts initiatives helped them make peace with their larger commitment to cultural transformation. Rather than being at odds with Americanization, their enthusiasm for immigrant gifts was an enabling concession. The immigrant gifts movement made Americanization more palatable by suggesting that it did not demand choices between homogeneity and difference, modernity and tradition, or social control and individual expression. Like the women who sampled the foreign goodies at Americanization teas, the consumers at the pinnacle of the American empire could have their cake and eat it too.

Conclusion

*The Global Production of
American Domesticity*

Looking back to the years between the Civil War and World War I, no one can deny the ascendant military and political power of the United States or the impressive volume and dollar value of its exports. William Stead was certainly on to something when he predicted the Americanization of the world. But his view of the United States as an expansive colossus tells us as much (if not more) about his own concerns and politics as it does about the United States in global context. Yes, U.S. manufactures took the world by storm, challenging the commercial supremacy of Britain and lesser European powers. But the currents that carried U.S. goods to foreign ports also circled back, carrying the bounty of the world to U.S. harbors.

The previous chapters counter the Americanization-of-the-world narrative that has shaped our perceptions of the United States at the dawn of the "American century." In contrast to Stead and those who have followed in his footsteps, this book reminds us that making a mark on the world did not mean remaining impervious to international influences. To the contrary, the more the United States expanded its commercial, political, military, and cultural presence, the more it brought home. The United States imported consumer goods and culture as well as people. And it did so not only from Europe but also from Asia, Latin America, the Middle East, Africa, Canada, the Caribbean, and the Pacific.

Rather than arguing that its ascendant power enabled the United States to stand aloof, this book argues that the richer and more powerful the

United States became, the more it could afford to import. Along with obtaining the wherewithal to purchase foreign treasures, a growing number of Americans developed imperial sensibilities. They came to see themselves as having needs that could no longer be satisfied and stature that could be no longer be sustained merely by home production. Rather than asserting their nationalism through buying American, countless U.S. consumers—women prominent among them—did so through buying into empire. Imports are often associated with weakness and exports with strength. But just as exports on unfavorable terms may reveal relations of dependency, imports on favorable terms can reveal the exercise of power. That is the case for the fin-de-siècle consumers' imperium.

It is not surprising that Stead missed this story, situated as he was across the Atlantic. If the *Titanic* had only avoided the iceberg, he might have gone on to write a very different account that placed the United States in a larger history of world-shrinking imperial networks. Yet even if Stead had made it to New York, I suspect that he would have dismissed the subjects covered by this book as mere curiosities. It was not until the end of the Cold War, well after Stead's untimely death, that the concept of globalization opened up the intellectual space to regard these developments as evidence of international relations.

Rather than fault Stead for his myopia, we should ask why his narrative has had such staying power. Why, more than a quarter century after the United States started running up large trade deficits, have we continued to neglect its history as an importing nation? Several explanations come to mind. First, the U.S. rise to superpower status after World War II helped underscore Stead's assessment of its clout. Second, the United States has been a preeminent exporter of mass culture, something with higher visibility than, say, copper ore and luxury items. Third, in contrast to other peoples who have had to come to grips with U.S. dominance, Americans have not regarded any one nation as capable of colonizing them. Hence even as U.S. historians have written about imports from particular countries and traced the paths of particular commodities, they have hesitated to proclaim the Japanization or Italianization of the United States. Finally, the staggering number of links between the United States and the wider world and the overwhelming range of goods that made it to U.S. shores have made it difficult to get a sense of the big picture.

Indeed, as my research took me from crockery to playground festivals, I was tempted to settle on a single site of consumption. Focusing on one topic—such as household decoration or food—would have made it easier to get a grasp on the corresponding literature and to track down elusive leads.

It would have enabled me to cover a broader expanse of years and thus to address change over time more fully. I could have paid significant attention to foreign producers and their labor, placed the United States in comparative perspective, considered government policy, grappled with men's roles in domestic consumption, and fleshed out the characters who people this account (or so I told myself when pondering how to proceed). And, conceivably, I could have done all this without abandoning any of the themes—ranging from secondhand empire to imperialist nostalgia—that provide revealing insights into this book's central concerns: the popularity of imports, the politics of cosmopolitanism, and the imperial aspects of domestic consumption.

True, each realm of consumption I studied suggested a different line of interpretation. Orientalist cosey corners patterned after European salons brought the issue of secondhand empire to mind more than Swiss travelogues and Swedish folk dances. Fashion pages suggested imagined communities exceptionally well because of their gossipy tone, and cooking writings drew my attention to popular geography because of their ethnographic bent. Just as travel club records prompted conclusions about the rise of a tourist mentality, immigrant gifts events made it hard to avoid thinking about nostalgia.

Although different realms of consumption suggested different lines of analysis, there are nevertheless plenty of resonances between them. The attractions of secondhand empire can be found not only in household furnishings but also in Orientalist fashions, curried eggs, lectures on the Taj Mahal, and native arts displays. The desire to affiliate with the global elite influenced not only choices in dress but also the cachet of French cuisine, ersatz visits to European watering spots, the royal patronage of lace-making classes, and the aristocratic tastes of Gilded Age decorators. American women faked foreignness in club meetings, ethnic pageants, theme rooms, and boudoir wear as well as in Dutch teas; they revealed a tourist mentality in their folk productions, souvenir collections, Spanish mantillas, and chop suey meals as well as in their armchair journeys. As for nostalgia, it permeated not only arts and crafts of the homelands exhibits but also eclectic handicraft ensembles, gauze renditions of peasant blouses, efforts to diversify industrialized diets, and the search for authentic tourist experiences. I may not have latched on to the same array of themes if I had focused on a particular realm of consumption, but, looking back, it seems I could have.

Yet even if I had approached the subject from a comparable number of interpretive angles, focusing on one realm of consumption would have resulted in a very different book. However much I insisted that it was about imports, cosmopolitanism, and empire, it would have been at heart a book about furniture or fashion or ethnic arts. Because it assays a range of topics—from macaroni eating to the touristic commodification of entire cultures—this book reveals something larger than the sum of its parts: the global production of American domesticity.

What does the global production of American domesticity imply? First, it took the world to produce American domesticity. Foreign workers made the rugs that lay in Chicago mansions, the porcelain found in Gopher Prairie china cabinets. They wove the silks and embroidered the underwear worn by well-to-do women in New York. They grew the coffee beans, sorted the tea leaves, and bottled the condiments that appeared in California cupboards. They changed the linens, loaded the baggage, and captured the eye when Americans turned tourist. And foreign-born performers provided some of the most colorful entertainment in Fourth of July celebrations and other community gatherings. This book shows that long before our own global age, U.S. domesticity depended on the labor of foreign producers, that the U.S. standard of living was a thoroughly imperial standard.

This book illuminates the global production of American domesticity in a second sense as well. It shows how white, native-born, well-to-do American women produced the globe. They fabricated foreignness in their national theme rooms, hat trimmings, Mexican fiestas, stereopticon expeditions, and playground festivals. The imaginary world they conjured up centered on self-gratification and fantasy fulfillment. It deflected attention from the real world, with its real conflicts, real inequities, and real commercial, social, political, and military interconnections. Despite the self-centered nature of these geographies, they had significant implications for global consciousness. They contributed to the illusion that the world could be known through an assortment of decontextualized things. They advanced the tendency to see the world as an imperial bazaar, as a global midway that existed for the pleasure of entitled consumers.

Whereas the first meaning of the global production of American domesticity centers on commercial relations, the second centers on a world view. But material and imaginative life cannot be separated so easily: while the consumption of imports led to the production of meaning, the production of meaning added to the attractions of imports. To appreciate this dynamic, we can trace a sample circuit, starting with imported foodstuffs. These, as we have seen, taught geographic lessons. Geographic consciousness in turn added to the allure of armchair travel. Fictive journeys encouraged touristic outlooks. The tourist mentality prompted reformers to see immigrants as cultural resources. Immigrant gifts events fostered nostalgic longings for a world untouched by the Americanizing juggernaut. Feelings of nostalgia enhanced the appeal of handmade foreign curios. And so on, in countless permutations. As objects and meanings encircled each other, they created an ever-expanding vortex. Though animated by the same ascendant national power as the Americanization surge, this vortex created an oppositional dynamic. Instead of flowing out, it spiraled in, stirring up the insatiable appetites and distorted world views of the consumers' imperium.

To their credit, the consumers who bought into this imperium felt a sense of engagement with the world beyond the United States—a conviction that it had much to offer. They wanted to be part of global currents; they appreciated foreign cultural production. They were curious about other peoples and customs. They valued broad-mindedness over narrow-mindedness, urbane internationalism over xenophobic nationalism. But despite their cosmopolitan aspirations, which stand out all the more starkly in the context of their times, they could not escape the insularity that marked their detractors, much less their imperial ambitions. They may not have struggled to keep the world at bay or to remake it in their own image, but they did want it to serve their interests.

This book shows that countless women in the late nineteenth- and early twentieth-century United States dealt with the confines of domesticity by turning their homes into imperial outposts and by escaping—if only imaginatively—into the wider world. However distressing their second-class citizenship, they could take comfort in being world-class consumers. They softened their subordination by luxuriating in the trappings of power. Yes, the various chapters show a yearning for connectedness, but they also show only superficial connections, mediated through goods and staged performances. Yes, they show a passion for imports, but they also show a greater valuation of products than the workers who made them. Yes, they show transnational affiliative impulses, but they also show a desire for differentiation. The consumers of this account appropriated the foreign to assert standing and mark status. From their privileged perspectives it seemed inconceivable that authority could ever accrue to foreign producers, whom they regarded as servile, if they regarded them at all, or that consumption had costs not easily measured in dollars. From the shelter of their well-stuffed cosey corners, it was easy to overlook how domestic pleasures had concrete consequences for international relations; how domestic consumption produced a world of enabling workers. Although the women who bought into the consumers' imperium prided themselves on their cosmopolitan perspectives, from the center of the vortex it was hard to see beyond their own desires, circling around and around.

Appendix of Travel Clubs

Club Name	Known Dates through 1920	Number of Members	Known Destinations through 1920	Source(s)
Alabama				
Highland Book Club, Birmingham	1894–98		"Countries"	Croly, *History of the Woman's Club Movement*
Thursday Literary Club, Selma	1890–98	12	"Foreign cities"	Croly, *History of the Woman's Club Movement*
Arizona				
Monday Club, Prescott	1895		France	GFWC State Federation Records
Sahuara Club, Safford	1901–12	20	Bay View course	GFWC State Federation Records
Self Culture Club, Glendale	1901	7	Bay View course	GFWC State Federation Records
Arkansas				
Aesthetic Club, Little Rock	1900		Paris	1900 GFWC convention
Bay View Reading Circle, Little Rock	1903–20	25		GFWC Local Club Records
Hawthorne Club, Little Rock	1886–98		"Travels"	Croly, *History of the Woman's Club Movement*
Quid Nunc Club, Little Rock	1897–1900		"Comprehensive studies of various countries," France, Holland	1900 GFWC convention; Croly, *History of the Woman's Club Movement*
Waverly Book Club	1898		"Travel"	Croly, *History of the Woman's Club Movement*
California				
Tourist section of the Ebell Society, Oakland	1876–98			Croly, *History of the Woman's Club Movement*
Travel Club, Los Angeles	1913–18	34–45	Russia	Winslow, *Official Register, Los Angeles Times*, Feb. 3, 1918
Travellers' Club, San Jacinto	1903–8	22		Winslow, *Official Register*

Colorado

Club	Years	No.	Places/Notes	Source
Bay View Reading Circle, Fort Morgan	1910–11	25		GFWC *Directory*, 1911
Current Event and Travel Club, Fort Collins	1913–18	23–25		Winslow, *Official Register*
Fortnightly Club, Longmont	1894–98	40	"Tourist club"	Croly, *History of the Woman's Club Movement*
Isabella Tourist Club, Gunnison	1908–18	25–30		Winslow, *Official Register*
Isabelle Tourist Club, Grand Junction	1892–95			GFWC Local Club Records
Monday Literary Club	1885–94		Continental Europe, including England, Holland, Hungary, Italy, Germany, Russia, Scandinavia	Croly, *History of the Woman's Club Movement*
Sphinx Club, Denver	1895–98	25	England, France, Germany, Italy, Portugal, Scotland, Spain, Switzerland, Wales	Croly, *History of the Woman's Club Movement*
Tourist Club, Trinidad	1891–1966	16–30	"Foreign countries"	GFWC Local Club Records; Winslow, *Official Register; List of Officers*, 1899
Woman's Club of Denver, art and literature department	1896–98		Holland, Spain	Croly, *History of the Woman's Club Movement*
Woman's Club, Fowler	1905	15	Followed Stoddard's Lectures	GFWC Local Club Records
Woman's Club, Ouray	1897–98	25	"Different countries"	Croly, *History of the Woman's Club Movement*

Connecticut

Club	Years	No.	Places/Notes	Source
English Literary Club, Bridgeport	1879–98		"Occasional evenings of travel, and short trips, as one from Damascus to Jerusalem"; Australia, Holland	Croly, *History of the Woman's Club Movement*
Four-Corners Club	1898		Germany	Croly, *History of the Woman's Club Movement*
Traveler's Club, Danbury	1876–1918	15–40		Winslow, *Official Register;* GFWC Local Club Records
Woman's Club of New Britain	1875–98		Egypt, Mexico, USA	Croly, *History of the Woman's Club Movement*

(continued)

Club Name	Known Dates through 1920	Number of Members	Known Destinations through 1920	Source(s)
Georgia				
Travel Study Club, Atlanta	1913	24		Winslow, *Official Register*
Illinois				
Heliades Club	1881–91		Abyssinia, Afghanistan, Arabia, "Atlantic islands," Australia, Austria, Belgium, Beloochistan, British India, China, Cochin-China, the Congo, Denmark, "east coast of Africa," East India, Egypt, England, European Russia, France, "Grahams Land," Greece, Guineas, Holland, Ireland, Italy, Japan, Madagascar, Manchuria, Melanesia, Micronesia, New Zealand, North Pole, Norway, Nubia, Patagonia, Persia, Polynesia, Portugal, Prussia, Sahara, Scotland, Senegambia, Siberia, Soudan, southern Africa, Spain, Sweden, Switzerland, Toorkistan, Turkey, Wales	Croly, *History of the Woman's Club Movement*
Highland Park Woman's Club	1900		Holland, Ireland, Norway, Poland	1900 GFWC convention
Hull-House Women's Club	1898		Lectures on "foreign cities"	*Hull-House Bulletin*
Hyde Park Travel Club	1874–1918	70–250	"Through the Heart of Africa," "Across Africa and down the Congo," Algiers, Andora, Arabia, Argentina, Australia, Austria, Belgium, Bermuda, Bolivia, Brazil, Burma, Canada, Ceylon, Chile, China, Colombia, Cuba, Denmark, Ecuador, Egypt, England, France, Germany, Greece, Holland, India, Italy, Ireland, Jamaica, Japan, Korea, Mexico,	Winslow, *Official Register*; Hyde Park Travel Club Records, Chicago Historical Society

Club	Dates	Number	Study topic / countries	Source
Kenwood Fortnightly Club	1893–96		Morocco, New Guinea, Norway, Palestine, Panama, Persia, Peru, Philippines, Portugal, Puerto Rico, Russia, Sandwich Islands, Scotland, Siam, Spain, Sweden, Switzerland, Syria, Turkey, USA, Wales	1896 GFWC convention; *New Cycle*
Klio Club, Chicago	1893		"Great cities of the world," Japan	*New Cycle*
Lawndale Woman's Club, Chicago	1878–98	40	India	Croly, *History of the Woman's Club Movement*
Millard Avenue Club	1896		"Girdled the earth in the study of different countries," France	1896 GFWC convention
Tourist Club, Lewistown	1895–1999	12–35	India, China, Japan, France	GFWC notebook; Tourist Club Records in Rasmussen Museum, Lewistown, Illinois
Travel Class, Chicago	1903–13	131	Argentina, Austria-Hungary, Belgium, Bermuda, Bolivia, Brazil, Canada, Chile, China, England, France, Germany, Hawaii, Holland, Iceland, India, Ireland, Italy, Japan, Korea, Mexico, Norway, Panama, Peru, Philippines, Poland, Porto Rico, Russia, Scotland, Spain, Sweden, Switzerland, USA, Venezuela, Wales	Winslow, *Official Register*
Travelers' Club, Greenfield	1913	20		Winslow, *Official Register*
Travelers' Club, Virginia	1903–18	24–30		Winslow, *Official Register*
Travellers, Kankakee	1903	35		Winslow, *Official Register*
Tuesday Art and Travel Class, Chicago	1908–18	406–500		*Chicago Tribune*, Jan. 16, 1916; Winslow, *Official Register*
Wednesday Club, Jacksonville			"Travel"	Croly, *History of the Woman's Club Movement*
Woman's Club, Aurora	1889–90	28		Croly, *History of the Woman's Club Movement*
Woman's Club, Austin	1896–99	70	Travel	*List of Officers and Directors*, 1899
Woman's Club, Evanston	1889–98		Finland, Russia	Croly, *History of the Woman's Club Movement*

(continued)

Club Name	Known Dates through 1920	Number of Members	Known Destinations through 1920	Source(s)
Indiana				
Amaranth Club, New Albany	1892–93		Germany	Croly, *History of the Woman's Club Movement*
Bay View Reading Circle, Mooresville	1914	25		GFWC *Directory*, 1914
Mary-Martha Club	1891–98	25	Denmark, England, France, Holland, USA	Croly, *History of the Woman's Club Movement*
Round Table Club	1898	20	Africa, Cuba, Greece, Ireland, Mexico, Scotland	Croly, *History of the Woman's Club Movement*
Tourist Club, Des Moines	1895–99	25		*List of Officers and Directors*, 1901
Tourist Club, Evansville	1913–18	20		Winslow, *Official Register*
Tourist Club, Frankfort	1889–1918	30	Italy, Switzerland, "systematic study of the different countries of the world"	*New Cycle*; *Woman's Cycle*; Winslow, *Official Register*; Croly, *History of the Woman's Club Movement*
Tourist Club, Lebanon	1918	15–20		Winslow, *Official Register*
Tourist Club, Muncie	1900–1903	12		1900 GFWC Convention; Winslow, *Official Register*; *Club Woman*
Tourist Club, Noblesville	1918	30		Winslow, *Official Register*
Tourist Club, Portland	1913–18	16–20		Winslow, *Official Register*
Tourist Club, Princeton	1918	18		Winslow, *Official Register*
Tourist Club, Shelbyville	1908	12		Winslow, *Official Register*
Tourist Club, Sheridan	1913–18	16–20		Winslow, *Official Register*
Travelers' Club, Huntington	1913–18	15		Winslow, *Official Register*
Woman's Study Club, Michigan City	1900–1904	60	Travel	*List of Officers and Directors*, 1904
Iowa				
Bay View Club, Goldfield	1917		GFWC Local Club Records	
Federated Woman's Club, Fonda	1900–1914		Bay View Program	GFWC Local Club Records
Friends in Council, Cresco	1897	13	British Isles, Norway	GFWC Local Club Records
History and Travel Club, Hawkeye	1900–1918	22–31		Winslow, *Official Register*

Club	Dates	No.	Places studied	Sources
O.O.P. Club, Marion	1900		Foreign lands	GFWC Local Club Records
Tourist Club, Cedar Rapids	1881–87	30	"Imaginary tour of the world, country by country"	Winslow, *Official Register;* Croly, *History of the Woman's Club Movement*
Tourist Club, Des Moines	1892–1918	20–30		Winslow, *Official Register;* Croly, *History of the Woman's Club Movement*
Tourist Club, Fairbank	1908–15	27		GFWC notebook; Winslow, *Official Register*
Tourist Club, Forest City	1908–18	27–37		Winslow, *Official Register*
Tourist Club, Lamont	1913–18	16–37		Winslow, *Official Register*
Tourist Club, McGregor	1894–1990	26–40	Scotland, all Europe "except Poland and the Balkan States," USA, "far places"	GFWC notebook; Winslow, *Official Register;* clipping sent by Elizabeth F. Moe, McGregor, Iowa
Tourist Club, Manchester	1892–1903	20	Egypt	Winslow, *Official Register;* Croly, *History of the Woman's Club Movement*
Tourist Club, Marcus	1912–18	31	Great Britain	GFWC notebook; Winslow, *Official Register;* letter from Madge V. Drefke, Marcus, Iowa
Tourist Club, Mason City	1918	18		Winslow, *Official Register*
Tourist Club, Ottumwa	1891–1918	15		Winslow, *Official Register*
Tourist Club, Rockwell City	1908–18	30–44		Winslow, *Official Register*
Tourist Club, Sioux City	1913	15		Winslow, *Official Register*
Tourist Club, West Union	1894–1918	25–50	Constantinople, England, France, Japan, Rome, Russia	1896 GFWC convention; *New Cycle;* Winslow, *Official Register;* Croly, *History of the Woman's Club Movement*
Tourists, Cedar Rapids	1894		*New Cycle*	
Travel Club, Sheldon	1897–1918	19–35		Winslow, *Official Register*
Travel Club, Webster City	1913–18	12		Winslow, *Official Register*
Tuesday Tourist Club, Oelwein	1893–1918	25–35		Winslow, *Official Register*
Woman's Club, Dallas Center	1896	20	Canada, Central America, Mexico, Netherlands, Palestine, Scandinavian countries	GFWC Local Club Records

(continued)

Club Name	Known Dates through 1920	Number of Members	Known Destinations through 1920	Source(s)
Woman's Club, Marshalltown, travel department	1885–98			Croly, *History of the Woman's Club Movement*
Kansas				
Monday Tourist Club, Topeka	1903–8	17		Winslow, *Official Register*
Tourist Club, Neosho Falls	1903	17		Winslow, *Official Register*
Tourist Club, Wakeeney	1908–18	15		Winslow, *Official Register*
Travelers' Club, Burlington	1903	21		Winslow, *Official Register*; Croly, *History of the Woman's Club Movement*
Travelers' Club, Edna	1903–8	12		Winslow, *Official Register*
Travelers' Club, Kansas City	1882–1913	31–34		1900 GFWC Convention; Official Register
Travelers' Club, Topeka	1903–8	23		Winslow, *Official Register*
Kentucky				
The Tourist, Louisville	1913–18	32–35		*Official Register*
Tourist's Club, Louisville	1903–8	25–29		Winslow, *Official Register*
Travelers' Club, Shelbyville	1896–1908	18–25		1896 GFWC Convention; Winslow, *Official Register*; Croly, *History of the Woman's Club Movement*
Louisiana				
Woman's Club of New Orleans	1898		London, Zulu Land	Croly, *History of the Woman's Club Movement*
Maine				
Barton Reading Club, Norway	1892–98		"Travel"	Croly, *History of the Woman's Club Movement*
Clionea Club, Fairfield	1894–98	12	Paris	Croly, *History of the Woman's Club Movement*
Cosmopolitan Club, Gorham	1896–98	20	"Travellers' club"; USA	Croly, *History of the Woman's Club Movement*
Crescent Club	1884–98	12	England	Croly, *History of the Woman's Club Movement*
Dial Club, Fairfield	1897–98		England	Croly, *History of the Woman's Club Movement*
Fortnightly Club, Bath	1891–92	40	Europe	Croly, *History of the Woman's Club Movement*

Club	Date	Page	Location/Topic	Source
October Club, Bucksport	1895–98	59	England	Croly, *History of the Woman's Club Movement*
Ricker Travel Class, Houlton	1903–18	19–25		Winslow, *Official Register*
Sorosis, Lewiston	1898	96	England, Ireland, Scotland	Croly, *History of the Woman's Club Movement*
Sorosis, Skowhegan	1886	50–75	Egypt, Ireland, Land of the Midnight Sun	Croly, *History of the Woman's Club Movement*
Travelers' Club, Belfast	1908–18	18–19		Winslow, *Official Register*
Travelers' Club, Portland	1882–1918	14	Spain, Germany, Switzerland, Italy, USA	1896 GFWC convention; Official Register
Tuesday Club, Oakland	1897–98	25	Germany	Croly, *History of the Woman's Club Movement*
Venice Club	1897		Venice	Croly, *History of the Woman's Club Movement*
Woman's Club, Orono	1898	25	"A travel trip"	Croly, *History of the Woman's Club Movement*
Woman's Club, Skowhegan	1896–97	60–75	Egypt	Croly, *History of the Woman's Club Movement*
Woman's Literary Club, Dexter	1896–98	50	British Isles, France, Germany, Mexico, Portugal, Scandinavia, Spain, Switzerland	Croly, *History of the Woman's Club Movement*
Woman's Literary Club, Fryeburg, standing committee on history and travel	1890–98	8		Croly, *History of the Woman's Club Movement*
Woman's Literary Club, Waterville	1893–98	76	"Occasional travel trips"	Croly, *History of the Woman's Club Movement*
Maryland				
Lend-a-Hand Club, Mount Washington	1888–98		"Papers on travel"	Croly, *History of the Woman's Club Movement*
Massachusetts				
All-Around Dickens Club, Boston	1894–98		England	Croly, *History of the Woman's Club Movement*
Castilian Club, Boston	1888–98	13–125	Spain	Croly, *History of the Woman's Club Movement*
Clinton Woman's Club, tourists class	1896–98	27–76		Croly, *History of the Woman's Club Movement*
Educational Club, West Newton, travel class	1890–1920		"Papers on foreign travel," Sicily, Spain	GFWC State Federation Records; *Woman's Cycle*

(continued)

Club Name	Known Dates through 1920	Number of Members	Known Destinations through 1920	Source(s)
1884 Club, Lynn, tourists section	1884–98	60		Croly, *History of the Woman's Club Movement*
Fortnightly Club, Winchester, committee on history and travel	1881–98		"Travels in Europe," France, Morocco, Germany	*Woman's Cycle*; Croly, *History of the Woman's Club Movement*
Home Club, Worcester	1896	30	Italy	Croly, *History of the Woman's Club Movement*
Home Travel Club, Framingham	1908–18	15–21		Winslow, *Official Register*
Lothrop Club, Beverly, history and travel committee	1895–98	19–150		Croly, *History of the Woman's Club Movement*
Sorosis, Nantucket	1872–98	30	Japan	Croly, *History of the Woman's Club Movement*
Traveler's Club, Lawrence	1918	15		Winslow, *Official Register*
Wednesday Morning Club, Boston	1870–98		Assyria, Egypt, Greece, Italy	Croly, *History of the Woman's Club Movement*
Woman's Club, Arlington, tourist class	1896	15		1896 GFWC convention
Women's Club of Brockon, department of art and travel	1901–4		France	*Club Woman*; *General Federation Bulletin*
Woman's Club, Newburyport, travel class	1896–98	200		Croly, *History of the Woman's Club Movement*
Michigan				
Bay View Club, Saginaw	1898		Bay View program	Croly, *History of the Woman's Club Movement*
Detroit Woman's Club	1877–98		England, Egypt, France, Germany, Italy, Scotland, Switzerland, USA	*Woman's Cycle*; Croly, *History of the Woman's Club Movement*
Ladies' Literary Club, Kalamazoo	1892		Mexico	*New Cycle*
Monday Reading Club, Saginaw	1898		South America	Croly, *History of the Woman's Club Movement*
Research Club, Saginaw	1898		Germany	Croly, *History of the Woman's Club Movement*
Tourist Club, Dowagiac	1913–18	25		Winslow, *Official Register*

Club	Years	Pages	Places/Topics	Sources
Tourist Club, Jackson	1888–94	27–175	Belgium, England, France, Germany, Holland, Ireland, Russia, Scandinavia, Scotland, Switzerland	*New Cycle*; Winslow, *Official Register*; Croly, *History of the Woman's Club Movement*
Tourist Club, Pigeon	1913–18	25		Winslow, *Official Register*
Tourist Club, Saginaw	1898		"Travels on paper the year through"	Croly, *History of the Woman's Club Movement*
Tuesday Club, Saginaw	1898		France	Croly, *History of the Woman's Club Movement*
Woman's Club, Mendon	1889–98		"Some of the Eastern countries," Russia, South America	Croly, *History of the Woman's Club Movement*
Minnesota				
Art and Travel Club, Austin	1913	30		Winslow, *Official Register*
Disco Club, Albert Lea	1902–3		France	Tourist Club of Minneapolis Records, Minnesota Historical Society
Saturday Club, Duluth	1898		"Travels," England	Croly, *History of the Woman's Club Movement*
Tourist Club, Adrian	1894–1913	13–22		GFWC 1896 convention; Official Register
Tourist Club, Graceville	1901–13	15–25		Winslow, *Official Register*
Tourist Club, Henderson	1898–1913	20	China, England, Germany, Ireland, Japan, USA	GFWC Local Club Records; Winslow, *Official Register*
Tourist Club, Heron Lake	1902–13	14–18		Winslow, *Official Register*
Tourist Club, Luverne	1896–1913	25–27		Winslow, *Official Register*
Tourist Club, Mankato	1913	15		Winslow, *Official Register*
Tourist Club, Minneapolis	1891–1913	30–35	Belgium, China, Egypt, England, France, Germany, Greece, Holland, India, Ireland, Italy, Mexico, Morocco, Russia, Scotland, Spain, Switzerland, USA, Wales	1896 GFWC convention; Winslow, *Official Register*; Croly, *History of the Woman's Club Movement*; club records in the Minnesota Historical Society
Tourist Club, Ortonville	1895–1913	15–20		Winslow, *Official Register*
Tourist Club, Pipestone	1896		1896 GFWC convention	Winslow, *Official Register*
Tourist Club, Rochester	1908–13	20		Winslow, *Official Register*
Tourist Club, Spring Valley	1898–1908	19		Winslow, *Official Register*

(continued)

Club Name	Known Dates through 1920	Number of Members	Known Destinations through 1920	Source(s)
Tourist Club, Windom	1895–1913	25–29	"Every foreign country"	GFWC Local Club Records; Winslow, *Official Register*
Tourist Club, Worthington	1900–1913	12		Winslow, *Official Register*
Town and Country Club, Northfield	1895–98	75	Italy	Croly, *History of the Woman's Club Movement*
Travel Class, Albert Lea	1890–1913	21–29	Europe	GFWC Local Club Records; 1896 GFWC convention; *Official Register*
Travel Class, Fairmont	1891–1913	25		Winslow, *Official Register*
Travel Class, Sherburn	1899–1913	30		Winslow, *Official Register*
Travel Club, Glencoe	1913	25		Winslow, *Official Register*
Travelers Club, Faribault	1892–1913	32–33		Winslow, *Official Register*; Croly, *History of the Woman's Club Movement*
Travelers' Club, Minneapolis	1896–1913	30–35		Winslow, *Official Register*
Travelers' Club, Plainview	1908	25		Winslow, *Official Register*
Woman's Club, Lake City	1896–98		Chili, Cuba, Mexico, Peru, South America	Croly, *History of the Woman's Club Movement*
Missouri				
Bay View Reading Circle, Marceline	1914	14		GFWC *Directory*, 1914
Bay View Reading Circle, Piedmont	1914	15		GFWC *Directory*, 1914
Bay View Reading Circle, St. Louis	1910–14	35		GFWC *Directory*, 1914
81 Club, Kansas City	1881–91		Egypt, Europe	Croly, *History of the Woman's Club Movement*
Ladies' Saturday Club, Springfield	1879–98	40	Paris	Croly, *History of the Woman's Club Movement*
Monday Club, Webster Grove	1896			*Club Woman*
Sorosis, Springfield, tourist department	1897–98	60	Spain	Croly, *History of the Woman's Club Movement*

Club	Date	No.	Topic	Source
Tourist Club, Brookfield	1903–13	15–16		Winslow, *Official Register*
Tourist Club, Clinton	1903	22		Winslow, *Official Register*
Tourist Club, Nevada	1903	20		Winslow, *Official Register*
Travel Club, St. Joseph	1908–13	6		Winslow, *Official Register*
Montana				
Nineteenth Century Club, Kalispell	1893–94	12	England, Ireland, Scotland, the Continent	Croly, *History of the Woman's Club Movement*
Travel Club, Great Falls	1903–18	37–65		Winslow, *Official Register*
Travel Club, White Sulphur Springs	1913			Winslow, *Official Register*
Woman's Club of Butte	1898–99	75	Japan	*List of Officers and Directors, 1899*
Nebraska				
Bay View Reading Circle, Greeley	1914	25		*GFWC Directory, 1914*
Travel Club, Washington	1880–98		"Different countries"	Croly, *History of the Woman's Club Movement*
New Hampshire				
Fortnightly Club, Concord	1896–98	25	Paris	Croly, *History of the Woman's Club Movement*
Friday Club, Littleton	1889–98	10	Famous cities	Croly, *History of the Woman's Club Movement*
Graffort Club, Portsmouth	1898–99	134	Travel	*List of Officers and Directors, 1901*
Ladies' Literary Society, Hanover	1887–98	30	Famous cities	Croly, *History of the Woman's Club Movement*
Nashaway Woman's Club, Nashua	1896–98	200	Switzerland	Croly, *History of the Woman's Club Movement*
Robinson Seminary Alumna Association	1890–98	190	"Journals of foreign travel"	Croly, *History of the Woman's Club Movement*
Somersworth Woman's Club, tourist department	1895–98	125		Croly, *History of the Woman's Club Movement*
Tuesday Afternoon Club, Durham	1893		"Leading Cities of the World"	Croly, *History of the Woman's Club Movement*

(continued)

Club Name	Known Dates through 1920	Number of Members	Known Destinations through 1920	Source(s)
Tourist Club, Keene	1897–1918	30–50	United States	Winslow, *Official Register*; Croly, *History of the Woman's Club Movement*
Woman's Club, Milford	1895–98	150	"Traveling club"	Croly, *History of the Woman's Club Movement*
Woman's Club, Somersworth, tourist department	1895–98	61–125		Croly, *History of the Woman's Club Movement*
New Jersey				
Athena Club, Bayonne	1892–98	24	"Travel"	Croly, *History of the Woman's Club Movement*
Charlotte Emerson Brown Club, East Orange	1898–1900		Russia, Japan, "America's new territory"	1900 GFWC convention
El Mora Literary and Social Club	1891		Japan	Croly, *History of the Woman's Club Movement*
Fortnightly Jaunts Club, Madison	1890–98	12	Germany, Ionia, Italy, Russia, Scandinavia; "lands far to the north, east, south, and west"	Croly, *History of the Woman's Club Movement*
Odd Volumes, Jersey City	1888–98		Italy, Holland	Croly, *History of the Woman's Club Movement*
Shrewsbury Reading Club, Eatontown	1877–98		"Tourist trips"	Croly, *History of the Woman's Club Movement*
Travelers' Club of Roseville, Newark	1898–1918	27–33		Winslow, *Official Register*; Croly, *History of the Woman's Club Movement*
Woman's Reading Club, Rutherford	1889–98	150	Italy, Germany	Croly, *History of the Woman's Club Movement*
New Mexico				
Bay View Reading Circle, Tucumcari	1910–11	24		GFWC *Directory*, 1911
New York				
Belmont Tourist Club, Allegany County	1898			Croly, *History of the Woman's Club Movement*
Cambridge Club, Brooklyn	1890–98	50	Africa, India, "isles of the sea"	Croly, *History of the Woman's Club Movement*
Clio Club, New York City	1894		Lake Country	*New Cycle*

Club	Years	Members	Places	Source
Clionian Circle, Corning	1903–14		Africa, Holland, India, Mexico, Russia	GFWC Local Club Records
Columbian Club, Groton	1892–98	20	Greece, "Eastern countries"	Croly, *History of the Woman's Club Movement*
Friendly Tourists' Club, Brooklyn	1895–1918	16–20	Austria, British Isles, France, Germany, Italy, Portugal, Russia, Spain, Switzerland	*Club Woman; Club Women of New York;* Winslow, *Official Register*
Friendship Travellers' Club, Allegany	1898			Croly, *History of the Woman's Club Movement*
Home Travelers' Club, New York City	1900–1904	13–25	"Places of interest at home and abroad"	*Club Woman; Club Women of New York;* Winslow, *Official Register*
Literary Club of the Church of the Messiah, Buffalo	1880–98	40–150	Britain, Ireland, France	Croly, *History of the Woman's Club Movement*
Motley Club, Brooklyn	1898	25	England	Croly, *History of the Woman's Club Movement*
Progress Club, Oneida	1889–98	25	England, France, Germany, Italy	Croly, *History of the Woman's Club Movement*
Prospect Club, Brooklyn	1897	38	Belgium, Britain, France, Germany, Switzerland	Croly, *History of the Woman's Club Movement*
Tourist Club, Belmont	1903–8	18–20		Winslow, *Official Register*
Tourist Club, Middletown	1918	15		Winslow, *Official Register*
Tourist Club, Port Jervis	1913–18	35–40		Winslow, *Official Register*
Tourist Club, Syracuse	1908	25		Winslow, *Official Register*
Travel Club of Elmira	1904–2000	25–30	Belgian Congo, China, England, Italy, Spain, Turkey, USA	GFWC Local Club Records; Winslow, *Official Register;* letter from Helen Covey, Horseheads, New York
Travelers' At Home Circle, Saratoga	1892–1918	20		Winslow, *Official Register*
Travelers' Club, Ilion	1891–1918	35–49		Winslow, *Official Register*
Travelers' Club, Middletown	1918	17		Winslow, *Official Register*
Travelers' Club, Olean	1884–1908	30		Winslow, *Official Register*
Travellers' Club, Friendship	1898–1908			Croly, *History of the Woman's Club Movement;* Winslow, *Official Register*
Travellers' Club, Waterville	1893–1918	17–20		Winslow, *Official Register*

(continued)

Club Name	Known Dates through 1920	Number of Members	Known Destinations through 1920	Source(s)
Travellers' Club, Wellsville	1918			Winslow, *Official Register*
Watertown Wanderlust Club	1918	30		Winslow, *Official Register*
Woman's Club, Brooklyn	1869–98	150	Italy	Croly, *History of the Woman's Club Movement*
Women's Literary Club, Dunkirk	1885–98	50	America, England, France, Germany, Ireland, Italy	Croly, *History of the Woman's Club Movement*
North Carolina				
Travelers' Club, Asheville	1918	16		Winslow, *Official Register*
Travelers' Club, Salisbury	1913–18	12		Winslow, *Official Register*
North Dakota				
Tourist Club, Grand Forks	1897–1908	12	Holy Land, Mexico	Winslow, *Official Register*; Croly, *History of the Woman's Club Movement*
Travelers at Home Club, Milton	1913	8		Winslow, *Official Register*
Ohio				
Les Voyageurs, Avondale				
Baedeker Club, East Liverpool	1908–18	25		Winslow, *Official Register*
Bay View Reading Club, Lima	1914	14		GFWC Directory, 1914
Carpe Diem Club, Findlay	1896	10	France	Croly, *History of the Woman's Club Movement*
Conversational Club, Cleveland	1878–98		China, Egypt, India, Japan, Turkey	Croly, *History of the Woman's Club Movement*
Cosmopolitan Club, Fremont	1895–1920, but travel emphasis lasted only from 1895 to 1907 with another tour 1915–16	16–25	Argentina, Bolivia, Brazil, Chile, Colombia, Ecuador, Egypt, France, Germany, Greenland, Iceland, Ireland, Italy, Netherlands, Panama, Paraguay, Peru, Russia, Russian Poland, Scandinavia, Scotland, Uruguay, USA, Venezuela, Wales	Records of the Fremont Cosmopolitan Club, Rutherford B. Hayes Presidential Center; GFWC Directory, 1911
Faculty Woman's Club, Columbus	1897		Holland	Croly, *History of the Woman's Club Movement*

Club	Years	Members	Places/Topics	Source
Fortnightly Travel Club, Milan	1918	40		Winslow, *Official Register*
Les Voyageurs, Avondale	1889–98	30	"Germany and elsewhere"	1896 GFWC convention; Croly, *History of the Woman's Club Movement*
Les Voyageurs, Cincinnati	1889–1903	36		Winslow, *Official Register*
Monday Club, Mount Vernon	1894–98		Travel, including Germany	Croly, *History of the Woman's Club Movement*
Nomad Club, Mansfield	1888		England, Scotland, Wales	Croly, *History of the Woman's Club Movement*
Nomads, Walnut Hills	1887–98	25	France, Germany, USA	Croly, *History of the Woman's Club Movement*
Pilgrims, Avondale	1897	17–25	Portugal, Spain	Croly, *History of the Woman's Club Movement*
Pilgrims, Cincinnati	1894–1904	25		*List of Officers and Directors*, 1904
Society of Art and History, Cleveland	1898	50	"Flying trip through Holland"	*Club Woman*
Sorosis, Cleveland	1891–98	57–400	Russia	Croly, *History of the Woman's Club Movement*
Tourist Club, Barnesville	1896–1918	17–21		Winslow, *Official Register*
Tourist Club, Cincinnati	1908–18	25–35		Winslow, *Official Register*
Tourist Club, Logan	1908–18	20–31		Winslow, *Official Register*
Tourist Club, Mansfield	1913–18	30		Winslow, *Official Register*
Tourist Club, Mechanicsburg	1894–1913	55		Winslow, *Official Register*
Tourist Club, New Philadelphia	1890–1918	16–19		Winslow, *Official Register*
Tourist Club, Steubenville	1918	23		Winslow, *Official Register*
Tourist Club, Uhrichsville	1892–1918	20–24		Winslow, *Official Register*
Tourist Club, West Union	1892		Constantinople	*New Cycle*
Tourist Club, Youngstown	1918	31		*New Cycle*; Winslow, *Official Register*
Tourists, Price Hill, Cincinnati	1884–1913	25	Canada, China, England, Egypt, Germany, India, Italy, Japan, Mexico, South America, USA	1896 GFWC convention; *New Cycle*; Winslow, *Official Register*; Croly, *History of the Woman's Club Movement*
Tourists, Sidney	1898		"Foreign travel"	Croly, *History of the Woman's Club Movement*
Tourists' Club, Kinsman	1918	20		Winslow, *Official Register*
Travel Class, Bluffton	1913–18	15–22		Winslow, *Official Register*

(continued)

Club Name	Known Dates through 1920	Number of Members	Known Destinations through 1920	Source(s)
Travelers' Club, East Liverpool	1918	20		Winslow, *Official Register*
Travelers' Club, Granville	1913	30		Winslow, *Official Register*
Travelers' Club, Kent	1918	46		Winslow, *Official Register*
Traveler's Club, Mansfield	1887–1918	21–49	British Isles, Egypt, France, Germany, Greece, Italy, Spain, Switzerland	*New Cycle*; 1896 GFWC convention; Winslow, *Official Register*; Croly, *History of the Woman's Club Movement*
Traveler's Club, Salem	1918	50		Winslow, *Official Register*
Travelers' Club, Wooster	1891–1918	21–28		*Official Register*
Traveller's Club, Springfield	1888–96	40	America, England, France, Gibraltar, Portugal, Scotland, Spain, Wales	1896 GFWC convention; *New Cycle*; Croly, *History of the Woman's Club Movement*
Tuesday Tourist Club, Berlin Heights	1918	36		Winslow, *Official Register*
Women's Tourist Club, Mechanicsburg	1894–1990	50		GFWC Local Club Records; Official Register
Oklahoma				
Travel Club, McAlester	1913			Winslow, *Official Register*
Oregon				
Modern Travelers, Albany	1900–1908	30	Russia	1900 GFWC convention; Winslow, *Official Register*
Twentieth Century Club, Portland	1893–98	10	Austria, Spain, "the different countries of the world"	Croly, *History of the Woman's Club Movement*
Pennsylvania				
New Century Club, Philadelphia	1890		Africa, Spain	*Woman's Cycle*
Reading Circle, Newcastle	1897	40	France, Germany, Holland, Italy	Croly, *History of the Woman's Club Movement*
Schuylkill Shakespeare Students' Club, Pottsville	1875–98	25	England, France	Croly, *History of the Woman's Club Movement*; *New Cycle*
Tourist Club, Hollidaysburg	1908–18	19–20		Winslow, *Official Register*

Club	Years	Members	Places	Source
Tourist Club, Pittsburgh	1903–18	24–48		Winslow, *Official Register*
Travel Club, Bristol	1908–18	36–41		Winslow, *Official Register*
Travel Club, Irwin	1918	30		Winslow, *Official Register*
Traveler's Club, Pittsburgh	1896–1918	48–75		1896 GFWC convention; *Official Register*
Travelers' Club, Smethport	1903–18	50–65		Winslow, *Official Register*
Travelers' Club, Zelienople	1913–18	26–40		Winslow, *Official Register*
Traveller's Club, Allegheny	1890–92		*England, Scotland*	*New Cycle*
Travellers' Club, Carlisle	1903	22		*Official Register*
Travellers' Club, Meadville	1903	15		*Official Register*
Wednesday Club, Franklin	1889–98	35	England, Germany, France, Italy	Croly, *History of the Woman's Club Movement*
Woman's Club, Bradford	1894–95		The Orient	Croly, *History of the Woman's Club Movement*
Woman's Club, Media, department of travel	1894–98	150		Croly, *History of the Woman's Club Movement*
Woman's Club, Titusville	1897	60	Greece	Croly, *History of the Woman's Club Movement*
Woman's Literary Club, Meadville	1890–98	40	England, France	Croly, *History of the Woman's Club Movement*
South Dakota				
GFWC Travelers Club, Chamberlain	1906–2006	12–21	Austria, Belgium, Brazil, Canada, Cuba, Denmark, England, France, Germany, Greece, Holland, India, Ireland, Italy, Jerusalem, Malta, Mexico, Norway, Panama, Poland, Russia, Scotland, Spain, Sweden, Switzerland, Turkey, Venezuela, West Indies	GFWC notebook; Winslow, *Official Register*; Papers of the Chamberlain Travelers Club provided by Lillian Johnsson
Travelers' Club, Hot Springs	1903–18	15		Winslow, *Official Register*
Tennessee				
Art and Travel Club, Jackson	1913–18	28		Winslow, *Official Register*

(continued)

Club Name	Known Dates through 1920	Number of Members	Known Destinations through 1920	Source(s)
Utah				
Ladies Literary Club, Salt Lake City, tourist committee	1877–98			Croly, *History of the Woman's Club Movement*
Vermont				
Fortnightly Club, Bennington, standing committee on history and travel	1892–98	200	"Advantages of Travel"; USA	Croly, *History of the Woman's Club Movement*
Washington, D.C.				
Travel Club	1890		Mexico, "all countries by proxy"	*Woman's Cycle*
West Virginia				
The Traveler's Club, Morgantown	1918	22		Winslow, *Official Register*
Wisconsin				
Bay View Reading Circle, Ripon	1914	30		GFWC *Directory, 1914*
Bay View Reading Circle, Tomah	1914	15		GFWC *Directory, 1914*
Friends in Council, Berlin	1873–98	25	France, India, "Foreign countries"	Croly, *History of the Woman's Club Movement*
Ladies' Travel Class, Marshfield	1908	63		Winslow, *Official Register*
Ramblers, Fond du Lac	1898	12	Caribbean, Mexico, South America	Croly, *History of the Woman's Club Movement*
Tourist Club, Platteville	1908–18	31–45		Winslow, *Official Register*
Tourist Club, Superior	1908	12		Winslow, *Official Register*
Tourists' Club, Fond du Lac	1880–98		Belgium, England, Egypt, France, Greece, Italy, Palestine, up the Rhine, Scotland, Switzerland	Croly, *History of the Woman's Club Movement*
Travel Club, Durand	1918	20		Winslow, *Official Register*
Travel Club, Grand Rapids	1903–18	16–22		Winslow, *Official Register*
Travel Club, Milwaukee	1918	35		Winslow, *Official Register*

Travelers' Club, Columbus	1903–13	17–30		Winslow, *Official Register*
Woman's Club, Steven's Point	1894–1904	40	Japan	*List of Officers and Directors*, 1904
Wyoming				
Tourist Club, Lander	1913			Winslow, *Official Register*
Woman's Club, Cheyenne	1896–1901	20	Germany, Holland	Croly, *History of the Woman's Club Movement; Club Woman*

Other Clubs with a Travel Component, Not Known to Be Affiliated with the GFWC

African American Club Mentioned by the Woman's Era

Oak and Ivy Club, Springfield	1895		China	*Woman's Era*, May 1895

Bay View Clubs

Bay View Clubs, across the country with particularly heavy representation in the Midwest, most not known to be affiliated with the GFWC	1893–1922	25,000 members in 1914	Abyssinia, Algeria, Argentina, Ashanti, Australia, Austria-Hungary, Belgium, Bolivia, Britain, Brazil, Canada, Central Asia, Ceylon, Chile, China, Congo, Cuba, Dahomey, Denmark, Ecuador, Egypt, Finland, France, Germany, Greece, Haiti, Holland, India, Ireland, Italy, Japan, Kaffirland, Kamerun, Liberia, Luxemburg, Madagascar, Mexico, Morocco, New Zealand, Nigeria, Norway, Panama, Paraguay, Persia, Peru, Philippines, Poland, Russia, Santo Domingo, Sierra Leone, South Africa, Spain, Sudan, Sweden, Switzerland, Tripoli, Tunisia, Uganda, USA, Venezuela, Zanzibar	*Bay View Magazine*, 1896–1916; Fennimore, *Heritage of Bay View*

(continued)

Club Name	Known Dates through 1920	Number of Members	Known Destinations through 1920	Source(s)
Massachusetts Club Located via Archives USA, Not Found in GFWC Records				
Travelers Club, Pocasset	1905–2000	18–40	"Along the Danube," "Along the Euphrates," "Along the Jordan," "On a whaling voyage," Algeria, Australia, Brazil, Canada, China, Denmark, Egypt, England, Finland, France, Germany, Greece, Guam, Iceland, India, Italy, Japan, Jerusalem, Mexico, Morocco, Norway, Panama, Peru, Philippines, Portugal, Russia, Sandwich Islands, Spain, Sweden, Switzerland, Syria, Turkey, USA	Papers located in Jonathan Bourne Historical Center, Bourne, Mass.

Notes

Abbreviations

BVM	*Bay View Magazine*
CC	Cosmopolitan Club of Freemont, Ohio
CW	*Club Woman*
DF	*Decorator and Furnisher*
GFB	*General Federation Bulletin*
GFM	*General Federation Magazine*
GFWC	General Federation of Women's Clubs
GH	*Good Housekeeping*
HB	*House Beautiful*
HG	*House and Garden*
HHB	*Hull-House Bulletin*
HPTC	Hyde Park Travel Club (also known as Hyde Park Travel Class)
IIL	International Institute of Lewiston, Maine
IINWI	International Institute of Northwest Indiana
LHJ	*Ladies' Home Journal*
LITC	Lewistown, Illinois, Tourist Club
NGM	*National Geographic Magazine*
TCC	GFWC Travelers Club of Chamberlain, South Dakota
TCM	Tourist Club of Minneapolis
YWCA	Young Women's Christian Association

Beyond Main Street

1 Stead, *The Americanisation of the World*, 126.

2 Ibid., 6–9, 73.

3 Thwaite, "The American Invasion"; M. Prager, "Die Amerikanische Gefahr," cited in C. Campbell, *Special Interests*, 5; *Le peril américain*, cited in Orty, "From Baudelaire to Duhamel," 42–54; Heindel, *The American Impact on Great Britain*, 17, 138–39, 323, 330–51; McKenzie, *The American Invaders*, 1, 142.

4 Tomlinson, *Cultural Imperialism*, 2, dates the term "cultural imperialism" to the 1960s; Gienow-Hecht, "Shame on US?"

5 Plesur, *America's Outward Thrust*; Davies, *Peacefully Working to Conquer the World*; Rosenberg, *Spreading the American Dream*; Thompson, *Exporting Entertainment*; Healy, *Drive to Hegemony*. See also LaFeber, *The American Search for Opportunity*. Some notable exceptions to this narrative include Wilkins, *The History of Foreign Investment*; Iriye, *The Globalizing of America*; and Rodgers, *Atlantic Crossings*.

6 Langley, *The Banana Wars*; Pérez, *The War of 1898*; Rosenberg, *Financial Missionaries*; Cabán, *Constructing a Colonial People*; Ninkovich, *The United States and Imperialism*. Recent scholarship on U.S. imperialism has been greatly influenced by social and cultural history. See, for example, Findlay, *Imposing Decency*; Renda, *Taking Haiti*; Briggs, *Reproducing Empire*. On informal empire, see LaFeber, *The New Empire*; Wilkins and Hill, *American Business Abroad*; W. Williams, *The Roots of the Modern American Empire*; Wilkins, *The Emergence of Multinational Enterprise*; T. O'Brien, *The Revolutionary Mission*; Pletcher, *The Diplomacy of Trade and Investment*; Ayala, *American Sugar Kingdom*; Curti, *American Philanthropy Abroad*; J. Hunter, *The Gospel of Gentility*; P. Hill, *The World Their Household*; Boyd, *Emissaries*; Berghahn, "Philanthropy and Diplomacy"; Chin, "Beneficent Imperialists." On cultural exports, see Slotkin, "Buffalo Bill's 'Wild West'"; Wagnleitner and May, *"Here, There and Everywhere"*; Hart, *Empire and Revolution*; Cody, *Exporting American Architecture*; Rydell and Kroes, *Buffalo Bill in Bologna*.

7 See, for example, Bigsby, *Superculture*; Costigliola, *Awkward Dominion*; Wagnleitner, *Coca-Colonization*; Bell and Bell, *Americanization and Australia*; Willett, *The Americanization of Germany*; Kuisel, *Seducing the French*; Nolan, *Visions of Modernity*; Haddow, *Pavilions of Plenty*; Pells, *Not Like Us*; Dower, *Embracing Defeat*; Fehrenbach and Poiger, *Transactions, Transgressions, Transformations*; de Grazia, *Irresistible Empire*; LaFeber, *Michael Jordan and the New Global Capitalism*; Zeiler, "Just Do It!"; N. Smith, *American Empire*, 4; Eckes and Zeiler, *Globalization and the American Century*; Beck, Sznaider, and Winter, *Global America?*

8 For a critique of American exceptionalism, see Tyrrell, "American Exceptionalism."

9   Kupperman, "International at the Creation," 105. On travel, see Dulles, *Americans Abroad*; Stowe, *European Travel*; Levenstein, *Seductive Journey*; on Shakespeare, see Levine, *Highbrow, Lowbrow*; on films, see Abel, *The Red Rooster Scare*. See also Mead, *Atlantic Legacy*; H. Jones, *The Age of Energy*, chap. 7; Howe, *Victorian America*; Crunden, *American Salons*; Shi, *Facing Facts*, 108, 154–58, 173–75; Landsman, *From Colonials to Provincials*; Bowers, *Foreign Influences in American Life*.

10 Lancaster, *The Japanese Influence*; Impey, *Chinoiserie*; Carrott, *The Egyptian Revival*; J. F. Kasson, *Amusing the Million*; E. Denker, *After the Chinese Taste*; Hosley, *The Japan Idea*; Tweed, *The American Encounter with Buddhism*; J. Curl, *Egyptomania*; MacKenzie, *Orientalism*; R. Lewis, *Gendering Orientalism*; Kuklick, *Puritans in Babylon*; Brody, "Fantasy Realized"; Tchen, *New York before Chinatown*; Lee, *Picturing Chinatown*; Snodgrass, *Presenting Japanese Buddhism*; Yoshihara, *Embracing the East*; Kim, "Being Modern"; Moses, *The Golden Age of Black Nationalism*; Moses, *Afrotopia*; Adeleke, *UnAfrican Americans*; Gallicchio, *The African American Encounter*; Rodgers, *Atlantic Crossings*.

11 The influence of immigrants on U.S. culture can be seen, for example, in the literature on food ways. See Gabaccia, *We Are What We Eat*; Pillsbury, *No Foreign Food*. Jacobson, *Barbarian Virtues*, 56.

12 Higham, *Strangers in the Land*, 43, 324.

13 Wyman, *Round-Trip to America*, 127; Gabaccia, *Italy's Many Diasporas*, 96–99.

14 Robert Crunden periodized American culture as local prior to 1815, sectional from 1815 to 1901, national from 1901 to 1941, and cosmopolitan from 1941 to the present, in *A Brief History of American Culture*, 9–11; John Agnew stresses the incorporation of the United States into the world economy prior to 1890 and the dominance of the United States in the world economy after 1890, in *The United States in the World-Economy*. Foner, "American Freedom in a Global Age," 4.

15 On tariffs, see Goldstein, *Ideas, Interests, and American Trade Policy*, 102–22; Frank, *Buy American*, chap. 2; Wolman, *Most Favored Nation*; on rain forests, see Tucker, *Insatiable Appetite*; on Singer, see Davies, *Peacefully Working*; Domosh, "A 'Civilized' Commerce." An excellent book on U.S. banana consumption, Jenkins, *Bananas*, has recently joined the literature on U.S. enterprise in the Caribbean.

16 S. Lewis, *Main Street*, 6, 233.

17 Ibid., 259.

18 Ibid., 258.

19 Hollinger, *In the American Province*, ix; on provincialism as localism and marginality, see Dawley, *Changing the World*, 62; on the similarities between cosmopolitanism and provincialism, see Landsman, *From Colonials to Provincials*, 62.

20 S. Lewis, *Main Street*, 9–11, 15–17.

21 Ibid., 49, 69–81.

22 Ibid., 102, 134, 137, 197, 208, 228, 232, 238, 258, 262, 408.

23 On the problematic nature of the home-away dichotomy, see Kaplan and Pease, *Cultures of United States Imperialism*; Wexler, *Tender Violence*; Kaplan, *The Anarchy of Empire*, chap. 1; Burton, "Feminism, Empire, and the Fate of National Histories," 41.

24 Neverdon-Morton, *Afro-American Women*, 197–201; Tyrrell, *Woman's World*; Alonso, *Peace as a Women's Issue*; Rupp, *Worlds of Women*; DuBois, *Harriot Stanton Blatch*; Schott, *Reconstructing Women's Thoughts*; Alonso, *The Women's Peace Union*; McFadden, *Golden Cables of Sympathy*; Kaplan, Alarcón, and Moallem, *Between Woman and Nation*; Berkovitch, *From Motherhood to Citizenship*; D'Itri, *Cross Currents*; B. S. Anderson, *Joyous Greetings*; Laville, *Cold War Women*, 9. On patriotic motherhood, see Kennedy, *Disloyal Mothers*, 16; on tensions between cosmopolitanism and more limited outlooks, see Weber, "Unveiling Scheherazde."

25 Cohen, *A Consumers' Republic*. On consumption and nation building, see Breen, *The Marketplace of Revolution*.

Chapter 1

1 De Wolfe, *The House in Good Taste*, 18–21. Leavitt, *From Catharine Beecher*, 9.

2 Blanchard, "Mrs. Potter Palmer's Castle"; Ross, *Silhouette in Diamonds*, 1, 32, 53–56.

3 On household consumption and class status, see Bushman, *The Refinement of America*; Blumin, *The Emergence of the Middle Class*, esp. chap. 5; Walton, *France at the Crystal Palace*. See "The Vanderbilt House," *DF* 2 (May 1883): 44; "Residence of Jay Gould," *DF* 2 (July 1883): 131; Ada Conf, "A Notable New York House," *DF* 11 (Mar. 1888): 209–12. Harrison, "Worrosquoyacke," 73. On cosmopolitanism and the signification of wealth, see Colley, *Britons*, 166.

4 "The Cosey Corner," *DF* 27 (Mar. 1896): 182.

5 On cosmopolitanism, see Landsman, *From Colonials to Provincials*, 62; Hollinger, *Postethnic America*; Crunden, *American Salons*, 33–61; Wood, *The Radicalism of the American Revolution*, 221–24; Hollinger, *In the American Province*; H. Jones, *The Age of Energy*, chap. 7; Mead, *Atlantic Legacy*; Kim, "Being Modern," 383; on declining cosmopolitanism after 1890, see Handlin, *One World*, 4; Peyser, *Utopia and Cosmopolis*; K. O'Brien, *Narratives of Enlightenment*; Hannerz, "Cosmopolitans and Locals"; Cheah and Robbins, *Cosmopolitics*.

6 Ware, *Home Life*, 23, 85. Marsh, *Suburban Lives*, 147; Van de Wetering, "The Popular Concept of 'Home.'" On considering the domestic vis-à-vis the foreign,

see Amy Kaplan, "Manifest Domesticity," 581–82; on domesticity as a protective membrane, see Wexler, *Tender Violence*, 211.

7   Victorian writers argued that the home was the "church and State in embryo"; see Grier, *Culture and Comfort*, 4. See also Sklar, *Catherine Beecher*, xii, 158; Clark, *The American Family Home*, 29; Cott, *The Bonds of Womanhood*, 94–96; Irving, *Immigrant Mothers*, 10. On foreign design revivals before 1850, see Carrott, *The Egyptian Revival*; J. Curl, *Egyptomania*; Seale, *The Tasteful Interlude*, 14. On houses influenced by the China trade, see Downs, *The Golden Ghetto*, 248, 251; on commercial incursions into Victorian homes, see Loeb, *Consuming Angels*, 129; on cosmopolitan interiors, see also R. Wilson, "Cultural Conditions," 28–32.

8   F. O. H., "The French Note," *Art Interchange* 23 (July 6, 1889): 3.

9   Eastlake, *Hints on Household Taste*, vi–ix. On Eastlake, see also Williams and Jones, *Beautiful Homes*, 9; "Eastlake and His Ideas," *Art Amateur* 2 (May 1880): 126–27. On country homes, see Edwin L. Lutyens, "Berrydown Court," *HG* 6 (Oct. 1904): 157; P. H. Ditchfield, "Houses with a History, Longleat," *HG* 13 (May 1908): 149.

10 "A Dining Room in the English Style," *DF* 31 (Aug. 1898): 178; "An Italian Renaissance Dining-Room," *DF* 29 (Dec. 1896): 69; "A Dutch Corner," *DF* 30 (Sept. 1897): 165; Jonathan A. Rawson Jr., "A Consistent Dutch Dining-Room," *Country Life in America* 22 (Oct. 1, 1912): 48; F. J. Wiley, "Original Design for a Dining Room in the German Renaissance," *DF* 19 (Feb. 1892): 213. On German influences, see also Greenleaf, "Decorating and Furnishing," 68; J. Miller, "Planning the Kitchen," 123; on a Russian room, see *DF* 30 (June 1897): 87; on French, English, Japanese, and Mooresque boudoirs, see *DF* 19 (Feb. 1892): 163. Elizabeth Walling, "The House of Mrs. Ole Bull," *DF* 28 (May 1896): 43–44.

11 Laura B. Starr, "An Indian Room," *DF* 14 (May 1889): 38; "The Closing Days of the Exposition," *Atlanta Constitution*, Jan. 5, 1896; Wade, "The Ethnic Art Market"; Jensen, *One Foot on the Rockies*; Dilworth, *Imagining Indians*.

12 Spofford, *Art Decoration*, 162.

13 "A Dainty Japanese Room," *Times-Picayune*, Sept. 6, 1996. See also Lancaster, *The Japanese Influence*, 51–52, 62; Hosley, *The Japan Idea*; Meech and Weisberg, *Japonisme*; Yoshihara, *Embracing the East*, chap. 1.

14 Mary Rutherfurd Jay, "A Bungalow in Japanese Spirit," *HB* 32 (Aug. 1912): 72.

15 Barnard, Sumner and Putnam Co., *The Artistic Home.* Carrie May Ashton, "Home Workshop. Cosey Corners," *DF* 19 (Oct. 1891): 29; "Home Workshop. Cosey Corners," *DF* 19 (Nov. 1891): 69; Charlotte Robinson, "A Moorish Recess," *DF* 20 (Aug. 1892): 189–90; Marion A. McBride, "Cosy Corners," *DF* 25 (Oct. 1894): 18; Laura B. Starr, "Cosy Nooks and Corners," *DF* 15 (Nov. 1889): 43; "Cosey

Corner on Stair Landing," *DF* 27 (Jan. 1896): 118; "An Oriental Cosey Corner," *DF* 28 (May 1896): 47. See also Lichten, *Decorative Art*, 244; Mayhew and Myers, *A Documentary History of American Interiors*, 252; B. Gordon, "Cozy, Charming, and Artistic," 127; Butler, "The Decorative Arts," 323; G. Wright, *Moralism and the Model Home*, 35, 242; Halttunen, "From Parlor to Living Room," 164; Burns, "The Price of Beauty," 233; S. Leavitt, *From Catharine Beecher*, 125. The popularity of cosey corners underscores Katherine Grier's finding that nineteenth-century Americans "became cosmopolitan in a modest way through . . . consumer culture," *Culture and Comfort*, 74.

16 On New York, Denver, and Montana ones, see Seale, *The Tasteful Interlude*, 158, 173, 210; on New York and Chicago interiors, see Johnson, *Inside of One Hundred Homes*, 44, 54; on Houston corner, see Brooks, "Clarity, Contrast, and Simplicity," 20; on shipboard, see Howard, *In Distant Climes*, 47.

17 "The Bride's Primer," *GH* 41 (Oct. 1905): 385.

18 On ballast, see Chaudhuri, *Trade and Civilisation*, 53. Honor, *Chinoiserie*; Impey, *Chinoiserie*; E. Denker, *After the Chinese Taste*; Nelson, *Directly from China*; P. Hunter, *Purchasing Identity*, 117. Earlier examples of Orientalist architecture include Longwood, built in Mississippi in 1860, in Norton, "Architecture," 93; and P. T. Barnum's Connecticut house, Iranistan, erected in 1848, in Mayhew and Myers, *A Documentary History of American Interiors*, 253; Van Rensselaer, "The Development of American Homes," 49. John Sweetman finds that the remoteness of Islamic contacts, the enthusiasm for English classicism as a means to associate with Europe, an emphasis on national self-reliance, and lingering Puritanism inhibited Islamic styles in the United States prior to 1825; see *The Oriental Obsession*, 217, 244.

19 Harriet Monroe, "A Successful House," *HB* 6 (Nov. 1899): 266–75, 271–74; on the ceiling ensemble, see "House of W. A. Hammond, M.D.," *DF* 6 (June 1885): 81–82; on the grillwork ensemble, see "A Typical American Interior," *DF* 20 (July 1892): 140–43. See also R. Wright, *Inside the House*, iv; R. Wilson, "Cultural Conditions," 28, 32, 34; Ella Rodman Church, "How Two Houses Were Furnished," *Art Amateur* 12 (Mar. 1885): 87; Mayhew and Myers, *A Documentary History of American Interiors*, 211.

20 Hester M. Poole, "Elegance, Taste and Art in the Home," *GH* 3 (May 15, 1886): 1–5, 3.

21 Helen M. Chamberlin, "A Small City Apartment," *HB* 4 (June 1898): 18–21; *DF* 7 (Jan. 1886): 109.

22 Higham, *Strangers in the Land*, 20, 39, 43, 64, 98; Takaki, *Strangers from a Different Shore*, chaps. 5–6; R. Daniels, *The Politics of Prejudice*, 11, 15, 44, 68; Beisel, *Imperiled Innocents*, 105; Parker, *Purifying America*, 115, 129.

23 Wexler, *Tender Violence*, 107; Rhoads, "The Colonial Revival," 361; Hoy, *Chasing*

Dirt, 115; Shah, "Cleansing Motherhood," 25; Cohen, "Embellishing a Life of Labor," 324–28; J. Hunter, *The Gospel of Gentility*, 129; Rafael, "Colonial Domesticity."

24 R. Herrick, *The Common Lot*, 133.

25 "Egyptian Pottery," *Harper's Weekly* 26 (Apr. 29, 1882): 263; Maud Going, "A West-Indian Cruise," *Harper's Weekly* 50 (June 30, 1906): 912–14; "Pekin Is a Good Place to Shop," *Chicago Tribune*, Jan. 1, 1904; *New York Tribune*, Jan. 2, 1904. Mrs. S. B. Putnam, "The Shop of Far-Away-Moses," *DF* 19 (Mar. 1892): 205–6; Dewing, *Beauty in the Household*, 25.

26 On travelers, expatriates, and their possessions, see Margaret Greenleaf, "Chinese Spirit in Furnishing," *HB* 36 (June 1914): 32; "An Attractive Studio," *DF* 7 (Nov. 1885): 50–51; William R. Bradshaw, "Mr. George A. Kessler's Bachelor Apartments," *DF* 25 (Mar. 1895): 207; Mary Rutherfurd Jay, "A Bungalow in Japanese Spirit," *HB* 32 (July 1912): 72–73; French, *Homes and Their Decoration*, 191. On goods brought back by diplomats to China, see Hester M. Poole, "House Decoration Rich and Rare," *GH* 1 (Sept. 19, 1885): 2. On the Grants, see Feller, "The China Trade," 293.

27 On the primacy of the domestic market for pottery, see Blaszczyk, *Imagining Consumers*, 118. On shipping falling by more than 60 percent during the war, see Cochran and Miller, *The Age of Enterprise*, 111. For trade figures, see Department of the Treasury, *Commerce and Navigation of the United States* (1865), 243, 345, 350–51, (1900), 69, 77; Department of Commerce, *Commerce and Navigation of the United States* (1920), 40–41, 100, 101–2. I have not come up with a total figure for household imports because the Treasury and Commerce Department reports do not, in many cases, distinguish between goods imported for industrial and household use. Furthermore, their categories—including "household and personal effects, and wearing apparel in use, etc. of persons arriving from foreign countries"—can be very broad. Overall U.S. imports rose from $354 million in 1860 to $1.9 billion in 1914. In the same period, exports rose from $316 million to $2.4 billion. Bruchey, *Enterprise*, 296–300; Wilkins, *The History of Foreign Investment*, 142. The consumer price index is from the Global Financial Data Web site, http://www2.globalfinancialdata.com/index.php3?action=detaile dinfo&id=2624 (accessed Nov. 7, 2006).

28 "Imported Argentine Lamp Shade Covers," *Chicago Tribune*, Aug. 1, 1920; on relics see "Kamel's Kurious Kurios," *Los Angeles Times*, Nov. 4, 1892; on linen, see *DF* 25 (Jan. 1895): 124; on glass, see "Levy's Palais Royal Bazaar," *Times-Picayune*, Feb. 1, 1880; on hammocks, see "Veranda Decoration," *New York Tribune*, June 28, 1896; on furniture, see "Montgomery and Co.," *Times-Picayune*, June 5, 1884; on cooking ware, see "In Metropolitan Shops," *HB* 27 (May 1910): 176; on pitchers, see "For Christmas Buyers," *Art Interchange* 23 (Nov. 23, 1889):

193; on batik, see Priestman, *Art and Economy*, 122; on pottery, see "The Shopping Guide," *HB* 28 (Nov. 1910): iv; on drawn work, see "The Shopping Guide," *HB* 43 (Jan. 1918): 69; on malacca, see *Fiber Rush Imported Malacca*, 173; on baskets, see "The Shopping Guide," *HB* 28 (Aug. 1910); for quotation, see "The Hunt for Gifts," *New York Tribune*, Apr. 7, 1912.

29 "In Metropolitan Shops," *HB* 24 (Jan. 1908): 38.

30 On Vantines and other importers, see Yoshihara, *Embracing the East*, 31–38; Sharf, "Bunkio Matsuki"; Hosley, *The Japan Idea*, 43; C. Harrison, "Woman's Handiwork," 265; "Interiors in the Oriental Style," *DF* 27 (Jan. 1896): 104; "The First Japanese M'f'g & T'd'g Co.," *New York Tribune*, Dec. 9, 1888; "F. P. Bhumgara & Co.'s Oriental Interiors," *DF* 27 (Mar. 1896): 185; on the Vantine's inventory, see *Entrance to Vantine's*, 5–11, 76–77. On Chicago branch, see "Vantine's," *Chicago Tribune*, June 2, 1908. On Palmer, see Mar. 1891; Feb. 11 and 12, 1890; May 21, 1892, Account Book 6, 1889–1894, Potter Palmer Papers. On New Orleans, see the ads in the *Times-Picayune*, Jan. 6, 1890; Dec. 1, 1884; "Grand Oriental Exhibition," *Times-Picayune*, Dec. 6, 1884; see also Brandimarte, "Japanese Novelty Stores."

31 On visiting Chinatown, see "The Shopping Guide," *HB* 31 (Jan. 1912): vii; Eberlein, McClure, and Holloway, *The Practical Book of Interior Decoration*, 365; "Gathered Here and There," *New York Tribune*, Dec. 20, 1908. On East Side bargains, see Mary Alden Hopkins, *HB* 46 (Dec. 1919): 388–89; on slums as shopping destinations, see Cocks, *Doing the Town*, 200; on fairs, see "The Closing Days of the Exposition," *Atlanta Constitution*, Jan. 5, 1896; McCabe, *The Illustrated History of the Centennial Exhibition*, 465; "Oriental Bazaar of G. A. Coudsi and A. Andalaft," "The Japan Village," "Guide to the Irish Industrial Village," folders .53–.63, .64–.71, box 1, World's Columbian Exposition Collection.

32 "There Is No Denying," *New York Tribune*, Oct. 30, 1892. *Vantine's Catalog*, 1; *Wanamaker's Catalog*, 8; Matsumoto-Do, *The Book of Genuine Things Japanese*.

33 On curio shops, see S. Leavitt, *From Catharine Beecher*, 161. Francis E. Lester Co., *Catalogue*; on peddlers, see Naff, *Becoming American*, 130, 170–73, 180.

34 Cowles, *Artistic Home Furnishing*, 155.

35 John M. MacKenzie finds that Victorians and Edwardians were "massively eclectic" because "theirs was the first age in which almost all the cultures of the world had been made available"; *Orientalism*, xii. On museums, see Virginia Robie, "Spanish and Moorish Furniture," *HB* 27 (Mar. 1910): 89–90, 112; Quinn, *Planning and Furnishing the Home*, 73; Leach, *Land of Desire*, 169–72. On fairs, see "Indian Art in Metal and Wood," *DF* 25 (Jan. 1895); Mrs. S. A. Brock Putnam, "Russian Embroideries and Laces," *DF* 26 (July 1895): 138; Yoshihara, *Embracing the East*, 18–20; Crinson, *Empire Building*, 64–65; MacKenzie, *Orientalism*, 62, 86–88; *DF* 26 (Apr. 1895) 4. On missionary exhibits, see "Many Industries,"

New York Tribune, Feb. 11, 1900; on manufacturing displays, see "Come and See," *New York Times*, Sept. 8, 1912; on writing, see Morse, *Japanese Homes*. On the bazaar, see McCabe, *The Illustrated History of the Centennial Exhibition*, 449.

36 "A Visit to the Sevres Porcelain Manufactory," *Hearth and Home* 4, Dec. 7, 1872, 900. On travel, see C. Harrison, "Woman's Handiwork," 265; Annetta Josefa Halliday-Antona, "The Paris of China (Canton)," *Outing* 26 (Apr. 1895): 120–23; quotation from "Interiors in the Oriental Style," *DF* 27 (Jan. 1896): 103.

37 Mrs. Oliver Bell Bunce, "Virginia Brush, The Able Decorator," *DF* 28 (Sept. 1896): 168–69. On decorators and travel, see Jackson and Jackson, *The Study of Interior Decoration*, 450; Throop, *Furnishing the Home*, ii. On interior decorating, see Seale, *The Tasteful Interlude*, 22; W. R. Bradshaw, "A Leading Brooklyn Decorator," *DF* 16 (Sept. 1890): 186–89.

38 On earlier nationalism, see G. Wright, *Moralism and the Model Home*, 11; Amy Kaplan, "Manifest Domesticity," 591. On the cachet of imports even in the mid-nineteenth century, see Pulos, *American Design Ethic*, 119. On the importance of printed media in disseminating fashions, see Purdy, *The Tyranny of Elegance*, ix; Ewen and Ewen, *Channels of Desire*, 124.

39 "Cozy Corners for Parlors," *LHJ* 7 (July 1890): ii; Cowles, *Artistic Home Furnishing*, 155, 161, 163.

40 On shawls, see "Some Pictures of Quaint Things"; on piano, see James Thomason, "Piano Decorations," *DF* 25 (Oct. 1894): 31. This idea was repeated in Cooke, *Our Social Manual*, 483.

41 "Oriental Rugs and Why They Are So Highly Valued," *New York Tribune*, Sept. 22, 1912. On Bukhara rugs, see Spooner, "Weavers and Dealers," 197; George Leland Hunter, "Oriental Rugs for $50 and Less," *HG* 16 (Dec. 1909): 204; Ormsbee, *The House Comfortable*.

42 "M'Brides," *Atlanta Constitution*, Mar. 4, 1884; on Cairo rug, see Hester M. Poole, "Household Decoration," *Home-Maker* 2 (July 1889): 288; Francis E. Lester Co., *Catalogue*, 17.

43 *Wanamaker's Catalog*, inside cover; "F. P. Bhumgara and Co.," *DF* 29 (Oct. 1896): 31.

44 Matsumoto-Do, *The Book of Genuine Things Japanese*, i.

45 Frank T. Robinson, "Bedroom Furniture," *DF* 5 (Dec. 1884): 90. See also the Gent's Turkish Chairs in M. Grossman and Son, *Illustrated Catalogue*.

46 On exotic arts and distinctiveness, see Graburn, "Introduction: Arts of the Fourth World," 2.

47 Spofford, *Art Decoration*, 162.

48 "A Japanese or a Japanesque Room," *Art Interchange* 22 (Apr. 13, 1889): 123; on greatest charm, see "An Interior in the Turkish Style," *DF* 25 (Oct. 1894): 16.

49 Williams and Jones, *Beautiful Homes*, 9.

50 *DF* 7 (Dec. 1885): 69.

51 *DF* 5 (Dec. 1884): 77.

52 "Pushman Brothers" and "Alexander H. Revell and Co.," *Chicago Tribune*, Dec. 3, 1920; Dec. 6, 1920; Dec. 1, 1920; "Whittall Rugs," *HB* 28(Oct. 1910): xiii (illustration); "Whittall Rugs," *HB* 28 (Nov. 1910): xxvii. Likewise, a Vantine's catalog featured Eastern scenes that overshadowed pictures of the goods being sold; see A. A. Vantine and Co., *The Wonder Book*. D. H. Holmes Co., a New Orleans retailer, advertised its Eastern products with pictures of Pacific Island women doing needlework, Chinese men sailing junks, Japanese women tying a bundle, and Arab men on camels; see "Holmes Brings to You the Products of the Industrious East," *Times-Picayune*, Apr. 3, 1920.

53 "A Roman Studio," *DF* 5 (Dec. 1884): 87; Burns, "The Price of Beauty," 210–12. Sato and Watanabe, "The Aesthetic Dialogue Examined," 19, note that it was unusual for a British artist from the 1870s onward *not* to own Japanese objects. See also "An Attractive Studio," *DF* 7 (Nov. 1885): 50–51; Eleanor Evans, "The Atelier of Mr. Clyde Fitch," *HB* 3 (Dec. 1897): 5–9; Anne H. Wharton, "Some Philadelphia Studios," *DF* 8 (May 1886): 38–39; Frank T. Robinson, "Boston Artists' Studios," *DF* 5 (Oct. 1884): 6–9; McCarthy, *Women's Culture*, 95–97, 107.

54 Maurice Guillemot, "Sarah Bernhardt at Home," *DF* 18 (June 1891): 98–100. On Bernhardt's tours, see Glenn, *Female Spectacle*, 10. Rudnick, *Utopian Vistas*, 39–41. Many outlandish interiors of the late nineteenth century emerged from the aesthetic movement; see Blanchard, *Oscar Wilde's America*, 107, 118.

55 On bohemians' "ambivalence toward their own social identities," see Seigel, *Bohemian Paris*, 11.

56 "How to Sit on a Divan," *DF* 19 (Oct. 1891): 8. Caroline B. Le Row, "A Proper Way to Sit," *LHJ* 9 (May 1892): 4. On aesthetic interiors as "a way out of the dead ends of conventional domestic life," see Blanchard, *Oscar Wilde's America*, xiii. On the hedonism of late nineteenth-century consumption, see Loeb, *Consuming Angels*, vii, 4; on the carnivalesque aspect of exotic goods, see Lears, *Fables of Abundance*, 51–52. On the indolence associated with the Moorish style, see J. C. Brown, "The 'Japanese Taste,'" 143. On the association of Chinese styles with sensuality, violence, and melancholy, see Spence, *The Chan's Great Continent*, 146.

57 "Miss Muffin and Mr. Turk," *HB* 41 (Mar. 1917): 219.

58 Mrs. Reginald De Coven, "Social Life in Chicago," *LHJ* 9 (Apr. 1892): 4.

59 [Mrs. Frona E. Wait], "The Flood Palace at San Francisco," *GH* 3 (Oct. 30, 1886): 316.

60 S. Lewis, *Main Street*, 16, 69–71, 76, 86, 89, 97, 262, 408–9.

61 Maude Annulet Andrews, "More Dining Rooms," *Atlanta Constitution*, Dec. 2, 1888.

62 On amusement parks, see J. F. Kasson, *Amusing the Million*; on department

stores, see Leach, *Land of Desire*, 70, 79, 83; on amusement halls, see W. L. D. O' Grady, "Influence of Oriental Art on Modern American Decoration," *DF* 4 (Nov. 1884): 211. "The New York Casino," *DF* 4 (Apr. 1884): 11; "Hyde and Behman's New Theatre," *DF* 17 (Dec. 1890): 96–97; "The Star Theatre, New York," *DF* 27 (Mar. 1896): 169–70; "The Montana Club," *DF* 25 (Mar. 1895): 215–17. On the Armory, see Blanchard, *Oscar Wilde's America*, 26; on temples, see Moore, "From Lodge Room to Theatre," 39. On Murray's, see Bevington, *New York Plaisance*. "Decoration of the Hoffman House," *DF* 5 (Nov. 1884): 42; "Turkish Salon in the Waldorf Hotel," *DF* 26 (Sept. 1895): 209. On the Palmer House, see Ross, *Silhouette in Diamonds*, 39.

63 Isabel Floyd-Jones, "The Potters of Golfe-Juan and Vallauris," *GH* 50 (Mar. 1910): 347–51.

64 Oliver Coleman, "Taste," *HB* 12 (Sept. 1902): 242–44.

65 *The Housekeeper's Quest*, 6.

66 On cultural capital, see Bourdieu, *Distinction*.

67 *Potter Family Collections*, 7, 8; Saarinen, *The Proud Possessors*, 16, 20; on European residences, Drury, *Old Chicago Houses*, 130; Palmer, *Addresses and Reports*, 116.

68 W. P. Pond, "A Zulu Woman's Mansion," *LHJ* 8 (Mar. 1891): 9.

69 On Yankees, see "Japanese Art Works," *DF* 5 (Jan. 1885): 144; on quickness, see Humphreys, "House Decoration and Furnishing," 168.

70 Alice Van leer Carrick, "The Furniture of the Allies: Japanese Furniture," *HB* 45 (June 1919): 366–68.

71 Helen Watterson, "On Over-Decoration," *Atlanta Constitution*, Mar. 6, 1892.

72 Frédéric Vors, "House Japanese Decoration," *Art Amateur* 1 (July 1879): 53–55.

73 Bederman, *Manliness and Civilization*, 31; J. C. Brown, "The 'Japanese Taste,'" 155.

74 Said, *Orientalism*, 204; Yoshihara, *Embracing the East*, 26. My argument is more in line with Reina Lewis's argument that Western women "registered difference less pejoratively and less absolutely than was implied by Said's original formulation"; see *Gendering Orientalism*, 4. See also MacKenzie, *Orientalism*, xii. On Lowe, see "The Closing Days of the Exposition," *Atlanta Constitution*, Jan. 5, 1896.

75 Ralph A. Cram, "Interior Decoration of City Houses," *DF* 8, June 1886.

76 Laura B. Starr, "Cairene Furniture," *DF* 26 (May 1895): 48; John Kimberly Mumford, "Glimpses of Modern Persia," *HG* 2 (Aug. 1902): 361–73. This fits with the Orientalist tendency to regard the Orient as unchanging; see T. Mitchell, "Orientalism," 289. On imperialists' regret at the transformations they have wrought, see Rosaldo, *Culture and Truth*, chap. 3.

77 Walter E. Browne, "Modern Indian Rugs," *HB* 1 (Apr. 1897): 22–24, 24. On artis-

tic degradation, see A. L. Liberty, "The Industrial Arts of Japan," *DF* 17 (Nov. 1890): 65.

78   Frank, *Buy American*, chap. 2; on patriotism, see Kinne and Cooley, *Shelter and Clothing*, 1, 5; S. Leavitt, *From Catharine Beecher*, 22.

79   Auslander, *Taste and Power*, 141, 378; Cooper, *The Opulent Eye*, 9, 17; Van Rensselaer, "The Development of American Homes," 37. On eliminating maids, see Pattison, *Principles of Domestic Engineering*, 1. On servants, see Katzman, *Seven Days a Week*, 27, 72, 78. Amelia Muir Baldwin, "Interior Decoration, A Form of Expression," folder 15, box 1, Amelia Muir Baldwin Papers; Cohen, "Embellishing a Life of Labor," 346.

80   On the purity of style in other parts of the world, see Laura B. Starr, "The Houses of Various Nations—Norwegian Homes," *HB* 4 (Oct. 1898): 151–56, 151; *DF* 26 (July 1895): 123. On Americans as conglomerate, see Parsons, *Interior Decoration*, 54, 235.

81   *DF* 25 (Oct. 1894): 4. In contrast to the idea that eclecticism offered wider possibilities, T. J. Jackson Lears finds it intensified feelings of artificiality that "contributed to the symbolic impoverishment of Western culture"; see *No Place of Grace*, 33, 302.

82   On mass, see *DF* 19 (Mar. 1892): 203; on intimacies, see Wheeler, *Principles of Home Decoration*, 162–63; on households as museums, see "Odds and Ends," *DF* 3 (Oct. 1883): 24; Jeannette M. Dougherty, "Individuality in Artistic Furnishing," *HB* 6 (July 1899): 76; Rose Standish Nichols, "Individuality in Interior Decoration," *HB* 28 (June 1910): 6–10.

83   Carter, *Millionaire Households*, 108.

84   Jackson and Jackson, *The Study of Interior Decoration*, 41–42. On objections to foreign styles of architecture, see "The Work of Messrs. Carrère and Hastings," *Architectural Record* 27 (Jan. 1910): 3.

85   Walter E. Browne, "How to Buy Rugs," *HB* 5 (Jan. 1899): 67–70, 68.

86   "The American Idea," *DF* 14 (Sept. 1889): 168; J. A. Price, "Maizart," *DF* 14 (June 1889): 70; "The Price 'Maize' Competition," *DF* 15 (Feb. 1890): 138. Candace Wheeler, a specialist in decorative needlework, also promoted Indian corn as an American art form; see Blanchard, *Oscar Wilde's America*, 58, 67; Florine Thayer McCray, "Distinguished American Women—Mrs. Candace Wheeler," *LHJ* 5, July 1888, 3. On the colonial revival, see Seale, *The Tasteful Interlude*, 23; Ames, *Death in the Dining Room*, 237. David Eric Brody sees both Orientalist and colonial revival interiors as conducive to imperialism: the former for instilling colonial fantasies, the latter for manifesting American patriotism; see "Fantasy Realized," 1, 48. Helen Anderson, "American versus Foreign Art," *DF* 16 (July 1890): 136.

87 Hester M. Poole, "The Home of Mrs. John A. Logan," *DF* 18 (July 1891): 132–33.

88 Brooks, "Clarity, Contrast, and Simplicity," 34. Ames, introduction, 10.

89 Richard Bach cited in Taylor and Bokides, *New Mexican Furniture*, 217.

90 Cumming and Kaplan, *The Arts and Crafts Movement*, 107; Boris, *Art and Labor*; Seale, *The Tasteful Interlude*, 25; Pulos, *American Design Ethic*, 296.

91 Ralph Prescott Heard, "The Chinese Influence in Home Furnishings," *HB* 41 (May 1917): 357–59, 414. On the English roots of the craftsman ideal, see Boris, *Art and Labor*, chap. 2.

92 N. Tomes, *The Gospel of Germs*, 160–61; on home economics, see also Frederick, *Household Engineering*, 99. On scientific households, see G. Wright, *Moralism and the Model Home*, 3, 197.

93 Burns, "The Price of Beauty," 236–37.

94 L. Mead, *To Whom Much Is Given*, 10–11.

95 "The Poor Taste of the Rich," *HB* 17 (Feb. 1905): 18–21; on eclecticism as inimical to democracy, see also "Something New under the Sun," *HB* 38 (Aug. 1915): 81.

96 Samuel Dauchy, "An Architectural Censorship," *HB* 1 (Jan. 1897): 18–21.

97 *DF* 27 (Oct. 1895): 3.

98 Quoted in Auslander, *Taste and Power*, 224.

99 Needell, *A Tropical Belle Epoque*, 154, 176; Orlove, *The Allure of the Foreign*.

100 Florence Finch Kelly, "Bungalow Furnishings and Fitments," *HB* 36 (June 1914): 24–28, 27.

101 Katherine Louise Smith, "Oriental Carpets and Rugs," *HB* 6 (Sept. 1899): 171–178, 171; "The Romance of the Rug," *DF* 14 (Apr. 1889): 11; "The Famine in Persia," *Times-Picayune*, Mar. 4, 1880.

102 On ransacked, see W. L. D. O'Grady, "Influence of Oriental Art on Modern American Decoration," *DF* 4 (Nov. 1884): 211; on armed, see Varney, *Our Homes*, 280; on plunder, see Laura B. Starr, "An Indian Room," *DF* 14 (May 1889): 38; on trophies, see Humphreys, "House Decoration and Furnishing," 144; Hester M. Poole, "The City Residence of Geo. W. Childs, Esq.," *DF* 14 (June 1889): 69; John Kimberly Mumford, "Glimpses of Modern Persia," *HG* 2 (Sept. 1902): 429–36, 433.

103 H. Brown, *Book of Home Building*, 63. On low wages, see also Humphreys, "House Decoration and Furnishing," 166; on consumption and U.S. commercial power, see McCarthy, *Women's Culture*, 54; Emma Thacker Holliday, "Oriental Carpets," *DF* 27 (Nov. 1895): 47–48.

104 Hester M. Poole, "House Decoration Rich and Rare," *GH* 1 (Sept. 19, 1885): 2.

105 Topik and Wells, introduction to *The Second Conquest*, 11; Tucker, *Insatiable Appetite*, 351; S. G. Benjamin, "How Persian Rugs Are Made," *DF* 29 (Nov. 1891): 56;

Francis E. Lester Co., *Catalogue*, 3; see also "The Romance of the Rug," *DF* 14 (Apr. 1889): 11.

106 "Come and See," *New York Times*, Sept. 8, 1912.

107 Mrs. S. A. Brock Putnam, "Mexican Drawn Work," *DF* 26 (Aug. 1895): 178.

108 Mrs. S. A. Brock Putnam, "Embroideries of the Turkish Compassionate Fund," *DF* 25 (Mar. 1895): 220–21; Mrs. S. A. Brock Putnam, "Russian Embroideries and Laces," *DF* 26 (July 1895): 138; Mrs. Oliver Bell Bunce, "The Turkish Compassionate Fund," *DF* 30 (Sept. 1897): 172–74; "Ancient Irish Filigrees," *New York Tribune*, Feb. 8, 1908. On seeing mingling as an act of benevolence, see Price, *Primitive Art*, 25; *Furniture of To-Day*; on spenders, see Laura Jean Libbey, "Praying for a Husband," *Atlanta Constitution*, Nov. 17, 1912.

109 Stocking, *Objects and Others*; Conn, *Museums*, 89; Florence Finch Kelly, "Bungalow Furnishings and Fitments," *HB* 36 (June 1914): 24–28, 27–28.

110 Yoshihara, *Embracing the East*, 43. An article on acquiring a Russian samovar illustrates the ethnographic knowledge conveyed by shopping essays: it provided information on keeping a kosher household; "In Metropolitan Shops," *HB* 24 (Jan. 1908): 38. "Eastern Rugs and Carpets," *DF* 2 (May 1883): 56; "Salon in a Private Residence in Cairo in the Moorish Style," *DF* 27 (Nov. 1895): 52.

111 "An Oriental Interior," *DF* 18 (Aug. 1891): 172–73.

112 Mary Parmele, "Some Thoughts upon Life and Art," *DF* 4 (May 1884): 63.

113 Rosenberg, *Financial Missionaries*, 203.

114 On expression, see Parsons, *Interior Decoration*, 235. On preferring genuineness, see "Among Novelties in Oriental Shops," *New York Tribune*, Feb. 7, 1892; "The Most Characteristic," *New York Tribune*, Feb. 7, 1892; Hester M. Poole, "House Decoration Rich and Rare," *GH* 1 (Sept. 19): 1885, 2; Matsumoto-Do, *The Book of Genuine Things Japanese*. On cosmopolitanism as a signifier of leisure, education, and wealth, see Colley, *Britons*, 166.

115 Gardner Teall, "Collecting Antiques of Persia and India," *HG* 36 (July 1919): 18–19.

116 Emmeline Lott, *The Grand Pacha's Cruise*, 1:276, 2:23; Holmes, *Burton Holmes Travelogues*, 2:217; Eugene Clute, "Japanese Homes of Today," *HG* 35 (June 1919): 39. On the Westernization of Japanese interiors, see Sand, *House and Home*; Rydell, "The Culture of Imperial Abundance," 198.

117 "A Paris Mania," *Cottage Hearth* 2 (June 1875): 161. On European eclecticism, see also Cooper, *The Opulent Eye*, 8; Tiersten, *Marianne in the Market*, 167–68. "French Home Interiors," *Art Amateur* 18 (Mar. 1888): 88.

118 Bacon, *Central Asians*, 104; Fieldhouse, *The Colonial Empires*, 183, 195, 220, 229, 272, 283.

119 Bacon, *Central Asians*, 67. On the role of imperialism in exposing Westerners to non-Western goods, see W. L. D. O'Grady, "Indian Metal Work," *DF* 4 (July

1884): 140; "Oriental Carpets, Rugs, and Embroideries," *DF* 19 (Jan. 1892): 128; on imperialism and Western control of production and trade, see Humphreys, "House Decoration," 166; Wills, "European Consumption." Not coincidentally, after the U.S. occupation of the Philippines, American shoppers encountered more Philippine handiwork; see "Filipino Industries," *New York Tribune*, Feb. 18, 1900. Spofford, *Art Decoration*, 161.

120 Laverton and Co., *New Illustrated Catalog*, 145, 155; Maude Adams, "Maude Adams in London," *Atlanta Constitution*, July 5, 1896.

121 W. L. D. O'Grady, "Oriental Rugs and Carpets," *DF* 3 (Dec. 1883): 95.

122 W. L. D. O'Grady, "Oriental Brasswork," *DF* 8 (Aug. 1886): 140. On prison labor, see also "Rugs of Antique Make," *New York Tribune*, Feb. 5, 1900; Duncan, *The House Beautiful*, 194.

123 Frank Chaffee, "Bachelor Bits," *Home-Maker* 1 (Feb. 1899): 354. See also William R. Bradshaw, "Mr. George A. Kessler's Bachelor Apartments," *DF* 25 (Mar. 1895): 207; W. L. D. O'Grady, "Influence of Oriental Art on Modern American Decoration," *DF* 4 (Nov. 1884): 211; "A Turkish Smoking-Room," *DF* 6 (June 1885): 90. On the banker's apartment, see "A Typical American Interior," *DF* 20 (July 1892): 140–43.

124 *DF* 30 (May 1897): 37; Seale, *The Tasteful Interlude*, 233.

125 "The Closing Days of the Exposition," *Atlanta Constitution*, Jan. 5, 1896; Hichens, *The Garden of Allah*, 63; Brumberg, "Zenanas and Girlless Villages"; Hatem, "Through Each Other's Eyes," 183–98. Reina Lewis and Janaki Nair find that Western women also depicted the harem positively, but I have found this to be rare in U.S. newspaper and magazine reports; see R. Lewis, *Gendering Orientalism*, 152; Nair, "Uncovering the Zenana."

126 Fannie S. Benjamin, "Home Life in Iran," *Home-Maker* 4 (June 1890): 199–202.

127 Field, *America and the Mediterranean World*, 307, 339, 347, 445.

128 Ross, *Silhouette in Diamonds*, 41.

129 On Brighton and British Orientalism, see MacKenzie, *Orientalism*, 81. Stoddard, *Red-Letter Days Abroad*, 145. On French Orientalism, see Troy, *Modernism and the Decorative Arts*, 11, 13; Theodore Child, "French House Furnishing," *DF* 4 (Apr. 1884): 22–23, 23; "The Modern Chinese Style," *DF* 19 (Nov. 1891): 50; *DF* 20 (June 1892): 84; on British Orientalism, see Laura B. Starr, "Sir Frederick Leighton's Arab Hall," *DF* 27 (Mar. 1896): 171–72; *DF* 16 (July 1890): 131; Sato and Watanabe, *Japan and Britain*; Sweetman, *The Oriental Obsession*, 192–97; Maude Andrews, "Maude Andrews in London," *Atlanta Constitution*, July 12, 1896.

130 "The Exhibition of Rooms at the Crystal Palace, London," *DF* 20 (June 1892): 97.

131 On the English connotations of Japanese products, see J. C. Brown, "The 'Japanese Taste,'" 38; Bennett, "The Exhibitionary Complex," 123–54; on the second-hand appeal of "Japonisme," see Meech and Weisberg, *Japonisme*, 16, 22–26, 35–36.

132 George, "Homes in the Empire," 97; Nair, "Uncovering the Zenana," 10. On the privileged life-style available even to missionaries, see Isaacs, *Scratches on Our Minds*, 153. "What She Does in India," *New York Tribune*, June 14, 1896.

133 Rydell, "The Culture of Imperial Abundance," 192.

134 On the inequalities of what she terms "interculturism," see Bharucha, *Theatre and the World*, 1; on commercial supremacy, see T. Mitchell, *Colonising Egypt*, 166.

135 L. Hughes, *The Big Sea*, 112.

Chapter 2

1 J. M. H., "American Girls and Titled Husbands," *Chicago Tribune*, Sept. 5, 1880.

2 Montgomery, "*Gilded Prostitution*," 10; Montgomery, *Displaying Women*, 68.

3 B. Anderson, *Imagined Communities*.

4 Yarwood, *European Costume*, 206, 215; Banner, *American Beauty*, 66. Although European women looked to Paris at the turn of the nineteenth century, American women often looked to London early in the century, regarding British fashions as more modest; see Halttunen, *Confidence Men*, 72; Jenny June (Jane C. Croly), "Renaissance of Fashion," *Times-Picayune*, Nov. 4, 1888. On June, see Walsh, "The Democratization of Fashion," 310.

5 "French Fashion Openings," *New York Tribune*, Aug. 25, 1912.

6 On Paquin, see Steele, *Paris Fashion*, 235. Grace Corneau, "Fashion's Dictates from Paris," *Chicago Tribune*, Jan. 3, 1904; Mary Brush Williams, "The Last Word in Paris Fashions," *Chicago Tribune*, May 2, 1920; "Seen in the Shops of Paris," *Atlanta Constitution*, May 2, 1912; "Paris Notes," *Chicago Tribune*, Mar. 3, 1912; "Seasonable Styles," *Delineator* 28, Nov. 1886, 313.

7 "J. P. Allen & Co.," *Atlanta Constitution*, Mar. 3, 1912.

8 "Bonwit Teller & Co.," *New York Tribune*, Apr. 9, 1916; "Bonwit Teller & Co.," *New York Tribune*, Nov. 5, 1916; "Miss J. C. Morrison," *Atlanta Constitution*, Sept. 22, 1912. "French Model Gowns . . . Lord and Taylor," *Vogue* 25, Apr. 13, 1905, ix; "J. M. Gidding & Co.," *New York Tribune*, Jan. 4, 1916.

9 "John Wanamaker," *New York Tribune*, Jan. 3, 1916; "Keely Company," *Atlanta Constitution*, Mar. 8, 1896.

10 By the 1860s women's outerwear (cloaks and so forth) was commonly ready-made, but in the 1870s custom dressmaking was still the norm. In the 1880s wealthy women continued to order custom-made clothing, and other women ordered custom clothing for special events; see Baron and Klepp, "'If I Didn't

Have My Sewing Machine,'" 27, 47, 50; Schorman, *Selling Style*, 5; "Nicole de Paris," *New York Tribune*, Apr. 9, 1916; on accent, see "Nicole de Paris," *New York Tribune*, Apr. 16, 1916; "Nicole de Paris," *New York Tribune*, May 7, 1916.

11   "Mrs. M. M. Merchant," *Atlanta Constitution*, May 17, 1890.

12   Constance Astor Choate, "Paris and New York Fashions," *American Woman* 7 (Aug. 1897): 11.

13   Gamber, *The Female Economy*, 111. On low earnings for sewing women, see Baron and Klepp, "'If I Didn't Have My Sewing Machine,'" 22; Hay, "Introduction: A. & L. Tirocchi," 13, 20; Parmel, "Line, Color, Detail, Distinction, Individuality," 27–35; Hay, "Paris to Providence," 173.

14   See "Mlle. Enright," *Atlanta Constitution*, Jan. 14, 1912. On the non-French origins of most "Parisian" modistes in the United States, see Gamber, *The Female Economy*, 34; Milbank, *New York Fashion*, 25. On Demorest, see Lynes, *The Tastemakers*, 77–78; Ross, *Crusades and Crinolines*, 2, 21. "Madame La Modiste," *Atlanta Constitution*, Nov. 22, 1896.

15   On walking jackets, see E. Butterick and Co., *Pattern Catalogue*, 3; on riding habits, see "Franklin Simon & Co.," *New York Tribune*, Mar. 3, 1918; on English jacket suits, see "Tailor-Made Costumes," *New York Tribune*, Jan. 19, 1896; "Wheelwomen's Costumes," *New York Tribune*, Apr. 9, 1996; "London Party Dresses," *Chicago Tribune*, July 4, 1880; on theater wear, see "How English Women Dress," *New York Tribune*, Jan. 12, 1896; on Brussels, see "Paris Fashions," *New York Tribune*, Apr. 12, 1896; on Vienna, see *The Godiva Riding Habit*; on Nice, see "Paris Fashions," *New York Tribune*, Apr. 12, 1896; on Monte Carlo, see "Who Wears the Loveliest Gowns at Monaco," *Vogue* 41 (Mar. 1, 1913): 25; on Cannes, see "An International Country Club," *Vogue* 41 (Mar. 1, 1913): 29.

16   "German Fashions," *Demorest's Monthly Magazine*, Mar. 1868, 90; Flora McDonald Thompson, "Lessons in Economical Dressing," *Harper's Bazar*, May 1907, 350–354, 351.

17   Severa, *Dressed for the Photographer*, 4, 185, 474.

18   Schreier, *Becoming American Women*, 66, 74, 108; Enstad, *Ladies of Labor*, 30, 67, 80; Peiss, *Cheap Amusements*, 48, 63–65.

19   Glenn, *Daughters of the Shtetl*, 160; Heinze, *Adapting to Abundance*, 90; Ewen and Ewen, *Channels of Desire*, 158; Schreier, *Becoming American Women*, 59–64. On Chinese and Mexican women, see Heinze, *Adapting to Abundance*, 4, 89–93. On work, see Enstad, *Ladies of Labor*, 9, 61; Ewen, *Immigrant Women*, 68–69.

20   On black women, see P. Hunt, "Clothing as an Expression of History," 397; White and White, *Stylin'*, 128, 168, 169, 210; on rural women, see Jensen, "Needlework as Art," 12; on upstate New York, see Bruère and Bruère, *Increasing Home Efficiency*, 6.

21   Ewen and Ewen, *Channels of Desire*.

22 E. Wilson, *Adorned in Dreams*, 76; Green, *Ready-to-Wear*, 2, 23, 46, 118; on shirt-waists, see Banner, *American Beauty*, 4, 148. On tailored suits, see Steele, *Paris Fashion*, 173; "Hickson," *New York Tribune*, Apr. 16, 1916.

23 Cahan, *The Rise of David Levinsky*; E. Wilson, *Adorned in Dreams*, 76; Ewen, *Immigrant Women*, 25.

24 Ross, *Crusades and Crinolines*, 21, 115; on 1871, see Walsh, "The Democratization of Fashion," 304; Lynes, *The Tastemakers*, 77–78; Barker, *Catalogue of Mme. Demorest's Reliable Patterns*.

25 Walsh, "The Democratization of Fashion," 303, 307; quotation, E. Butterick and Co., *Catalogue for Fall*.

26 *Delineator* 60 (Apr. 1898): 382. On the Metropolitan Catalog, see *Delineator* 60 (Apr. 1898): 384. On challenge, see E. Butterick and Co., *Catalogue for Fall*.

27 Department of Commerce, *Commerce and Navigation* (1870), 1523; (1920), 215–18, 258–59, 383–84, 419; Department of Commerce and Labor, *Foreign Commerce and Navigation*, (1911), 839, 845. This figure does not include laces, furs, leather products, or goods listed under "all other." On Mexico and U.S. fashion, see Bunker, "'Consumers of Good Taste,'" 254.

28 B. Altman and Co., *Catalogue of Fall and Winter Fashions*, 2.

29 *Vogue* 7 (May 21, 1896): 348; Frances Faulkner, "Our Skirts and Sleeves," *Ladies' World*, Oct. 1895, 13.

30 On New York, see Gamber, *The Female Economy*, 111. Department of Commerce, *Commerce and Navigation* (1910), 214, 217, 331–34, 374–75, 839, 841. By the year ending June 30, 1915, import figures had fallen to roughly $22 million, whereas export figures had risen to roughly $26 million; see Department of Commerce, *Foreign Commerce and Navigation* (1916), xviii–xxvii.

31 "Gimbels," *New York Tribune*, Mar. 26, 1916; "Silk Dresses," *New York Tribune*, Mar. 5, 1916.

32 On pirating, see E. Wilson, *Adorned in Dreams*, 87. Barker, *Catalogue of Mme. Demorest's Reliable Patterns*.

33 E. Butterick and Co., *Catalogue for Fall*; Walsh, "The Democratization of Fashion," 300, 312.

34 Maude Andrews, "The Question as to Where," *Atlanta Constitution*, Dec. 27, 1896.

35 Quoted in Milbank, *New York Fashion*, 59.

36 On authentic, see "Gidding," *New York Tribune*, Mar. 23, 1916; on characteristically, see Ada Bache Cone, "Evening Gowns," *Atlanta Constitution*, Jan. 3, 1892; on home sewers, see Margaret Bisland, "Fashions and Fabrics," *GH*, Oct. 1899, 171, cited in Schorman, *Selling Style*, 53; on Frenchy, see "Parisian Fall Styles in Women's Dresses at the Frohsin Store!" *Atlanta Constitution*, Sept. 8, 1912.

37 Steele, *Paris Fashion*, 140; Saunders, *The Age of Worth*, 46, 95, 112; Perrot, *Fash-*

ioning the Bourgeoisie, 184; E. Wilson, *Adorned in Dreams*, 32; Hay, "Introduction: A. and L. Tirocchi," 20–21. On new money, see de Marly, *The History of Haute Couture*, 24.

38 "Far From Being Frivolous, Clothes Are a Serious Matter," *New York Tribune*, June 9, 1912; "The English Wife," *Atlanta Constitution*, June 21, 1896. On the attribution of French tastefulness to discriminating consumers, see Walton, *France at the Crystal Palace*, 222.

39 On the abandonment of ethnic dress among peasants, see Ruane, "Subjects into Citizens," 53, 70. On Russian influences on fashion, see "Notes from Our Foreign Correspondent," *Godey's* 109 (Sept. 1884): 306–7; "Dress in Paris," *New York Tribune*, Apr. 8, 1888; on Spanish themes, see Mrs. John W. Bishop, "Latest Fashions," *LHJ* 7 (Mar. 1890): 13; on Greek influences, see Anne Rittenhouse, "French and American Designers are Working in Harmony," *New York Tribune*, Apr. 14, 1918.

40 "Fashions in Paris," *Delineator* 7 (Jan. 1876): 35.

41 On hats, see "The Frilled Hat," *Los Angeles Times*, Oct. 4, 1896. Ann Rittenhouse, "What Well-Dressed Women Will Wear," *New York Tribune*, Feb. 10, 1918 (illustration); and same column Feb. 17, 1918; Mar. 3, 1918; Mar. 10, 1918.

42 Steele, *Paris Fashion*, 74, 221; "Chitchat on Fashions for March," *Godey's* 100 (Mar. 1880): 283–86, 285; "Chitchat on Fashions for Apr.," *Godey's* 100 (Apr. 1880): 379.

43 "The Frilled Hat," *Los Angeles Times*, Oct. 4, 1896.

44 On the war, see Yarwood, *European Costume*, 255; Virginia Ralston, "What Mrs. Ralston Saw in Paris," *LHJ* 24 (Sept. 1907): 75; on the ballets, see Braun-Ronsdorf, *Mirror of Fashion*, 175. "One Step from Savage," *Times-Picayune*, May 3, 1920.

45 On Breton bonnets, see "Hats This Year," *New York Tribune*, July 28, 1912; on mantillas, see "Society Gossip," *Chicago Tribune*, July 18, 1880; on cloaks, see "Autumn Wraps," *New York Tribune*, Sept. 9, 1888; on embroidery, see "Latest Styles," *Times-Picayune*, Sept. 2, 1900; on ruffles and shawls, see B. Altman and Co., *Catalogue of Fall and Winter Fashions*, 14, 21.

46 Augusta Reimer, "The New Spanish Dresses," *LHJ* 31 (Mar. 1914): 29.

47 On colors, see "The Fashions," *New York Tribune*, Sept. 2, 1888; on bricolage, see "Never Before," *New York Tribune*, Dec. 4, 1892.

48 On the newest and best, see "High's," *Atlanta Constitution*, Sept. 6, 1896; on fame, see "J. M. Gidding & Co.," *New York Tribune*, Mar. 21, 1916.

49 Wolf von Schierbrand, "The Women of Russia," *Delineator* 63 (Sept. 1904): 358; on Russian debates over fashion and Westernization, see Ruane, "Clothes Shopping in Imperial Russia," 765–82.

50 Holmes, *Burton Holmes Travelogues*, 3:23. "Influence of Paris Fashion," *Atlanta*

Constitution, June 2, 1912. On French influence in Germany, see also Purdy, *The Tyranny of Elegance*, 7, 13.

51 "Home and Society," *New York Tribune*, Oct. 23, 1892.

52 "Here Is a 'bit,'" *New York Tribune*, Sept. 18, 1892.

53 Holmes, *Burton Holmes Travelogues*, 13:149; on Paquin, see de Marly, *The History of Haute Couture*, 50. On Latin Americans and European fashions, see Needell, *A Tropical Belle Epoque*, 158; Orlove, *The Allure of the Foreign*, 5, 40, 42, 75, 103; Bauer, *Goods, Power, History*, 13, 153–54.

54 "Havana a Second, Almost a Gayer, Riviera," *New York Tribune*, Jan. 23, 1916.

55 Gail Hamilton, "New Year Suggestion," *Los Angeles Times*, Jan. 3, 1888. On proving Westernization through clothing, see Perrot, *Fashioning the Bourgeoisie*, 79.

56 On the empress, see de Marly, *The History of Haute Couture*, 132; on Young Turks, see "The Naked Truth about the Turk and His Harem," *Chicago Tribune*, Oct. 6, 1912. On Paris fashions in the Ottoman Empire, see Jirousek, "The Transition to Mass Fashion System Dress," 234–36. On Hawaiian royals, see Silva, *Aloha Betrayed*, 177–80; Maxwell, *Colonial Photography*, 194; Desmond, *Staging Tourism*, 50.

57 Mrs. Jas. H. Lambert, "Dress Material," *LHJ* 6 (June 1889): 12; Mrs. Mallon, "For Woman's Wear," *LHJ* 8 (Dec. 1890): 23.

58 Anne Rittenhouse, "Fashion Stages a Fantasy," *Vanity Fair* 2 (Apr. 1914): 61.

59 "Why Parisian Ladies Do Not Wear Black," *Demorest's Illustrated Monthly* 13 (Sept. 1877): 487.

60 Blum, *Victorian Fashions*, 66, 249, 269. On casino gowns, see *Vogue* 7 (May 21, 1896): 366; on the unsuitability of fashion for maternity wear, see Crane, *Fashion*, 108.

61 "The Origin of Fashion," *Cosmopolitan* 1 (June 1886): 252.

62 On citing dressmakers, see "London Frocks for This Summer to Be Explosive," *Times-Picayune*, Apr. 4, 1920. Pink Hyacinth, "London Fashions," *Godey's* 116 (Mar. 1888): 262–65, 265; "Horse Show Gowns at Ostend," *New York Tribune*, Sept. 20, 1908; "Toilets Won at the Riviera," *New York Tribune*, Feb. 23, 1908; on the opera, see M. T. K., "Paris Fashions," *Demorest's Monthly Magazine* 19 (June 1883): 520; on teas, see "Unusual Individuality in Gowns," *New York Tribune*, Apr. 26, 1908; on promenades, see Grace Corneau, "Paris Women Imitate Men's Fashions," *Chicago Tribune*, Mar. 6, 1904; on idle set, see "A Glimpse of Paris Tea Rooms," *New York Tribune* Feb. 9, 1908.

63 On exposition wear, see "Charms of the Separate Coat as Worn by Parisiennes," *New York Tribune*, June 9, 1912; on theater wear, see "Beautifully Gowned Women," *New York Tribune*, Mar. 22, 1908. "London Correspondence," *Frank Leslie's Gazette* 4 (Nov. 1855): 82; "Paris," *Vogue* 8 (July 16, 1896): 46.

64 Comtesse de Champdoce, "Paris," *Vogue* 6 (July 25, 1895): 65; Baroness Salssee, "Vienna," *Vogue* 8 (July 30, 1896): 78; Lady Duff-Gordon, "Gaby's New Clothes," *Atlanta Constitution*, June 23, 1912.

65 "Letter from Abroad," *Demorest's Illustrated Monthly*, Nov. 1869, 407; "London Correspondence," *Frank Leslie's Gazette* 4 (Nov. 1855): 82; "Coronets behind the Counter," *Vogue* 30 (Dec. 5, 1907): 804. On Czartorisky, see "Paris: The Fashionable World Still Lingering at Watering-Places," *Chicago Tribune*, Oct. 9, 1880. "From the Faubourg St. Germain," *Vogue* 30 (Dec. 5, 1907): 812; "Chitchat on Fashions for May," *Godey's* 92 (May 1876): 486.

66 Steele, *Women of Fashion*, 29, 40; Perrot, *Fashioning the Bourgeoisie*, 168; "Sarah Bernhardt," *Chicago Tribune*, Oct. 31, 1880. On aristocrats' marriages to actresses in the early 1900s, see Cannadine, *The Decline and Fall*, 348. On the stage as a source for fashion, see Rappaport, *Shopping for Pleasure*, 185–86. On actresses and fashion, see also "Charms of the Separate Coat as Worn by Parisiennes," *New York Tribune*, June 9, 1912; Lady Duff-Gordon, "Gaby's New Clothes," *Atlanta Constitution*, June 23, 1912; "The Last Word in Paris Fashions," *Chicago Tribune*, Feb. 1, 1920.

67 "The Parisian in Chic Rôles," *Vanity Fair* 2 (Apr. 1914): 60; "What They Wear in Vanity Fair," *Vanity Fair* 1 (Feb. 1914): 57.

68 Nancy M. W. Woodrow, "How Fashions are Set," *Cosmopolitan* 33 (July 1902): 253–61.

69 On outdoor wear, see Gow, *Good Morals*, 187, 190; M. E. W. Sherwood, "The Dress of an American Woman," *LHJ* 6 (Aug. 1889): 2.

70 Jensen, "Needlework as Art," 8; Walsh, "The Democratization of Fashion," 313; Kidwell and Christman, *Suiting Everyone*, 17.

71 U.S. Constitution, article 1, section 9; Wood, *The Creation of the American Republic*, 71–72, 208, 400. On exploitation, see Maude Andrews, "I have seen a king," *Atlanta Constitution*, Sept. 6, 1896; on marital infidelity, see "Seeks to Annul Marriage," *Chicago Tribune*, Jan. 4, 1904. Eliot, *Heiresses and Coronets*, 175.

72 On demimonde, see Widow, *Intimacies of Court*, 149; on affair, see "'Women Should Wear More Modest Clothes,'" *Atlanta Constitution*, Feb. 4, 1912. Woolson, *Dress-Reform*, xii.

73 "Queening It over Ireland," *Vogue* 46 (Aug. 1, 1915): 43.

74 Davidoff, *The Best Circles*, 54, 102.

75 "A Devoted King," *New York Tribune*, Jan. 5, 1896; "The Princess of Bulgaria," *New York Tribune*, Jan. 26, 1896; "Prince D'Orleans Is Married," *Chicago Tribune*, Nov. 5, 1908; on Victor, see "Prince Refutes Baby Jo's Action," *Chicago Tribune*, Apr. 2, 1908; on Louise, see "Princess and Gems Go," *Chicago Tribune*, Sept. 1, 1904; on the Swedish queen, see "The Daily Picayune," *Times-Picayune*, Apr. 2, 1876. "The Tsarita Is Much Improved," *Atlanta Constitution*, Jan. 14, 1912;

"Royalty United," *Los Angeles Times*, May 4, 1908; "Swindles Large Sum Then Elopes," *Atlanta Constitution*, Aug. 25, 1912; on the annulment, see Emil Andrassy, "By Atlantic Cable," *Los Angeles Times*, Nov. 3, 1912; "Finds Her Friend a Suicide," *Chicago Tribune*, Sept. 4, 1904.

76   Mrs. John Van Vorst, "Dress and Gossip of Paris," *Delineator* 63 (Mar. 1904): 363 (this was the running title of her column).

77   E. M. R., "From the Faubourg St. Germain," *Vogue* 30 (Nov. 7, 1907): 636.

78   Princess gown was a common fashion term; on empress walking-suit, see "Mirror of Fashions," *Demorest's Illustrated Monthly*, May 1870, 151; on Queen Margot, see "Fashions in Paris," *Delineator* 7 (Jan. 1876): 34; on duchesse, see "What She Wears," *Vogue* 6 (July 25, 1895): 60. On czarina, see *Stern Brothers Fashion Catalogue*, 52. "Princess Chic Supporter," *Vogue* 29 (May 23, 1907): 814; "The Empress Skirt," *Vogue* 11 (Jan. 20, 1898): iv.

79   On shades, see "Chitchat on Fashions for November," *Godey's* 77 (Nov. 1868): 465; on royalty, see "J. M. Gidding & Co.," *New York Tribune*, Feb. 27, 1916; on courts, see "J. M. Gidding & Co.," *New York Tribune*, Feb. 14, 1916; on overcoats, see Smith, Gray, and Co., *New York Times*, Jan. 9, 1913.

80   Fowler, *In a Gilded Cage*, xiii; M. E. W. Sherwood, "How Shall Our Girls Behave?" *LHJ* 5 (Oct. 1888): 2.

81   Mrs. Burton Harrison, "Social Life at Six Centres," *LHJ* 9 (Jan. 1892): 2.

82   Hester Donaldson Jenkins, "Bulgaria and Its Women," *NGM* 27 (Apr. 1916): 377–400, 382.

83   Darrah, *The World of Stereographs*, 49; "Costumes of All Nations," Singer Mfg. Co., folder .110–.118, box 1, World's Columbian Exposition Collection. On the Singer Company's efforts to cast itself as a herald of civilization, see also Brandon, *A Capitalist Romance*, 140. Ironically, Singer was no model of "civilized" morality: in 1860 it emerged that he had been maintaining three families simultaneously, not to mention his legitimate one, 164.

84   "Dutch Meccas of Modern Artists," *Vogue* 39 (May 15, 1912): 23.

85   "Swiss Costumes," *Godey's* 92 (Feb. 1876): 19; M. E. W. Sherwood, "The Dress of an American Woman," *LHJ* 6 (Aug. 1889): 2.

86   "A Forecast of Fall Fashions in the Balkan War Zone," *Vanity Fair* 3 (Sept. 1914): 38.

87   "Fair Women as Well as Brave Men Dwell in Rugged Balkan Hills," *New York Tribune*, Nov. 17 1912. "Pictures from Roumania," *Demorest's Monthly Magazine* 19 (June 1883): 492–503.

88   Frank G. Carpenter, "Russian Girls," *Los Angeles Times*, Oct. 2, 1892.

89   "Easter Millinery in Other Lands," *Chicago Tribune*, Apr. 7, 1912.

90   Jean Urquhardt, "A Girl's Life in Old Mexico," *Ladies' World*, Oct. 1897, 13. On

foreigners' disdain for Mexican peasant dress, see Beezley, *Judas at the Jockey Club*, 70–71.

91 Holmes, *Burton Holmes Travelogues*, 11:11.

92 "The Feet of Chinese Women," *Chicago Tribune*, Oct. 16, 1880; on veils, see "Costume of Persian Ladies," *Cottage Hearth* 1 (Oct. 1874): 276; on beatings, see "Back to Solitude Go Turkish Women," *Atlanta Constitution*, Sept. 1, 1912; "The Fashionable Kaffir," *New York Tribune*, Jan. 11, 1880; "Women of the Transvaal," *New York Tribune*, Feb. 18, 1900. Quotation in Kramer, "Making Concessions," 98.

93 On missionary women's efforts to clothe Hawaiians, see Grimshaw, *Paths of Duty*, 164.

94 Veblen, *The Theory of the Leisure Class*, 175.

95 Frances E. Fryatt, "A Modern Juggernaut," *Ladies' World*, Feb. 1897, 13.

96 "Autumn Days," *Atlanta Constitution* Sept. 4, 1892.

97 Gail Hamilton, "New Year Suggestion," *Los Angeles Times*, Jan. 3, 1888.

98 Blanchard, *Oscar Wilde's America*, 142.

99 Frances Faulkner, "Our Skirts and Sleeves," *Ladies' World*, Oct. 1895, 13.

100 "At Vantine's," *New York Tribune*, Jan. 19, 1896; "Simpson Crawford Co.," *New York Tribune*, Jan. 12, 1908; "Mme. Najla Mogabgab," *Vogue* 38 (Nov. 1, 1911): 117.

101 "The Fashions," *New York Tribune*, Sept. 2, 1888.

102 "Superb Chinese Coat," *Vogue* 29 (Feb. 7, 1907): 189.

103 "Gathered Here and There," *New York Tribune*, Oct. 15, 1908; Alice Long, "What I See on Fifth Avenue," *LHJ* 31 (Jan. 1914): 24.

104 "The Allen Exhibit of Paris Fashions," *Atlanta Constitution*, Sept. 29, 1912.

105 "Bonwit Teller & Co.," *New York Tribune*, Oct. 1, 1916; Anne Rittenhouse, "Mid-Season Sees Some New French Gowns to Promote Trade," *New York Tribune*, Jan. 6, 1918. See also "Mandel Brothers, Nikko Shop," *Chicago Tribune* Dec. 4, 1918.

106 "Women Can Look," *New York Tribune*, July 7, 1912.

107 On authenticity, see "A Special Easter-Sale," *New York Tribune*, Apr. 16, 1916; Edna Kent Forbes, "Beauty Chats," *Times-Picayune*, July 3, 1916.

108 Montgomery Ward and Co., *Catalogue*, 81:59; *The 1902 Edition of the Sears Roebuck Catalogue*, 1069; "The Tribune Pattern," *New York Tribune*, June 3, 1908; Anna Ash, "A Lady's Crocheted Kimono," *GH* 41 (Sept. 1905): 290.

109 Newman, *White Women's Rights*, 102–7; Boisseau, *White Queen*.

110 "A Woman in Darkest Africa," *Housekeeper's Weekly* 2 (May 28, 1892): 2.

111 Department of Commerce, *Foreign Commerce and Navigation* (1916), xvii–xix, 45, 96.

112 *Boggs and Buhl Fashion Catalogue.* "Bonwit Teller and Co.," *Vogue* 39 (Apr. 15, 1912): 9; *The 1902 Edition of the Sears Roebuck Catalogue*, 851; "John Forsythe," *Vogue* 29 (Apr. 18, 1907): 665; "Revillon Frères in the Orient," *Vanity Fair* 11 (Nov. 1918): 78–79; "Where Vantine's Buy," *New York Tribune*, Feb. 2, 1896; on imported textiles in the colonial period, see Baumgarten, *What Clothes Reveal*, 81–82.

113 Li, "The Silk Export Trade," 78–79, 81.

114 I am indebted to Laura Wexler for suggesting this terminology.

115 "Japanese Wraps," *Harper's Bazar*, Aug. 1904, 792–795, 795.

116 "McCallum Silk Hosiery," *Vanity Fair* 10 (Oct. 1918): 105.

117 Laura B. Starr, "My Oriental Dressmaker," *Harper's Bazar*, Aug. 1904, 768–771.

118 Widow, *Intimacies of Court*, 327–28.

119 "Fashions for Spring," *Atlanta Constitution*, Feb. 7, 1892.

120 Department of Commerce, *Commerce and Navigation* (1920), xviii, xxiv.

121 "Bonwit Teller and Co.," *New York Tribune*, Jan. 16, 1916.

122 "Bonwit Teller and Co.," *Vogue* 49 (May 1, 1917): 5.

123 "John Wanamaker," *New York Tribune*, Jan. 1, 1918; Bulatao, "Iloilo," 47.

124 "B. Altman & Co.," *New York Tribune*, Jan. 8, 1918. On lingerie from Puerto Rico and the Philippines, see also "Mandel Brothers," *Chicago Tribune*, Mar. 1, 1918; Department of Commerce and Labor, *Foreign Commerce and Navigation* (1911), 22; on teachers, see Azize-Vargas, "The Emergence of Feminism in Puerto Rico," 261.

125 "Bonwit Teller and Co.," *Vogue* 49 (May 1, 1917): 5.

126 Knoblauch, *My Lady's Dress*, 134; "My Lady's Dress," *Vanity Fair* 3 (Dec. 1914): 38.

127 Knoblauch, *My Lady's Dress*, 14; McCarthy, *Women's Culture*, 224.

128 "'My Lady's Dress' Most Interesting," *New York Times*, Oct. 12, 1914.

129 Ecob, *The Well-Dressed Woman*, 146, 236.

130 Ethel H. Traphagen, "The American Indian Dress," *LHJ* 31 (Jan. 1914): 31; quotation from Lauer and Lauer, *Fashion Power*, 58.

131 Quoted in Lauer and Lauer, *Fashion Power*, 178.

132 Mrs. John C. Hessler, "Better Dress Standards," *The General Federation of Women's Clubs, Eleventh Biennial Convention*, 1912, 160–67, folder: 11th Biennial, box: Convention Records (Proceedings-Reports), 1912–1916, GFWC.

133 On nationalism and U.S. fashion in this period, see Joselit, *A Perfect Fit*, 2; Schorman, *Selling Style*, 103–27; on bodies as metaphors for the nation, see Irving, *Immigrant Mothers*, 10; on the American girl, see Banta, *Imaging American Women*, 2, 206, 211, 500, 557; on distinctiveness, see J. Jackson, *American Womanhood*,

10. Thomas L. Masson, "The White Woman's Burden," *New York Times*, May 16, 1909.

134   "Never Before," *New York Tribune*, Dec. 4, 1892; [Edward Bok], "Thus Far, but No Farther," *LHJ* 31 (Apr. 1914): 5.

135   "Our Home Department: Dress and Its Relation to Life," *Craftsman* 11 (Nov. 1906): 269–71, 269.

136   Braun-Ronsdorf, *Mirror of Fashion*, 139; Holland, "Fashioning Cuba"; Bayly, "The Origins of Swadesi," 310.

137   M. D. C. Crawford, "Women's Costumes in War Time," *GFWC Magazine* 17 (Oct. 1918): 20–21, 20.

138   "Royalty to Honor American," *Chicago Tribune*, Oct. 2, 1904; quotation: Widow, *Intimacies of Court*, 294.

139   "Reopening of Parliament Makes London Socially Gay," *Chicago Tribune*, Feb. 7, 1904; on Paget, see "American Duchess to Teach King George How to Fish," *Atlanta Constitution*, Aug. 18, 1912. "Countess of Yarmouth Granted a Divorce," *Times-Picayune*, Feb. 6, 1908; "Horse Show Gowns at Ostend," *New York Tribune*, Sept. 20, 1908.

140   Maude Andrews, "I Have Seen a King," *Atlanta Constitution*, Sept. 6, 1896.

141   *The Bazar Book of Decorum*, 163.

142   Maude Andrews, "Back in London," *Atlanta Constitution*, Aug. 30, 1896.

143   "Chitchat upon New York and Philadelphia Fashions," *Godey's* 76 (Jan. 1868): 107.

144   "The Story of the Fashion Fête," *Vogue* 44 (Nov. 1, 1914): 35–37, 37.

Chapter 3

1   Simmons, *American Cookery*, 33, 40, 44–45, 47, 51. For a similar account of eighteenth-century New England cookery, see Gardiner, *Mrs. Gardiner's Receipts*. On colonial food, see also S. Booth, *Hung, Strung, and Potted*; Hess, *Martha Washington's Booke*; McMahon, "'A Comfortable Subsistence.'"

2   Harland et al., *The New England Cook Book*. On cookbook nationalism, see Fordyce, "Cookbooks of the 1800s," 93; Pilcher, "'Recipes for *Patria*.'" Harland, *Cookery for Beginners*, 60, 99, 108–10, 113.

3   Simmons, *American Cookery*, 20, 39, 45, 47, 80. On culinary mixing, see Gabaccia, *We Are What We Eat*, 34; Pillsbury, *No Foreign Food*, 5. On the madeira trade, see Hancock, "'A Revolution in the Trade.'"

4   On rice and garum, see Toussaint-Samat, *A History of Food*, 153, 373; Jenkins, *Bananas*, 1; A. Smith, *The Tomato in America*, 15; Schivelbusch, *Tastes of Paradise*, 5–6. On the history of food as a history of mixing, see Bell and Valentine, *Consuming Geographies*, 168.

5   Sokolov, *Why We Eat What We Eat*, 11–12 (quotation), 38, 53, 83, 100. See also Mintz, *Sweetness and Power*; Shammas, "Changes in English and Anglo-American Consumption"; Camporesi, *Exotic Brew*, 74, 87; Mazumdar, "The Impact of New World Food Crops"; Pelto and Pelto, "Diet and Delocalization," 309–30; Mintz, *Tasting Food*; Wilk, "Food and Nationalism," 67–89; Weatherford, *Indian Givers*, 103, 105; Mennell, *All Manners of Food*, 175–76, 188; Freeman, *Mutton and Oysters*, 32, 74, 86; Pilcher, "'Recipes for *Patria*,'" 205; Camporesi, *The Magic Harvest*, 193.

6   On the African and West Indian origins of southern cooking, see K. Hess, *The Carolina Rice Kitchen*, 95, 109, 111–12; Carney, *Black Rice*. On the food nationalism of antebellum cookbooks, see Fordyce, "Cookbooks of the 1800s," 93. On culinary conservatism, see Gabaccia, *We Are What We Eat*, 37. Crowfield [Stowe], *House and Home Papers*, 265.

7   J. Hill, *Practical Cooking*, 636; "Home Interests," *New York Tribune*, Mar. 14, 1880.

8   On peas, see "Kitchen," *Demorest's Monthly Magazine* 19 (June 1883): 513; on fish, see "What to Eat and How," *LHJ* 28 (Mar. 1, 1911): 32; on goulash, see Baxter, *Housekeeper's Handy Book*, 36; on piroga and haddocks, see *Breakfast, Dinner, and Tea*, 100–101; on pudding, fritters, bread, and eggs, see Harland et al., *The New England Cook Book*; on liver dumplings, see Rice, *Dainty Dishes*, 31–35; on olla podrida, see Pechin, *The 3-6-5 Cook Book*. Laura Shapiro, *Perfection Salad*, 212, acknowledges "adventurous perspectives" on food in this period, but she emphasizes culinary nationalism on the part of domestic scientists. Similarly, Mary Drake McFeely argues that in the late nineteenth century, "mainstream American culture scorned ethnic cooking"; see *Can She Bake a Cherry Pie?*, 37.

9   Farmer, *The Boston Cooking-School Cook Book*, 101; on French "international culinary hegemony," see Mennell, *All Manners of Food*, 134.

10 C. Herrick, *What to Eat How to Serve It*, 108, 192–93; Corson, *Miss Corson's Practical American Cookery*, 113; Catherine Owen, "French Terms Used in Cooking," *GH* 2 (Mar. 20, 1886): 287–88.

11 On 1918 manual, see Baxter, *Housekeeper's Handy Book*, 30–31, 33–34, 38, 41, 43, 47–48, 70; on salad, Marion Mackenzie, "Salads for Light Summer Lunches," *Woman's World* 32 (July 1916): 18; on chantisa, *Breakfast, Dinner, and Tea*, 40; on koumiss, Willard H. Morse, "Koumiss and Imitation Koumiss," *GH* 2 (Mar. 20, 1886): 299; on radishes, Eleanor Van Horn, "Recipes of Society Cooks," *GH* 50 (Jan. 1910): 119; on chop suey, Rice, *Dainty Dishes*, 51.

12 Constance D. Borrowe, "A Mexican Dinner," *GH* 50 (Feb. 1910): 271. On chilies, see Women of the Central Presbyterian Church, *Housekeeper's Favorites*, 104, 129; on peppers, see Baxter, *Housekeeper's Handy Book*, 37; on gaspacho, see Rice, *Dainty Dishes*, 51; on enchiladas, see Wilcox, *Buckeye Cookery*, 286; on pollo

and tamales, see Shulman, *Favorite Dishes*, 72, 190. Emma Hays Brown, "Curries," *Ladies' World*, June 1899.

13 Parloa, *Miss Parloa's Kitchen Companion*, 88–91, 435. On vanilla, see Austin, *Dr. Austin's Indispensable Hand-book*, 298; on olives and oil, see L. Wilson, *Handbook of Domestic Science*, 201; on chutney, see Ellet, *The New Cyclopaedia*, 135.

14 On ginger, "At Vantine's," *New York Tribune*, Jan. 19, 1896; "Lyons's Norwegian Cod Liver Oil," *Times-Picayune*, Mar. 3, 1880; *Vantine's Catalog*, 45–46. On water, see "Celestins Vichy," *Atlanta Constitution*, Jan. 3, 1912. On Macy's, see Leach, *Land of Desire*, 23.

15 Quotation: "Prices in the Markets," *New York Tribune*, Oct. 21, 1884. On yams and smelts, see "Home Interests," *New York Tribune*, Jan. 20, 1884; on bananas and drilichinuts, see "Home Interests," *New York Tribune*, Apr. 27, 1884; on persimmons and cantaloupes, see "Rare Fruits and How to Serve Them," *New York Tribune*, Dec. 30, 1908; on other products, see "Home Interests," *New York Tribune*, Nov. 16, 1884. A. R. Ward, "Landing Tropical Fruits at Burling Slip," *Harper's Weekly* 14 (June 1870): 388.

16 J. Williams, *The Way We Ate*, 78; Conlin, *Bacon, Beans and Galantines*, 79; Sears, Roebuck, *Your Grocery Store*, 10, 14, 29–31, 40–43, 53, 57.

17 *The Grocer's Manual*, nutmegs, 9–10, almonds, 42, 63. By 1900 California growers supplied the United States with many of its almonds and olives; see Vaught, *Cultivating California*, 14. Ward, *The Grocer's Encyclopedia*, 44, 115, 124, 265, 313, 318, 374, 465, 480, 513, 517, 670. On curry ingredients, see Leslie, *Miss Leslie's New Cookery Book*.

18 These numbers should be regarded as rough because of the nature of the government categories. I did not include live animal imports in the total, because I could not tell if these were intended for consumption, breeding, or other purposes. Nor did I include things that may have been foodstuffs but were listed under other categories—such as the mustard seeds listed under seeds. However, I did include vegetable oils, even though some of these may have had nonfood uses. Department of the Treasury, *Commerce and Navigation* (1865), 526–536; (1900) 66–78; Department of Commerce, *Foreign Commerce and Navigation* (1921), xv–xxvi; vanilla, 31; fish, 47; bananas, 48; cheese, 72; pickles and sauces, 96. On coffee imports, see also Jiménez, "'From Plantation to Cup,'" 40.

19 On names, see "Home Interests," *New York Tribune*, Jan. 20, 1884; on tapioca, see Lyman and Lyman, *The Philosophy of House-Keeping*, 31; on turtle, see J. Hill, *Practical Cooking*, 108. Farmer, *The Boston Cooking-School Cook Book*, 14; on potatoes, see *Breakfast, Dinner, and Tea*, 133–34.

20 William Joseph Showalter, "How the World Is Fed," *NGM* 29 (Jan. 1916): 2–110, 104–5.

21 On industrial food, see Goody, *Cooking, Cuisine and Class*, 160–74; Strasser,

Never Done. Barrett, *Work and Community*, 15, 56. On refrigeration, see S. Williams, *Savory Suppers*, 93. On canning, see R. Cummings, *The American and His Food*, 67, 106–7, 116; Stoll, *The Fruits of Natural Advantage*, 55; on Del Monte, see J. Denker, *The World on a Plate*, 8.

22 Strasser, *Never Done*, 259.

23 On apples, Hess and Hess, *The Taste of America*, 43. On standardization and variety, see Gabaccia, *We Are What We Eat*, 37.

24 S. J. White, *Housekeepers*, 86. Eleanor Van Horn, "Recipes of Society Cooks," *GH* 50 (Jan. 1910): 119.

25 "Nellie Murray on European Cooking," *Times Picayune*, Dec. 4, 1896; Leach, *Land of Desire*, 82; on the cachet of French food, see Dudden, *Serving Women*, 134; S. Williams, *Savory Suppers*, 24; Levenstein, *Revolution at the Table*, 10; A. Escoffier, "Six Ways to Cook a Chicken," *Atlanta Constitution*, Mar. 10, 1912.

26 *Visitor's Guide to the Centennial Exhibition*, 18; Bolotin and Laing, *The World's Columbian Exposition*, 82–83; W. Carson, *Mexico*, 49–50.

27 "A Mexican Market," *New York Tribune*, Oct. 31, 1880; "The Chinese Cuisine," *New York Tribune*, Feb. 1, 1880; Jane Eddington, "The World's Cooks," *Chicago Tribune*, Dec. 7, 1912; Weigley, *Sarah Tyson Rorer*, 92, 96–97.

28 Quotation: Flora Michaelis, "Anglo-Indian Pickles and Chutneys," *Delineator* 74 (Oct. 1909): 322. On labels, see "A Curry," *New York Tribune*, June 19, 1892. On colonialism and curry, see Chaudhuri, "Shawls, Jewelry, Curry, and Rice," 238; Appadurai, "How to Make a National Cuisine," 18; Collingham, *Curry*, 115–18; on the imperial dimensions to tea consumption, see Chatterjee, *A Time for Tea*, 49.

29 Edith Bradford Gird, "Spanish-California Cookery," *GH* 50 (Feb. 1910): 272–73; on later interventions, see G. Cooper, "Love, War, and Chocolate," 76. Anna Barrows, "In Place of Meat, What?" *GH* 50 (Feb. 1910): 268–71, 271.

30 Mary Hamilton Talbott, "'New' Fruits and Vegetables," *GH* 51 (Aug. 1910): 213. On overseas USDA researchers, see Charles, "Searching for Gold in Guacamole," 133.

31 "Home Interests," *New York Tribune*, Mar. 14, 1880.

32 Jenkins, *Bananas*, 5; Healy, *Drive to Hegemony*, 22.

33 Collins, *America's Favorite Food*, 66, 69, 70, 86. On manufacturers and new foods, see Gabaccia, *We Are What We Eat*, 37; on chili, see J. Denker, *The World on a Plate*, 142. "Recipes," *Everyland* 1 (Dec. 1909): 65.

34 Condit and Long, *How to Cook and Why*, 2.

35 Mrs. Monachesi, "The Italian Way of Cooking It," *GH* 3 (Oct. 30, 1886): 319.

36 Kander, *The "Settlement" Cook Book*, 14, 83, 145, 217. The 1903 version of this cookbook seems more heavily weighted toward old New England fare. Kander and Schoenfeld, *The "Settlement" Cook Book*, 1903. Frederick, *Household Engi-*

neering, 447. She praises the cooking abilities of Italian, Polish-Lithuanian, and French immigrants. See also Mary Hungerford, "Fanchon, My Cook," *LHJ* 6 (July 1889): 15. On anxieties about the health menace posed by immigrant cooks, see J. Leavitt, *Typhoid Mary,* 117.

37 Weigley, *Sarah Tyson Rorer,* 31; Starr cited in S. Jackson, *Lines of Activity,* 56.

38 "International Institute Committee Minutes, May 1923," and "International Institute Board Meeting, Tues., June 26th, 1923," both in folder: "Board of Directors Minutes with Annual Report-1923," box 1, International Institute of San Francisco Records.

39 Ewen, *Immigrant Women,* 84; Elizabeth Howe, Report, Mar. 1920, and Report, May 1920, folder 2, International Institute of Niagara Falls Records.

40 Ruth Crawford Mitchell Diary, Oct. 27, 1916.

41 "Russian Meals an Adventure," *New York Tribune,* Apr. 7, 1918. On ethnic restaurants, see Gabaccia, *We Are What We Eat,* 95–101; Batterberry and Batterberry, *On the Town in New York,* 129, 218; Pillsbury, *From Boarding House to Bistro,* 52, 165.

42 R. Hughes, *The Real New York,* 252, 268.

43 *Standard Guide to Los Angeles,* 51–52, 111; *Historical Sketch Book and Guide to New Orleans,* 84.

44 On Chicago, see Ernest Poole, "A Mixing Bowl for Nations," *Everybody's Magazine* 23 (Oct. 1910): 554–64, 556, 558, 562; Morley, *Travels in Philadelphia,* 17.

45 Jane Eddington, "Mrs. Eddington's Kitchen Hints," *Atlanta Constitution,* Apr. 14, 1912; "Garcia Cafe," *Atlanta Constitution,* Jan. 28, 1912; "Bouchees de Dames," *New York Tribune,* Apr. 12, 1912.

46 On rat eating, see Tchen, *New York before Chinatown,* 265; Light, "From Vice District," 384. Lui, "'The Real Yellow Peril'"; on gravy, see William Brown Meloney, "Slumming in New York's Chinatown," *Munsey's Magazine* 41 (Sept. 1909): 818–30, 824–25. Charles H. Shinn, "A Chinese Dinner of Six Courses," *GH* 10 (Feb. 1, 1890): 149.

47 Herbert Copeland, "Rice as the Chinese Prepare It," *LHJ* 25 (June 1908): 50. On immigrant foods as a nonthreatening way to engage with cultural variety, see Bramen, "The Urban Picturesque."

48 Corson, *Family Living,* 38.

49 Rice, *Dainty Dishes,* 11. On procuring Parmesan from Italian grocers, see Bush, *What to Have,* 213.

50 Jeannette Young Norton, "Going Marketing in 'Little Italy,'" *New York Tribune,* July 23, 1916; Jeannette Young Norton, "When Madame Goes Marketing in Chinatown," *New York Tribune,* Oct. 8, 1916; Rice, *Dainty Dishes,* 54.

51 On Tuscan peddlers and delis, see J. Denker, *The World on a Plate,* 7, 69, 73; on kohlrabi, see Corson, *Family Living,* 128; on brioche, see Parloa, *Miss Parloa's*

Kitchen Companion, 546; Gabaccia, *We Are What We Eat*, 64, 66; "Home Interests," *New York Tribune*, Apr. 27, 1884. On tamales, see Strasser, *Never Done*, 15.

52 On male clientele, see Levenstein, *Revolution at the Table*, 185; on etiquette, see Dusselier, "Bonbons," 22; on relishes, see "A curry," *New York Tribune*, June 19, 1892. "Try a Cup of Real Indian Tea," *Vogue* 44 (Nov. 14, 1914): 113; William Joseph Showalter, "How the World Is Fed," *NGM* 29 (Jan. 1916): 2–110, 110.

53 On culling "from each system the best," see Mary Barrett Brown, *LHJ* 8 (Apr. 1891): 26. On cooking Indian dishes as a way for working-class British women to "share in the imperial experience," see Chaudhuri, "Shawls, Jewelry, Curry, and Rice," 242.

54 "Don't Drink Slave Cocoa," *Survey*, Nov. 6, 1909; on forced labor on Guatemalan coffee plantations in this period, see Stolcke, "The Labors of Coffee in Latin America," 84.

55 Topik, "Coffee," 58–59.

56 Dean, *With Broadax and Firebrand*, 191; Tucker, *Insatiable Appetite*, 16–60, 182–84. Ayala, *American Sugar Kingdom*, 245. U.S. companies produced roughly half the sugar on Cuba in 1920, Healy, *Drive to Hegemony*, 203–6. On sugar and slavery, see Mintz, *Sweetness and Power*. Dosal, *Doing Business with the Dictators*, 6, 13, 37, 38, 50. On Honduran strikes, see T. O'Brien, *The Revolutionary Mission*, 93.

57 Seller, "The Education of the Immigrant Woman," 311; Strasser, *Never Done*, 204–12; Ewen, *Immigrant Women*, 84–91, 172–75; L. Shapiro, *Perfection Salad*; Levenstein, *Revolution at the Table*, 103–8; on domestic science in Europe, see Mennell, *All Manners of Food*, 230–31.

58 Amanda B. Harris, "Coffee," *GH* 12 (Apr. 1891): 195. On invitations, see Helen Campbell, "The American Housekeeper in Norway," *HB* 10 (Aug. 1901): 156–58, 156. Food writers proudly recalled dinners eaten in foreign homes as evidence of their expertise on foreign food ways; see "An Arab Dinner," *Household* 12 (May 1879): 104; "A Chinese Dinner in High Life," *GH* 2 (Feb. 20, 1886): 238.

59 Campbell, *The Easiest Way*, 7; Pechin, *The 3-6-5 Cook Book*, vii. On the home economic movement, Stage and Vincenti, *Rethinking Home Economics*.

60 "German-American Housekeeping," *Chautauquan* 3 (May 1883): 442–45, 444.

61 "All Good Epicureans Go to Paris before They Die," *Vogue* 44 (Aug. 1, 1914): 40.

62 Estelline Bennett, "What the French Eat in the North," *Table Talk* 42 (Feb. 1917): 15–16.

63 G. N. Collins, "Dumboy, the National Dish of Liberia," *NGM* 22 (Jan. 1911): 84–88, 85.

64 Daniel F. Randolph, "Life in Other Lands: Japan," *Ladies' World*, Mar. 1899, 7.

65 Crowfield [Stowe], *House and Home Papers*, 232–33; S. Solomons, "Letters from

an American Woman Physician Abroad," *Chautauquan* 23 (Sept. 1896): 756–60, 757.

66 "West African Diet," *GH* 3 (May 29, 1886): 49; on Hindu women, see *Breakfast, Dinner, and Tea*, 255. Harland and Van de Water, *Everyday Etiquette*, 165.

67 On miso, see K. Sano, "How a Japanese Lady Keeps House," *HB* 14 (Nov. 1903): 351–54, 352–53. Alice M. Ivimy, "A Norwegian Morning Meal," *GH* 51 (Aug. 1910): 221; "The Cuisine in Sweden," *Household* 12 (July 1879): 152; on port, Austin, *Dr. Austin's Indispensable Hand-book*, 320; on mats, see "Some Japanese Etiquette," *GH* 2 (Mar. 20, 1886): ii.

68 On cannibalism, Fernández-Armesto, *Near a Thousand Tables*, 22. *Breakfast, Dinner, and Tea*, 265. On eating jellyfish, see "Some Japanese Etiquette," *GH* 2 (Mar. 20, 1886): ii.

69 Lyman and Lyman, *The Philosophy of House-Keeping*, 39.

70 From bats to fins, see *Breakfast, Dinner, and Tea*, 258–59; "A Dinner of Rat, Cat, and Tipsy Shrimps," *New York Tribune*, Feb. 15, 1880.

71 "Snails as an Article of Food," *Household* 12 (Jan. 1879): 8; on horse flesh, see Corson, *Family Living*, 89; on patés, *Breakfast, Dinner, and Tea*, 117.

72 *Breakfast, Dinner, and Tea*, 263; Emma Shaw Colcleugh, "The Eskimo Woman as I Found Her," *Ladies' World*, Dec. 1896, 10; "Some Japanese Etiquette," *GH* 2 (Mar. 20, 1886): ii; on steaming lumps, see Rice, *Dainty Dishes*, 8.

73 On butter, "Human Food," *Cottage Hearth* 2 (Mar. 1875): 71. "The Chinese Cuisine," *New York Tribune*, Feb. 1, 1880; Alice M. Ivimy, "A Norwegian Morning Meal," *GH* 51 (Aug. 1910): 221; "Parisian Restaurants," *New York Tribune*, July 25, 1880; "The Cuisine in Sweden," *Household* 12 (July 1879): 152; on veal, "Home Interests," *New York Tribune*, Oct. 5, 1884.

74 On odors, see L. Wilson, *Handbook of Domestic Science*, 73; "Macaroni," *GH* 9 (Aug. 17, 1889): 170; on washing, see Corson, *Family Living*, 39.

75 Bainbridge, *Round the World Letters*, 178.

76 "Ceylon and India Tea," *Ladies' World*, Feb. 1897, 7.

77 Parloa, *Miss Parloa's Kitchen Companion*, 86; New England Grocer Office, *The Grocer's Companion*, 7. On food rumors and unease about global capitalism, see Derby, "Gringo Chickens with Worms"; Burke, "Cannibal Margarine." A. Smith, *Pure Ketchup*, 35, 59, 64, 67; Sinclair, *The Jungle*.

78 "Household Notes," *New York Tribune*, Oct. 3, 1880.

79 Nesbitt, *Household Management*, 64–65, 101; on national cuisine, L. Shapiro, *Perfection Salad*, 63.

80 Helen Campbell, "The American Housekeeper in Italian Kitchens," *HB* 10 (June 1901): 9–11, 9.

81 "German Cookery," *GH* 2 (Jan. 9, 1886): 143; "The English Inn," *New York Tribune*, Jan. 7, 1912.

82 "Home Interests," *New York Tribune*, Apr. 4, 1880.

83 "How England Is Fed," *New York Tribune*, Oct. 31, 1880.

84 "Quaker Oats," *Vogue* 43 (Feb. 1, 1914): 74. On fruit exports, see Stoll, *The Fruits of Natural Advantage*, 55. On U.S. foodstuffs, see also Domosh, "Pickles and Purity"; "Heinz Spaghetti," *General Federation Magazine* 11 (Oct. 1913): 33.

85 "An Arab Dinner," *Household* 12 (May 1879): 104.

86 "A Chinese Dinner in High Life," *GH* 2 (Feb. 20, 1886): 238.

87 Helen Campbell, "The American Housekeeper in Norway," *HB* 10 (Aug. 1901): 156–158, 157.

88 On national attributes, see Campbell, *The Easiest Way*, 77. J. Hunter, *The Gospel of Gentility*,134; Stocking, *Race, Culture, and Evolution*, 243. Quotation from Levenstein, *Revolution at the Table*, 90.

89 Emilia Custer, "German Cookery," *GH* 3 (May 15, 1886): 13.

90 On wasteful cooking, see Mary C. Hungerford, "Fanchon, My Cook," *LHJ* 6 (July 1889): 15; on undervaluation, see R. Tomes, *The Bazar Book of Decorum*, 183.

91 On the Occidental, see Saint Nihal Singh, "The Cooking of Vegetables as Done by the Hindu," *GH* 50 (Mar. 1910): 544–46. On dyspepsia, see Laura A. Smith, "Why the French Menu Has Become So Universally Popular," *New York Times*, May 16, 1909. On regard, see Mrs. John D. Sherman, "Conservation and Americanization," in *Americanization Programs*, 11.

92 "The Book Review," *GFB* 1 (Jan. 1904): 57; on thriftiness, see Cora Moore, "Little French Dinners for a Week," *New York Tribune*, Mar. 10, 1918.

93 Rebecca Middleton Samson, "The Art of Little Things," *GH* 60 (Nov. 1910): 616–17.

94 "Recipes from East and West," *New York Tribune*, Oct. 6, 1912; "The Book Review," *GFB* 1 (Jan. 1904): 57.

95 Pratt, *Imperial Eyes*, 201–8.

96 On curry, see Ellet, *The New Cyclopaedia*, 221; on sauce, see Lemcke, *European and American Cuisine*, 94. On the regional associations conveyed by food, see de Wit, "Food-Place Associations."

97 Rice, *Dainty Dishes*, 46, 56–57. For a testimonial, see Mrs. D. A. Lincoln, *Mrs. Lincoln's Boston Cook Book*, 140.

98 On spaghetti, Mrs. D. A. Lincoln, *Mrs. Lincoln's Boston Cook Book*, 309; on chop sticks, Dawson and Telford, *The Book of Parties*, 168–69; on tea cups, "Chat," *Demorest's Family Magazine* 29 (Nov. 1892): 51; on theme meals, "Church Socials from Over the Seas," *LHJ* 31 (Feb. 1914): 73; quotation in Ada Marie Peck, "Salads," *GH* 7 (June 23, 1888): 76–77, 88.

99 As Jessamyn Neuhaus notes, cookbooks tell us more about efforts to establish norms than about lived experience; see *Manly Meals*, 4.

100 On dinner parties, see Levenstein, *Revolution at the Table*, 61; Halttunen, *Confidence Men*, 174–75.

101 Mitchell, *All on a Mardi Gras Day*, 53, 107.

102 McAllister, *Society as I Have Found It*, 326, 336–37, 370.

103 "Miss Emily Bissell as a Turkish Girl," *Chicago Tribune*, Jan. 1, 1900; "Maryland Society Belle Was Fair Senorita at Ball," *Times-Picayune*, Feb. 7, 1916; "Big Oriental Ball," *Los Angeles Times*, Mar. 2, 1916.

104 Sarah Leyburn Coe, "A Personality Party," *Vogue* 35 (Feb. 12, 1910): 12.

105 Gordon, *Bazaars and Fair Ladies*, 131; Benton, *Fairs and Fetes*; see also "'Dutch Girls' at the Peck Bazaar," *Chicago Tribune*, Dec. 4, 1904.

106 "Second Day of the Fair," *Times Picayune*, Feb. 3, 1896; on Chicago, see "Church Socials from Over the Seas," *LHJ* 31 (Feb. 1914): 73; on New York, see M. E. W. Sherwood, "Some Society Tableaux," *Cosmopolitan* 24 (Jan. 1898): 235–46. See also "Tableaux of Foreign Nations," *Chicago Tribune*, Apr. 3, 1904.

107 On immigrant festivals, see Hoelscher, *Heritage on Stage*. "Germans Prepare Charity Bazaar," *Chicago Tribune*, Nov. 4, 1904; "Crowd at the Bazaar," *New York Tribune*, Nov. 14, 1908.

108 "Fancy Costumes," *Delineator* 7 (Jan. 1876): 37–38, 37; "Masquerade Costumes," *Metropolitan* 9 (Dec. 1872): 407–9, 409; on Dutch and Japanese costumes, see "Fancy Dress," *Vogue* 14 (Dec. 28, 1899): 447; on Spanish and Portuguese costumes, see Lady Candour, "The Choice of Part and Period in Fancy Dress," *Vogue* 35 (Feb. 12, 1910): 10–11.

109 Holt, *Fancy Dresses Described*; Peiss, *Hope in a Jar*, 146.

110 On Kaffeeklatches, Anna Wentworth Sears, "Midwinter Entertainments," *Harper's Bazar*, Jan. 1904, 88–89; on Tyrolean singers, C. Harrison, "Society and Social Usages," 154.

111 On the pageant, see "A Weaver of India's Spell," *Chicago Tribune* Dec. 5, 1900. "Oriental Markets at Bazaar," *Chicago Tribune*, Feb. 5, 1904; "Rogers Park Club Women Have Lesson in Japanese Etiquette," *Chicago Tribune*, Nov. 2, 1904.

112 "A Japanese Party," *Los Angeles Times*, May 3, 1896; "La Paloma Club," *Los Angeles Times*, May 1, 1904; "A Dainty Japanese Room," *Times Picayune*, Nov. 6, 1896; Anna Wentworth Sears, "Midwinter Entertainments," *Harper's Bazar*, Jan. 1904, 88–89. On international theme parties, see Hammond, "Novelty in Entertaining," 37.

113 "Chat," *Demorest's Family Magazine* 29 (Nov. 1892): 51.

114 On clubwomen, see "A Japanese Tea," *Woman's Era* 1 (Mar. 24, 1894): 12; "The Japanese Tea," *Woman's Era* 3 (June 1896): 5; on Texas women, see Brandimarte, "Japanese Novelty Stores," 21. Glover, *"Dame Curtsey's" Book*, 209.

115 "The Closing Days of the Exposition," *Atlanta Constitution*, Jan. 5, 1896.

116 B. Shackman and Co., *Catalog*, 38, 141, 153–54, 159.

117 Gordon, *Bazaars and Fair Ladies*, 131; on chop suey, see "Oriental Markets at Bazaar," *Chicago Tribune*, Feb. 5, 1904. For all the other booth descriptions, see Benton, *Fairs and Fetes*, 129–33.

118 On Macon Society, see "Japanese Tea-Drinking," *Atlanta Constitution*, Dec. 7, 1884. "Federation of Women," *New York Tribune*, May 2, 1900. See also Winnifred Fales, "The New Wall-Paper Bazar Booths," *LHJ* 28 (Oct. 1911): 49. Another benefit fair included South American and Chinese booths; see "Some Who Are Working for the Cuban Fair," *New York Tribune*, Apr. 21, 1900.

119 Benton, *Fairs and Fetes*, 145–47.

120 Dawson and Telford, *The Book of Parties*, 266.

121 On Japanese, St. Patrick's, and Spain, see Glover, *"Dame Curtsey's" Book*, 35, 192; on Kaffeeklatches, see Anna Wentworth Sears, "Midwinter Entertainments," *Harper's Bazar* 36 (Jan. 1904): 88–89. On bread, "Just among Ourselves," *BVM* 12 (Feb. 1905): 301; on spaghetti, "Just among Ourselves," *BVM* 16 (Jan. 1909): 266; on chop suey, "Just among Ourselves," *BVM* 18 (Jan. 1911): 224. Sears, Roebuck, *Your Grocery Store*, 38. On food as a form of symbolic ethnicity, see Magliocco, "Playing with Food," 146.

122 Glover, *"Dame Courtsey's" Book*, 249. On an around-the-world dinner, see "Just among Ourselves," *BVM* 16 (May 1909): 600.

123 Dawson and Telford, *The Book of Parties*, 168–69.

124 Marie Gozzaldi, "Macaroni, and How to Cook It," *GH* 9 (Mar. 1, 1890): 205–6, 205; Olive Logan, "About English Dinners," *American Cookery* 1 (Dec. 1876): 195–96, 196.

125 Jones and Williams, *Household Elegancies*, 258. On eating as fictive travel, see Zelinsky, "You Are Where You Eat"; Spang, "All the World's a Restaurant," 79–80.

126 On studying pictures, Hewitt, *Queen of Home*, 337; on Japanese customs, Blain, *Games for All Occasions*, 65; on interviewing, Dawson and Telford, *The Book of Parties*, 169.

127 On jumbled letters and postcard parties, "Church Socials from Over the Seas," *LHJ* 31 (Feb. 1914): 73; on Dutch games, Dawson and Telford, *The Book of Parties*, 16.

128 "Just among Ourselves," *BVM* 11 (Jan. 1904): 228.

129 Glover, *"Dame Curtsey's" Book*, 192.

130 On kangaroos, see Holt, *Fancy Dresses Described*, 16; on Dutch treat, see Dawson and Telford, *The Book of Parties*, 16.

131 On chop suey, see Light, "From Vice District," 384; on curry, see Collingham, *Curry*, 115–18; Chaudhuri, "Shawls, Jewelry, Curry, and Rice," 239; on sauce, see Eleanor Van Horn, "Recipes of Society Cooks," *GH* 50 (Jan. 1910): 119. Willard H.

Morse, "Koumiss and Imitation Koumiss," *GH* 2 (Mar. 20, 1886): 299. C. Miller, *Joy from Japan*, 193.

132 Mrs. Monachesi, "The Italian Way of Cooking It," *GH* 3 (Oct. 30, 1886): 319; Bosson, *Aunt Mena's Recipe Book*; "Society in Calcutta," *New York Tribune*, Nov. 28, 1880. On Americanizing food, see L. Shapiro, *Perfection Salad*, 213; Pillsbury, *No Foreign Food*, 5, 98, 208; Levenstein, *Paradox of Plenty*, 122.

133 Diner, *Hungering for America*, 45–46, 49, 54; Kaplan, Hoover, and More, "Introduction: On Ethnic Foodways," 123.

134 Rice, *Dainty Dishes*, 8. On cookbooks and international understanding, see Theophano, "Home Cooking," 145.

135 As Beverly Gordon has written of fund-raising fairs, "Nonwhites were either ignored, represented as the childlike, primitive, or savage 'other,' or reduced to 'humorous' stereotypes. The only booths that ever represented Africa, for example, had Moorish or Egyptian themes; white Americans could not imagine themselves as blacks"; see *Bazaars and Fair Ladies*, 132. Harvey Levenstein *Paradox of Plenty*, 216, has argued that Italian and Chinese foods were most popular in areas without Little Italies and Chinatowns.

136 "The Book Review," *GFB* 1 (Jan. 1904): 57.

137 Eric Lott, *Love and Theft*; Rogin, *Blackface, White Noise*, 12, 19; Deloria, *Playing Indian*.

138 Gabaccia, *We Are What We Eat*, 51, 121–23, 128, 227; Levenstein, *Revolution at the Table*, 103–4; Theophano, "Home Cooking," 149; Diner, *Hungering for America*, 204; Tuchman and Levine, "New York Jews and Chinese Food"; Seller, "The Education of the Immigrant Woman," 311. On haddock, see L. Shapiro, *Perfection Salad*, 62.

139 Thomas Nast, "Uncle Sam's Thanksgiving Dinner," *Harper's Weekly* 13 (Nov. 20, 1869): 745.

140 "Report of the Executive of the International Institute, St. Louis, Mo., Dec. 1919," folder 14: "Executive Reports, 1919–1920," box 2, International Institute of St. Louis Records; quotation, "Report of Miss Elizabeth Howe, International Institute, Jan. 1920," folder 2, International Institute of Niagara Falls Records. Howe eventually persuaded a leader of Niagara Falls society to invite some of her immigrant clients to a party. But this event was more the exception than the rule.

141 Lutz and Collins, *Reading National Geographic*, 21.

Chapter 4

1 Bly's real name was Elizabeth Cochrane. Kroeger, *Nellie Bly*; Rittenhouse, *The Amazing Nellie Bly*, 15, 155–214; I. Peck, *Nellie Bly's Book*, 7. Elisabeth Bisland, "A

Flying Trip around the World," *Cosmopolitan* 9 (May 1890): 50–61; (June 1890): 173–84; (July 1890): 533–45; (Aug. 1890): 401–13; (Oct. 1890): 666–77. On technology, time, and space, see Kern, *The Culture of Time and Space*.

2   H. Smith, *American Travellers Abroad*, 5, 79, 130, 141, 146. Periodicals, too, published round-the-world accounts. For example, see Mary Low Dickinson, "A Tour Round the World," *Chautauquan* 3 (Nov. 1882): 99–101; on Conner, see "Women of Many Lands," *New York Tribune*, Jan. 19, 1900. Mabel Loomis Todd, "A Circumnavigation Story," *CW* 9 (Oct. 1901): 9; "Cupid Nabs Fair Tourist," *Chicago Tribune*, Jan. 6, 1908. See also Sweetser, *One Way Round the World*; on suffragists, see M. Peck, *Carrie Chapman Catt*, 181–208; Van Voris, *Carrie Chapman Catt*, 80–106.

3   Edward Frank Allen, "Around the World in a Motor-Car," *Travel* 16 (Dec. 1910): 74–77, 88; Madeline Z. Doty, "Japan: A Land Unawakened," *GH* (Mar. 1918): 16–17; on Bainbridge, see Schriber, *Telling Travels*, 205; on Ackerman, see "Suffrage in Australia," *Times-Picayune*, July 7, 1908; on the forty-minute trip, see "Travel Class 1911–1912," 28, Yearbooks, HPTC Records.

4   On a Scottish program, see Lena Myers, "Through The Years," McGregor Tourist Club Records. On costumery in a Turkish program, see L. H. W. T., "An Afternoon at Constantinople," *New Cycle* 5 (July–Aug. 1892): 79; on Pfannkuchen, see "Just among Ourselves," *BVM* 5 (Apr. 1898): 242; on Burgos soup, see "Just among Ourselves," *BVM* 6 (Apr. 1899): 251; on Persian lecture, see Dec. 9, 1901, Club and Board Minutes, 1899–1903, box 1, HPTC Records; on scrapbooks, see "Around the Study Lamp," *BVM* 5 (Dec. 1897): 81.

5   See Robertson, "Mapping the Global Condition"; Pratt, *Imperial Eyes*, esp. chap. 2; Geyer and Bright, "World History"; Appadurai, *Modernity at Large*, 6, 31; Peyser, *Utopia and Cosmopolis*, x, 26; Rothschild, "Globalization"; Held and McGrew, "The Great Globalization Debate"; Iriye, *Global Community*, 8–9. On geography, see Schulten, *The Geographical Imagination*; N. Smith, *American Empire*, 3.

6   Croly, *The History of the Woman's Club Movement*, 733, 745; Mrs. George O. Welch, *The General Federation of Women's Clubs, Eleventh Biennial Convention, 1912*, 53, folder: 11th Biennial, box: Convention Records (Proceedings-Reports), 1912–1916, GFWC.

7   On the estimation that only 5 to 10 percent of U.S. women's clubs belonged to the GFWC circa 1906, see Martin, *Sound of Our Own Voices*, 3; on the Thursday Literary Club, see Croly, *The History of the Woman's Club Movement*, 233; "Kalamazoo, Michigan," *New Cycle* 5 (July, Aug. 1892): 79. Many large women's clubs had several study classes. For example, the women's club of Hinsdale, Illinois, had five: history, literature, current topics, the Bible, and foreign travel; see *Third Biennial*, 70.

8 "Two Hundred and Three Clubs Adopt the Bay View Course," *BVM* 9 (Dec. 1901): 119–20; on 8,000, see "Around the Study Lamp," *BVM* 9 (Apr. 1902): 341. "The Classical, of Washington, Ind.," *BVM* 6 (June 1899): 372. On Athens, see "Around the Study Lamp," *BVM* 9 (May 1902): 406.

9 Fennimore, *The Heritage of Bay View*, 126.

10 On the Bridgeport and Eatontown clubs, see Croly, *The History of the Woman's Club Movement*, 305, 850; on the Cleveland club, see May Alden Ward, "Club Study Department," *CW* 2 (June 1898): 81. Knupfer, *Toward a Tenderer Humanity*, 108. On the foreign study topics covered by one African American women's club, the Book Lovers of Kansas City, Missouri, see E. Davis, *Lifting as They Climb*, 414.

11 "Report of the New Century Club," *Woman's Cycle* 1 (May 1, 1890): 8; "Hull-House Women's Club," *HHB* 3 (Apr.–May 1898): 6; on Constantinople, see "Hull-House Woman's Club," *HHB* 5, no. 1 (1902): 7–8. Winslow, *Official Register and Directory* (1903 and 1918 editions).

12 Clipping, "Agnes Taaffe over the Breakfast Table"; Mrs. J. A. A. Burnquist, essay on Martha Wells; "I Remember Me," all in folder 11, box 2, TCM Papers.

13 Edith R. Daniels, "Poem for 40th Anniversary of Tourists," box 1, file 2, TCM Papers.

14 Clipping, "Mrs. Buchanan Is Dead"; Isabella R. Coffin, "An Appreciation of Isabella Reid Buchanan," both in folder 11, box 2, TCM Papers.

15 Clipping, "Elizabeth Fish Rites Friday," Aug. 8, 1934, folder 11, box 2; on wash day, see Edith R. Daniels, "Poem for 40th Anniversary of Tourists," box 1, file 2, both in TCM Papers.

16 "Just among Ourselves," *BVM* 10 (Jan. 1903): 192.

17 "The Oak and Ivy Club," *Woman's Era* 2 (May 1895): 13. E. Davis, *Lifting as They Climb*, 47; National Association of Colored Women's Clubs, *A History of the Club Movement*, 49; Welke, *Recasting American Liberty*, 255–61, 319.

18 Lena Myers, "Through The Years," Dec. 7, 1944 clipping, McGregor Tourist Club records; "Just among Ourselves," *BVM* 5, May 1898, 283; on Watson, see Lillian Johnsson's interview of Adelaide Dannenbring, June 30, 2000. On Bay View club members, see "Just among Ourselves," *BVM* 5 (Mar. 1898): 201; 5 (May 1898): 283; 6 (Jan. 1899): 125.

19 On charges, see Mrs. Cyrus W. Wells, "Playlet for the Fortieth Anniversary of the Organization"; on shredded wheat, see Edith R. Daniels, "Poem for 40th Anniversary of Tourists," both in file 2, box 1, TCM Papers.

20 "The Tourist Club, Lewistown, Illinois, Program Book, 1907–1908," LITC Records.

21 On witness, see "Travel Class, Report of Secretary, Season 1895–1896," Miscellaneous pamphlets, HPTC Records; on pride, see "Program of the Lewistown Tourist Club, 1916–1917," LITC Records.

22 Blair, *The Clubwoman as Feminist*, 27, 99; Martin, *Sound of Our Own Voices*; Scott, *Natural Allies*; Blair, *The Torchbearers*; Knupfer, *Toward a Tenderer Humanity*; Hendricks, *Gender, Race, and Politics*; D. White, *Too Heavy a Load*. On real travel and breaking free, see Dolan, *Ladies of the Grand Tour*, 8.

23 Stoddard, *John L. Stoddard's Lectures* (1925), 1:3; Stoddard, *John L. Stoddard's Lectures* (1897–98), 10 vols.; Stoddard, *John L. Stoddard's Lectures*, supplementary vols., nos. 1–4; Stoddard, *Sunny Lands*; Stoddard, *Scenic America*.

24 On cost, see Stoddard, *Portfolio of Photographs*, inside back cover; on forming a club after purchasing his books, see Undated Report, TCC Records. On club use of Stoddard's photographs, see "Just among Ourselves," *BVM* 5 (May 1898): 284.

25 Wallace, introduction, 11–22.

26 Holmes, *Burton Holmes Travelogues*, 1:3; Holmes, *Burton Holmes Travelogues* (1908–17), vols. 1–14; on charm, see "Burton Holmes Travelogues," *Travel* 13 (June 1908): 390.

27 On the Chautauqua affiliation, see Aron, *Working at Play*, 113; Fennimore, *The Heritage of Bay View*, 103–15; Mott, *A History of American Magazines*, 54; Parmele, *A Short History of Russia*; Parmele, *A Short History of Rome and Italy*; Clough, *South American Life*; W. M. Taylor, "Swiss Life and Scenery," *BVM* 9 (June 1902): 417; R. S. Macarthur, "Moscow and St. Petersburg," *BVM* 5 (Feb. 1898): 155–60.

28 "Just among Ourselves," *BVM* 6 (Dec. 1898): 80.

29 On conferences, see "The Circle's Summer Meetings," *BVM* 6 (June 1899): 251; on helps, see "Bay View Reading Courses," *CW* 8 (Apr. 1901): 33. The summer encampment offered more than just travel courses. On founding libraries, see Lillian Johnsson, "GFWC Travelers Club: Ninety Years of Service," TCC Records; Lena Myers, "Through the Years," Dec. 7, 1944 clipping, McGregor Tourist Club Records; "History of the Traveler's Club," Apr. 15, 1965, 4, Pocasset Travelers Club Records; "Women's Clubs and Libraries," *GFB* 4 (Mar. 1907): 220–21.

30 On using the *Mentor* in club work, see "Mrs. Quinn's History of the Marcus Woman's Club," folder: Marcus Woman's Study Club, Iowa, box 1, Local Club Records (Club Histories) Iowa, GFWC; *Mentor* 2 (Mar. 16, 1914): 12; "The Open Letter," *Mentor* 4 (Aug. 15, 1916): 12. Dwight L. Elmendorf, "Scotland: The Land of Song and Scenery," *Mentor* 1 (Apr. 21, 1913); Dwight L. Elmendorf, "Paris, the Incomparable," *Mentor* 1 (June 16, 1913); Dwight L. Elmendorf, "Egypt, the Land of Mystery," *Mentor* 1 (Dec. 1, 1913). On Elmendorf, see Musser, *The Emergence of Cinema*, 222.

31 Editorial, *Mentor* 1 (Feb. 9, 1914): 12; Frederick Palmer, "Mexico," *Mentor* 2 (Mar. 2, 1914); Albert Bushnell Hart, "The Story of the Danube," *Mentor* 3 (Nov. 1,

1915); Ruth Kedzie Wood, "The Canadian Rockies," *Mentor* 5 (Oct. 1, 1917); E. M. Newman, "Korea and Its People," *Mentor* 8, serial number 201 (1920 [no month given]). On subscribers, see "The Open Letter," *Mentor* 4 (May 1, 1916): 12.

32 Club and Board Minutes, Membership List, 1891–1896, Apr. 13, 1891, box 1, HPTC Records.

33 On Kennan, see "Directory of Club Lectures," *CW* 6 (May 1900): 87; on watercolors, see "Portfolio Travel Talks," *CW* 10 (June and July 1903): 385; on stereopticon projections, see "Directory of Club Lectures," *CW* 6 (May 1900): 87. The 1918 *Official Register and Directory* included six ads for travel lecturers. Its speakers directory listed fourteen names under the "travel" heading. Additional speakers were listed under national headings such as Ireland, Japan, Mexico, and Russia; see Winslow, *Official Register and Directory*, xv–xxxv. On travel lectures, see also "Exquisitely Illustrated Stereopticon Lectures," *CW* 11 (Sept. 1904): ii; "Travel Talks," *CW* 2 (Aug. 1898): 167; "Brittany and How to See It," *CW* 2 (Aug. 1898): 167; "Fraulein Antoinie Stolle," *CW* 4 (June 1899): 107.

34 Ruth B. Lord, *A History of Hyde Park Travel Club, 1888–1935*; Mar. 11, 1895, and Mar. 14, 1898, entries, Club and Board Minutes, Membership List, box 1; Oct. 30, 1900, entry, Club and Board Minutes, 1899–1903, box 1; "Hyde Park Travel Club, 1914–1915," 27, Yearbooks, all in HPTC Records.

35 On travel cultures, see Koshar, *German Travel Cultures*.

36 On seventeenth-century literature, see Towner, *An Historical Geography*, 101; on eighteenth-century guides, see Levenstein, *Seductive Journey*, 32; on numbers of travel books, see H. Smith, *American Travellers Abroad*; on circulation figures, see Zboray, *A Fictive People*, 176. Missionary memoirs sold tens of thousands of copies in the antebellum period; see Brumberg, *Mission for Life*, 16.

37 Bode, *The American Lyceum*, 218; Oettermann, *The Panorama*, 314. Perry, *Boats against the Current*, 129.

38 On the minister, see Strout, *The American Image of the Old World*, 111. On Baedeker, see Dulles, *Americans Abroad*, 104; Edwin Asa Dix, "Baedeker and His Guide Books," *Travel* 13 (June 1908): 403–4. For a small sampling of the voluminous travel literature of the era, see Mrs. Joseph Cook, "A Tour Round the World," *Chautauquan* 3 (June 1883): 510–14; Mrs. A. R. Ramsey, "How to Go Abroad," *LHJ* 6 (June 1889): 4; Maude Andrews, "Maude Andrews in London," *Atlanta Constitution*, July 5, 1896; Mary Sargent Hopkins, "Bicycling through Picturesque Europe," *Ladies' World*, Feb. 1897, 10; Walter Germain Robinson, "The American Colony in Paris," *Cosmopolitan* 29 (Oct. 1900): 575–84; Flora McDonald Thompson, "Our Paris Letter," *Harper's Bazar*, Jan. 1904, 49–51; Charles Newton Hood, "European Pensions," *GH* 11 (June 1905): 595–99, 596; "At the German Resorts," "Americans in Lucerne," and "Americans in France," *New York Tribune*, Sept. 8, 1912.

39 E. H. Blichfeldt, "A Reading Journey through Mexico," *Chautauquan* 63 (Aug. 1911): 251–72; Percy Holmes Boynton, "A Reading Journey in London," *Chautauquan* 62 (May 1911): 329–53. On *Around the World*, see Mott, *A History of American Magazines*, 224. *Travel Magazine* and *Outing* are more widely available; Champney, *Three Vassar Girls in the Tyrol*; "Are You Going to Europe?" *LHJ* 8 (Apr. 1891): 16.

40 Burton Holmes, "With Burton Holmes through the Austrian Tyrol," *LHJ* 24 (July 1907): 7; Edward W. Bok, "At Home with the Editor," *LHJ* 8 (August 1891): 10. Elizabeth Bisland, "A Flying Trip around the World," *Cosmopolitan* 9 (June 1890): 173–84, 181; Bisland, "The Art of Travel."

41 I. Peck, *Nellie Bly's Book*, 7; "Lettie Lane's Around the World Party," *LHJ* 28 (Apr. 1, 1911): 25; "Coffee. Advertiser: Arbuckle Brothers," Album 24, "Advertising Cards (national) teas-coffees," box 1, Amusements-Footwear," Trade Card Collection, Downs Collection.

42 *The 1902 Edition of the Sears Roebuck Catalogue*, 1018–22; Glover, *"Dame Curtsey's" Book*, 186; Hall, *The Correct Thing*, 186; "For the Hostess: A 'Bon Voyage' Supper," *Vogue* 39 (May 15, 1912): 72. On well-wishers, see Dulles, *Americans Abroad*, 142. P. Hill, *The World Their Household*, 63.

43 "Special European Columns," *New York Tribune*, Jan. 2, 1904; "Steamships," *Times-Picayune*, Oct. 1, 1900; "The Royal Mail Steam Packet Co.," advertisement, *Travel* 13 (Jan. 1908): 161. On Cook agencies, see *Cook's American Tours*, inside cover; for a Thomas Cook ad, see "Japan-China Tours," *Los Angeles Times*, Feb. 2, 1908; on conducting, see "Europe," *Atlanta Constitution*, Jan. 21, 1912.

44 Adams, *Ocean Steamers*; on ocean crossings, see Withey, *Grand Tours*, 172; Stoddard, *John L. Stoddard's Lectures*, 3:7.

45 Buzard, *The Beaten Track*, 78–79; on Holmes, see Musser in collaboration with Nelson, *High-Class Moving Pictures*, 126. Stoddard, *John L. Stoddard's Lectures*, 3:7. Brendon, *Thomas Cook*, 151; Hamburg American Line, "Around the World," *Travel* 5 (Mar. 1912): 57.

46 Levenstein, *Seductive Journey*, 129. From the 1820s to 1850s, about 2,000 to 8,000 a year made the trip, Dulles, *Americans Abroad*, 27.

47 Charles Newton Hood, "European Pensions," *GH* 11 (June 1905): 595–99, 595; on trips for teachers, see Levenstein, *Seductive Journey*, 160; "How We Went Abroad," *LHJ* 6 (Aug. 1889): 4.

48 Helen R. Norton, "The Story of the Women's Rest Tour Association," 4–5, folder 1; *A Summer in England with a Continental Supplement, A Handbook of Travel*, 5th rev. ed. (Boston: Published for the Women's Rest Tour Association by A. J. Ochs, 1900), 7–69, both in Women's Rest Tour Association Records.

49 "Women's Rest Tour Association," 8–10; "Our Traveling Fund," Jan. 1913;

Helen R. Norton, "The Story of the Women's Rest Tour Association," 16–18, folder 1; List of Members of the Women's Rest Tour Association, Jan. 1910, all in the Women's Rest Tour Association Records.

50 On passenger lists, see *Vogue* 21 (May 21, 1896): inside front page; "Hundreds off for Europe," *New York Tribune*, Apr. 29, 1888; "Where Atlantians Are Summering," *Atlanta Constitution*, Aug. 9, 1896; on seeing compatriots, "Paris Pencilings," *Times-Picayune*, July 7, 1884; on flourishing colonies, see "Americans Who Go Abroad," *Atlanta Constitution*, Oct. 11, 1896.

51 "New Trip to Europe Competition," *Vogue* 30 (Oct. 19, 1907): 518; Ad, *Travel* 13 (May 1908): 347; readers could obtain a discount if they subscribed to both *Travel* and *Vogue* magazines, *Travel* 13 (Aug. 1908): 483. Recruitment letter cited in Choy, *Empire of Care*, 29.

52 Woody, "International Postcards," 13; on very German, see Postcards of Hilda Haines Hess, 1912–1915, Downs Collection. Mathur, "Wanted Native Views," 99, 112.

53 "Sunday Evening Lectures," *HHB* 5, no. 2 (1902): 2. Among the travel lectures presented in the Hull-House Auditorium the following season was a six-part series on the capitals of Europe, "Entertainments in the Auditorium," *HHB* 6 (Midwinter 1903–4): 1. On other destinations covered in Hull-House lectures, see "Public Entertainments," *HHB* 2, no. 2 (Feb. 1, 1897): 1; "Public Entertainments," *HHB* 2, no. 4 (Apr. 1, 1897): 1; "Observations of an African Traveler," *HHB* 2, no. 3 (Mar. 1, 1897): 1. "Where to Go To-Day," *New York Tribune*, Apr. 5, 1900; "The Summer Assemblies," *Chautauquan* 14 (Oct. 1891): 113–21, 115; Aron, *Working at Play*, 117; Schultz, *The Romance of Small-Town Chautauquas*, 105–6. On Industrial School, see Bevier and Usher, *The Home Economics Movement*, 54–58.

54 "Thirteenth Annual Report, Year 1903–4," vol. 6, box 3, TCM Papers; Board Meeting, Sept. 4, 1901, Club and Board Minutes, 1899–1903, box 1: Minute Books 1891–1906, HPTC Records.

55 On talks by government officials and a Mexican minister, see "One of the Most Interesting Clubs," *Woman's Cycle* 1 (Apr. 17, 1890): 20. L'Alliance Française was founded in Paris in 1883 to propagate the French language. There were 135 branches of the Alliance in the United States around the turn of the century; see Clipping, "Alliance Française," folder 14, box 2, TCM Papers; P. Hill, *The World Their Household*, 85; "Y.W.C.A. Notes," *Atlanta Constitution*, Jan. 7, 1912.

56 "Magic Lantern," *LHJ* 8 (Feb. 1891): 3; *The 1902 Edition of the Sears Roebuck Catalogue*, 165; on Arctic to Sahara, see *Hall's Illustrated Catalogue*; *Classified Catalogue of Magic Lantern Slides*, 3. On "Parlor Tours of the Holy Land," see Long, *Imagining the Holy Land*, chap. 3.

57 Milligan, *Illustrated Catalogue*, 53; *The 1902 Edition of the Sears Roebuck Catalogue*, 166; on dime museums and their magic lantern shows, see Dennett, *Weird and Wonderful*, 7, 41, 118.

58 *Original Stereographs Catalogue*, 3. On stereoscopes, see also *Light on Stereographs*, 8–13.

59 *Original Stereographs Catalogue*, 3–4.

60 *Light on Stereographs*, inside of front and back covers.

61 Underwood and Underwood, *Catalogue 28*, 9; Darrah, *The World of Stereographs*, 48.

62 *Original Stereographs Catalogue*, 5–14, 59–60, 91, 130–34.

63 On antebellum cycloramas, dioramas, and panoramas, see Sears, *Sacred Places*, 50–51; on the popularity of cycloramas in the 1880s, see Oettermann, *The Panorama*, 342; Long, *Imagining the Holy Land*, 17; on Paris by night, see *A Succinct Description*, 3, 6. On cycloramas, see Oettermann, *The Panorama*, 343.

64 Maxwell, *Colonial Photography*, 11; J. K. Brown, *Making Culture Visible*, 165; Gibson, *London*; Gibson, *Sketches in Egypt*; Henry Bacon, *On Shipboard*; Bullington, "Henry Bacon's Imaging of Transatlantic Travel."

65 Oberdeck, *The Evangelist and the Impresario*, 103; Musser, *The Emergence of Cinema*, 300, 313, 445–46; Abel, *The Red Rooster Scare*, 98.

66 Musser in collaboration with Nelson, *High-Class Moving Pictures*, 3, 9, 132, 174, 177, 233–34; Wallace, introduction.

67 "Go to France Today!" *Times Picayune*, Sept. 7, 1918.

68 Musser in collaboration with Nelson, *High-Class Moving Pictures*, 182.

69 *The Artistic Guide to Chicago*, 277, 327–32; on national exhibits, see Greenhalgh, *Ephemeral Vistas*, 105. On pleasure grounds, see Shaw, *World's Fair Notes*, 57–59; Burg, *Chicago's White City*, 216–19; on the Electric Theatre, see Bolotin and Laing, *The World's Columbian Exposition*, 128. "Laying out the Model of the City of Paris," *Frank Leslie's Illustrated Historical Register*, 74.

70 Shaw, *World's Fair Notes*, 42, 56. On the one-tenth figure, see J. Gilbert, *Perfect Cities*, 1. On the Chicago and other fairs, see Rydell, *All the World's a Fair*.

71 Haraway, "Teddy Bear Patriarchy"; Zboray and Zboray, "Between 'Crockerydom' and Barnum"; Kirshenblatt-Gimblett, "Objects of Ethnography," 404; Fitzhugh, "Ambassadors in Sealskins"; Wonders, "Habitat Dioramas," 106.

72 Hanson, *Animal Attractions*, 15–16, 100, 131, 143–44; Rothfels, *Savages and Beasts*, 143. Hertrich, *The Huntington Botanical Gardens*, 28, 78–79; Solit, *History of the United States Botanic Garden*, 38; for a list of botanical gardens, see McCracken, *Gardens of Empire*, 218; on European displays, see Preson, "The Scenery of the Torrid Zone."

73 "P. T. Barnum's Great Traveling World's Fair," *Hearth and Home* 5 (Apr. 5, 1873): 226; J. Davis, *The Circus Age*, 112, 118, 220, quotation 131; Slotkin, "Buffalo Bill's

'Wild West'"; J. S. Kasson, *Buffalo Bill's Wild West*, 55, 251–54, quotation 253; Hirshler, "'Gondola Days,'" 125. On representing empire through consumer culture, see Baranowski and Furlough, introduction, 20.

74 J. F. Kasson, *Amusing the Million*, 53, 69, 86; R. Hughes, *The Real New York*, 312–13; Register, *The Kid of Coney Island*, 92–93, 98; on Bantocs, see Cross and Walton, *The Playful Crowd*, 89.

75 "Oriental Interiors in New York," *DF* 25 (Nov. 1894): 51; "Interiors in the Oriental Style," *DF* 27 (Jan. 1896): 103; Leach, *Land of Desire*, 70, 79–83, 102–3, 145.

76 Leach, *Land of Desire*, 137; *Entrance to Vantine's*, 5; on Murray's, see Bevington, *New York Plaisance*.

77 On the Hotel New Netherlands, in New York, see *DF* 29 (Nov. 1896): 40; "Turkish Salon in the Waldorf Hotel, New York," *DF* 26 (Sept. 1895): 209; on a Japanese room at the Southern Hotel, St. Louis, see *DF* 30 (July 1897): 115.

78 "A Japanese Village," *DF* 7 (Jan. 1886): 116; "Old London," *DF* 10 (July 1887): 115; George Full et al., "Around the World in Ninety Minutes," *LHJ* 25 (Oct. 1908): 33; Long, *Imagining the Holy Land*, 8; "Onteora's Own County Fair," *LHJ* 21 (July 1904): 19.

79 *A Guide to the City of Chicago*, 25; on the Land Show, see "United States Land Show," *Chicago Tribune*, Dec. 4, 1912. Nasaw, *Going Out*, 65; Light, "From Vice District"; William Brown Meloney, "Slumming in New York's Chinatown," *Munsey's Magazine* 41 (Sept. 1909): 818–30, 820; Beck, *New York's Chinatown*; Kirshenblatt-Gimblett, *Destination Culture*, 112; Cocks, "The Chamber of Commerce's Carnival"; Cocks, *Doing the Town*, 188, 197, 201–2.

80 Gelernter, *A History of American Architecture*, 136, 148, 161–63, 169, 198–99; Andrews, *Architecture, Ambition, and Americans*, 100, 103, 146, 171, 188; on the Italianate look, see Devlin, *Portraits of American Architecture*, 82; Roth, *American Architecture*, 152, 184–86, 212, 218, 286–87; Sloane, *The Last Great Necessity*, 104.

81 Frederic Harrison, "An Englishman on American Architecture," *HB* 10 (Oct. 1901): 282–84, 283.

82 Curl, *Mizner's Florida*, 43, 64; Gebhard, *Santa Barbara*, 13–15. On castellated forms, Devlin, *Portraits of American Architecture*, 58; on art museums, Steffensen-Bruce, *Marble Palaces*, 199; Bryant, "Cathedrals, Castles, and Roman Baths," 195; B. Wilson, *The Parthenon*; Sweetman, *The Oriental Obsession*, 236–37; "Hyde and Behman's New Theatre," *DF* 17 (Dec. 1890): 96–97.

83 Schneer, *London 1900*, 7–10; Driver and Gilbert, "Imperial Cities."

84 Mar. 6, 1910, entry, Hyde Park Travel Club Minutes 1908–1911, box 2, HPTC Records.

85 "Travel Class 1911–1912," 25, Yearbooks, HPTC Records; Stoddard, *John L. Stoddard's Lectures* (1918), 1:6.

86   On monotony, see "Just among Ourselves," *BVM* 5 (Jan. 1898): 124; on brightest spots, see "Just among Ourselves," *BVM* 9 (May 1902): 409.

87   "Cosmopolitan Club. Scandinavia and The Netherlands, Season 1898–1899," CC Records; "The Tourist Club in India, 1897–8," annual programs, box 3; Minutes of Nov. 23, 1891, vol. 2, box 3, both in TCM Records; "The Hyde Park Travel Class," 1895–1896, Miscellaneous pamphlets, HPTC Records.

88   On grand tours, see Leed, *The Mind of the Traveler*, 59; Edward W. Bok, "At Home with the Editor," *LHJ* 8 (August 1891): 10.

89   *Original Stereographs Catalogue*, 4; "Travel Club of America," *Travel* 28 (Mar. 1917): 37.

90   "Women's Clubs and Libraries," *GFB* 4 (Mar. 1907): 220–21. On real travel as a means to acquire refinement, see Dolan, *Ladies of the Grand Tour*, 6.

91   Mrs. H. M. Bushnell, "A Defense of the Study Club," *GFB* 3 (Dec. 1905): 122; Martin, *Sound of our Own Voices*, 46; on the postgraduate function of women's clubs, see Gere, *Intimate Practices*, 35; Fanny H. Carpenter, "Are New York Club Women Shallow," *GFB* 4 (Nov. 1906): 57–59, 58.

92   "After Fifteen Years," Feb. 16, 1910, clipping, "The Tourist Club, Lewistown, Illinois, Program notes," LITC Records; Lena Myers, "Through The Years," McGregor Tourist Club Records; "Report of the Tourist Club, of Frankfort, Ind.," *Woman's Cycle* 1 (May 15, 1890): 28; "Around the Study Lamp," *BVM* 5 (Dec. 1897): 57, 81.

93   On Johnson, see Cora B. Eichelberger, "The Travellers' Club," *New Cycle* 6 (Feb.–Mar. 1893): 332; on price, see Mary Low Dickinson, "A Tour Round the World," *Chautauquan* 3 (Nov. 1882): 99–101, 100.

94   Margaret Wheeler Ross, *History of the Arizona Federation of Women's Clubs and Its Forerunners* (1946), 33–34, 36, State Federation Records, GFWC.

95   *The Sociable*, 243; Adelaide Westcott Hatch, "A Trip around the World," *CW* 11 (Sept. 1904): 56.

96   "The General Federation," *CW* 2 (Sept. 1898): 184.

97   Helen Elise Villard, "The Berlin Industrial Exposition," *Woman's Era* 3 (Aug. 1896): 6; Harley, "Mary Church Terrell," 310; "Social Notes," *Woman's Era* 2 (Apr. 1895): 12.

98   "The Tourist Club, 1891–1931," folder 2, box 1, TCM Records.

99   "Just among Ourselves," *BVM* 5 (Jan. 1898): 122; 9 (Dec. 1901): 116; 9 (Mar. 1902): 292; on acquaintance, see "Notes from All Points," *GFB* 8 (Apr. 1911): 390.

100 "The Story of a European Tour," *CW* 8 (Sept. 1901): 181; May Alden Ward, "Club Study Department," *CW* 3 (Jan. 1899): 127; May Alden Ward, "Club Study Department," *CW* 4 (Apr. 1899): 18; "Atlas Mail Steamship Co.," *CW* 5 (Jan. 1900): 183; "The Story of a European Tour," *CW* 8 (Aug. 1901): 157; "You Are Invited to

Join One of the Boston Travel Society Journeys," *GFB* 6 (Apr. 1909): 195; "World Art and Travel Clubs," *GFM* 12 (June 1914): 95.

101 "Send Your Daughter to Europe," *GFB* 7 (Feb. 1910): 172; "Europe and the Exposition," *CW* 5 (Jan. 1900): 185.

102 "History of Travel Class," folder: Travel Class, Albert Lea, Minnesota, Local Club Records, GFWC.

103 L. Mead, *To Whom Much Is Given*, 35.

104 Nov. 15, 1907, "The Tourist Club, Lewistown, Illinois, Program Book, 1907–1908," LITC Records. On tourism and class distinction, see D. Brown, *Inventing New England*, 7; Stowe, *European Travel*, 5–6; Endy, "Travel and World Power."

105 On the cachet of travel in settler societies, see Pesman, *Duty Free*, 26; on the Ducal Palace, see Stoddard, *A Trip around the World*. As Stoddard said of Paris, "Hither come yearly hundreds of thousands of pleasure-seekers from every quarter of the globe"; see Stoddard, *Portfolio of Photographs*. On Cook, see Withey, *Grand Tours*, 285; on Farrar, see June 15, 1891, entry, Club and Board Minutes, Membership List, 1891–1896, box 1, HPTC Records.

106 Hamburg-American Line, "Around World Cruises," *Travel* 16 (Nov. 1910): 41.

107 Endy, "Travel and World Power," 573; "Around the Study Lamp," *BVM* 6 (May 1899): 301.

108 On companionship, see Mrs. Robert J. Burdette, "Remnant Corner," *CW* 11 (May 1904): 6; on intellectual activity, see "To Our Readers," *Woman's Cycle* 1 (Sept. 19, 1889): 3. "Hyde Park Travel Club, 1913–1914," 5, Yearbooks, HPTC Records.

109 Lena Myers, "Through The Years," Dec. 7, 1944, McGregor Tourist Club Records; on afternoon in Spain, see "Just among Ourselves," *BVM* 6 (Apr. 1899): 252; on German banquet, see "Just among Ourselves," *BVM* 6 (Nov. 1898): 37; on school rooms, see *Fifth Biennial of the General Federation of Women's Clubs*, 92, folder: 5th Biennial, box: Convention Records (Proceedings-Reports), 1896–1904, GFWC; on entertainment, see Croly, *The History of the Woman's Club Movement*, 269.

110 On differences between tourism and ethnography, see MacCannell, *The Tourist*; on other modes of viewing the world in this period, see Brumberg, "Zenanas and Girlless Villages"; M. Hunt, *Ideology and U.S. Foreign Policy*; Rydell, *All the World's a Fair*; Lutz and Collins, *Reading National Geographic*; Conn, "An Epistemology for Empire"; Jacobson, *Barbarian Virtues*; on tourism and consumption, see D. Brown, *Inventing New England*, 6. On atlases, see Schulten, *The Geographical Imagination*, 199.

111 Jan. 26, 1891, Feb. 16, 1891, Club and Board Minutes, Membership List, 1891–1896, box 1, HPTC Records; Mary G. Palmer, "For the Tourist Club," Nov. 23, 1907, poem, folder 2, box 1, TCM Records; Lena Myers, "Through The Years," McGregor Tourist Club Records.

112 On Spain, see "Around the Study Lamp," *BVM* 6 (Nov. 1898): 36; on Russia and the Netherlands, see "Early Announcement," *BVM* 6 (Apr. 1899): 249; on Italy, Greece, and Switzerland, see *BVM* 9 (1901–2). On programs, see *BVM*, 1896–1922. *The General Federation of Women's Clubs Thirteenth Biennial Convention: 1916*, 85, 168, folder: 13th Biennial, New York, box: Convention Records (Proceedings-Reports), 1912–1916, GFWC.

113 On Ewan, see "The Tourist club. Lewistown, Illinois, notebook," 7, LITC Records; "Hyde Park Travel Club, 1913–1914," 4, Yearbooks, HPTC Records.

114 Croly, *The History of the Woman's Club Movement*, 394.

115 "Cosmopolitan Club. The Pan-American Republics, 1915–1916," CC Records.

116 "Just among Ourselves," *BVM* 6 (Feb. 1899): 165; on contests, "Just among Ourselves," *BVM* 6 (Jan. 1899): 123; "The Tourist Club in India, 1897–8," annual programs, box 3, TCM Records.

117 On Switzerland, see Oct. 15, 1900, entry, Club and Board Minutes, 1899–1903, box 1, HPTC Records; on Italy, see Nov. 26, 1900, meeting, Club and Board Minutes, 1899–1903, box 1: Minute Books 1891–1906, HPTC Records.

118 Dec. 3, 1909, "The Tourist Club, Lewistown, Illinois, 1909–1910 Program," LITC Records; Mar. 6, 1910, entry, Hyde Park Travel Club Minutes 1908–1911, box 2, HPTC Records. The poem is attributed to Tomonori, Nov. 14, 1919, 1919–1920 Tourist Club Year Book, LITC Records.

119 "Travel Class 1898–1899," 14, Yearbooks, HPTC Records. On Eiffel, Oct. 29, 1897, "The Tourist Club, Lewistown, Illinois, Program notes," LITC Records; on pyramids, Feb. 18, 1907, "Cosmopolitan Club. Egypt. 1906–1907," CC Records; on Agra, "The Tourist Club in India, 1897–8," annual programs, box 3, TCM Records; on resorts, see Mar. 22, 1897, "Cosmopolitan Club. Germany. Season 1896–1897," CC Records.

120 "Travel Class 1902–1903," 25, Yearbooks, HPTC Records.

121 "Around the World with Burton Holmes," *Travel* 18 (Nov. 1911): 59. "Travel Class, 1907–1908," Yearbooks, HPTC Records. On guidebooks' depiction of the world as easily knowable, see Stowe, *European Travel*, 48–50.

122 "Around the Study Lamp," *BVM* 9 (May 1902): 406; "The Travel Class 1901–1902," Yearbooks, HPTC Records.

123 Jan. 14, 1901, entry, Club and Board Minutes, 1899–1903, box 1, HPTC Records; Jan. 11, 1907, "The Tourist Club, Lewistown, Illinois, Program Book, 1906–1907"; on music, Mar. 9, 1906, "The Tourist Club, Lewistown, Illinois, Program Book, 1905–1906," both in LITC Records.

124 On Indian talks, see "The Tourist Club in India, 1897–8," annual programs, box 3, TCM Records; on sagas, Jan. 26, 1906; on Canadian West, Apr. 6, 1906, both in "The Tourist Club, Lewistown, Illinois, Program Book, 1905–1906"; on festivals, Dec. 3, 1909, "The Tourist Club, Lewistown, Illinois, 1909–1910 Pro-

gram," all in LITC Records. On Germans, Oct. 5, 1896, "Cosmopolitan Club. Germany. Season 1896–1897," CC Records. "The Tourist Club in India, 1897–8," annual programs, box 3, TCM Records.

125 Geo. De Haven, "A Day in the Mexican Capital," *Outing* 16 (Sept. 1890): 419–29; on Italy, see "Just among Ourselves," *BVM* 9 (Dec. 1901): 117.

126 On classes, see Dec. 5, 1898, entry, Club and Board Minutes, Membership List, 1891–1896 [*sic*]; on Luzerne, see Oct. 22, 1900, entry, Club and Board Minutes, 1899–1903, both in box 1, HPTC Records.

127 On women of Brittany, see Nov. 28, 1904, entry, Club and Board Minutes, 1903–1906, box 1; on women of Spain, see "Travel Class, 1908–1909," 25, Yearbooks, both in HPTC Records.

128 Minutes, Feb. 16, 1911, Pocasset Travelers Club Records; Oct. 18, 1918, 1918–1919 Tourist Club Year Book, LITC Records. Housekeeping in Japan, Nov. 14, 1919, 1919–1920 Tourist Club Year Book; Home Life of Russian People, Apr. 5, 1907, "The Tourist Club, Lewistown, Illinois, Program Book, 1906–1907," both in LITC Records; on Russia, see Jan. 24, 1898, entry, Club and Board Minutes, Membership List; on Dutch and Irish domesticity, see Mar. 20, 1905, and Nov. 6, 1905, entries, Club and Board Minutes, 1899–1903, both in box 1, HPTC Records.

129 On Japan, see Mar. 6, 1910, entry, Hyde Park Travel Club Minutes 1908–1911; on Palestine, see Mar. 11, 1912, entry, Hyde Park Travel Club Minutes 1911–1914, both in box 2, HPTC Records.

130 On Jamaica, see Mar. 15, 1909, entry, Hyde Park Travel Club Minutes 1908–1911; on Morocco, see Oct. 8, 1907, entry, Hyde Park Travel Club Minutes 1906–1908; on the Philippines, see Mar. 15, 1909, entry, Hyde Park Travel Club Minutes 1908–1911; on Mexicans, see Feb. 8, 1909, entry, Hyde Park Travel Club Minutes 1908–1911, all in box 2, HPTC Records. On the hierarchies of civilization stressed in geographical education, see Schulten, *The Geographical Imagination*, 11.

131 Stoddard, *Red-Letter Days Abroad*, 13, 174.

132 Dec. 15, 1913, entry, Hyde Park Travel Club Minutes 1911–1914, box 2, HPTC Records; clipping from the *Winona Independent*, May 15, 1900, folder 10, box 2, TCM Records.

133 Edward S. Farwell, "A Pedestrian Tour in the Scottish Highlands," *Outing* 7 (Jan. 1886): 436–43; George Horton, "Modern Athens," *BVM* 9 (May 1902): 364; "Women as Travellers," *Godey's* 92 (May 1876): 473–74; Stoddard, *John L. Stoddard's Lectures*, 3:34, 165, 183, 334.

134 Stoddard, *John L. Stoddard's Lectures*, 3:183; W. Carson, *Mexico*, 105.

135 On Mexican coffee production, Feb. 8, 1909, entry; on the Japanese tea industry, Mar. 6, 1910, entry; on Havana harbor, Mar. 15, 1909, entry; on electrifica-

tion and transportation in Algiers, Mar. 6, 1910, entry, all in Hyde Park Travel Club Minutes 1908–1911; on European seaports, Nov. 16, 1914, entry, Hyde Park Travel Club Minutes 1911–1914, all in box 2, HPTC Records. On Peruvian staircase farms, Feb. 21, 1919, Tourist Club Year Book, 1918–1919; "Japan Learns to Do Business," Jan. 9, 1920, Tourist Club Year Book, 1919–1920, both in LITC Records; on tea plantations, "The Tourist Club in India, 1897–8," annual programs, box 3, TCM Records.

136   On commercial expansion, see Oct. 5, 1908, entry and Mar. 15, 1909, entry, Hyde Park Travel Club Minutes 1908–1911, box 2, HPTC Records; on the romance of rubber, see Jan. 24, 1919, Tourist Club Year Book, 1918–1919, LITC Records; on preserving local color, see Nov. 19, 1900, entry, Club and Board Minutes, 1899–1903, box 1, HPTC Records.

137   On Cairo road, Feb. 19, 1912, entry, Hyde Park Travel Club Minutes 1911–1914, box 2, HPTC Records; on trains and steamers, Oct. 18, 1907, The Tourist Club, Lewistown, Illinois, Program Book, 1907–1908, LITC Records. On gondolas see Feb. 7, 1905, "Cosmopolitan Club. Italy. 1905–1906"; on Dresden potteries, Apr. 5, 1897, "Cosmopolitan Club. Germany. Season 1896–1897"; on Delft wares, Feb. 20, 1899 (Amsterdam), Mar. 6, 1899 (Delft), "Cosmopolitan Club. Scandinavia and The Netherlands, Season 1898–1899," all in CC Records. On shopping opportunities, Feb. 19, 1912, entry, Hyde Park Travel Club Minutes 1911–1914, box 2, HPTC Records; Ada Cone, "The Rendezvous of Parisian Fashion," BVM 13 (Jan. 1906): 241–44.

138   "Our Relation with Canada," Mar. 25, 1910, "The Tourist Club, Lewistown, Illinois, 1909–1910 Program," LITC Records; "The Egypt of Today," Mar. 4, 1907, "Cosmopolitan Club. Egypt. 1906–1907"; "School Systems in Norway and Sweden," Nov. 14, 1898, "Cosmopolitan Club. Scandinavia and the Netherlands, Season 1898–1899," both in CC Records; May Alden Ward, "Club Study Department," CW 6 (May 1900): 63; "English Law and Legislation," "The Tourist Club in India, 1897–8," annual programs, box 3, TCM Papers.

139   Oct. 10, 1904, entry, Club and Board Minutes, 1903–1906, box 1, HPTC Records; Ida Vera Simonton, "The Belgian Congo or the Congo Free State," BVM 19 (Jan. 1912): 198–203, 199.

140   On Holland, see Mar. 20, 1905, entry, Club and Board Minutes, 1903–1906, box 1; on Morocco, see Oct. 8, 1907, entry, Hyde Park Travel Club Minutes 1906–1908, box 2; on Japan, see "Travel Class 1914–1915," 28, Yearbooks, all in HPTC Records.

141   Sara Cary, "Corning Clionian Circle, 1881–1981," folder: Local Records (Club Histories) 1881–1981, Corning Clionian Circle, New York, box: Local Club Records, New York, GFWC; Lillian Johnsson, "GFWC Travelers Club: Ninety

Years of Service," TCC Records; Feb. 5, 1906 meeting, Club and Board Minutes, 1903–1906, box 1: Minute Books 1891–1906, HPTC Records.

142 "Hyde Park Travel Club, 1918–1919," 36, Yearbooks; Nov. 9, 1914, entry, Hyde Park Travel Club Minutes 1911–1914, box 2; "Hyde Park Travel Club, 1916–1917," 30, Yearbooks, all in HPTC Records.

143 Lillian Johnsson's interview of Adelaide Dannenbring, June 30, 2000.

144 On Bavaria, see Nov. 22, 1909, entry, Hyde Park Travel Club Minutes 1908–1911; on Paris, see Jan. 27, 1908, entry, Hyde Park Travel Club Minutes 1906–1908, both in box 2, HPTC Records. This speaker took her material verbatim from Stoddard. See Stoddard, *John L. Stoddard's Lectures*, 5:7.

145 On Spain, see "Just among Ourselves," *BVM* 6 (Apr. 1899): 251. On tourists as the center of a circumscribed world, see Turner and Ash, *The Golden Hordes*, 90.

146 Stoddard, *Portfolio of Photographs*.

147 Higham, "Social Discrimination against Jews," 239; Hale, *Making Whiteness*, 126. On segregation in Europe, see Levenstein, *Seductive Journey*, 264.

148 May 6, 1910, "The Tourist Club, Lewistown, Illinois,1909–1910 Program," LITC Records; on choice spirits, see "Around the Study Lamp," *BVM* 9 (Jan. 1902): 156.

149 Dwight L. Elmendorf, "The Mediterranean," *Mentor* 1 (Nov. 10, 1913): prefatory plate; E. M. Newman, "The Virgin Islands of the United States of America," *Mentor* 6 (Aug. 15, 1918). Angela Woollacott has found that traveling to Britain taught Australian women about empire; see "'All This Is the Empire,'" 1004. On travel and empire, see also Endy, "Travel and World Power," 565–94; Newman, *White Women's Rights*, chap. 4. On Hawaii, see Jan. 26, 1917, *The Tourist Club Year Book, 1917–1918*, LITC Records. This paper likely came from an article with the same title: Homer Croy, "Hawaii, a New Winter Resort," *Travel* 28 (Nov. 1916): 22–25.

150 Stoddard, *China*, 46; on the Philippines, see Holmes, *Burton Holmes Travelogues*, 11:119; on China, see Holmes, *Burton Holmes Travelogues*, 9:265. "Hyde Park Travel Club, 1914–1915," 27–29, Yearbooks, HPTC Records.

151 Holmes, *Burton Holmes Travelogues*, 11:336; "Just among Ourselves," *BVM* 6 (Nov. 1898): 38.

152 Nov. 9, 1914, entry, Hyde Park Travel Club Minutes 1911–1914, box 2; "Hyde Park Travel Club, 1916–1917," 30, Yearbooks, both in HPTC Records; Endy, "Travel and World Power," 592.

153 Mar. 6, 1910, entry, Hyde Park Travel Club Minutes 1908–1911, box 2; on "America" see Oct. 15, 1917, entry, Hyde Park Travel Club Minutes 1916–1921, box 3, both in HPTC Records.

154 R. Elson, *Guardians of Tradition*, 339; Clough, *South American Life*, 7.

155 On relief, see "Hyde Park Travel Club, 1918–1919," 36, Yearbooks, HPTC Records. Lillian Johnsson, "GFWC Travelers Club: Ninety Years of Service," TCC Records; on aiding "National Defense," see Oct. 8, 1917, entry, Hyde Park Travel Club Minutes 1916–1921, box 3, HPTC Records.

156 On World War I as a boost for U.S. tourism, see Dulles, *Americans Abroad*, 152; Oct. 5, Oct. 19, Dec. 14, 1917, *The Tourist Club Year Book, 1917–1918*, LITC Records.

157 On Russia, see "Just among Ourselves," *BVM* 9 (Jan. 1902): 157; on Germany, "Just among Ourselves," *BVM* 5 (May 1898): 284. On wandering at will, see "Hyde Park Travel Class. Season 1894–1895," Miscellaneous pamphlets; on peaks, see Oct. 15, 1900, entry, Club and Board Minutes, 1899–1903, box 1; on matter of days, see "Travel Class 1901–1902," 6, Yearbooks, all in HPTC Records.

158 On some of the tribulations of real travelers, see Mrs. Joseph Cook, "A Tour Round the World," *Chautauquan* 3 (June 1883): 510–14, 513; Sweetser, *One Way Round the World*, 52; on tourists' insulation from local life, see Brendon, *Thomas Cook*, 227.

159 Edith R. Daniels, "Poem for 40th Anniversary of Tourists," file 2, box 1, TCM Records. On men's anxieties that women travelers thought their homes inadequate, see Dolan, *Ladies of the Grand Tour*, 9; on travel as a threat to home values, see Frawley, *A Wider Range*, 27. On criticisms of women's study clubs in general, see Martin, *Sound of Our Own Voices*, 119–23; Gere, *Intimate Practices*, 257–64.

160 Shaffer, "Seeing the Nature of America," 155.

161 "Constitution," LITC Records. On travel as a male endeavor, see Leed, *The Mind of the Traveler*, 113.

162 Bessie Leach Priddy, "Thoughts on the Club Program," *GFM* 18 (July 1919): 15; Martin, *Sound of Our Own Voices*, 4; Blair, *The Clubwoman as Feminist*, 99, 103–5.

163 Lena Myers, "Through the Years," McGregor Tourist Club Records; "Tourist Club Observes Seventy-fifth Birthday," *Fulton Democrat*, Feb. 11, 1917, LITC Records.

164 On scholarship, see Mar. 6, 1905, meeting, Club and Board Minutes, 1903–1906, box 1: Minute Books 1891–1906, on philanthropy, see "Hyde Park Travel Club, 1913–1914," 34, Yearbooks; on political activism, see Mar. 6, 1905, meeting, Club and Board Minutes, 1903–1906, box 1: Minute Books 1891–1906, all in HPTC Records.

165 Blair, *The Clubwoman as Feminist*, 119; Muncy, *Creating a Female Dominion*, 64; Evans, *Born For Liberty*, 150.

166   On prejudices, see "Around the Study Lamp," *BVM* 9 (Apr. 1902): 341; on enthusiasm, see "Just among Ourselves," *BVM* 5 (Mar. 1898): 202; on Spaniards, see "Around the Study Lamp," *BVM* 6 (Apr. 1899): 248.

167   Mar. 4, 1901, entry, Club and Board Minutes, 1899–1903, box 1, HPTC Records; "Just among Ourselves," *BVM* 9 (Apr. 1902): 342.

168   "Around the Study Lamp," *BVM* 6 (May 1899): 303.

Chapter 5

1   "6,000 Foreign-Born Americans Renew Pledge," *Chicago Herald*, July 5, 1916. On public holidays as invented traditions aimed at constructing national identity, see Litwicki, *America's Public Holidays*, 2–3.

2   McClymer, *War and Welfare*, 99–107; McClymer, "The Americanization Movement."

3   Hartmann, *The Movement to Americanize the Immigrant*, 31, 33, 136; Reimers, *Unwelcome Strangers*; General Federation of Women's Clubs, "A Suggested Program for Americanization," 3; "Americanization Plans of the GFWC," *GFM* 18 (Aug. 1919): 5; "Americanization," *GFM* 17 (Nov. 1918): 20. State federations likewise took up the Americanization banner, see Taaffe, *The History of the Missouri Federation*, 72, 81; Maw, *A History of the Michigan State Federation*, 88; Buffum and Thurston, *History of the Iowa Federation*, 104; Courtney, *History Indiana Federation*, 272; Laws, *History of the Ohio Federation*, 276, 300, 302, 309, 312.

4   Hartmann, *The Movement to Americanize the Immigrant*, 24, 36, 38, 56–57, 146, 160, 204–5, 228; Korman, *Industrialization, Immigrants and Americanizers*. "The Women's Christian Temperance Union Trains Workers for Americanization Centers," *Foreign-Born* 1 (Nov. 1919): 19; "Jewish Women and Americanization," *American Hebrew* 106 (Nov. 21, 1919): 16; "Council of Jewish Women Will Extend Americanization Work," *American Hebrew* 106 (Mar. 5, 1920): 485; Archdeacon, *Becoming American*, 167; Crocker, *Social Work*. On the Bureaus of Naturalization and Education, see Van Nuys, *Americanizing the West*, 148–71. On educators, see Seller, "The Education of the Immigrant Woman"; Weiss, *American Education*. On ethnic groups, see Glenn, *Daughters of the Shtetl*, 57; Barrett, "Americanization."

5   On acculturation, see Ewen, *Immigrant Women*, 15; Peiss, *Cheap Amusements*, 31; Barrett, "Americanization," 997; Enstad, *Ladies of Labor*. Korman, *Industrialization, Immigrants and Americanizers*, 136; Van Nuys, *Americanizing the West*, 109; Barrett, *Work and Community*, 138–43. On various strains in the Americanization movement, see Higham, *Strangers in the Land*; Crawford, *Hold Your Tongue*, 47; on Americanization as improving working and housing conditions, see General Federation of Women's Clubs, *A Suggested Program for Americanization*, 7.

6   On teaching English, see Martha S. F. Bent, "Talk to Leaders of Public Opinion," in *A Suggested Program for Americanization*, 31–33; on patriotic rituals, see "Citizenship Day Program." On sound immigration laws, see Mary Wood, "Legislation and Americanization," in *Americanization Programs*, 14–15. On 1 percent, see "In reply," *GFM* 18 (Aug. 1919): 36.

7   On cultural conformity, see Ruiz, *From Out of the Shadows*, 34; Hartmann, *The Movement to Americanize the Immigrant*, 253–54; McClymer, "The Americanization Movement"; Archdeacon, *Becoming American*, 93. On the melting pot, see Gleason, "The Melting Pot," 34–38; Kraut, *The Huddled Masses*, 170–71; Van Nuys, *Americanizing the West*, 35–36, 68; King, *Making Americans*, 16, 27, 85; on the tension between Anglo-Saxonism and cosmopolitanism, see Lissak, *Pluralism and Progressives*, 3.

8   Sanchez, "'Go After the Women.'"

9   J. Hunter, *The Gospel of Gentility*; P. Hill, *The World Their Household*; Flemming, *Women's Work for Women*; Chin, "Beneficent Imperialists," 340. K. Hansen, *African Encounters*; Findlay, *Imposing Decency*, 111; Rafael, *White Love*, chap. 2; Cabán, "Subjects and Immigrants"; "American Progress in Habana," *NGM* 13 (Mar. 1902): 97–108. On links between Americanization efforts in the Philippines and Minnesota, see Soderstrom, "Family Trees." Flora McDonald Thompson, "Our Paris Letter," *Harper's Bazar* 38 (June 1904): 594–96.

10 Davies, *Peacefully Working to Conquer the World*; Rosenberg, *Spreading the American Dream*; Rosenberg, "Consuming Women"; Domosh, "Pickles and Purity"; Cody, *Exporting American Architecture*, 5.

11 Ewen, *Immigrant Women*, 175; Nesbitt, *Household Management*, 106–7, 111; Seller, "The Education of the Immigrant Woman," 311; on resistance to such measures, see Diner, *Hungering for America*, 78. Jacobson, *Barbarian Virtues*, 14, 56.

12 On immigrant gifts and pluralism, see Fisher, "The People's Institute," 89–90.

13 On costumes, "No Hyphen Here," *Chicago Herald*, July 5, 1916; "Pageants and Picnics Are to Mark Fourth," *Chicago Daily News*, July 3, 1916; "Citizens of Foreign Birth to Carry Flags," *Chicago Evening Post*, July 3, 1916. On culture as an appropriately female realm, see Blair, *The Torchbearers*, 2.

14 "Music," *GFM* 18 (Mar. 1919): 19. On ethnic music see Vaillant, *Sounds of Reform*, 26–29, 32.

15 "Music Festival by 2,000 Germans," *Chicago Tribune*, Oct. 5, 1908; "Good Music Will Grace Mexicans' Celebration," *Los Angeles Times*, Sept. 3, 1916.

16 The Gary International Institute Y.W.C.A., "Europe in America in Folk Songs and Dances," folder 10: "Program/Publicity, Europe in America in Folk Songs and Dances," ca. 1920; box 4, IINWI Records. I would like to thank Maria Todorova and John Randolph for their translations and for their observations on

other transliteration possibilities. On ethnic and European records, see Greene, *A Passion for Polka*, 69–70, 72.

17 "The Second Annual Playground Congress," *Playground* 2 (Oct. 1908): 3–5; "Chicago's Third Play Festival," *Survey* 23 (Nov. 6, 1909): 195–200; on the 1908 festival, see Graham Romeyn Taylor, "The Chicago Play Festival," *Charities and the Commons* 20 (Aug. 1, 1908): 539–45; see also "'Dutch Dancers' in Dance of All Nations," *Chicago Tribune*, Feb. 2, 1912. "Italians Observe Independence Day with Big Festival," *Times-Picayune*, June 7, 1920.

18 Alfred G. Arvold, "The Little Country Theatre," *Immigrants in America Review* 1 (June 1915): 31–35, 33.

19 Addams, *Twenty Years at Hull-House*, 268; S. Jackson, *Lines of Activity*, 228–29, 233; Lissak, *Pluralism and Progressives*, 41, 45; M. Carson, *Settlement Folk*, 116.

20 On pageants, see Glassberg, "History and the Public," 965; Glassberg, *American Historical Pageantry*, 131; see also "Foreign Girls in Pageant," *New York Tribune*, Feb. 24, 1916.

21 "A Pageant of the Melting Pot," *Survey* 32, July 4, 1914, 356.

22 Perkins, "Influence of Art," 7.

23 Ibid., 8.

24 "The Labor Museum," *HHB* 4 (Autumn 1900): 8; "Hull-House Labor Museum," *HHB* 5, no. 1, semi-annual (1902): 12; "Hull-House Labor Museum," *HHB* 6 (Midwinter 1903–4): 12; Lissak, *Pluralism and Progressives*, 41.

25 On Annunziata, see "Chicago Arts and Crafts Society," *HHB* 4 (Autumn 1900): 8. Boris, "Crossing Boundaries," 40. "Immigrant Arts at Greenwich House," *Charities and the Commons* 20 (May 2, 1908): 146. On the Cincinnati and other homelands exhibitions, see Kirshenblatt-Gimblett, *Destination Culture*, 112–17.

26 Conzen et al., "The Invention of Ethnicity," 24. On immigrant celebrations as opportunities to bolster ethnicity and claims to belonging, see Øverland, *Immigrant Minds*, 2. On spectators, see Kirshenblatt-Gimblett, *Destination Culture*, 78. Remben Crawford, "Sweet Senoritas," *Atlantic Constitution*, Mar. 29, 1896; Hoelscher, *Heritage on Stage*, 35, 48.

27 Mrs. Edward W. Bemis, "Council of Foreign Language Women," *GFM* 18 (Mar. 1919): 22. On dispelling prejudice, see Eaton, *Immigrant Gifts*. On the value of ethnic difference, see Conzen et al., "The Invention of Ethnicity," 10.

28 On the struggles of ethnic nationalists, see Litwicki, *America's Public Holidays*, 139. On echoing jeremiads, see Eaton, *Immigrant Gifts*, 27, 34; Laws, *History of the Ohio Federation*, 276; "A Pageant of the Nations in New York," *Survey* 32 (May 23, 1914): 209–10; on preservation, see Melvin, "Building Muscles and Civics," 94.

29 "Report of Immigration Secretary for June 1918," folder 4, IIL Records; "Hull-House Music School," *HHB* 5, no. 1 (1902): 5; Gulick, *The Healthful Art*, 7, 66–

68; Eleanor Smith taught European folk songs at the Hull-House music school; see Vaillant, *Sounds of Reform*, 107. On costumes, see J. Lincoln, *The Festival Book*, 28; on teaching crafts, see Randilla Willard, "Annual Report, Immigration Secretary, 1920," folder 3, IIL Records. On embroideries, see Luba Tzvetanova, "Report of Mar., 1921," folder 15: Monthly Reports, 1921; box 2, IINWI Records. On Greenwich House, see "Immigrant Arts at Greenwich House," *Charities and the Commons* 20 (May 2, 1908): 146.

30 On dances, see State Commission, *A Manual for Home Teachers*, 45. Elson, *Folk Songs*, v; Gilbert, *One Hundred Folk-Songs*, 4; Faulkner, *Americanization Songs*, 2. On performing dances from other ethnic groups, see "Dances of All Nations," *HHB* 4 (Midwinter 1900): 3. On authenticity, see Graham Romeyn Taylor, "The Chicago Play Festival," *Charities and the Commons* 20 (Aug. 1, 1908): 539–45, 541.

31 Ellen Litwicki notes that native-born whites attended Europeans' celebrations more than they attended African Americans' celebrations, in *America's Public Holidays*, 141; on excluding African Americans from the urban picturesque, see Bramen, "The Urban Picturesque," 448–49; on African Americans' absence from the Hull-House stage, see S. Jackson, *Lines of Activity*, 228; on settlements' segregationist practices, see Lasch-Quinn, *Black Neighbors*, 3, 25. On anti-Semitism, see Lissak, *Pluralism and Progressives*, 163.

32 "Gay Little Foreigners," *New York Tribune*, Jan. 14, 1908; "Syrian Girls' Club," *Times-Picayune*, Feb. 3, 1918; on Mexican handicrafts, see Lida Wilson Jones, "A Model Club's Social Service," *GFM* 16 (May 1917): 27; on Chicago celebration, see "The New Independence Day," *Survey* 40 (July 13, 1918): 419–21; on Columbus Day pageant, see E. B. Mero, "The Holiday as a Builder of Citizenship," *Playground* 8 (June 1914): 101–2.

33 "Customs and Dances of All Nations in Harvest Pageant," *Gary Evening Post*, Nov. 13, 1920, folder 9: "Program/Publicity, Harvest Pageant, 1920"; Gary International Institute, YWCA, "Europe in America in Folk Songs and Dances," folder 10: "Program/Publicity, Europe in America in Folk Songs and Dances," ca. 1920; both in box 4, IINWI Records.

34 Gulick, *The Healthful Art*, 39. On gifts from allied nations, see "'All Nations' Tonight," *Chicago Tribune*, Dec. 7, 1918. On the belief that only "white" immigrants were assimilable, see Van Nuys, *Americanizing the West*, 6, 35. On pan-Europeanism and whiteness, see Jacobson, *Whiteness*, 75, 210, 241.

35 For sample Americanization programs with "Gifts of the Nations" components, see State Commission, *A Manual for Home Teachers*, 45; Priddy, "Civics and Americanization," 9; "Program for Americanization Day, July 4, 1919," *GFM* 18 (June 1919): 21.

36 M. Carson, *Settlement Folk*, quotation 103, 159–60. Although Ruth Crocker and Rivka Shpak Lissak emphasize settlement houses' efforts to eradicate immigrant culture, they also provide examples of their cultural preservation efforts; see Crocker, *Social Work and Social Order*, 30, 57–58, 66, 214; Lissak, *Pluralism and Progressives*, 6, 25, 30, 45, 47, 164.

37 On Denison House, see M. Carson, *Settlement Folk*, 104, 108. Siegel, *Lillian Wald*, 93, 111; "A Pageant of America in the Making," *Survey* 38 (Sept. 15, 1917): 529.

38 Jane Addams, quoted in *General Federation of Women's Clubs, Eighth Biennial Convention, 1906*, 166, folder: 8th Biennial, St. Paul, Minnesota, box: Convention Records (Proceedings-Reports), 1906–1910, GFWC.

39 Hedger, "What Is an Americanization Institute?" 5; see also Perkins, "Influence of Art."

40 On immigrant gifts, see also "Americanization," *GFM* 18 (Aug. 1919): 19; GFWC Division of Americanization, 1922–1924, "Americans All," folder: Program Records, 1920–1924 (Pamphlets), Department of American Citizenship, box: Program Records, Winter 1920–1924, GFWC.

41 On Albany event, see Mrs. Charles W. Greene, "Making the Ideal of the American Home," in *Americanization Programs*, 12–13. Anne Walker, "An Americanization Tea," *Woman's Home Companion* 47 (Jan. 1920): 29, 34.

42 Charlotte W. Foster, "International Institute, Report of New Bedford, Mass., Dec. 15, 1918 to Jan. 15, 1919," folder 3, International Institute of New Bedford Records.

43 Bremer, "'Foreign Community and Immigration Work'"; Eaton, *Immigrant Gifts*, 92–93; Mohl and Betten, "Ethnic Adjustment"; Mohl, "The International Institutes," 118–22, 126; Mohl, "Cultural Pluralism," 111–37; on handicraft instructors, see Harriette M. Dills, "Report of International Institute Committee, Oct. 1, 1919," folder 3, International Institute of New Bedford Records. *Foreign-Born* 1 (Sept.–Oct. 1920): 1, 3, 18.

44 On Bremer's experience, see Mohl, "The International Institutes," 119. On names, see Bremer, "'Foreign Community and Immigration Work,'" 7–8.

45 "Report of the Executive of the International Institute, St. Louis Missouri, Nov. 1919," folder 14, box 2, IINWI Records.

46 Quotation in "Report of Immigration Secretary—May, 1918," folder 4; see also "Annual Report, Immigration Secretary, 1918," folder 3; on display, see "January, 1918, Report of Immigration Secretary," folder 4; on international party, see "Annual Report, Immigration Secretary, 1918," folder 3; on entertainment, see "Report of Immigration Secretary, Dec. 1919," folder 4, all in IIL Records.

47 Mohl, "The International Institutes," quotation 121–22, 129.

48 Addams cited in Lissak, *Pluralism and Progressives*, 48, 55. John Collier, "Caliban of the Yellow Sands," *Survey* 36 (July 1, 1916): 343–50, 345; H. Gilbert, *One Hundred Folk-Songs*, 4.

49 Gulick, preface, vii; Gulick, *The Healthful Art*, 7, 22, 66, 130; Melvin, "Building Muscles," 89–99.

50 "Dubuque, Iowa," *Playground* 8 (Dec. 1914): 306; "Pittsburgh Play Festival," *Playground* 3 (May 1909): 34; "Playground Festival, Providence, R.I.," *Playground* 3 (Oct. 1909): 8–11; on the Chicago festival, see Ida M. Tarbell, "An Old World Fete in Industrial America," *Charities and the Commons* 20 (Aug. 1, 1908): 546.

51 Du Mont, *Reform and Reaction*, 101; P. Jones, *Libraries, Immigrants*, 21; on the Mt. Vernon library, see John Foster Carr, "What the Library Can Do for Our Foreign-Born," *Library Journal* 38 (Oct. 1913): 566–68, 567; on the Cedar Rapids library, see Sarka Hrbek, "The Library and the Foreign-Born Citizen," *Public Libraries* 15 (Mar. 1910): 98–104, 103; on helping with community pageants, see Adelaide B. Maltby, "Immigrants as Contributors to Library Progress," *Bulletin of the American Library Association* 7 (July 1913): 150–54, 152.

52 Eaton, *Immigrant Gifts*, 30–33. See also Kirshenblatt-Gimblett, "Objects of Ethnography," 433.

53 Eaton, *Immigrant Gifts*, 36, 39–50, illustration plate after p. 42.

54 Ibid., 53–63.

55 "Dances of All Nations," *HHB* 4 (Midwinter 1900): 3; "Report on the Executive of the International Institute, St. Louis, Missouri, May 1920," folder 14: "Executive Records 1919–1920," box 2, International Institute of St. Louis Records; "Report of Miss Elizabeth Howe, Nov. 1920," folder 2, International Institute of Niagara Falls Records.

56 Walker, "An Americanization Tea," *Woman's Home Companion* 47 (Jan. 1920): 29, 34; on the Buffalo exhibit, see Eaton, *Immigrant Gifts*, 64. On the commercial value of ethnic difference, see Cocks, *Doing the Town*, 190.

57 On their own kind, see Raymond Morley, foreword to *The Jugoslavs of Cleveland* by Eleanor E. Ledbetter (Cleveland: The Mayor's Advisory War Committee, 1918), in folder 11, box 12, Immigrants' Protective League Records. On the belief that fostering an appreciation of their cultures would lead immigrants to respond more warmly to Americanization efforts, see Kirshenblatt-Gimblett, *Destination Culture*, 111; Melvin, "Building Muscles," 91, 96; Eaton, *Immigrant Gifts*, 29; Lissak, *Pluralism and Progressives*, 31, 34, 41.

58 Hazel MacKaye, "Americanization Via Pageantry," *GFM* 18 (June 1919): 19–20, 19; "What Some State Federations Are Doing," *GFM* 18 (Mar. 1919): 23–26, 24. The GFWC's chairman of art urged clubwomen to promote immigrant handicrafts because "The contact with the foreign women through this work will

do much for their education in Americanization"; see Perkins, "Influence of Art," 7.

59 On anthem, see "Getting Acquainted through Song," *Playground* 9 (Dec. 1915): 300. Hazel MacKaye, "Americanization Via Pageantry," *GFM* 18 (June 1919): 19–20, 19; clipping, "To Gary's Foreign Born," folder 10: "Program/Publicity, Europe in America in Folk Songs and Dances," ca. 1920, box 4, IINWI Records.

60 "A Pageant of the Nations in New York," *Survey* 32 (May 23, 1914): 209–10.

61 On altar, see Eaton, *Immigrant Gifts*, 36; on representatives, see William Norman Guthrie, "Foreign Literature and the New Citizen," in *General Federation of Women's Clubs Thirteenth Biennial Convention, 1916*, ed. Mrs. Harry L. Keefe, 298–93, 291, folder: 13th Biennial, New York, box: Convention Records (Proceedings-Reports), 1912–1916, GWFC.

62 Bridges, *On Becoming an American*, 27; on exchange, see Hazel MacKaye, "Americanization Via Pageantry," *GFM* 18 (June 1919): 19–20, 19.

63 On mass culture, see Higham, *Send These to Me*, 26; on the tendency to depreciate commercial culture in the immigrant gifts movement, see J. Gilbert, *Perfect Cities*, 216; on depicting immigrants as premodern, see Bramen, "The Urban Picturesque," 463; on modernity and pageants, Jacobson, *Barbarian Virtues*, 114. "Hull-House Labor Museum," *HHB* 6 (Midwinter 1903–4): 12; on urban tourism, see Cocks, *Doing the Town*, 197.

64 Lilian Brandt, "A Transplanted Birthright," *Charities* 12 (May 7, 1904): 494–99, 496. On the belief that Mexicans had natural artistic abilities, see Garcia, *A World of Its Own*, 67. On manual education and subordination, see Seller, "The Education of the Immigrant Woman," 311.

65 On managing "ethnicization" see Conzen et al., "The Invention of Ethnicity"; Lissak, *Pluralism and Progressives*, 130, 165; Henry R. Mussey, "The 'Ajax' in New York," *Charities* 12 (Apr. 2, 1904): 325.

66 Orsi, *The Madonna of 115th Street*; on nationalist politics, see Litwicki, *America's Public Holidays*, 121. Melvin, "Building Muscles," 97. On ethnic preservation, see Lissak, *Pluralism and Progressives*, 131.

67 Kirshenblatt-Gimblett, "Objects of Ethnography," 433.

68 On changing into factory-made outfits, see Litwicki, *America's Public Holidays*, 193. Speaking of gifts pageants, Barbara Kirshenblatt-Gimblett notes that "the very form that these celebrations took, wherein individual immigrant groups pledged their loyalty as ethnic groups, undermined the drive for 100 percent Americanism"; see "Objects of Ethnography," 419.

69 On Kallen as "the chief author of the theory of cultural pluralism," see Higham, *Send These to Me*, 205. See also M. Gordon, *Assimilation*, 141–44; Hollinger, *Postethnic America*, 11, 92; Jacobson, *Whiteness*, 214–15; King, *Making Americans*, 27,

115; Akam, *Transnational America*, 45, 56; on Kallen (and others) as "cosmopolitan patriots," see J. Hansen, *The Lost Promise of Patriotism*, xiv, 105. Hansen finds that unlike Kallen, other cosmopolitan patriots believed that individuals could choose their cultural affiliation and that this voluntarism made cosmopolitanism different from pluralism (93). Kallen, *Culture and Democracy*. On cultural pluralism in the Progressive Era, see G. White, "Social Settlements"; Litwicki, *America's Public Holidays*, 220; M. Carson, *Settlement Folk*, 101. On the educational value of festivals, see Tanen, "Festivals and Diplomacy," 367.

70 Bremer quoted in Mohl, "The International Institutes," 119; Esther Johnston cited in Dain, *The New York Public Library*, 65; on soil, see Lingle, "Industrial and Social Conditions," 14.

71 Bremer, "Foreign Community and Immigration Work"; on homes, see Mrs. J. E. Church, cited in *General Federation of Women's Clubs, Fifteenth Biennial Convention, 1920*, ed. Mrs. Adam Weiss, folder: Convention Records (Proceedings, Reports), 1920, box: Convention Records (Proceedings-Reports), 1918–1924, GFWC.

72 Hedger, "What Is an Americanization Institute?"

73 On sympathetic knowledge, see Mrs. True Worthy White, "Department of Literature and Library Extension," *GFM* 17 (Feb. 1918): 39; on studying customs, see GFWC, *A Suggested Program for Americanization*, 20; Lingle, "A Course on Americanization," 9–10; on knowing immigrant races, see Mrs. True Worthy White, "Americanization as Related to Literature," 16.

74 Martha S. F. Bent, "Suggested Outlines for Speakers on Americanization," in *A Suggested Program for Americanization*, 30; Richardson, "A Study of One National Group."

75 Mrs. Harry L. Keefe, ed., *General Federation of Women's Clubs Thirteenth Biennial Convention, 1916*, 457–70; folder: 13th Biennial, New York, New York, box: Convention Records (Proceedings-Reports), 1912–1916, GFWC; on bibliography, see *Americanization Programs*, 21. On inviting immigrants to meetings, see Richardson, "A Study of One National Group." On referrals, see Hedger, "What Is an Americanization Institute?" On teachers as conduits of knowledge to and from immigrants, see State Commission, *A Manual for Home Teachers*, 18.

76 On ethnic knowledge as a means to Americanization, see Hedger, "What Is an Americanization Institute?"; on beginning with ourselves, see "What Is an American?" *GFM* 18 (Aug. 1919): 4.

77 On fellowship, see *Americanization Programs*, 3; on wisdom, see Hedger, "What Is an Americanization Institute?"

78 Anne Rhodes, "What Women's Clubs Can Do," *GFM* 18 (Mar. 1919): 14; "Literature and Library Extension," *GFM* 18 (Mar. 1919): 18–19.

79 Mrs. W. I. McFarland, *General Federation of Women's Clubs, Fourteenth Biennial Convention, 1918*, folder: Convention Records (Proceedings-Reports), 1918, box: Convention Records (Proceedings-Reports), 1918–1924, GFWC.

80 On doctrine, see "What Some State Federations Are Doing," *GFM* 18 (Mar. 1919): 23–26, 23; on inferiors, see Hazel MacKaye, "Americanization via Pageantry," *GFM* 18 (June 1919): 19–20.

81 Randilla Willard, "Annual Report, Immigration Secretary, 1920," folder 3, IIL Records; "Elementary Adult Education," 73.

82 Hazel MacKaye, "Americanization via Pageantry," *GFM* 18 (June 1919): 19–20.

83 "A Pageant of the Nations in New York," *Survey* 32 (May 23, 1914): 209–10.

84 Hazel MacKaye, "Americanization via Pageantry," *GFM* 18 (June 1919): 19–20, 19.

85 Quoted in Eaton, *Immigrant Gifts*, 65.

86 Addams, "The New Internationalism," 57. See also Herman, *Eleven against War*, chap. 5.

87 Boyd, *Emissaries*, 6; on international government work, see "International Institute Committee Minutes, May 1923," folder: Board of Directors Minutes with Annual Report—1923," box 1, International Institute of San Francisco Records; *General Federation of Women's Clubs Thirteenth Biennial Convention, 1916*, ed. Mrs. Harry L. Keefe, 168–69, folder: 13th Biennial, New York, New York, box: Convention Records (Proceedings-Reports), 1912–1916, GFWC; William Norman Guthrie, "Address—Foreign Literature and the New Citizen," in ibid., 289–93, 293.

88 Lucia Ames Mead, "Club Programs in the World Crisis," *GFM* 17 (Dec. 1918): 14.

89 Drachsler, *Democracy and Assimilation*, 195.

90 Mary Gibson, "Americanization," in *A Suggested Program for Americanization*, 5–13, 12; GFWC, *A Suggested Program for Americanization*, 33–34; on Bohemians, see Ethel Richardson, "A Study of One National Group," in *A Suggested Program for Americanization*, 20–21.

91 On slime, see Aronovici, *Americanization*, 28; on Polish, see Graham Taylor, "Enforcing English by Proclamation," *Survey* 40 (July 6, 1918): 394–95.

92 Abbott, *The Immigrant*, 277–78.

93 Randilla Willard, "February, 1918, Report of Immigration Secretary," folder 4, IIL Records.

94 J. J. Whittle, "Cosy Corners," *Charities* 4 (Feb. 3, 1900): 14; "Fancy Linens from Italy at McCutcheon's," *Survey* 40 (May 4, 1918): 133; A Catalogue of the Second Exhibition of the Chicago Arts and Crafts Society, 1909, Addams, *Jane Addams Papers*, reel 52; Marion Foster Washburne, "A Labor Museum," *Craftsman* 6

(Sept. 1904): 570–80, 577; *Hull-House Year Book*, 1907, 12, *Jane Addams Papers*, reel 53. On immigrant handicrafts, see also "Hull-House Labor Museum," *HHB* 5, semiannual (1902): 12; also Addams, *Twenty Years at Hull-House*, 183–84.

95 General Federation of Women's Clubs, Division on Americanization, 1918– 1920, "Americanization Programs," 7, folder: Program Records, 1918–1920 (pamphlets), American Citizenship Department, Americanization Committee, box: Program Records, 1904–1920, GFWC.

96 Steward, "Tourism in Late Imperial Austria," 116; Löfgren, "Know Your Country," 139. On museums, see Eaton, *Immigrant Gifts*, 156; Granlund, "Sweden," 3; Bilachevsky, "The Peasant Art of Little Russia," 17. On festivals and dances in Germany, see Mosse, *The Nationalization of the Masses*.

97 Cohn, "Representing Authority in Victorian India," 183; on Western women's cultural endeavors, see Jayawardena, *The White Woman's Other Burden*, 108; on Canada, see Eaton, *Immigrant Gifts*, 112–13. Hobsbawm, "Introduction: Inventing Traditions."

98 Bovbjerg, *Danish Folk Dances*, 3; "The Italian Industrial School," *Vogue* 29 (Apr. 18, 1907): 650.

99 On prizes, see Eaton, *Immigrant Gifts*, 39, 48; on festivals, see Needham, *Folk Festivals*, 45–46, 125–31; Glassberg, *American Historical Pageantry*, 43, 111; on Scotland and England, see Addams, *The Spirit of Youth*, 102.

100 On aristocratic patronage of handicraft schools, see Churchill, "Introductory Note," 5; on Princess Alexandre Sidamon-Eristoff's collection of peasant art, see Holme, *Peasant Art in Russia*, iii; on museums, see Levetus, "Austria," 2; on the spindle, see Ricci, "Women's Crafts," 18.

101 Gulick, *The Healthful Art*, 196, 270. On Abbey Players, S. Jackson, *Lines of Activity*, 206.

102 "Report of Miss Elizabeth Howe, Apr. 1920," folder 2, International Institute of Niagara Falls Records; G. Ricciardi, "Torrone," *Foreign-Born* 2 (Dec. 1920): 67; "$2,000 for Girls' League," *New York Tribune*, Feb. 24, 1912.

103 On traveling with an open mind, see Edward W. Bok, "At Home with the Editor," *LHJ* 8 (Aug. 1891): 10; "Going Abroad—Thoughts on Travel," *Hearth and Home* 3 (May 20, 1871): 382; on local folk culture, see Stoddard, *Japan*, 5; Holmes, *Burton Holmes Travelogues*, 7:184, 189; on traveling third class to better observe ordinary people, see "How We Went Abroad," *LHJ* 6 (Aug. 1889): 4. Luther Hasley Gulick, "Exhibition of Folk and National Dances," in "Descriptive Program Second Annual Congress Playground Association of America, New York City," folder: 1908 NRA Congress, box 14, National Recreation Association Records.

104 "International Institute for Alien Women," folder 1, International Institute of Niagara Falls Records.

105 Mary Wood Hinman cited in "Proceedings of the Third Annual Congress of

the Playground Association of America," folder: 1909—NRA Congress, box 14, National Recreation Association Records; Dec. 12, "Scandinavia and The Netherlands," Cosmopolitan Club program, 1898–1899, Program Booklets, 1895–1920, Cosmopolitan Club Records; on ethnic tourism, see Light "From Vice District," 367–94; Cocks, *Doing the Town*, 190–202.

106 Hughes, *The Real New York*, 234. On the urban picturesque as a means to transform immigrants from social threats to cultural resources, see Bramen, "The Urban Picturesque," 446. "International Institution for Youth's Educational Travel," *Charities* 2 (May 20, 1899): 24; "Going Abroad?," *Charities* 2 (May 20, 1899): 25; Gulick, *The Healthful Art*, 72; on the Labor Museum, see Marion Foster Washburne, "A Labor Museum," *Craftsman* 6 (Sept. 1904): 570–80, 577.

107 On uniting parents and children, see Bremer, "'Foreign Community and Immigration Work,'" 16; G. White, "Social Settlements," 65; S. Jackson, *Lines of Activity*, 256; Lissak, *Pluralism and Progressives*, 57. Mary E. McDowell, "Making the Foreign Born One of Us," *Survey* 40 (May 25, 1918); 213–15, 213. Addams, *Twenty Years at Hull-House*, 171.

108 On Milwaukee, see "Does This Apply to Your City?" *Playground* 9 (July 1915): 121–24; on Addams, see M. Carson, *Settlement Folk*, 114; Addams, *The Spirit of Youth*, 6. On reformers' concerns about commercial amusements, see Peiss, *Cheap Amusements*, 164; on the appeal of ethnic and tourist arts as a counterpoint to standardized, mass-produced products, see Graburn, "Introduction: Arts of the Fourth World," 2.

109 Jane Addams, "The Public School and the Immigrant Child," *Journal of Proceedings and Addresses of the National Education Association* 46 (July 1908): 99–102, 101–2.

110 Addams, "Introduction. Immigration," 13.

111 "Dances of All Nations," *HHB* 4 (Midwinter 1900): 3; on modern life, see Gulick, preface, vii.

112 On settlement workers' concerns about excessive commercialism, see M. Carson, *Settlement Folk*, 108; on preserving handicrafts, see Perkins, "Influence of Art," in *Americanization Programs*, 7–8; on preventing loss, see Eaton, *Immigrant Gifts*, 62; "Immigrant Arts at Greenwich House," *Charities and the Commons* 20 (May 2, 1908): 146. Wald, "New Americans and Our Policies," 435.

113 "A Pageant of the Nations in New York," *Survey* 32 (May 23, 1914): 209–10; Nesbitt, *Household Management*, 23–24.

114 On other manifestations of antimodernism, see Lears, *No Place of Grace*, xv, xix, 4, 7; H. Shapiro, *Appalachia on Our Mind*, xiii, 220, 248–52; D. Whisnant, *All That Is Native and Fine*, 6, 8, 48, 54.

115 Wilkins, *The Emergence of Multinational Enterprise*, 70–71; Wyman, *Round-Trip to America*, 182–86; Gabaccia, *Italy's Many Diasporas*, 96–100. On views of the

United States, see Heindel, *The American Impact on Great Britain*; Strauss, *Menace in the West*, 38, 176; Orty, "From Baudelaire to Duhamel"; Bell and Bell, "Introduction: The Dilemmas of 'Americanization,'" 4–6; Matthews, "Which America?," 17; Woodward, *The Old World's New World*, 81; Wagnleitner, *Coca-Colonization*; Pells, *Not Like Us*, 9; Wagnleitner and May, *"Here, There, and Everywhere,"* 4, 5.

116 Gulick, *The Healthful Art*, 195; on Americanization overseas, see W. Carson, *Mexico*, vi; Holmes, *Burton Holmes Travelogues*, 4:194; Stoddard, *John L. Stoddard's Lectures* (1918), 1:68.

117 Eaton, *Immigrant Gifts*, 154–55.

118 Rosaldo, "Imperialist Nostalgia," 69, 86.

Bibliography

Newspapers and Periodicals

American Cookery: A Monthly Dining
  Room Magazine
American Hebrew and Jewish Messenger
American Woman
Architectural Record
Art Amateur
Art Interchange
Atlanta Constitution
Bay View Magazine
Bulletin of the American Library
  Association
Charities
Charities and the Commons
Chautauquan
Chicago Daily News
Chicago Evening Post
Chicago Herald
Chicago Tribune
Club Woman
Cosmopolitan
Cottage Hearth
Country Life in America
Craftsman
Decorator and Furnisher
Delineator
Demorest's Family Magazine
Demorest's Illustrated Monthly
Demorest's Monthly Magazine
Everybody's Magazine
Everyland

Foreign-Born
Frank Leslie's Gazette of Fashions and
  the Beau Monde
General Federation Bulletin
General Federation of Women's Clubs
  Magazine (General Federation
  Magazine)
Godey's
Good Housekeeping
Harper's Bazar
Harper's Weekly
Hearth and Home
Home-Maker
House and Garden
House Beautiful
Household
Housekeeper's Weekly
Hull-House Bulletin
Immigrants in America Review
Journal of Proceedings and Addresses of
  the National Education Association
Ladies' Home Journal
Ladies' World
Library Journal
Los Angeles Times
Mentor
Metropolitan
Munsey's Magazine
National Geographic Magazine
New Cycle

New York Times

New York Tribune

Outing

Playground

Public Libraries

Survey

Table Talk: The National Food Magazine, including the International Culinary Magazine

Times-Picayune (New Orleans)

Travel Magazine (Travel)

Vanity Fair

Vogue

Woman's Cycle

Woman's Era

Woman's Home Companion

Archival Collections

Elmer L. Andersen Library, University of Minnesota, Minneapolis

 Immigration History Research Center

  International Institute of Lewiston Records (Lewiston-Auburn Maine)

  International Institute of New Bedford Records, microfilm edition prepared by Lynn Schweitzer

  International Institute of Niagara Falls Records, microfilm edition prepared by Lynn Schweitzer

  International Institute of St. Louis Records

  International Institute of San Francisco Records

  Ruth Crawford Mitchell Diary

 Social Welfare History Archives

  National Recreation Association Records

Jonathan Bourne Historical Center, Bourne, Massachusetts

 Pocasset Travelers Club Records

Calumet Gary Regional Archives, Indiana University Northwest Library, Gary

 International Institute of Northwest Indiana Records

Chicago Historical Society

 Hyde Park Travel Club (also referred to as the Hyde Park Travel Class) Records

 Bertha H. Palmer Papers

 Potter Palmer Papers

General Federation of Women's Clubs, Washington, D.C.

 Convention Records (Proceedings-Reports)

 Local Club Records

 Program Records

 State Federation Records

Rutherford B. Hayes Presidential Center, Fremont, Ohio

 Cosmopolitan Club Records

Minnesota Historical Society, St. Paul

 Tourist Club of Minneapolis Records

Rasmussen Blacksmith Shop Museum, Lewistown, Illinois

    Lewistown, Illinois, Tourist Club Records

Arthur and Elizabeth Schlesinger Library on the History of Women in America, Cambridge, Massachusetts

    Amelia Muir Baldwin Papers

    Women's Rest Tour Association Records

Travel Club Records (in the author's possession and held by individuals)

    GFWC Travelers Club of Chamberlain, South Dakota, copies sent to the author by Lillian Johnsson

    Lillian Johnsson's interview of Adelaide Dannenbring, June 30, 2000, tape and transcript in possession of the author

    McGregor, Iowa, Tourist Club, copies sent to the author by Elizabeth F. Moe

University of Illinois, Chicago

    Immigrants' Protective League Records

Winterthur Library, Winterthur, Delaware

    Downs Collection

        Postcards of Hilda Haines Hess

        Trade Card Collection

    World's Columbian Exposition Collection

Published Materials

Abbott, Grace. *The Immigrant and the Community.* New York: The Century Co., 1917.

Abel, Richard. *The Red Rooster Scare: Making Cinema American, 1900–1910.* Berkeley: University of California Press, 1999.

Adams, John. *Ocean Steamers: A History of Ocean-going Passenger Steamships, 1820–1970.* London: New Cavendish Books, 1993.

Addams, Jane. "Introduction. Immigration: A Field Neglected by the Scholar." In *Immigration and Americanization: Selected Readings*, ed. Philip Davis and Bertha Schwartz, 3–22. Boston: Ginn and Co., 1920.

———. *The Jane Addams Papers.* Ed. Mary Lynn McCree Bryan et al. Ann Arbor: University Microfilms International, 1984.

———. "The New Internationalism." 1907. In *Jane Addams on Peace, War, and International Understanding, 1899–1932*, ed. Allen F. Davis, 56–59. New York: Garland, 1976.

———. *The Spirit of Youth and the City Streets.* New York: Macmillan, 1911.

———. *Twenty Years at Hull-House.* 1910. New York: Penguin Books, 1981.

Adeleke, Tunde. *UnAfrican Americans: Nineteenth-Century Black Nationalists and the Civilizing Mission.* Lexington: University Press of Kentucky, 1998.

Agnew, John. *The United States in the World-Economy: A Regional Geography.* Cambridge: Cambridge University Press, 1987.

Akam, Everett Helmut. *Transnational America: Cultural Pluralist Thought in the Twentieth Century.* New York: Rowman and Littlefield, 2002.

Alonso, Harriet Hyman. *Peace as a Women's Issue: A History of the U.S. Movement for World Peace and Women's Rights.* Syracuse: Syracuse University Press, 1993.

———. *The Women's Peace Union and the Outlawry of War, 1921–1942.* 1989. Reprint, Syracuse: Syracuse University Press, 1997.

Americanization Programs. N.p.: General Federation of Women's Clubs [1919–20].

Ames, Kenneth L. *Death in the Dining Room and Other Tales of Victorian Culture.* Philadelphia: Temple University Press, 1992.

———. Introduction to *The Colonial Revival in America,* ed. Alan Axelrod, 1–14. New York: W. W. Norton, 1985.

Anderson, Benedict. *Imagined Communities: Reflections on the Origin and Spread of Nationalism.* 1983. Rev. ed. New York: Verso, 1991.

Anderson, Bonnie S. *Joyous Greetings: The First International Women's Movement, 1830–1860.* New York: Oxford, 2000.

Andrews, Wayne. *Architecture, Ambition, and Americans: A Social History of American Architecture.* New York: Free Press, 1978.

Appadurai, Arjun. "How to Make a National Cuisine: Cookbooks in Contemporary India." *Comparative Studies in Society and History* 30 (Jan. 1988): 3–24.

———. *Modernity at Large: Cultural Dimensions of Globalization.* Minneapolis: University of Minnesota Press, 1996.

Archdeacon, Thomas J. *Becoming American: An Ethnic History.* New York: Free Press, 1983.

Aron, Cindy S. *Working at Play: A History of Vacations in the United States.* New York: Oxford University Press, 1999.

Aronovici, Carol. *Americanization.* St. Paul: Keller Publishing Co., 1919.

The Artistic Guide to Chicago and the World's Columbian Exposition. N.p.: Columbian Art Co., 1892.

Auslander, Leora. *Taste and Power: Furnishing Modern France.* Berkeley: University of California Press, 1996.

Austin, George L. *Dr. Austin's Indispensable Hand-book and General Educator.* Portland, Maine: George Stinson and Co., 1885.

Ayala, César J. *American Sugar Kingdom: The Plantation Economy of the Spanish Caribbean, 1898–1934.* Chapel Hill: University of North Carolina Press, 1999.

Azize-Vargas, Yamila. "The Emergence of Feminism in Puerto Rico, 1870–1930." In *Unequal Sisters: A Multicultural Reader in U.S. Women's History,* ed. Vicki L. Ruiz and Ellen Carol DuBois, 260–67. 2nd ed. New York: Routledge, 1994.

B. Altman and Co. *Catalogue of Fall and Winter Fashions.* New York: B. Altman and Co., 1880.

B. Shackman and Co. Importers. *Catalog.* New York: B. Shackman and Co., 1912.

Bacon, Elizabeth E. *Central Asians Under Russian Rule: A Study in Cultural Change.* Ithaca: Cornell University Press, 1966.

Bainbridge, Lucy S. *Round the World Letters.* 1881. Reprint, Boston: D. Lothrop and Co., 1882.

Banner, Lois. *American Beauty.* New York: Alfred A. Knopf, 1983.

Barker, Mrs. C. C. *Catalogue of Mme. Demorest's Reliable Patterns of the Fashions.* Saratoga Springs: W. Demorest, 1874.

Barnard, Sumner, and Putnam Co. *The Artistic Home.* Worcester, Mass.: n.p., 1903.

Banta, Martha. *Imaging American Women: Idea and Ideas in Cultural History.* New York: Columbia University Press, 1987.

Baranowski, Shelley, and Ellen Furlough. Introduction to *Being Elsewhere: Tourism, Consumer Culture, and Identity in Modern Europe and North America,* 1–31. Ann Arbor: University of Michigan Press, 2001.

Baron, Ava, and Susan E. Klepp. "'If I Didn't Have My Sewing Machine . . .': Women and Sewing-Machine Technology." In *A Needle, a Bobbin, a Strike: Women Needleworkers in America,* ed. Joan M. Jensen and Sue Davidson, 20–59. Philadelphia: Temple University Press, 1984.

Barrett, James R. "Americanization from the Bottom Up: Immigration and the Remaking of the Working Class in the United States, 1880–1930." *Journal of American History* 79 (Dec. 1992): 996–1020.

———. *Work and Community in the Jungle: Chicago's Packinghouse Workers, 1894–1922.* Urbana: University of Illinois Press, 1987.

Batterberry, Michael, and Ariane Batterberry. *On the Town in New York: The Landmark History of Eating, Drinking, and Entertainments from the American Revolution to the Food Revolution.* New York: Routledge, 1999.

Bauer, Arnold J. *Goods, Power, History: Latin America's Material Culture.* Cambridge: Cambridge University Press, 2001.

Baumgarten, Linda. *What Clothes Reveal: The Language of Clothing in Colonial and Federal America.* New Haven: Yale University Press, 2002.

Baxter, Lucia Millet. *Housekeeper's Handy Book.* Boston: The House Beautiful Publishing Co., 1918.

Bayly, C. A. "The Origins of Swadesi (Home Industry): Cloth and Indian Society, 1700–1930." In *The Social Life of Things: Commodities in Cultural Perspective,* ed. Arjun Appadurai, 285–322. Cambridge: Cambridge University Press, 1986.

Beck, Louis J. *New York's Chinatown.* New York: Bohemia Publishing Co., 1898.

Beck, Ulrich, Natan Sznaider, and Rainer Winter, eds. *Global America? The Cultural Consequences of Globalization.* Liverpool: Liverpool University Press, 2003.

Bederman, Gail. *Manliness and Civilization: A Cultural History of Gender and Race in the United States, 1880–1917.* Chicago: University of Chicago Press, 1995.

Beezley, William H. *Judas at the Jockey Club and Other Episodes of Porfirian Mexico.* Lincoln: University of Nebraska Press, 1987.

Beisel, Nicola. *Imperiled Innocents: Anthony Comstock and Family Reproduction in Victorian America.* Princeton: Princeton University Press, 1997.

Bell, David, and Gill Valentine. *Consuming Geographies: We Are Where We Eat.* New York: Routledge, 1997.

Bell, Philip, and Roger Bell, eds. *Americanization and Australia.* Sydney: University of New South Wales Press, 1988.

———. "Introduction: The Dilemmas of 'Americanization.'" In *Americanization and Australia*, ed. Philip Bell and Roger Bell, 1–14. Sydney: University of New South Wales Press, 1988.

Bennett, Tony. "The Exhibitionary Complex." In *Culture/Power/ History: A Reader in Contemporary Social Theory*, ed. Nicholas B. Dirks, Geoff Eley, and Sherry B. Ortner, 123–54. Princeton: Princeton University Press, 1994.

Bent, Martha S. F. "Talk to Leaders of Public Opinion." In *A Suggested Program for Americanization*, 31–33. N.p.: General Federation of Women's Clubs, [1918].

Benton, Caroline French. *Fairs and Fetes.* Boston: Dana Estes and Co., 1912.

Berghahn, Volker R. "Philanthropy and Diplomacy in the 'American Century.'" *Diplomatic History* 23 (Summer 1999): 393–419.

Berkovitch, Nitza. *From Motherhood to Citizenship: Women's Rights and International Organizations.* Baltimore: Johns Hopkins University Press, 1999.

Bevier, Isabel, and Susannah Usher. *The Home Economics Movement, Part I.* Boston: Whitcomb & Barrows, 1906.

Bevington, Charles R. *New York Plaisance, an Illustrated Series of New York Places of Amusement.* New York: Rogers and Co., 1908.

Bharucha, Rustom. *Theatre and the World: Performance and the Politics of Culture.* New York: Routledge, 1990.

Bigsby, C. W. E., ed. *Superculture: American Popular Culture and Europe.* Bowling Green: Bowling Green University Popular Press, 1975.

Bilachevsky, N. "The Peasant Art of Little Russia (the Ukraine)." Trans. V. Stepan Kowsky. In *Peasant Art in Russia*, ed. Charles Holme, 15–31. London: The Studio, 1912.

Bisland, Elizabeth. "The Art of Travel." In *The House and Home, a Practical Book, in two volumes*, vol. 1, ed. Lyman Abbott et al., 371–400. New York: Charles Scribner's Sons, 1896.

Blain, Mary E. *Games for All Occasions.* New York: Barse and Hopkins, 1909.

Blair, Karen J. *The Clubwoman as Feminist: True Womanhood Redefined, 1868–1914.* New York: Holmes and Meier Publishers, 1980.

———. *The Torchbearers: Women and Their Amateur Arts Associations in America, 1890–1930.* Bloomington: Indiana University Press, 1994.

Blanchard, Mary W. "Mrs. Potter Palmer's Castle." *Nest: A Magazine of Interiors*, Winter 2002–3, 80–93.

———. *Oscar Wilde's America: Counterculture in the Gilded Age*. New Haven: Yale University Press, 1998.

Blaszczyk, Regina Lee. *Imagining Consumers: Design and Innovation from Wedgwood to Corning*. Baltimore: Johns Hopkins University Press, 2000.

Blum, Stella, ed. *Victorian Fashions and Costumes from Harper's Bazar, 1867–1898*. New York: Dover Publications, 1974.

Blumin, Stuart M. *The Emergence of the Middle Class: Social Experience in the American City, 1760–1900*. Cambridge: Cambridge University Press, 1989.

Bode, Carl. *The American Lyceum: Town Meeting of the Mind*. New York: Oxford University Press, 1956.

Boggs and Buhl Fashion Catalogue, Fall and Winter, 1888–9. Pittsburgh: Shaw Brothers, [1888].

Boisseau, Tracey Jean. *White Queen: May French-Sheldon and the Imperial Origins of American Feminist Identity*. Bloomington: Indiana University Press, 2004.

Bolotin, Norman, and Christine Laing. *The World's Columbian Exposition: The Chicago World's Fair of 1893*. Urbana: University of Illinois Press, 2002.

Booth, Michael R. *Victorian Spectacular Theatre, 1850–1910*. Boston: Routledge and Kegan Paul, 1981.

Booth, Sally Smith. *Hung, Strung, and Potted: A History of Eating in Colonial America*. New York: Clarkson N. Potter, 1971.

Boris, Eileen. *Art and Labor: Ruskin, Morris, and the Craftsman Ideal in America*. Philadelphia: Temple University Press, 1986.

———. "Crossing Boundaries: The Gendered Meaning of the Arts and Crafts." In *The Ideal Home, 1900–1920: The History of Twentieth-Century American Craft*, ed. Janet Kardon, 32–45. New York: Harry N. Abrams, 1993.

Bosson, M. B. *Aunt Mena's Recipe Book*. Philadelphia: The National Baptist, 1888.

Bourdieu, Pierre. *Distinction: A Social Critique of the Judgement of Taste*. Trans. Richard Nice. Cambridge: Harvard University Press, 1984.

Bovbjerg, Viggo. *Danish Folk Dances*. Chicago: Viggo Bovbjerg, 1917.

Bowers, David F., ed. *Foreign Influences in American Life*. Princeton: Princeton University Press, 1944.

Boyd, Nancy. *Emissaries: The Overseas Work of the American YWCA, 1895–1970*. New York: Woman's Press, 1986.

Bramen, Carrie Tirado. "The Urban Picturesque and the Spectacle of Americanization." *American Quarterly* 52 (Sept. 2000): 444–77.

Brandimarte, Cynthia A. "Japanese Novelty Stores." *Winterthur Portfolio* 26 (Spring 1991): 1–26.

Brandon, Ruth. *A Capitalist Romance: Singer and the Sewing Machine.* Philadelphia: J. B. Lippincott, 1977.

Braun-Ronsdorf, Margarete. *Mirror of Fashion: A History of European Costume, 1789–1929.* Trans. Oliver Coburn. New York: McGraw-Hill, 1964.

Breakfast, Dinner, and Tea: Viewed Classically, Poetically, and Practically, Containing Numerous Curious Dishes and Feasts of All Times and All Countries. New York: D. Appleton and Co., 1875. Breen, T. H. *The Marketplace of Revolution: How Consumer Politics Shaped American Independence.* New York: Oxford University Press, 2004.

Bremer, Edith Terry. "'Foreign Community and Immigration Work' of the National Young Women's Christian Association." Reprint from Jan. 1916 issue of *Immigrants in America Review.* New York: National Board of Young Women's Christian Associations, [1916].

Brendon, Piers. *Thomas Cook: 150 Years of Popular Tourism.* London: Secker and Warburg, 1991.

Brewer, John, and Roy Porter, eds. *Consumption and the World of Goods.* New York: Routledge, 1993.

Bridges, Horace J. *On Becoming an American.* Boston: Marshall Jones Co., 1909.

Briggs, Laura. *Reproducing Empire: Race, Sex, Science, and U.S. Imperialism in Puerto Rico.* Berkeley: University of California Press, 2002.

Brody, David Eric. "Fantasy Realized: The Philippines, Orientalism, and Imperialism in Turn-of-the-Century American Visual Culture." Ph.D. diss., Boston University, 1997.

Brooks, Bradley C. "Clarity, Contrast, and Simplicity: Changes in American Interiors, 1880–1930." In *The Arts and the American Home, 1890–1930,* ed. Jessica H. Foy and Karal Ann Marling, 14–43. Knoxville: University of Tennessee Press, 1994.

Brown, Dona. *Inventing New England: Regional Tourism in the Nineteenth Century.* Washington, D.C.: Smithsonian Institution Press, 1995.

Brown, Henry Collins. *Book of Home Building and Decoration.* Garden City, N.Y.: Doubleday, Page & Co., 1912.

Brown, Jane Converse. "'Fine Arts and Fine People': The Japanese Taste in the American Home, 1876–1916." In *Making the American Home: Middle-Class Women and Domestic Material Culture, 1840–1940,* ed. Marilyn Ferris Motz and Pat Browne, 121–139. Bowling Green: Bowling Green State University Press, 1988.
———. "The 'Japanese Taste:' Its Role in the Mission of the American Home and in the Family's Presentation of Itself to the Public as Expressed in Published Sources, 1876–1916." Ph.D. diss., University of Wisconsin, Madison, 1987.

Brown, Julie K. *Making Culture Visible: The Public Display of Photography at Fairs, Expositions and Exhibitions in the United States, 1847–1900.* Amsterdam: Harwood Academic Publishers, 2001.

Bruchey, Stuart Weems. *Enterprise: The Dynamic Economy of a Free People*. Cambridge: Harvard University Press, 1990.

Bruère, Martha Bensley, and Robert W. Bruère. *Increasing Home Efficiency*. New York: Macmillan, 1912.

Brumberg, Joan Jacobs. *Mission for Life*. New York: Free Press, 1980.

———. "Zenanas and Girlless Villages: The Ethnology of American Evangelical Women, 1870–1910." *Journal of American History* 69 (Sept. 1982): 347–71.

Bryan, Mary Lynn McCree, ed. *The Jane Addams Papers*. Ann Arbor: University Microfilms International, 1984.

Bryant, Keith L., Jr., "Cathedrals, Castles, and Roman Baths: Railway Station Architecture in the Urban South." *Journal of Urban History* 2 (Feb. 1976): 195–230.

Buffum, Mrs. Hugh, and Mrs. Lloyd Thurston. *History of the Iowa Federation of Women's Clubs, 1893–1968*. Hartley, Iowa: Sentinel Publishing, 1968.

Bulatao, Beth. "Iloilo." In *Of Common Cloth: Women in the Global Textile Industry*, ed. W. Chapkis and Cynthia Enloe, 47. Washington, D.C.: Transnational Institute, 1983.

Bullington, Judy. "Henry Bacon's Imaging of Transatlantic Travel in the Gilded Age." *Nineteenth Century Studies* 14 (2000): 63–91.

Bunker, Steven B. "'Consumers of Good Taste': Marketing Modernity in Northern Mexico, 1890–1910." *Mexican Studies/Estudios Mexicanos* 13 (Summer 1997): 227–69.

Burchenal, Elizabeth. *Folk-Dances and Singing Games*. New York: G. Schirmer, 1909.

Burg, David F. *Chicago's White City of 1893*. Lexington: University Press of Kentucky, 1976.

Burke, Timothy. "Cannibal Margarine and Reactionary Snapple: A Comparative Examination of Rumors about Commodities." *International Journal of Cultural Studies* 1 (Aug. 1998): 253–70.

Burns, Sarah. "The Price of Beauty: Art, Commerce, and the Late Nineteenth-Century Studio Interior." In *American Iconology: New Approaches to Nineteenth-Century Art and Literature*, ed. David C. Miller, 209–38. New Haven: Yale University Press, 1993.

Burton, Antoinette. *At the Heart of the Empire: Indians and the Colonial Encounter in Late-Victorian Britain*. Berkeley: University of California Press, 1998.

———. "Feminism, Empire, and the Fate of National Histories: The Case of Victorian Britain." In *Exploring Women's Studies: Looking Forward, Looking Back*, ed. Carol R. Berkin, Judith L. Pinch, and Carole S. Appel, 38–52. Upper Saddle River, N.J.: Pearson Prentice Hall, 2006.

Bush, R. G. T. [Rebecca Gibbons Tatnall]. *What to Have and How to Cook It, A*

Practical Cook Book for Every Day Living. Wilmington: New Amstel Magazine
Company, 1911.

Bushman, Richard L. *The Refinement of America: Persons, Houses, Cities.* New York:
Vintage, 1993.

Butler, Joseph T. "The Decorative Arts." In *The Arts in America: The Nineteenth
Century,* by Wendell D. Garrett, Paul F. Norton, Alan Gowans, and Joseph T.
Butler, 285–384. New York: Charles Scribner's Sons, 1969.

Buzard, James. *The Beaten Track: European Tourism, Literature, and the Ways to
Culture, 1800–1918.* Oxford: Clarendon Press, 1993.

Cabán, Pedro A. *Constructing a Colonial People: Puerto Rico and the United States,
1898–1932.* Boulder: Westview Press, 1999.

———. "Subjects and Immigrants during the Progressive Era." *Discourse* 23 (Fall
2001): 24–51.

Cahan, Abraham. *The Rise of David Levinsky.* 1917. New York: Penguin Books, 1993.

Campbell, Charles S., Jr. *Special Interests and the Open Door Policy.* New Haven: Yale
University Press, 1951.

Campbell, Helen. *The Easiest Way in Housekeeping and Cooking.* New York: Fords,
Howard, & Hulbert, 1881.

Camporesi, Piero. *Exotic Brew: The Art of Living in the Age of Enlightenment.* Trans.
Christopher Woodall. Cambridge: Polity Press, 1994.

———. *The Magic Harvest: Food, Folklore, and Society.* Trans. Joan Krakover Hall.
Cambridge: Polity Press, 1993.

Cannadine, David. *The Decline and Fall of the British Aristocracy.* New Haven: Yale,
1990.

Carney, Judith A. *Black Rice: The African Origins of Rice Cultivation in the Americas.*
Cambridge: Harvard University Press, 2001.

Carrott, Richard G. *The Egyptian Revival: Its Sources, Monuments, and Meaning, 1808–
1858.* Berkeley: University of California Press, 1978.

Carson, Mina. *Settlement Folk: Social Thought and the American Settlement Movement,
1995–1930.* Chicago: University of Chicago Press, 1990.

Carson, W. E. [William English]. *Mexico: The Wonderland of the South.* 1909. Rev. ed.
New York: Macmillan for the Bay View Reading Club, 1914.

Carter, Mary Elizabeth. *Millionaire Households and Their Domestic Economy.* New
York: D. Appleton, 1903.

Chalif, Louis H. "Góralski Tanić." New York: Louis H. Chalif Normal School of
Dancing, 1914.

Champney, Elizabeth W. *Three Vassar Girls in the Tyrol.* Boston: Estes and Lauriat,
1891.

———. *Three Vassar Girls on the Rhine.* Boston: Estes and Lauriat, 1887.

Charles, Jeffrey. "Searching for Gold in Guacamole: California Growers Market the

Avocado, 1910–1914." In *Food Nations: Selling Taste in Consumer Societies*, ed.
Warren Belasco and Philip Scranton, 131–54. New York: Routledge, 2002.

Chatterjee, Piya. *A Time for Tea: Women, Labor and Post/Colonial Politics on an Indian Plantation*. Durham: Duke University Press, 2001.

Chaudhuri, K. N. *Trade and Civilisation in the Indian Ocean: An Economic History from the Rise of Islam to 1750*. Cambridge: Cambridge University Press, 1985.

Chaudhuri, Nupur. "Shawls, Jewelry, Curry, and Rice in Victorian Britain." In *Western Women and Imperialism: Complicity and Resistance*, ed. Nupur Chaudhuri and Margaret Strobel, 231–46. Bloomington: Indiana University Press, 1992.

Cheah, Pheng, and Bruce Robbins, eds. *Cosmopolitics: Thinking and Feeling Beyond the Nation*. Minneapolis: University of Minnesota Press, 1998.

Chin, Carol C. "Beneficent Imperialists: American Women Missionaries in China at the Turn of the Twentieth Century." *Diplomatic History* 27 (June 2003): 327–52.

Choy, Catherine Ceniza. *Empire of Care: Nursing and Migration in Filipino American History*. Durham: Duke University Press, 2003.

Churchill, Sidney J. A. "Introductory Note." In *Peasant Art in Italy*, ed. Charles Holme, 1–8. London: The Studio, 1913.

"Citizenship Day Program." Washington, D.C.: General Federation of Women's Clubs, [1920].

Clark, Clifford Edward, Jr. *The American Family Home, 1800–1960*. Chapel Hill: University of North Carolina Press, 1986.

Classified Catalogue of Magic Lantern Slides and Transparencies for the Stereoscope. Philadelphia: Benerman and Wilson, 1874.

Clough, Ethlyn T. *South American Life*. Detroit: Bay View Reading Club, 1912.

Club Women of New York. New York: Club Women of New York Co., 1918.

Clute, Eugene. *The Treatment of Interiors*. New York: Pencil Points Press, 1926.

Cochran, Thomas C., and William Miller. *The Age of Enterprise: A Social History of Industrial America*. New York: Macmillan, 1942.

Cocks, Catherine. "The Chamber of Commerce's Carnival: City Festivals and Urban Tourism in the United States, 1890–1915." In *Being Elsewhere: Tourism, Consumer Culture, and Identity in Modern Europe and North America*, ed. Shelley Baranowski and Ellen Furlough, 89–107. Ann Arbor: University of Michigan Press, 2001.

———. *Doing the Town: The Rise of Urban Tourism in the United States, 1850–1915*. Berkeley: University of California Press, 2001.

Cody, Jeffrey W. *Exporting American Architecture, 1870–2000*. New York: Routledge, 2003.

Cohen, Lizabeth A. *A Consumers' Republic: The Politics of Mass Consumption in Postwar America*. New York: Alfred A. Knopf, 2003.

———. "Embellishing a Life of Labor: An Interpretation of the Material Culture of American Working-Class Homes, 1885–1915." In *Labor Migration in the Atlantic*

Economies: The European and North American Working Classes during the Period of Industrialization, ed. Dirk Hoerder, 321–52. Westport, Conn.: Greenwood Press, 1985.

Cohn, Bernard S. "Representing Authority in Victorian India." In *The Invention of Tradition*, ed. Eric Hobsbawm and Terence Ranger, 165–209. 1983. Reprint, Cambridge: Cambridge University Press, 1984.

Colley, Linda. *Britons: Forging the Nation, 1707–1837*. New Haven: Yale University Press, 1992.

Collingham, Lizzie. *Curry: A Tale of Cooks and Conquerors*. New York: Oxford University Press, 2006.

Collins, Douglas. *America's Favorite Food: The Story of Campbell Soup Company*. New York: Harry N. Abrams, 1994.

Condit, Elizabeth, and Jessie A. Long. *How to Cook and Why*. New York: Harper and Brothers, 1914.

Conlin, Joseph R. *Bacon, Beans and Galantines: Food and Foodways on the Western Mining Frontier*. Reno: University of Nevada Press, 1986.

Conn, Steven. "An Epistemology for Empire: The Philadelphia Commercial Museum, 1893–1896." *Diplomatic History* 22 (Fall 1998): 533–63.

———. *Museums and American Intellectual Life, 1876–1926*. Chicago: University of Chicago Press, 1998.

Conzen, Kathleen Neils, et al. "The Invention of Ethnicity: A Perspective from the U.S.A." *Journal of American Ethnic History* 12 (Fall 1992): 3–41.

Cooke, Maud C. *Our Social Manual for All Occasions or Approved Etiquette of To-Day*. Chicago: Monarch Book Co., 1896.

Cook's American Tours. New York: Thomas Cook and Son, 1896.

Cooper, Gail. "Love, War, and Chocolate: Gender and the American Candy Industry, 1880–1930." In *His and Hers: Gender, Consumption, and Technology*, ed. Roger Horowitz and Arwen Mohun, 67–94. Charlottesville: University Press of Virginia, 1998.

Cooper, Nicholas. *The Opulent Eye: Late Victorian and Edwardian Taste in Interior Design*. London: Architectural Press, 1976.

Corson, Juliet. *Family Living on $500 a Year*. New York: Harper and Brothers, 1888.

———. *Miss Corson's Practical American Cookery and Household Management*. New York: Dodd, Mead, and Co., 1885.

Costigliola, Frank. *Awkward Dominion: American Political, Economic, and Cultural Relations with Europe, 1919–1933*. Ithaca: Cornell University Press, 1984.

Cott, Nancy F. *The Bonds of Womanhood: "Woman's Sphere" in New England, 1780–1835*. New Haven: Yale University Press, 1977.

Courtney, Grace Gates. *History Indiana Federation of Clubs*. Fort Wayne: Fort Wayne Printing, 1939.

Cowles, Julia Darrow. *Artistic Home Furnishing for People of Moderate Means*. New York: F. M. Lupton, 1898.

Crane, Diana. *Fashion and Its Social Agendas: Class, Gender, and Identity in Clothing*. Chicago: University of Chicago Press, 2000.

Crawford, James. *Hold Your Tongue: Bilingualism and the Politics of "English Only."* New York: Addison-Wesley, 1992.

Crinson, Mark. *Empire Building: Orientalism and Victorian Architecture*. London: Routledge, 1996.

Crocker, Ruth Hutchinson. *Social Work and Social Order: The Settlement Movement in Two Industrial Cities, 1889–1930*. Urbana: University of Illinois Press, 1992.

Croly, Jennie June. *The History of the Woman's Club Movement in America*. New York: Henry G. Allen and Co., 1898.

Cross, Gary S., and John K. Walton. *The Playful Crowd: Pleasure Places in the Twentieth Century*. New York: Columbia University Press, 2005.

Crowfield, Christophe [Harriet Elizabeth Beecher Stowe]. *House and Home Papers*. 1864. Reprint, Boston: James R. Osgood and Co., 1872.

Crunden, Robert M. *American Salons: Encounters with European Modernism, 1885–1917*. New York: Oxford University Press, 1993.

———. *A Brief History of American Culture*. Helsinki: SHS, 1990.

Cumming, Elizabeth, and Wendy Kaplan. *The Arts and Crafts Movement*. London: Thames and Hudson, 1991.

Cummings, Richard Osborn. *The American and His Food: A History of Food Habits in the United States*. Chicago: University of Chicago Press, 1940.

Curl, Donald W. *Mizner's Florida: American Resort Architecture*. Cambridge: MIT Press, 1984.

Curl, James Stevens. *Egyptomania: The Egyptian Revival, a Recurring Theme in the History of Taste*. New York: Manchester University Press, 1994.

Curti, Merle. *American Philanthropy Abroad: A History*. New Brunswick: Rutgers University Press, 1963.

Dain, Phyllis. *The New York Public Library: A Universe of Knowledge*. New York: New York Public Library, 2000.

Daniels, John. *America via the Neighborhood*. New York: Harper and Brothers, 1920.

Daniels, Roger. *The Politics of Prejudice: The Anti-Japanese Movement in California and the Struggle for Japanese Exclusion*. Gloucester, Mass.: Peter Smith, 1966.

Darrah, William C. *The World of Stereographs*. Gettysburg: W. C. Darrah, 1977.

Davidoff, Leonore. *The Best Circles: Women and Society in Victorian England*. Totowa, N.J.: Rowman and Littlefield, 1973.

Davies, Robert Bruce. *Peacefully Working to Conquer the World: Singer Sewing Machines in Foreign Markets, 1854–1920*. New York: Arno Press, 1976.

Davis, Elizabeth Lindsay. *Lifting as They Climb*. 1933. Reprint, New York: G. K. Hall, 1996.

Davis, Janet M. *The Circus Age: Culture and Society under the American Big Top*. Chapel Hill: University of North Carolina Press, 2002.

Dawley, Alan. *Changing the World: American Progressives in War and Revolution*. Princeton: Princeton University Press, 2003.

Dawson, Mary, and Emma Paddock Telford. *The Book of Parties and Pastimes*. New York: William Rickey and Co., 1912.

Dean, Warren. *With Broadax and Firebrand: The Destruction of the Brazilian Atlantic Forest*. Berkeley: University of California Press, 1995.

de Grazia, Victoria. *Irresistible Empire: America's Advance through Twentieth-Century Europe*. Cambridge: Belknap Press of Harvard University Press, 2005.

Deloria, Philip J. *Playing Indian*. New Haven: Yale University Press, 1998.

de Marly, Diana. *The History of Haute Couture, 1850–1950*. New York: Holmes and Meier, 1980.

Denker, Ellen Paul. *After the Chinese Taste: China's Influence in America, 1730–1930*. Salem: Peabody Museum of Salem, 1985.

Denker, Joel. *The World on a Plate: A Tour through the History of America's Ethnic Cuisines*. Boulder: Westview Press, 2003.

Dennett, Andrea Stulman, *Weird and Wonderful: The Dime Museum in America*. New York: New York University Press, 1997.

Dennis, Matthew. *Red, White, and Blue Letter Days: An American Calendar*. Ithaca: Cornell University Press, 2002.

Department of Commerce. *The Commerce and Navigation of the United States*. Washington, D.C.: Government Printing Office, 1870.

———. *The Commerce and Navigation of the United States*. Washington, D.C.: Government Printing Office, 1910.

———. *The Commerce and Navigation of the United States*. Washington, D.C.: Government Printing Office, 1920.

———. *Foreign Commerce and Navigation of the United States*. Washington, D.C.: Government Printing Office, 1916.

———. *Foreign Commerce and Navigation of the United States*. Washington, D.C.: Government Printing Office, 1921.

Department of Commerce and Labor. *Foreign Commerce and Navigation of the United States*. Washington, D.C.: Government Printing Office, 1911.

Department of the Treasury. *The Commerce and Navigation of the United States*. Washington, D.C.: Department of the Treasury, 1900.

———. *The Commerce and Navigation of the United States*. Washington, D.C.: Department of the Treasury, 1865.

Derby, Lauren. "Gringo Chickens with Worms: Food and Nationalism in the

Dominican Republic." In *Close Encounters of Empire: Writing the Cultural History of U.S.-Latin American Relations*, ed. Gilbert M. Joseph, Catherine C. LeGrand, and Ricardo D. Salvatore, 451–93. Durham: Duke University Press, 1998.

Desmond, Jane C. *Staging Tourism: Bodies on Display from Waikiki to Sea World*. Chicago: University of Chicago Press, 1999.

Devlin, Harry. *Portraits of American Architecture: Monuments to a Romantic Mood, 1830–1900*. Boston: David R. Godine, 1989.

Dewing, Mrs. T. W. [Maria]. *Beauty in the Household*. New York: Harper and Brothers, 1882.

de Wit, Cary W. "Food-Place Associations on American Product Labels." In *The Taste of American Place: A Reader on Regional and Ethnic Foods*, ed. Barbara G. Shortridge and James R. Shortridge, 101–9. New York: Rowman and Littlefield, 1998.

de Wolfe, Elsie. *The House in Good Taste*. New York: The Century Co., 1913.

Dilworth, Leah. *Imagining Indians in the Southwest: Persistent Visions of a Primitive Past*. Washington, D.C.: Smithsonian Institution Press, 1996.

Diner, Hasia R. *Hungering for America: Italian, Irish, and Jewish Foodways in the Age of Migration*. Cambridge: Harvard University Press, 2001.

D'Itri, Patricia Ward. *Cross Currents in the International Women's Movement, 1848–1948*. Bowling Green: Bowling Green State University Popular Press, 1999.

Dolan, Brian. *Ladies of the Grand Tour: British Women in Pursuit of Enlightenment and Adventure in Eighteenth-Century Europe*. New York: Harper Collins, 2001.

Domosh, Mona. "A 'Civilized' Commerce: Gender, 'Race,' and Empire at the 1893 Chicago Exposition." *Cultural Geographies* 9 (April 2002): 181–201.

———. "Pickles and Purity: Discourses of Food, Empire and Work in Turn-of-the-century U.S.A." *Cultural Geography* 4 (March 2003): 7–26.

Dosal, Paul J. *Doing Business with the Dictators: A Political History of United Fruit in Guatemala, 1899–1944*. Wilmington: Scholarly Resources, 1993.

Dower, John W. *Embracing Defeat: Japan in the Wake of World War II*. New York: W. W. Norton, 1999.

Downs, Jacques M. *The Golden Ghetto: The American Commercial Community at Canton and the Shaping of American China Policy, 1784–1844*. Bethlehem: Lehigh University Press, 1997.

Drachsler, Julius. *Democracy and Assimilation: The Blending of Immigrant Heritages in America*. 1920. Westport, Conn.: Negro Universities Press, 1970.

Driver, Felix, and David Gilbert. "Imperial Cities: Overlapping Territories, Intertwined Histories." In *Imperial Cities: Landscape, Display, and Identity*, ed. Felix Driver and David Gilbert, 1–17. New York: Manchester University Press, 1999.

Drury, John. *Old Chicago Houses*. 1941. Reprint, Chicago: University of Chicago Press, 1976.

DuBois, Ellen Carol. *Harriot Stanton Blatch and the Winning of Woman Suffrage*. New Haven: Yale University Press, 1997.

Dudden, Faye E. *Serving Women: Household Service in Nineteenth-Century America*. Middletown, Conn.: Wesleyan University Press, 1983.

Dulles, Foster Rhea. *Americans Abroad: Two Centuries of European Travel*. Ann Arbor: University of Michigan Press, 1964.

Du Mont, Rosemary Ruhig. *Reform and Reaction: The Big City Public Library in American Life*. Westport, Conn.: Greenwood Press, 1977.

Duncan, J. H. Elder. *The House Beautiful and Useful*. New York: Cassell and Co., 1911.

Dusselier, Jane. "Bonbons, Lemon Drops, and Oh Henry! Bars: Candy, Consumer Culture, and the Construction of Gender, 1895–1920." In *Kitchen Culture in America: Popular Representations of Food, Gender, and Race*, ed. Sherrie A. Innes, 15–50. Philadelphia: University of Pennsylvania Press, 2001.

E. Butterick and Co. *Pattern Catalogue*. New York: John De Vries and Co., [1880].
————. *Catalogue for Fall*. New York: E. Butterick and Co., 1874.

Eastlake, Charles L. *Hints on Household Taste*. [1868] 1878. Introduction by John Gloag. New York: Dover, 1964.

Eaton, Allen H. *Immigrant Gifts to American Life: Some Experiments in Appreciation of the Contributions of Our Foreign-Born Citizens to American Culture*. New York: Russell Sage Foundation, 1932.

Eberlein, Harold Donaldson, Abbot McClure, and Edward Stratton Holloway. *The Practical Book of Interior Decoration*. Philadelphia: J. B. Lippincott, 1919.

Eckes, Alfred E., Jr., and Thomas W. Zeiler. *Globalization and the American Century*. New York: Cambridge University Press, 2003.

Ecob, Helen Gilbert. *The Well-Dressed Woman*. New York: Fowler and Wells, 1892.

"Elementary Adult Education." Los Angeles: Los Angeles City School District, 1919.

Eliot, Elizabeth. *Heiresses and Coronets: The Story of Lovely Ladies and Noble Men*. New York: McDowell, Obolensky, 1959.

Ellet, Mrs. E. F., ed. *The New Cyclopaedia of Domestic Economy and Practical Housekeeper*. Norwich, Conn.: Henry Bill Publishing Co., 1873.

Elson, Louis C., ed. *Folk Songs of Many Nations*. Cincinnati: The John Church Co., 1905.

Elson, Ruth Miller. *Guardians of Tradition: American Schoolbooks of the Nineteenth Century*. Lincoln: University of Nebraska Press, 1964.

Endy, Christopher. "Travel and World Power: Americans in Europe, 1890–1917." *Diplomatic History* 22 (Fall 1998): 565–94.

Enstad, Nan. *Ladies of Labor, Girls of Adventure: Working Women, Popular Culture, and*

Labor Politics at the Turn of the Twentieth Century. New York: Columbia University Press, 1999.

Entrance to Vantine's, the House of the Orient. New York: A. A. Vantine, n.d.

Evans, Sarah M. *Born For Liberty: A History of Women in America*. New York: Free Press, 1989.

Ewen, Elizabeth. *Immigrant Women in the Land of Dollars: Life and Culture on the Lower East Side, 1890–1925*. New York: Monthly Review Press, 1985.

Ewen, Stuart, and Elizabeth Ewen. *Channels of Desire: Mass Images and the Shaping of American Consciousness*. Minneapolis: University of Minnesota Press, 1992.

A Facsimile of Frank Leslie's Illustrated Historical Register of the Centennial Exposition, 1876. New York: Paddington Press, 1974.

Farmer, Fannie Merritt. *The Boston Cooking-School Cook Book*. 1896. Reprint, New York: Signet, 1984.

Faulkner, Anne Shaw, ed. *Americanization Songs: Liberty Chorus Song Book for Home, School and Community Singing*. Chicago: McKinley Music Co., 1920.

Fehrenbach, Heide, and Uta G. Poiger, eds. *Transactions, Transgressions, Transformations: American Culture in Western Europe and Japan*. New York: Berghahn Books, 2000.

Feller, John Quentin. "The China Trade and the Asiatic Squadron." *Winterthur Portfolio* 18 (Winter 1983): 291–300.

Fennimore, Keith J. *The Heritage of Bay View, 1875–1975*. Grand Rapids: William B. Eerdmans, 1975.

Fernández-Armesto, Felipe. *Near a Thousand Tables: A History of Food*. New York: Free Press, 2002.

Fiber Rush Imported Malacca and Mission Furniture. Chicago: J. S. Ford, Johnson & Co., 1904.

Field, James A., Jr. *America and the Mediterranean World, 1776–1882*. Princeton: Princeton University Press, 1969.

Fieldhouse, D. K. *The Colonial Empires: A Comparative Survey from the Eighteenth Century*. 2nd ed. New York: Dell, 1982.

Findlay, Eileen J. Suárez. *Imposing Decency: The Politics of Sexuality and Race in Puerto Rico, 1870–1920*. Durham: Duke University Press, 1999.

Fisher, Robert Bruce. "The People's Institute of New York City, 1897–1934: Culture, Progressive Democracy, and the People." Ph.D. diss., New York University, 1974.

Fitzhugh, William W. "Ambassadors in Sealskins: Exhibiting Eskimos at the Smithsonian." In *Exhibiting Dilemmas: Issues of Representation at the Smithsonian*, ed. Amy Henderson and Adrienne L. Kaeppler, 206–45. Washington, D.C.: Smithsonian Institution Press, 1997.

Flemming, Leslie A., ed. *Women's Work for Women: Missionaries and Social Change in Asia*. Boulder: Westview Press, 1989.

Foner, Eric. "American Freedom in a Global Age." *American Historical Review* 106 (Feb. 2001): 1–16.

Fordyce, Eleanor T. "Cookbooks of the 1800s." In *Dining in America, 1850–1900*, ed. Kathryn Grover, 85–113. Amherst: University of Massachusetts Press and the Margaret Woodbury Strong Museum of Rochester, New York, 1987.

Fowler, Marian. *In a Gilded Cage: From Heiress to Duchess*. New York: St. Martin's Press, 1993.

Francis E. Lester Co. *Catalogue*. Mesilla Park, N.M., 1904.

Frank, Dana. *Buy American: The Untold Story of Economic Nationalism*. Boston: Beacon Press, 1999.

Frawley, Maria H. *A Wider Range: Travel Writing by Women in Victorian England*. London: Associated University Presses, 1994.

Frederick, Christine. *Household Engineering: Scientific Management in the Home*. Chicago: American School of Home Economics, 1921.

Freeman, Sarah. *Mutton and Oysters: The Victorians and Their Food*. London: Victor Gollancz, 1989.

French, Lillie Hamilton. *Homes and Their Decoration*. New York: Dodd, Mead, and Co., 1903.

Furniture of To-Day. Philadelphia: John Wanamaker, n.d.

Gabaccia, Donna R. *Italy's Many Diasporas*. Seattle: University of Washington Press, 2002.

———. *We Are What We Eat: Ethnic Food and the Making of Americans*. Cambridge: Harvard University Press, 1998.

Gallicchio, Marc. *The African American Encounter with Japan and China: Black Internationalism in Asia, 1895–1945*. Chapel Hill: University of North Carolina Press, 2000.

Gamber, Wendy. *The Female Economy: The Millinery and Dressmaking Trades, 1860–1930*. Urbana: University of Illinois Press, 1997.

Garcia, Matt. *A World of Its Own: Race, Labor, and Citrus in the Making of Greater Los Angeles, 1900–1970*. Chapel Hill: University of North Carolina Press, 2001.

Gardiner, Anne Gibbons. *Mrs. Gardiner's Receipts from 1763*. Hallowell, Maine: White & Horne Co., 1938.

Gebhard, David. *Santa Barbara — The Creation of a New Spain in America*. Santa Barbara: University Art Museum, University of California, Santa Barbara, 1982.

Gelernter, Mark. *A History of American Architecture: Buildings in Their Cultural and Technological Context*. Hanover: University Press of New England, 1999.

General Federation of Women's Clubs, Americanization Committee 1918–20. *A Suggested Program for Americanization*. San Francisco: California Commission of Immigration and Housing, reprinted by permission of the G.F.W.C., [1920].

General Federation of Women's Clubs, Directory. N.p., Oct. 1911.

————. N.p., Nov. 1914.

George, Rosemary Marangoly. "Homes in the Empire, Empires in the Home."
    Cultural Critique, Winter 1993–94, 95–127.

Gere, Anne Ruggles. *Intimate Practices: Literacy and Cultural Work in U.S. Women's
    Clubs, 1880–1920*. Urbana: University of Illinois Press, 1997.

Geyer, Michael, and Charles Bright. "World History in a Global Age." *American
    Historical Review* 100 (Oct. 1995): 1034–60.

Gibson, Charles Dana. *London as Seen by Charles Dana Gibson*. New York: Charles
    Scribner's Sons, 1897.

————. *Sketches in Egypt*. New York: Doubleday and McClure, 1899.

Gienow-Hecht, Jessica E. E. "Shame on US? Academics, Cultural Transfer, and the
    Cold War: A Critical Review." *Diplomatic History* 24 (Summer 2000): 465–94.

Gilbert, Henry F., ed. *One Hundred Folk-Songs from Many Countries*. Boston: C. C.
    Birchard and Co., 1910.

Gilbert, James. *Perfect Cities: Chicago's Utopias of 1893*. Chicago: University of Chicago
    Press, 1991.

Glassberg, David. *American Historical Pageantry: The Uses of Tradition in the Early
    Twentieth Century*. Chapel Hill: University of North Carolina Press, 1990.

————. "History and the Public: Legacies of the Progressive Era." *Journal of American
    History* 73 (Mar. 1987): 957–80.

Gleason, Philip. "The Melting Pot: Symbol of Fusion or Confusion?" *American
    Quarterly* 16 (Spring 1964): 20–46.

Glenn, Susan A. *Daughters of the Shtetl: Life and Labor in the Immigrant Generation*.
    Ithaca: Cornell University Press, 1990.

————. *Female Spectacle: The Theatrical Roots of Modern Feminism*. Cambridge:
    Harvard University Press, 2000.

Glover, Ellye Howell. *"Dame Curtsey's" Book of Party Pastimes for the Up-to-Date
    Hostess*. Chicago: A. C. McClurg and Co., 1912.

The Godiva Riding Habit. New York: S&S Goldberg, n.d.

Goldstein, Judith. *Ideas, Interests, and American Trade Policy*. Ithaca: Cornell
    University Press, 1993.

Goody, Jack. *Cooking, Cuisine and Class: A Study in Comparative Sociology*. Cambridge:
    Cambridge University Press, 1982.

Gordon, Beverly. *Bazaars and Fair Ladies: The History of the American Fundraising
    Fair*. Knoxville: University of Tennessee Press, 1998.

————. "Cozy, Charming, and Artistic: Stitching Together the American Home."
    In *The Arts and the American Home, 1890–1930*, ed. Jessica H. Foy and Karal Ann
    Marlin, 124–48. Knoxville: University of Tennessee Press, 1994.

Gordon, Milton M. *Assimilation in American Life: The Role of Race, Religion, and
    National Origins*. New York: Oxford University Press, 1964.

Gow, Alex M. *Good Morals and Gentle Manners*. Cincinnati: Van Antwerp, Bragg and Co., 1873.

Graburn, Nelson H. H. "Introduction: Arts of the Fourth World." In *Ethnic and Tourist Arts: Cultural Expressions from the Fourth World*, ed. Nelson H. H. Graburn, 1–32. Berkeley: University of California Press, 1976.

Granlund, Sten. "Sweden." In *Peasant Art in Sweden, Lapland and Iceland*, ed. Charles Holme, 3–34. London: The Studio, 1910.

Green, Nancy L., *Ready-to-Wear and Ready-to-Work: A Century of Industry and Immigrants in Paris and New York*. Durham: Duke, 1997.

Greene, Mrs. Charles W. "Making the Ideal of the American Home." In *Americanization Programs*, 12–13. N.p.: General Federation of Women's Clubs [1919–20].

Greene, Victor. *A Passion for Polka: Old-Time Ethnic Music in America*. Berkeley: University of California Press, 1992.

Greenhalgh, Paul. *Ephemeral Vistas: The Expositions Universelles, Great Exhibitions, and World's Fairs, 1851–1939*. Manchester: Manchester University Press, 1988.

Greenleaf, Margaret. "Decorating and Furnishing the Bedroom." In *A Book of Distinctive Interiors*, ed. William A. Vollmer, 68–86. New York: McBride, Nast & Co., 1912.

Grier, Katherine C. *Culture and Comfort: Parlor Making and Middle-Class Identity, 1850–1930*. Washington, D.C.: Smithsonian Institution Press, 1997.

Grimshaw, Patricia. *Paths of Duty: American Missionary Wives in Nineteenth-Century Hawaii*. Honolulu: University of Hawaii Press, 1989.

The Grocer's Manual. Claremont, N.H.: Claremont Manufacturing Co., 1898.

A Guide to the City of Chicago. Chicago: Chicago Association of Commerce, 1909.

Gulick, Luther H. *The Healthful Art of Dancing*. New York: Doubleday, Page, and Co., 1911.

———. Preface to *Folk-Dances and Singing Games*, by Elizabeth Burchenal, vii. New York: G. Schirmer, 1909.

Haddow, Robert H. *Pavilions of Plenty: Exhibiting American Culture Abroad in the 1950s*. Washington, D.C.: Smithsonian Institution Press, 1997.

Hale, Grace. *Making Whiteness: The Culture of Segregation in the South, 1890–1940*. New York: Vintage Books, 1998.

Hall, Florence Howe. *The Correct Thing in Good Society*. Boston: Estes and Lauriat, 1888.

Hall's Illustrated Catalogue of Magic Lanterns. Boston, n.d.

Halttunen, Karen. *Confidence Men and Painted Women: A Study of Middle-class Culture in America, 1830–1870*. New Haven: Yale University Press, 1982.

———. "From Parlor to Living Room: Domestic Space, Interior Decoration, and the Culture of Personality." In *Consuming Visions: Accumulation and Display of Goods in America, 1880–1920*, ed. Simon J. Bronner, 157–90. New York: W. W. Norton, 1989.

Hammond, Jennifer Jo. "'Novelty in Entertaining . . . Easily and Artistically Arranged': Middle-Class Women and Themed Parties in America, 1880–1915." M.A. thesis, University of Delaware, 1997.

Hancock, David. "'A Revolution in the Trade': Wine Distribution and the Development of the Infrastructure of the Atlantic Market Economy, 1703–1807." In *The Early Modern Atlantic Economy*, ed. John J. McCusker and Kenneth Morgan, 105–53. Cambridge: Cambridge University Press, 2000.

Handlin, Oscar. *One World: The Origins of an American Concept*. Oxford: Clarendon Press, 1974.

Hannerz, Ulf. "Cosmopolitans and Locals in World Culture." In *Global Culture: Nationalism, Globalization and Modernity*, ed. Mike Featherstone, 237–51. London: Sage, 1990.

Hansen, Jonathan M. *The Lost Promise of Patriotism: Debating American Identity, 1890–1920*. Chicago: University of Chicago Press, 2003.

Hansen, Karen Tranberg, ed. *African Encounters with Domesticity*. New Brunswick: Rutgers University Press, 1992.

Hanson, Elizabeth. *Animal Attractions: Nature on Display in American Zoos*. Princeton: Princeton University Press, 2002.

Haraway, Donna. "Teddy Bear Patriarchy: Taxidermy in the Garden of Eden, New York City, 1908–1936." In *Cultures of United States Imperialism*, ed. Amy Kaplan and Donald E. Pease, 237–91. Durham: Duke University Press, 1993.

Harland, Marion. *Cookery for Beginners*. Boston: D. Lothrop and Co., 1884.

Harland, Marion, M. Parloa, Mrs. D. A. Lincoln, Thomas J. Murrey and many other authorities. *The New England Cook Book*. Boston: Chas. E. Brown Publishing Co., 1905.

Harland, Marion, and Virginia Van de Water. *Everyday Etiquette: A Practical Manual of Social Usages*. Indianapolis: The Bobbs-Merrill Co., 1905.

Harley, Sharon. "Mary Church Terrell: Genteel Militant." In *Black Leaders of the Nineteenth Century*, ed. Leon Litwack and August Meier, 307–22. Urbana: University of Illinois Press, 1988.

Harrison, Constance Cary. "Society and Social Usages." In *The House and Home*, vol. 1, ed. Dr. Lyman Abbott et al., 145–78. New York: Charles Scribner's Sons, 1896.

———. "Woman's Handiwork." In *The House and Home*, vol. 2, ed. Dr. Lyman Abbott et al., 217–74. New York: Charles Scribner's Sons, 1896.

Harrison, Mrs. Burton. "Worrosquoyacke." In *The Merry Maid of Arcady, His Lordship and Other Stories*, 51–116. Boston: Lamson, Wolffe and Co., 1897.

Hart, John Mason. *Empire and Revolution: The Americans in Mexico since the Civil War.* Berkeley: University of California Press, 2002.

Hartmann, Edward George. *The Movement to Americanize the Immigrant.* New York: AMS Press, 1967.

Hatem, Mervat. "Through Each Other's Eyes: Egyptian, Levantine-Egyptian, and European Women's Images of Themselves and of Each Other (1862–1920)." *Women's Studies International Forum* 12, no. 2 (1989): 183–98.

Hay, Susan. "Introduction: A. & L. Tirocchi; A Time Capsule Discovered." In *From Paris to Providence: Fashion, Art, and the Tirocchi Dressmakers' Shop, 1915–1947*, ed. Susan Hay, 13–22. Providence: Rhode Island School of Design, 2000.

———. "Paris to Providence: French Couture and the Tirocchi Shop." In *From Paris to Providence: Fashion, Art, and the Tirocchi Dressmakers' Shop, 1915–1947*, ed. Suan Hay, 133–71. Providence: Rhode Island School of Design, 2000.

Healy, David. *Drive to Hegemony: The United States in the Caribbean, 1898–1917.* Madison: University of Wisconsin Press, 1988.

Hedger, Caroline. "What Is an Americanization Institute?" In *Americanization Programs*, 4–6. N.p.: General Federation of Women's Clubs [1919–20].

Heindel, Richard Heathcote. *The American Impact on Great Britain.* Philadelphia: University of Pennsylvania Press, 1940.

Heinze, Andrew R. *Adapting to Abundance: Jewish Immigrants, Mass Consumption, and the Search for American Identity.* New York: Columbia University Press, 1990.

Held, David, and Anthony McGrew. "The Great Globalization Debate: An Introduction." In *The Global Transformations Reader: An Introduction to the Globalization Debate*, ed. David Held and Anthony McGrew, 1–45. Cambridge: Polity Press, 2000.

Hendricks, Wanda A. *Gender, Race, and Politics in the Midwest: Black Club Women in Illinois.* Bloomington: Indiana University Press, 1998.

Herman, Sondra R. *Eleven against War: Studies in American Internationalist Thought, 1898–1921.* Stanford: Hoover Institution Press, 1969.

Herrick, Christine Terhune. *What to Eat, How to Serve It.* New York: Harper and Brothers, 1905.

Herrick, Robert. *The Common Lot.* 1904. Upper Saddle River, N.J.: Gregg Press, 1968.

Hertrich, William. *The Huntington Botanical Gardens, 1905–1949.* San Marino, Calif.: Huntington Library, 1949.

Hess, John L., and Karen Hess. *The Taste of America.* New York: Grossman Publishers, 1977.

Hess, Karen. *The Carolina Rice Kitchen: The African Connection.* Columbia: University of South Carolina Press, 1992.

———. *Martha Washington's Booke of Cookery.* New York: Columbia University Press, 1981.

Hewitt, Emma Churchman. *Queen of Home*. Oakland, Calif.: H. J. Smith and Co., 1889.

Hichens, Robert. *The Garden of Allah*. New York: Grosset and Dunlap, 1904.

Higham, John. *Send These to Me: Immigrants in Urban America*. 1975. Baltimore: Johns Hopkins University Press, 1984.

Higham, John. "Social Discrimination against Jews in America, 1830–1930." In *Anti-Semitism in America*, part 1, *American Jewish History*, vol. 6, ed. Jeffrey S. Gurock, 229–61. New York: Routledge, 1998.

———. *Strangers in the Land: Patterns of American Nativism 1860–1925*. 1955. Reprint, New York: Atheneum, 1970.

Hill, Janet McKenzie. *Practical Cooking and Serving: A Complete Manual of How to Select, Prepare, and Serve Food*. New York: Doubleday, Page, and Co., 1915.

Hill, Patricia R. *The World Their Household: The American Woman's Foreign Mission Movement and Cultural Transformation, 1870–1920*. Ann Arbor: University of Michigan Press, 1985.

Hirshler, Erica E. "'Gondola Days': American Painters in Venice." In *The Lure of Italy: American Artists and the Italian Experience, 1760–1914*, ed. Theodore E. Stebbins Jr., 112–28. New York: Museum of Fine Arts Boston in association with Harry N. Abrams, 1992.

Historical Sketch Book and Guide to New Orleans. New York: Will H. Coleman, 1885.

Hobsbawm, Eric. "Introduction: Inventing Traditions." In *The Invention of Tradition*, ed. Eric Hobsbawm and Terence Ranger, 1–14. 1983. Cambridge: Cambridge University Press, 1984.

Hoelscher, Steven. *Heritage on Stage: The Invention of Ethnic Place in America's Little Switzerland*. Madison: University of Wisconsin Press, 1998.

Holland, Norman S. "Fashioning Cuba." In *Nationalisms and Sexualities*, ed. Andrew Parker, Mary Russo, Doris Sommer, and Patricia Yaeger, 147–56. New York: Routledge, 1992.

Hollinger, David A. *In the American Province: Studies in the History and Historiography of Ideas*. Bloomington: Indiana University Press, 1985.

———. *Postethnic America: Beyond Multiculturalism*. New York: BasicBooks, 1995.

Holloway, Edward Stratton. *The Practical Book of Furnishing the Small House and Apartment*. Philadelphia: J. B. Lippincott, 1922.

Holme, Charles, ed. *Peasant Art in Russia*. London: The Studio, 1912.

Holmes, Burton. *Burton Holmes Travelogues*. Vol. 1, 1908, 1914, 1917, 1919. Chicago: The Travelogue Bureau, 1920.

———. *Burton Holmes Travelogues*. Vol. 2, 1908. Chicago: The Travelogue Bureau, 1920.

———. *Burton Holmes Travelogues*. Vol. 3, 1910. Chicago: The Travelogue Bureau, 1920.

————. *Burton Holmes Travelogues*. Vol. 4, 1908. Chicago: The Travelogue Bureau, 1920.

————. *Burton Holmes Travelogues*. Vol. 7, 1910. Chicago: The Travelogue Bureaus, 1920.

————. *Burton Holmes Travelogues*. Vol. 9, 1908. Chicago: The Travelogue Bureau, 1920.

————. *Burton Holmes Travelogues*. Vol. 11, 1910. Chicago: The Travelogue Bureau, 1920.

————. *Burton Holmes Travelogues*. Vol. 13, 1917. Chicago: The Travelogue Bureau, 1920.

Holt, Ardern. *Fancy Dresses Described*. 6th ed. London: Debenham and Freebody, n.d.

Honor, Hugh. *Chinoiserie: The Vision of Cathay*. London: John Murray, 1961.

Hosley, William. *The Japan Idea: Art and Life in Victorian America*. Hartford: Wadsworth Atheneum, 1990.

The Housekeeper's Quest: Where to Find Pretty Things. New York: Sypher and Co., 1885.

Howard, Jennie E. *In Distant Climes and Other Years*. Buenos Aires: The American Press, 1931.

Howe, Daniel Walker, ed. *Victorian America*. Philadelphia: University of Pennsylvania Press, 1976.

Hoxie, Frederick E. *A Final Promise: The Campaign to Assimilate the Indians, 1880–1920*. Lincoln: University of Nebraska Press, 1984.

Hoy, Suellen. *Chasing Dirt: The American Pursuit of Cleanliness*. New York: Oxford University Press, 1995.

Hughes, Langston. *The Big Sea*. New York: Hill and Wang, 1940.

Hughes, Rupert. *The Real New York*. New York: The Smart Set Publishing Co., 1904.

Humphreys, Mary Gay. "House Decoration and Furnishing." In *The House and Home, a Practical Book, in two volumes*, vol. 2, ed. Lyman Abbott et al., 103–78. New York: Charles Scribner's Sons, 1896.

Hunt, Michael H. *Ideology and U.S. Foreign Policy*. New Haven: Yale University Press, 1987.

Hunt, Patricia K. "Clothing as an Expression of History: The Dress of African-American Women in Georgia, 1880–1915." In *"We Specialize in the Wholly Impossible": A Reader in Black Women's History*, ed. Darlene Clark Hine, Wilma King, and Linda Reed, 393–404. Brooklyn: Carlson Publishing, 1995.

Hunter, Jane. *The Gospel of Gentility: American Women Missionaries in Turn-of-the-Century China*. New Haven: Yale University Press, 1984.

Hunter, Phyllis Whitman. *Purchasing Identity in the Atlantic World: Massachusetts Merchants, 1670–1780*. Ithaca: Cornell University Press, 2001.

Impey, Oliver. *Chinoiserie: The Impact of Oriental Styles on Western Art and Decoration*. New York: Charles Scribner's Sons, 1977.

Iriye, Akira. *The Cambridge History of American Foreign Relations*. Vol. 3, *The Globalizing of America, 1913–1945*. 1993. Reprint, Cambridge: Cambridge University Press, 1997.

———. *Global Community: The Role of International Organizations in the Making of the Contemporary World*. Berkeley: University of California Press, 2002.

Irving, Katrina. *Immigrant Mothers: Narratives of Race and Maternity, 1890–1925*. Urbana: University of Illinois Press, 2000.

Isaacs, Harold R. *Scratches on Our Minds: American Images of China and India*. New York: John Day, 1957.

Jackson, Alice, and Bettina Jackson. *The Study of Interior Decoration*. New York: Doubleday, Doran & Co., 1928.

Jackson, James C. *American Womanhood: Its Peculiarities and Necessities*. 2nd ed. New York: Austin, Jackson and Co., 1870.

Jackson, Shannon. *Lines of Activity: Performance, Historiography, Hull-House Domesticity*. Ann Arbor: University of Michigan Press, 2000.

Jacobson, Matthew Frye. *Barbarian Virtues: The United States Encounters Foreign Peoples at Home and Abroad, 1876–1917*. New York: Hill and Wang, 2000.

———. *Whiteness of a Different Color: European Immigrants and the Alchemy of Race*. Cambridge: Harvard University Press, 1998.

Jayawardena, Kumari. *The White Woman's Other Burden: Western Women and South Asia during British Colonial Rule*. New York: Routledge, 1995.

Jenkins, Virginia Scott. *Bananas: An American History*. Washington, D.C.: Smithsonian Institution Press, 2000.

Jensen, Joan M. "Needlework as Art, Craft, and Livelihood before 1900." In *A Needle, a Bobbin, a Strike: Women Needleworkers in America*, ed. Joan M. Jensen and Sue Davidson, 1–19. Philadelphia: Temple University Press, 1984.

———. *One Foot on the Rockies: Women and Creativity in the Modern American West*. Albuquerque: University of New Mexico Press, 1995.

Jiménez, Michael F. "'From Plantation to Cup': Coffee and Capitalism in the United States, 1830–1930." In *Coffee, Society, and Power in Latin America*, ed. William Roseberry, Lowell Gudmundson, and Mario Samper Kutschbach, 38–64. Baltimore: Johns Hopkins University Press, 1995.

Jirousek, Charlotte. "The Transition to Mass Fashion System Dress in the Later Ottoman Empire." In *Consumption Studies and the History of the Ottoman Empire, 1550–1922*, ed. Donald Quataert, 201–42. Albany: State University of New York Press, 2000.

Johnson, William Martin. *Inside of One Hundred Homes*. Philadelphia: Curtis Publishing, 1898.

Jones, Mrs. C. S., and Henry T. Williams. *Household Elegancies, Suggestions in Household Art and Tasteful Home Decorations*. New York: Henry T. Williams, 1875.

Jones, Howard Mumford. *The Age of Energy: Varieties of American Experience, 1865–1915.* New York: Viking, 1970.

Jones, Plummer Alston, Jr. *Libraries, Immigrants, and the American Experience.* Westport, Conn.: Greenwood Press, 1999.

Joselit, Jenna Weissman. *A Perfect Fit: Clothes, Character, and the Promise of America.* New York: Metropolitan Books, 2001.

Joseph, Gilbert M., Catherine C. LeGrand, and Ricardo D. Salvatore, eds. *Close Encounters of Empire: Writing the Cultural History of U.S.-Latin American Relations.* Durham: Duke University Press, 1998.

Kallen, Horace M. *Culture and Democracy in the United States.* New York: Boni and Liveright, 1924.

Kander, Mrs. Simon. *The "Settlement" Cook Book.* Milwaukee: J. H. Yewdale and Sons, 1910.

Kander, Mrs. Simon, and Mrs. Henry Schoenfeld. *The "Settlement" Cook Book, 1903: The Way to a Man's Heart.* 1903. Reprint, New York: Hugh Lauter Levin, 1984.

Kaplan, Amy. *The Anarchy of Empire in the Making of U.S. Culture.* Cambridge: Harvard University Press, 2002.

———. "Manifest Domesticity." *American Literature* 70 (Sept. 1998): 581–606.

Kaplan, Amy, and Donald E. Pease, eds. *Cultures of United States Imperialism.* Durham: Duke University Press, 1993.

Kaplan, Anne R., Marjorie A. Hoover, and Willard B. More. "Introduction: On Ethnic Foodways." In *The Taste of American Place: A Reader on Regional and Ethnic Foods,* ed. Barbara G. Shortridge and James R. Shortridge, 121–33. New York: Rowman and Littlefield, 1998.

Kaplan, Caren, Norma Alarcón, and Minoo Moallem. *Between Woman and Nation: Nationalisms, Transnational Feminisms, and the State.* Durham: Duke University Press, 1999.

Kasson, John F. *Amusing the Million: Coney Island at the Turn of the Century.* New York: Hill and Wang, 1978.

Kasson, Joy S. *Buffalo Bill's Wild West: Celebrity, Memory, and Popular History.* New York: Hill and Wang, 2000.

Katzman, David M. *Seven Days a Week: Women and Domestic Service in Industrializing America.* Urbana: University of Illinois Press, 1981.

Kennedy, Kathleen. *Disloyal Mothers and Scurrilous Citizens: Women and Subversion during World War I.* Bloomington: Indiana University Press, 1999.

Kern, Stephen. *The Culture of Time and Space, 1880–1918.* Cambridge: Harvard University Press, 1983.

Kidwell, Claudia B., and Margaret C. Christman. *Suiting Everyone: The Democratization of Clothing in America.* Washington, D.C.: Smithsonian Institution Press, 1974.

Kim, Thomas W. "Being Modern: The Circulation of Oriental Objects." *American Quarterly* 58 (June 2006): 379–406.

King, Desmond. *Making Americans: Immigration, Race, and the Origins of the Diverse Democracy.* Cambridge: Harvard University Press, 2000.

Kinne, Helen, and Anna M. Cooley. *Shelter and Clothing.* New York: Macmillan, 1915.

Kirshenblatt-Gimblett, Barbara. *Destination Culture: Tourism, Museums, and Heritage.* Berkeley: University of California Press, 1998.

———. "Objects of Ethnography." In *Exhibiting Cultures: The Poetics and Politics of Museum Display,* ed. Ivan Karp and Steven D. Lavine, 386–443. Washington, D.C.: Smithsonian Institution Press, 1991.

Knoblauch, Edward. *My Lady's Dress.* New York: Doubleday, Page & Co., 1916.

Knupfer, Anne Meis. *Toward a Tenderer Humanity and a Nobler Womanhood: African American Women's Clubs in Turn-of-the-Century Chicago.* New York: New York University Press, 1996.

Korman, Gerd. *Industrialization, Immigrants and Americanizers: The View from Milwaukee, 1866–1921.* Madison: State Historical Society of Wisconsin, 1967.

Koshar, Rudy. *German Travel Cultures.* New York: Berg, 2000.

Kramer, Paul. "Making Concessions: Race and Empire Revisited at the Philippine Exposition, St. Louis, 1901–1905." *Radical History Review* 73 (Winter 1999): 74–114.

Kraut, Alan M. *The Huddled Masses: The Immigrant in American Society, 1880–1921.* 1982. 2nd ed. Wheeling, Ill.: Harlan Davidson, 2001.

Kroeger, Brooke. *Nellie Bly: Daredevil, Reporter, Feminist.* New York: Random House, 1994.

Kuklick, Bruce. *Puritans in Babylon: The Ancient Near East and American Intellectual Life, 1880–1930.* Princeton: Princeton University Press, 1996.

Kuisel, Richard F. *Seducing the French: The Dilemma of Americanization.* Berkeley: University of California Press, 1993.

Kupperman, Karen Ordahl. "International at the Creation: Early Modern American History." In *Rethinking American History in a Global Age,* ed. Thomas Bender, 103–22. Berkeley: University of California Press, 2002.

LaFeber, Walter. *The Cambridge History of American Foreign Relations.* Vol. 2, *The American Search for Opportunity, 1865–1913.* Cambridge: Cambridge University Press, 1993.

———. *Michael Jordan and the New Global Capitalism.* New York: W. W. Norton, 1999.

———. *The New Empire: An Interpretation of American Expansion, 1860–1898.* Ithaca: Cornell University Press, 1963.

Lancaster, Clay. *The Japanese Influence in America.* New York: Walton H. Rawls, 1963.

Landsman, Ned C. *From Colonials to Provincials: American Thought and Culture, 1680–1760.* New York: Twayne, 1997.

Langley, Lester D. *The Banana Wars: United States Intervention in the Caribbean, 1898–1934.* 1983. Wilmington: Scholarly Resources, 2002.

Lasch-Quinn, Elisabeth. *Black Neighbors: Race and the Limits of Reform in the American Settlement House Movement, 1890–1945.* Chapel Hill: University of North Carolina Press, 1993.

Lauer, Jeanette C., and Robert H. Lauer. *Fashion Power: The Meaning of Fashion in American Society.* Englewood Cliffs, N.J.: Prentice-Hall, 1981.

Laverton and Co. *New Illustrated Catalog of Furniture.* Bristol: n.p., 1875.

Laville, Helen. *Cold War Women: The International Activities of American Women's Organisations.* New York: Manchester University Press, 2002.

Laws, Annie. *History of the Ohio Federation of Women's Clubs for the First Thirty Years, 1894–1924.* Cincinnati: Ebbert and Richardson Co., [1924].

Leach, William. *Land of Desire: Merchants, Power, and the Rise of a New American Culture.* New York: Pantheon Books, 1993.

Lears, T. J. Jackson. *Fables of Abundance: A Cultural History of Advertising in America.* New York: BasicBooks, 1994.

———. *No Place of Grace: Antimodernism and the Transformation of American Culture, 1880–1920.* New York: Pantheon Books, 1981.

Leavitt, Judith Walzer. *Typhoid Mary: Captive to the Public's Health.* Boston: Beacon Press, 1996.

Leavitt, Sarah A. *From Catharine Beecher to Martha Stewart: A Cultural History of Domestic Advice.* Chapel Hill: University of North Carolina Press, 2002.

Lee, Anthony W. *Picturing Chinatown: Art and Orientalism in San Francisco.* Berkeley: University of California Press, 2001.

Leed, Eric J. *The Mind of the Traveler: From Gilgamesh to Global Tourism.* New York: Basic Books, 1991.

Lemcke, Gesine. *European and American Cuisine.* New York: D. Appleton and Co., 1906.

Leslie, Eliza. *Miss Leslie's New Cookery Book.* Philadelphia: T. B. Peterson, 1857.

Levenstein, Harvey A. *Paradox of Plenty: A Social History of Eating in Modern America.* New York: Oxford, 1993.

———. *Revolution at the Table: The Transformation of the American Diet.* New York: Oxford University Press, 1988.

———. *Seductive Journey: American Tourists in France from Jefferson to the Jazz Age.* Chicago: University of Chicago Press, 1998.

Levetus, A. S. "Austria." In *Peasant Art in Austria and Hungary,* ed. Charles Holme, 1–14. London: The Studio, 1911.

Levine, Lawrence W. *Highbrow, Lowbrow: The Emergence of Cultural Hierarchy in America*. Cambridge: Harvard University Press, 1988.

Lewis, Reina. *Gendering Orientalism: Race, Femininity and Representation*. New York: Routledge, 1996.

Lewis, Sinclair. *Main Street*. 1920. Reprint, New York: Signet Classic, 1980.

Li, Lillian M. "The Silk Export Trade and Economic Modernization in China and Japan." In *America's China Trade in Historical Perspective: The Chinese and American Performance*, ed. Ernest R. May and John K. Fairbank, 77–99. Cambridge: Harvard University Press, 1986.

Lichten, Frances. *Decorative Art of Victoria's Era*. New York: Charles Scribner's Sons, 1950.

Light, Ivan. "From Vice District to Tourist Attraction: The Moral Career of American Chinatowns, 1880–1940." *Pacific Historical Review* 43 (Aug. 1974): 367–94.

Light on Stereographs. New York: Underwood and Underwood, 1902.

Lincoln, Mrs. D. A. [Mary Johnson Bailey Lincoln]. *Mrs. Lincoln's Boston Cook Book*. Boston: Roberts Brothers, 1888.

Lincoln, Jennette Emeline Carpenter. *The Festival Book: May-Day Pastime and the May-Pole*. New York: A. S. Barnes Co., 1912.

Lingle, Mrs. Thomas W. [Clara Souther]. "A Course on Americanization." Chapel Hill: University of North Carolina, 1919.

―――. "Industrial and Social Conditions and Americanization." In *Americanization Programs*, 13–14. N.p.: General Federation of Women's Clubs [1919–20].

Lissak, Rivka Shpak. *Pluralism and Progressives: Hull House and the New Immigrants, 1890–1919*. Chicago: University of Chicago Press, 1989.

List of Officers and Directors, Committees, State Federations, Federation Secretaries and Federation Clubs of the General Federation of Women's Clubs. Charleston: Walker, Evans, and Cogswell, 1904.

List of Officers and Directors, Federation Secretaries and Committees, State Federations, and List of Federated Clubs of G.F.W.C. Philadelphia: John R. McFetridge and Sons, 1901.

List of Officers and Directors, State Chairmen of Correspondence, State Federations, and List of Federated Clubs of G.F.W.C. N.p., 1899.

Litwicki, Ellen M. *America's Public Holidays, 1865–1920*. Washington, D.C.: Smithsonian Institution Press, 2000.

Loeb, Lori Anne. *Consuming Angels: Advertising and Victorian Women*. New York: Oxford, 1994.

Löfgren, Orvar. "Know Your Country: A Comparative Perspective on Tourism and Nation Building in Sweden." In *Being Elsewhere: Tourism, Consumer Culture, and Identity in Modern Europe and North America*, ed. Shelley Baranowski and Ellen Furlough, 137–54. Ann Arbor: University of Michigan Press, 2001.

Long, Burke O. *Imagining the Holy Land: Maps, Models, and Fantasy Travels.*
Bloomington: Indiana University Press, 2003.

Lott, Emmeline. *The Grand Pacha's Cruise on the Nile in the Viceroy of Egypt's Yacht.*
2 vols. London: T. Cautley Newby, 1869.

Lott, Eric. *Love and Theft: Blackface Minstrelsy and the American Working Class.* New
York: Oxford University Press, 1993.

Lui, Mary Ting Yi. "'The Real Yellow Peril': Mapping Racial and Gender Boundaries
in New York City's Chinatown, 1870–1910." *Hitting Critical Mass* 5 (Spring 1998):
107–26.

Lutz, Catherine A., and Jane L. Collins. *Reading National Geographic.* Chicago:
University of Chicago Press, 1993.

Lyman, Joseph B., and Laura E. Lyman. *The Philosophy of House-Keeping: A Scientific
and Practical Manual.* Hartford: Goodwin and Betts, 1867.

Lynes, Russell. *The Tastemakers.* New York: Grosset and Dunlap, 1949.

M. Grossman and Son. *Illustrated Catalogue of Parlor Furniture.* New York: B. Hasper,
n.d.

MacCannell, Dean. *The Tourist: A New Theory of the Leisure Class.* 1976. Rev. ed.
Berkeley: University of California Press, 1999.

MacKenzie, John M. *Orientalism: History, Theory and the Arts.* Manchester:
Manchester University Press, 1995.

Magliocco, Sabina. "Playing with Food: The Negotiation of Identity in the Ethnic
Display Event by Italian Americans in Clinton, Indiana." In *The Taste of American
Place: A Reader on Regional and Ethnic Foods,* ed. Barbara G. Shortridge and
James R. Shortridge, 145–61. New York: Rowman and Littlefield, 1998.

Marsh, Margaret. *Suburban Lives.* New Brunswick: Rutgers University Press, 1990.

Martin, Theodora Penny. *The Sound of Our Own Voices: Women's Study Clubs, 1860–
1910.* Boston: Beacon Press, 1987.

Matthews, Jill Julius. "Which America?" In *Americanization and Australia,* ed. Philip
Bell and Roger Bell, 15–31. Sydney: University of New South Wales Press, 1988.

Mathur, Saloni. "Wanted Native Views: Collecting Colonial Postcards of India." In
Gender, Sexuality, and Colonial Modernity, ed. Antoinette Burton, 95–115. London:
Routledge, 1999.

Matsumoto-Do. *The Book of Genuine Things Japanese.* Tokyo: The Matsumoto-Do
[ca. 1911].

Maw, Blanche Blynn. *A History of the Michigan State Federation of Women's Clubs,
1895–1953.* Ann Arbor: Ann Arbor Press, 1953.

Maxwell, Anne. *Colonial Photography and Exhibitions: Representations of the "Native"
and the Making of European Identities.* London: Leicester University Press, 1999.

Mayhew, Edgar de N., and Minor Myers Jr. *A Documentary History of American
Interiors, from the Colonial Era to 1915.* New York: Charles Scribner's Sons, 1980.

Mazumdar, Sucheta. "The Impact of New World Food Crops on the Diet and Economy of China and India, 1600–1900." In *Food in Global History*, ed. Raymond Grew, 58–78. Boulder: Westview Press, 1999.

McAllister, Ward. *Society as I Have Found It*. New York: Cassell Publishing, 1890.

McCabe, James D. *The Illustrated History of the Centennial Exhibition*. Philadelphia: National Publishing Co., 1876.

McCarthy, Kathleen D. *Women's Culture: American Philanthropy and Art, 1830–1930*. Chicago: University of Chicago Press, 1991.

McClymer, John F. "The Americanization Movement and the Education of the Foreign-Born Adult, 1914–1925." In *American Education and the European Immigrant: 1840–1940*, ed. Bernard J. Weiss, 96–116. Urbana: University of Illinois Press, 1982.

———. *War and Welfare: Social Engineering in America, 1890–1925*. Westport, Conn.: Greenwood Press, 1980.

McCracken, Donald P. *Gardens of Empire: Botanical Institutions of the Victorian British Empire*. London: Leicester University Press, 1997.

McFadden, Margaret H. *Golden Cables of Sympathy: The Transatlantic Sources of Nineteenth-Century Feminism*. Lexington: University Press of Kentucky, 1999.

McFeely, Mary Drake. *Can She Bake a Cherry Pie? American Women and the Kitchen in the Twentieth Century*. Amherst: University of Massachusetts Press, 2000.

McKenzie, F. A. *The American Invaders*. London: Grant Richards, 1902.

McMahon, Sarah Francis. "'A Comfortable Subsistence': A History of Diet in New England, 1630–1850." Ph.D. diss., Brandeis, 1982.

Mead, Lucia Ames. *To Whom Much Is Given*. New York: Thomas Y. Crowell, 1899.

Mead, Robert O. *Atlantic Legacy: Essays in American-European Cultural History*. New York: New York University Press, 1969.

Meech, Julia, and Gabriel Weisberg. *Japonisme Comes to America: The Japanese Impact on the Graphic Arts, 1876–1925*. New York: Harry N. Abrams, 1990.

Melvin, Patricia Mooney. "Building Muscles and Civics: Folk Dancing, Ethnic Diversity and the Playground Association of America." *American Studies* 24 (Spring 1983): 89–99.

Mennell, Stephen. *All Manners of Food: Eating and Taste in England and France from the Middle Ages to the Present*. 2nd ed. Urbana: University of Illinois Press, 1996.

Milbank, Caroline Rennolds. *New York Fashion: The Evolution of American Style*. New York: Harry N. Abrams, 1989.

Miller, Catherine Atkinson. *Joy from Japan, Recreation Programs*. Philadelphia: Heidelberg Press, 1923.

Miller, James Earle. "Planning the Kitchen." In *A Book of Distinctive Interiors*, ed. William A. Vollmer, 116–28. New York: McBride, Nast & Co., 1912.

Milligan, C. T. *Illustrated Catalogue of Stereo-Panopticons*. Philadelphia: Grant, Faires, and Rodgers, [1881].

Mintz, Sidney W. *Sweetness and Power: The Place of Sugar in Modern History*. New York: Viking, 1985.

———. *Tasting Food, Tasting Freedom: Excursions into Eating, Culture, and the Past*. Boston: Beacon Press, 1996.

Mitchell, Reid. *All on a Mardi Gras Day: Episodes in the History of New Orleans Carnival*. Cambridge: Harvard University Press, 1995.

Mitchell, Timothy. *Colonising Egypt*. Cambridge: Cambridge University Press, 1988.

———. "Orientalism and the Exhibitionary Order." In *Colonialism and Culture*, ed. Nicholas B. Dirks, 289–318. Ann Arbor: University of Michigan Press, 1992.

Mohl, Raymond A. "Cultural Pluralism in Immigrant Education: The YWCA's International Institutes, 1910–1940." In *Men and Women Adrift: The YMCA and the YWCA in the City*, ed. Nina Mjagkij and Margaret Spratt, 111–37. New York: New York University Press, 1997.

———. "The International Institutes and Immigrant Education, 1910–40." In *American Education and the European Immigrant: 1840–1940*, ed. Bernard J. Weiss, 117–41. Urbana: University of Illinois Press, 1982.

Mohl, Raymond A., and Neil Betten. "Ethnic Adjustment in the Industrial City: The International Institute of Gary, 1919–1940." *International Migration Review* 6 (Winter 1972): 361–76.

Montgomery, Maureen E. *Displaying Women: Spectacles of Leisure in Edith Wharton's New York*. New York: Routledge, 1998.

———. *"Gilded Prostitution": Status, Money, and Transatlantic Marriages, 1870–1914*. London: Routledge, 1989.

Montgomery Ward and Co. *Catalogue*. No. 81. Chicago: Montgomery Ward and Co., 1912.

Moore, William D. "From Lodge Room to Theatre: Meeting Spaces of the Scottish Rite." In *Theatre of the Fraternity: Staging the Ritual Space of the Scottish Rite of Freemasonry, 1896–1929*, ed. C. Lance Brockman, 31–51. Jackson: University Press of Mississippi, 1996.

Morley, Christopher. *Travels in Philadelphia*. 1920. Reprint, Philadelphia: David McKay Co., 1921.

Morse, Edward S. *Japanese Homes and Their Surroundings*. 1886. New York: Dover Publications, 1961.

Moses, Wilson Jeremiah. *Afrotopia: The Roots of African American Popular History*. New York: Cambridge University Press, 1998.

———. *The Golden Age of Black Nationalism, 1850–1925*. Hamden, Conn.: Archon Books, 1978.

Mosse, George L. *The Nationalization of the Masses: Political Symbolism and Mass*

Movements in Germany from the Napoleonic Wars through the Third Reich. New York: Howard Fertig, 1975.

Mott, Frank Luther. *A History of American Magazines, 1885–1905*. Cambridge: Belknap Press of Harvard University Press, 1957.

Muncy, Robyn. *Creating a Female Dominion in American Reform, 1890–1935*. New York: Oxford University Press, 1991.

Musser, Charles. *The Emergence of Cinema: The American Screen to 1907*. Berkeley: University of California Press, 1990.

Musser, Charles, in collaboration with Carol Nelson. *High-Class Moving Pictures: Lyman H. Howe and the Forgotten Era of Traveling Exhibition, 1880–1920*. Princeton: Princeton University Press, 1991.

Naff, Alixa. *Becoming American: The Early Arab Immigrant Experience*. Carbondale: Southern Illinois University Press, 1985.

Nair, Janaki. "Uncovering the Zenana: Visions of Indian Womanhood in Englishwomen's Writings, 1813–1940." *Journal of Women's History* 2 (Spring 1990): 8–34.

Nasaw, David. *Going Out: The Rise and Fall of Public Amusements*. New York: Harper Collins, 1993.

National Association of Colored Women's Clubs. *A History of the Club Movement among the Colored Women of the United States of America*. 1902. Reprint, Washington, D.C.: National Association of Colored Women's Clubs, 1978.

Needell, Jeffrey D. *A Tropical Belle Epoque: Elite Culture and Society in Turn-of-the-Century Rio de Janeiro*. New York: Cambridge University Press, 1987.

Needham, Mary Master. *Folk Festivals: Their Growth and How to Give Them*. New York: B. W. Huebsch, 1912.

Nelson, Christina H. *Directly from China: Export Goods for the American Market, 1784–1930*. Salem: Peabody Museum of Salem, 1985.

Nesbitt, Florence. *Household Management*. New York: Russell Sage Foundation, 1918.

Neuhaus, Jessamyn. *Manly Meals and Mom's Home Cooking: Cookbooks and Gender in Modern America*. Baltimore: Johns Hopkins University Press, 2003.

Neverdon-Morton, Cynthia. *Afro-American Women of the South and the Advancement of the Race, 1895–1925*. Knoxville: University of Tennessee Press, 1989.

New England Grocer Office. *The Grocer's Companion and Merchant's Hand-Book*. Boston: Benjamin Johnson, Publisher, 1883.

Newman, Louise Michele. *White Women's Rights: The Racial Origins of Feminism in the United States*. New York: Oxford, 1999.

The 1902 Edition of the Sears Roebuck Catalogue. With an introduction by Cleveland Amory. New York: Bounty Books, 1969.

Ninkovich, Frank. *The United States and Imperialism*. Malden, Mass.: Blackwell Publishers, 2001.

Nolan, Mary. *Visions of Modernity: American Business and the Modernization of Germany.* New York: Oxford University Press, 1994.

Norton, Paul F. "Architecture." In *The Arts in America: The Nineteenth Century*, by Wendell D. Garrett, Paul F. Norton, Alan Gowans, and Joseph T. Butler, 39–174. New York: Charles Scribner's Sons, 1969.

Oberdeck, Kathryn J. *The Evangelist and the Impresario: Religion, Entertainment, and Cultural Politics in America, 1884–1914.* Baltimore: Johns Hopkins University Press, 1999.

O'Brien, Karen. *Narratives of Enlightenment: Cosmopolitan History from Voltaire to Gibbon.* Cambridge: Cambridge University Press, 1997.

O'Brien, Thomas F. *The Revolutionary Mission: American Enterprise in Latin America, 1900–1945.* Cambridge: Cambridge University Press, 1996.

Oettermann, Stephan. *The Panorama: History of a Mass Medium.* Trans. Deborah Lucas Schneider. New York: Zone Books, 1997.

Original Stereographs Catalogue No. 25. New York: Underwood and Underwood, 1905.

Ormsbee, Agnes Bailey. *The House Comfortable.* New York: Harper and Brothers, 1892.

Orlove, Benjamin, ed. *The Allure of the Foreign: Imported Goods in Postcolonial Latin America.* Ann Arbor: University of Michigan Press, 1997.

Orsi, Robert Anthony. *The Madonna of 115th Street: Faith and Community in Italian Harlem, 1880–1950.* New Haven: Yale University Press, 1985.

Orty, Pascal. "From Baudelaire to Duhamel: An Unlikely Antipathy." In *The Rise and Fall of Anti-Americanism: A Century of French Perception*, ed. Denis Lacorne, Jacques Rupnik, Marie-France Toinet, 42–54. Trans. Gerry Turner. 1986. New York: St. Martin's, 1990.

Øverland, Orm. *Immigrant Minds, American Identities: Making the United States Home, 1870–1930.* Urbana: University of Illinois Press, 2000.

Palmer, Mrs. Potter [Bertha]. *Addresses and Reports.* Chicago: Rand, McNally, 1894.

Parker, Alison M. *Purifying America: Women, Cultural Reform and Pro-Censorship Activism, 1873–1933.* Urbana: University of Illinois, 1997.

Parloa, Maria. *Miss Parloa's Kitchen Companion.* Boston: Estes and Lauriat, 1887.

Parmel, Pamela A. "Line, Color, Detail, Distinction, Individuality: A. & L. Tirocchi, Providence Dressmakers." In *From Paris to Providence: Fashion, Art, and the Tirocchi Dressmakers' Shop, 1915–1947*, ed. Susan Hay, 25–49. Providence: Rhode Island School of Design, 2000.

Parmele, Mary Platt. *A Short History of Rome and Italy.* Detroit: Published for the Bay View Reading Club by Charles Scribner's Sons, 1908.

———. *A Short History of Russia.* Detroit: Published for the Bay View Reading Club by Charles Scribner's Sons, 1904.

Parsons, Frank Alvah. *Interior Decoration: Its Principles and Practice*. New York: Doubleday, Page, and Co., 1916.

Pattison, Mary. *Principles of Domestic Engineering*. New York: Trow Press, 1915.

Pechin, Mary Shelley. *The 3-6-5 Cook Book for Use 365 Days in the Year*. Cleveland: The Helman-Taylor Co., 1899.

Peck, Ira, ed. *Nellie Bly's Book: Around the World in 72 Days*. Brookfield, Conn.: Twenty-first Century Books, 1998.

Peck, Mary Gray. *Carrie Chapman Catt: A Biography*. New York: H. W. Wilson Company, 1944.

Peiss, Kathy. *Cheap Amusements: Working Women and Leisure in Turn-of-the-Century New York*. Philadelphia: Temple University Press, 1986.

———. *Hope in a Jar: The Making of America's Beauty Culture*. New York: Metropolitan Books, 1998.

Pells, Richard. *Not Like Us: How Europeans Have Loved, Hated, and Transformed American Culture Since World War II*. New York: Basic Books, 1997.

Pelto, Gretel H., and Pertti J. Pelto. "Diet and Delocalization: Dietary Changes since 1750." In *Hunger and History: The Impact of Changing Food Production and Consumption Patterns on Society*, ed. Robert I. Rotberg and Theodore K. Rabb, 309–30. Cambridge: Cambridge University Press, 1983.

Pérez, Louis A., Jr. *The War of 1898: The United States and Cuba in History and Historiography*. Chapel Hill: University of North Carolina Press, 1998.

Perkins, Mrs. Cyrus E. "Influence of Art in Americanization." In *Americanization Programs*, 7–8. N.p.: General Federation of Women's Clubs [1919–20].

Perrot, Philippe. *Fashioning the Bourgeoisie: A History of Clothing in the Nineteenth Century*. Trans. Richard Bienvenu. Princeton: Princeton University Press, 1994.

Perry, Lewis. *Boats against the Current: American Culture Between Revolution and Modernity, 1820–1860*. New York: Oxford, 1993.

Pesman, Ros. *Duty Free: Australian Women Abroad*. Oxford: Oxford University Press, 1996.

Peyser, Thomas. *Utopia and Cosmopolis: Globalization in the Era of American Literary Realism*. Durham: Duke University Press, 1998.

Pilcher, Jeffrey M. "Recipes for *Patria*: Cuisine, Gender, and Nation in Nineteenth-Century Mexico." In *Recipes for Reading: Community Cookbooks, Stories, Histories*, ed. Anne L. Bower, 200–215. Amherst: University of Massachusetts Press, 1997.

Pillsbury, Richard. *From Boarding House to Bistro: The American Restaurant Then and Now*. Boston: Unwin Hyman, 1990.

———. *No Foreign Food: The American Diet in Time and Place*. Boulder: Westview Press, 1998.

Plesur, Milton. *America's Outward Thrust: Approaches to Foreign Affairs, 1865–1890*. DeKalb: Northern Illinois University Press, 1971.

Pletcher, David M. *The Diplomacy of Trade and Investment: American Economic Expansion in the Hemisphere, 1865–1900*. Columbia: University of Missouri Press, 1998.

Potter Family Collections. Sarasota: Ringling Museum of Art, 1963.

Pratt, Mary Louise. *Imperial Eyes: Travel Writing and Transculturation*. New York: Routledge, 1992.

Preson, Rebecca. "'The Scenery of the Torrid Zone': Imagined Travels and the Culture of Exotics in Nineteenth-Century British Gardens." In *Imperial Cities: Landscape, Display, and Identity*, ed. Felix Driver and David Gilbert, 194–211. Manchester: Manchester University Press, 1999.

Price, Sally. *Primitive Art in Civilized Places*. Chicago: University of Chicago Press, 1989.

Priddy, Bessie Leach. "Civics and Americanization." In *Americanization Programs*, 8–9. N.p.: General Federation of Women's Clubs [1919-20].

Priestman, Mabel Tuke. *Art and Economy in Home Decoration*. New York: John Lane, 1908.

Pulos, Arthur J. *American Design Ethic: A History of Industrial Design to 1940*. Cambridge: MIT Press, 1983.

Purdy, Daniel L. *The Tyranny of Elegance: Consumer Cosmopolitanism in the Era of Goethe*. Baltimore: Johns Hopkins University Press, 1998.

Quinn, Mary J. *Planning and Furnishing the Home*. New York: Harper and Brothers 1914.

Rafael, Vicente L. "Colonial Domesticity: White Women and United States Rule in the Philippines." *American Literature* 67 (Dec. 1995): 639–66.

———. *White Love and Other Events in Filipino History*. Durham: Duke University Press, 2000.

Rappaport, Erika Diane. *Shopping for Pleasure: Women in the Making of London's West End*. Princeton: Princeton University Press, 2000.

Register, Woody. *The Kid of Coney Island: Fred Thompson and the Rise of American Amusements*. New York: Oxford, 2001.

Reimers, D. M. *Unwelcome Strangers: American Identity and the Turn against Immigration*. New York: Columbia, 1998.

Renda, Mary A. *Taking Haiti: Military Occupation and the Culture of U.S. Imperialism, 1915–1940*. Chapel Hill: University of North Carolina Press, 2001.

Rhoads, William B. "The Colonial Revival and the Americanization of Immigrants." In *The Colonial Revival in America*, ed. Alan Axelrod, 341–61. New York: W. W. Norton, 1985.

Ricci, Elisa. "Women's Crafts." In *Peasant Art in Italy*, ed. Charles Holme, 17–32. London: The Studio: 1913.

Rice, Louise. *Dainty Dishes from Foreign Lands*. Chicago: A. C. McClurg & Co., 1911.

Richardson, Ethel. "A Study of One National Group." In *A Suggested Program for Americanization*, 20–21. N.p.: General Federation of Women's Clubs, [1918].

Rittenhouse, Mignon. *The Amazing Nellie Bly*. 1956. Reprint, Freeport, New York: Books for Libraries Press, 1971.

Robertson, Roland. "Mapping the Global Condition: Globalization as the Central Concept." In *Global Culture: Nationalism, Globalization and Modernity*, ed. Mike Featherstone, 15–30. London: Sage, 1990.

Rodgers, Daniel T. *Atlantic Crossings: Social Politics in a Progressive Age*. Cambridge: Belknap Press of Harvard University Press, 1998.

Rogin, Michael. *Blackface, White Noise: Jewish Immigrants in the Hollywood Melting Pot*. Berkeley: University of California Press, 1996.

Rosaldo, Renato. *Culture and Truth: The Remaking of Social Analysis*. Boston: Beacon Press, 1989.

———. "Imperialist Nostalgia." In *Culture and Truth: The Remaking of Social Analysis*, 68–87. 1989. Reprint, Boston: Beacon Press, 1993.

Rosenberg, Emily S. "Consuming Women: Images of Americanization in the 'American Century.'" *Diplomatic History* 23 (Summer 1999): 479–97.

———. *Financial Missionaries to the World: The Politics and Culture of Dollar Diplomacy, 1900–1930*. Cambridge: Harvard University Press, 1999.

———. *Spreading the American Dream: American Economic and Cultural Expansion, 1890–1945*. New York: Hill and Wang, 1982.

Ross, Ishbel. *Crusades and Crinolines: The Life and Times of Ellen Curtis Demorest and William Jennings Demorest*. New York: Harper and Row, 1963.

———. *Silhouette in Diamonds: The Life of Mrs. Potter Palmer*. New York: Arno Press, 1975.

Roth, Leland M. *American Architecture: A History*. Boulder: Westview Press, 2001.

Rothfels, Nigel. *Savages and Beasts: The Birth of the Modern Zoo*. Baltimore: John Hopkins University Press, 2002.

Rothschild, Emma. "Globalization and the Return of History." *Foreign Policy* 115 (Summer 1999): 106–16.

Ruane, Christine. "Clothes Shopping in Imperial Russia: The Development of a Consumer Culture." *Journal of Social History* 28 (Summer 1995): 765–82.

———. "Subjects into Citizens: The Politics of Clothing in Imperial Russia." In *Fashioning the Body Politic: Dress, Gender, Citizenship*, ed. Wendy Parkins, 49–70. New York: Oxford University Press, 2002.

Rudnick, Lois Palken. *Utopian Vistas: The Mabel Dodge Luhan House and the American Counterculture*. Albuquerque: University of New Mexico Press, 1996.

Ruiz, Vicki L. *From Out of the Shadows: Mexican Women in Twentieth-Century America*. New York: Oxford University Press, 1998.

Rupp, Leila J. *Worlds of Women: The Making of an International Women's Movement.* Princeton: Princeton University Press, 1997.

Rydell, Robert W. *All the World's a Fair: Visions of Empire at American International Expositions, 1876–1916.* Chicago: University of Chicago Press, 1984.

———. "The Culture of Imperial Abundance: World's Fairs in the Making of American Culture." In *Consuming Visions: Accumulation and Display of Goods in America, 1880–1920,* ed. Simon J. Bronner, 191–216. New York: W. W. Norton, 1989.

Rydell, Robert W., and Rob Kroes. *Buffalo Bill in Bologna: The Americanization of the World, 1869–1922.* Chicago: University of Chicago Press, 2005.

Saarinen, Aline B. *The Proud Possessors: The Lives, Times and Tastes of Some Adventurous American Art Collectors.* New York: Random House, 1958.

Said, Edward W. *Orientalism.* 1978. Reprint, New York: Vintage Books, 1979.

Sanchez, George J. "'Go After the Women': Americanization and the Mexican Immigrant Woman, 1915–1929." In *Unequal Sisters: A Multi-Cultural Reader in U.S. Women's History,* ed. Ellen Carol DuBois and Vicki L. Ruiz, 250–63. New York: Routledge, 1990.

Sand, Jordan. *House and Home in Modern Japan: Architecture, Domestic Space and Bourgeois Culture, 1880–1930.* Cambridge: Harvard University Press, 2003.

Sato, Tomoko, and Toshio Watanabe. "The Aesthetic Dialogue Examined: Japan and Britain, 1850–1930." In *Japan and Britain: An Aesthetic Dialogue, 1850–1930,* ed. Tomoko Sato and Toshio Watanabe, 14–53. London: Lund Humphries, 1991.

———, eds. *Japan and Britain: An Aesthetic Dialogue, 1850–1930.* London: Lund Humphries, 1991.

Saunders, Edith. *The Age of Worth: Couturier to the Empress Eugénie.* Bloomington: Indiana University Press, 1955.

Schivelbusch, Wolfgang. *Tastes of Paradise: A Social History of Spices, Stimulants, and Intoxicants.* Trans. David Jacobson. New York: Pantheon Books, 1992.

Schneer, Jonathan. *London 1900: The Imperial Metropolis.* New Haven: Yale University Press, 1999.

Schorman, Rob. *Selling Style: Clothing and Social Change at the Turn of the Century.* Philadelphia: University of Pennsylvania Press, 2003.

Schott, Linda K. *Reconstructing Women's Thoughts: The Women's International League for Peace and Freedom before World War II.* Stanford: Stanford University Press, 1997.

Schreier, Barbara A. *Becoming American Women: Clothing and the Jewish Immigrant Experience, 1880–1920.* Chicago: Chicago Historical Society, 1994.

Schriber, Mary Suzanne, ed. *Telling Travels: Selected Writings by Nineteenth-Century American Women Abroad.* Dekalb: Northern Illinois University Press, 1995.

Schulten, Susan. *The Geographical Imagination in America, 1880–1950*. Chicago: University of Chicago Press, 2001.

Schultz, James R. *The Romance of Small-Town Chautauquas*. Columbia: University of Missouri Press, 2002.

Scott, Anne Firor. *Natural Allies: Women's Associations in American History*. Urbana: University of Illinois Press, 1993.

Seale, William. *The Tasteful Interlude: American Interiors through the Camera's Eye, 1860–1917*. 2nd ed. Nashville: American Association for State and Local History, 1981.

Sears, John F. *Sacred Places: American Tourist Attractions in the Nineteenth Century*. New York: Oxford, 1989.

Sears, Roebuck, and Co. *Your Grocery Store*. Chicago: Sears, Roebuck, and Co., 1916.

Seigel, Jerrol. *Bohemian Paris: Culture, Politics, and the Boundaries of Bourgeois Life, 1830–1930*. New York: Viking, 1986.

Seller, Maxine. "The Education of the Immigrant Woman, 1900–1935." *Journal of Urban History* 4 (May 1978): 307–30.

Severa, Joan L. *Dressed for the Photographer: Ordinary Americans and Fashion, 1840–1900*. Kent, Ohio: Kent State University Press, 1995.

Shaffer, Marguerite S. "Seeing the Nature of America: The National Parks as National Assets, 1914–1929." In *Being Elsewhere: Tourism, Consumer Culture, and Identity in Modern Europe and North America*, ed. Shelley Baranowski and Ellen Furlough, 155–81. Ann Arbor: University of Michigan Press, 2001.

Sharf, Frederic A. "Bunkio Matsuki: Salem's Most Prominent Japanese Citizen." *Essex Institute Historical Collection* 129 (April 1993): 135–61.

Shah, Nayan. "Cleansing Motherhood: Hygiene and the Culture of Domesticity in San Francisco's Chinatown, 1875–1900." In *Gender, Sexuality and Colonial Modernities*, ed. Antoinette Burton, 19–34. London: Routledge, 1999.

Shammas, Carole. "Changes in English and Anglo-American Consumption from 1550–1800." In *Consumption and the World of Goods*, ed. John Brewer and Roy Porter, 177–205. New York: Routledge, 1993.

Shapiro, Henry D. *Appalachia on Our Mind: The Southern Mountains and Mountaineers in the American Consciousness, 1870–1920*. Chapel Hill: University of North Carolina Press, 1978.

Shapiro, Laura. *Perfection Salad: Women and Cooking at the Turn of the Century*. New York: Farrar, Straus, and Giroux, 1986.

Shaw, Marian. *World's Fair Notes: A Woman Journalist Views Chicago's 1893 Columbian Exposition*. N.p.: Pogo Press, 1992.

Sherman, Mrs. John D. "Conservation and Americanization." In *Americanization Programs*, 11. N.p.: General Federation of Women's Clubs, [1919–20].

Shi, David E. *Facing Facts: Realism in American Thought and Culture, 1850–1920*. New York: Oxford, 1995.

Shulman, Carrie V. *Favorite Dishes: A Columbian Autograph Souvenir Cookery Book*. 1893. Reprint, Urbana: University of Illinois Press, 2001.

Siegel, Beatrice. *Lillian Wald of Henry Street*. New York: Macmillan, 1983.

Silva, Noenoe K. *Aloha Betrayed: Native Hawaiian Resistance to American Colonialism*. Durham: Duke University Press, 2004.

Simmons, Amelia. *American Cookery*. 1796. Reprint, Grand Rapids: William B. Eerdmans, 1965.

Sinclair, Upton. *The Jungle*. New York: Doubleday, Page, and Co., 1906.

Sklar, Kathryn Kish. *Catherine Beecher: A Study in American Domesticity*. New Haven: Yale University Press, 1973.

Sloane, David Charles. *The Last Great Necessity: Cemeteries in American History*. Baltimore: Johns Hopkins University Press, 1991.

Slotkin, Richard. "Buffalo Bill's 'Wild West' and the Mythologization of the American Empire." In *Cultures of United States Imperialism*, ed. Amy Kaplan and Donald E. Pease, 164–81. Durham: Duke University Press, 1993.

Smith, Andrew F. *Pure Ketchup: A History of America's National Condiment with Recipes*. Columbia: University of South Carolina Press, 1996.

———. *The Tomato in America: Early History, Culture, and Cookery*. Urbana: University of Illinois Press, 2001.

Smith, Harold F. *American Travellers Abroad: A Bibliography of Accounts Published before 1900*. Carbondale-Edwardsville: Southern Illinois University Press, 1969.

Smith, Neil. *American Empire: Roosevelt's Geographer and the Prelude to Globalization*. Berkeley: University of California Press, 2003.

Snodgrass, Judith. *Presenting Japanese Buddhism to the West: Orientalism, Occidentalism, and the Columbian Exposition*. Chapel Hill: University of North Carolina Press, 2003.

The Sociable; or, One Thousand and One Home Amusements. New York: Dick and Fitzgerald, 1858.

Soderstrom, Mark. "Family Trees and Timber Rights: Albert E. Jenks, Americanization, and the Rise of Anthropology at the University of Minnesota." *Journal of the Gilded Age and Progressive Era* 3 (April 2004): 176–204.

Sokolov, Raymond. *Why We Eat What We Eat: How the Encounter between the New World and the Old Changed the Way Everyone on the Planet Eats*. New York: Summit Books, 1991.

Solit, Karen D. *History of the United States Botanic Garden, 1816–1991*. Washington, D.C.: Government Printing Office, 1993.

Some Pictures of Quaint Things Which Are Sold at the Sign of the "Popular Shop." New York: Joseph P. McHugh, 1898.

Spang, Rebecca L. "All the World's a Restaurant: On the Global Gastronomics of Tourism and Travel." In *Food in Global History*, ed. Raymond Grew, 79–91. Boulder: Westview Press, 1999.

Spence, Jonathan D. *The Chan's Great Continent: China in Western Minds.* New York: W. W. Norton, 1998.

Spofford, Harriet Prescott. *Art Decoration Applied to Furniture.* New York: Harper and Bros., 1877.

Spooner, Brian. "Weavers and Dealers: The Authenticity of an Oriental Carpet." In *The Social Life of Things: Commodities in Cultural Perspective*, ed. Arjun Appadurai, 195–235. Cambridge: Cambridge University Press, 1986.

Stage, Sarah, and Virginia B. Vincenti, eds. *Rethinking Home Economics: Women and the History of a Profession.* Ithaca: Cornell University Press, 1997.

Standard Guide to Los Angeles, San Diego, and the Panama-California Exposition. San Francisco: North American Press Association, 1914.

State Commission of Immigration and Housing of California. *A Manual for Home Teachers.* Sacramento: California State Printing Office, 1919.

Stead, W. T. *The Americanisation of the World.* London: Review of Reviews, 1902.

Steele, Valerie. *Paris Fashion: A Cultural History.* 2nd ed. New York: Berg, 1998.

Steffensen-Bruce, Ingrid A. *Marble Palaces, Temples of Art: Art Museums, Architecture, and American Culture, 1890–1930.* Lewisburg: Bucknell University Press, 1998.

Stern Brothers Fashion Catalogue. Fall and Winter 1900–1901. New York: Stern Brothers, 1900.

Steward, Jill. "Tourism in Late Imperial Austria: The Development of Tourist Cultures and their Associated Images of Place." In *Being Elsewhere: Tourism, Consumer Culture, and Identity in Modern Europe and North America*, ed. Shelley Baranowski and Ellen Furlough, 108–34. Ann Arbor: University of Michigan Press, 2001.

Stocking, George W., Jr., ed. *Objects and Others: Essays on Museums and Material Culture.* Madison: University of Wisconsin Press, 1985.

———. *Race, Culture, and Evolution: Essays in the History of Anthropology.* New York: Free Press, 1968.

Stoddard, John L. *China.* Chicago: Belford, Middlebrook and Co., 1897.

———. *Japan.* Chicago: Belford, Middlebrook and Co., 1897.

———. *John L. Stoddard's Lectures.* Vol. 1, 1897. Chicago: Geo. L. Shuman and Co., 1918.

———. *John L. Stoddard's Lectures.* Vol. 1, 1897. Rev. ed. Chicago: Geo. L. Shuman and Co., 1925.

———. *John L. Stoddard's Lectures.* Vol. 3, 1897. Chicago: Geo. L. Shuman and Co., 1917.

———. *John L. Stoddard's Lectures.* Vol. 5, 1898. Boston: Balch Brothers Co., 1899.

———. *John L. Stoddard's Lectures.* Vol. 7, 1898. Chicago: Geo. L. Shuman and Co., 1917.

———. *John L. Stoddard's Lectures.* Supplementary volumes, nos. 1–4. Chicago: Geo. L. Shuman and Co., 1917.

———. *Portfolio of Photographs.* Chicago: Educational Publishing Co., 1893.

———. *Red-Letter Days Abroad.* Boston: James R. Osgood and Co., 1884.

———. *Scenic America: The Beauties of the Western Hemisphere.* Chicago: The Werner Co., [189?].

———. *Sunny Lands of the Eastern Continent: A Pictorial Journey through the Tropical Countries of the Eastern Hemisphere.* New York: The Werner Company, 1899.

———. *A Trip around the World.* Chicago: The Werner Co., 1894.

Stolke, Verena. "The Labors of Coffee in Latin America: The Hidden Charm of Family Labor and Self-Provisioning." In *Coffee, Society, and Power in Latin America,* ed. William Roseberry, Lowell Gudmundson, and Mario Samper Kutschbach, 65–93. Baltimore: Johns Hopkins University Press, 1995.

Stoll, Steven. *The Fruits of Natural Advantage: Making the Industrial Countryside in California.* Berkeley: University of California Press, 1998.

Stowe, William W. *European Travel in Nineteenth-Century American Culture.* Princeton: Princeton University Press, 1994.

Strasser, Susan. *Never Done: A History of American Housework.* New York: Pantheon Books, 1982.

Strauss, David. *Menace in the West: The Rise of French Anti-Americanism in Modern Times.* Westport, Conn.: Greenwood Press, 1978.

Strout, Cushing. *The American Image of the Old World.* New York: Harper and Row, 1963.

A Succinct Description of the Great Cycloramic Illusion, Paris by Night. Chicago: Evening Journal Book and Job Printing House, 1874.

A Suggested Program for Americanization. N.p.: General Federation of Women's Clubs, [1918].

Sweetman, John. *The Oriental Obsession: Islamic Inspiration in British and American Art and Architecture, 1500–1920.* Cambridge: Cambridge University Press, 1988.

Sweetser, Delight. *One Way Round the World.* Indianapolis: The Bowen-Merrill Company, 1899.

Taaffe, Martha Coffin. *The History of the Missouri Federation of Women's Clubs.* N.p.: Missouri Federation of Women's Clubs, 1946.

Takaki, Ronald. *Strangers from a Different Shore: A History of Asian Americans.* New York: Penguin Books, 1989.

Tanen, Ted M. G. "Festivals and Diplomacy." In *Exhibiting Cultures: The Poetics and Politics of Museum Display,* ed. Karp and Steven D. Lavine, 366–72. Washington, D.C.: Smithsonian Institution Press, 1991.

Taylor, Lonn, and Dessa Bokides. *New Mexican Furniture, 1600–1940: The Origins, Survival, and Revival of Furniture Making in the Hispanic Southwest.* Santa Fe: Museum of New Mexico Press, 1987.

Tchen, John Kuo Wei. *New York before Chinatown: Orientalism and the Shaping of American Culture, 1776–1882.* Baltimore: Johns Hopkins University Press, 1999.

Theophano, Janet. "Home Cooking: Boston Baked Beans and Sizzling Rice Soup as Recipes for Pride and Prejudice." In *Kitchen Culture in America: Popular Representations of Food, Gender, and Race,* ed. Sherrie A. Innes, 139–56. Philadelphia: University of Pennsylvania Press, 2001.

Third Biennial of the General Federation of Women's Clubs, Official Proceedings. Louisville: John P. Morton and Co., 1896.

Thompson, Kristin. *Exporting Entertainment: America in the World Film Market, 1907–34.* London: British Film Institute, 1985.

Throop, Lucy Abbot. *Furnishing the Home of Good Taste.* New York: McBride, Nast & Co., 1912.

Thwaite, B. H. "The American Invasion; or, England's Commercial Danger." Wilmington, N.C.: Hugh MacRae and Co., 1902.

Tiersten, Lisa. *Marianne in the Market: Envisioning Consumer Society in Fin-de-Siècle France.* Berkeley: University of California Press, 2001.

Tomes, Nancy. *The Gospel of Germs: Men, Women, and the Microbe in American Life.* Cambridge: Harvard University Press, 1998.

Tomes, Robert. *The Bazar Book of Decorum.* New York: Harper and Brothers, 1870.

Tomlinson, John. *Cultural Imperialism: An Introduction.* Baltimore: Johns Hopkins University Press, 1991.

Topik, Steven C. "Coffee." In *The Second Conquest of Latin America: Coffee, Henequen, and Oil during the Export Boom, 1850–1930,* ed. Steven C. Topik and Allen Wells, 37–84. Austin: University of Texas Press, 1998.

Topik, Steven C., and Allen Wells, eds. *The Second Conquest of Latin America: Coffee, Henequen, and Oil during the Export Boom, 1850–1930.* Austin: University of Texas Press, 1998.

Toussaint-Samat, Maguelonne. *A History of Food.* Trans. Anthea Bell. Cambridge: Blackwell Publishers, 1992.

Towner, John. *An Historical Geography of Recreation and Tourism in the Western World, 1540–1940.* New York: John Wiley & Sons, 1996.

Troy, Nancy J. *Modernism and the Decorative Arts in France: Art Nouveau to Le Corbusier.* New Haven: Yale, 1991.

Tuchman, Gayle, and Harry Gene Levine. "New York Jews and Chinese Food: The Social Construction of an Ethnic Pattern." In *The Taste of American Place: A Reader on Regional and Ethnic Foods,* ed. Barbara G. Shortridge and James R. Shortridge, 163–84. New York: Rowman and Littlefield, 1998.

Tucker, Richard P. *Insatiable Appetite: The United States and the Ecological Degradation of the Tropical World*. Berkeley: University of California Press, 2000.

Turner, Louis, and John Ash. *The Golden Hordes: International Tourism and the Pleasure Periphery*. New York: St. Martin's Press, 1976.

Tweed, Thomas A. *The American Encounter with Buddhism, 1844–1912: Victorian Culture and the Limits of Dissent*. Bloomington: Indiana University Press, 1992.

Tyrrell, Ian. "American Exceptionalism in an Age of International History." *American Historical Review* 96 (Oct. 1991): 1031–73.

―――. *Woman's World, Woman's Empire: The Woman's Christian Temperance Union in International Perspective, 1880–1930*. Chapel Hill: University of North Carolina Press, 1991.

Underwood and Underwood. *Catalogue 28 — The Underwood Travel System*. New York: Underwood and Underwood, n.d.

Vaillant, Derek. *Sounds of Reform: Progressivism and Music in Chicago, 1873–1935*. Chapel Hill: University of North Carolina Press, 2003.

Van de Wetering, Maxine. "The Popular Concept of 'Home' in Nineteenth-Century America." *Journal of American Studies* 18 (Apr. 1984): 5–28.

Van Nuys, Frank. *Americanizing the West: Race, Immigrants, and Citizenship, 1890–1930*. Lawrence: University Press of Kansas, 2002.

Van Rensselaer, Mrs. M. G. "The Development of American Homes." In *Household Art*, ed. Candace Wheeler, 35–55. New York: Harper and Brothers, 1893.

Vantine's Catalog. New York: A. A. Vantine, 1914.

Van Voris, Jacqueline. *Carrie Chapman Catt: A Public Life*. New York: Feminist Press at the City University of New York, 1987.

Varney, Almon C. *Our Homes and Their Adornments*. Detroit: J. C. Chilton, 1882.

Vaught, David. *Cultivating California: Growers, Specialty Crops, and Labor, 1875–1920*. Baltimore: Johns Hopkins University Press, 1999.

Veblen, Thorstein. *The Theory of the Leisure Class: An Economic Study of Institutions*. New York: Modern Library, 1899.

Visitor's Guide to the Centennial Exhibition and Philadelphia. Philadelphia: J. B. Lippincott, 1876.

Vollmer, William A., ed. *A Book of Distinctive Interiors*. New York: McBride, Nast & Co., 1912.

Wade, Edwin L. "The Ethnic Art Market in the American Southwest, 1880–1980." In *Objects and Others: Essays on Museums and Material Culture*, ed. George W. Stocking Jr., 167–91. Madison: University of Wisconsin Press, 1985.

Wagnleitner, Reinhold. *Coca-Colonization and the Cold War: The Cultural Mission of the United States in Austria after the Second World War*. Trans. Diana M. Wolf. Chapel Hill: University of North Carolina Press, 1994.

Wagnleitner, Reinhold, and Elaine Tyler May, eds. *"Here, There and Everywhere": The*

Foreign Politics of American Popular Culture. Hanover: University Press of New England, 2000.

Wald, Lillian D. "New Americans and Our Policies." In *Immigration and Americanization: Selected Readings*, ed. Philip Davis and Bertha Schwartz, 427–39. Boston: Ginn and Co., 1920.

Wallace, Irving. Introduction to *The Man Who Photographed the World: Burton Holmes Travelogues, 1886–1938*, ed. Genoa Caldwell, 11–22. New York: Harry N. Abrams, 1977.

Walsh, Margaret. "The Democratization of Fashion: The Emergence of the Women's Dress Pattern Industry." *Journal of American History* 66 (Sept. 1979): 299–313.

Walton, Whitney. *France at the Crystal Palace: Bourgeois Taste and Artisan Manufacture in the Nineteenth Century*. Berkeley: University of California Press, 1992.

Wanamaker's Catalog. Philadelphia: John Wanamaker's, 1908.

Ward, Artemas. *The Grocer's Encyclopedia*. New York: The James Kempster Printing Co., 1911.

Ware, John F. W. *Home Life: What It Is, and What It Needs*. Boston: Wm. V. Spencer, 1866.

Weatherford, Jack. *Indian Givers: How the Indians of the Americas Transformed the World*. New York: Fawcett Columbine, 1988.

Weber, Charlotte. "Unveiling Scheherazde: Feminist Orientalism in the International Alliance of Women, 1911–1950." *Feminist Studies* 27 (Spring 2001): 125–57.

Weigley, Emma Seifrit. *Sarah Tyson Rorer: The Nation's Instructress in Dietetics and Cookery*. Philadelphia: American Philosophical Society, 1977.

Weiss, Bernard J., ed. *American Education and the European Immigrant: 1840–1940*. Urbana: University of Illinois Press, 1982.

Welke, Barbara Young. *Recasting American Liberty: Gender, Race, Law, and the Railroad Revolution, 1865–1920*. Cambridge: Cambridge University Press, 2001.

Wexler, Laura. *Tender Violence: Domestic Visions in an Age of U.S. Imperialism*. Chapel Hill: University of North Carolina Press, 2000.

Wheeler, Candace. *Principles of Home Decoration with Practical Examples*. New York: Doubleday, Page, 1908.

Whisnant, David E. *All That Is Native and Fine: The Politics of Culture in an American Region*. Chapel Hill: University of North Carolina Press, 1983.

White, Deborah Gray. *Too Heavy a Load: Black Women in Defense of Themselves, 1894–1994*. New York: W. W. Norton, 1999.

White, George Cary. "Social Settlements and Immigrant Neighbors, 1886–1914." *Social Service Review* 33 (March 1959): 55–66.

White, Sallie Joy. *Housekeepers and Home-Makers*. Boston: Jordan, Marsh & Co., 1888.

White, Shane, and Graham White. *Stylin': African American Expressive Culture from its Beginnings to the Zoot Suit*. Ithaca: Cornell, 1998.

White, Mrs. True Worthy. "Americanization as Related to Literature and Library Extension." In *Americanization Programs*, 15–17. N.p.: General Federation of Women's Clubs [1919–20].

The Widow of an American Diplomat. *Intimacies of Court and Society: An Unconventional Narrative of Unofficial Days*. New York: Dodd, Mead, and Co., 1912.

Wilcox, Estelle Woods. *Buckeye Cookery and Practical Housekeeping*. Marysville, Ohio: Buckeye Publishing Co., 1877.

Wilk, Richard R. "Food and Nationalism: The Origins of 'Belizean Food.'" In *Food Nations: Selling Taste in Consumer Societies*, ed. Warren Belasco and Philip Scranton, 67–89. New York: Routledge, 2002.

Wilkins, Mira. *The Emergence of Multinational Enterprise: American Business Abroad from the Colonial Era to 1914*. Cambridge: Harvard University Press, 1970.

———. *The History of Foreign Investment in the United States to 1914*. Cambridge: Harvard University Press, 1989.

Wilkins, Mira, and Frank Ernest Hill. *American Business Abroad: Ford on Six Continents*. Detroit: Wayne State University Press, 1964.

Willett, Ralph. *The Americanization of Germany, 1945–1949*. London: Routledge, 1989.

Williams, Henry T., and Mrs. C. S. Jones. *Beautiful Homes*. New York: Henry T. Williams, 1878.

Williams, Jacqueline B. *The Way We Ate: Pacific Northwest Cooking, 1843–1900*. Pullman: Washington State University Press, 1996.

Williams, Susan. *Savory Suppers and Fashionable Feasts: Dining in Victorian America*. New York: Pantheon Books, 1985.

Williams, William Appleman. *The Roots of the Modern American Empire: A Study of the Growth and Shaping of Social Consciousness in a Marketplace Society*. New York: Random House, 1969.

Wills, John E., Jr. "European Consumption and Asian Production in the Seventeenth and Eighteenth Centuries." *Consumption and the World of Goods*, ed. John Brewer and Roy Porter, 133–47. New York: Routledge, 1993.

Wilson, Benjamin Franklin, III. *The Parthenon at Athens, Greece and at Nashville, Tennessee*. Nashville: John T. Benson Co., 1941.

Wilson, Elizabeth. *Adorned in Dreams: Fashion and Modernity*. 1985. Rev. ed. New Brunswick: Rutgers University Press, 2003.

Wilson, Lucy Langdon Williams, ed. *Handbook of Domestic Science and Household Arts for Use in Elementary Schools*. New York: Macmillan, 1900.

Wilson, Richard Guy. "Cultural Conditions." In *The American Renaissance, 1876–1917*, 27–37. New York: Brooklyn Museum, 1979.

Winslow, Helen M., ed. *Official Register and Directory of the Women's Clubs in America*. Boston: Helen M. Winslow, 1903.

———. *Official Register and Directory of Women's Clubs in America.* Shirley, Mass.: Helen M. Winslow, 1918.

Withey, Lynne. *Grand Tours and Cooks Tours: A History of Leisure Travel, 1750 to 1915.* New York: William Morrow, 1997.

Wolman, Paul. *Most Favored Nation: The Republican Revisionists and U.S. Tariff Policy, 1897–1912.* Chapel Hill: University of North Carolina Press, 1992.

Women of the Central Presbyterian Church of Downington, Pennsylvania. *Housekeeper's Favorites.* Oxford, Pa.: The News Print, 1910.

The Wonder Book. New York: A. A. Vantine and Co., n.d.

Wonders, Karen. "Habitat Dioramas: Illusions of Wilderness in Museums of Natural History." Acta Universitatis Upsaliensis. *Figura Nova Series* 25. Uppsala: Almqvist and Wiksell, 1993.

Wood, Gordon S. *The Creation of the American Republic, 1776–1787.* New York: W. W. Norton, 1969.

———. *The Radicalism of the American Revolution.* New York: Vintage, 1991.

Wood, Mary. "Legislation and Americanization." In *Americanization Programs,* 14–15. N.p.: General Federation of Women's Clubs, [1919–20].

Woodward, C. Vann. *The Old World's New World.* New York: Oxford University Press, 1991.

Woody, Howard. "International Postcards: Their History, Production, and Distribution (circa 1895 to 1915)." In *Delivering Views: Distant Cultures in Early Postcards,* ed. Christraud M. Geary and Virginia-Lee Webb, 13–45. Washington, D.C.: Smithsonian Institution Press, 1998.

Woollacott, Angela. "'All This Is the Empire, I Told Myself': Australian Women's Voyages 'Home' and the Articulation of Colonial Whiteness." *American Historical Review* 102 (Oct. 1997): 1003–29.

Woolson, Abba Goold, ed. *Dress-Reform: A Series of Lectures Delivered in Boston.* Boston: Roberts Brothers, 1871.

Wright, Gwendolyn. *Moralism and the Model Home: Domestic Architecture and Cultural Conflict in Chicago, 1873–1913.* Chicago: University of Chicago Press, 1980.

Wright, Richardson, ed. *Inside the House of Good Taste.* New York: McBride, Nast and Co., 1915.

Wyman, Mark. *Round-Trip to America: The Immigrants Return to Europe, 1880–1930.* Ithaca: Cornell University Press, 1993.

Yarwood, Doreen. *European Costume: 4000 Years of Fashion.* New York: Larousse and Co., 1975.

Yoshihara, Mari. *Embracing the East: White Women and American Orientalism.* New York: Oxford University Press, 2003.

Zboray, Ronald J. *A Fictive People: Antebellum Economic Development and the American Reading Public.* New York: Oxford University Press, 1993.

Zboray, Ronald J., and Mary Saracino Zboray. "Between 'Crockery-dom' and Barnum: Boston's Chinese Museum, 1845–47." *American Quarterly* 56 (June 2004): 271–307.

Zeiler, Thomas W. "Just Do It! Globalization for Diplomatic Historians." *Diplomatic History* 25 (Fall 2001): 529–51.

Zelinsky, Wilbur. "You Are Where You Eat." In *The Taste of American Place: A Reader on Regional and Ethnic Foods*, ed. Barbara G. Shortridge and James R. Shortridge, 243–50. New York: Rowman and Littlefield, 1998.

Index

Campbell's Soup Company, 115

Chamberlain, South Dakota, Travel Club, 159–60, 198, 203, 275

Chautauqua Literary and Scientific Circle, 162, 166, 173, 175, 180

Chili, 108, 114, 115, 119, 146

Chinatowns, 23, 118, 138, 181, 313 (n. 135)

Chinoiserie, 4, 17–19, 53. *See also* Cultural production and goods—Chinese

Chop suey, 108, 118, 142, 143, 144, 146, 147

Citizenship, 10, 38, 211, 237, 255. *See also* Pluralism

Civilizational distinctions, 5; and interior decoration, 36, 39–42, 55; and fashion, 80–87, 90–92, 103–4; and cuisine, 124–35; and travel, 187, 190; and immigrant gifts, 220. *See also* Racial distinctions, global; Western civilization

Class distinctions: and interior decoration, 14, 41, 53–55, 57–58; and fashion, 61–62, 65, 67, 71–86, 93–95, 99; and cooking, 113, 120, 150; and travel, 158–60, 172, 184–88, 200; and immigrant gifts, 230–31, 235

Clothing, folk: masquerade costumes, 7, 37, 99, 137–49; ethnic dress, 61, 80–87, 92, 100, 168–245 passim; elements in Paris fashion, 65–67, 88–90, 94–95, 179. *See also* Cultural production and goods; Fashion, Paris; Kimonos

Coffee, 109, 110, 112, 116, 117, 140, 142, 143, 146, 177; production of, 121; improper use of, 130; cards from Arbuckle Brothers, 168

Colonial revival, 39–41, 43, 46, 54, 142

Consumers' imperium, 11–12, 252–55; and imported consumer goods, 22;

and fashionable world, 58, 104; and culinary geographies, 111, 113, 120–21, 134, 151; and tourist mentality, 166, 183, 188, 190, 198, 200, 208; appropriative tendencies of, 212, 217, 240, 245

Consumption, 8–12, 251–55; environmental implications of, 5, 45, 113, 121; and international relations, 11, 54, 189; decoration-related, 13–56; and modernity, 35, 49, 70–71, 82–87, 103, 149; and whiteness, 40, 80, 91, 99–100, 186–88, 200; fashion-related, 67–104; culinary, 109–51; touristic, 154–208, 245; of immigrant cultural production, 212–49. *See also* Consumers' imperium; Cultural production and goods; Decoration, interior; Fashion, Paris; Food and cooking; Immigrant gifts; Imports into United States; Shopping; Travel

Cosey corners, 14, 16–17, 24, 26, 34, 39, 51, 53–55, 138, 142, 240, 253

Cosmopolitan Club, 192, 244

Cosmopolitanism, 6–12, 253–55; and distinctions (racial, national, class, and civilizational), 14, 41–56, 67, 71–87, 90–95, 99–104, 113, 120, 124–35, 148–50, 184–88, 200, 230–31, 255; and interior decoration, 14–38, 43–56, 195, 241; opposition to, 21, 33, 37–43, 204–5, 211; and modernity, 35, 49, 70–71, 82–87, 103, 149; and popular geography, 35, 206; and nationalism, 54–55, 95, 101–4, 220–41; and fashion, 71–80, 88–92, 98, 101–4, 243; culinary, 105–21, 133–51, 222, 224, 228, 235, 243; travel-related, 187–88, 204–8; and immigrant gifts, 212–

94, 288 (n. 52); and world's fairs, 46, 49, 85, 177–79; and culture of travel, 49, 175–79, 194–96, 244; of harems, 51–52; and dress, 70–71, 80–87; as counterpoint to high society writing, 92; of immigrants, 233–35. *See also* Geography, popular

Exceptionalism, U.S., 3–5, 102–3

Exports, U.S., 1–5, 48, 61, 63–64, 129, 131, 211–12, 247, 251

Fairs, fund-raising, 138–43, 180, 222, 228

Farrar, Charles, 164–65, 188, 190

Fashion, Paris, 9, 142; and nationalism, 57–58, 74, 99–104; and imagined communities, 58, 67–80, 97–104; exclusionary functions of, 58, 71–87, 90–99, 104; cosmopolitanism of, 58–80, 88–92, 98, 101–4, 243; and U.S. industry, 59–64; and immigrants, 60–62, 138; and African American women, 61–62; and class distinctions, 61–62, 65, 67, 71–86, 93–95, 99; appropriative nature of, 65–67, 87–90, 94–95, 103; and Orientalism, 66, 87–90, 95–100; aristocratic connotations of, 72–80, 91, 98–99; and high society gossip, 73–80, 92, 101; and actresses, 74–75, 78; critiques of, 76, 85–86, 99–102; and racial distinctions, 76–77, 80–82, 86, 90, 92–95, 99–100; and civilizational distinctions, 80–87, 90–92, 103–4; and travel, 82, 90–91, 102; as means of asserting power, 90–91, 100–101; and imperialism, 91, 95–97. *See also* Clothing, folk; Cultural production and goods; Kimonos; Lingerie; Silk

Fictive travel. *See* Travel—fictive

Fish, Elizabeth, 159

Folk traditions. *See* Arts and crafts of homelands; Clothing, folk; Dance: folk; Handicrafts; Music, folk

Food and cooking, 10, 105–52; and U.S. production, 2, 106, 111–13, 115, 118, 129, 131; and nationalism, 105–6, 122, 127–34, 149–50; and cosmopolitanism, 105–21, 133–51, 222, 224, 228, 235, 243; and imperialism, 106, 114–15, 120–21, 148; imported items for, 106–15, 118–22, 128–29, 142–45, 151; and particular appeal of French cuisine, 107; and popular geography, 108, 111–51; and class distinction, 113, 120, 150; and travel, 113–14, 117–18, 130, 145; and immigrants, 115–22, 130, 147, 149–50; and home economics, 122–24, 130, 133–34, 149; and racial distinctions, 124–25, 131, 133, 148; as determinant of identity, 124–33; and civilizational distinction, 124–35; and etiquette, 126–27, 132, 141; and contamination scares, 128–29; and foreign entertainments, 135–48. *See also* Chili; Chop suey; Coffee; Cultural production and goods; Curry; Entertainments, foreign; Fairs, fund-raising; Macaroni; Restaurants; Sugar; Tea

Gender: and foreign relations, 10; of goods and cultural production, 32, 41, 51, 108, 120; and aristocratic display, 77; and geography, 90–91, 123–24; and nationalism, 102–3; and travel, 186–88, 204–5

General Federation of Women's Clubs (GFWC), 156, 158, 185, 186, 191, 205–38 passim. *See also* Travel clubs

of, 219–20; and social distinctions, 219–20, 229–31, 235; and women's clubs, 222–38 passim; and educators, 225–26; and librarians, 226; and antimodernism, 231, 241–42, 245–49; and internationalism, 237–40; and imperialism, 239, 247; and consumerist sensibilities, 240–45; and generational reconciliation, 245; and nostalgia, 249

Immigrants: Americanization of, 4, 6, 21, 38, 61, 122, 150, 209–12, 217, 220–40, 245–49; and immigrant gifts, 6, 209–40, 246–49; as servants, 7, 15, 38, 116, 130, 138, 150, 236; and U.S. domesticity, 15, 38, 54, 55; as vendors, 23, 24, 118–19, 147, 240; and fashion, 60–62; and food and cooking, 115–22, 130, 147, 149–50; and foreign entertainments, 139; and fictive travel, 159, 180–82, 194, 201, 243–44

Immigration, 40; restriction of, 4, 20–21, 90, 198, 200, 210

Imperialism, 12; cultural, 2, 211; and decoration, 14, 43, 46, 48–55; critiques of, 37, 41–42, 55, 99, 101, 198; and fashion, 91, 95; and food and cooking, 106, 114–15, 120–21, 148; and travel, 170, 178–79, 182–83, 198, 201; and immigrant gifts, 239, 247. *See also* British Empire; Consumers' imperium; Empire, secondhand
—U.S., 2–4, 8, 11, 95, 211, 247, 252–55; in Philippines, 21, 142, 154, 170–71, 172, 175, 201–2, 249; formal, 95–97, 114–15, 133, 142, 148, 170, 172, 175, 179, 201–2, 203; in Puerto Rico, 96–97, 211; in Panama, 115; informal, 115, 121, 188, 197, 212, 251. *See also* Buy-in, imperial; Consumers' imperium; Em-

pire, secondhand; Nostalgia; Spanish-American War

Imperialist nostalgia. *See* Nostalgia

Imports into United States, 11–12, 251–55; decoration-related, 13–54, 285 (n. 27); fashion-related, 59–62, 64, 87–88, 91–99, 305 (n. 18); food related, 106–15, 118–22, 128–29, 142–45, 151. *See also* Cultural production and goods; Trade

Ingersoll, Agnes, 165, 193

Interior decorators, professional, 25, 26, 33, 41. *See also* Decoration, interior

International Institutes, 116, 150, 222–25, 228, 229, 235, 237, 239, 243

Internationalism, 148, 206, 223, 237–40, 255

International relations, 3, 10–11, 54, 189, 197–99, 202, 252, 255. *See also* Political economy, international

Kennicott, Carol, 6, 12, 33

Kimonos, 66, 88–89, 140

Knoblauch, Edward, 97–99

Labor, conditions of, 37, 44–46, 50–51, 93, 121–22, 210, 215. *See also* Production; Workers

Lewistown Tourist Club, 184, 187, 192, 195, 200, 203, 205

Librarians, 7, 164, 175, 226, 233

Lili'uokalani (queen of Hawaii), 71, 85

Lingerie, 88–90, 95

Localism: denigration of, 33, 35, 48–49, 80–87, 95, 103, 149, 151, 187–88; of antebellum food supply, 106; ethnography of, 123; of clubwomen, 201, 205–6; and nationalism, 237, 241, 243; and over-Americanization, 247–48. *See also* Provincialism, U.S.

34, 37, 47, 51; English, 13; Flemish, 13; French, 13; German, 15, 43; Indian, 33, 34, 53, 179; Italian, 15, 179; Japanese, 16, 30, 33, 43, 141, 179; Moorish, 13, 14, 34, 53, 179; Native American, 16; Norwegian, 16; Orientalist, 14, 33, 34, 37, 39, 50–54, 141, 142, 179; Persian, 179; Russian, 15; Scandinavian, 15; Spanish, 13, 15, 43; Turkish, 34, 38, 51, 53, 179. *See also* Cosey corners

Tourism. *See* Travel

Tourist Club of Minneapolis, 158–60, 173, 186, 190–91, 192, 194, 195, 204

Tourist mentality, 7, 10, 155, 190–205, 243, 245, 253; and commodification of world, 183, 199–200

Trade, 17, 43–46, 50, 54, 92, 106, 111–13, 120–22, 252; data on, 22, 63–64, 91, 95, 110. *See also* Exports, U.S.; Imports into United States

Travel: educational value of, 7; and decoration, 21–26, 28, 33–35, 42, 44, 49, 59; and shopping, 21–26, 34, 44, 70, 173, 197; as conducive to cosmopolitanism, 24; and fashion, 82, 90–91, 102; and food and cooking, 113–14, 117–18, 130, 145; enabling developments, 170–72, 197; obstacles to, 200; as professional credential, 243

—fictive, 10; and exotic interiors, 19, 53; and lectures, 90–91, 153, 157, 161–66, 173, 174, 176, 190, 317 (n. 33); and foreign entertainments and fund-raising fairs, 135–48, 180; visual component of, 143, 155, 161–65, 173–76, 226; and women's travel clubs, 154–65, 183–208; and culture of travel, 155, 165–208, 243–46; and popular geography, 155, 167, 173–85, 188–206; and tourist

mentality, 155, 190–205, 243, 245, 253; and class distinction, 158–60, 172, 184–88, 200; and racial distinction, 159, 200; and gender transgression, 160, 186–87, 204–8; and dissatisfaction with domesticity, 161; as preparation for real travel, 161, 184–86, 193; and moving pictures, 162, 176–77; and print culture, 166–68, 171–72; and material culture, 168, 172; and travel industry, 168–71, 188; and stereopticons, 173–74; and stereoscopes, 174–75; and cycloramic pictures, 175, 180; and world's fairs and exhibits, 177–79; and retail establishments, 179; and restaurants, 179, 182; and immigrant cultural production, 180–82, 218, 224, 227–28, 231, 243–46; and built environment, 182; and imperialism, 182–83; and cultural literacy, 185–86; and cosmopolitanism, 187–88, 204–8; and nationalism, 188–89, 200, 202–4; and civilizational distinction, 200; and empowerment, 200. *See also* Elmendorf, Dwight L.; Farrar, Charles; Holmes, Burton; Stoddard, John; Theme rooms; Travel clubs; Travel destinations, real and fictive

Travel clubs, 10, 35, 145–46, 154–65, 171–72, 183–208; criticisms of, 204–5. *See also* Bay View Reading Circle; Chamberlain, South Dakota, Travel Club; Cosmopolitan Club; Heliades Club; Hyde Park Travel Club; Lewistown Tourist Club; McGregor Tourist Club; Tourist Club of Minneapolis

Travel destinations, real and fictive

—Africa, 35, 157, 176; Algeria, 49, 173,

177; Barbary Coast, 201; Congo, 191; Dahomey, 177; Egypt, 22, 32, 49, 114, 164, 175, 176, 177, 179, 192; Liberia, 124–25; Madagascar, 191; Morocco, 195, 198; Sahara, 174; South Africa, 23, 173, 179; Zanzibar, 90–91, 191
—Arctic, 174
—Around the world, 142–44, 153–55, 161–64, 168–93 passim, 207, 243
—Australia and New Zealand, 176, 191
—Caribbean, 168, 203; Cuba, 175, 179; Haiti, 191; Jamaica, 165, 195; Martinique, 22; Puerto Rico, 175; Virgin Islands, 201
—Central and South America, 163, 171, 191, 192, 203; Argentina, 17, 70; Brazil, 177; Guatemala, 179; Mexico, 114, 156, 164, 166, 173, 175, 191, 192, 194, 195, 196; Panama, 175, 191, 201; Peru, 191
—East Asia: China, 22, 24, 114, 132, 142, 159, 175, 177, 179, 191, 193, 195, 196, 201; Japan, 16, 141, 142, 154, 162, 175–98 passim; Java, 177; Korea, 164, 175; Manchuria, 175; Philippines, 85, 142, 170, 172, 173, 175, 179, 191, 195, 201–2, 203
—Europe, 21, 22, 23, 35, 59, 113, 158–92 passim, 242, 243, 248; Austria, 26, 114, 175, 177; Belgium, 198; Black Sea, 176; Bohemia, 226; Britain, 26, 35, 59, 114, 143, 154–96 passim; the Danube, 164; France, 26, 35, 59, 114, 142, 143, 154–99 passim, 243; Germany, 59, 130–206 passim; Greece, 70, 156, 191; Ireland, 114, 175, 176, 177, 179, 243; Italy, 162–94 passim, 207, 234, 243; Netherlands, 142, 143, 157, 179, 183, 190, 191, 198; Norway, 132, 175, 176; Poland, 114, 193; Portugal, 146; Rus-

sia, 154, 163, 165, 191, 195, 243; Scandinavia, 181, 183, 193, 244; Spain, 146, 157, 164, 175, 191, 194, 195, 200, 206; Sweden, 244; Switzerland, 82, 114, 143, 177, 179, 180, 191, 192, 194
—Middle East, 85, 179; Black Sea, 176; Holy Land, 175; Palestine, 175, 180, 195; Turkey, 31, 142, 176, 177, 179
—North America: Canada, 6, 164, 172, 176, 191, 193, 202; Eskimo lands, 179
—Pacific Islands, 176, 177, 203; Fiji, 176; Hawaii, 85, 201; Java, 177; Solomon Isles, 7
—South and Central Asia: Ceylon, 175; India, 176, 179, 183, 191, 192, 193, 194

Underwood and Underwood, 174–75, 184
United Fruit Company, 5, 115
United States: power of, 1–6, 42–46, 54, 100–103, 183, 188, 200, 212, 248, 251–52, 255; cultural deference to Europe of, 3, 15, 35, 42, 63, 72, 75–76, 100, 102–4, 182, 241–42; exceptionalism of, 3–5, 102–3; provincialism of, 3–9, 20, 33, 42, 102, 132, 187, 204, 212; assumed superiority of, 5, 62, 102–4, 127–33, 203, 229, 240; globalization of, 10, 12, 110–11, 251–52; standard of living in, 11, 130, 210, 252, 254; as small part of world, 35; as normative, 127–28; as culturally deficient, 215, 222, 246; as exemplar of modernity, 230–32, 248. See also Imperialism—U.S.; Nationalism; Provincialism, U.S.

Vantines, 23, 44, 87, 92, 179
Veblen, Thorstein, 85–86

Watson, Cora M., 160, 199

Wells, Martha C., 158

Western civilization: United States as climax of, 5; assumed superiority of, 36, 55, 71, 84–87, 92, 188; critiques of, 37, 85–86; identification with, 39, 48–49, 53–56, 103, 182, 188, 200. *See also* Empire, secondhand

Whiteness, 195; and masquerade, 37, 148; and consumption, 40, 80, 91, 99–100, 125, 186–88, 200; and immigrant gifts, 219–20, 227, 237. *See also* Racial distinctions, global; Racism in U.S. context

Women

—foreign: Orientalist depictions of, 29, 51; as models to U.S. women, 31, 35–36, 77, 85–86; oppressed status of, 44, 51–52, 85; as workers, 44, 93, 96–99, 194; as markers of civilizational status, 70–71, 80–86; femininity, assumed universality of, 71, 98; and national distinctiveness, 81–83, 100, 139, 175; and domesticity, 175, 195. *See also* Aristocracy, European; Ethnography; Imagined communities

—U.S.: and dissatisfaction with domesticity, 7, 15, 31–33, 52, 135, 161, 183–85, 204–8, 255; privileged status of white, native-born, middle-class, 8; agency of, 8, 12, 30, 189–90; as symbols of domesticity, 8, 15, 38, 154, 204–5; and social reproduction, 8–9, 38, 146, 189–90; and Americanization, 9; and distinctions (racial, national, class, civilizational), 9, 12, 31, 41, 58, 77, 95, 100–104, 131–32, 149–50, 187, 255; provincialism of, 9, 20; transnational activism of, 9, 121, 237; as privileged consumers in global context, 9–10, 12,

44–48, 53–55, 122, 135, 149, 183, 195, 200, 238, 254–55; subordination of, 12, 52, 77, 205, 255; and gender transgression, 31–33, 120, 154, 160, 186–87, 204–8; liberation of, 41, 86, 154, 205; assumed superiority of, 48, 100–104, 130, 188; and valuation of social capital, 102–3; and geographical knowledge, 123–24, 126, 151, 155; and travel culture, 155–208; as leaders in immigrant gifts movement, 212, 221–26; as exponents of pluralism, 232–33

Women's English Rest Tour Association, 171–72

Workers: immigrants to United States as, 4, 230; and global production of American domesticity, 11, 254–55; relegation to consumers' social unconscious, 12, 121–22, 230; assessments of, 21, 37–38, 44, 94, 128–29, 255; women as, 44, 93, 96–99, 160, 194; exclusion from imagined communities of consumption, 45–48, 50, 54–55, 91–99, 121–22, 149–50; compelled labor of, 50, 121–22; in U.S. fashion industry, 59–64; as service providers, 72, 120. *See also* Labor, conditions of; Production; Servants

World-class status: expressed through consumption, 48, 67–72, 79, 90, 92, 102–3, 120, 188, 255; expressed through production, 62–63, 102–3, 131; as standard of measurement, 106, 108

World's fairs, 35–36; and shopping, 23, 24, 51, 142; and ethnographic displays, 46, 49, 85, 177–79; and exposure to decoration styles, 53, 177; and eating, 113–14; and fictive travel, 177–79, 182

World War I: and consumption; 83, 96, 134; and fictive travel, 176, 191, 199, 201, 202–4; and Americanization, 209–10, 232, 238–39

Worth, Charles Frederick, 65, 70, 74

Young Women's Christian Association (YWCA), 116, 150, 173, 218, 219, 222–25, 235, 237, 243. *See also* International Institutes